D1302867

REMOVED FROM
E.S. FARLEY LIBRARY
WILKES UNIVERSITY
COLLECTION

Pharmaceutical R&D: Costs, Risks and Rewards

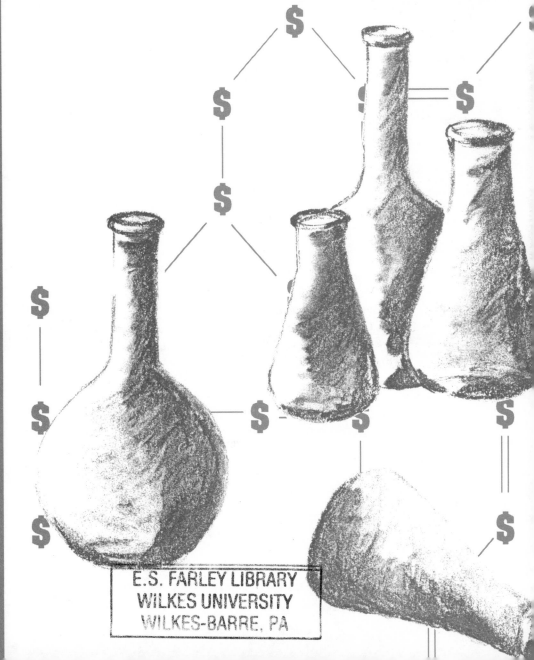

**Office of
Technology
Assessment**

E.S. FARLEY LIBRARY
WILKES UNIVERSITY
WILKES-BARRE, PA

RM 301.25
P42

Recommended Citation:

U.S. Congress, Office of Technology Assessment, *Pharmaceutical R&D: Costs, Risks and Rewards*, OTA-H-522 (Washington, DC: U.S. Government Printing Office, February 1993).

For sale by the U.S. Government Printing Office
Superintendent of Documents, Mail Stop: SSOP, Washington, DC 20402-9328
ISBN 0-16-041658-2

Foreword

Pharmaceutical costs are among the fastest growing components of health care costs today. Although increases in the inflation-adjusted prices of ethical drugs and perceived high prices of new drugs have been a concern of congressional committees for over 30 years, the growing Federal role in paying for prescription drugs has increased the concern over the appropriateness of prices relative to the costs of bringing new drugs to market. Specific policies of U.S. and other governments can alter the delicate balance between costs and returns to pharmaceutical R&D, with ramifications for the future health of Americans, for health care costs, and for the future of the U.S. pharmaceutical industry.

OTA's report focuses mainly on the economic side of the R&D process. Pharmaceutical R&D is an investment, and the principal characteristic of an investment is that money is spent today in the hopes of generating even more money in the future. Pharmaceutical R&D is a risky investment; therefore, high financial returns are necessary to induce companies to invest in researching new chemical entities. Changes in Federal policy that affect the cost, uncertainty and returns of pharmaceutical R&D may have dramatic effects on the investment patterns of the industry. Given this sensitivity to policy changes, careful consideration of the effects on R&D is needed.

The specific request for this study came from the House Committee on Energy and Commerce and its Subcommittee on Health and the Environment. The Senate Committee on the Judiciary's Subcommittee on Antitrust, Monopolies, and Business Rights endorsed the study.

OTA was assisted in this study by an advisory panel of business, consumer, and academic leaders chaired by Frederick M. Scherer, Ph.D., Professor of Economics, John F. Kennedy School of Government at Harvard University.

OTA gratefully acknowledges the contribution of each of these individuals. As with all OTA reports, the final responsibility for the content of the assessment rests with OTA.

Roger Herdman, Acting Director

94-190497

Advisory Panel

Frederick M. Scherer, Chair
Professor of Economics
John F. Kennedy School of
    Government
Harvard University
Cambridge, MA

Jerome Avorn
Director
Program for Analysis of Clinical
    Strategies
School of Medicine
Harvard University
Boston, MA

Nancy L. Buc
Partner
Weil Gotshal & Manges
Washington, DC

Martin Neil Baily
Professor of Economics
University of Maryland
College Park, MD

William S. Comanor
Professor of Economics
University of California
Santa Barbara, CA

Lewis A. Engman
Partner
Winston & Strawn
Washington, DC

Thomas Q. Garvey, III
President
Garvey Associates Inc.
Potomac, MD

Frederic Greenberg
Partner
EGS Partners
New York, NY

Robert Helms
Resident Scholar
American Enterprise Institute
Washington, DC

Gene Kimmelman
Legislative Director
Consumer Federation of America
Washington, DC

Jeffrey Levi
Director of Government Affairs
AIDS Action Council
Washington, DC

Judy C. Lewent
Senior Vice President and Chief
    Financial Officer
Merck & Company, Inc.
Whitehouse Station, NJ

George B. Rathmann
Chairman of the Board
ICOS
Bothell, WA

Shyam Sunder
Professor of Management and
    Economics
School of Industrial Administration
Carnegie-Mellon University
Pittsburgh, PA

Jacob C. Stucki
Retired Vice President for
    Pharmaceutical Research
The Upjohn Company
Kalamazoo, MI

W. Leigh Thompson
Executive Vice President
Eli Lilly & Company
Indianapolis, IN

NOTE: OTA appreciates and is grateful for the valuable assistance and thoughtful critiques provided by the advisory panel members. The panel does not, however, necessarily approve, disapprove, or endorse this report. OTA assumes full responsibility for the report and the accuracy of its contents.

Project Staff

Roger C. Herdman
Assistant Director
OTA Health and Life Sciences
Division

Clyde J. Behney
Health Program Manager

PRINCIPAL STAFF

JUDITH L. WAGNER
Project Director

Michael E. Gluck
Senior Analyst

Penelope Pollard
Senior Analyst[1]

Timothy W. Brogan
Research Assistant[2]

Lara Jakubowski
Research Assistant[3]

David J. Kaufman
Research Assistant

Arna M. Lane
Research Analyst

OTHER CONTRIBUTING STAFF

Jacqueline C. Corrigan
Senior Analyst

Philip T. Polishuk
Research Assistant

ADMINISTRATIVE STAFF

Beckie Erickson
Office Administrator

Eileen Murphy
P.C. Specialist

Carolyn Martin
Secretary

PRINCIPAL CONTRACTORS

Roseanne Altshuler
Rutgers University

William R. Baber
George Washington University

Lester Chadwick
University of Delaware

Robert Cook-Deegan
Consultant

Joseph DiMasi
Tufts University

W. Gary Flamm
SRS International, Inc.

Richard Frank
The Johns Hopkins University

Alan Garber
Palo Alto Department of Veteran Affairs
and Stanford University

Elizabeth Jensen
Hamilton College

Albert Link
University of North Carolina at Greensboro

Stewart C. Myers
Massachusetts Institute of Technology

Lynn Powers
Editorial Consultant

Stephen W. Schondelmeyer
University of Minnesota

Gordon Sick
University of Calgary

Ellen S. Smith
Consultant

Steven J. Wiggins
Texas A&M University

---

[1] From September 1989 to September 1991.

[2] From February 1991 to February 1992.

[3] From August 1989 to July 1991.

Contents

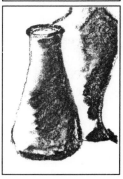

Summary | 1

I n this assessment, the Office of Technology Assessment examined the costs of pharmaceutical research and development (R&D), the economic rewards from that investment, and the impact of public policies on both costs and returns. Below is a brief synopsis of the study's major conclusions:

SUMMARY OF FINDINGS

- Pharmaceutical R&D is a costly and risky business, but in recent years the financial rewards from R&D have more than offset its costs and risks.
- The average aftertax R&D cash outlay for each new drug that reached the market in the 1980s was about $65 million (in 1990 dollars). The R&D process took 12 years on average. The full aftertax cost of these outlays, compounded to their value on the day of market approval, was roughly $194 million (1990 dollars).
- The cost of bringing a new drug to market is very sensitive to changes in science and technology, shifts in the kinds of drugs under development and changes in the regulatory environment. All of these changes are occurring fast. Consequently, it is impossible to predict the cost of bringing a new drug to market today from estimated costs for drugs whose development began more than a decade ago.
- Each new drug introduced to the U.S. market between 1981 and 1983 returned, net of taxes, at least $36 million more to its investors than was needed to pay off the R&D investment. This surplus return amounts to about 4.3 percent of the price of each drug over its product life.

- Dollar returns on R&D are highly volatile over time. Changes in R&D costs, tax rates, and revenues from new drugs are the most important factors influencing net returns. Drugs approved for marketing in 1984-88 had much higher sales revenues (in constant dollars) in the early years after approval than did drugs approved in 1981-83. On the other hand, R&D costs may be increasing and generic competition could be much stiffer for these drugs after they lose patent protection.

- Over a longer span of time, economic returns to the pharmaceutical industry as whole exceeded returns to corporations in other industries by about 2 to 3 percentage points per year from 1976 to 1987, after adjusting for differences in risk among industries. A risk-adjusted difference of this magnitude is sufficient to induce substantial new investment in the pharmaceutical industry.

- The rapid increase in revenues for new drugs throughout the 1980s sent signals that more investment would be rewarded handsomely. The pharmaceutical industry responded as expected, by increasing its investment in R&D. Industrywide investment in R&D accelerated in the 1980s, rising at a rate of 10 percent per year (in constant dollars).

- The rapid increase in new drug revenues was made possible in part by expanding health insurance coverage for prescription drugs in the United States through most of the 1980s. Health insurance makes patients and their prescribing physicians relatively insensitive to the price of a drug. The number of people with prescription drug coverage increased, and the quality of coverage improved.

- Almost all private health insurance plans covering prescription drugs are obligated to pay their share of the price of virtually any FDA-approved use of a prescription drug. FDA approval acts as a *de facto* coverage guideline for prescription drugs. Most health insurers have almost no power to influence prescribing behavior or to control the prices they pay for patented drugs.

- Manufacturers of drugs that are therapeutically similar to one another compete for business primarily on quality factors, such as ease of use, side-effect profiles and therapeutic effect. With price-conscious buyers such as health maintenance organizations (HMOs) and hospitals, however, they have engaged in more vigorous price competition.

- If price competition among therapeutically similar compounds became more common, the directions of R&D would change and the total amount of R&D would probably decline. Whether a decrease in R&D would be good or bad for the public interest is hard to judge. It is impossible to know whether today's level of pharmaceutical R&D is unquestionably worth its costs to society.

- The National Institutes of Health (NIH) and other Public Health Service laboratories have no mechanism to protect the public's investment in drug discovery, development and evaluation. These agencies lack the expertise and sufficient legal authority to negotiate limits on prices to be charged for drugs discovered or developed with Federal funds.

INTRODUCTION

Pharmaceutical R&D is the process of discovering, developing, and bringing to market new ethical drug products.[1] Most pharmaceutical R&D is undertaken by private industrial firms, and this report is about how and why industrial pharmaceutical companies make decisions to undertake R&D, what they stand to gain from such investments, and how they are helped or hindered by public policies that influence the process.

Industrial R&D is a scientific and an economic process. R&D decisions are always made with both considerations in mind. Science defines the opportunities and constraints, but economics determines which opportunities and scientific challenges will be addressed through industrial research.

This report focuses mainly, but not entirely, on the economic side of the R&D process. In this perspective, **pharmaceutical R&D is an investment**. The principal characteristic of an investment is that money is spent today in the hope that even more money will be returned to the investors sometime in the future. If investors (or the corporate R&D managers who act on their behalf) believe that the potential profits from R&D are worth the investment's cost and risks, then they will invest in it. Otherwise, they will not.

ORIGINS AND SCOPE OF OTA'S STUDY

OTA's study of pharmaceutical R&D grew out of a long-standing congressional debate over the prices of ethical drugs. Increases in real (inflation-adjusted) drug prices and perceived high prices for new drugs have been a concern of congressional committees for more than 30 years.

The industry's collective response to charges that drug prices are too high or are increasing too fast has been to point to the high and increasing cost of pharmaceutical R&D and their need to repay investors for their substantial and risky investments (325,326,505). Industry representatives have pointed to academic studies of the

Photo credit: ELI LILLY AND COMPANY

Pharmaceutical research and development is both a scientific and an economic process. Personnel, equipment and facilities come together in sophisticated organizations required for R&D.

average cost of bringing a new pharmaceutical compound to the market (324,326). One objective of OTA's report is to evaluate the accuracy of the industry's claims by examining the data and methods used to reach such conclusions.

By itself, the average cost of pharmaceutical R&D tells little about whether drug prices are too high or are increasing too fast. A more important question is whether the dollar returns on R&D investments are higher or lower than what is needed to induce investors to make these investments. The long-run persistence of higher dollar returns in the industry as a whole than the amount needed to justify the cost and risk of R&D is evidence of unnecessary pricing power for ethical pharmaceuticals (366). OTA examined the economic returns to investors in pharmaceutical R&D.

The U.S. Federal Government is anything but a passive observer of the industrial pharmaceutical R&D process. The Federal Government subsidizes private R&D, regulates the introduction and

---

[1] Ethical drugs are biological and medicinal chemicals advertised and promoted primarily to the medical, pharmacy, and allied professions. Ethical drugs include products available only by prescription as well as some over-the-counter drugs (320). Strictly speaking, ethical drugs include diagnostic as well as therapeutic products, but this report concentrates on R&D for therapeutic ethical drugs.

Box 1-A—The Content of Pharmaceutical R&D

Synthesis and Extraction—*The process of identifying new molecules with the potential to produce a desired change in a biological system (e.g., to inhibit or stimulate an important enzyme, to alter a metabolic pathway, or to change cellular structure).* The process may require: 1) research on the fundamental mechanisms of disease or biological processes; 2) research on the action of known therapeutic agents; or 3) random selection and broad biological screening. New molecules can be produced through artificial synthesis or extracted from natural sources (plant, mineral, or animal). The number of compounds that can be produced based on the same general chemical structure runs into the hundreds of millions.

Biological Screening and Pharmacological Testing—*Studies to explore the pharmacological activity and therapeutic potential of compounds.* These tests involve the use of animals, isolated cell cultures and tissues, enzymes and cloned receptor sites as well as computer models. If the results of the tests suggest potential beneficial activity, related compounds—each a unique structural modification of the original—are tested to see which version of the molecule produces the highest level of pharmacological activity and demonstrates the most therapeutic promise, with the smallest number of potentially harmful biological properties.

Pharmaceutical Dosage Formulation and Stability Testing—*The process of turning an active compound into a form and strength suitable for human use.* A pharmaceutical product can take any one of a number of dosage forms (i.e., liquid, tablets, capsules, ointments, sprays, patches) and dosage strengths (i.e., 50, 100, 250, 500 mg). The final formulation will include substances other than the active ingredient, called excipients. Excipients are added to improve the taste of an oral product, to allow the active ingredient to be compounded into stable tablets, to delay the drug's absorption into

---

marketing of new drugs, and pays for many drugs through Federal health care programs. Federal tax policies also alter R&D costs and returns. OTA assessed how Federal policies affect R&D costs and returns and how well Federal agencies protect the direct and indirect Federal investment in pharmaceutical R&D.

ISSUES BEYOND THE SCOPE OF THIS STUDY

OTA did not examine the implications for the competitiveness of the U.S.-based pharmaceutical industry of Federal policies affecting pharmaceutical R&D. The U.S.-based industry is a leader in the discovery and development of new drugs, particularly important new drugs with global markets. The U.S.-based industry has introduced roughly one out of every four new compounds introduced to the world market since 1961 (68,342) and is so far unchallenged as the leader

in biotechnology-based drugs and vaccines. All of the 15 biotechnology-based drugs and vaccines approved in the United States as of August 1991 were developed by U.S.-based firms (453).

Federal policies affecting R&D obviously affect the U.S.-based industry, but their influence on the relative competitiveness of the U.S.-based industry is much more difficult to predict. Most of the U.S. Federal policies in place today that affect drug R&D are neutral with respect to the drug's country of origin. Whether the United States should adopt policies that explicitly encourage U.S.-based R&D or manufacturing is beyond the scope of this project.[2]

THE NATURE OF PHARMACEUTICAL R&D INVESTMENTS

■ Pharmaceutical R&D's Two Objectives: New Drugs and New Markets

Pharmaceutical R&D includes many different scientific and clinical activities (see box 1-A).

---

[2] For an examination of the competitiveness of U.S.-based dedicated biotechnology companies, see OTA's recent report on the subject (453).

the body, or to prevent bacterial growth in liquid or cream preparations. The impact of each on the human body must be tested.

Toxicology and Safety Testing—*Tests to determine the potential risk a compound poses to man and the environment.* These studies involve the use of animals, tissue cultures, and other test systems to examine the relationship between factors such as dose level, frequency of administration, and duration of exposure to both the short- and long-term survival of living organisms. Tests provide information on the dose-response pattern of the compound and its toxic effects. Most toxicology and safety testing is conducted on new molecular entities prior to their human introduction, but companies can choose to delay long-term toxicity testing until after the therapeutic potential of the product is established.

Regulatory Review: Investigational New Drug (IND) Application—*An application filed with the U.S. FDA prior to human testing.* The IND application is a compilation of all known information about the compound. It also includes a description of the clinical research plan for the product and the specific protocol for phase I study. Unless the FDA says no, the IND is automatically approved after 30 days and clinical tests can begin.

Phase I Clinical Evaluation—*The first testing of a new compound in human subjects, for the purpose of establishing the tolerance of healthy human subjects at different doses, defining its pharmacologic effects at anticipated therapeutic levels, and studying its absorption, distribution, metabolism, and excretion patterns in humans.*

Phase II Clinical Evaluation—*Controlled clinical trials of a compound's potential usefulness and short term risks.* A relatively small number of patients, usually no more than several hundred subjects, enrolled in phase II studies.

Phase III Clinical Evaluation—*Controlled and uncontrolled clinical trials of a drug's safety and effectiveness in hospital and outpatient settings.* Phase III studies gather precise information on the drug's effectiveness for specific indications, determine whether the drug produces a broader range of adverse effects than those exhibited in the smaller study populations of phase I and II studies, and identify the best way of administering and using the drug for the purpose intended. If the drug is approved, this information forms the basis for deciding the content of the product label. Phase III studies can involve several hundred to several thousand subjects.

Process Development for Manufacturing and Quality Control—*Engineering and manufacturing design activities to establish a company's capacity to produce a product in large volume and development of procedures to ensure chemical stability, batch-to-batch uniformity, and overall product quality.*

Bioavailability Studies: *The use of healthy volunteers to document the rate of absorption and excretion from the body of a compound's active ingredients.* Companies conduct bioavailability studies both at the beginning of human testing and just prior to marketing to show that the formulation used to demonstrate safety and efficacy in clinical trials is equivalent to the product that will be distributed for sale. Companies also conduct bioavailability studies on marketed products whenever they change the method used to administer the drug (e.g., from injection to oral dose form), the composition of the drug, the concentration of the active ingredient, or the manufacturing process used to product the drug.

Regulatory Review: New Drug Application (NDA)—*An application to the FDA for approval to market a new drug.* All information about the drug gathered during the drug discovery and development process is assembled in the NDA. During the review period, the FDA may ask the company for additional information about the product or seek clarification of the data contained in the application.

Postapproval Research—*Experimental studies and surveillance activities undertaken after a drug is approved for marketing.* Clinical trials conducted after a drug is marketed (referred to as phase IV Studies in the United States) are an important source of information on as yet undetected adverse outcomes, especially in populations that may not have been involved in the premarketing trials (i.e., children, elderly, pregnant women) and the drug's long-term morbidity and mortality profile. Regulatory authorities can require companies to conduct Phase IV studies as a condition of market approval. Companies often conduct post-marketing studies in the absence of a regulatory mandate.

SOURCE: Office of Technology Assessment, 1993; based on Pharmaceutical Manufacturers Association Annual Survey Reports.

Before any new therapeutic ethical pharmaceutical product can be introduced to the market in the United States and most other industrialized countries, some R&D must be undertaken, but the specific activities and required R&D expenditures vary enormously with the kind of product under development. New therapeutic ethical pharmaceutical products fall into four broad categories:

- **New chemical entities (NCEs)**—new therapeutic molecular compounds that have never before been used or tested in humans.[3]
- **Drug delivery mechanisms**—new approaches to delivering therapeutic agents at the desired dose to the desired site in the body.
- **Follow-on products**—new combinations, formulations, dosing forms, or dosing strengths of existing compounds that must be tested in humans before market introduction.
- **Generic products**—copies of drugs that are not protected by patents or other exclusive marketing rights.

R&D is needed to bring all of these products to the market. National regulatory policies determine some of the required R&D, but some R&D would be undertaken even if there were no new drug regulation.

NCEs are discovered either through screening existing compounds or designing new molecules; once synthesized, they must undergo rigorous preclinical testing in laboratories and animals and clinical testing in humans to establish safety and effectiveness. The same is true for novel drug delivery mechanisms, such as monoclonal antibodies or implantable drug infusion pumps. Follow-on products also must undergo preclinical and clinical testing before they can be marketed, but the amount of R&D required to prove safety and effectiveness is usually less than for the original compound.

Even after a new drug has been approved and introduced to the market, clinical R&D may continue. Some of this postapproval clinical evaluation is required by regulatory agencies as a condition of approval, but other clinical research projects are designed to expand the market for the drug. For example, much clinical research is done to test new therapeutic uses for a drug already on the market or to compare its effectiveness with that of a competing product.

The research required on a generic product is typically much less than on the original compound it copies. In the United States, the makers of generic products must show the U.S. Food and Drug Administration (FDA) that the drug is therapeutically equivalent to the original compound, not that the compound itself is effective against the disease. This involves much less R&D than is necessary to introduce either NCEs or follow-on products.

The discovery and development of NCEs is the heart of pharmaceutical R&D, because the developers of follow-on or generic products build on the knowledge produced in the course of developing them. The market for the compound and all its follow-on products or generic copies in future years rests on the R&D that led to its initial introduction to the market. Most of the money spent on pharmaceutical R&D goes to the discovery and development of NCEs. Companies responding to the Pharmaceutical Manufacturers Association's (PMA) annual survey estimated that 83 percent of total U.S. R&D dollars in 1989 were spent in "the advancement of scientific knowledge and development of new products" versus "significant improvements and/or modifications of existing products" (320).[4]

---

[3] Another term frequently used to refer to newly developed compounds is "new molecular entity" (NME). The U.S. Food and Drug Administration (FDA) coined the term for use in its published statistical reports (474). The FDA includes some diagnostic agents and excludes therapeutic biologicals in data they present on NMEs, whereas in this report the term NCE is used to refer to therapeutic drugs and biologicals but not to diagnostic products. OTA uses the term NME only when discussing work that specifically employs FDA's definition of that term.

[4] How responding firms defined new products or modifications of existing products is unclear, however, and the accuracy or reliability of these estimates cannot be verified.

A patent on an NCE gives its owner the right to invest in further R&D to test new therapeutic uses or produce follow-on products. This continuing R&D may extend the compound's life in the market or increase its market size. Therefore, a complete analysis of returns on R&D for NCEs should encompass the costs of and returns on these subsequent investments as well.

NCEs comprise two poorly-defined subcategories: **pioneer** drugs and **"me-too"** drugs. Pioneer NCEs have molecular structures or mechanisms of action that are very different from all previously existing drugs in a therapeutic area. The first compound to inhibit the action of a specific enzyme, for example, is a pioneer drug. Me-too drugs are introduced after the pioneer and are similar but not identical to pioneer compounds in molecular structure and mechanism of action. Many me-too drugs are developed through deliberate imitation of the pioneer compound and have a shorter and more certain discovery period (158). But, the R&D cost advantage gained by imitation is typically met by a reduction in potential dollar returns from being a late entrant to the market (55,158).

The distinction between pioneers and me-toos is fuzzy, and not all me-too drugs are imitative. Although it is rational for pharmaceutical firms to imitate an existing product in order to share in a potentially lucrative market (102,298,346,363,418), much of the R&D on me-too drugs is not imitative but competitive. Companies race to be first to the market. The race has one winner and often a field of followers. The R&D costs of those who lose the race but manage ultimately to produce a product may be as high as or even higher than the costs of developing the pioneer compound.

For example, substantial R&D activity is currently underway in several pharmaceutical companies to develop new asthma therapies based on leukotriene inhibitors (403). A total of 25 compounds are now under investigation. How the research will proceed, which research programs will yield products that can be tested in humans, and which of those products will ultimately meet the tests of efficacy and safety required for market approval are anyone's guess. Already, research has been discontinued on at least three such products because of unanticipated safety problems in animal or clinical studies (378,379).

▋ The Three Most Important Components of R&D Investment: Money, Time, and Risk

Investors spend money today to make more money in the future. The less money required for the investment and the more that is expected in the future, the better the investment is. But **money** is only the first component of the R&D investment. Not only do investors care about how much money is required and the potential dollar returns that may result, but they also care about the second component: the **timing** of money outflows and inflows. The longer the investor must wait to get money back, the more he or she expects to get. Stated another way, money that will come in tomorrow, even with complete certainty, is not worth as much as the same amount in hand today.[5]

For risk-free investments, such as U.S. Treasury bills, the required return (as a percent of the capital invested) is determined by supply and demand in the money markets. If the going risk-free interest rate is 5 percent per year, for example, an investor who puts up $100 expects to get at least $105 back next year. From another point of view, $100 promised for delivery next year is worth only $95.23 today, because the investor could take that $95.23, invest it in a risk-free security, and have the $100 a year hence. Not having access to the $95.23 today essentially deprives the investor of the opportunity to invest at the going interest rate.

The interest rate required to induce the investor to permit his or her money to be used is referred to as the **opportunity cost of capital**. The value today (e.g., $95.23) of money promised for delivery sometime in the future (e.g., $100), evaluated at the opportunity cost of capital (e.g.,

---

[5] This principle lies behind the payment of interest on safe investments like insured bank deposits or U.S. Treasury bills.

5 percent), is referred to as the **present value** of money.

Like all investments, R&D investments must return enough money in the future so that the present value of those returns (evaluated at the investment's cost of capital) is at least as great as the amount of the investment.

Risk is the third component of the R&D investment. Riskier investments require higher dollar returns; otherwise investors would put their money in safe investments like U.S. Treasury bills. Thus, the opportunity cost of capital for R&D investments must be higher than the cost of capital for risk-free investments. And, the present value of $100 that is expected next year but with a great deal of uncertainty is even lower than the present value of a risk-free investment. How much higher the opportunity cost of capital for an R&D investment is, and how much lower the present value of future expected returns is, depends on the riskiness of the R&D investment.

Pharmaceutical industry executives often emphasize the particular riskiness of R&D. Analogies to drilling for oil are common: R&D involves many dry holes and a few gushers. According to one industry executive, pharmaceutical R&D is like "wildcatting in Texas (188)." Data on the dropout rate for drugs under development support these notions that R&D is, indeed, an uncertain and risky undertaking.

The risk that is accounted for in the opportunity cost of capital is different from these conventional notions about the risks of R&D. Modern finance theory distinguishes between two different kinds of investor risk: diversifiable risk and undiversifiable risk (59). The "wildcatting" risks of drug R&D are diversifiable: the investor can invest in a large diversified portfolio of R&D projects (or firms undertaking such projects) and obtain, on average, an expected dollar return that is very predictable.

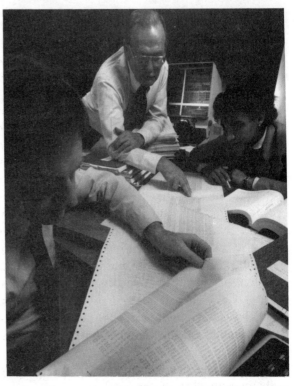

Photo credit: BRISTOL-MYERS SQUIBB COMPANY

Pharmaceutical R&D is risky business. Clinical testing of thousands of patients can result in the failure of a new compound to reach the market. Company scientists review detailed clinical data on many patients to determine the therapeutic benefit of a new agent.

For example, suppose the average NCE entering clinical testing has a 1-in-5 chance of ultimately reaching the market. If it does, it will make on average $100 million for the company. The expected dollar return, then, is $20 million.[6] If investors diversify their portfolios across a large enough number of R&D projects, they can be fairly certain that they will make, on average, about $20 million per project. Thus, the variation in returns due to the low probability of successful drug development can be eliminated by diversify-

---

[6] The expected value is the average return weighted by the probability of each potential outcome: $100(0.20) + $0(0.80) = $20.

ing the investment portfolio across a large number of projects.[7]

Some kinds of risk cannot be diversified away. Suppose, for example, prescription drug sales were closely linked to the state of the economy, perhaps because high unemployment produces more people who are uninsured and cannot afford prescription drugs. Pharmaceutical R&D would then have a great deal of undiversifiable risk because returns on R&D would depend on the state of the economy as a whole, and investors cannot diversify away these economywide risks.

The central finding of modern finance theory is that the cost of capital for a given investment must be adjusted only for the portion of risk that is undiversifiable. (See appendix C for an explanation.) The technical risks of project failure that weigh so heavily on the minds of R&D managers and executives do not raise the opportunity cost of capital.

OTA used standard financial techniques to obtain estimates of the cost of capital in the pharmaceutical industry as a whole and the cost of capital for pharmaceutical R&D investments in particular. We relied on techniques and data provided in a contract report by Stuart Myers and Lakshmi Shyam-Sunder (285). The cost of capital varies over time and across firms, but over the past 15 years the cost of capital in the pharmaceutical industry as a whole varied in the neighborhood of roughly 10 percent after adjusting for investors' inflation expectations (see appendix C).

Pharmaceutical firms are collections of investments, some very risky and others much less so. The undiversifiable risks of R&D projects are higher than those of other investments that drug companies must make, for reasons that are outlined in appendix C. R&D investments are riskier the earlier in the R&D process they are. How much riskier is difficult to assess, but OTA concluded that the cost of capital for the earliest stages of R&D may be up to 4 percentage points higher than the cost of capital for pharmaceutical companies as a whole.

■ Investors Look Ahead

In making R&D decisions, investors try to predict the possible future outcomes as accurately as they can. They assess the present value of their investments based on these predictions, not on the basis of past performance or profits.[8] An industry's past performance is informative to an investor only to the extent that technology and market conditions remain stable.

If investors always look ahead, then profits from today's drugs (which were developed with yesterday's R&D) do not determine how much will be invested in R&D. R&D managers do not invest in R&D simply because they have the cash on hand; they invest when the prospects for future returns look promising.

This conclusion seems to contradict the industry's contention that today's profits are needed to fund today's R&D (356). The success of the health-care oriented biotechnology industry in raising external capital proves that companies can

---

[7] The portfolio diversification need not occur within each individual company; investors can just as easily hold a diverse portfolio of companies in the industry. Within-company diversification may be important for managers whose professional and financial futures may rest with their own firm's performance, however. To the extent that managers seek to diversify their company's investments for their own purposes, they are not representing the interests of the firm's owners.

[8] In interviews with executives and R&D directors of eight pharmaceutical firms, OTA learned that few companies do formal present value analyses to select R&D projects or to determine how much R&D should be conducted in any year. What is true for the pharmaceutical industry may be true more generally. Scherer surveyed executives of Fortune 100 companies about their investment decisions and found that only about 30 percent of the responding companies used present value analysis in decisions regarding R&D (364). The high level of technical uncertainty may lead to other decision rules for R&D. Total R&D budgets appear to be based on current and recent earnings, managers' intuitive assessments of technical opportunities, and constraints on the rate of growth of R&D operations.

Despite the fact that formal investment analysis is infrequently used in R&D decisions, the present value of dollar returns to R&D across the entire industry should approximate the present value of R&D costs. Although R&D managers may not follow strict rules, companies whose investments do not return enough to cover the cost of capital will ultimately fail, while those whose investments return more than enough to cover the cost of capital will gradually expand their investments.

raise substantial R&D capital in external capital markets when future prospects look promising. Between July 1990 and July 1991, over $2.6 billion was raised by the biotechnology industry from external financing sources, almost all of it for health care applications (65).[9]

Established pharmaceutical firms do fund almost all of their investment needs, not just R&D, with internal cash flows from current operations (285). Internal funds may carry a lower cost of capital for complex investments like R&D, because outside investors are at a disadvantage in being able to assess the potential returns on R&D projects and will therefore demand a higher expected return on their money to cover the risk of being misled by company managers (170,189). The more complex the R&D, the more these information disparities are likely to raise the cost of external sources of capital.

A higher cost of external capital than of internal funds would explain companies' clear preference for internally generated cash flows when they have access to them. If the effective cost of capital is lower for firms that have high cash flows, more R&D projects would pass the present value test and be undertaken. Thus, the availability of internally generated funds may increase the amount of R&D that is performed over what the R&D levels would be if all such funds had to be raised in external capital markets.

How much more R&D is conducted because established pharmaceutical firms use cash flows to fund their investments depends on how much higher the cost of capital for outside funds is. The size of external capital market investments in the biotechnology industry (which has low current operating cash flows) suggests that much of the R&D currently financed in established firms through internally generated cash would be undertaken even if these cash flows were unavailable.

R&D COSTS: THE EVIDENCE

Although the investor always looks ahead in making R&D decisions, R&D cost estimates are retrospective. R&D costs can change quickly as underlying scientific, technical or regulatory conditions change, so it is dangerous to predict much about the future, or even about the costs of projects under way today, from studies of past R&D costs. OTA looked at the existing studies of R&D costs and also at recent trends in some critical components of the cost of bringing new drugs to market.

The costs of bringing a new drug to market rightly include those for projects that were abandoned along the way. Since investors could not have known beforehand which projects would succeed and would not knowingly have invested in the losers, these "dead-end" costs are unavoidable costs of R&D.

The full cost of bringing a new drug to market can be thought of as the minimal payoff required from the drugs that successfully reach the market required to induce investors to lay out the money at each step of the way. To measure the full cost of past R&D projects, all outlays required to achieve the successes must be compounded (or capitalized) to their present value on the day of market approval at an interest rate equal to the cost of capital.

The full cost of bringing a new drug to market calculated in this way is much higher than the amount of money companies must actually raise to fund R&D projects. To pursue R&D, companies must raise only enough money to cover the actual outlays for successful and unsuccessful projects. Estimating the full cost of bringing a new drug to market, by contrast, provides a way of gauging how much money must be earned from the successful drugs, once they reach the market, to justify the research outlays.

---

[9] The sources of external financing used by biotechnology firms change from year to year. In the past, R&D Limited Partnerships were an attractive financing mechanism, but changes in federal tax law took away their advantage. In 1991, initial public offerings were the major source of funds. Venture capital was less important than in previous years. Small biotechnology companies look to strategic alliances with traditional pharmaceutical firms for sources of financing when other sources are unavailable (65).

The present value of full R&D costs has three components:

- Cash outlays required to produce the successes (and to pay for the abandoned projects along the way),
- Timing of the cash outlays, and
- Opportunity cost of capital for each specific R&D investment.

There is only one way to get information on both the amount and timing of cash outlays required to produce a successful NCE: take a large and representative sample of R&D projects and, for each project, record incurred costs month-by-month until the project is either abandoned or approved for marketing. Then, outlays over time can be converted to their present value in a particular reference year at the appropriate cost of capital. The present value of outlays per approved NCE is the average cost of bringing an NCE to market.

This project-level approach was used in a pair of studies pioneered by Ronald Hansen (175) and updated and extended by Joseph DiMasi and colleagues (109). The frequent contention by industry spokesmen that it costs $231 million (in 1987 constant dollars) to bring an NCE to market (326) is the central result of the DiMasi study (109). In 1990 constant dollars, the cost would be $259 million.[10]

The main problem with this approach is that accurate data on the costs and time required to reach specific milestones in the R&D process, and rates of success or abandonment along the way, are proprietary. Researchers must depend on the ability and willingness of companies to supply detailed data on R&D project costs and histories. Hansen and DiMasi relied on surveys of 14 and 12 U.S.-based pharmaceutical firms, respectively, that were willing to provide estimates of R&D outlays and timing for the samples of newly synthesized NCEs. The researchers could not audit these estimates for accuracy or consistency across companies.

Early in this assessment, OTA determined that it would be infeasible to mount an independent project-level study of R&D costs. Although Congress has the power to subpoena company data, pharmaceutical companies have actively resisted providing it to congressional agencies. In the past, the U.S. General Accounting Office (GAO) tried to obtain data on pharmaceutical R&D (and other) costs but was ultimately foiled after many years of effort that involved decisions in the U.S. Supreme Court. (See appendix D for a legal analysis of congressional access to financial data.) Although business confidentiality arguments are not sufficient to block a congressional subpoena (423), such arguments can result in protracted negotiations over whether or not the information will be kept confidential and the scope of the documents that must be turned over. The pursuit of data from a number of companies would be very costly and take many years.

OTA's approach to R&D cost assessment relied on a detailed analysis of the validity of the Hansen and DiMasi studies. First, OTA examined the validity of the methods used to estimate each component of R&D costs (cash outlays, project time profiles, and success rates). Second, OTA tested the consistency of the resulting estimates with corroborative studies. Third, OTA examined whether the rate of increase in real (i.e., inflation-adjusted) R&D cost implied by the two studies is consistent with data on trends in major cost drivers, such as the number of subjects of clinical trials, biomedical research personnel costs, and animal research costs.

■ Cash Costs Per Success

Hansen examined a probability sample of about 67 NCEs originated by U.S.-based pharmaceutical companies first entering human clinical trials from 1963 through 1975. DiMasi and colleagues studied a sample of 93 such NCEs first entering human trials from 1970 through 1982.

---

[10] In this OTA report, all estimates of R&D costs and returns are expressed in 1990 constant dollars and were calculated by OTA using the GNP implicit price deflator.

Total cash outlays per successful new NCE were estimated at $65.5 million (in 1990 dollars) by Hansen and at $127.2 million by DiMasi, a 94 percent increase in estimated outlays per successful new drug over the period of the two studies. The two studies suggest that real (inflation-adjusted) R&D cash outlays per successful NCE increased at an annual rate of about 9.5 percent.

The increase in cash outlays per success was moderated by an improvement in the success rate of NCEs over time. Whereas Hansen projected only 12.5 percent of the NCEs would ultimately get FDA approval for marketing, DiMasi and colleagues estimated that about 23 percent of the projects would be successful. Without this improvement, the reported increase in cash outlays per success would have been even higher.

OTA found two principal threats to validity of the methods used to estimate cash outlays per success: 1) the small number of NCEs in the samples, especially in the Hansen study; and 2) the reliance on unverifiable cost data that responding companies supplied. Although most companies were capable of estimating the costs associated with discovery and development of particular NCEs with reasonable accuracy, inherent differences in the structure of cost-accounting systems across companies introduce potential inconsistency and bias. More importantly, any company that understood the study methods and the potential policy uses of the study's conclusions could overestimate costs without any potential for discovery. Thus, the motivation to overestimate costs cannot be discounted.

Because of these threats to validity, OTA looked for corroborative evidence on cash outlays per success. Aggregate annual data on industry R&D spending and NCE approvals in the United States are readily available and reasonably verifiable. In a study using industry-level spending data, Wiggins estimated R&D cash outlays per successful NCE at $75 million (in 1990 dollars) (520).

Wiggins' sample of **approved** NCEs corresponds roughly in time to Hansen's sample of NCEs **first entering clinical testing**, but for technical reasons Wiggins' sample may be somewhat more recent and therefore more costly to develop than the drugs in Hansen's study. (See chapter 3 for an explanation.) On the other hand, Wiggins studied the costs of producing all NCEs, not just those originated by U.S.-based firms. NCEs licensed from other firms probably cost the firm that acquires them less to develop. Thus, Wiggins' estimate of R&D costs may be too low for self-originated drugs. OTA concluded, therefore, that Hansen's estimate of $65.5 million in cash outlays per successful drug is reasonably accurate and perhaps even slightly low.

A similar analysis was not available to cover the time period of DiMasi's study, but OTA checked the results of the DiMasi study against data on aggregate R&D spending by the U.S. industry and the total number of self-originated NCEs introduced by these companies. OTA's check revealed a substantial consistency between aggregate R&D spending estimates and the cash outlays per NCE estimated by DiMasi study (see chapter 3 for details).

OTA also examined whether trends in three R&D cost drivers—the costs of research personnel, the size of clinical trials, and the cost of animal research—were consistent with the estimated increases in cash R&D outlays per successful NCE between the periods that Hansen and DiMasi studied.

R&D PERSONNEL

The number of R&D personnel employed by PMA-member firms remained fairly constant throughout the 1970s but grew rapidly beginning in 1980 (figure 1-1). Most of this growth was in scientific and professional personnel, which numbered about 12,000 in 1977, but increased to almost 29,000 by 1989. At the same time, inflation-adjusted salaries of biological scientists did not increase.

How much of the increase in employment in the 1980s reflects increased labor inputs per successful NCE, versus adjustments for a larger field of NCEs entering each phase of clinical testing or a greater commitment to basic research,

Figure 1-1—Research and Development Personnel in Pharmaceutical Companies, 1970-89

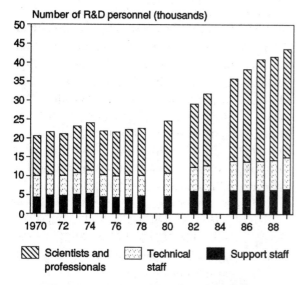

Number of R&D personnel (thousands)

SOURCE: Office of Technology Assessment, 1993, based on Pharmaceutical Manufacturers Association Annual Survey Reports.

cannot be answered with available data. The most that can be said is that trends in employment of research personnel are consistent with a substantial increase in R&D cash outlays per NCE for those NCEs first entering clinical research in the late 1970s and early 1980s, the later part of the period covered by the DiMasi study.

ANIMAL RESEARCH

Trends in the cost of animal research are even more difficult to gauge. Some tentative evidence suggests that the number of animals used in pharmaceutical research may have declined between the 1970s and the 1980s, especially in the earliest stages of pharmaceutical R&D, when compounds are being screened for their pharmacologic activity. Any decline in the use of animals was accompanied by a dramatic increase in the cost of conducting animal tests, however. Table 1-1 shows the inflation-adjusted cost of conducting specific animal studies in 1980 and 1990 in eight animal testing laboratories. The costs of virtually all kinds of animal studies increased dramatically over the period. These data suggest that the cost of studies involving animal subjects has increased dramatically, but the ultimate impact on the cash costs per successful NCE cannot be gauged because of uncertainties about trends in the volume of testing, about which there is little information.

Table 1-1—Price of Animal Studies[a] ($ 1990 thousands)[b]

Study	Estimated price in 1980	Price range in 1990	Fold increase	Number of Labs providing information
Acute rats....................	$ 0.8	$ 4 - 5	5 - 6.25	8
28-day toxicity in rats..........	15	30 - 65	2 - 4.3	6
Subchronic rats...............	38	55 - 143	1.4 - 3.8	8
2-year rat bioassay............	384	250 - 575	.7 - 1.5	5
Teratology rats...............	23	52 - 70	2.3 - 3.0	5
Acute monkey...............	14	39 - 62	2.8 - 4.4	6
Subchronic monkey...........	74	108 - 184	1.5 - 2.5	6
Acute dog....................	2.3	22 - 51	9.6 - 22.1	7
Subchronic dog...............	46	72 - 147	1.6 - 3.2	7

[a] Each laboratory surveyed was given an identical protocol on which the price is based. The "cost" includes profit as well as all direct and indirect costs. Laboratories surveyed were Hazleton, Bioresearch, IIT, TSI Mason, Bio/dynamics, Pharmakon, PRI, and IRDC.

[b] All prices were adjusted to 1990 dollars using GNP implicit price deflator.

SOURCE: Office of Technology Assessment, 1993, based on W.G. Flamm and M. Farrow, "Recent Trends in the Use and Cost of Animals in the Pharmaceutical Industry," contract report prepared for the Office of Technology Assessment, DC, April 1991.

CLINICAL TRIAL SIZES

Pharmaceutical executives claim that the number of people enrolled in clinical trials has increased dramatically over time. A rapid increase in trial sizes would be consistent with an increase in the estimated cost of phase III clinical trials from $5.7 million for each NCE entering the phase in Hansen's study to $14.3 million in DiMasi's study (in 1990 dollars). Part of the explanation for such an increase may be a change in the mix of drugs under testing from those for acute illness to those for chronic illness. Drugs for long-term use often require larger trial sizes.

Even within specific categories of drugs, however, the number of people enrolled in trials seems to have increased. OTA surveyed pharmaceutical companies for the size of clinical trials conducted prior to FDA approval for NCEs in three classes with a large number of approved drugs: antihypertensives, antimicrobials, and nonsteroidal anti-inflammatory drugs (NSAIDs). We compared NCEs approved for marketing 1978-83 with those approved between 1986 and 1990. Figure 1-2 shows the average number of subjects entered in trials up to the point of NDA submission.

Although the time periods covered in the clinical trial survey do not correspond exactly to the Hansen and DiMasi research periods,[11] the survey results do show that the number of subjects in clinical trials increased in the period between the later years of the Hansen study and the later years of the DiMasi study, even within reasonably homogeneous therapeutic categories.

That the number of subjects in foreign countries increased faster than did the number of U.S. subjects in two categories suggests that part of the observed increase in research costs is due to the globalization of research strategies over time. Other industrialized countries increased their requirements for premarket approval during the 1970s, and U.S. firms may have become more aggressive in seeking early approval for NCEs in other countries. These forces would gradually

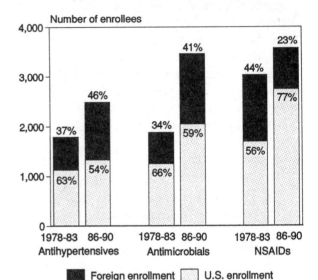

Figure 1-2—Mean Number of Subjects Enrolled in Clinical Trials Prior to Submission of NDA for NCEs Approved in 1978-83 and 1986-90

KEY: NCE = new chemical entity; NDA = new drug application; NSAIDs = nonsteroidal anti-inflammatory drugs

SOURCE: Office of Technology Assessment, 1993.

compress total R&D expenditures into the pre-NDA period.

The increase in clinical trial sizes within the therapeutic categories that OTA studied is not big enough to explain the almost three fold increase in the average cash outlay for NCEs that entered phase III clinical trials between the Hansen and DiMasi studies. Trial sizes were not very different across categories, even though antimicrobial drugs are more frequently for acute conditions, while antihypertensive drugs and NSAIDs are more frequently for chronic conditions. The per-patient cost of conducting trials must have increased dramatically. OTA could not independently verify whether this cost increased as fast as the Hansen and DiMasi studies imply.

OTA FINDINGS ON THE VALIDITY OF ESTIMATED CASH COSTS

OTA concluded from the corroborative evidence available at the aggregate spending level

---

[11] Hansen's study years (NCEs first entering testing between 1963-75) correspond roughly with introductions in 1970-81. DiMasi and colleagues' study years (1970-82) correspond roughly with introductions in 1978-90.

that the estimates of cash outlays per successful NCE made by DiMasi are reasonably accurate. Hansen's early estimate may have been too low, suggesting that the rate of increase in costs between the periods covered by the two studies may have been overstated. Data on rates of change in three illustrative components of R&D—personnel, animal research costs, and clinical trial size—are consistent with a substantial increase over the period covered by the studies in the real cash outlays required to bring a new drug to market.

▌ Present Value of Cash Outlays

The present value of the R&D cost at the point of market approval depends on the timing of R&D expenditures over the life of projects and the cost of capital for the investments over time. R&D outlays occur over a long and, according to the Hansen and DiMasi studies, lengthening period of time. Hansen estimated the total R&D time was 9.6 years; DiMasi, 11.8 years.

OTA concluded from a review of study methods that the length of the clinical research and the regulatory review periods estimated by Hansen and DiMasi are very accurate. Estimates of the length of the preclinical period (the time required to discover and prepare a compound for testing in humans) are much less precise and might even be a bit too short, especially in DiMasi's study.

Neither Hansen nor DiMasi adjusted the cost of capital for the greater risk of R&D projects. Both studies took the weighted average company cost of capital in established pharmaceutical firms as their basis for calculating the fully capitalized cost of R&D. Hansen assumed a real cost of capital of 8 percent; DiMasi, 9 percent. As discussed above, the average inflation-adjusted cost of capital for pharmaceutical firms as a whole varied throughout the period but was probably closer to 10 percent. The cost of capital for R&D projects is even higher and increases the earlier the stage of R&D.

OTA estimated that the cost of capital for early R&D may be up to 4 percent higher than the cost of capital for manufacturing plant and equipment. OTA recalculated the fully capitalized cost of R&D at the point of market approval with a cost of capital that decreases linearly from 14 to 10 percent from the beginning to the end of R&D projects.[12] The estimate for the DiMasi study increased from $259 million (in 1990 dollars) to $359 million. Thus, a reasonable upper bound on the fully capitalized cost of R&D per successful NCE at the time of market approval is $359 million.

▌ After-Tax Costs of R&D

The effective cost to a company of bringing a new drug to market is substantially less than the cost estimates discussed above because they do not account for the taxes the company is relieved of paying when it invests in R&D. The net cost of every dollar spent on research must be reduced by the amount of tax avoided by that expenditure. These tax savings result from both deductions and tax credits. (When R&D is successful and produces marketable products, the company will pay extra taxes as a result, and these dollar returns must also be reduced by the amount of the extra taxes.)

Like all business expenses, R&D is deductible from a firm's taxable income. This tax deduction reduces the cost of R&D by the amount of the company's marginal tax rate. Because of the size and sales of most major pharmaceutical firms, the bulk of their taxable income would fall into the highest tax bracket. This marginal tax rate fell from 48 to 46 percent between 1971 and 1986. At 46 percent, every dollar spent on R&D would cost the company only $0.54. With the passage of the Tax Reform Act of 1986 (Public Law 99-514), the marginal rate fell to 34 percent, thus effectively raising the cost of each dollar of R&D to $0.66. Corporations also pay State income taxes which also can be reduced with business deductions.

---

[12] Because 10 percent is a weighted average cost of capital across all of the company's investments, investments in manufacturing facilities probably have a cost of capital below 10 percent. Therefore, this estimate may overestimate the cost of capital for R&D at each stage.

Pharmaceutical firms can also use special tax credits available only for firms that perform certain kinds of R&D. Since 1981, the tax code has included a tax credit for increases in qualifying R&D expenses. This credit carried a statutory rate of 25 percent until 1986, when it was reduced to 20 percent. Quantifying the extent to which this credit reduces the cost of R&D for pharmaceutical firms is impossible for two reasons: 1) the credit depends on the amount that a firm increases R&D expenditures, not on the level of those expenses; and 2) expenditures on supervisory activities or overhead do not qualify for the credit.

When it can be used, the most powerful tax credit affecting pharmaceutical R&D is the Orphan Drug credit. The Orphan Drug Act of 1983 (Public Law 97-414) provides a 50-percent tax credit for qualifying clinical R&D on drugs that have received an orphan designation. An important limitation of the Orphan Drug credit, in addition to its being limited only to clinical R&D and orphan drugs, is that the credit cannot be saved and used in future years if the company has no current taxable income. Thus, small startup companies, often the developers of orphan drugs, cannot use it.

OTA recalculated DiMasi's estimate of R&D cost per NCE taking account of tax savings. The sample of NCEs that DiMasi studied underwent the great bulk of discovery and development at a time when the marginal tax rate was 48 or 46 percent. Adjusting for tax savings (using a 46 percent rate) without any other changes reduces the net cash outlays per NCE from $127.2 million to $65.5 million, and adjusting for tax savings reduces the total costs capitalized to the point of market approval at a 10 percent cost of capital from $259 million to $140 million (table 1-2). When the cost of capital is permitted to decrease linearly from 14 to 10 percent over the life of the R&D projects, the net after tax cost is $194 million. OTA concluded that for NCEs whose clinical research began in the period 1970-82— the time period of the DiMasi study—the upper bound on after-tax capitalized cost of

Table 1-2—After-Tax R&D Costs Estimated by DiMasi Under Different Assumptions About the Cost of Capital[a] ($ 1990 millions)

Cost of capital (%)	Before-tax savings	After-tax savings (46%)
9	$258,650	$139,671
10	279,112	151,045
Variable (10 - 14)	359,313	194,029

[a] All assumptions, given in 1990 dollars, were adjusted for inflation using GNP implicit price deflator.

SOURCE: Office of Technology Assessment, 1993, estimates adapted from J.A. DiMasi, R.W. Hansen, H.G. Grabowski, et al., "The Cost of Innovation in the Pharmaceutical Industry," *Journal of Health Economics 10:107-142, 1991.*

R&D required to bring an NCE to market is $194 million. The effect of the R&D tax credit, the U.S. investment tax credit and the orphan drug tax credit was not taken into account.

Had today's marginal corporate tax rate (34 percent) been in effect at the time the NCEs in DiMasi's study were developed, the net after-tax cash outlay per successful NCE would have been no more than $80.1 million, and the full cost capitalized at a 10 percent cost of capital would be $171 million. At today's tax rate, with a cost of capital decreasing from 14 to 10 percent over the life of the project, the average cost of developing a new drug would be no more than $237 million.

■ R&D Costs Today and in the Future

The fully capitalized cost of bringing a new drug to market is very sensitive to four components of the R&D process:

1. The preclinical cash outlays required to discover or design a potential therapeutic compound and then to determine whether it is worth testing in humans;
2. The success rate at which compounds move from phase to phase of clinical research and ultimately to the market;
3. The scope and size of clinical trials; and
4. The time a drug spends in regulatory review.

The studies of R&D costs that OTA reviewed were for compounds that entered human clinical testing in the 1960s and 1970s. Much has changed since then in the technical and regulatory conditions governing pharmaceutical R&D, making inappropriate any extrapolation from the experience of that generation of drugs to those entering clinical testing today.

The technology of drug discovery and design has changed enormously. Whereas researchers used to screen a large number of chemicals for the few that cause a desired chemical or biological reaction, they now frequently engage in a more deliberate process based on knowledge of biological function. (See chapter 5 for a description of trends in the science and technology of drug discovery.)

For example, many drugs are discovered today through analysis of drug receptors, molecules that bind with specific agents to change cellular function. Agents that can bind with the receptor or that inhibit the binding of a naturally occurring substance become potential drug candidates. The process of finding such molecules involves determining the shape of a receptor and designing the agents that will affect its function.

Understanding the structure of receptor molecules has become the key to many areas of drug discovery. Most receptors are large proteins with multiple regions of interest. Expensive analytic instruments and computers are necessary to define the shape of these molecules. Companies have justified investments in nuclear magnetic resonance spectroscopy and x-ray crystallography, two techniques for analyzing the shape of large molecules, as tools to determine the three-dimensional structure of receptor sites, a process that will improve the prospects for developing drugs that fit into the desired sites. These and other techniques of structure-activity analysis require massive computer power to analyze data and construct three-dimensional molecular images.

One outgrowth of the expanding base of knowledge about disease mechanisms is the endless supply of possible research directions that

Photo credit: BRISTOL-MYERS SQUIBB COMPANY

Computers facilitate the design of new enzyme inhibitors by enabling scientists to graphically visualize the structure of targeted molecules.

this knowledge creates. For example, drug receptors that reside on the surface of cells mediate many of the most important functions in the body and are extremely promising targets for future drug development. Enzymes that mediate biochemical reactions and genetic materials also offer up a plethora of drug development targets. There are too many possible targets, however, for scientists to understand the structure and function of each. Thus, at the same time that new research technology advances understanding, it expands the choices and increases the chances of dry holes in the discovery phase.

The impact of the rapid advances in the science and technology of drug discovery on the costs of R&D is impossible to predict. While investment in instrumentation and computers has clearly increased, the impact on the cost of R&D depends largely on what these advances do to the productivity of the discovery phase of R&D. If, dollar-for-dollar, the new drug discovery techniques produce more new drugs worthy of clinical testing, and if these new drugs are more likely to successfully jump the hurdles in each phase and

Figure 1-3—IND Applications Received by the Center for Drug Evaluation and Research

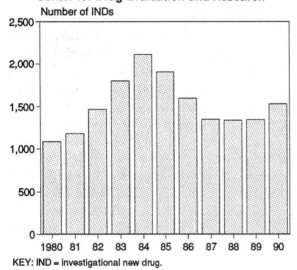

KEY: IND = investigational new drug.

SOURCE: Office of Technology Assessment, 1993 based on U.S. Department of Health and Human Services, Public Health Service, Food and Drug Administration, Center for Drug Evaluation and Research, *Office of Drug Evaluation Statistical Report: 1991*, U.S. Department of Health and Human Service, Rockville, MD, 1992.

Figure 1-4—IND Applications Received by the Center for Biologics Evaluation and Research

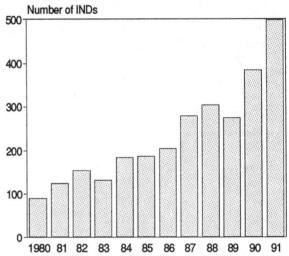

SOURCE: Federal Coordinating Council for Science, Engineering, and Technology, Office of Science and Technology Policy, Executive Office of the President, *Biotechnology for the 21st Century: A Report by the FCCSET Committee on Life Sciences and Health* (Washington, DC: U.S. Government Printing Office, February 1992), and data provided by the Center for Biologics Evaluation and Research, U.S. Food and Drug Administration.

reach the market, then the costs of R&D per successful drug could decline. On the other hand, if the explosion of possible research avenues makes the discovery process even more chancy, then the cost of bringing a new drug to market could increase. Both trends could occur at the same time, with unpredictable consequences for overall R&D costs.

The results of the changes under way in the process of drug discovery are evident in the number of investigational new drug (IND) applications submitted to the FDA in recent years. INDs increased throughout the 1980s, with the highest rate of growth coming in the investigation of biologicals (biotechnology drugs and other biological products) (figure 1-3 and figure 1-4). The shift in drug development toward biotechnology-based drugs means that discovery and development costs may be very different from those that

came before, but without better data on clinical trial sizes, regulatory delays, and other regulatory requirements, it is impossible to say whether on the whole the shift toward biotechnology-based drugs will increase or decrease the costs of R&D.

The most recently available data on the success rate from first filing of an IND application to FDA approval shows an improvement over time. At OTA's request, the FDA compiled information on INDs filed for new molecular entities (NMEs) in the periods 1976-78 and 1984-86.[13] The percent of NMEs that reached the NDA filing stage within 54 months of the first filing of a commercial IND increased from 6.8 to 11 percent, and although few drugs filing INDs in the later period have yet been approved, the percent reaching approval within 54 months is also higher for drugs entering testing in the later period. Improvements in

[13] FDA staff were very helpful to OTA and provided staff to collect and analyze IND data according to OTA's specifications. The amount of effort that FDA staff were required to spend on this analysis revealed some of the limitations of FDA's electronic databases for tracking trends in drug development. FDA's automated information system does not link applications for INDs with applications for NDAs, so any tracking of drugs from IND to approval, rejection or discontinuation of the project must be done by manual search of the IND and NDA files.

success rates can have a substantial moderating effect on realized R&D costs per success, but the data available so far are too limited to conclude much about ultimate success rates for drugs that recently entered testing.

OTA's data on the length of the regulatory period (from the NDA filing to approval) show no improvement in recent years, but efforts to harmonize the regulatory review process across countries and recently passed legislation that will increase FDA staff available for new drug review in return for "user fees" from sponsors (Public Law 102-571) could shorten the period overall. If the ultimate success rate for NCEs does not improve, getting successful drugs through the FDA regulatory period faster will only modestly reduce the capitalized cost of R&D.

In short, OTA cannot predict how R&D costs will change in the future. The rapid advances in science and technology, the shift in the nature of drugs under development, and the new FDA regulatory initiatives all promise to influence R&D costs, but the net direction of the effect of all of these influences together is beyond predicting.

RETURNS ON R&D: THE EVIDENCE

The costs of R&D are most meaningful in comparison with the dollar returns they produce. Measuring dollar returns accurately is difficult because the life of a new NCE may be 20 years or longer and the costs of producing, distributing and marketing the NCE can be estimated only imprecisely. Nevertheless, several authors have tried to measure the present value on the day of market approval of dollar returns on NCEs (159,215,500). The studies produced widely differing findings, ranging from high present values of dollar returns to present values that lie below the fully capitalized cost of R&D. The studies

differ widely because they each examined NCEs that came to market in different periods and made different assumptions about the value of product sales over the product life cycle and the cost of manufacturing, distribution and marketing.

OTA conducted an independent analysis of the dollar returns on R&D using recent data on annual revenues from NCEs and the costs of producing, marketing and distributing these products. OTA analyzed the return on NCEs introduced to the U.S. market in the years 1981-83. OTA chose this relatively brief period for two reasons. First, the period corresponds in time to the R&D period studied by DiMasi and colleagues. Second, we had access to data on drugstores and hospital sales only for this particular set of NCEs (97).[14]

■ The Sales Curve

Figure 1-5 shows U.S. sales to hospitals and drugstores in constant 1990 dollars in each year after market introduction for NCEs introduced in the years 1981-83 and, for the sake of comparison, in earlier and later periods as well. Although OTA had access to only 1 year of data on NCEs introduced from 1984 through 1988, that one data point suggests that, after adjusting for inflation, U.S. sales of NCEs in the early years after approval continued to steepen throughout the 1980s.

To predict the sales curve for the 1981-83 NCEs beyond the 9th year, OTA examined trends in effective patent lives and in the loss of revenue after patent expiration.

EFFECTIVE PATENT LIFE

The effective patent life is the elapsed time between FDA approval for marketing of a new drug and expiration of the last patent or market exclusivity provision that effectively protects the original compound from generic competition. Two new Federal laws passed in the 1980s, the

---

[14] Gaining access to sales data on NCEs was a major problem for OTA throughout the course of this study. Detailed data are collected by proprietary organizations on U.S. and worldwide sales of NCEs, and these data are sold to subscribers. IMS America, Inc. and IMS International, Inc. are market research firms that, among other activities, conduct ongoing surveys of pharmaceutical product sales and prescriptions for sale to subscribers. The cost to OTA would have been prohibitive, however. For example, IMS International, Inc. quoted a preliminary price to OTA for estimates of the total non-U.S. sales between 1981 and 1990 for NCEs introduced between 1981-83 at $75,000 to $125,000 (339).

Figure 1-5—Average U.S. Sales of New Chemical Entities Introduced in 1970-79, 1981-83, and 1984-88

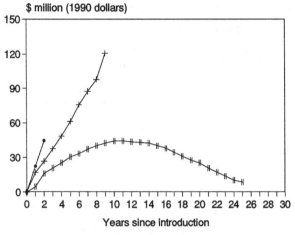

$ million (1990 dollars)

Years since introduction

—╫— 1970-1979   —+— 1981-1983   —•— 1984-1988

SOURCES: 1970-79: H.G. Grabowski and M. Vernon, "A New Look at the Returns and Risks to Pharmaceutical R&D," *Management Science* 36(7):804-821, July 1990. 1981-83: Coppinger, P., "Overview of the Competitiveness of the U.S. Pharmaceutical Industry," presentation to the Council in Competitiveness Working Group on the Drug Approval Process, Washington, DC, Dec. 12, 1990. 1984-88: IMS America, Inc., unpublished data prepared for the Office of Technology Assessment, 1991.

Drug Price Competition and Patent Term Restoration Act of 1984 (Public Law 98-417) and the Orphan Drug Act of 1983 (Public Law 97-414), increased the effective patent life for new compounds.

Figure 1-6 shows recent trends in the average effective patent life for NCEs. As expected, after declining steadily throughout the 1970s and early 1980s, effective patent life rebounded somewhat in the years since 1984.

The end of the effective patent life does not always mark the end of exclusive marketing for the NCE. Some compounds may not have generic competitors for several years after the patent expires, either because of delays in FDA approval of generic versions or because the total market for the drug is too small to induce generic manufacturers to enter the market. Occasionally a process patent issued after the original patents will protect a product for some time.

Product line extensions, such as new once-a-day dosage forms, have become increasingly important in protecting the original compound's market against generic competition. The 1984 Drug Price Competition and Patent Term Restoration Act (Public Law 98-417) granted a 3-year period of market exclusivity, regardless of patent status, to any product for which new clinical research is required. Thus, if a new sustained release formulation is developed and approved for the originator compound, the new dosage form has a 3-year period of market exclusivity from the date of its FDA approval regardless of the patent status of the compound itself.

Companies use the terms of the provision to extend the effective exclusivity period by managing the introduction of new dosage forms to coincide with the expiration of the patent on earlier generations of the compound. Physicians almost always prefer extended-release dosage forms because they increase patients' adherence to the prescription. Increasing company incentives to develop products with these benefits is the rationale for the 3-year exclusivity provision in

Figure 1-6—Effective Patent Life for Drugs Approved, 1968-89

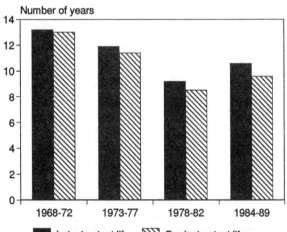

Number of years

■ Latest patent life   ▨ Product patent life

SOURCES: Office of Technology Assessment, 1993. Based on U.S. Congress, House of Representatives, Committee on Energy and Commerce, unpublished data, 1993; U.S. Department of Health and Human Services, Food and Drug Administration, unpublished data, 1991; U.S. Department of Commerce, Patent and Trademark Office, unpublished data, 1991.

the Drug Price Competition Act. Nevertheless, the introduction of these new products can keep the compound's revenues high for years after the effective patent life ends.

POSTPATENT REVENUES

The Drug Price Competition and Patent Term Restoration Act made FDA approval relatively easy for makers of generic copies of originator drugs after patents or market exclusivities expire. It is widely held that this law has led to rapid decline in the originator drug's market share following patent expiration.

OTA analyzed changes in the U.S. market for 35 therapeutic compounds that lost patent protection in from 1984 through 1987 and found that the sales decline is not nearly as steep as is commonly thought—at least not yet. Figures 1-7 and 1-8 show how the compounds' hospital and drugstore sales (in 1990 dollars) and physical units changed before and after the year in which patents expired. Three years after patent expiration, the mean annual dollar sales of the original compound were 83 percent of mean sales revenue in the year of

Figure 1-7—Originator Revenue[a] as a Percent of Originator Revenue in Year of Patent Expiration

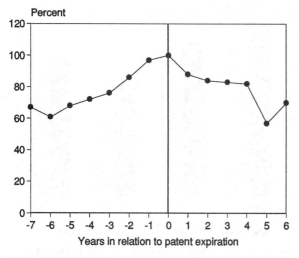

a Based on 1990 dollars.

SOURCE: Office of Technology Assessment, 1993, based on S.W. Schondelmeyer, "Economic Products," contract paper prepared for Office of Technology Assessment, December 1991.

Figure 1-8—Originator Unit Volume as a Percent of Originator Volume in Year of Patent Expiration

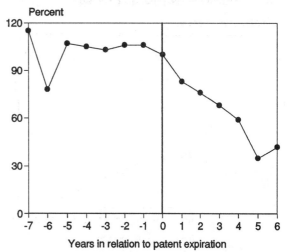

SOURCE: Office of Technology Assessment, 1993, based on S.W. Schondelmeyer, "Economic Products," contract paper prepared for Office of Technology Assessment, December 1991.

patent expiration, while the mean sales volume in physical units was 68 percent of its level in the year of patent expiration.

OTA extended the sales curve beyond the 9th year after U.S. market introduction based on these trends and also made adjustments for sales to other countries and to purchasers other than hospitals and drugstores (see chapter 4 for details). Figure 1-9 shows the projected worldwide sales for NCEs introduced in the United States from 1981 through 1983. OTA assumed that the originator compound would stay on the market only 20 years and that the products are not sold in other countries before they are approved in the United States. Overall, then, the assumptions used to build this projected sales curve were conservative.

■ Costs of Production

Sales revenues from new products must be reduced to reflect the cash outlays required to manufacture and sell them, and the ongoing R&D costs required to produce follow-on products or to justify new uses for the NCE. The net cash flows induce additional tax liabilities as well. OTA estimated these costs using data as available and subtracted them from the net sales revenues over the life of the compound. (See chapter 4 for details of OTA's method.)

■ Net Cash Flows

The 1981-83 NCEs deliver net cash flows of $341 million per compound (discounted to their present value in the year of FDA market approval at 9.8 percent per year). The net after-tax value of the cash flows projected for the 1981-83 cohort of new drugs is $230 million.

■ Net Return on Investment

These net postapproval cash flows must be compared with the present value of the investment in R&D required to discover and develop the compounds. An upper bound on the fully capitalized R&D costs of drugs introduced in the early 1980s is about $359 million before tax savings, or $194 million after tax savings are considered (table 1-2). Thus, **OTA concluded that the average NCE introduced to the U.S. market in the period 1981-83 can be expected to produce dollar returns whose present value is about $36 million more (after taxes) than would be required to bring forth the investment in the R&D.**

Some of the revenue and cost assumptions underlying this analysis were very uncertain, so OTA analyzed the sensitivity of the estimated returns to changes in critical assumptions. The results are somewhat sensitive to the ratio of global sales (about which we know relatively little) to U.S. sales (about which we know much more). If the ratio of global sales to U.S. sales is much greater than 2, as we have reason to believe it may be, the present value of the cash flows would be even more (after taxes) than is necessary to repay the R&D investment.

The results were not very sensitive to changes in the speed with which originator brand sales decline after patent expiration. If the average sales per compound were to decline by 20 percent per year after patent expiration, the present value of the cash flows would be $311 million before taxes and $209 million after taxes, still above the full after-tax cost of R&D. Fully 6 years after the

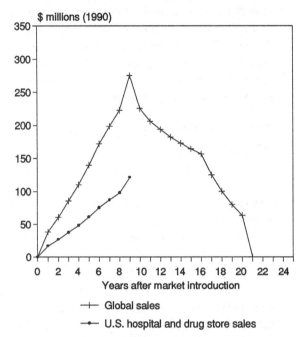

Figure 1-9—Estimated Average Global Sales Profile Per New Chemical Entity Introduced in the United States, 1981-83

SOURCE: Office of Technology Assessment, 1993; based on data from P. Coppinger, "Overview of the Competitiveness of the U.S. Pharmaceutical Industry," presentation to the Council on Competitiveness Working Group on the Drug Approval Process, Washington, DC, December 12, 1990.

passage of the Drug Price Competition and Patent Term Restoration Act there is no evidence that the rate of sales decline for originator compounds after patent expiration is approaching this rate.

What does it mean to have the average revenue per compound deliver $36 million more in present value than was needed to bring forth the research on the drugs in the cohort? **OTA estimated that excess returns over R&D costs would be eliminated if the annual revenue per compound was reduced by 4.3 percent over the product's life.**

These estimates are rough predictions of the actual returns that the 1981-83 cohort of NCE's will earn over their full product lives. OTA attempted to be conservative in measuring returns, but the estimate is subject to measurement error whose magnitude is not easily assessed.

More importantly, the analysis illustrates how volatile net returns can be for drugs introduced in different time periods. This report documents how rapidly both worldwide revenues and the average cost of R&D for each new NCE can change. The wide variation in R&D costs and sales revenues across individual drugs means that estimates of both average R&D costs and returns could vary over short periods of time.

TOTAL PHARMACEUTICAL INDUSTRY RETURNS

Another more indirect way to measure returns on R&D is to estimate the profitability of research-intensive pharmaceutical companies. Pharmaceutical firms invest in the discovery, development, production, marketing and distribution of many products, including some that are not ethical pharmaceuticals. The total profit or return on a company's investment in a given period is a mixture of returns on past investments made over many previous years on many different projects.

At the company level, the return on investment is defined by the internal rate of return (IRR), the interest rate at which the net present value of all cash flows into and out of the firm equals zero. If the IRR across all companies in an industry is greater than the industry's cost of capital, one would expect to see increased investment in the industry, including R&D, as investors enter to reap the high rewards. In a dynamically competitive industry, IRRs much greater than the cost of capital can not persist indefinitely. If abnormally high profits persist for a long time, one would suspect that barriers to entry or other forms of monopoly power (perhaps obtained through patent protection) might exist in the industry (86). On the other hand, a low IRR compared with the cost of capital would lead to disinvestment in the industry, including R&D.

The annual financial reports of public companies contain estimates of company profit rates based on accounting records. For example, net income as a percent of total "book value" of assets is a commonly used benchmark of firm profitability (301). Companies themselves report this ratio in their annual financial statements and compare their return on assets in one year with that in previous years. Other commonly used profit ratios, such as net operating income as a percent of sales, are also easily computed from company financial statements.

It is not surprising, then, that analysts would compare the accounting profit rates of firms in the industry with those of firms in other industries (301,457). The ready availability of publicly reported and independently audited data and the widespread use of these measures by companies themselves invites such comparisons. By these conventional accounting measures, the pharmaceutical industry looks very profitable compared with other industries (301,457). But these comparisons are limited in two important ways.

First, accounting profits are poor measures of true IRRs. Revenues and costs recognized in accounting statements don't correspond very well to actual cash flows. And, because profits are computed over a limited period, they don't adjust properly for the time profile of cash flows from various investments made in previous times or for payoffs that won't occur until after the profit measurement period.

Second, even if accounting profits are corrected to correspond more closely to IRRs, differences in rates of return among industries might reflect differences in their riskiness (and hence in the cost of capital). Simple comparisons that do not address differences in risk among industries can be misleading.

OTA commissioned a study comparing the IRR of 54 U.S.-based research-intensive pharmaceutical companies with the IRRs of two control groups, each with 54 firms, selected to be most similar to the pharmaceuticals on certain financial characteristics (27) (see chapter 4 for details). The accounting profit rate for the pharmaceutical companies was 4 to 6 percentage points per year higher in the study period (1976-87) than for the control firms.

The contractors used a new technique that adjusts accounting profits to obtain a closer approximation of IRRs. IRRs cannot be measured with precision, because assumptions are required about the time profile of returns on investments, but across a wide range of assumptions about timing of cash flows, the estimated internal rate of return in the pharmaceutical firms over the 12-year study period (1976-87) was on average 2 to 3 percentage points higher per year than the internal rate of return in either control group.

The contractors did not address the question of whether a 2 to 3 percentage point difference in internal rates of return can be explained by differences in the cost of capital between pharmaceuticals and control firms. If investment in the pharmaceutical industry is riskier than in the control firms, then the cost of capital will be higher. OTA calculated the difference in the cost of capital between the pharmaceutical industry and each of the two control samples. OTA found that the cost of capital for the pharmaceutical industry was higher by 0.7 percentage points per year than one of the control samples, but lower by 1.6 percentage points than the other.

The cost of capital can vary widely over time with underlying interest rates and expected inflation, so precise measurement of each group's cost of capital over the study period is impossible. In addition, OTA's method may be subject to biases in measurement. We used the same method consistently across all samples, however, so the biases would tend to cancel themselves out when examining differences in the cost of capital between pharmaceuticals and controls. Therefore, **OTA concluded that returns to the pharmaceutical industry as a whole over the 12-year period from 1976 to 1987 were higher by 2 to 3 percentage points per year than returns to nonpharmaceutical firms, after adjusting for differences in risk.**

INDUSTRY RESPONSE: INCREASING R&D

In an industry with a large number of active competitors, high returns (compared with the cost of capital) should attract new investment capital. Data on aggregate domestic and worldwide pharmaceutical R&D reveal a rapid increase in real R&D spending beginning in 1980 and continuing today. Total R&D conducted by U.S.-based pharmaceutical companies in 1975 was about $1.1 billion; by 1990, this spending had grown to between $7.9 billion and $8.1 billion (table 1-3). **After adjusting for inflation, U.S.-based companies' foreign and domestic R&D spending increased at about 9 percent per year between 1975 and 1990. The rate of increase accelerated over the period. Before 1980, U.S. companies' real worldwide R&D spending increased by only 5 to 6 percent per year. Between 1985 and**

Table 1-3—Aggregate Pharmaceutical Foreign and Domestic R&D, Selected Years ($ billions)

| | 1975 | 1980 | 1985 | 1987 | 1990 | Annual percent rate of change | | |
						1975-80	1980-85	1985-90
Compustat[TMa]								
Current dollars...............	$1.10	$2.08	$4.20	$5.53	$7.90	13.6%	15.1%	13.5%
Constant 1990 dollars[b].........	2.44	3.19	4.98	6.19	7.90	5.5	9.3	9.7
Pharmaceutical Manufacturers Association[c]								
Current dollars................	1.06	1.98	4.08	5.51	8.13	13.2	15.6	14.8
Constant 1990 dollars..........	2.36	3.03	4.83	6.17	8.13	5.2	9.8	10.9

[a] Figures are based on a total of 133 firms listed in the Compustat file under Standard Industrial Code (SIC) code 2834 in at least 1 year between 1971 and 1990. The number of firms vary from year to year due to firms' entry and exit from SIC 2834.
[b] Adjusted by GNP implicit price deflator.
[c] R&D expenditures reported by Pharmacuetical Manufacturers Association member firms.

SOURCE: Office of Technology Assessment, 1993, based on unpublished data provided by S.H. Kang, School of Industrial Administration, Carnegie-Mellon University, Pittsburgh, PA; Pharmaceutical Manufacturers Association, *Annual Survey Reports*, 1975-91 (Washington, DC: PMA, 1976-91).

Table 1-4—HMG-CoA Reductase Inhibitors Currently or Formerly Under Development

Compound	Sponsor	Approval Status
lovastatin	Merck	IND: April 1984. NDA: November 1986. Approval: August 1987.
pravastatin	Sankyo, Bristol-Myers Squibb	Launched in Canada, Europe, Japan, and Mexico. U.S. NDA: January 31, 1989. U.S. approval: November 31, 1991.
simvastatin	Merck	Launched in at least 17 countries worldwide, including most of Europe. U.S. NDA: November 1986. U.S. approval: December 1991.
colestolone	American Cyanamid	Entered U.S. clinical trials in 1987.
fluvastatin	Sandoz	U.S. NDA filed March 1992.
crilvastain	Pan Medica	Phase II clinical trials.
dalvastatin	Rhone-Poulenc Rorer	Phase III clinical trials.
BAYW6228	Bayer	Phase II clinical trials.
HR780	Hoeschst	Phase II clinical trials.
CI 981	Warner-Lambert	Phase I clinical trials.
BB-476	British Bio-technology	Series of compounds under development; preclinical.
BMY-22566	Bristol-Myers Squibb	Preclinical studies.
SQ-33600	Bristol-Myers Squibb	Preclinical studies, discontinued.
BMY-21950	Bristol-Myers Squibb	Phase I clinical trials.
GR-95030	Glaxo	Preclinical studies, discontinued.
SC-45355	Searle	Preclinical studies, discontinued.
L-659699	Merck	Preclinical studies.
L-669262	Merck	Preclinical studies.
CP-83101	Pfizer	Preclinical studies.

SOURCE: Office of Technology Assessment, 1993.

1990, they increased at about 10 percent per year.[15] These data do not even fully reflect the rapid increase in spending by small research-intensive biotechnology companies, a phenomenon that began in the early 1980s.

OTA's findings on returns to pharmaceutical R&D and to the industry as a whole explain why R&D expenditures have risen so fast throughout the 1980s. Investors followed the promise of high returns on future innovations. Ultimately investment in research is determined by expected revenues. The dramatic increase in real revenues to new drugs throughout the 1980s has sent signals to the industry that more investment will be rewarded handsomely. The industry has responded as expected, by increasing its commitment to investment, including R&D.

What will this increased investment mean for pharmaceutical returns in the future? Some of the research dollars are pursuing the development of me-too NCEs that will compete with similar products already on the market. For example, the first HMG-CoA reductase inhibitor—a new class of drugs that lowers cholesterol—was approved for marketing by the FDA in 1987. Today, three compounds are approved for marketing, one is awaiting approval, and 12 others are under active development (table 1-4). Over time, the entry of new products should dampen the potential returns on research into new NCEs in this class, as companies spend more and more money developing competing products and fighting for a share of the market.

Some research dollars are pursuing new classes of drugs, which may supplant older therapies or create new markets in areas where there was before no effective therapy. Several companies have current research programs on drugs for Alzheimer's disease, a major cause of dementia in older people, but so far no drug can offer substantial improvements in patient functioning. (See chapter 5, box 5-E for more information on

---

[15] Because spending in various countries must be converted into a common currency, exchange rate changes can affect reported spending. The devaluation of the dollar after 1985 may be responsible for some of the unusually high increase in total spending reported in recent years.

the status of research into drug therapies for Alzheimer's disease.) Successes in these areas could mean a new cycle of high returns to the pioneer and early me-too compounds but lower returns to the later entrants who must compete for market share in the class.

PAYMENT POLICY AND RETURNS ON R&D

Future returns to the research-intensive pharmaceutical industry depend not only on the opportunities created by scientific research, but also on the regulatory and market conditions that will govern the sale of pioneer and me-too products. OTA examined recent trends in payment policies that affect the market for new pharmaceuticals.

Sales of new ethical drugs depend on physicians' decisions to prescribe them and on patients' decisions to buy them. Physicians and patients base these decisions on judgments about a drug's quality and price compared with the quality and price of existing alternatives. The tradeoff between perceived quality and price depends on many factors, including the severity of the disease or condition for which a drug is intended, evidence of its effectiveness compared with alternative courses of action, the availability of close substitutes, and the effectiveness of advertising and promotion in convincing doctors the drug is the right choice for the patient (86).

■ Importance of Health Insurance in Determining Demand

When a patient's health insurance plan covers prescription drugs, the balance between perceived quality and price tips in favor of quality. While it protects consumers from uncontrollable and catastrophic expenses, health insurance also reduces the effective price of health care services and products. By reducing patients' out-of-pocket cost, health insurance makes them less sensitive to price than they would otherwise be (516).

Insurance coverage for prescription drugs in the United States changed during the 1980s in two ways that made the demand for prescription drugs

Table 1-5—Percent of U.S Population With Outpatient Prescription Drug Coverage, 1979 and 1987[a]

	1979	1987
People under 65..............	71-73	73-77
People 65 and over............	36	43-46
Total.......................	67-69%	70-74%

[a] A detailed memorandum describing OTA's methods in preparing this table is available upon request.

SOURCE: Office of Technology Assessment, 1993; based on sources listed in table 10-2.

even less sensitive to price than it was before. First, the percent of Americans with outpatient prescription drug benefits increased, albeit modestly, over the 1980s, from 67-69 percent in 1979 to 70-74 percent in 1987, the latest year for which good data are available (see table 1-5). Although few Americans had insurance plans that covered outpatient drugs in full, the mere existence of insurance coverage makes patients less sensitive to price than they would be without such coverage (294).

Second, the structure of outpatient prescription drug benefits changed markedly over the period. In the past, almost all nonelderly people with outpatient drug benefits had "major medical" plans with an overall annual deductible that had to be met before insurance would help pay for any services or drugs. By 1989, 30 percent of these people had policies that required fixed copayments for prescription drugs instead of including them in the overall deductible (table 1-6). The vast majority of people with fixed copayments per prescription in 1989 paid $5 or less per prescription (35). The insurance company picked up the rest of the bill regardless of its amount.

The switch from overall deductibles to fixed copayments for prescription drugs means a richer insurance benefit structure for prescription drugs. For people whose annual medical expenses lie below their plan's annual deductible (commonly $200 or $250 per year), a flat copayment for prescription drugs means lower out-of-pocket prescription drug costs than do major medical restrictions. Even when patients do meet the deductible in a year, many would have higher

Table 1-6—Limitations of Prescription Drug Benefits Among Nonelderly People With Private Health Insurance Covering Prescription Drugs

	1977[a]	1989/1990[b]
Full coverage	3%	3%
Separate limits (copayments)[c]	9	30
Overall limits (major medical)[d]	88	61
Other limits[e]		7

[a] Results based on 1977 National Medical Care Expenditure Study Survey of employers and insurers of individuals under 65 years of age.

[b] Results based on U.S. Bureau of Labor Statistics 1989 and 1990 surveys of employers.

[c] "Separate limits" refers to restrictions applicable only to prescription drugs, such as a copayment for each prescription.

[d] "Overall limits" refers to restrictions applicable to a broader set of medical services. For example, a major medical policy may carry a $100 deductible and 20-percent coinsurance rate that applies to all covered services, not just prescription drugs.

[e] Other limits include policies that combine fixed copayments with overall limits.

SOURCE: Office of Technology Assessment, 1993, based on data from P.J. Farley, *Private Health Insurance in the U.S. Data Preview #23*, DHHS Publication No. (PHS) 86-3406, 1986. U.S. Department of Health and Human Services, National Center for Health Services Research and Health Care Technology Assessment, September 1986; U.S. Department of Labor, Bureau of Labor Statistics, *Employee Benefits in Medium and Large Firms, 1989*, Bulletin 2363 (Washington, DC: U.S. Government Printing Office, June 1990); U.S. Department of Labor, Bureau of Labor Statistics, *Employee Benefits in Small Private Establishments, 1990*, Bulletin 2388 (Washington, DC: U.S. Government Printing Office, September 1991); U.S. Department of Labor, Bureau of Labor Statistics, *Employee Benefits in State and Local Governments, 1990* (Washington, DC: U.S. Government Printing Office, February 1992).

out-of-pocket prescription drug costs under a major medical plan than under a fixed copayment.[16]

The impact of these improvements in prescription drug insurance benefits shows up in insurance reimbursements. The percent of total outpatient prescription drug spending in the United States paid for by insurance increased substantially, from 28 to 44 percent, between 1977 and 1987 (figure 1-10). The same trend holds among elderly Americans, for whom private insurance paid for about 36 percent of outpatient prescription drug expenses in 1987 compared with only 23 percent in 1977.

Most private and public health insurers have little power to restrict physicians' prescribing decisions. Private insurers generally cover all prescription drugs the FDA has licensed for sale in the United States (35). Thus, FDA approval is a *de facto* insurance coverage guideline. If the physician orders a specific compound, the insurer routinely pays its share of the costs.

Despite the fact that many compounds, though protected from generic competition by patents or other market exclusivity provisions, compete for market share with similar compounds, that competition tends to focus on product characteristics, such as ease of use, favorable side-effect profiles, or therapeutic effects, and not on price.[17] Companies spend a great deal on this product competition. One major U.S. pharmaceutical company reported recently that about 28 percent of its sales went for marketing (advertising and promotion) expenses (119a).

Emphasizing product competition over price competition is a rational strategy for companies operating in a market that is not very sensitive to price differentials among similar compounds. If prescribing physicians will not be swayed by lower prices, it would be foolhardy for firms to set prices for their products much lower than those of competitors. Unless or until the demand for prescription drugs becomes more price sensitive, the benefits of the competitive R&D on prices will not be felt.

■ Different Buyers Pay Different Prices

Ethical drugs are sold through multiple distribution channels, and companies can set different

---

[16] In most major medical plans, the insured person is responsible for sharing 20 percent or more of the cost of services above the deductible. Under a 20 percent major-medical cost-sharing requirement, any prescription with a price greater than $25 would cost the insured person more than it would a patient with the most frequent separate copayment rate. For example, a $30 prescription would cost someone with a major medical policy and a 20-percent cost-sharing requirement $6, whereas the typical cost under a flat copayment would be only $5.

[17] This is not to say that price competition among competing brand-name compounds is entirely absent, or that prices of pioneer drugs are established without any concern for their effect on patient demand. Anecdotal reports suggest that new NCEs are often launched at lower prices compared with competing drugs, but the discounts are typically not high and they rarely lead the manufacturers of other compounds to meet price reductions.

Figure 1-10—Sources of Payment for Prescribed Medicines in the United States

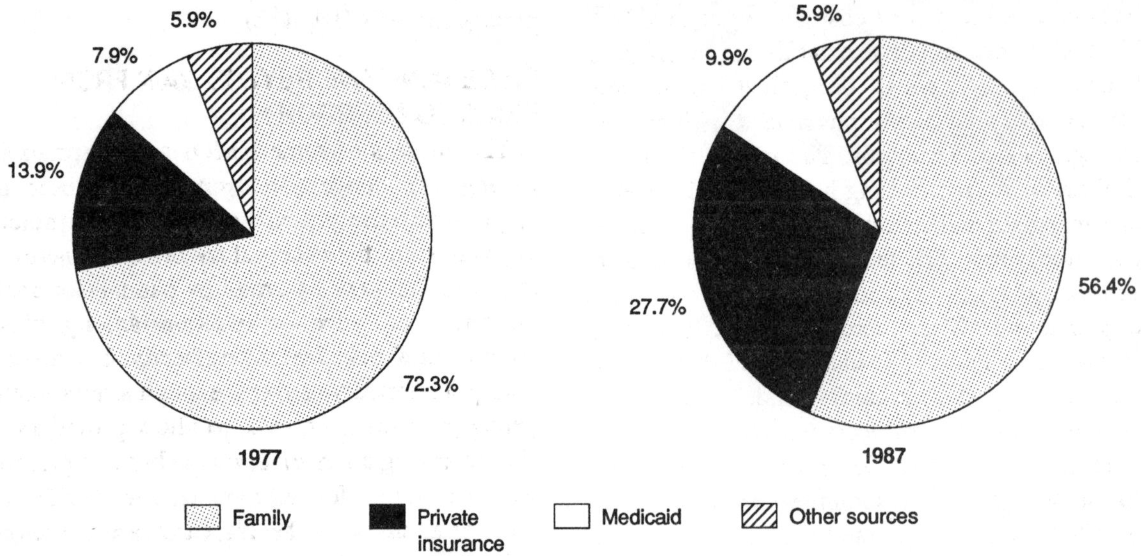

1977

1987

Family   Private insurance   Medicaid   Other sources

a Other sources include Workmen's Compensation, Medicare, other State and local programs, and any other source of payment.

SOURCE: Data from J.F. Moeller, Senior Project Director, U.S. Department of Health and Human Services, Public Health Service, Agency for Health Care Policy and Research, Rockville, MD, personal communication, Mar. 12, 1991; J.A. Kasper, Prescribed Medicines: Use, Expenditures, and Sources of Payment, Data Preview (Washington, DC: U.S. Department of Health and Human Services, National Center for Health Services Research, April 1982).

prices to different kinds of buyers. For example, companies can sell direct to HMOs[18] or large hospital chains and offer lower prices than they charge for drugs sold to community pharmacies. The ability to charge different prices to different kinds of buyers is referred to as **price discrimination**. Price discrimination increases profits by separating buyers who are price sensitive from those who are not.

Price discrimination in pharmaceutical markets takes its most extreme form when companies offer expensive drugs free or at reduced charge to people who cannot easily afford them because they lack insurance and have low incomes. Many pharmaceutical firms have developed such programs in recent years (327,458). In a separate background study under this project, OTA examined Ceredase™, a new drug for a rare inherited disease, whose high annual cost (at least $58,000

per year for the drug alone for the remainder of the patient's life) threatens to exhaust many patients' lifetime insurance benefits (141).[19] The company that makes Ceredase™ provides the drug free to patients who have exhausted their benefits or do not have health insurance. Although these programs respond in a compassionate way to a real need, they also separate the market into two components—one with very high price sensitivity (uninsured people) and one with very low price sensitivity (insured people). The Ceredase™ program is similar in its consequences to offering a patient a lifetime supply of the drug in exchange for the remaining value of his or her insurance coverage plus associated premiums.

PRICE-SENSITIVE BUYERS PAY LOWER PRICES

HMOs, particularly those with tight organizational structures, have both the incentive and the

[18] Unlike traditional fee-for-service insurance plans, HMOs (sometimes referred to as "prepaid health plans") collect a set premium for each member, but charge either nothing or a relatively small amount for each individual service. People enrolled in the HMO must receive their health care from providers designated by the HMO.

[19] Approximately 71 percent of private insurance policy beneficiaries face a lifetime maximum benefit of $1 million or less (491).

ability to influence physicians' prescribing practices to take account of cost as well as quality.[20] They can do this by establishing restrictive "formularies," lists of drugs that can be prescribed by participating physicians without special appeals or approvals. The power to impose limitations on prescribing has given HMOs purchasing clout with manufacturers and, over the past few years, has led manufacturers to offer substantial price discounts to some of these organizations. When there are several close substitutes in a therapeutic class, the HMO can use the formulary as a bargaining chip to exact price concessions from producers.[21]

Hospitals also have an incentive to establish formularies for drugs administered to inpatients. In 1983, Medicare adopted a new "prospective payment system" that pays hospitals on the basis of the admission, not the specific services each patient uses.[22] This system created incentives for hospitals to reduce both length of stay and the cost of services offered per stay, including drugs. The incentive to develop restrictive formularies is limited, however, because most insured nonelderly hospitalized people pay for hospital care on the basis of charges for individual products and services. Pharmacy charges are passed on to the private insurance company. Nevertheless, the number of hospital pharmacies adopting formularies increased steadily in the mid-1980s. The percent of hospitals with a well-controlled formulary increased from 54 percent in 1985 to 58 percent in 1989 (101,412).

PRICE-SENSITIVE BUYERS GAIN FROM PRICE COMPETITION

The success of some HMOs and hospitals in getting price concessions from manufacturers of single-source drugs (i.e., those with patent protection) attests to the potential for price competition to lower the cost of drugs to patients or their insurers. For price competition among close therapeutic alternatives to be effective in a market with price-sensitive buyers, enough similar competing products must exist to allow providers to choose among alternatives on the basis of price as well as quality. Me-too products, often derided as not contributing to health care, are therefore necessary to obtain the benefits of price competition in segments of the market that are price sensitive.

Most of the new drugs entering the world market in recent years have offered little therapeutic advantage over pre-existing competitors. A 1990 European study of the therapeutic value of new drugs first introduced in at least one of seven industrialized countries[23] between 1975 and 1989 found that only 30 percent of all NCEs were classified by a group of experts as "adding something to therapy" compared with compounds already on the market (37).[24] The rest fell into categories that could be called me-toos. About 42 percent of those NCEs originated in the

---

[20] Enrollment in HMOs grew from 4 percent of the population in 1980 to 14 percent in 1990 (209). But, many HMOs do not give their doctors incentives to economize in drug prescribing. A recent review of seven HMOs found the plans were structured so that the prescribing physician never bore financial risk for prescription drug costs (515). These HMOs were all individual practice associations or networks. These kinds of HMOs tend to have looser fiscal controls than staff-model HMOs, where physicians are either employees or partners in the organization. In 1990, pharmaceutical sales to staff-model HMOs made up 2.4 percent of the pharmaceutical market.

[21] The power of certain classes of purchasers to exact discounts was recognized by the framers of the 1990 Medicaid Rebate law (Public Law 101-508) which requires manufacturers to offer Medicaid the "best price" (i.e., lowest price) they offer to private purchasers if the manufacturer wants to sell its products to the Medicaid patient. The strategy may have backfired, however, because manufacturers eliminated many such discounts to HMOs and hospitals when they found that they would lose the amount of the discount on a large part of their total market (431). (Medicaid makes up 10 to 15 percent of the market for outpatient drugs.)

[22] Medicare beneficiaries accounted for 45.2 percent of inpatient hospital days in 1989 and for 33 percent of the discharges (164).

[23] The seven countries were the France, Germany, Great Britain, Italy, Japan, Switzerland, and the United States.

[24] Each product was evaluated by several experts, including doctors, pharmacists, chemists, and pharmacologists, each working within the therapeutic area of the new product. The study report contains little detail on the methods used to rate drugs, so the validity of the ratings has not been verified. Over 65 percent of all compounds introduced in 1980-84 and rated as offering added therapeutic benefit were marketed in at least four of the seven industrialized countries, compared with only 31 percent of the drugs judged to offer no additional benefits.

Table-1-7—New Chemical and Biological Entities Entering the World Market by Therapeutic Category, 1975-89

	1975-79		1980-84		1985-89	
	Total	% with therapeutic gain	Total	% with therapeutic gain	Total	% with therapeutic gain
Antibiotics	25	36%	27	44%	33	27%
Anticancer	14	64	16	50	14	36
Antivirus	3	33	2	50	8	75
Cardiovascular	35	43	36	33	68	27
Nervous System	29	35	32	25	24	17
Anti-ulcer	3	67	7	29	15	20
Hormones	12	17	13	39	10	50
Anti-inflammatory	26	23	30	13	19	5

SOURCE: P.E. Barral, "Fifteen Years of Pharmaceutical Research Results Throughout the World 1975-1989," (Antony, France: Foundation Rhone-Poulenc Sante, August 1990).

United States were judged to offer therapeutic benefits, so well over one-half of all drugs introduced in the United States were judged to offer no therapeutic benefit. Over the entire study period, the majority of drugs in almost every therapeutic category did not "add something to therapy" (see table 1-7). These results suggest the supply of therapeutic competitors is large and the potential for price competition in those segments of the market with price-sensitive buyers is potentially vast.

The problem with me-too drugs is not that they are sometimes imitative or of modest therapeutic benefit. Imitation is an important dimension of competition, and the more choices consumers have, the more intense will be the competition. The personal computer industry provides a clear illustration of how rapid improvements in quality can coincide with steep price reductions (46). The problem with me-too drugs is that a large part of the market in the United States is very insensitive to price and does not get the full benefits of price competition that would be expected from the availability of an array of similar products.

GENERIC COMPETITION GIVES INSURERS MORE CONTROL OVER DRUG PRICES

Once a drug loses patent protection, it is vulnerable to competition from copies whose therapeutic equivalence is verified by the FDA. These generic competitors compete largely on the basis of price, since they can claim no quality advantage over the brand-name drug.

Private and public health insurers have initiated programs to encourage dispensing of cheaper versions of multisource compounds (those with generic equivalents on the market). These strategies include using mail-order pharmacies, waiving beneficiaries' cost-sharing requirements when prescriptions are filled with generic versions, or refusing to pay more than a certain amount for a drug with a generic competitor. Medicaid, the health insurance program for the poor, mandates substitution with cheaper generic drugs unless the prescribing physician specifically prohibits it in writing on the prescription form.

These programs have substantially reduced brand-name compounds' unit sales and revenues, but it takes several years after the compound's patent expires for the full brunt of generic competition to be felt (see figures 1-7 and 1-8). Indeed, OTA found that 6 years after patent expiration, brand-name drugs still held over 50 percent of the market in physical units (table 1-8).

PRICING SYSTEMS DIFFER ACROSS COUNTRIES

Not only is the market for prescription drugs segmented among different classes of buyers in the United States, but it is also segmented internationally. Pharmaceutical companies

Table 1-8—Originator's Market Share for 35
Compounds Losing Patent Protection 1984-87

Year[a]	Dollar Sales	Unit Sales[b]
−7	100%	100%
−6	99	100
−5	99	100
−4	99	100
−3	99	100
−2	99	100
−1	99	100
0	95	94
+1	86	73
+2	84	65
+3	84	57
+4	85	51
+5	83	44
+6	85	62

[a] Year 0 is the year of patent expiration.
[b] Unit sales are measured in defined daily dose.

SOURCE: Office of Technology Assessment, 1993, based on S.W. Schondelmeyer, "Economic Impact of Multiple Source Competition on Originator Products," contract paper prepared for Office of Technology Assessment, U.S. Congress, December 1991.

charge different prices for the same drug in different countries (439a,457).

Most other industrialized countries have universal health insurance that includes prescription drugs, so patients' demand for drugs is not very sensitive to the price charged. Nevertheless, the prices paid tend to be more strictly controlled by the third-party payers in these countries than in the United States. Drug payment policy in each of these other countries is governed by two potentially conflicting objectives: minimization of health insurance prescription drug costs and encouragement of the domestic pharmaceutical industry. National prescription drug payment policies represent a blend between these objectives. In other industrialized countries, drug payment policy is generally developed with explicit recognition of the two policy objectives.

Virtually all of the five countries whose pharmaceutical reimbursement systems OTA reviewed—Australia, Canada, France, Japan, and the United Kingdom—use some mechanism for controlling the price of single-source as well as multiple-source drugs. Four of the five countries do so directly by setting payment rates for new drugs based on the cost of existing therapeutic alternatives. The pricing policies in these countries reward pioneer, or "breakthrough," drugs with higher prices than me-too drugs, although they accomplish this objective through different mechanisms, and the prices of breakthrough drugs may still be low in comparison with those obtained in the United States.

These countries obtain reduced prices for new drugs through pricing systems that do not use market mechanisms or price competition to determine the demand for prescription drugs. They use price regulation or price control as a substitute for price competition. The importance of politics in determining prices in countries with price controls is illustrated by the favorable prices explicitly granted to locally developed or manufactured products in some of the countries whose pharmaceutical payment systems OTA examined. In contrast, prices in the United States are determined in the market, but, because of the structure of health insurance, a large part of the market gives inadequate consideration to price in making prescribing and purchasing decisions.

■ Implications of Increasing Price Competition for R&D

If the price-sensitive segment of the market for health care services in the United States continues to grow, either through natural evolution or through a national health reform initiative, revenues from many existing and new drugs would fall as price competition expands. The United States accounts for 27 percent of total spending on ethical pharmaceuticals among countries in the Organization for Economic Cooperation and Development and is the largest single national market. Changes in the U.S. market therefore can have a major impact on worldwide pharmaceutical revenues.

A decline in expected revenues would reduce a drug's expected returns and would certainly cause R&D on some new drug products to be discontinued or reduced. The market may not support as many close competitors in a therapeutic class. R&D on me-too drugs could decline as firms come to realize that the makers of pioneer drugs will respond to competition with price reductions of their own.

Research on pioneer drugs could also decline as firms realize that the returns to the winner are likely to be reduced by early price competition from me-too drugs. Fewer competitors might follow each specific line of research, and companies might choose to specialize in certain scientific or medical areas. How such dynamic changes in the R&D environment might affect aggregate R&D investment is impossible to predict with any certainty. Much would depend on the supply of technological opportunities, regulatory barriers to new drugs, and the present availability of acceptable therapies for specific diseases. **It is likely, however, that industrywide investment in R&D would grow more slowly or even decline.**

Systems that control prices, especially those that control the launch prices of new drugs, also affect R&D, and it is even more difficult to predict the directions or overall magnitude of their effect on R&D. The effects would depend on how prices were set and how high they are. For example, a system that controlled only the prices of me-too drugs could have effects on R&D that are very different from a system that controlled all new drug prices. Price regulation adds an additional level of uncertainty to the process of R&D which, as a new risk, lowers expected returns from R&D investments.

Would a decline in R&D or a slowdown in its rate of growth be a bad thing? A widely accepted principle is that, left to its own devices, private industry invests too little in R&D. The patent system, which offers temporary monopolies over new products, processes, and uses, is built on this principle (366). The monopoly granted by patents allows firms to charge more for inventions than they could without such protection from competition. Other public policies, such as subsidies and tax policies that favor R&D, are predicated on the assumption that patents alone are insufficient to bring forth the level of R&D that maximizes the general welfare of society. The high direct

Federal subsidies of basic research and training of scientific personnel are a result of the principle that private industry has inadequate incentives to engage in basic research.

Despite this general principle, there is no theoretical basis for predicting that R&D is always lower than the socially optimal level. When R&D takes place under conditions of rivalry, as it certainly does in pharmaceuticals, that rivalry can lead to wasteful and duplicative R&D efforts and lower returns to the public as a whole than to private industry (102,170,222, 338,365,418). That is, the public can end up paying too much for the benefits it receives from the competitive R&D. The relationship between private and social returns depends on many factors, such as the cost of innovation, the profitability of existing products the innovation will replace, how easy it is for rivals to copy innovations, how easy it is for a new company to enter a particular field, and how rival companies react to each others' moves (222,365).

Statistical studies of the private and social rates of return on R&D in other industries generally find rates of return on R&D to the public as a whole substantially greater than private rates of return on R&D (166). Yet, in the pharmaceutical industry health insurance weakens the role of price competition, so findings from other industries are not germane to pharmaceuticals. **Because the "appropriate" level of demand for prescription drugs in the United States cannot be inferred from the existing level of demand, it is impossible to know whether on the whole there is too much R&D or too little R&D on new drugs.**

THE REGULATION OF PHARMACEUTICAL R&D

Numerous regulations at both the State and Federal level in the United States control the products of the pharmaceutical industry. But, the Federal Food, Drug, and Cosmetic (FD&C) Act has the greatest influence over the drug R&D process. As the agency charged with implementing this body of law and regulation, the FDA has slowly grown in importance since its inception in 1938.

Regulatory requirements unquestionably increase the cost and time necessary to bring a new drug to market. Because it is difficult to sort out the effects of regulation from other factors that could alter drug R&D time and costs, however, the effect cannot be quantified. Most studies of the impact of FDA regulation on the cost of bringing new drugs to market examined the effect of the 1962 Kefauver-Harris Amendments, which added the requirement that drugs must be shown to be effective as well as safe before they can be approved for marketing. Little attention has been paid to how more recent management and regulatory changes at the FDA altered the resources required for the drug R&D process.

Since 1977, the FDA has undertaken a number of initiatives to simplify and clarify the new drug review process and to expedite the review of new drugs identified by the agency as therapeutically important. Most of the initiatives were implemented in the late 1980s, so their effects, if any, on the cost or speed of the R&D process may not yet be discernible.

One initiative designed to make important but not-yet-approved drugs for life-threatening conditions available quickly to the public is the Treatment Investigational New Drug (IND) program. Established in 1987, the Treatment IND program codifies a long-standing agency practice of releasing investigational drugs to practicing physicians on a case-by-case basis for use in the treatment of immediately life-threatening diseases where no immediate alternative treatment exists. To date, 23 drugs have been made available under this program.

A unique feature of the Treatment IND program is that the sponsoring firm may sell the drug to patients under the program at a price that covers not only manufacturing and handling costs, but R&D as well. Five Treatment INDs have so far

Photo credit: *NATIONAL INSTITUTES OF HEALTH*

Aerial view of the National Institutes of Health campus in Bethesda, Maryland. Over $2 billion is spent each year on intramural research in Federal biomedical laboratories.

been supplied by the sponsor at a price. In the case of alglucerase, the drug's manufacturer generated $5 million in revenue through the Treatment IND while the drug was still in the R&D process (141).

Selling investigational new drugs under the Treatment IND program allows companies to generate returns on their R&D investment before the FDA has certified that the drug is safe and effective. The FDA, the agency responsible for reviewing companies' requests to charge under a Treatment IND, lacks the expertise and the authority to determine whether cost data provided by companies are accurate and justify the price they wish to charge. In the case of Ceredase™, the price charged under the Treatment IND ($3.00 per unit) was only slightly lower than the drug's price after the drug was approved for marketing ($3.06 per unit in 1991 net of free goods, uncollected revenues and rebates to the Medicaid program) (141).

FEDERAL TAX POLICIES AFFECTING PHARMACEUTICAL R&D

In 1987, drug companies claimed $1.4 billion in credits against their Federal income taxes.[25] Of

---

[25] This does not include over $900 million foreign tax credits. Unlike other tax credits which are designed to stimulate certain types of behavior among taxpayers, foreign tax credits are simply a mechanism to prevent U.S. firms from being taxed twice on income earned in another country.

this amount, only about $90 million was for credits whose specific purpose was to stimulate R&D. The tax credit for conducting business operations in U.S. possessions such as Puerto Rico accounted for over $1.3 billion in foregone taxes from the pharmaceutical industry in 1987. Pharmaceutical companies are the main beneficiary of this tax provision, claiming just over 50 percent of all dollars claimed under this credit in 1987. Overall, the tax credits reduced the amount of taxes drug companies would have otherwise owed the U.S. Government by 36 percent and equaled 15 percent of the industry's taxable U.S. income.

Although the aggregate value of R&D-oriented tax credits *earned* by the industry is relatively small ($105 million), the pharmaceutical industry is a major user of such credits (table 1-9). The pharmaceutical industry earned almost 10 percent of all R&D oriented tax credits in 1987. The industry's differential ability to use such credits attests to its greater research orientation than other industries and the rapid growth of its

research expenditures. These credits represent an indirect subsidy to the industry for undertaking activities deemed to be in the public interest.

FEDERAL SUPPORT FOR PHARMACEUTICAL R&D

The Federal Government is the mainstay of the country's health sciences enterprise. Health-related R&D reached almost $10 billion in 1990. Some of this money is spent in government laboratories on intramural research ($2.6 billion in 1990), but the vast majority of this federally sponsored health-related R&D is awarded to universities and private nonprofit laboratories through extramural grants and contracts. The money not only supports scientists but also has paid for much of the infrastructure of health research facilities in use today at American universities. The Federal Government also provides the bulk of support for training scientific personnel. Some of that training is paid for under research grants and contracts, but in 1989 alone

Table 1-9—Research Tax Credits Earned by the Pharmaceutical Industry in 1987[a]

	Aggregate credit claimed ($ thousands)	Number of firms claiming credit	Aggregate credit earned as a percent of aggregate earned by all industries
Research and experimentation tax credit[b]			
Firms with assets < $50 million..................	$ 6,455	147	3.1%
Firms with assets ≥ $50 million and < $250 million. .	2,042	9	2.0
Firms with assets of $250 million or more..........	88,878	28	12.6
All firms.....................................	97,375	184	9.6
University-based basic research tax credits			
Firms with assets < $50 million..................	3	90	17.3
Firms with assets ≥ $50 million and <$250 million. . .	0	39	0.0
Firms with assets of $250 million or more..........	2,257	43	10.7
All firms.....................................	2,260	990	6.4
Orphan drug tax credits			
Firms with assets < $50 million..................	0	0	—
Firms with assets ≥ $50 million and < $250 million. .	0	0	—
Firms with assets of $250 million or more..........	5,358	8	84.3
All firms.....................................	5,358	8	84.3

a Estimates for tax year 1987 are from the U.S. Treasury's Statistics of Income (SOI) sample weighted to reflect relevant populations. Pharmaceutical industry is defined as SOI industry group 2830 minus firms with assets of $250 million or more *and* known not to be involved in pharmaceuticals. Tax credits *earned* are not equivalent to tax credits *claimed* because the former does not reflect insufficient tax liability in current year, or carry-forwards from previous years.

b Research and experimentation credit estimates are net of university-based basic research credit.

SOURCE: Office of Technology Assessment, 1993. Estimates provided by U.S. Congress, Joint Committee on Taxation.

the NIH spent $256 million on 11,585 training awards in the life sciences.

Although most of the research supported by the NIH and other Federal health research organizations is aimed at understanding the basic mechanisms of health and disease, the Federal Government supports a substantial amount of research directly targeted to the development of new pharmaceuticals. OTA estimates that NIH and other Public Health Service (PHS) research organizations spent approximately $400 million in 1988 for preclinical pharmaceutical research and $250 million for clinical pharmaceutical R&D. This spending includes 13 targeted drug development programs whose specific mission is to develop new medications for particular diseases or conditions.

The pharmaceutical industry is particularly adept at mining the motherlode of knowledge created by government-sponsored biomedical research and training. The pharmaceutical industry benefits from the Federal investment in extramural and intramural research through its collaborations with universities and academic researchers and through its contacts with intramural researchers at NIH and other Federal health research laboratories. In the past decade, Federal technology transfer policies have provided new incentives for both federally supported academic researchers and government researchers to collaborate with private industry in bringing to the market patentable inventions arising from federally supported research.

∎ Federal Technology Transfer Policy

Today, any inventions arising out of the substantial Federal support to academic research are essentially the property of those institutions. The Bach-Dole Patent and Trademark Act of 1980 (Public Law 96-517) gave universities, nonprofit organizations and small businesses the rights to inventions resulting from research supported with Federal grants. This law was in part the impetus for the creation in the 1980s of university-sponsored enterprises whose purpose is to commercialize biomedical research findings.

Universities and nonprofit organizations can license their valuable inventions to commercial enterprises and share in the revenues the inventions generate.

Inventions arising from the $2.6 billion annual investment in intramural Federal research have also been encouraged by legislation whose purpose is to foster commercial innovation. The Stevenson-Wydler Technology Innovation Act of 1980 (Public Law 96-480) made the transfer of Federal technology to the private sector a national policy and a duty of Federal laboratories. Among its provisions, the act required that Federal laboratories spend at least 0.5 percent of their research budgets on efforts to transfer technology from the laboratory to the marketplace. Additional legislation in 1984 directed the Department of Commerce to issue regulations governing licensing of technologies developed in Federal laboratories (Public Law 98-620).

These initiatives proved insufficient to bring about the desired amount of formal interaction between government and industrial scientists. The Federal Technology Transfer (FTT) Act of 1986 (Public Law 99-502) followed with financial and professional incentives to Federal scientists to actively pursue the commercialization of their inventions. The act also requires Federal agencies to share at least 15 percent of royalties from any licensed invention with the inventing scientists, and it directs agencies to establish cash awards with other personnel involved in productive Federal technology transfer activities.

The legislation also permitted Federal laboratories to enter into formal cooperative research and development agreements (CRADAs) in which a Federal agency provides personnel, services, facilities, equipment or resources (but not money) and a private company provides money, personnel, services, facilities, equipment or other resources for R&D. The law leaves implementation of CRADA policy up to the research agency, but as part of a CRADA the Federal laboratory can agree in advance to grant licenses to the collaborating partner on any inventions resulting from research under the agreement.

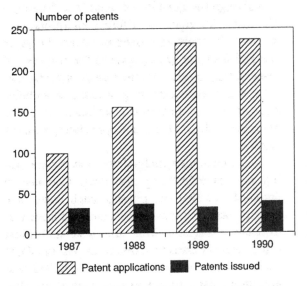

Figure 1-11—Public Health Service Patent Applications and Patents Issued, 1987-90

Number of patents

Patent applications   ▓ Patents issued

SOURCE: The Office of Technology Assessment, 1993. Based on data from U.S. Department of Health and Human Services, Public Health Service, National Institutes of Health, Office of Technology Transfer, 1991.

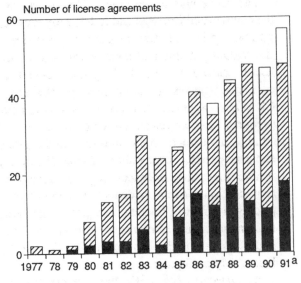

Figure 1-12—Licenses Issued by the U.S. Department of Health and Human Services, Fiscal Years 1977-91

Number of license agreements

Type of license

☐ Research/evaluation   ▓ Exclusive
▨ Nonexclusive

a Number in fiscal year 1991 annualized from the number of agreements reached during first 4 months of the year.

SOURCE: Office of Technology Assessment, 1993. Based on data from U.S. Department of Health and Human Services, Public Health Service, National Institutes of Health, Office of Technology Transfer, 1991.

Early data suggest that the FTT Act may be successful in increasing the patenting of inventions created in Federal biomedical research laboratories. The number of patents filed annually by the Public Health Service (which includes NIH) has grown dramatically since 1987, the first year for which data on PHS patents are available. The number of applications more than doubled between 1987 and 1989 alone (figure 1-11).

▌ Licensing Inventions from Federal Laboratories

The Federal government has steadily increased the number of licenses issued on its biomedical patents throughout the 1980s (figure 1-12). Royalties paid to the inventing agency typically do not exceed 5 to 8 percent of the resulting product sales. The PHS policy is to grant **exclusive** licenses only in cases where substantial additional risks, time and costs must be undertaken by a licensee prior to commercialization (484,486). Otherwise, PHS tries to negotiate nonexclusive

licenses. Firms collaborating with Federal health laboratories under CRADAs, however, may have built into the CRADA at its inception the right to negotiate an exclusive license to any invention arising out of the collaboration. The advent of CRADAS in recent years[26] may portend even more exclusive licenses in the future.

Royalty income to PHS agencies from licenses is a small fraction of the total PHS intramural budget. In 1988, the total NIH royalty income was just 0.03 percent of total NIH intramural spending. NIH takes the position that the purpose of royalties is to stimulate technology transfer by "offering an attractive incentive to encourage [PHS] scientists to participate in collaborations

---

26 109 separate agreements were signed by the end of fiscal year 1990.

with industry. . .'' rather than to augment or replace funds appropriated by Congress for research (75).

The net returns to both the NIH scientists and the commercial firm rise and fall directly with the ultimate price of the product to consumers (individual patients and their private and public health insurers). The PHS policy governing exclusive licenses, including those granted under CRADAs, requires that prices of commercial products be commensurate with the extent of ''public investment in the product, and the health and safety needs of the public'' (486). The policy further states that licensees may be required to provide ''reasonable evidence'' to support their pricing decisions. To date, this policy has been implemented only in one case—the antiviral ddI, manufactured under an exclusive license by Bristol-Myers Squibb.

At present, the PHS has no established mechanism or standards for reviewing the reasonableness of prices for products marketed under exclusive licenses and lacks the legal authority to enforce its policy in cases where prices would be deemed unreasonable.

The need for review of prices of drugs licensed from public agencies results from the failure of the market for prescription drugs to assign appropriate values to new technologies. Because most patients have health insurance policies that pay for a large fraction of the charges for covered drugs and other health care products and services, they may be willing to ''purchase'' such care even when it is worth less to them that what the seller charges. Insurers have little flexibility in choosing what pharmaceuticals to cover and what prices to pay.

Although the question of what is a ''reasonable'' price is subject to differing interpretations, the term is commonly used to mean the price charged does not greatly exceed the full cost of researching, developing, manufacturing, marketing and distributing the drug, where cost includes a return on the investment sufficient to cover investors' risks or failure and opportunity costs of capital.

OTA's contractor study of the costs of developing and manufacturing the drug Ceredase™ demonstrated that determining such costs is a difficult task. Expertise in cost analysis is critical to such a review. Even the best and most sophisticated efforts to assess costs will fall short if they are not based on an audit of detailed cost accounting data. Access to such data is possible only with full cooperation of the company producing the drug.

Implementing PHS's fair pricing clause for exclusive licenses in more than a cursory way could conflict with the Federal goals of technology transfer and the collaborative development of new medicines with industry. When faced with potential government scrutiny of their books and manufacturing processes, some firms may opt not to license drug technology developed at NIH. Whether such reactions would be frequent enough or universal enough to delay the availability of new therapies can only be judged through experience. So far, NIH has been reluctant to take on the task of demanding detailed cost information as part of its technology transfer function.

Research and
Development Expenditures | 2

T his chapter summarizes trends in pharmaceutical research and development (R&D) spending and compares
estimates from available data sources. In short, the
pharmaceutical industry invests more intensively in
R&D than do most industries, and expenditures in constant
dollars have risen at an astonishing rate of roughly 10 percent per
year. Since 1980, pharmaceutical firms in the United States and
abroad have devoted an increasing proportion of total sales to
R&D. How much is spent? What does this record of increasing
real investment in R&D say about the costs and returns to
pharmaceutical R&D, both in the past and in the future? This
chapter addresses these questions.

HOW TO MEASURE R&D SPENDING

There is no single comprehensive source of data on worldwide
spending for pharmaceutical R&D. Because the research-
intensive pharmaceutical industry is a mix of large multinational
companies and small research-oriented firms, it is difficult to
capture all R&D spending on human-use pharmaceuticals in one
data source. R&D data come from three main sources: industry
trade associations, governments, and companies themselves.

The Pharmaceutical Manufacturers Association (PMA) is the
main source of industry trade data on R&D conducted in the
United States by its member companies and abroad by its
U.S.-based businesses.[1] PMA publishes an annual survey of its
60 corporate members, representing about 100 business entities.

---

[1] Domestic R&D data are for PMA members that are U.S.-based companies and U.S.
subsidiaries of foreign companies. Data on foreign R&D expenditures reflect only PMA
members that are U.S.-based companies.

In addition, in 1991, the Centre for Medicines Research, an arm of the Association of the British Pharmaceutical Industry, conducted a survey of pharmaceutical industry trade associations in nine European countries, Japan and the United States (172).

U.S. Government data on domestic R&D expenditures by industry are available from the National Science Foundation (NSF) Survey of Industrial Research and Development conducted routinely since 1956. Each firm in the sample is classified by a three-digit Standard Industrial Classification (SIC) Code.[2] The U.S. Census Bureau on behalf of NSF collects data on total companywide domestic R&D expenditures. The estimates for drug companies (SIC 283) include all R&D conducted in the United States in company-owned and -operated facilities. Unfortunately, nonpharmaceutical R&D may be included in the estimates.

Also, the composition of firms in the pharmaceutical industry changes as mergers and acquisitions alter SIC codes. For example, the acquisition in 1985 of G.D. Searle Company by Monsanto Corporation, a chemical firm, probably caused Searle's spending on R&D to be counted in SIC 281 (chemicals) in subsequent years. Because the SIC classifications change with merger and acquisition activity, NSF is probably a less reliable source of industrywide R&D growth rates than is PMA.

Company data are also available from annual reports and filings with the Securities and Exchange Commission (SEC). Compustat™ [3] publishes audited company financial data for over 13,000 publicly traded companies in the United States. The data are organized by four-digit SIC code; firms are assigned to a primary SIC category by Compustat™ staff using industry definitions from the SIC manual, but there is no guarantee that firms will be given the same SIC code as the NSF survey (387). Like the NSF survey, Compustat™ data on R&D spending include companywide estimates, including both pharmaceutical and nonpharmaceutical R&D. The Compustat™ estimates include both foreign and domestic R&D conducted by the reporting companies. Between 1971 and 1990, 133 firms were listed as pharmaceutical companies during at least 1 year of that period.[4]

Estimates of total industry R&D expenditures built from individual companies' financial records (i.e., PMA and Compustat) may be overstated because of certain accounting practices that can lead to double counting of such costs at the industry level. The purchase of the right to further develop a product is considered a purchase of ''in-process R&D'' for accounting purposes. If one company synthesizes a new drug, for example, and licenses it to another company for clinical development and marketing, the company purchasing the right in exchange for an upfront cash payment and future royalty payments may ac-

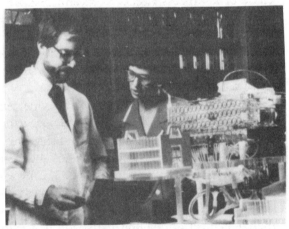

Photo credit: ELI LILLY AND COMPANY

The pharmaceutical industry's investment of approximately $6 billion on R&D is one of the most intensive of all the R&D-oriented industries.

---

[2] The Standard Industrial Classification system is a method used to assign firms to industries according to the products or services they sell (126).

[3] Compustat™ is a commercial on-line, time-series database service of Standard & Poor's, publisher of business reference books.

[4] Prior to 1975, uniform accounting standards did not exist for reporting R&D spending; hence, data are reported in this study only for the period beginning with 1975.

count for the upfront cash payment as the purchase of "in-process R&D" (144). This cash payment may bear no relation to the actual incurred research expenditures; it is the purchase price of a valuable asset, whose cost of development was already accounted for (in earlier years) in the R&D expenses of the first company. The purchase price may include not only the payback for R&D performed by the first company but also a payment for the potential market value of the drug in the future. (A drug with a large potential market, for example, will have a high licensing price, even if the R&D costs to date have been low.)

Conservative accounting practices require that such upfront payments be expensed, rather than capitalized as investments, because unapproved drugs are considered intangible assets of unproven value.[5] Some companies, particularly small ones for which such payments are a substantial part of their R&D expenses, may separately identify such transactions as "purchase of in-process R&D."[6] Nevertheless, even when such transactions are separately identified in annual financial statements, it is unclear how the transactions are treated when companies report their expenditures through surveys such as those conducted by PMA.

The potential magnitude of the overstatement of industrywide R&D costs in databases using company financial statements is illustrated by a recently-announced strategic alliance between Centocor, a biotechnology firm, and Eli Lilly and Company, a large pharmaceutical company. Lilly acquired the right to collaborate with Centocor on the commercialization and marketing of Centocor's promising anti-infective drug, Centoxin™ in exchange for purchase of Centocor stock and

$50 million in cash (121). The $50-million cash payment from Lilly to Centocor will probably be recorded as an R&D expense on Lilly's financial statements because Centoxin™ is not yet approved for marketing.[7] If Centocor uses the cash to fund continued R&D on the product, it, too, will report R&D expenses of $50 million. Then, industrywide estimates of R&D expenditures that include both firms' recorded R&D expenses would double count the actual R&D outlays associated with Centoxin.

The overestimate of R&D costs may have increased in the 1980s for two reasons. First, the percent of new chemical entities (NCEs) under development that are licensed from other companies increased in the 1980s (107). The increasing frequency of strategic alliances between pharmaceutical firms and small biotechnology firms in the late 1980s may have added to the trend. Second, between 1981 and 1987, the R&D limited partnership was an attractive financing vehicle for small biotechnology firms. Since the partnership actually owns the rights to the products of the research, purchase of in-process R&D by the company would be one way for the company to buy back the rights to products developed through the partnership before they are approved for marketing.

Despite these distortions, the Office of Technology Assessment believes that the overstatement in estimates based on company financial reports is still a small proportion of total industry R&D and does not account for much of the increase in the recorded rate of change of R&D in the 1980s, especially domestic R&D. First, PMA's membership does not include many small biotechnology companies, so the potential for double counting of R&D expenditures is reduced. (For example,

---

[5] Once a product is approved for marketing, however, the purchase of rights to market it can be treated as an investment. For example, when Genentech, Inc. purchased rights to market Protropin (its human growth hormone product) from the R&D limited partnership that owned rights, it accounted for the transaction as a "purchase of product technology" and amortized the cash outlay over a period of years (145).

[6] For example, when Genzyme, Inc. purchased the rights to further develop the orphan product alglucerase from an R&D limited partnership, it showed the $20-million price of buying out the partnership as a purchase of "in-process R&D" (141).

[7] The Office of Technology Assessment requested Eli Lilly and Company to confirm or correct this interpretation but the company declined to respond to OTA's inquiry.

Centocor is not a member of PMA and is also not included as a pharmaceutical firm in the Compustat database.) Second, although the R&D limited partnership grew in use over the 1980s, it represented a small proportion of the overall funding of pharmaceutical R&D, and few biotechnology based pharmaceutical products were actually marketed in the 1980s; therefore, few buyouts would have occurred in the period. Third, a review of annual reports of nine large U.S. pharmaceutical companies over the period 1978-89 found no disclosure of unusual R&D expenditures (such as those involving a large cash payment to another firm), suggesting that such expenses were not material in these firms (29).

Nevertheless, the overestimation bias could grow in the 1990s as cross-licensing and strategic alliances among pharmaceutical companies increase in frequency. The NSF survey does not suffer from the double counting problem, although its estimates are sensitive to mergers and acquisitions that change industry classifications. Because the magnitude of the effect of the limitations of each database on the resulting estimates is unclear, it is best to examine all such estimates together.

TRENDS IN DOMESTIC R&D SPENDING

PMA and NSF each report on R&D performed by pharmaceutical firms in the United States. Between 1977 and 1990, domestic R&D spending increased at an annual rate of 13.3 percent in the NSF survey and 15.1 percent in the PMA series (see figure 2-1). After adjusting for inflation, the annual increases were 7.6 percent for the NSF series and 9.4 percent for the PMA series. Table 2-1 shows the estimated domestic expenditures from 1975 through 1990. R&D spending increased from $1.1 billion in 1977 to between $5.7 billion (NSF) and $6.6 billion (PMA) in 1990.

Until 1986, the NSF estimates were higher than those of PMA. Because the NSF survey measures total company R&D, including R&D on both ethical pharmaceuticals and other lines of business, the difference is to be expected. Since 1986,

however, the PMA estimates have exceeded the NSF estimates. One possibility for this shift is the impact of mergers and acquisitions in the mid-1980s on industry classification in the NSF series.

Although the two data sources are not completely comparable, both reveal a shift in the speed of growth in domestic R&D spending by pharmaceutical companies beginning in the early 1980s. For example, according to NSF, inflation-adjusted R&D spending increased at about 7.7 percent per year between 1977 and 1980; between 1980 and 1985 it increased at 8.6 percent per year. However, between 1985 and 1990 real R&D spending in the NSF survey increased at only 6.5 percent. PMA data show more striking trends: between 1975 and 1980 real domestic R&D spending increased at a rate of 3.5 percent per year; between 1980 and 1985 it averaged 11 percent and between 1985 and 1990 it averaged 10.7 percent.

Figure 2-1—Domestic Pharmaceutical R&D Expenditures, 1977-90

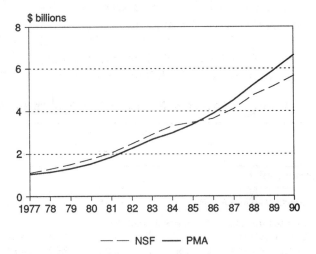

KEY: NSF = National Science Foundation; PMA = Pharmaceutical Manufacturers Association.

SOURCES: Pharmaceutical Manufacturers Association, *Annual Survey Reports*, 1975-91 (Washington, DC: PMA, 1976-91). National Science Foundation, Surveys of Science Resources Series, *Research and Development in Industry: 1987-1988*, Detailed Statistical Tables, NSF 89-323 (Washington, DC: NSF, 1989, 1990). National Science Foundation, *Selected Data on Research and Development in Industry: 1990*, NSF 92-317, Selected Data Tables (Washington, DC: NSF, 1992).

Table 2-1—Aggregate Domestic R&D Expenditures,[a] 1975-90 ($ billions)

	1975	1976	1977	1978	1979	1980	1981	1982	1983	1984	1985	1986	1987	1988	1989	1990[b]
National Science Foundation																
Current dollars....	NA	NA	1.1	1.3	1.5	1.8[c]	2.1[c]	2.5[c]	2.9[c]	3.3[c]	3.5	3.7	4.1	4.7	5.2	5.7
Constant 1990 dollars[d]........	NA	NA	2.2	2.4	2.5	2.7	2.9	3.3	3.7	4.0	4.1	4.2	4.6	5.1	5.4	5.7
Pharmaceutical Manufacturers Association																
Current dollars....	.9	1.0	1.1	1.2	1.3	1.5	1.9	2.2	2.7	3.0	3.3	3.9	4.5	5.2	6.0	6.6
Constant 1990 dollars[d]........	2.0	2.0	2.1	2.1	2.2	2.4	2.6	3.0	3.4	3.6	4.0	4.5	5.0	5.7	6.3	6.6

[a] Includes company, Federal and other funds for R&D.
[b] Budgeted amounts.
[c] Federal sources of R&D funds to companies are excluded in this year.
[d] Adjusted by GNP implicit price deflator.
KEY: NA = not available.
SOURCE: Office of Technology Assessment, 1993, based on Pharmaceutical Manufacturers Association, *Annual Survey Reports*, 1975-91 (Washington, DC: PMA, 1976-91). National Science Foundation, Surveys of Science Resources Series, *Research and Development in Industry: 1987-1988*, Detailed Statistical Tables, NSF 89-323 (Washington, DC: National Science Foundation, 1989, 1990).

TRENDS IN WORLDWIDE PHARMACEUTICAL R&D EXPENDITURES

Data on worldwide R&D expenditures by U.S.-based firms are available both from Compustat™ and PMA. Despite the difference between the two sources in coverage of R&D expenditures, total R&D conducted by U.S.-based pharmaceutical companies in 1975 was estimated at $1.1 billion by both PMA and Compustat™ (table 2-2). By 1990, this spending had grown to between $7.9 billion (Compustat™)

and $8.1 billion (PMA). These data suggest that after adjusting for inflation, foreign and domestic R&D spending by U.S.-based companies increased at approximately 8 to 8.5 percent per year between 1975 and 1990. The rate of increase appears to have accelerated, however. Before 1980, real worldwide R&D expenditures of U.S. firms increased only by 5 to 6 percent per year (table 2-2). Between 1985 and 1990, PMA data show a 10.9 percent annual rate of increase in real spending.[7] Compustat™ data show a rate of

Table 2-2—Aggregate Pharmaceutical Foreign and Domestic R&D, Selected Years ($ billions)

	1975	1980	1985	1987	1990	Annual percent rate of change		
						1975-80	1980-85	1985-90
Compustat[TMa]								
Current dollars..................	$1.10	$2.08	$4.20	$5.53	$7.90	13.6%	15.1%	13.5%
Constant 1990 dollars[b].........	2.44	3.19	4.98	6.19	7.90	5.5	9.3	9.7
Pharmaceutical Manufacturers Association[c]								
Current dollars.................	1.06	1.98	4.08	5.51	8.13	13.2	15.6	14.8
Constant 1990 dollars...........	2.36	3.03	4.83	6.17	8.13	5.2	9.8	10.9

[a] Figures are based on a total of 133 firms listed in the Compustat file under Standard Industrial Code (SIC) code 2834 in at least 1 year between 1971 and 1990. The number of firms vary from year to year due to firms' entry and exit from SIC 2834.
[b] Adjusted by GNP implicit price deflator.
[c] R&D expenditures reported by Pharmacuetical Manufacturers Association member firms.
SOURCE: Office of Technology Assessment, 1993, based on unpublished data provided by S.H. Kang, School of Industrial Administration, Carnegie-Mellon University, Pittsburgh, PA; Pharmaceutical Manufacturers Association, *Annual Survey Reports*, 1975-91 (Washington, DC: PMA, 1976-91).

---

[7] Because spending in various countries must be converted into a common currency, exchange rate changes can affect reported spending. The devaluation of the dollar after 1985 may be responsible for some of the unusually high increase in total spending reported in recent years.

growth in real spending of 9.2 percent per year between 1985 and 1990.

The Centre for Medicines Research estimates total expenditure on pharmaceutical R&D in 11 industrialized countries increased from $5.4 billion in 1981 to $15 billion in 1988 (172). Estimated spending (in current dollars) accelerated after 1985, increasing 22 percent per year between 1985 and 1988, compared with 10.5 percent per year between 1981 and 1985.

Thus, although a comprehensive source of data on worldwide R&D spending is unavailable, the existing data sources point to an accelerating rate of increase in real spending on R&D throughout the 1980s.

DIRECTIONS OF PHARMACEUTICAL R&D

Where have the increasing funds devoted to pharmaceutical R&D been applied? Have they been used increasingly for the advancement of scientific knowledge within companies? Have they been increasingly targeted to discovery and development of drugs that treat diseases through entirely new modes of action ("breakthrough" drugs) or have they been targeted to new drugs similar in structure and mode of action to products already on the market (so-called "me-too" drugs)? To what extent have they been used to support the development of product extensions or to research new uses of existing drugs?

The data available on trends in R&D do not provide answers to these questions. PMA is the only source of data on the allocation of R&D across different kinds of functions, and the PMA functional classification system is not germane to these questions (table 2-3). Unfortunately, these categories cut across all kinds of research and cannot even be used very accurately to estimate the proportion of R&D that is for drug discovery versus clinical testing. Spending by functional category has remained relatively stable over time. Companies reporting to PMA also provide estimates of the percent of R&D devoted to "the advancement of scientific knowledge and development of new products" versus "significant improvements and/or modifications of existing

Table 2-3—Distribution of R&D Expenditures by Function, Selected Years 1976-89[a] ($ millions)

Function	1976	1977	1978	1980	1982	1985	1987	1988	1989
Clinical evaluation: phases I,II,III	$20.2	$17.8	$16.5	$19.8	$19.9	$21.0	$24.0	$26.4	$26.7
Biological screening and pharmacological testing	19.5	18.7	18.8	18.6	17.9	16.6	16.8	16.7	16.9
Synthesis and extraction	16.6	17.2	16.3	15.4	11.6	11.6	10.3	10.3	9.8
Pharmaceutical dosage formulation and stability testing	9.1	9.7	10.1	9.2	10.4	9.3	9.1	9.1	9.4
Toxicology and safety testing	8.9	9.2	10.0	9.7	8.9	8.9	8.3	7.8	7.0
Process development for manufacturing and quality control	9.5	8.8	9.2	9.0	9.5	9.4	9.4	9.1	7.3
Clinical evaluation: phase IV	3.2	4.7	4.8	3.7	3.2	5.0	4.4	3.5	4.0
Regulatory, IND and NDA preparation, submission and processing	3.3	3.3	3.6	4.1	3.9	4.4	3.6	3.0	3.3
Bioavailability studies	2.2	2.3	2.2	2.1	2.8	2.9	3.0	2.8	2.6
Other	7.5	8.3	8.5	8.4	11.9	10.9	11.1	11.3	13.0
Percent of pharmaceutical R&D devoted developing new products	79%	80%	80%	81%	79%	82%	83%	82%	82%

[a] Based on R&D conducted in the United States by all PMA members.

KEY: IND = investigational new drug application; NA = not available; NDA = new drug application.

SOURCE: Pharmaceutical Manufacturers Association, *Annual Survey Reports*, 1975-91 (Washington, DC: PMA, 1976-91).

products'' (320). How firms define new products or modifications of existing products is unclear, however, and the reliability of these estimates cannot be verified. Nevertheless, the data do suggest a relatively stable mix of R&D over time—about 80 percent devoted to new-product R&D (table 2-3).

There is only sketchy information on trends in the allocation of new-product R&D between discovery research and clinical trials. DiMasi and colleagues asked 12 U.S. companies to estimate R&D expenditures for clinical and preclinical research on self-originated NCEs for the period 1970-86 (107). Over the entire period, 66.1 percent of research on self-originated drugs was reported as devoted to the preclinical phase. No clear trends were evident in the ratio over time (106), suggesting the allocation of R&D dollars has remained stable over time.

Early signs are emerging that the output of R&D—new products—is increasing modestly. Though the number of new molecular entities (NMEs)[9] approved by the U.S. Food and Drug Administration (FDA) remained fairly constant throughout the 1980s—at a mean of 22.5 per year, the number of commercial investigational new drug (IND) applications for initiation of clinical testing of NMEs has increased over the decade. From 1980 to 1982, the Center for Drug Evaluation and Research (CDER) of the FDA issued an average of 271 commercial INDs annually while during the 1988-90 period, the average rose to 349 per year (475). Because more than one IND can be filed for each compound, a better indicator of trends in productivity of research, especially early research, is the number of NCEs entering testing. Data from a sample of over 40 companies indicate that the number of INDs for NCEs increased from 210 per year between 1975 and 1978 to 299 per year between 1983 and 1986 (107).[10] The total

Photo credit: ELI LILLY AND COMPANY

The introduction of biotechnology-derived drugs has increased rapidly since the first FDA approval in 1982 of Lilly's recombinant DNA product, Humlin.

number of NCEs entering human testing in U.S.-based firms grew from 58 per year in the late 1970s to 67 per year between 1983 and 1986. Although INDs for NCEs originated in U.S.-based firms grew by 25 percent between the periods, the percent of all NCE INDs for self-originated U.S. drugs declined from 60 to 53 percent between the two periods. Licensed-in drugs and INDs submitted by foreign firms grew as a proportion of total NCE INDs submitted to the FDA.

The number of biotechnology drugs in development increased dramatically over the period. Between 1982—the year the FDA approved the first biotechnology-derived drug (Eli Lilly's recombinant human insulin)—and 1991, the FDA had approved a total of seven biotechnology drugs; however, as of October 1991 21 biotechnology drugs were awaiting FDA marketing approval (146). Chapter 6 discusses the potential backlog of approvals for biotechnology drugs in greater detail.

---

[9] The terms ''new chemical entity'' (NCE) and ''new molecular entity'' (NME) both refer to new drugs, although their precise definitions are somewhat different. DiMasi et al. define NCE as ''a new molecular compound not previously tested in humans.'' NME is a term used by the FDA that, unlike NCE, includes some diagnostic agents and excludes therapeutic biologicals (109,474). In keeping with DiMasi's definition, this report uses the term NCE to refer to both therapeutic drugs and biologicals. OTA uses the term NME only when discussing work that specifically employs FDA's definition of that term.

[10] DiMasi and colleagues also give information on the 1979-82 period. See chapter 6 for more detail.

INTERPRETING AGGREGATE TRENDS

Each new dollar spent on pharmaceutical R&D is an investment in a potential stream of future revenues. Although investors make mistakes, their decisions are a true reflection of expectations about the future. The rapid increase in total industrywide pharmaceutical R&D in constant dollars in the 1980s means that investors expected aggregate net revenues over the lifetimes of the new products would be sufficient to justify the additional investment with its attendant risks.

Little more can be concluded from an examination of R&D spending trends. For example, investors might or might not expect the number of drugs approved for marketing to increase in the future. The R&D could be directed toward fewer products with more lucrative markets, or it could be directed to the introduction of a large number of products, each with more modest market potential.

Some of the R&D might be directed to the development of "me-too" drugs that do not substantially enlarge the overall market but share an existing market with close therapeutic substitutes. The pursuit of "me-too" drugs is an attempt by rival firms to shave off part of the monopoly profits enjoyed by the maker of the pioneer drug in a therapeutic class.[11] The higher the initial monopoly profits, the more incentive rivals have to develop a similar competing drug (102,346,363,418). Thus, the increased R&D in the 1980s could in part be a response to high returns to pioneer drugs developed in the 1970s.

R&D dollars pursue returns, and the risks investors will take to obtain those returns depend on how great they promise to be. To understand the drivers behind the pharmaceutical R&D phenomenon of the 1980s, it is necessary to examine closely how the returns to these investments have been changing over time. Subsequent chapters of this report examine trends in the average cost of discovering and developing new ethical pharmaceuticals and the net returns to bringing these products to market.

---

[11] Pioneer and "me-too" drugs are granted monopolies by the United States and other countries' patent systems, which protect patented pharmaceutical compounds (or their manufacturing processes or uses) from copy for specific periods from the date of application or issue. Even with a strong patent, the monopoly may be limited by the availability of similar drugs in the therapeutic class, of competing classes of drugs, or of nonpharmaceutical therapies.

The Costs of
Pharmaceutical R&D | 3

his chapter brings together existing evidence on the cost
of bringing new pharmaceuticals to market. It begins
with background on how to measure such costs and then
moves to an assessment of existing studies of research
and development (R&D) costs. These studies are retrospective:
they estimate the costs of R&D for pharmaceutical products
developed and brought to market in the past. R&D costs can
change quickly as underlying scientific, technical, or regulatory
conditions change, so it is dangerous to predict much about the
future, or even about today's R&D costs, from studies of past
costs. In the last part of the chapter, the Office of Technology
Assessment (OTA) examines recent trends in some critical
components of the cost of bringing new drugs to market.

A FRAMEWORK FOR ESTIMATING R&D COSTS

R&D is an investment in a potential future stream of revenues
from the sale of successful new drugs. Unlike other kinds of
investments, such as a new manufacturing plant, the success of
a pharmaceutical R&D investment is highly uncertain and may
take many years to be realized. The investors in pharmaceutical
R&D must be able to ''expect'' not only to recoup their actual
cash outlays for R&D but also to be compensated for the risk they
took of losing their investment altogether and for the time they
spent waiting for the investment to pay off. Without such an
expectation, no investor would put his or her money on the line.

The full cost of the R&D investment can be thought of as the
minimal ''expected'' payoff required to induce the investor to lay
out the money at each step of the research project. The
''expected'' payoff does not mean an assured payoff; rather, it
means the minimal payoff required from the drugs that successfully reach the market after taking into account the chances of
success and failure and the expected development time involved.

The full cost of bringing a new drug to market, as defined above, is clearly higher than the cash outlays spent to discover and develop successful new drugs. It also includes the cash outlays spent on projects that fail.[1] And, it must include the *opportunity cost of capital,* the rate of interest that dollars invested at a given level of risk must earn in exchange for being tied up in the investment (59,285).

The opportunity cost of capital for pharmaceutical R&D is higher than the interest rate on safe investments, such as insured bank deposits or government bonds, but just how high the cost of capital for pharmaceutical R&D projects is depends on how investors evaluate the risks of these investments. (See appendix C for a detailed discussion of the cost of capital.) The risk and, therefore, the cost of capital varies across different projects and even within the same R&D project at different stages of development. The cost of capital for any investment also varies from year to year with underlying changes in the risk-free rate of interest (e.g., on bank deposits). Thus, the full cost of R&D varies widely over time and across projects.

To measure the full cost of bringing a new drug to market, all outlays required to achieve the successes (including spending on projects that fail) must be compounded (or capitalized) at an interest rate equal to the cost of capital, to their **present value (or capitalized value)** at the date of market approval. For example, $1 million invested 1 year ago should be worth $1.1 million today if the cost of capital for that investment was 10 percent per year.

Note again that the full cost of bringing a new drug to market is much higher than the amount of money companies must actually raise to fund R&D projects. To pursue R&D, companies must raise only enough cash to cover the actual outlays associated with the successful and unsuccessful

Photo credit: THE UPJOHN COMPANY

R&D expenditures include substantial investment in research facilities and equipment. The Upjohn Company recently built this new addition to its research facilities, the "white" building located at the top of the photograph. It encompasses more than 700,000 square feet, was constructed at a cost of $120,000 million, and will house more than 500 scientists.

projects. Estimating the full cost of bringing a new drug to market, by contrast, provides a way of gauging how much money must be earned from the successful drugs, once they reach the market, to justify the research outlays.

EXISTING STUDIES OF R&D COSTS

Two major approaches have been used to estimate the cost of bringing new drugs to market. One approach examines project-level data acquired from pharmaceutical firms. The second approach analyzes R&D expenditures and new products at the industry level. Table 3-1 contains a summary of selected pharmaceutical R&D cost studies of both kinds—project-level and industry-level—listed in the order of the R&D period studied.

Project-level studies try to measure costs incurred at each stage of development and the percent of drugs that will successfully pass each stage, and then use these calculations to arrive at a final cost estimate. The key advantage of the project-level approach is that, if sufficiently

---

[1] When the full cost of R&D is estimated with historical data, averaging of outlays across winners and losers must take place across the entire industry, or at least a good part of it, because individual companies may have unusual experiences. For example, a company could have mismanaged its research, leading to relatively few successes and high outlays per success. Though investors in that company might have lost money, they need not be rewarded for their bad judgment. The experience of the industry as a whole is a good basis for estimating the true (and uncontrollable) probability of success and failure of R&D projects.

Table 3-1—Summary of Selected Pharmaceutical R&D Cost Studies

Study	Sample years	Estimation method	Data source	Estimated R&D costs	Constant dollar year	Opportunity cost of capital	Preclinical costs	Treatment of unsuccessful projects
Project-level studies								
Schnee, 1972	1950-67 (market introductions)	Average development cost and time for 75 projects marketed in one large firm.	R&D project cost data reported by one firm.	NCEs: $534,000.	Current dollars	0%	Not included	Not included
Hansen, 1979	1963-75 (projects entering human testing)	R&D expenditure profile built for sample of approximately 67 self-originated NCEs, not all successful.	NCE sample and R&D project expenditures from 14-firm survey.	$54 million	1976	8%	Assumed to be 53% (allocated over 3 years prior to IND filing).	Estimated 12.5% NCE success rate.
DiMasi et al., 1991	1970-82 (projects entering human testing)	R&D expenditure profile built for sample of 93 self-originated NCEs, not all successful.	NCE sample and R&D project expenditures from 12-firm survey.	$231 million	1987	9%	Estimates from reported preclinical and clinical period expenditures.	Estimated success rate by phase for sample NCEs.
Industry-level studies								
Baily, 1972	1949-69 (market introductions)	Regression of total U.S. drug introductions in U.S. firms 1949-69 on total research expenditures (lagged 5 years), FDA regulation stringency, and a measure of depletion of research opportunities.	Total R&D data: PMA survey. New drug introductions: Paul de Haen, Inc.	Pre-1962: $2.5 million. Post-1962: $6 million.	1958	0%	Implicit	Implicit
Schwartzman, 1976	1966-72 (NCE approvals)	Allocation of total R&D expenditures (lagged 5 years) to NCEs introduced in 1966-72.	R&D expenditures: PMA survey.	$24.4 million	1973	0%	Assumed to be 50%.	Implicit
Wiggins, 1987	1970-85 (NCE approvals)	Regression of NCE introductions on total R&D expenditures (lagged 4 years); FDA approval times, by therapeutic class. Adjusted for Hansen's time profile.	NCEs: FDA. R&D expenditures: PMA surveys.	$108 million[a]	1986	8%	Implicit	Implicit
Grabowski & Vernon, 1989	1970-79 (NCE approvals)	Analysis of industry R&D expenditures and NCE production. R&D time profiles modified from regression estimates.	NCEs: FDA. Total R&D expenditures: PMA surveys.	$125 million	1986	9%	Implicit	Implicit

a Wiggins originally reported $125 million; adjustment for technical error changes the number to $108 million (DiMasi et al; 1991).

KEY: NCE = new chemical entity; IND = investigational new drug; FDA = U.S. Food and Drug Administration; PMA = Pharmaceutical Manufacturers Association.

SOURCES: J.E. Schnee, "Development Cost: Determinants and Overruns," *Journal of Business* 45(3):347-374, 1972. M.N. Baily, "Research and Development Costs and Returns: The U.S. Pharmaceutical Industry," *Journal of Political Economy* 80(1):70-85, 1972. D. Schwartzman, *The Expected Return From Pharmaceutical Research* (Washington, DC: American Enterprise Institute, 1975). R. Hansen, "The Pharmaceutical Development Process: Estimates of Development Costs and Times and the Effect of Proposed Regulatory Changes," *Issues in Pharmaceutical Economics,* R.A. Chien (ed.) (Lexington, MA: D.C. Heath and Co., 1979). S.N. Wiggins, *The Cost of Developing a New Drug* (Washington, DC: Pharmaceutical Manufacturers Association, 1987). H.G. Grabowski and J.M. Vernon, "A New Look at the Returns and Risks to Pharmaceutical R&D," *Management Science* 36(7):804-821, July 1990. J.A. DiMasi, R.W. Hansen, H.G. Grabowski, et al., "The Cost of Innovation in the Pharmaceutical Industry," *Journal of Health Economics* 10:107-142, 1991.

reliable data can be obtained, it provides the most detailed view of the costs of particular projects and overall development costs. These studies look at a sample of new product introductions (virtually always new chemical entities (NCEs)[2]) and use project cost data obtained from companies to estimate the average cost of bringing a product to market. Although Clymer (79) and Schnee (367) took this project-level approach in early studies, they calculated only the cash R&D outlays of a single firm, and Schnee did not consider the cost of failures. These studies are therefore not considered further.

The prototype of project-level R&D cost estimation is a pair of studies published by Hansen in 1979 and DiMasi and colleagues in 1991 (109,175). They used very similar methods and data sources to estimate the present value in the year of U.S. market approval of the costs of discovering and developing NCEs. The results of these studies have been used to estimate net returns to R&D and to estimate recent changes in the cost of developing new drugs.

Industry-level studies examine the relationship between new product introductions and industry research expenditures. An estimated regression equation that predicts NCE introductions as a function of R&D expenditures in previous years as well as other external factors (such as regulatory controls) is then solved for the R&D expenditures required to bring one additional NCE to market.[3]

The advantage of these industry-level studies is that data on product introductions and research expenditures are verifiable and readily available at the industry level. The disadvantage is that the introduction of NCEs in any year must be related to a pattern of past R&D expenditures that is complex and often beyond estimation with the limited number of years of data available. This approach was pioneered by Baily (32), but the cost estimate from that study is based on very old data that are not converted to present values.

A recent estimate based on a study by Wiggins (520) is the most comprehensive analysis using this approach. Wiggins followed the general method first used by Baily, but Wiggins had more data at hand and used less restrictive assumptions about the nature of the relationship between expenditures and new drug production. Therefore, this chapter focuses on the Wiggins study.

Grabowski and Vernon (159) also used published aggregate R&D expenditure data to estimate the cost of successful drug development. Though Grabowski and Vernon did not estimate development time profiles with statistical analysis, their estimate provides another point of reference for comparison among methods, and it is also summarized here.

■ The Hansen and DiMasi Studies

METHODS

The two studies by Hansen (175) and DiMasi (109) are based on samples of NCEs first entering human testing in specified time periods. The sample of NCEs for each study was selected from a set of data on NCEs constructed and maintained by the Tufts University Center for the Study of Drug Development (CSDD) from an ongoing triennial survey of over 40 pharmaceutical firms. The early study examined approximately 67 NCEs, discovered and developed by 14 U.S. pharmaceutical firms that first entered human trials between 1963 and 1975. The second study

---

[2] DiMasi defines "NCE" as "a new molecular compound not previously tested in humans" (107). In keeping with DiMasi's definition, this report uses the term NCE to refer to both therapeutic drugs and biologicals.

[3] Industry-level analyses are therefore estimates of marginal costs of NCE production. As DiMasi observed, marginal costs and average costs are not likely to be equal unless R&D is subject to constant returns to scale (109). In an R&D-intensive pharmaceutical firm, there may be substantial economies of scale, particularly at low levels of expenditure. However, from the standpoint of the industry as a whole, marginal costs may more closely approximate average costs. A more important criticism of the marginal cost measure is that the marginal NCE (i.e., the next one that would be brought forth by an infusion of new R&D expenditures) is not determined by costs alone but by the present value of net returns. The marginal NCE might be a low-cost project with low revenue prospects. Therefore, marginal research cost does not have much meaning from the standpoint of R&D decisions.

examined 93 NCEs, discovered and developed by 12 U.S. firms, that were first tested in humans between 1970 and 1982 (109).

Both studies looked only at NCEs that were actually discovered by the firms themselves (i.e., self-originated), not licensed from other companies, and the samples in both studies included unsuccessful as well as successful NCEs. Products acquired through joint ventures or licenses were excluded because part of the costs of these R&D projects would have been borne by other firms and could not be measured easily.

The study authors surveyed the firms sponsoring the sampled NCEs for information about the costs incurred from year to year as each NCE traveled through the drug development process. Many of the sampled products were abandoned during the clinical testing phase, and the costs were adjusted for these abandonments. With year-by-year estimates of spending for each project, the authors could build a time profile of expenditures throughout the development period. These time profiles were then combined with information about the survival experience of the NCEs under study to estimate the average cash outlays[4] for clinical research.

A portion of R&D cost is devoted to the discovery of NCEs. These basic and preclinical research activities cannot be allocated to specific NCEs, so the authors of each study asked firms to report information that would allow estimation of preclinical research expenditures. In the early study, firms were asked to report total NCE R&D expenditures in the United States between 1962 and 1975 as well as ''basic research'' expenditures.[5] Overall, firms reported that 51 percent of all NCE R&D expenditures were for basic re-

search, so Hansen assumed an amount equal to the total average development period cost went to basic research in the preclinical period, spread equally over 3 years prior to the initiation of clinical testing.

DiMasi used a more involved methodology to estimate both the amount of preclinical cost and the timing of those costs. Firms reported total **self-originated NCE R&D** expenditures and preclinical research expenditures between 1970 and 1986. Preclinical expenses averaged 66 percent of total self-originated NCE research. This estimate was revised to 58 percent to account for trends in the data over the time period on which the estimate was based.[6] These estimated preclinical costs were spread evenly over 42.6 months prior to the initiation of the clinical period.[7]

The estimated cash outflows, spread over the discovery and development periods according to the time profile reported by companies, were converted to their present value in the year of market approval. The early study used a real (inflation-adjusted) cost of capital of 8 percent; the later study used 9 percent.

RESULTS

Table 3-2 shows how the actual estimated cash expenditures (in 1990 constant dollars) changed between the two studies. Total cash outlays per successful new NCE were estimated at $65.5 million (1990 dollars) by Hansen and at $127.2 million by DiMasi, a 94 percent increase in estimated real (inflation-adjusted) outlays per successful new drug over the period of the two studies. If the midpoint of the study years is used to calculate the rate of increase in cash outlays,

---

[4] The reported expenditures don't correspond exactly to cash outlays because charges for indirect costs, overhead, or capital equipment and facilities may be made using allocation or depreciation methods that don't correspond in time to actual cash outlays. The term ''cash costs'' is used here to differentiate the reported expenditures from their present values in the year of market approval.

[5] Development costs included clinical costs and short-term preclinical animal studies.

[6] Since clinical period expenditures occur later than preclinical expenditures, the ratio of preclinical period real R&D to total real R&D expenditures overestimates the true preclinical period contribution when total expenditures are rising (109).

[7] The length of the preclincial period was estimated from data in the CSDD database on NCEs approved for marketing by the U.S. Food and Drug Administration (FDA) in the years of the study. The preclinical period is defined in that database as the length of time from synthesis of a drug to the beginning of human clinical studies.

Table 3-2—Cash Outlays per Successful New Chemical Entity:
Hansen and DiMasi ($ 1990 millions)[a]

| Study | Study years (midpoint) | Clinical cost | Preclinical/discovery | | Total cash outlays per success |
			Cost	As percent of total cost	
Hansen, 1979........	1963-75 (1969)	$29.9	$35.6	54%	$65.5
DiMasi et al., 1991....	1970-82 (1976)	53.8	73.4	58	127.2
Rate of increase (%)...		79	106		94

[a] All estimates were adjusted for inflation using the GNP implicit price deflator.

SOURCE: Office of Technology Assessment, 1993, adapted from R. Hansen, "The Pharmaceutical Development Process: Estimates of Development Costs and Times and the Effect of Proposed Regulatory Changes," *Issues in Pharmaceutical Economics*, R.A. Chien (ed.) (Lexington, MA: D.C. Heath and Co., 1979); J.A. DiMasi, R.W. Hansen, H.G. Grabowski, et al., "The Cost of Innovation in the Pharmaceutical Industry," *Journal of Health Economics* 10:107-142, 1991.

this pair of studies suggests that real R&D cash outlays per successful NCE increased at an annual rate of about 9.5 percent in the study years.[8]

The increase in cash outlays per success is moderated by an improvement in the success rate of the drugs in the two study cohorts. Whereas Hansen projected an ultimate success rate from human testing to approval by the U.S. Food and Drug Administration (FDA) of 12.5 percent, DiMasi and colleagues estimated about 23 percent of the projects would be successful. Without this improvement, the increase in cash outlays per success would be even higher.

Because the estimated ratio of preclinical costs to clinical costs was higher in the later study than in the early study, the increase in real cash outlays is somewhat greater for preclinical costs than for clinical period costs, but the annual rates of increase were not very different—10.3 percent per year for preclinical costs compared with 8.3 percent per year for clinical period costs.

Total R&D costs capitalized to the date of approval for marketing increased from $108 million to $259 million (in 1990 dollars) over the course of the two study periods, an inflation-adjusted increase of 139 percent, or 12.4 percent per year from the midpoint of the early study (1969) to the midpoint of the later study (1976). The even more rapid increase in fully capitalized costs was due to cost-increasing changes in two components of the estimates:

- An increase in the estimated cost of capital from 8 percent in the early study to 9 percent in the later study.
- An increase in the total development time from 9.6 to 11.8 years, led by a longer preclinical period in the later study (42.6 months, compared with 36 months) and a longer period of regulatory review once a new drug application (NDA) is filed with the FDA (30.3 months compared with 24 months).

The change in the assumed cost of capital alone would account for little of the increase in total capitalized costs. OTA reconstructed Hansen's cost analysis using a 9 percent cost of capital. This change, in the absence of any others, increased Hansen's total cost estimate by only 5 percent to

---

[8] Comparison of the midpoints of the study years may understate the true difference in time between the studies and may therefore overstate the rate of change over the time period. Although the database from which the sample of NCEs in each study was drawn shows the median years for self-originated NCEs receiving investigational new drugs in the two studies were 7 years apart (107), the cost estimates in the early study were based more heavily on the older NCEs in the sample than were the cost estimates in the second study (176). If a steady upward trend in the real cost of R&D was occurring throughout the decades of the two studies, the cost estimates of the early study would be biased downward.

approximately $114.8 million (in 1990 dollars). Increasing the discovery/development period to match that of the DiMasi study without any other changes would increase Hansen's total cost estimate to $122.7 million (13 percent higher than the baseline estimate). Together, a higher cost of capital and a longer R&D time profile (in the absence of any other changes) increased Hansen's estimated cost to $132.9 million (in 1990 dollars), only 23 percent higher than the baseline estimate. Thus, without the very large changes in estimated cash outlays over the two periods, the inflation-adjusted rise between the two periods in R&D costs per success would have been relatively modest.

■ The Wiggins Study

Wiggins regressed the total number of NCEs that the FDA approved between 1970 and 1985 on the estimated total NCE-oriented research spending in previous years[9] and on the average delay in NDA approval times for drugs approved 5 years earlier. The regression equation was then transformed into an estimate of the extra cash research outlay required to bring forth one additional NCE. This estimate of marginal R&D cash outlay per additional NCE was $75 million in 1990 dollars.

Wiggins' analysis is based on NCE approvals for marketing, not NCEs entering human testing. If the average time from the filing of an investigational new drug (IND) application to approval of the drug by the FDA was 6.5 years (as Hansen's early survey indicated), then Wiggins' sample corresponds to NCEs first entering clinical testing between roughly 1963 and 1979, a period that overlaps substantially with the Hansen study (1963 to 1975). Thus, Wiggins' estimate of $75

million in cash costs is roughly in line with Hansen's estimate of $65.5 million, especially when one considers Wiggins' analysis probably covers a somewhat more recent population of NCEs than does Hansen's.

Wiggins' NCE sample is different from Hansen's, however, because it includes licensed-in products as well as self-originated NCEs. It is unknown how the full costs of discovery and development for licensed-in products compare with those of self-originated drugs. Though the cost of developing licensed-in products is likely to be lower for the licensee, if the licensor is a Pharmaceutical Manufacturers Association (PMA)-member company, then Wiggins' method would have captured the early costs.

Although Wiggins converted cash R&D costs to their present value at the time of market approval, he did so by assuming the cash costs followed Hansen's estimated time profile.[10] Like Hansen, Wiggins used an 8 percent cost of capital. Starting with higher out-of-pocket expenses, Wiggins necessarily concluded the full cost of bringing an NCE to market is higher than Hansen predicted. In 1990 dollars, Wiggins' estimated cost of discovery and development of a new NCE is $123.4 million[11] compared with $108 million estimated by Hansen (175).

■ The Grabowski and Vernon Study

Grabowski and Vernon (160) also used annual aggregate R&D data reported by PMA to estimate the average cost of developing new NCEs approved by the FDA for marketing during the 1970s. Like Wiggins, Grabowski and Vernon estimated the cost per NCE for both self-originated and licensed-in drugs. They assigned

---

[9] The average research expenditures for NCEs in the third, fourth, and fifth year prior to FDA market approval as reported to the Pharmaceutical Manufacturers Association was used as the measure of research expenditure.

[10] Since Wiggins' analysis included licensed-in as well as self-originated drugs, he should have used a different, and probably shorter, time profile for the licensed-in drugs. Data on development times for approved licensed-in drugs suggest they are substantially shorter than the development times for approved self-originated products (107), which suggests lower costs to the licensee. Had Wiggins applied a different profile to the licensed-in drugs, his estimate of total capitalized cost would have been lower.

[11] This value disagrees with Wiggins' estimate, $144 million in 1990 dollars. As discussed by Woltman (524) and DiMasi et al. (109), Wiggins made an error in calculating the total capitalized cost. OTA's re-estimate, $123.4 million, is slightly lower than DiMasi's recalculation, $124.7 million in 1990 dollars, because of differences in price indexes used.

R&D expenditures in each year between 1962 and 1978 to product introductions in the years 1970-79 using assumptions about the application of each year's expenditures to the future years' introductions. For example, Grabowski and Vernon assumed that in 1965, 10 percent of R&D expenditures for NCEs was spent on drugs introduced in 1970, 10 percent on drugs introduced in 1971, etc.[12]

This weighting scheme was then used to estimate the cost of introductions in each year. Compounding these values to the date of market introduction at 9 percent, Grabowski and Vernon estimated the mean cost per successful NCE approved by the FDA between 1970 and 1979 was $142 million in 1990 dollars. Because the weighting scheme assumes a total discovery/development period of 8 to 12 years (lengthening over the period of study), this estimate corresponds to NCEs first entering human testing in the period roughly bounded by 1965 and 1972. This period falls within the bounds of Hansen's study years.

Whereas Hansen's total estimated cost in 1990 dollars with a 9-percent discount rate is $114.8 million for drugs entering testing in the period, Grabowski and Vernon estimated an average cost of $142 million. For NCEs approved in 1975, Grabowski and Vernon estimated cash R&D outlays of $86.7 million in 1990 dollars compared with $65.5 million estimated by Hansen.

■ Comparison of Estimates

The studies discussed above are best compared by standardizing for constant dollar year and cost of capital, chosen here to be 1990 and 9 percent. Table 3-3 shows the estimates from each reviewed study.

The three studies of research conducted on NCEs first entering clinical testing in the 1960s and early 1970s use different methods and arrive

Table 3-3—Estimates of the Full Cost of Bringing a New Chemical Entity to Market[a] ($ 1990 millions)

Study	First year of clinical testing (midpoint)	
	1963-75 (1969)	1970-82 (1976)
Hansen, 1979................	$114.8	—
DiMasi et al., 1991.............	—	$259
Wiggins, 1987................	131.5	—
Grabowski and Vernon, 1990....	142	—

[a] All estimates were adjusted for inflation using the GNP implicit price deflator and were calculated at 9 percent cost of capital.

SOURCE: Office of Technology Assessment, 1993.

at estimates differing by up to 25 percent. Since the methods used in each study are not completely independent,[13] more congruence might have been expected.

Because neither Wiggins nor Grabowski and Vernon differentiated between licensed-in and self-originated drugs, their estimates should be lower, or at least no higher, than those of Hansen. Yet the cash outlays estimated in both industry-level studies are higher than those of Hansen. Hansen estimated cash outlays per successful NCE of $65 million; Wiggins estimated $75 million; and Grabowski and Vernon estimated $86.7 million.

VALIDITY OF R&D COST ESTIMATES

All of the R&D cost studies described above begin with estimates of R&D cash outlays in each phase of development, the time required to complete each phase, and the success rate for projects in each phase of the process. These estimated cash flows are then capitalized with a cost of capital that differs among studies. The validity of the studies rests ultimately on the accuracy of the estimates of cash outlays and the timing of those outlays. In this section, OTA analyzes the validity of the estimates of cash

---

[12] These assumptions were based in part on a regression estimate Thomas made in 1986 (421).

[13] Hansen used the sample firms' self-reported data on R&D expenditures to estimate basic research costs to their present value; Wiggins used Hansen's time profile generated from a survey of companies' NCE introductions to capitalize costs, and Grabowski and Vernon's time profiles were based largely on data supplied by the CSDD NCE database, the same database from which Hansen's sample was drawn and from which estimates of Hansen's R&D time profile were partially drawn.

outlays, their timing, and the success rates from stage to stage in the development process.

Are the estimates of cash outlays accurate? OTA addressed this question in two ways. First, we critically assessed the validity of the methods and data sources used to arrive at the estimates and the potential importance of departures from full validity. Second, we attempted to corroborate the findings with data from independent or semi-independent sources.

The assessment of validity of the methods concentrates on the project-level studies of Hansen (175) and DiMasi (109) for two reasons. First, the DiMasi study offers the most recent estimate which industry representatives and others have quoted widely as the definitive estimate of research costs (325). Second, the other studies based on aggregate R&D expenditures draw from the project-level analyses of Hansen and DiMasi for estimates of the time profile of development and are therefore partially dependent on them.

▮ Validity of Study Methods

The validity of the project-level studies depends on three aspects of the study methods:

- Sample of firms;
- Sample of NCEs; and
- Accuracy of survey responses regarding:
  1. clinical period cash outlays,
  2. preclinical period cash outlays,
  3. phase-specific development times, and
  4. phase-specific success rates.

THE SAMPLE OF FIRMS

Both Hansen and DiMasi examined NCEs originated at U.S.-owned, research-intensive pharmaceutical firms. Hansen's early study included 14 firms willing to respond to the survey; DiMasi's later study included 12. Because the samples were predominantly large well-

established companies in both surveys, the reported R&D costs may not reflect the cost experience of small and relatively young firms,[14] although the direction of potential biases between large and small firms is unknown.[15] Even if systematic differences in R&D costs by firm size or total R&D commitment do exist, they should not survive for long, for the industry would gradually reorganize to operate at the most efficient level. The responding firms in the DiMasi study represented 40 percent of domestic R&D, as measured by PMA, and the distribution of R&D by therapeutic class in these firms was virtually identical to the distribution of R&D in the U.S. pharmaceutical industry as a whole.[16] Thus, the sample of firms appears to pose no serious threat to the validity of the study.

THE SAMPLE OF NCES

Both studies selected a sample of NCEs that originated within the company's U.S. research organizations. NCEs were selected from a database maintained by CSDD of new products under development. Probability samples were drawn from the universe of NCEs in the CSDD database, but some nonresponding companies could have biased the sample. Furthermore, neither study reported the within-firm response rate. If firms failed to provide data on some NCEs for which data were poor, or if they selectively reported on NCEs for some other reason, the sample of NCEs could be biased. Again, the effect of such potential biases on cost estimates cannot be judged.

The adequacy of the sample size to reliably predict costs is determined by the underlying variation in the costs to be measured. The sample size in the Hansen study was 65 to 70 NCEs. The precise NCE sample size was not reported. DiMasi examined 93 NCEs. The higher the

---

[14] The emergence of dozens of small biotechnology firms performing pharmaceutical research in the 1980s would make this point more salient for periods later than those studied by Hansen and DiMasi.

[15] Pharmaceutical firms may experience decreasing returns to scale of R&D at low levels of R&D (213). Comanor found the marginal productivity of research personnel is inversely related to the size of the firm (85), but after controlling for R&D levels, Jensen did not find such a relationship (213).

[16] Hansen did not provide estimates of the proportion of domestic R&D accounted for by the 14 firms in his sample.

Table 3-4—Confidence Intervals for Clinical Period Cash Outlays in DiMasi Study
($ 1987 millions)

Phase	Mean cost[a]	Standard deviation	95% confidence interval for mean	Probability that true mean is within 10 percent of estimated mean
I.	$2,134	$4,519	$1,184 - 3,084	0.34
II.	3,954	5,230	1,729 - 4,179	0.36
III.	12,801	13,974	8,236 - 17,366	0.41
Long-term animal.	2,155	2,411	1,480 - 2,830	0.46
Other animal.	648	1,183	49 - 1246	0.17

[a] Calculated for all new chemical entities entering the phase.

SOURCE: Office of Technology Assessment, 1993, based on data provided in J.A. DiMasi, R.W. Hansen, H.G. Grabowski, et al., "The Cost of Innovation in the Pharmaceutical Industry," *Journal of Health Economics* 10:107-142, 1991.

underlying variation in costs, the larger the sample size must be to meet any required level of precision. Hansen did not report on the observed variation in costs among NCEs, so there is no way to evaluate the precision of his estimate.

DiMasi did report the sample standard deviation of cash outlays in each phase of the clinical period. Table 3-4 shows the standard deviations, the 95-percent confidence intervals[17] for the true mean cash outlay in each clinical phase, and the estimated probability that the true mean cash outlay in each phase lies within 10 percent of the estimated mean. The chance that the true mean cost is no more than 10 percent greater or less than the estimated cost of each phase ranges from 17 to 46 percent over the different clinical phases. To have a higher chance of estimating the mean costs with no more than a 10-percent error in either direction, the sample size must be bigger.

Because the cost of one phase may be correlated with the cost of another, the precision of the estimate of total cash costs cannot be computed with the existing data (106). Thus, the precision of the total cost estimate is unknown.

ACCURACY OF SURVEY RESPONSES

The project-level studies depend on data supplied by responding companies that are unavailable from other sources. The accuracy of such data depends on two factors: the ability of firms to provide accurate data (i.e., does the company have access to accurate information?), and the motivation of firms to provide accurate data.

Clinical Period Cash Outlays—OTA's interviews with pharmaceutical company managers indicated that, once projects reach the clinical stage, virtually all companies have project-level cost accounting systems that keep track of funds spent on specific projects, generally identified by the chemical or biological compound. Therefore, most firms have the ability to report data on overall clinical period outlays.

OTA was unable to obtain much information about the structure of such accounting systems; hence, the ability of firms to identify expenditures by clinical phase is unclear. All companies would have an accurate picture of monthly charges to individual project accounts, however, and the dates at which phase I, phase II, and phase III trials began are available to companies, so allocation of costs by date is a reasonable approach to estimating the distribution of costs by phase. If companies responded to survey questions with this approach, the phase-specific estimates would be reasonably accurate.

Companies responding to either survey may have handled indirect, overhead, and capital costs in inconsistent or biased ways.[18] For example, in some companies the costs of a central computer may be billed to specific projects based on actual use; in others, these costs are charged to projects based on a predetermined allocation formula.

---

[17] A 95-percent confidence interval means there is a 5 percent chance the true mean will lie outside the interval.

Such differences in cost allocation conventions may explain part of the high variation in reported phase-specific costs among NCEs.

The money spent to acquire capital equipment and facilities used in research (referred to as capital expenditures) sometimes is not allocated to project-level management cost accounts. How companies allocated these expenses to specific NCEs for the purpose of the survey is unknown. If a responding company estimated only direct expenditures in its clinical period R&D, but included R&D capital expenditures in its total R&D expenditures, the costs in the clinical period would be underestimated, but the ratio of preclinical period costs to total R&D costs would be overestimated. Because clinical period costs occur later, the total capitalized cost would appear higher using this method. On the other hand, plant and equipment costs are always accounted for with depreciation formulas, which spread costs out for a number of years subsequent to the actual capital expenditure.[19] Because a proper cost estimate should be based on actual cash outlays, the delay in accounting for capital costs will skew expenditures toward the end of the period and will cause the total costs of R&D capitalized to the point of market introduction to be underestimated.

One hypothetical scenario that a pharmaceutical firm presented to OTA estimated that total costs capitalized to the point of market introduction could be underestimated by as much as 12 percent because of depreciation methods, but the size of the underestimate depends critically on assumptions about the initial cost of facilities and equipment, their useful life, the length of time such assets are used for the project, their remain-

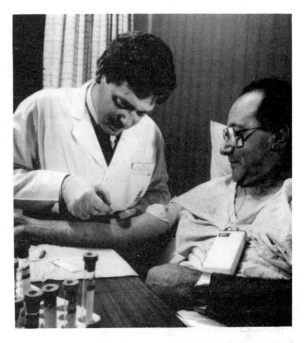

Photo credit: THE UPJOHN COMPANY

The cost of testing NCEs in humans has risen rapidly in recent years. New diagnostic tests make for more expensive and larger clinical trials.

ing value at the end of the project, and the extent of shared use among different research projects.

Preclinical Cash Outlays—Both of the project-level studies estimated the preclinical cash outlays for each sampled NCE from company survey responses to similar (but not identical) questions about annual expenditures for total NCE-oriented R&D and preclinical NCE-oriented R&D.[20] In DiMasi's study the reported ratio of preclinical to total expenditures was 66 percent, but DiMasi adjusted this estimate to 58 percent to account for trends in total spending over time. In Hansen's study the reported ratio of basic to total NCE

---

[18] Although the survey questionnaires did contain questions about the methods of estimating overhead, indirect, and capital costs associated with research projects, the questions were structured broadly and the study authors have provided no details about how such costing methods may have varied (109,175).

[19] If a piece of equipment, bought new, has a 10-year life, for example, the company might charge this expenditure off at 10 percent of its initial cost each year over the next 10 years. This annual depreciation charge would then be allocated across the projects that shared in use of the capital equipment.

[20] DiMasi asked companies to report total expenditures for self-originated NCE R&D and preclinical expenditures for self-originated NCE R&D in the period 1970-86. Hansen asked companies to provide estimates of total and "basic" NCE-oriented R&D conducted in the United States in the years 1962-75.

research was 51 percent. When basic research is combined with short-term preclinical animal research (estimated separately in Hansen's study) to obtain an estimate of the percent of preclinical expenditures (i.e., comparable to DiMasi), the resulting ratio is 54 percent.

The accuracy of these estimates depends both on the capability of firms to separate preclinical expenditures for NCEs from those of other products (such as combination drugs, new formulations, new drug delivery systems, etc.) and on their motivation to report such expenditures accurately.

The capability of firms to identify such preclinical expenditures would depend on the structure of their cost accounting systems. Although OTA did not have access to information on the structure of these systems in any firm, virtually all companies of reasonable size have in place project-level cost accounting systems. Projects to extend product lines of existing NCEs are probably separately identified. Any project to develop a licensed-in drug is also likely to have its own account. Separating projects among the categories required to estimate the preclinical ratio would require categorizing these projects, which can be done with a reasonable level of effort by knowledgeable personnel. Thus, it is reasonable to assume companies can slot R&D expenditures into the detailed categories needed for the estimate.

Motivation is another matter. Because the estimated ratio of preclinical cost to total R&D cost cannot be verified without an independent audit of cost accounting information, a company that understood the use to which the data would be put and with a strategic incentive to overestimate the preclinical ratio could do so without potential for discovery.

Although the firms responding to the early study may not have been aware of the potential policy uses of the study's conclusions, those responding to the later study would surely have been aware of the use to which the data would be put and its potential use in political debates. A brief review of the methods and findings of the early study could alert respondents to the importance of preclinical costs to the final full cost estimate. Thus, the motivation to overestimate this percentage cannot be discounted, especially in DiMasi's later study.

If companies responding to the DiMasi survey overestimated the percent of self-originated U.S. R&D expenditures devoted to preclinical research by 5 percentage points, so that the true percent was 53, as in Hansen's study, the estimated total cost of developing a new NCE would be $228 million in 1990 dollars, 12 percent less than the $259 million estimated by DiMasi et al.

Phase-Specific Development Times—The studies used identical methods to estimate a typical development time profile for NCEs in their sample. Responding companies reported the start date and ending date for each NCE entering a phase. The study researchers then calculated the mean phase length for all NCEs entering the phase.[21] Not only do companies have accurate archival records to provide these dates, but companies also must report on the start and progress of clinical testing to the FDA. Although data reported to the FDA are not in the public domain unless an NCE is ultimately approved for marketing, it is unlikely companies would deliberately misreport such data in survey responses.

The length of the period from submission of a new drug application to FDA approval was not estimated from the company survey; rather, the authors estimated average new drug application review times from the CSDD NCE database. In the early study, Hansen used the reported mean time from NDA submission to approval of all approved NCEs in the database, 24 months. DiMasi used the reported mean NDA review time for approved self-originated NCEs first tested in humans between 1970 and 1982, 30.2 months.

OTA re-estimated the NDA review period for all self-originated U.S. NCEs in the CSDD

---

[21] The mean phase lengths were weighted to take account of sampling probabilities.

database approved between 1967 and 1979, the time corresponding to Hansen's sample of NCEs (107).[22] The estimated approval time was 26 months. Thus, Hansen may have slightly underestimated the review time in the early study. The effect on total costs is negligible, however. Hansen's estimate would increase from $108 million to $110 million.

Companies also did not report the length of the preclinical period, but the studies' authors estimated it through other means. DiMasi used the CSDD database on approved NCEs which contains company reports on the date of first synthesis of a compound and the date of first human clinical testing. Because NCEs can be identified as self-originated or licensed-in, DiMasi was able to estimate the preclinical period for the large sample in the CSDD database of approved self-originated NCEs that U.S. firms developed during the study period. The mean estimated length of the preclinical period was 42.7 months.[23]

Hansen had no information at hand with which to estimate the length of the preclinical period. He simply assumed that the period was 36 months in length. OTA analyzed published CSDD data on NCEs approved between 1969 and 1982 and found the mean reported preclinical period was about 30 months. (107). A shorter preclinical period would reduce Hansen's estimated costs slightly (see table 3-5).

The preclinical period as defined by DiMasi (107) begins at the point of synthesis of a compound. Since firms must screen multiple products to obtain a lead compound (399) and engage in basic research to understand disease pathways before synthesizing a new product, this period could understate the length of the true preclinical period. If the true mean preclinical

Table 3-5—Effects of R&D Time Profile on Costs of R&D in Project-Level Studies[a] ($ 1990 millions)

Study	Capitalized cost	Percent increase (decrease) from baseline
Hansen (1979)[b]		
● Baseline estimate	$108	—
● NDA review time		
26 months	109	0.9%
● Preclinical time		
30 months	106	(1.8)
43 months	109	0.9
60 months	114	5.5
● NDA review time/preclinical time		
26 months/30 months	108	0
26 months/43 months	110	1.8
26 months/60 months	115	6.4
DiMasi et al. (1991)[c]		
● Baseline estimate	259	—
● Preclinical time		
60 months	270	4.2

[a] Estimates were adjusted for inflation using the GNP implicit price deflator.
[b] Cost of capital is 8 percent.
[c] Cost of capital is 9 percent.

KEY: NDA = new drug application.

SOURCE: Office of Technology Assessment, 1993, based on data provided in J.A. DiMasi, R.W. Hansen, H.G. Grabowski, et al., "The Cost of Innovation in the Pharmaceutical Industry," *Journal of Health Economics* 10:107-142, 1991; R. Hansen, "The Pharmaceutical Development Process: Estimates of Development Costs and Times and the Effect of Proposed Regulatory Changes," *Issues in Pharmaceutical Economics*, R.A. Chien (ed.) (Lexington, MA: D.C. Heath and Co., 1979).

period was 5 years, the cost estimates would increase modestly (see table 3-5).

The combined impact on total capitalized costs of potential changes in the NDA review times in the Hansen study and a longer preclinical period is shown in table 3-5. The estimated capitalized costs increase modestly—by about 4 to 6 percent in both studies—as a result of these potential errors in timing.

---

[22] Hansen estimated a mean 4.5-year lag between IND and NDA submission and a 2-year period from NDA submission to approval. Therefore, the Hansen study period for NCEs first entering human trials in 1963-75 would correspond roughly to NCEs reaching approval between 1969 and 1982.

[23] Although the preclinical period for drugs that were ultimately not approved may have been different from the period for drugs that were, OTA is unaware of any potential systematic differences that would suggest a bias in the estimate.

Success Rates—The estimated probability of reaching each clinical phase was based on survey responses. These data are both available and likely to have been reported accurately by survey respondents. Both studies predicted final approval rates not from the study sample, but from a large sample of NCEs in the CSDD database. DiMasi estimated the ultimate approval rate—23 percent—for the population of survey firm NCEs in the CSDD database that met the survey inclusion criteria. Hansen's estimated approval rate—12.5 percent—was based on all NCEs in the CSDD database covering the years of his study.[24]

Recently published data from the CSDD database suggest that Hansen's predicted success rate for his cohort of NCEs may have been slightly low. After 17 years of experience, approximately 14 percent of self-originated U.S. NCEs first investigated in humans between 1964 and 1975 had been approved, and further approvals were obtained later (107). A 14 percent success rate (rather than a 12.5 percent rate) would reduce Hansen's estimated capitalized cost per successful NCE by 11 percent, from $108 million to $96.2 million in 1990 dollars.

It is too early to tell whether DiMasi's predicted overall success rate will be borne out by history. The effect of the 1.5 percentage point difference in success rate on the estimated cost of Hansen's NCE sample reflects the importance of small errors either way in success rates on the ultimate cost of R&D.

▮ Corroborating Evidence

The estimates of R&D cash outlays and capitalized costs in the project-level studies are imprecise and potentially biased, but the magnitude and net direction of these errors cannot be predicted. Therefore, OTA looked for estimates of R&D costs from independent data sources to provide additional confidence about the accuracy of the estimates from the project-level studies.

Occasionally anecdotal data come to light on the cash outlays required for the development of specific NCEs. For example, in depositions filed for a patent infringement lawsuit, Genentech claimed it had spent $45 million to develop Protropin™, its human growth hormone product, (494) and Eli Lilly certified that it had spent $16 million between 1980 and 1987 on its effort to develop its version of the drug (495). In another example, a 1980 report of the development cost of an oral systemic drug for chronic use estimated $21 million in outlays in the clinical period (226). Unfortunately, anecdotal estimates of this kind do not help verify industrywide costs, because they are self-selected and do not reflect the cost of failures or basic research.

OTA attempted to corroborate the estimates of R&D costs with two approaches. First, the industry-level studies reviewed in the previous section produced independent estimates of R&D cash outlays per success. The consistency of these studies' findings on cash outlays with those of the project-level studies is examined below. Second, data on trends in important components of R&D costs are examined to determine whether they are consistent with the rapid rise in real cash outlays implied by the two project-level studies of R&D costs.

INDUSTRY-LEVEL STUDIES

The industry-level studies help to verify the reasonableness of total cash outlays required to produce an NCE. These studies begin with aggregate R&D spending reported to PMA by its member companies (320). Because Wiggins' estimate of cash outlays per successful NCE is completely independent of data obtained in the project-level study, Wiggins is a good corroborative source.[25]

---

[24] Both studies used Kaplan-Meier survival curve analysis (219,225) to estimate the ultimate success rate in the NCE cohort under study.

[25] Grabowski and Vernon's estimate of R&D cash costs is less useful for corroborative purposes than Wiggins' estimate because the estimated cash outlays are built from an assumed relationship between NCE approvals in 1 year and R&D expenditures in previous years.

Wiggins estimated cash outlays per successful NCE at $75 million (in 1990 dollars) compared with Hansen's estimate of $65.5 million (in 1990 dollars). Because Wiggins was estimating the cost of developing all NCEs, not just self-originated NCEs, his cost estimate should be conservative. The population of NCEs entering testing was somewhat more recent than Hansen's, however, and Hansen's cost estimates are based more heavily on drugs entering human testing in the earlier years of his sample. Overall, then, Wiggins' study suggests Hansen's estimated cash outlays are not out of line with the true costs and may even be slightly underestimated.

However, before one can conclude that Hansen's estimate of cash outlays is too low, it is necessary to assess the validity of the aggregate R&D data reported to and compiled by PMA and used by Wiggins in his analysis. Are these company-generated estimates accurate? PMA does not audit its member companies' reported R&D expenditures, but comparison of PMA data with publicly available financial statements suggests that R&D spending reported to PMA has increased at rates very similar to those recorded in companies' financial statements. (See chapter 2.) Although OTA cannot rule out the possibility that PMA-member firms systematically overestimate human pharmaceutical research by the same percent each year, this congruence in rates of change with audited financial records suggests the PMA aggregate R&D data are reasonably sound estimates of total R&D spending.

The total R&D spending reported to PMA includes spending not only on new drug products but also on modifications and extensions of existing products. PMA publishes the firms' reported percent of R&D devoted to new products in most years. Between 1973 and 1987 this reported percentage varied in the range of 79 to 82. Wiggins used 80 percent as an estimate of the proportion of total PMA spending devoted to NCE R&D. The accuracy of the reported expenditures cannot be verified. How companies define "new products" is unclear; if they include follow-on products such as new formulations, the estimate could be inflated for the purpose of estimating NCE expenditures. If it is too high, then the cash outlays estimated by Wiggins would be slightly high.[26]

Although there are no industry-level studies available to corroborate DiMasi's project-level analysis, DiMasi conducted his own check on his estimates using aggregate PMA data. He allocated a portion of U.S. firms' aggregate NCE R&D costs in each year of the period 1967 to 1987 to the production of NCEs in subsequent years. Using this approach he estimated the cash outlays per successful new drug at $155 million (in 1990 dollars) compared with the survey-based method of $127.2 million. This allocation technique assumed that the production of self-originated successful NCEs would continue into future years at an average rate of 7.9 per year, despite the fact that real R&D spending rose rapidly over the period. The validity of this assumption is tenuous.

OTA did a quasi-independent check of the results of the DiMasi study using data on aggregate R&D spending by the U.S. pharmaceutical industry and the total number of self-originated NCEs introduced by pharmaceutical companies. OTA used DiMasi's estimates (109) of aggregate R&D spending on self-originated NCEs by the U.S.-based industry between 1967 and 1987, which were obtained from PMA. The total cash R&D outlays estimated in the DiMasi study ($127 million in 1990 dollars) were attributed to each self-originated NCE approved between 1979 and 1989, spread out over the time profile estimated in DiMasi's study. Total self-originated R&D expenditures for the U.S. pharmaceutical industry in 1977[27] calculated in this way were just

---

[26] Followup R&D conducted on existing products that have already been approved for marketing represents a real R&D cost that is not included in any of the empirical studies but which affect the company's net returns. This issue will be discussed in the next chapter on measuring returns.

[27] The year 1977 was the only one in which all self-originated NCE research would be for NCEs approved in the 1979-89 period.

5 percent less than PMA's aggregate spending estimates for that year. This result would suggest the costs, time profiles, and ratios of self-o~ ~ted to total R&D found in the DiMasi proj~ct-level study are at least internally consistent with one another.

UNDERLYING COMPONENTS OF OUT-OF-POCKET COSTS

The Hansen/DiMasi studies imply that real cash outlays per successful NCE almost doubled in the 7-year period separating the midpoints of their study years, from $65.5 million to $127.2 million (in 1990 dollars). The increase would have been even greater had the ultimate success rate not improved markedly. The two surveys cover NCEs first entering human testing in 1963-75 and 1970-82. Is there any evidence to support such a rapid increase in the real costs of conducting research between the two periods? OTA examined data on three inputs to pharmaceutical R&D—research personnel, animal research subjects, and human research subjects—to learn more about the factors driving the increase in costs per successful NCE.

Research Personnel—The number of R&D personnel that PMA member firms employ remained fairly stable throughout the 1970s but began to grow rapidly in 1980 (figure 3-1). Most of this growth was in scientific and professional personnel, which numbered about 12,000 in 1977, but increased to almost 29,000 by 1989. Greater detail is unavailable on the kinds of jobs these new employees performed.

As the R&D workforce grew, so grew the salaries of biomedical research personnel employed by industry (figure 3-2); however, after adjusting for general inflation,[28] salaries actually decreased a bit. From 1973 to 1979, the median annual salary of biological scientists employed by business and industry decreased from $59,961 to $52,545 (in 1990 dollars), and from 1981 to 1989 it rebounded from a low of $49,176 to $56,600.

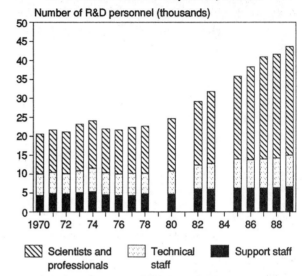

Figure 3-1—Research and Development Personnel in Pharmaceutical Companies, 1970-89

Number of R&D personnel (thousands)

Legend: Scientists and professionals | Technical staff | Support staff

SOURCE: Office of Technology Assessment, 1993, based on Pharmaceutical Manufacturers Association Annual Survey Reports.

If labor costs boosted the cost of bringing new drugs to market, it was largely due to the increased labor input per NCE, not wages.[29] How much of the increase in employment in the 1980s reflects increased labor inputs per successful NCE, versus adjustments for a larger field of NCEs entering each phase of clinical testing, or a greater commitment to basic research, is unknown. The most that can be said is that the trends in research personnel are not inconsistent with a substantial increase in R&D cash outlays per NCE for those NCEs first entering clinical research in the late 1970s and early 1980s.

Animal Research—Although data indicate the number of some types of animals used in pharmaceutical R&D may have decreased over the last decade, other evidence is consistent with increases in the per unit costs of animal testing.

One drug company, Hoffman-La Roche, reported that the number of animals it used fell from 1 million in 1979 to just under 250,000 in 1988 (204). Data collected by the U.S. Department of Agriculture (USDA) also shows a significant

---

[28] Inflation adjustments were made using the GNP implicit price deflator.

[29] The salary data do not reflect the costs of employee benefits, however, which may have increased in real terms over the period.

Figure 3-2—Median Annual Salary of Doctoral Biological Scientists[a]

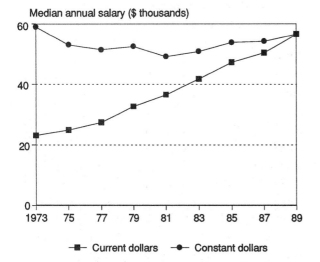

Median annual salary ($ thousands)

— ■ — Current dollars   — ● — Constant dollars

[a] Employed in business and industry.

SOURCE: National Science Foundation, Surveys of Science Resource Series, *Research and Development in Industry: 1987*, Detailed Statistical Tables, NSF 89-323 (Washington, DC: U.S. Government Printing Office, 1989). National Science Foundation, Surveys of Science Resource Series, *Research and Development in Industry, 1988*, Detailed Statistical Tables, NSF 90-319 (Washington, DC: U.S. Government Printing Office, 1990).

decline in absolute and relative use of animals for experimentation between 1975 and 1988 in States with a disproportionate number of industrial pharmaceutical R&D laboratories (459,460). However, these data are not definitive, since many pharmaceutical firms contract with other facilities to conduct their animal tests in other States. In addition, the USDA numbers do not include rodents, which make up the bulk of all animals employed in drug R&D, especially in the early efficacy and safety testing of potential drug candidates that companies ultimately abandon (133).

Beyond these few facts, several forces have been at work over the last 10 years to both increase and decrease the use of animals in pharmaceutical research. Because early testing involves the greatest number of animals, it also has the greatest potential for reduction. Hoffman-

La Roche said most of its reduction in the use of animals came from these early phases of the R&D process. Also, improvements in *in-vitro* testing and other innovations like computer modeling (described in chapter 5) may decrease some of the demand for rodents (133).

On the other hand, an earlier OTA report concluded that alternatives to many types of animal testing are limited (447). Also, pharmaceutical executives interviewed by OTA suggested any efficiencies brought about by such innovations in the R&D process are counterbalanced by the increased number of compounds to be tested for pharmaceutical activity. In addition, the number of animals used in later safety testing is largely governed by regulatory standards.[30]

Any possible decline in the number of animals used in drug R&D in the past decade was met by significant increases in the cost of acquiring animals and conducting tests in animals. An OTA contractor surveyed 3 major commercial breeders of animals used in drug R&D and 11 laboratories that perform such research for pharmaceutical firms. Table 3-6 shows trends in the costs of

Table 3-6—Trends in the Cost of Acquiring Research Animals ($ 1990)

Species	Cost per animal				Fold Increase
	1977	1980	1987	1990	
Rats.........	—	5.29	—	8.45	1.6
Mice..........	—	0.92	—	1.35	1.5
Guinea pigs....	—	—	—	25.30	—
Rabbits........	8	—	33.6	—	4.2
Dogs..........	195	—	—	300-500	1.5-2.6
Monkeys.......	391	—	—	1,000	2.6

NOTE: All costs were adjusted using the GNP implicit price deflator. Facilities surveyed were Charles River, Taconic Farms, and Hazleton. These facilities focus on breeding only. Although Hazleton conducts testing, it is carried out in a separate division.

SOURCE: Office of Technology Assessment, 1993, based on W.G. Flamm and M. Farrow, "Recent Trends in the Use and Cost of Animals in the Pharmaceutical Industry," contract report prepared for the Office of Technology Assessment, April 1991.

---

[30] See table 6-1 in chapter 6 for estimates of the number of animals typically used in each category of pharmaceutical safety testing.

Table 3-7—Price of Animal Studies[a] ($ 1990 thousands)[b]

Study	Estimated price in 1980	Price range in 1990	Fold increase	Number of Labs providing information
Acute rats..................	$ 0.8	$ 4 - 5	5 - 6.25	8
28-day toxicity in rats.........	15	30 - 65	2 - 4.3	6
Subchronic rats..............	38	55 - 143	1.4 - 3.8	8
2-year rat bioassay...........	384	250 - 575	.7 - 1.5	5
Teratology rats...............	23	52 - 70	2.3 - 3.0	5
Acute monkey..............	14	39 - 62	2.8 - 4.4	6
Subchronic monkey...........	74	108 - 184	1.5 - 2.5	6
Acute dog...................	2.3	22 - 51	9.6 - 22.1	7
Subchronic dog..............	46	72 - 147	1.6 - 3.2	7

[a] Each laboratory surveyed was given an identical protocol on which the price is based. The "cost" includes profit as well as all direct and indirect costs. Laboratories surveyed were Hazleton, Bioresearch, IIT, TSI Mason, Bio/dynamics, Pharmakon, PRI, and IRDC.

[b] All prices were adjusted to 1990 dollars using GNP implicit price deflator.

SOURCE: Office of Technology Assessment, 1993, based on W.G. Flamm and M. Farrow, "Recent Trends in the Use and Cost of Animals in the Pharmaceutical Industry," contract report prepared for the Office of Technology Assessment, DC, April 1991.

commonly used species.[31] The data indicate a significant upward trend in the real cost of acquiring all species of animals examined, with especially large increases in the costs of non-rodents.

OTA's contractor also surveyed eight facilities that conduct toxicological animals studies about the increases in their fees for tests involving various species. The results (shown in table 3-7) suggest the total costs of testing, which implicitly includes the cost of the animals' breeding, has also risen significantly over the last 10 years.

Another indicator of the potential increase in animal costs is PMA member firms' spending for safety and toxicological tests, R&D functions that use animals heavily. Between 1980 and 1989, spending for these functions went from $102 million to $565 million in 1989 dollars. Spending for safety testing increased from 7 to 10 percent of all R&D spending on human pharmaceuticals over the same 1980-89 period (321,324). However, these measures are imperfect, since not all animal testing is for safety and toxicology and not all safety and toxicology testing involves animals. The increase could reflect the increase in the number of NMEs tested for safety and toxicological effects during the 1980s.

Among the suggested reasons for animal cost increases in the OTA survey of animal research facilities are: 1) increased demands that animals be healthy and virus-free, largely eliminating the use of pound animals and explaining the particularly large increase in costs of some studies involving dogs; 2) stricter regulation of animals' living conditions under the Animal Welfare Act (most recently amended by Public Law 99-198), other government guidelines, and professional standards set by the American Association for Accreditation of Laboratory Animal Care; and 3) increased security for facilities housing animal research (133).

Research on Human Subjects—Pharmaceutical executives claim that the size of human clinical trials has increased dramatically over time. A rapid increase in trial sizes is consistent with an increase in the estimated cost of phase III clinical trials from $5.7 million (in 1990 dollars) for each new chemical entity (NCE) entering the phase in Hansen's study to $14.3 million (in 1990 dollars) in DiMasi's study. Part of the explanation

---

[31] Because each surveyed laboratory specializes in particular species, cost data for each type of animal are drawn from only one laboratory (except for dogs, which are represented by data from two breeders).

for such a large increase may be a change in the mix of drugs being tested from those for acute illness to those for chronic illness. Drugs for chronic use often require larger trial sizes.

Even within specific categories of drugs, however, the size of trials appears to have increased. OTA surveyed pharmaceutical companies for the size of clinical trials conducted prior to FDA approval for NCEs in three classes: antihypertensives, antimicrobials, and nonsteroidal anti-inflammatory drugs (NSAIDs). (See chapter 6 for a more detailed discussion of the survey and its findings.) Drugs in each class approved for marketing between 1978 and 1983 were compared with those approved between 1986 and 1990.[32] Table 3-8 shows the total number of subjects entered in trials up to the point of NDA submission. The average number of subjects increased between the two periods, with the largest increase occurring in research conducted outside the United States.

Although the drugs examined in the clinical trial survey do not correspond very well to the Hansen/DiMasi research periods (only the later years of the Hansen study correspond to the approved drugs in the 1978-83 period), they do show convincingly that the number of subjects in clinical trials increased in the period between the later years of the Hansen study and the later years of the DiMasi study.

The rapid increase in the number of foreign subjects suggests that the rising cost of preapproval research may be explained in part by the globalization of research strategies over time. If U.S. firms began to prepare self-originated NCEs for entry into foreign markets earlier, and if foreign governments increased their requirements for premarket approval over time, as they did during the 1970s, the estimated cost of developing NCEs in the IND-NDA period would increase even though part of the cost increase was for approval in other markets.

■ Conclusions About Validity of Existing Estimates

Although the cost estimates of bringing an NCE to market are imprecise and potentially biased, corroborative evidence from the aggregate studies suggests they are not grossly overestimated. The Hansen/DiMasi studies suggest: 1) the cost of developing NCEs rose rapidly in the 1970s and 1980s, and 2) increases in the numbers of employed research personnel, the size of clinical trials and the cost of animals are potentially important causes of this rise.

Some of the observed cost increase may be due to the restructuring of R&D into an integrated global process in the 1970s and early 1980s. U.S.-based firms became more aggressive in conducting the development required for approval of NCEs in other countries, thus compressing R&D expenditures into the pre-NDA approval phase. Nevertheless, these R&D costs, which may have been undercounted in the earlier studies because they occurred after the FDA approval date, are justifiable R&D outlays. Although the actual cash outlays required to bring a new drug to all of its potential markets may not have increased as rapidly as the studies suggest,

Table 3-8—Mean Enrollment in Clinical Trials Prior to New Drug Application, 1978-83 and 1986-90 (number of drugs in parentheses)

	1978-83	1986-90	Ratio of period 2 to period 1
Antihypertension drugs. . .	1,791 (9)	2,485 (9)	1.39
U.S. studies.	1,126 (8)	1,355 (9)	1.19
Foreign studies.	665 (8)	1,150 (9)	1.73
Antimicrobials.	1,885 (15)	3,461 (12)	1.84
U.S. studies.	1,248 (15)	2,049 (11)	1.64
Foreign studies.	637 (15)	1,412 (11)	2.22
Nonsteroidal antiflammatory drugs.	3,036 (4)	3,575 (4)	1.18
U.S. studies.	1,698 (4)	2,745 (4)	1.62
Foreign studies.	1,338 (4)	830 (4)	0.62

SOURCE: Office of Technology Assessment, 1993.

---

[32] Hansen's study years (NCEs first entering testing between 1963 and 1975) corresponds roughly with introductions between 1970 and 1981. DiMasi and colleagues' study years (1970-82) corresponds roughly with introductions between 1978 and 1990.

the recent estimates of DiMasi and colleagues of the pre-FDA approval cash outlays are reasonably accurate.

Can more or different kinds of studies improve on the existing estimates? More careful analysis of project cost accounts and adjustment of estimates for different cost allocation rules would give a more consistent estimate across firms, but it is unlikely the resulting estimates of cash outlays would be very different, and probably not lower.

Gaining access to proprietary company management cost accounts in a large enough number of companies would be very costly and would take many years. Although Congress has the power to subpoena financial data, pharmaceutical companies have demonstrated a willingness to actively resist providing access to this proprietary data. Past efforts of the U.S. General Accounting Office to obtain data on pharmaceutical costs were ultimately unsuccessful after many years of effort that ultimately involved decisions in the U.S. Supreme Court. (See appendix D for a history of the court cases and a legal analysis of congressional access to pharmaceutical companies' financial data.)

To summarize, the estimates by DiMasi and colleagues of the cash outlays required to bring a new drug to market and the time profile of those costs provide a reasonably accurate picture of the mean R&D cash outlays for NCEs first tested in humans between 1970 and 1982. The rapid increase in inflation-adjusted R&D cash outlays over the relatively short observed time span separating Hansen's and DiMasi's studies illustrates how quickly such costs can change and how sensitive such costs are to changes in R&D success rates over time.

OTHER FACTORS AFFECTING VALIDITY

■ The Cost of Capital

Capitalizing costs to their present value in the year of market approval more than doubles the cost of R&D as estimated by DiMasi and colleagues, from $127 million (in 1990 dollars) for

cash R&D outlays per successful drug to $259 million (at a 9 percent interest rate). While the practice of capitalizing costs to their present value in the year of market approval is a valid approach to measuring R&D costs, little is known about the appropriate cost of capital for R&D projects.

A completely accurate measurement of capitalized cost would require the analyst to know, for each dollar spent on the particular sample of NCEs studied by DiMasi, the cost of capital that pertained to that investment at the time it was made. Even though these are retrospective studies, the cost of capital that should be assigned is the cost the investors actually faced at the time they made their investments.

The cost of capital varies widely across types of research projects and with successive investments as the project progresses toward the market. (See appendix C for an explanation.) It also changes from day to day as the risk-free interest rate changes. But detailed data on the actual riskiness of particular projects invested at specific times simply do not exist. Consequently, the fully capitalized cost of R&D associated with the NCEs entering testing in DiMasi's study can be only crudely approximated.

All of the R&D cost studies reviewed in this chapter assumed the cost of capital for R&D investments was constant across all projects and over the entire period during which the R&D spending on the sampled NCEs was taking place. Myers and Shyam-Sunder estimated for OTA the inflation-adjusted weighted average cost of capital for a sample of pharmaceutical firms at three points in time, January 1, 1980, January 1, 1985, and January 1, 1990, at 9.9, 10.7 and 10.2 percent respectively (285). For pharmaceutical companies as a whole, then, a reasonably rough approximation for the cost of capital over the period of DiMasi's study would be 9 to 10 percent. (The higher the cost of capital, the higher would be the estimated R&D cost, so DiMasi's choice of 9 percent is conservative in that regard.)

Pharmaceutical firms can be thought of as collections of investments, some with high risk and some with low risk. R&D investments are riskier than other investments pharmaceutical companies make, but for reasons that are different from conventional ideas about risk (see appendix C for explanation). The earlier in the R&D process the investment is (e.g., at the preclinical phase of research), the higher its cost of capital is likely to be. How much riskier R&D investments are than the other investments of the firm cannot be precisely estimated with existing data, however. The best that can be done to get a quantitative estimate of the cost of capital for pharmaceutical R&D projects is to examine the cost of capital for firms investing largely in R&D and having relatively little investment in ongoing operations.

Myers and Shyam-Sunder estimated the real cost of capital for seven small pharmaceutical firms, three of which were biotechnology firms, at 14 percent, 4 percentage points higher than the cost of capital for 15 large pharmaceutical companies. In an unrelated study, Stewart (409) estimated the cost of capital for business risk for 1,000 publicly traded companies in the United States and Canada. Companies whose main business was providing R&D services (R&D laboratories) had a cost of capital for business risk approximately 4.5 percentage points higher than the cost of capital for business risk for the drug companies in Myers and Shyam-Sunder's sample. Shyam-Sunder's recent update of the Myers and Shyam-Sunder paper found a 2.6 percent difference in the net cost of capital between 30 biotechnology firms and 19 large pharmaceutical firms (390).[33] The results of these studies suggest that a 4 percent differential in the cost of capital from the beginning to the end of the research process is a reasonable upper bound for the capitalized costs of early R&D.

The weighted average cost of capital for pharmaceutical firms with ongoing operations (after adjusting for inflation expectations) was roughly 9 to 10 percent over the past 15 years. Investments in manufacturing capacity should therefore be below that value, while R&D investments should be above it. A reasonable upper bound on the true cost of capital for early pharmaceutical R&D can be constructed by assuming investments in a manufacturing plant have a 10 percent cost of capital (a high estimate). Applying the 4 percent spread (a relatively high estimate) to the 10 percent cost of capital, the real cost of capital for early R&D would be no greater than 14 percent.

OTA recalculated DiMasi's study with a cost of capital that decreases linearly over the life of R&D projects from 14 to 10 percent. The resulting capitalized cost in DiMasi's study increases from $259 million to $359 million (in 1990 dollars). Thus, an upper bound on the full cost of bringing NCEs to market in the 1970s is roughly $359 million. These calculations highlight the sensitivity of the estimate of fully capitalized R&D costs to assumptions about the cost of capital for R&D.

TAX SAVINGS FROM R&D

A company's effective cost of bringing a new drug to market is substantially reduced by tax savings the company (or its investors) receives when it invests in R&D. The net cost of every dollar spent on research must be reduced by the amount of tax avoided by that expenditure. These tax savings from R&D come about both from deductions and from tax credits that reduce a company's tax liability when it spends money on R&D.[34]

---

[33] A 1989 survey of approximately 145 biotechnology firms engaged in therapeutic health markets reported R&D expenses accounted for 67 percent of product sales (64).

[34] Companies get tax breaks from a number of provisions in the Federal tax code that effectively reduce the amount of taxes they owe on earned income. (See chapter 8 for details.) Some of these tax savings are not influenced by the amount of money the company invests in R&D. For example, companies that manufacture products in Puerto Rico and other U.S. possessions can take advantage of a tax credit on income from those operations (see chapter 8). The amount of the possessions tax credit that can be claimed is unaffected by how much R&D the company performs. Thus, the effect of taxes on the cost of R&D must be computed as if the possessions tax credit did not exist. Only those tax savings that come about from conduct of R&D should be included in the analysis.

Table 3-9—U.S. Corporate Marginal Tax Rates, 1971-91

Taxable income ($)	1971-74	1975-78	1979-81	1982	1983	1984-86	1987[a]	1988-91
0-25,000............	22	20	17	16	15	15	15.0	16
25,000-50,000.......	48	22	20	19	18	18	16.5	16
50,000-75,000.......	48	48	30	30	30	30	27.5	25
75,000-100,000.......	48	48	40	40	40	40	37.0	34
100,00-335,000.......	48	48	48	46	46	46	42.5	39
335,000-1,000,000....	48	48	48	46	46	46	40.0	34
1,000,000-1,405,000..	48	48	48	46	46	51	42.5	34
1,405,000+..........	48	48	48	46	46	47	40.0	34

[a] 1987 tax rates were based on average rates paid in 1986 and 1988. Figures shown are the average or rates paid by all firms in 1987.

SOURCE: U.S. House of Representatives, U.S. Congress, "The Overview of the Federal Tax System," 102d Congress (Washington, DC: U.S. Government Printing Office, April 10, 1991).

Under section 174 of the Federal tax code, qualifying R&D expenses are deductible from taxable income. This tax deduction reduces the cost of qualifying R&D by the amount of the company's marginal tax rate.[35] Table 3-9 presents the U.S. corporate marginal tax rates for the years 1971 to 1991. Because of the size and sales of most major pharmaceutical firms, the bulk of their taxable income would fall into the highest tax bracket.[36] Hence, in the simplest analysis, the cost of R&D spending should be reduced by the top tax rate.[37] Between 1971 and 1991, this marginal tax rate fell from 48 to 34 percent, thus effectively raising the cost of R&D. (It also raised the after-tax revenues from products resulting from the R&D, so the importance of taxes is not nearly as great when measuring net R&D returns, rather than R&D costs in isolation.)

In the R&D period covered by DiMasi (1970-87), the rate declined from 48 to 46 percent. With a 46-percent tax rate, the after-tax cost of $1.00 of R&D undertaken at the time of DiMasi's study would be: $1.00 - $0.46 = $0.54.[38] Today, the net cost of a dollar of R&D undertaken by an established company with positive net income would be $0.66.[39]

During the 1980s two tax credits were put into effect that reduce the cost of pharmaceutical R&D. In 1981, Federal tax law was amended to include a tax credit for any firm when it increases "qualifying" R&D expenses. This credit carried a statutory credit rate of 25 percent of qualifying

---

[35] If a firm conducts R&D in other countries that allow R&D to be deducted from taxable income but have tax rates that differ from those in the United States, the company may realize a different net rate of reduction in the cost of its R&D.

[36] Since the firms studied by Hansen and DiMasi made up 40 percent of domestic R&D, they were probably composed largely of well established pharmaceutical firms.

[37] Unlike other R&D expenses that are deducted in the year they are made, capital expenditures for R&D, such as new R&D equipment or facilities, are depreciated from taxable income over several years. The shorter the period of depreciation, the greater will be the effect of tax savings on the cost of R&D. Prior to 1981, Federal law required firms to deduct R&D capital expenditures in equal amounts over the useful life of the equipment or building, which could be 10 years or more. Beginning in 1981, firms could fully depreciate R&D capital expenditures within 3 years, although in 1986 Congress raised the period to 5 years. Not much is known about the depreciation schedules used to estimate R&D costs in the Hansen and DiMasi studies. Depreciation schedules on tax returns may be different from those for financial statements, and without more detailed information it is impossible to know whether the net tax savings for R&D capital expenditures are higher or lower than the statutory marginal rate. OTA assumed for the analyses here that R&D capital expenditures are taxed at the marginal tax rate.

[38] As explained in chapter 8, not all R&D expenses meet the definition of "qualifying" laid out in section 174 of the tax code. This definition becomes important for calculating the orphan and R&D tax credits discussed below. However, it is not important here for calculating the deduction, because R&D expenses not deductible under section 174 are nonetheless deductible as other business expenses.

[39] Small startup biotechnology firms may have little or no taxable income, but tax losses can be carried forward into future years. Still some firms may never become profitable, and the value of future tax benefits is less than those that can be used immediately. Therefore, the net cost of research to such small firms may be higher than for established pharmaceutical firms.

expenses until 1986, when the rate was reduced to 20 percent. The credit pertains only to increases in R&D, not to actual expenditure levels, so the extent to which it actually reduces the cost of R&D would depend on research spending trends in firms themselves. Because pharmaceutical R&D grew rapidly in the 1980s, the pharmaceutical industry may have benefited more than other industries from the R&D tax credit.

The Orphan Drug Act of 1983 (Public Law 97-414) provided a 50-percent tax credit for qualifying clinical R&D on investigational drugs that have been granted orphan status by the FDA. The credit is available only for "qualifying" clinical research, not for animal or laboratory research and not for supervisory or other kinds of R&D expenditures typically disallowed by the Internal Revenue Service. Also, when the credit is applied, the expenses cannot be deducted, so the net cost of a dollar of qualifying research under this credit is effectively $0.50. Companies without current taxable income cannot save the credit for use in future years, however, so startup research-based firms may not have access to this credit.

Because these credits are of recent vintage and would not apply to the vast part of the research undertaken in the time periods studied by Hansen and DiMasi, they would not affect the net costs of that research. Chapter 8 contains estimates of the extent to which these credits have been claimed in recent years.

To illustrate how important tax savings are to net R&D costs, OTA recalculated the R&D cost per new chemical entity from DiMasi's estimates (table 3-10). The sample of NCEs that DiMasi studied underwent the great bulk of discovery and development at a time when the marginal tax rate was 46 to 48 percent. Adjusting for tax savings (using a 46-percent rate) without any other changes reduces the net cash outlays per NCE from $127.2 million to $65.5 million, and it reduces the total costs capitalized to the point of market introduction from $259 million to $140 million. When the cost of capital was permitted to decrease linearly from 14 to 10 percent over the

Table 3-10—After-Tax R&D Costs Estimated by DiMasi Under Different Assumptions About the Cost of Capital[a] ($ 1990 millions)

Cost of capital (%)	Before-tax savings	After-tax savings (46%)
9	$258,650	$139,671
10	279,112	151,045
Variable (10 - 14)	359,313	194,029

[a] All assumptions, given in 1990 dollars, were adjusted for inflation using GNP implicit price deflator.

SOURCE: Office of Technology Assessment, 1993, estimates adapted from J.A. DiMasi, R.W. Hansen, H.G. Grabowski, et al., "The Cost of Innovation in the Pharmaceutical Industry," *Journal of Health Economics* 10:107-142, 1991.

life of the R&D projects, the net after-tax cost was $194 million. This estimate is an upper bound on the cost of bringing new drugs to market for products that first entered human testing in the 1970s.

Lower tax rates in the 1980s would raise the net costs of research, all other things being equal, to as much as $237 million in after-tax dollars, but because R&D outlays per successful drug are extremely sensitive to changes in technical and regulatory conditions, it is impossible to predict the cost of R&D for projects beginning today. The rising number of biotechnology-based drugs under investigation in recent years (see below) may radically alter the time and expenditure profile in ways that can not be predicted from the DiMasi study.

RECENT TRENDS IN THE COST OF R&D

The studies of R&D costs reviewed in this chapter examined NCEs that entered testing in the 1960s and 1970s. There are few data sources, outside of aggregate R&D expenditures, to establish trends for drugs that entered clinical research in the 1980s. As the previous chapter described, R&D spending climbed dramatically in real terms throughout the 1980s, but the ultimate impact of these spending increases on the cost of developing NCEs will depend on the productivity of the research in bringing promising NCEs into clinical testing and ultimately to market.

OTA compared recent data (from the 1980s) on the outputs of pharmaceutical research, the length of the development period and success rates for NCEs with data from the 1970s. Overall, the data suggest the output of preclinical research—the submission of investigational new drug applications for new molecular entities—has increased in the 1980s. Moreover, the rate of success in reaching the NDA stage or market approval has improved for NCEs introduced in the 1980s. However, the higher success rates for NCEs may be partly driven by an increase in the proportion of INDs for licensed-in drugs.

∎ Trends in Commercial INDs for NCEs

Data published by the FDA Center for Drug Evaluation and Research show the total number of commercial INDs handled by the Center increased from an average of 253 per year between 1975 and 1980 to 334 per year between 1981 and 1990.[40] (See chapter 6 for more detail.) Because the same NCE may have multiple INDs, and new uses or formulations of existing drugs also require INDs, the total number of INDs is not a perfect indicator of increases in the number of NCEs entering clinical development. Data from CSDD's NCE survey of over 40 companies indicate the number of INDs for NCEs increased from 210 per year in 1975-78 to 299 per year in 1983-86 (107).[41] Although INDs for U.S. self-originated NCEs grew by 25 percent between the periods, the percent of all NCE INDs that was for self-originated drugs declined from 60 to 53 percent between the two periods. Licensed-in drugs and INDs submitted by foreign firms grew as a proportion of total NCE INDs submitted to the FDA.

Not only did the number of INDs increase rapidly throughout the 1980s, but the makeup of the drugs shifted from chemically synthesized compounds to biotechnology drugs (see figure 3-3) (66). This substantial shift means that the technologic and regulatory conditions that influence drug R&D costs have changed in the decade

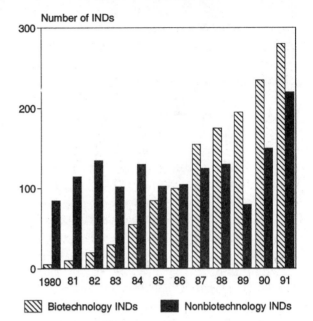

Figure 3-3—Biologic Applications for Investigational New Drugs, Fiscal Years 1980-91

Number of INDs

Biotechnology INDs ▨   Nonbiotechnology INDs ■

SOURCE: Federal Coordinating Council for Science, Engineering, and Technology, Office of Science and Technology Policy, Executive Office of the President, *Biotechnology for the 21st Century: A Report by the FCCSET Committee on Life Sciences and Health* (Washington, DC: U.S. Government Printing Office, February 1992).

of the 1980s. Success rates, regulatory delays, the length of the preclinical and clinical period, and costs of clinical research may be vastly different for these new drugs. Prediction of today's cost of bringing a new drug to market on the basis of the kinds of drugs that were being tested in the 1970s —the period of DiMasi's study—is bound to be inaccurate.

∎ Trends in Success Rates

Data CSDD supplied on NCEs developed by companies responding to its ongoing survey indicate the probability of reaching the NDA stage was higher for NCEs first entering clinical testing between 1980 and 1982 than it was for NCEs first entering clinical testing in the 1970s.

---

[40] The published IND numbers do not include biologicals, because the Center for Biologics does not compile such data. Biological products under development were few in the 1970s, but grew rapidly in the 1980s.

[41] DiMasi and colleagues also give information on the 1979-82 period. See chapter 6 for more detail.

Table 3-11 shows the proportion of NCEs in the CSDD sample for which an NDA was filed within 48 or 60 months of IND filing for four cohorts of NCEs first entering clinical testing.[42] In addition, the FDA supplied OTA with more recent data on a sample of NCEs whose first commercial INDs were filed in the 1984-86 period that were compared with an earlier published FDA analysis of a similar group of INDs first filed 1976-78. INDs reaching the NDA filing stage within 54 months increased from 6.8 to 11 percent. (Though few NMEs were approved from the 1984-86 cohort, the overall approval rate was also higher. See chapter 6 for more detail.)

Although overall success rates have improved in the recent past, the improvement may be due in part to a shift in NCEs from self-originated to licensed-in. Licensed-in drugs have higher success rates than do self-originated drugs, probably because they are self-selected for success. For example, of NCEs entering testing between 1970 and 1982, an NDA was submitted within 48 months for 7 percent of self-originated drugs, compared with 21 percent of licensed-in drugs (427). At 60 months, 28 percent of licensed-in NCEs had reached NDA submission compared with 9 percent of self-originated drugs. Of NCEs entering human testing among U.S. companies, those licensed-in grew from about 21 percent in 1975-78 to 27 percent in 1983-86 (107). Thus, the improvement in success rates for drugs first entering testing in the 1980s is at least partly due to the changing source of NCEs.

▌ Recent Development of Orphan Drugs

Since 1983, Federal law has stimulated the development of orphan products through a series of incentives and subsidies, including the tax credit for clinical research on designated orphans drugs. (See chapters 8 and 9 for more detail.) These products may have a very different cost

Table 3-11—Percent of NCEs Reaching NDA/PLA Submission in Given Time Intervals

Year in which NCE entered clinical trials	Percent filing NDA/PLA within:	
	48 months	60 months
1965-69	4.6%	7.0%
1970-74	8.0	12.0
1975-79	10.0	13.0
1980-82	12.0	17.0

KEY: NCE = new chemical entity; NDA = new drug application; PLA = product license application.

SOURCE: Office of Technology Assessment, 1993, based on data supplied by Tufts University Center for the Study of Drug Development from its database of NCEs reported by 41 pharmaceutical firms.

structure from other NCEs, not only because of the tax credit but also because they may involve smaller and shorter clinical trials than other drugs. Although FDA approval standards are no different for this class of drugs than for others, orphan drugs are likely to have smaller and quicker clinical research studies than other studies because of the relative rarity of the diseases studied.

The FDA provided OTA with confidential data on new molecular entities (NMEs) whose first commercial IND was filed in the years 1984-86. (See chapter 6 for more detail on this sample of drugs.) Within 54 months of the IND filing, an NDA had been filed for 11 percent of all INDs, and 3.8 percent had been approved (see chapter 6), whereas for NMEs that had orphan designations, an NDA had been filed within 54 months for 33 percent, and 11 percent had been approved.[43]

Regulatory approval times also appear to be shorter for orphan drugs. For example, during the period 1985-90, the average approval time for approved drugs without orphan designation was 29.3 months, while for approved orphan drugs it was 27.4 drugs (168). For products classified as ''A'' by the FDA, the approval time for non-orphans was 25.7 months, while for orphans it

---

[42] A regression of NDA filing rates on time indicated the increase shown in the table was statistically significant at the 10 percent level of significance for both the 48-month and 60-month success rates.

[43] OTA identified nine NMEs for which the first commercial IND had been filed in 1984-86, and which had been granted an orphan designation. An additional four NMEs in the IND cohort had orphan designations, but data on the sponsoring company were inconsistent and they were not used. (Exclusion of the four NMEs did not change the results materially.)

was 18.1 months (168). Although it is impossible to know whether the ultimate success rate for orphan products will be higher or lower than for nonorphans, the sensitivity of development costs to success rates suggests orphan drugs may have a substantial cost advantage.

CONCLUSIONS

The increase in the inflation-adjusted cost of developing a new drug from the early 1970s to the late 1970s is dramatic. Real cash outlays per successful NCE increased by almost 100 percent in the period. The evidence suggests that, in 1990 dollars, the mean cash outlay required to bring a new drug to market (including the costs of failures along the way) was in the neighborhood of $127 million for drugs first entering human testing in the 1970s. The size of this required cash investment depends on the rate of success at each stage of development and the ultimate productivity of the research enterprise. Small differences in the ultimate success rate can make a big difference in the cost per approved NCE. Other factors, such as changes in R&D technology and regulatory conditions, can also have dramatic and rapid impacts on costs. Thus, the estimates of the R&D cost per successful product are inherently unstable over time.

The fully capitalized cost of bringing a new drug to market cannot be measured with great accuracy because the cost of capital for R&D investments is unknown. The best evidence suggests, however, that for drugs first entering human testing in 1970-82, the after-tax cost per successful drug, capitalized to the point of FDA approval for market, was somewhere between $140 million and $194 million (in 1990 dollars).

Returns on Pharmaceutical R&D | 4

T he cash outlays spent in bringing a new product to the point of approval for marketing in the United States increased in the 1970s and early 1980s. These cash outlays occurred over a substantial period of time, an average of 12 or more years.

A company makes these investments expecting that the financial returns from successful drugs will be high enough to justify the money, time, and risk involved. If the expected financial returns are too low to repay investors, then research and development (R&D) will decline as fewer projects are pursued. On the other hand, if overall returns on drugs introduced in the past are more than enough to repay investors for the cost, time, and risk involved, then consumers are paying too much. Evidence of long-run persistence of higher returns for new drugs over what is necessary to justify the cost and risk of R&D would imply unnecessary pricing power for new drugs (366).[1]

In an industry with active competition, pharmaceutical R&D investment will follow expected returns on new products. The introduction of a ''pioneer'' drug, the first product introduced within a family of compounds, should and often does lead to R&D by rival firms intent on introducing a similar therapeutic alternative, or ''me-too'' drug (158,298), which can share the market with the leader. Box 4-A describes the intense competition among rival firms for the development of compounds in an important new class of drugs for the treatment of high cholesterol.

---

[1]The rationale for patent protection is based on the need for providing a return on the R&D necessary to bring an innovation to the market (366). In the absence of patent protection (or some other form of protection from imitation), competitors would copy the innovation at a fraction of the cost to the innovator and sell the product at prices that are insufficient to recover the initial R&D investment. Thus, incentives to invest in innovation would be compromised (242).

Box 4-A—HMG-CoA Reductase Inhibitors

In August 1987, the first of a newly discovered class of cholesterol-lowering drug compounds known as HMG-CoA reductase inhibitors was approved for marketing in the United States. The drug, lovastatin, developed by Merck & Company, generated higher first-year sales than any previously introduced prescription medicine. Today, lovastatin has annual sales exceeding $1 billion and maintains a 60 percent share of the U.S. market for all cholesterol-lowering drugs.

The competitive drive to bring the first HMG-CoA reductase inhibitor to market highlights the intense research and development (R&D) rivalry that frequently precedes the debut of an innovative new drug. Although Merck was the first company to win U.S. marketing approval for a drug in that class, Merck was not the first to synthesize and clinically test such an agent. The prototype HMG-CoA reductase inhibitor, mevastatin, was isolated in 1976 by researchers at Japan's Sankyo. Mevastatin entered phase I clinical trials in Japan and other countries in 1978. At that time, Mevastatin showed much promise in significantly reducing low-density lipoprotein (LDL) cholesterol levels with few side effects. Meanwhile, scientists at Merck isolated a related compound, lovastatin, early in 1979. Merck filed for a U.S. patent on lovastatin just months after Sankyo filed for a Japanese patent on mevastatin.

Foreign clinical trials with lovastatin began in April 1980 but were suspended just 5 months later because, according to a Merck spokesman, "a similar compound had caused a toxic reaction in animals at another lab." Although it was not announced at the time, the "similar compound" was Sankyo's mevastatin, which had been quickly withdrawn after intestinal lymphomas were found in 50 percent of laboratory dogs undergoing tests with the drug.

In 1982, Merck allowed several clinicians to file individually sponsored investigational new drug applications (INDs) for lovastatin in order to treat patients with severely high cholesterol unresponsive to existing therapies. The drug dramatically lowered LDL cholesterol with very few observed side effects. The results prompted Merck to reinstitute animal studies, and in May 1984 the company filed a commercial IND, allowing lovastatin to enter phase I clinical trials.

HMG-CoA reductase inhibitors drew more attention in 1985, as Dr. Michael S. Brown and Dr. Joseph S. Goldstein of the University of Texas won the Nobel prize for medicine for their work on LDL receptors. By November 14, 1986, Merck had finished its clinical and long-term animal studies and sent its new drug application (NDA) to the Food and Drug Administration (FDA). Lovastatin, with a IND/NDA classification of 1A, was approved within 9 months, bringing its total review time (from IND to NDA approval) to 1,204 days, making it one of the most rapidly approved drugs in the history of the FDA.

Meanwhile, the industry's R&D race produced additional HMG-CoA reductase agents. Sankyo's second HMG-CoA reductase inhibitor, pravastatin, licensed to Bristol-Myers Squibb, entered phase III clinical trials in Japan at the same time lovastatin entered phase III clinical trials in the United States. In October 1990, 21 months after Bristol-Myers Squibb submitted the NDA on January 31, 1989, FDA's Endocrinologic and Metabolic Advisory Committee unanimously recommended pravastatin be approved. On October 31, 1991, 3 years after approval in Japan, the FDA approved pravastatin with a "1C" rating, a new molecular entity (NME) with little or no therapeutic gain over existing therapies. Bristol-Myers Squibb initially offered pravastatin at a direct price discount of 5 percent and a 10 percent discount to wholesalers of lovastatin. By 1993, pravastatin's sales are estimated to reach $500 million.

Simvastatin, Merck's successor product to lovastatin, was recommended for approval by FDA's Endocrinologic and Metabolic Advisory Committee in February 1991 and was approved for marketing on December 21, 1991. As with pravastatin, the FDA gave simvastatin a "1C" rating, and it has been offered at a 5 to 10 percent discount to lovastatin. Unlike the breakthrough compound lovastatin, simvastatin has worldwide patent protection. Marketed outside the United States since 1988, simvastatin has been prescribed to over 1 million patients in 30 countries, and already ranks among the world's 50 top-selling drugs.

A list of HMG-CoA reductase inhibitors currently or formerly under development follows.

Compound	Sponsor	Approval Status
lovastatin	Merck	IND: April 1984. NDA: November 1986. Approval: August 1987.
pravastatin	Sankyo, Bristol-Myers Squibb	Launched in Canada, Europe, Japan, and Mexico. U.S. NDA: January 31, 1989. U.S. approval: November 31, 1991.
simvastatin	Merck	Launched in at least 17 countries worldwide, including most of Europe. U.S. NDA: November 1986. U.S. approval: December 1991.
colestolone	American Cyanamid	Entered U.S. clinical trials in 1987.
fluvastatin	Sandoz	U.S. NDA filed March 1992.
crilvastatin	Pan Medica	Phase II clinical trials.
dalvastatin	Rhone-Poulenc Rorer	Phase III clinical trials.
BAYW6228	Bayer	Phase II clinical trials.
HR780	Hoeschst	Phase II clinical trials.
CI 981	Warner-Lambert	Phase I clinical trials.
BB-476	British Bio-technology	Series of compounds under development; preclinical.
BMY-22566	Bristol-Myers Squibb	Preclinical studies.
SQ-33600	Bristol-Myers Squibb	Preclinical studies, discontinued.
BMY-21950	Bristol-Myers Squibb	Phase I clinical trials.
GR-95030	Glaxo	Preclinical studies, discontinued.
SC-45355	Searle	Preclinical studies, discontinued.
L-659699	Merck	Preclinical studies.
L-669262	Merck	Preclinical studies.
CP-83101	Pfizer	Preclinical studies.

Safety issues may lengthen the review period for successor products. As it considered pravastatin, the FDA's Endocrinologic and Metabolic Advisory Committee weighed increasing general concerns over the potential carcinogenicity of HMG-CoA reductase inhibitors against the need to maintain equitable review criteria for competing products. One FDA reviewer noted that too much emphasis on carcinogenicity data in pravastatin's review would "prevent a level playing field" with lovastatin. The approval of pravastatin and simvastatin suggest that comparable safety criteria continue to be used for successor HMG-CoA reductase agents.

The market potential for HMG-CoA reductase inhibitors is vast. In the United States alone, as many as 60 million people are estimated to have high cholesterol, but fewer than 1 million people currently receive drug therapy. As a result, the pharmaceutical industry continues to devote substantial R&D expenditures toward cholesterol-lowering drugs.

SOURCES: J. De Pass, "The World's Top 50 Prescription Drugs," *Medical Marketing & Media*, 26:21, August 1991. *F-D-C Reports: Health News Daily*, "Bristol-Myers Squibb Launching Pravachol in Mid-November," *F-D-C Reports: Health News Daily*, Nov. 4, 1991, p. 4-5. *F-D-C Reports: Prescription and OTC Pharmaceuticals*, "Rep. Weiss' Subcommittee Investigating Regulation of Merck's Mevacor, Roche's Versed, W-L's THA; Dec. 1 Subpoena Deadline Set for FDA, OMB Documents," *F-D-C Reports: Prescription and OTC Pharmaceuticals*, Nov. 23, 1987, p. 6-7. *F-D-C Reports: Prescription and OTC Pharmaceuticals*, "FDA Approves 15 of 21 New Molecular Entities in December; Commissioner Young Says Approvals Will Be More Evenly Distributed in Coming Years," *F-D-C Reports: Prescription and OTC Pharmaceuticals*, Jan. 11, 1988, p. 10-13. *F-D-C Reports: Prescription and OTC Pharmaceuticals*, "Bristol-Myers Squibb Pravachol (Pravastatin) Recommended for Approval by FDA Advisory Committee," *F-D-C Reports: Prescription and OTC Pharmaceuticals*, Oct. 29, 1990, p. 8-10. *F-D-C Reports: Prescription and OTC Pharmaceuticals*, "Cholesterol-Lowering Trials for New Classes of Drugs Should Include Clinical Endpoints," *F-D-C Reports: Prescription and OTC Pharmaceuticals*, Mar. 11, 1991, p. 7. *F-D-C Reports: Prescription and OTC Pharmaceuticals*, "Merck's Zocor (Simvastatin) Will Be Promoted by 1,230 Sales Reps Jointly With Smithkline Beecham," *F-D-C Reports: Prescription and OTC Pharmaceuticals*, Jan. 6, 1992. A. Garber, Assistant Professor, School of Medicine, Stanford University, Palo Alto, CA, personal communication, Jan. 5, 1993. N. Ishida, Finance Manager, Sankyo USA, New York, NY, personal communication, Oct. 17, 1991. M. Malkin, Merck & Company,Inc., Rahway, NJ, personal communication, Oct. 21, 1991. *Pharmaprojects* (Surrey, United Kingdom: P.J.B. Publications Ltd., 1991). R.L. Pierce, Food and Drug Administration, Public Health Service, U.S. Department of Health and Human Services, Rockville, MD, personal communication, Jul. 18, 1991. *Scrip World Pharmaceutical News*, "Sankyo's Compactin Effective in Familial Hypercholesterolaemia," *Scrip World Pharmaceutical News* 624:13, 1981. *Scrip World Pharmaceutical News*, "Blockbusters in R&D," *Scrip World Pharmaceutical News* 1104:24, 1986. *Scrip World Pharmaceutical News*, "Merck & Co. Products Lead World Markets," *Scrip World Pharmaceutical News* 1397:16-17, 1989. P.R. Vagelos, "Are Prescription Drug Prices High?" *Science* 252:1080-1084, 1991. M. Waldholz, "FDA Clears Sale of Bristol-Myers Cholesterol Drug," *New York Times*, Nov. 4, 1991, p. B5.

New drugs need not be very similar in molecular structure to compete in a therapeutic category. For example, new medicinal approaches to the treatment of hypertension proliferated during the 1980s, as calcium channel blockers and angiotensin converting enzyme inhibitors have competed with beta-blockers and diuretics (4). Thus, the opportunities for competitive R&D are numerous, and in an industry with a large number of competing research-intensive firms, this competition should reduce industrywide returns on pharmaceutical R&D as competing products are introduced to share existing markets.

This chapter examines the returns on pharmaceutical R&D. It provides two kinds of evidence on returns: the present value of dollar returns on new chemical entities (NCEs) introduced during a selected time interval (which can be compared with the present value of the R&D costs required to produce the NCEs); and the net internal rate of return (IRR), or economic profit, from all business activities of firms whose primary line of business is the development, manufacture, and sale of ethical pharmaceuticals.

RETURNS ON R&D: THE EVIDENCE

■ Overview of Methods

In chapter 3, the Office of Technology Assessment (OTA) reviewed the evidence on the full (or capitalized) cost of R&D at the point of market approval for drugs first entering clinical testing in the 1970s and early 1980s. The full cost of R&D can be thought of as the average value on the day the products are launched that successful drugs must have if they are to provide investors an adequate payback for the cash outlays, risk, and time spent in bringing the drugs to market.

The value of the potential income from successful drugs on the day of product launch depends on the complete product life cycle expected for these compounds. Figure 4-1 shows a hypothetical life cycle of R&D investment and revenues for an industry.

Suppose the industry starts from scratch with new companies 15 years before marketable products can be expected. The firms build or rent

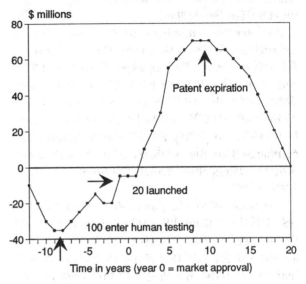

Figure 4-1—Cash-Flow Profile of 100 Drug Candidates

$ millions

Patent expiration

20 launched

100 enter human testing

Time in years (year 0 = market approval)

SOURCE: Office of Technology Assessment, 1993.

research facilities, then embark on programs to discover a group of candidate compounds for further research. Further laboratory and animal testing of these lead compounds over the next 3 to 4 years results in, say, 100 drug candidates that merit clinical testing. These 100 candidates then undergo rigorous testing to determine their safety and effectiveness in humans. More money is invested to fund the testing required to bring these drug candidates to market. As the testing process continues over the next 9 years, some compounds are found to be unsafe or ineffective and are abandoned. Ultimately, suppose only 20 of the 100 candidates jump all the hurdles and reach the market.

As the originators of the winning 20 compounds prepare for market entry, the firms developing them must invest again, this time in plant and equipment to manufacture the products. Once they are approved and launched, the new drugs start earning revenues (minus the costs of producing, marketing, and distributing them). Net revenues grow over the next few years and then flatten out. After 10 years or so, patents expire, and net revenues begin to decline as generic copies of the drugs are introduced. Ultimately, perhaps after 20 years, new generations of medical technology render the products obsolete, and they are removed from the market.

As figure 4-1 illustrates, in the early years of industry operation, cash flows out of the firms in the industry in the form of expenditures on R&D and manufacturing capacity. Years later, cash flows back into the firms as some of the investments paid off. Whether the NCEs pay off enough in revenues to justify the investment requires a comparison of the outflows of cash with their inflows, taking into account the timing of those cash flows.

The issue for this section is how to measure the net cash flows from the point of market approval to the end of the product's life cycle, taking account of the fact that revenues are uncertain, that costs must be incurred to manufacture, market and distribute the products, and that income delayed is worth less to investors than income today. Once the net income from the sale of successful drugs over their lifetime is appropriately measured, it must be compared with the fully capitalized cost of the R&D spent to bring them to market.

Just as the R&D investments in various years were compounded to their full net present value (NPV) in the year of market approval at an interest rate equal to the opportunity cost of capital, the future revenues (net of costs) must be discounted back to their NPV at the time of market approval, using an appropriate opportunity cost of capital. After that is done, the NPV of the fully capitalized costs of R&D can be subtracted from the NPV of the net revenues. If the difference is greater than zero, then the overall investment in R&D returned more than was necessary to repay the investors for the time their money was tied up and the risk they took. If the NPV of the investment as a whole was less than zero, then investors did not, on average, recover their cost of capital and could have done better by investing their funds in other industries.

Ideally, analysis of NPV should be based on actual cash flows, not on what financial accounting statements report. For example, when it builds a $50-million manufacturing facility, a company spends the money at the time of construction, but the firm's income statements will recognize the expense only gradually through depreciation charges. The actual investment in the facility was made at the time it was built, not as it was recognized in depreciation expenses. At the end of the product's life, the firm may "sell" the facility to a new group of projects at its current (or salvage) value. The salvage value of the facility should be reflected as a positive cash flow at the end of the product's life.

The analysis should also reflect the effect of taxes on cash flows. R&D expenses result in tax deductions and other credits that reduce taxes, while the net revenues from sales must be reduced by the taxes they cause to be paid.

Sales are highly uneven across drugs, with a few very successful drugs providing the bulk of the revenues (160). Some firms in the industry may not have any winners; others may be highly successful. At the industry level, analysis of returns on R&D is blind to the distribution of revenues across R&D projects or firms. Indeed, investors in startup firms or R&D projects expect many ventures to fail. It is the promise of the occasional big success that attracts the investment dollars. Nevertheless, across a large number of R&D projects, when winners and losers are averaged together, the NPV of the investment, at the appropriate cost of capital, should be in the neighborhood of zero.

■ Past Studies

Several researchers have tried to measure the net returns on R&D for new chemical entities by predicting the shape of the cash-flow profile (as illustrated in figure 4-1) for a group of drugs reaching the market in a given period. The researchers piece together information from a variety of sources about R&D outlays, the shape of the cash flow curve for new drugs, and the costs of producing and selling the products over the course of their life in the market.

These estimates are necessarily imprecise, because information on the full life cycle of a group of drugs introduced in the study period may not yet be available, and data on production, marketing, and distribution costs are typically available only for the company as a whole, not for individual products or even lines of business.

Three such studies are reviewed here.[2] Joglekar and Paterson (215), Grabowski and Vernon (160) and Virts and Weston (500) estimated the NPV of returns on R&D investment in different samples of NCEs. Table 4-1 summarizes the main assumptions and findings of each study.

Joglekar and Paterson used the sales histories of 218 NCEs introduced in the United States between 1962 and 1977 (adjusted for inflation) as the basis for predicting the revenues to an "average" NCE expected to be introduced in 1988. The researchers made assumptions about the cost of producing and distributing the NCEs over their product lives. R&D cash outlays were based on Hansen's study of R&D costs (175), adjusted for inflation.[3] Joglekar and Paterson calculated the NPV of the investment using a 6 percent cost of capital; the estimated average after-tax NPV was $75 million per NCE (in 1976 dollars).

Grabowski and Vernon used the sales history of NCEs introduced between 1970 and 1979 to estimate the returns on this group of NCEs. The researchers estimated the total R&D cost (capitalized to the point of market approval at 9 percent) for this group of NCEs at $125 million (in 1986 dollars). Grabowski and Vernon's assumptions about production and distribution costs are similar in many respects to those of Joglekar and Paterson's, but Grabowski and Vernon included substantial extra costs in the early years of product life to cover expenditures for facilities, equipment, advertising, and promotion associated with the launch of a new product. Using a 9 percent cost of capital, the estimated after-tax NPV of overall investment in NCEs was just $1.3 million (in 1986 dollars).

Virts and Weston (500) multiplied U.S. hospital and drugstore prescription volume data on 119 NCEs introduced between 1967 and 1976 by the average selling price of the drugs and a prescription volume growth factor of 2 percent per year to estimate the revenue curve for these drugs. The market life was assumed to be 10 years, after which revenues would decline immediately to zero. Tax effects were not considered. The costs of R&D were based on Hansen's study (175), and all costs and revenues were discounted at 8 percent per year. The pretax NPV of the investment was negative: -$16 million per drug (in 1978 dollars).

The differences among the three studies in net returns on R&D illustrate the importance of assumptions about the level and the timing of revenues and expenditures as well as the cost of capital. Table 4-1 summarizes the main assumptions and finding of each study.

The Virts and Weston study underestimated lifetime revenues by limiting the product life to 10 years, clearly much below the actual experience of drugs introduced throughout the period covered by their study. Grabowski and Vernon used more realistic estimates of revenues for the cohort of drugs introduced in the 1970s, but they assumed revenues would decline sharply after the loss of patent protection and foreign sales of new drugs would be in the same ratio to U.S. sales as are foreign sales of all pharmaceuticals. Joglekar and Paterson, on the other hand, may have overestimated worldwide revenues and underestimated the cost of capital.

---

[2] Earlier studies by Baily (32), Schwartzman (372), and Statman (401) also examined returns on R&D, but these studies used industry-level data on R&D expenditures, production of NCEs, and sales. These studies also cover an earlier period; consequently, they are not reviewed in this report. Another study by Grabowski and Vernon (157) is essentially an early version of their study reviewed here.

[3] Joglekar and Paterson spread the total R&D period out longer than Hansen's analysis projected. Between the discovery phase and the clinical testing phase, Joglekar and Paterson inserted time for preclinical animal tests and Investigational New Drug application filing time (a total of 14 months). Hansen had included the cost of preclinical animal tests, but his analysis assumed such tests would be undertaken concurrently with the last part of the discovery phase. Thus, Joglekar's and Paterson's capitalized R&D costs are higher than Hansen's study implied.

Table 4-1—Three Studies of Returns on Pharmaceutical R&D

	Grabowski & Vernon (1990)	Joglekar & Paterson (1986)	Virts & Weston (1980)
Assumptions			
Revenues			
U.S. revenues	▪ IMS[a] drugstore and hospital sales for NCEs introduced 1970-79 ▪ Postpatent loss of sales 60% over 5 years.	IMS[a] drugstore and hospital sales for 218 NCEs introduced in U.S. 1962-77—extrapolated with regression out to 24 years after introduction; expressed in 1976 dollars.	▪ IMS[a] outpatient prescriptions for 119 NCE's introduced 1967-76. Multiplied by average selling price. ▪ Revenues = 0 after year 10. ▪ 6% per year inflation in drug price over cost.
Worldwide sales (as a multiple of U.S. hospital and drugstore sales)	1.9	Increasing from 1.86 to 2.44 over the life of the drug (extrapolated from PMA data for 1954-78.)	1.6
Tax rate	35%	35%	0
Production and distribution costs	(see below)	(see below)	Cost per unit = 60% of selling price.
Contribution margin (operating profit + R&D as a percent of sales)[b]	Varied: 33%-40% (40% in 1980s) + 4% adjustment for depreciation.	45% (excludes depreciation and interest on working capital).	
Plant and equipment expenditures	50% of 10th year sales, 2/3 spent evenly in 2 years prior to product launch. Remainder spent evenly over years 2 to 10 after product launch.	24% of 5th year sales, spent evenly 4, 3, and 2 years prior to market launch. (Investment depreciates over time and remaining book value is written off in the last year of analysis.)	
Working capital	12.5% of annual sales, recovered in final year of product life.	24% of fifth year sales, invested evenly 3, 2, and 1 years prior to market launch. Withdrawn in last year of analysis.	
Inventories	41.6% of annual sales, valued at manufacturing cost.	[included in working capital]	
Promotion & advertising costs	100% of year 1 sales 50% of year 2 sales 25% of year 3 sales	[included in contribution margin]	[included in cost percentage]
R&D costs	$125 million (1986 dollars)	$32 million (1976 dollars) distributed according to Hansen, 1979.	$59 million (1978 dollars) based on Hansen, 1979

(Continued on next page)

Table 4-1—Three Studies of Returns on Pharmaceutical R&D—(Continued)

	Grabowski & Vernon (1990)	Joglekar & Paterson (1986)	Virts & Weston (1980)
Discount rate: (cost of capital)	9%	6%	8%
Results			
NPV of investment	+ $1.5 million (1986 dollars)	+ $75 million (1976 dollars)	- $16 million (1978 dollars)
	+ $1.73 million (1990 dollars)	+ $168 million (1990 dollars)	- $29 million (1990 dollars)

a IMS America, Inc., is a market research firm that conducts ongoing surveys of hospital and drugstore purchases of pharmaceuticals in the United States.
b Variable costs: 1=contribution margin. The contribution margin as defined in these studies equals operating profit and R&D as a percent of sales.

KEY: NCEs = new chemical entities; NPV = net present value.

SOURCE: Office of Technology Assessment, 1993. Based on data from H.G. Grabowski and J.M. Vernon, "A New Look at the Returns and Risks to Pharmaceutical R&D," *Management Science* 36(7):804-821, July 1990; P. Joglekar and M.L. Paterson, "A Closer Look at the Returns and Risks of Pharmaceutical R&D," *Journal of Health Economics* 5:153-177, 1986; J.R. Virts and J.F. Weston, "Returns to Research and Development in the U.S. Pharmaceutical Industry," *Managerial and Decision Economics* 1(3):103-111, 1980.

Assumptions about the cost of production, distribution, and marketing differed widely among the studies. Virts and Weston simply assumed that on average the full cost of producing and selling the drugs in any year is 60 percent of their selling price. Grabowski and Vernon and Joglekar and Patterson used a modified "contribution margin" to estimate these costs. The "contribution margin" is formally defined as the percent of a company's sales that contributes to paying off the fixed costs (such as investments in facilities, plant and equipment) and profits of the enterprise after the direct costs of producing, marketing and distributing the product are deducted (205). Fixed costs do not vary with the amount of drug that is sold. The contribution margin is the percent of sales left over after the direct variable costs have been deducted. The direct cost of production and distribution as a percent of sales (the estimate required to determine net cash flows) is therefore one minus the contribution margin.[4]

The firm's operating profit is calculated net of the costs of advertising and promotion, but these costs reflect the full line of products that the firm sells. Expenditures for promotion and advertising are heavier in the years immediately following product launch, so the contribution margin based on pharmaceutical companies' operating profits underestimates new products' share of advertising and promotion expenses and overestimates such expenditures for products as they age. Joglekar and Paterson did not account for the difference in timing of this major component of expenses but assumed the contribution margin was an accurate reflection of the expenses for new

NCEs. Grabowski and Vernon, on the other hand, added a substantial expense in the first 3 years of product sales to cover the additional advertising and promotion expenditures associated with product launch, but adjusted the contribution margin to reflect lower expenses in later years (154).

Finally, assumptions about actual cash outlays for manufacturing plant and equipment vary widely among the studies. Grabowski and Vernon effectively assumed a much higher total investment than did the authors of either of the other studies.

▮ OTA Analysis of Returns on R&D

OTA estimated the return on R&D for NCEs approved for marketing in the United States in the years 1981-83. OTA chose this relatively brief period for analysis because we had access to U.S. sales data only for these years. These NCEs include all newly introduced compounds regardless of their country of origin or licensing status within the sponsoring company.

OTA's approach is similar to Grabowski and Vernon's (160), but OTA's assumptions vary in important respects. Where the available data are imprecise or scant, OTA used a range of estimates reflecting the best available evidence. In addition, when uncertainty was high, OTA used conservative assumptions that would tend to understate returns on R&D.

THE SALES CURVE

Figure 4-2 shows U.S. sales to hospitals and drugstores in constant 1990 dollars for NCEs introduced in 1981-83 and, for the sake of

---

[4] In theory, the contribution margin should be calculated gross of charges for depreciation on facilities and equipment, R&D and other investments. These investments should be recognized separately at the time they are made. Information on product-specific direct production, distribution and marketing costs is hard to come by, however, and the closest approximation to the contribution margin that is available from companies' financial statements is operating profit plus R&D expenditures. Joglekar and Paterson explicitly recognized expenditures for plant and equipment as cash outlays in the year they would be expended and adjusted the contribution margin accordingly (215). Grabowski and Vernon also adjusted after-tax income for depreciation expenses, which had the effect of raising the contribution margin by about 4 percentage points (154).

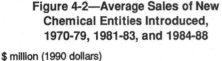

Figure 4-2—Average Sales of New Chemical Entities Introduced, 1970-79, 1981-83, and 1984-88

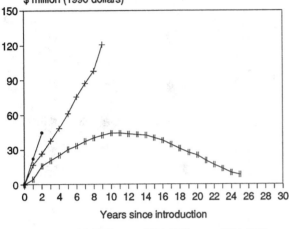

SOURCES: **1970-79:** H.G. Grabowski and M. Vernon, "A New Look at the Returns and Risks to Pharmaceutical R&D," *Management Science* 36(7):804-821, July 1990. **1981-83:** Coppinger, P., "Overview of the Competitiveness of the U.S. Pharmaceutical Industry," presentation to the Council in Competitiveness Working Group on the Drug Approval Process, Washington, DC, Dec. 12, 1990. **1984-88:** IMS America, Inc., unpublished data prepared for the Office of Technology Assessment, 1991.

comparison, in earlier and later years as well.[5] Although OTA had only 1 year of data for NCEs introduced in 1984-88, that one data point suggests that, after adjusting for inflation, U.S. sales of new NCEs in the early years after approval continued to steepen throughout the 1980s.

Sales to hospitals and drugstores account for the majority of, but not all, ethical pharmaceutical sales in the United States. Staff-model health maintenance organizations (HMOs) and mail-

order pharmacies account for a growing proportion (2.4 percent and 5.9 percent in 1991 respectively) of total pharmaceutical sales. Sales to clinics and nursing homes account for another 6 percent of pharmaceutical sales (128). Together, sales to these other distribution channels were 14 percent of total sales, or 19 percent of sales to drugstores and hospitals.[6] Therefore, OTA increased domestic hospital and drugstore sales in each year by 19 percent to account for these additional channels of distribution.

Hospital and drugstore sales data are based on retail invoices and therefore do not reflect the amount manufacturers actually receive. About 71 percent of ethical pharmaceutical sales were distributed through wholesalers in 1991 (320). For these drugs, the manufacturer received approximately 6.3 percent less revenue than the invoice price.[7] OTA therefore reduced the sales estimates by 4.5 percent to reflect the difference between sales at the wholesale level and manufacturers' revenues.

OTA had access to data on U.S. sales revenue only for the first 9 years of marketing for the 1981-83 drugs. To predict the revenue curve beyond those years, OTA examined trends in effective patent lives and in the loss of revenue after patent expiration.

Effective Patent Life—The effective patent life is defined here as the elapsed time between the U.S. Food and Drug Administration (FDA) approval for marketing of a new drug and the expiration of the last patent or market exclusivity provision that effectively protects the original compound from competition from bioequivalent

---

[5] Data on mean annual hospital and drugstore sales per NCE introduced in 1981-83 were supplied by the Food and Drug Administration (97). Data for the 1970s are taken from Grabowski's and Vernon's study (159), and OTA obtained 1 year's worth of data for the 1984-88 NCEs from IMS America Inc., a market research firm that conducts ongoing surveys of hospital and drugstore sales.

The data on sales for the 1984-88 cohort of drugs are for NCEs approved in the period, not necessarily introduced; the data for the 1970s cohort are for NCEs both approved and introduced in the period; and the data for the 1981-83 cohort are for NCEs introduced in the period. Of the 60 therapeutic NMEs first introduced to the U.S. market in 1981-83, 54 were approved during the same period. Three others were approved in 1979 and 1980 and are included in the analysis. Six therapeutic NMEs approved during 1981-83 were excluded from the analysis because one was never marketed and the other five were not introduced to the market until at least 5 years after 1983.

[6] Data supplied to OTA by Medco Containment Services, Inc., showed that new drugs constituted the same percentage of total sales (in physical units) in the mail-order business as in community pharmacies (255).

[7] The 1991 average wholesalers' gross margins were approximately 6.8 percent of net sales. Income obtained from interest, payment for direct services to retailers, and other sources accounted for 0.63 percent of sales (362).

generic products.[8] The longer this period, the more years the firm has a monopoly over its product. Though this monopoly is imperfect because close substitutes exist for many patented drug products, generic competition has the potential for rapidly transforming the originating company's brand-name product into a standardized commodity with consequent rapid declines in market revenues.

The greatest threat to the effective U.S. patent life of a new compound is the delay between patent issuance and FDA's approval to market the product. Since the passage of the Drug Price Competition and Patent Term Restoration Act of 1984 (Public Law 98-417), new drugs have been eligible to receive patent term extensions of up to 5 years (with total patent life not to exceed 14 years as a result of the extensions) to compensate for regulatory delays. In addition, the Orphan Drug Act of 1983 (Public Law 97-414) granted 7 years of exclusive marketing rights for new drug products designed to treat rare conditions.

OTA analyzed the effective patent life of NCEs approved for marketing between 1984 and 1989 and compared the results with an analysis of effective patent life conducted in 1983 for the U.S. House of Representatives as part of the legislative debate over the Drug Price Competition and Patent Term Restoration Act (440). OTA calculated two measures of effective patent life: the life of the patent protecting the product itself, and the longest period of protection indicated by any exclusivity provision or any patent covering a drug and listed in FDA's ''Orange Book'' (473).[9] Data from the U.S. Patent Office were used to update patent extension information not yet published in the most recent supplement to the Orange Book. The results are shown in figure 4-3.

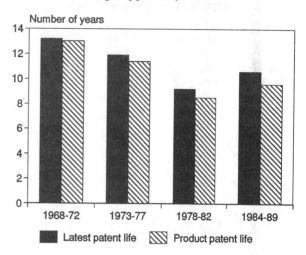

Figure 4-3—Effective Patent Life for Drugs Approved, 1968-89

SOURCES: Office of Technology Assessment, 1993. Based on U.S. Congress, House of Representatives, Committee on Energy and Commerce, unpublished data, 1993; U.S. Department of Health and Human Services, Food and Drug Administration, unpublished data, 1991; U.S. Department of Commerce, Patent and Trademark Office, unpublished data, 1991.

After declining steadily throughout the 1970s and early 1980s, effective patent life has rebounded somewhat in the years since 1984.

The simple average patent life data shown in figure 4-3 may actually understate the effective period of market exclusivity for originator compounds first marketed in 1981-83 and beyond. Firms may manage the patent period more carefully when the potential revenues from a drug are greater.[10]

To test this hypothesis, OTA obtained data on hospital and community pharmacy sales of all 1984-88 NCEs 2 calendar years after the calendar year of FDA approval (201). Table 4-2 shows the relationship between sales and effective patent life for NCEs by sales volume in the second year

---

[8] The term ''effective patent life'' may be a misnomer, since it refers to all kinds of market exclusivities. In this report it is used merely to indicate how long after entry to the market the compound in its original dosage form is formally protected from generic competition.

[9] Any patent listed in the Orange Book serves as a barrier to the approval of a generic version of the listed product. Under the 1984 Act, a generic manufacturer must provide a certification of patent invalidity or noninfringement as to any listed patent. The cost of researching such claims is high, and litigation is always a threat for a potential generic competitor (124).

[10] Patent terms in other industrialized countries run for 20 years from the date of application. In the United States, patent terms run for 17 years from the date of issuance. Firms have substantial opportunities to delay the date of issuance, and anecdotal evidence suggests pharmaceutical firms have taken advantage of those opportunities in the past (123).

Table 4-2—Mean and Median Effective Patent Life as a Function of Sales for New Chemical Entities Approved 1985-89

	Latest patent	NCE patent
Mean, total sample (113 drugs)........	10.6	9.6
Mean, nonorphans (94 drugs).........	10.7	9.5
Breakdown by sales[a]		
Mean for drugs with sales data available (69 drugs)..............	10.5	9.2
Standard deviation.............	4.0	3.8
$0-20 million (43 drugs)...........	9.8	8.4
Standard deviation.............	4.0	3.6
$20-$50 million (9 drugs)..........	10.6	8.4
Standard deviation.............	2.9	3.2
$50-$100 million (8 drugs).........	11.9	11.2
Standard deviation.............	3.4	2.7
>$100 million (9 drugs)...........	13.1	11.7
Standard deviation.............	4.0	4.2
Median effective patent life...........	10.7	10.0

[a] Sales are measured in the second calender year after the calendar year of approval. Sales data are in 1989 dollars, converted using GNP implicit price deflator.

KEY: NCE = new chemical entity.

SOURCE: Office of Technology Assessment, 1993. Sales data obtained from IMS America, Inc.

after approval (in 1989 dollars). A pattern of longer patent life for drugs with higher sales is evident in the table and was found to be statistically significant in a regression analysis.[11] This analysis suggests that, on average, each additional $100 million in sales is associated with 400 additional days of effective patent life.

The estimated period of effective patent protection reflects only the period during which the original compound is formally protected from competition by patent or other laws. The expiration of patent protection on the original compound may not mark the end of exclusive marketing, however. Some compounds may not experience generic competition for several years after the patent expires, either because of delays in FDA approval of generic copies or because the total market for the drug is too small to induce generic manufacturers to enter the market. Even more important, process patents that are issued after the original patents sometimes may be effective in keeping generic products out of the market (see box 4-B). And, other product-line extensions occurring late in the original patent life may partly protect the originator compound from competition. The 1984 Drug Price Competition and Patent Term Restoration Act granted a 3-year period of exclusivity, regardless of patent status, to any existing product for which an additional full NDA or supplemental NDA requiring new clinical research is approved by the FDA[12] (83). Thus, if a new dosage form, such as a sustained release formulation, is developed and approved for the originator product, the new dosage form has a 3-year period of market exclusivity from the date of its FDA approval regardless of the patent status of the product itself.[13]

As box 4-C illustrates, companies can and do use the terms of the provision to extend the effective period of exclusivity for the compound by managing the introduction of new dosage forms to coincide with the expiration of patents on earlier generations of a compound. Originator companies have a natural advantage in developing new dosage forms prior to the expiration of the original compound patents, because the patent

---

[11] The estimated regression model is $P_I = 3684.589 + .000004S_I$, where P_I is effective patent life for drug i expressed in days and S_I is sales for drug i expressed in dollars. The estimated coefficient on sales has a t-statistic of 2.0 with 67 degrees of freedom which is significant at the 5-percent level in a two-tailed test. The proportion of variation in effective patent life explained by this model (R^2) is .05.

[12] Generic companies can apply for a full NDA (undertaking all of the preclinical and clinical research required of the originator company) to avoid the exclusivity provision, provided the patent on the originator drug has expired, but they cannot receive approval under abbreviated new drug applications (ANDAs) to market the drug. The time and cost involved with full NDA submission effectively eliminates this avenue of competition.

[13] Supplemental NDAs also can be submitted for new indications or new dosing regimens, resulting in a new label for the originator product, but under FDA's current interpretation of the law, the sponsor of a generic drug can still submit an ANDA for the original label. Some legal experts claim this interpretation is potentially subject to court challenge, because FDA would be treating the generic drug and the newly labelled originator drug as completely interchangeable, thus impairing the exclusivity right (83).

Box 4-B—Postpatent Generic Competition: Opportunities and Obstacles

"Generic Erosion for Ceclor?"

"When Lilly's Ceclor (cefaclor) comes off patent in the U.S. in 1992, unit sales of the antibiotic, which account for roughly 15 percent of the company's total sales, could be eroded by 70-80 percent by generic competition in the first 18 months, according to Kidder, Peabody analyst James Flynn.

This erosion will take place despite the fact that Lilly holds process patent for Ceclor which expire between 1994 and 2006, and plans to introduce a sustained-release formulation, Ceclor AF, the analyst predicts.

Recent legal action in Japan, where Lilly has filed suit against ten companies for alleged infringement of its cefaclor patent, suggests that the company intends to defend its patents vigorously... However, Mr. Flynn argues that Lilly's process patents will not be recognized in a number of countries (e.g. Italy) which are likely to be used as manufacturing sites for generic companies planning to import formulations of cefaclor on expiration of the product patent.

Barr and Biocraft, which have valid cephalosporin manufacturing facilities in the U.S., may also try to "skirt" Lilly's process patents, Mr. Flynn says. Such a strategy would give these companies a "meaningful cost advantage" over importing firms, he adds.

Ceclor AF is unlikely to be introduced in the United States much before the cefaclor product patent expires, Mr. Flynn says. A preferred dosing regimen is the only benefit he is aware Ceclor AF would have over generic competition. The analyst notes that Lilly's Keftabs formulation of Keflex (cefalexin) gained less than 15 percent of Keflex' sales after the 1987 product patent expire."

"Ceclor Market Dominance Will Continue Past Dec. 1992 Patent Expiration, Lilly Contends: Process Protection Thru 1994"

"Lilly's dominant position in the oral antibiotic market will survive the expiration of the U.S. patent on Ceclor in December 1992, the company maintained at a meeting with financial analysts in New York on Feb. 28. Based on a process protection for cefaclor and a pending NDA application for the follow-up compound loracarbef, Lilly is forcefully declaring its intention to hold its place in the oral antibiotic field...

Asked to comment on the impact of the upcoming patent expiration on Ceclor sales, Lilly Pharmaceutical President Gene Step said the relevant questions should be what will be Lilly's overall position in the oral antibiotic market and what is the likelihood of generic versions of cefaclor reaching the market.

"You really have to [ask] what is our participation in the oral antibiotic market and to what extent will that be affected" by generic cefaclor or "by other products that we may or may not be selling" in the future, Step said.

Lilly is emphasizing the *de facto* protection of a difficult production process and a patent position on a late-stage intermediate... Step declared that when all factors are considered Ceclor should "remain a viable product for Eli Lilly beyond expiration of the patent."

As the company often has been pointing out recently, Step told the Feb. 28 meeting that Ceclor has yet to face generic competition outside the U.S., even in markets where there is no patent protection. "While we cannot know what the actions of everybody else in the world will be," Step said, "it is very interesting to observe that while there isn't patent coverage in a large part of the world for Ceclor, there isn't any generic Ceclor."

Lilly Research Labs President Mel Perelman, Phd, explained the process protection during question-and-answer. "The Ceclor synthetic route is so long and so complex," that it will be difficult to duplicate, Perelman said...

A producer of cefaclor can take a number of different routes to get to the intermediate, Perelman explained, "but they can't go through it without violating our patent. So an ethical or legal end-run seems extremely imprrobable." The patent on the intermediate runs until December 1994. Step further pointed out that establishing a cefaclor manufacturing process "will require very considerable capital investment...we have haven't seen that yet"...

SOURCES: Generic erosion: Quote from "Generic Erosion for Ceclor," *Scrip World Pharmaceutical News* 1594:25, 1991. Ceclor market: Quoted from "Ceclor Market Dominance Will Continue Past Dec. 1992 Patent Expiration, Lilly Contends: Process Protection Thru 1994, Lorabid NDA Filed as Backup," *F-D-C Reports: Prescription and OTC Pharmaceuticals*, Mar. 4, 1991, p. 15.

Box 4-C—"*Cardizem QD* 1991 Approval Is Key to Successful *Cardizem* Switch Before Patent Expiry in 1992"

"Marion Merrell Dow is counting on a late 1991 approval of *Cardizem QD* to give it time to convert patents from the immediate-release form of the diltiazem calcium channel blocker before the patent expires Nov. 5, 1992, company management indicated at a Feb. 27 meeting with securities analysts in Kansas City, Missouri.

Calling the approval of Cardizem QD Marion Merrell Dow's "number one new product priority," MMD President Fred Lyons said: "I think it's possible that QD could be approved this year and introduced by the first of next year."

The Cardizem QD NDA for hypertension was filed in February 1990 and is scheduled to go before FDA's Cardiovascular and Renal Drugs Advisory Committee on March 14.

To protect its $745 mil. *Cardizem* franchise, Marion Merrell Dow apparently intends to follow a strategy similar to the one Pfizer used to protect its nifedipine franchise from generics with sustained-release *Procardia XL*. Pfizer's strategy called for discounting the new generation product by 25 percent and promoting the price savings directly to consumers. Pfizer told analysts last fall that Procardia XL accounted for nearly two-thirds of all Procardia scripts one year after its launch in October 1989 ("The Pink Sheet" Nov. 5, p. 8).

Marion Merrell Dow Prescription Products Division President David Roche outlined his company's strategy to convert patents from immediate-release Cardizem to the once-a-day formulation by pointing to his own experience in Canada as head of MMD's Nordic Labs subsidiary. Cardizem went off-patent in July 1988, the same time that *Cardizem SR* twice-a-day was approved. By discounting the sustained-release product by 5 percent and aggressively promoting it, Roche said, Nordic was able to maintain the total number of Cardizem prescriptions through 1990.

Roche also said, that like Pfizer, Marion Merrell Dow would seek to "build patent brand loyalty" to its Cardizem products. In addition, Roche said, Cardizem products will constitute "50 percent plus" of the combined 1,100-person sales force's detail time in 1991.

Cardizem QD initially will be indicated only for hypertension, while Cardizem is approved for both hypertension and angina. However, Cardizem SR, which has been available since early 1989, is indicated for angina only, so the two products combined may replace the original. . ."

SOURCE: Quoted from "Cardizem QD 1991 Approval Is Key to Successful Cardizem Switch Before Patent Expiry in 1992," *F-D-C Reports: Prescription and OTC Pharmaceuticals*, Mar. 4, 1991, p. 12.

---

laws prohibit other companies from conducting research with commercial value using a patented product. (Appendix E contains a summary of the patent protection available to pharmaceutical products, including biotechnology drugs.)

New dosage forms typically offer important medical benefits to patients by making compliance easier or making dosing more convenient and sometimes less uncomfortable. Increasing company incentives to develop products with these benefits is the rationale for the 3-year exclusivity provision of the Drug Price Competition and Patent Term Restoration Act (Public Law 98-417). The issue raised here is not whether such provisions are good public policy, but what the magnitude of their potential impact on the complete life cycle of revenues may be for an originator NCE.

For NCEs approved in the 1981-83 period, OTA assumed that the average effective patent life is 9 years. As figure 4-3 shows, the simple average effective patent life for drugs approved in the period 1978-82 was between 8 and 9 years. Because patent life is positively correlated with sales revenue, it is appropriate to slightly increase the patent life for total revenues from the new drugs approved between 1981 and 1983. This estimate of patent life does not include any additional market exclusivity granted for new dosage forms.

Postpatent Revenues—After a drug loses patent protection, it becomes vulnerable to competition from generic copies. The Drug Price Competition and Patent Term Restoration Act of 1984 made FDA approval relatively easy for makers of generic copies of originator drugs.[14] It is widely held that this law has led to rapid decline in the originator drug's market share following patent expiration. In their analysis of returns on R&D for NCEs approved between 1970 and 1979, Grabowski and Vernon assumed that the originator drug would hold only 40 percent of total revenue in the market 5 years after patent expiration, but they predicted that increased generic competition in future years could reduce the originator's market share to 20 percent of the total domestic market revenue within 6 years of loss of patent or exclusive marketing protection (160).

OTA analyzed changes in the U.S. market for therapeutic compounds losing patent protection in the years 1984-87. An OTA contractor obtained data for the years 1980-90 on hospital and drugstore sales for 35 noninjectable, noninfusible, therapeutic molecular compounds that lost patent protection in the period 1984-87 (368,369). Details of sample selection, methods, and results are presented in appendix F. Sales (in revenue and

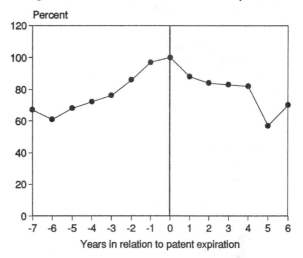

Figure 4-4—Originator Revenue[a] as a Percent of Originator Revenue in Year of Patent Expiration

Percent

Years in relation to patent expiration

a Based on 1990 dollars.

SOURCE: Office of Technology Assessment, 1993, based on S.W. Schondelmeyer, "Economic Products," contract paper prepared for Office of Technology Assessment, December 1991.

physical units) were recorded for all strengths and dosage forms of the compound. (Sales volume for each form of the compound was converted into a standardized physical volume measure, the defined daily dose (DDD)).

Figures 4-4 and 4-5 show how the annual sales in 1990 dollars and in physical units of the originator compound changed before and after the year in which the patent expired. Three years after patent expiration, the originator's annual dollar sales (in 1990 dollars) were 83 percent of sales in the year of patent expiration, while the originator's unit sales were 68 percent of its sales in the year of patent expiration.[15]

---

[14] Manufacturers seeking to market a generic version of an originator product could file an ANDA, showing only bioequivalence with the originator product, and not needing to prove anew that the generic copy is effective.

[15] A recent analysis of generic competition by Grabowski and Vernon reported different results (161). Grabowski and Vernon examined 18 compounds with annual sales of $50 million dollars or more, 16 of whose patents expired in the 1984-87 period. (Two drugs had patent expiration dates in the early 1980s.) They then examined the originator product's market share for *the most commonly prescribed dosage form*. They did not report market share data on revenues, but they did report on market shares in physical units of the most frequently prescribed dosage form. Within 2 years of the first generic entry, the originator's market share in physical units had fallen to 49 percent. (In OTA's sample of compounds, the originator's market share in physical units 2 years *after patent expiration* was 65 percent.) The difference in market shares can be explained in part by: 1) the inclusion in OTA's sample of compounds with lower annual sales, which may draw less competition from generics; 2) OTA's inclusion of sales of all strengths and dosage forms; and 3) delays between patent expiration and the entry of generic competition, during which the originator product maintains an exclusive marketing position.

Figure 4-5—Originator Unit Volume as a Percent of Originator Volume in Year of Patent Expiration

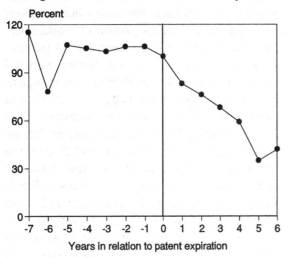

SOURCE: Office of Technology Assessment, 1993, based on S.W. Schondelmeyer, "Economic Products," contract paper prepared for Office of Technology Assessment, December 1991.

The slower decline of the originator's dollar sales than of physical units following patent expiration means that the price of originator products increased after patents expired. This finding is surprising to many people who would expect brand-name prices to decline in the face of active competition from generic competitors. Yet it makes sense for the manufacturer of an originator product to raise its price as generic competitors enter if a high enough proportion of the people who prescribe and buy the drug do not care very much about price when they choose between brand-name and generic products (136).

The sample excluded drugs not generally distributed through drugstores. Products sold exclusively to hospitals or other institutional settings, such as infusible or injectable drugs, would be likely to lose revenue more quickly after entry by generic competitors than products offered through drugstores (158). (See chapter 10 for a discussion.) OTA estimated that these drugs constitute roughly 14 percent of market sales (in dollars) in the year of patent expiration (see appendix F).

The data on the U.S. postpatent sales decline also do not include sales made to several kinds of purchasers that can be expected to switch to generic versions of drugs very soon after they are available. First, sales made through mail-order pharmacies, a small but growing channel of distribution comprising 5.9 percent of domestic pharmaceutical sales in 1991 (128) are not included. Generic versions of multisource drugs[16] constitute a somewhat higher proportion of dollar sales to mail-order pharmacies than to community-based pharmacies (see appendix F).

Second, sales to Federal Government purchasers, such as the Department of Veterans Affairs and the Military, are not included in these data. These purchasers can be expected to switch to generic versions of compounds soon after they are available. The Department of Veterans Affairs spent approximately $500 million for outpatient prescription drugs in 1991 (312). This sum is approximately 1 percent of total domestic pharmaceutical sales (128,320).

Third, staff-model HMOs, which represented about 2.4 percent of ethical pharmaceutical sales in 1991, switch to generics relatively quickly (515). Thus, the rate of decline in revenues after patent expiration is understated in these data. OTA adjusted the rate of decline in sales after patent expiration to take account of these and other limitations of the data (see appendix F for details).

For the analysis of the returns on NCEs approved in the 1981-83 period, OTA assumed that the originator drug's revenues would decline after patent expiration at annual rates shown in table 4-3. The generics data available to OTA gave no guidance on losses after the 6th year following patent expiration. OTA assumed that revenues would fall by 20 percent per year in the 8th to 11th year after patent expiration. Sales would fall to zero after 12 years following patent expiration or after 20 years following the original approval of the NCE.

---

[16] Multisource drugs are those with generic competition on the market.

Table 4-3—OTA's Assumptions About Changes in Sales of Originator Drugs After Patent Expiration

Year after patent expiration	Percent change in dollar sales
1	-18%
2	-8.5
3	-6.0
4	-6.0
5	-5.0
6	-5.0
7	-5.0
8	-20.0
9	-20.0
10	-100.0

SOURCE: Office of Technology Assessment, 1993; based on sources and assumptions outlined in appendix F.

Future changes in the health care system may increase the speed with which purchasers switch to generic products.[17] For illustrative purposes, OTA examined the sensitivity of measured returns on R&D to a decline in revenues at an annual rate of 20 percent from the date of patent expiration until the 20th year following approval of the drug.

Worldwide Sales—Revenues come from sales in other countries as well as in the United States, so the revenue curve must be adjusted accordingly. Although data on worldwide sales of pharmaceutical products are collected by IMS International, Inc., OTA did not have access to its data.[18] The only data available to OTA are aggregate estimates of the U.S. and foreign markets for all ethical pharmaceuticals (or for all pharmaceuticals). These aggregate estimates are available from industry trade organizations and from the annual reports of individual firms.

Glaxo, a British pharmaceutical company, estimates the total world market and the share of each country in its annual report. Glaxo bases its estimates on data from IMS International and other sources. According to Glaxo the United States accounts for 27 percent of world sales, and 10 other industrialized and newly industrialized countries account for 54 percent of world sales. The rest of the world accounts for 19 percent. Japan comprises the second largest national market, with an 18-percent share. These aggregate industry sales figures suggest a ratio of total world sales to U.S. sales of approximately 3.7 to 1. If only the top 10 countries are included (on the assumption that the "rest of the world" does not constitute a large market for new chemical entities), the ratio of total to U.S. sales is 3 to 1. Many of the drugs sold in other countries are never launched in the United States, so it is difficult to draw conclusions from these worldwide aggregate sales figures about how new chemical entities that are medically important enough to seek and receive U.S. FDA approval would fare.

The Pharmaceutical Manufacturers Association (PMA) collects sales data of its member firms in an annual survey. U.S.-owned PMA member firms reported that the ratio of total worldwide sales to domestic sales was 1.765 to 1 in 1990 (317). These companies are likely to have a lower percent of sales outside the United States than are foreign-owned firms that launch new products in the United States, and the ratio is based on drugs that have lost patent protection as well as those that are covered by patents. Thus, this ratio is too conservative.

Grabowski and Vernon, using estimates based on IMS International data, assumed that the ratio of total world revenues to U.S. revenues for drugs introduced in the 1970s, was 1.9 to 1 throughout the life of the NCE (160). Joglekar and Paterson estimated the trend in the global sales ratio over the period 1954-78 based on IMS data and predicted that the ratio for drugs introduced

---

[17] For example, HMOs and other managed care plans with comprehensive pharmaceutical benefits typically either mandate generic prescribing or offer incentives to users for purchase of generic brands (515). If managed care grows in the United States in the future, the speed with which generic substitution occurs may increase. See chapter 10 for a discussion of trends in insurance and payment.

[18] IMS International, Inc. indicated the cost to OTA of obtaining worldwide sales data for these drugs would be between $75,000 and $150,000 (339).

between 1962 and 1977 would increase from 1.86 to 1 to 2.44 to 1 between 1985 and 2044.

Lacking more detailed data on the ratio of total world sales for specific NCEs over their product life cycle, OTA assumed that the ratio is 2 to 1. OTA has reason to believe that this ratio is on the low side, based on informal discussions with researchers who have access to unpublished data.

Application of a worldwide sales ratio beginning with FDA approval ignores the revenues that accrue when products are launched in other countries before the FDA approves them.[19] Figure 4-6 charts the frequency of early approval in other countries for the NCEs approved by FDA in 1981-83. Over 25 percent of drugs approved in the United States in this period were first approved at least 5 years earlier in another country. The revenues realized in the years before FDA approval are potentially very significant in terms of the present value of revenues, but without access to foreign sales data it is impossible to estimate their size. To be conservative, OTA excluded early foreign sales from the analysis.

COST OF MANUFACTURING, MARKETING, AND DISTRIBUTING NCES

Sales revenues from new products must be reduced by the cash outlays required to make and sell them. Accurate measurement of product-specific costs of manufacture, marketing, distribution, and administration is difficult for multi-product companies, and publicly available financial statements offer only rough estimates of the magnitude of these costs.

OTA estimated manufacturing, distribution, marketing and administrative costs from a variety of sources, including the existing literature and annual reports of six U.S.-owned companies with pharmaceutical sales comprising at least 65 per-

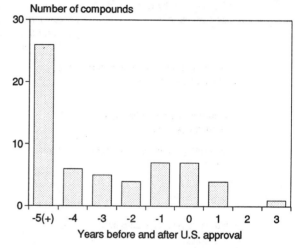

Figure 4-6—Year of First Entry to the Market for New Molecular Entities Approved in the United States, 1981-83

SOURCE: Office of Technology Assessment, 1993, based on unpublished data from the Office of Planning and Evaluation, Office of the Commissioner, U.S Food and Drug Administration.

cent of total company sales.[20] The method and estimates are described in detail in appendix G.

Marketing costs were assumed to be higher in the early years of product life and low after patent expiration, but over the lifetime of the product they average 22.5 percent of total sales.

OTA also accounted for high initial cash outlays for capital expenditures on manufacturing capacity as well as ongoing manufacturing costs. Initial expenditures for plant and equipment for each compound were assumed to be $25 million, spread evenly across the 2 years before and the year of product approval.[21] The sensitivity of the results to an increase in this cost to $35 million was also tested.

OTA assumed that the full value of plant and equipment would be consumed in the production of the single product and that at the end of the 20 years of product life, the salvage value would be

---

[19] OTA's analysis also ignores the revenues from products that remained unapproved in the United States but were accepted and launched in other countries. The foreign revenues from these drugs that are never approved in the United States help offset the R&D costs associated with each successful U.S. entry.

[20] The six firms are Merck, Eli Lilly, Syntex, Schering-Plough, Upjohn and Pfizer.

[21] In addition to this initial capital expenditure, OTA included all ongoing depreciation expenses for manufacturing facilities (which are embedded in cost-of-sales ratios) in excess of the depreciation that could be taken on the $25-million capital expenditure.

Table 4-4—Cost Assumptions in OTA's Analysis of Returns on R&D

Cost component	Year after product launch	Base case
Capital expenditures for plant and equipment	Total over life cycle 2 years before approval 1 year before approval Year of approval	$25 million $8.33 million $8.33 million $8.33 million
Manufacturing and distribution (as a percent of sales)	1-20	25.5% of sales less adjustment for depreciation charges on plant and equipment (20-year life)
General and administrative costs as percent of sales	1-20	11.1% of sales
Marketing costs as percent of sales	Average over life cycle 1 2 3-9 10-20	22.6% of sales 100.0% of sales 50.0% of sales 40.9% of sales 6.5% of sales
Value of inventory as percent of sales	1-20	12.7% of sales
Working capital as percent of sales	1-20	17.0% of sales
Ongoing R&D costs	Total over life cycle 1-9	$31.2 million $3.46 million

SOURCE: Office of Technology Assessment, 1993.

zero, also a conservative assumption. Table 4-4 contains a summary of OTA's base case assumptions regarding costs of production, distribution, administration and marketing.

R&D COSTS

The NCEs introduced in the period from 1981 to 1983 began clinical testing roughly 8 years earlier (1973-75), the midpoint of the study years in DiMasi's R&D cost study (109). OTA assumed that DiMasi's cash outlays (in constant 1990 dollars), success rates, and development time profile represent the experience of the NCEs approved between 1981 and 1983.

In addition to the costs required to bring a compound to market, OTA's analysis also explicitly recognized ongoing R&D costs after the product is launched. These R&D expenditures may be intended to explore the usefulness of the drug in new conditions or to develop new dosing strengths, formulations, or dosage forms. OTA's method for estimating the ongoing costs of R&D is outlined in appendix G. Total ongoing R&D

expenditure was assumed to be $31.7 million per compound (in 1990 dollars), evenly distributed over the first 9 years of product life.

TAXES

To measure the net after-tax returns on R&D, the cash flows generated by the sale of each product in the years following market launch must be reduced by the amount of taxes they cause to be paid. Ideally, the reduction in cash flows would be equal to the extra tax paid in each year of the product's life as a direct result of manufacturing and selling the product.

Precise measurement of these extra tax payments is difficult for three reasons. First, taxes owed or payable are based not only on cash flows from the product but on rules in tax codes governing what can be deducted, and when. Expenditures to build manufacturing facilities, for example, cannot be deducted in full in the year they are made for U.S. income tax purposes; they must be depreciated over a specified number of years. (OTA assumed that investments in plant and equipment would be depreciated for tax purposes on a straight-line basis over 10 years.)

Second, taxes owed or payable depend not only on what is manufactured and sold but also on where it is manufactured. Drug companies can and do make decisions to manufacture products in jurisdictions that will afford them the best profile of after-tax cash flows. The availability of tax credits for locating manufacturing operations in U.S. possessions, such as Puerto Rico, substantially reduces the tax liability of pharmaceutical companies. (See chapter 8 for more detail.) Thus, the opportunity to make a new product in a low-tax jurisdiction means that the extra taxes incurred as a result of the introduction of a new group of products will certainly fall short of the statutory marginal corporate tax rate.

Third, tax payments in any year depend not only on taxable income in that year but also on the profit and loss history of the company. Some current tax liabilities can be applied to previous years if the company lost money in the past. Similarly, payment of some taxes can be deferred to future years. Income tax expenses can remain higher or lower than actual payments over a long period of time if an industry as a whole is, or has been, in a period of eligibility for tax deferments.

Taken together, these measurement problems imply that the U.S. marginal corporate tax rate is too high a rate to apply to the cash flows associated with a new product after it is introduced to the market. A better approximation of the tax burden would be based on the ratio of taxes paid to income from ongoing pharmaceutical operations.[22]

Three estimates of this ratio are available for the pharmaceutical industry. All of them were made at the firm level and therefore include nonpharmaceutical operations. Also, each estimate is based on: 1) a different sample of firms, 2) a different definition of tax liability, and 3) a different definition of income.

- The General Accounting Office and the congressional Joint Committee on Taxation calculated taxes payable each year as a percent of firms' pretax net income (net of extraordinary income) in that year. (Tax liabilities that are deferred to future years were not included, but payments made as a result of past deferments were.) For five U.S.-based pharmaceutical firms in the sample, the effective worldwide tax rate on worldwide income was 34.3 percent in 1987 (438). The rate varied between 1981 and 1987, starting higher (41.3 percent) in 1981 and reaching a low in 1983 (32.1 percent), but climbing again to a high of 37.1 percent in 1986.

- Baber and Kang calculated worldwide income taxes paid as a percent of net income before depreciation and taxes (as reported in financial statements) between 1975 and 1987 for 54 U.S. pharmaceutical firms with R&D expenses greater than 5 percent of sales (24,224). Table 4-5 shows the income tax rates from 1981-87. Taxes paid for this sample of firms was in the range of 29 to 34 percent of income until 1987, when taxes paid jumped to 39.7 percent of income.

Table 4-5—Taxes Paid as a Percent of Net Income for 54 R&D-Intensive Pharmaceutical Companies

Year	Tax rate (percent)
1981	31.8%
1982	31.0
1983	31.7
1984	32.5
1985	29.1
1986	33.7
1987	39.1

SOURCE: The Office of Technology Assessment, 1993, based on unpublished computations by S-H. Kang for pharmaceutical firms in W.R. Baber and S.-H. Kang, "Accounting-Based Measure as Estimates of Economic Rates of Return: An Empirical Study of the U.S. Pharmaceutical Industry 1976-87, draft report prepared for the Office of Technology Assessment, March 1991.

---

[22] This ratio is also referred to as the effective tax rate (see chapter 8 for details).

• Tax Analysts, Inc., a tax research group, calculated current taxes payable, not including paybacks of past deferments but including a proportion of incurred tax liability that will be paid in future years,[23] as a percent of income from ongoing operations (257). The effective worldwide tax rate for 15 U.S.-based pharmaceutical firms under these criteria was 32 percent in 1987 (257,258).

The average effective tax rate for the industry after 1987 is likely to decline because the Tax Reform Act of 1986 reduced the U.S. corporate marginal tax rate after 1986. In 1987, the top Federal statutory marginal tax rate was 40 percent, compared with 46 percent in 1986, and it dropped to 34 percent in 1988. Therefore, when the effect of tax credits and deferments is taken into account, the average effective tax rate is likely to be even lower than 32 percent in years after 1987. For the drugs approved in 1981-83, the lower tax rate would have gone into effect in the 4th to 7th year after product launch.[24]

After taking into account the information summarized above, OTA assumed that taxes would constitute 32 percent of net pretax cash flows throughout the life of new drugs introduced between 1981 and 1983.

THE COST OF CAPITAL

The real (inflation-adjusted) weighted average company cost of capital for pharmaceutical firms varied roughly in the neighborhood of 10 percent in the 1980s (285). OTA assumed that the real cost of capital for investments made after product approval is 9.8 percent, because 10 percent is too high for investments made on existing products. The cost of capital for investments in ongoing operations is lower than the cost of capital for investments in R&D (285), and the weighted average cost of capital for the firm as a whole strikes a balance among different kinds of investments. OTA therefore adjusted the cost of capital for investments in ongoing operations slightly downward from 10 percent.

RESULTS

Table 4-6 shows the NPV of the net returns in the years following market approval (in 1990 dollars) under the base case. The NCEs of 1981-83 deliver cash flows equal to net present value of $341 million per compound. After taxes, the present value in the year of FDA approval of this net revenue is reduced to approximately $230 million. These net revenues must be compared with the present value of the investment in R&D required to discover and develop the compounds. An upper bound on the fully capitalized R&D costs is about $359 million before tax savings, or $194 million after tax savings are considered (see table 3-10 in chapter 3). Thus, under the base-case scenario, on average, each compound can be expected to return a net present value of at least $36 million more (after taxes) than would be required to bring forth the investment in the R&D.

The results are somewhat sensitive to the global sales multiplier, which is in turn very uncertain but likely to be higher than the ratio used in the base case. If the ratio were much higher than 2 to 1, the net present value of the

Table 4-6—Net Present Value[a] of Postlaunch Returns to R&D for NCEs Approved 1981-83 (1990 $ millions)

Pretax............................	$341
After tax............................	$230

[a] Net present value is calculated with a 9.9 percent cost of capital.
KEY: NCE = new chemical entity.
SOURCE: Office of Technology Assessment, 1993.

---

[23] According to Tax Analysts, Inc., a proportion of deferred taxes are never likely to be paid. This portion of deferred taxes is not counted in the tax rate.

[24] The reduction in U.S. corporate income taxes resulting from the Tax Reform Act represents a one-time windfall for returns on drugs discovered and developed before 1987. While taxes on net income from the manufacture and sale of new products will continue to stay as they are unless a new law changes them, the after-tax cost of R&D conducted after 1987 increased from approximately 54 percent of cash R&D outlays to 66 percent. Thus in the future the increased after-tax income from successful new drugs resulting from the Tax Reform Act of 1986 will be offset to some extent by increased after-tax costs of R&D.

investment would be even greater than the base case indicates.

Changes in the initial investment in plant and equipment slightly affect estimated returns. A $35-million investment in plant and equipment reduces the net present value of pretax net revenues to $336 million and the NPV of after-tax net revenues to $225 million.[25] The average capital expenditures for plant and equipment would have to be as high as $100 million for the NPV of after-tax cash flows to equal the NPV of after-tax R&D costs.

The results are not very sensitive to changes in the speed with which the originator's brand sales decline after patent expiration. If the average sales per compound were to decline by 20 percent per year beginning with the year of patent expiration (instead of according to the schedule shown in table 4-3), the present value of dollar returns would be $311 million before taxes and $209 million after taxes. The after-tax return still lies above the upper bound on R&D costs.

A decline of 20 percent per year in originator revenues from the date of patent loss would mean that within 3 years after patent expiration, originator sales revenue would be just 51 percent of its sales in the year of patent expiration. Fully 6 years after the passage of the Drug Price Competition and Patent Term Restoration Act of 1984 (Public Law 98-417) there is no evidence that the rate of revenue loss for originator compounds is approaching this rate. For the NPV of returns on R&D to equal zero, the postpatent decline in revenues would have to be over 30 percent per year from the year of patent expiration.

What does it mean to have the average revenue per compound deliver $36 million more in NPV than was needed to bring forth the research on the drugs introduced in 1981-83? This excess would be eliminated if the annual revenue per compound was reduced by 4.3 percent. If demand for the drugs is totally insensitive to changes in price,

then the average price could be reduced throughout the product life cycle by 4.3 percent without reducing returns below the amounts necessary to repay R&D investors. To the extent that demand for a compound increases as its price decreases, prices could have been reduced more than 4.3 percent in each year.

These estimates are rough approximations of the actual returns that the 1981-83 class of NCEs will earn. OTA attempted to be conservative in measuring returns, but the estimate is subject to measurement error whose magnitude is not easily assessed. They illustrate how volatile net returns can be over time and how sensitive they are to:

1. The cost of R&D, which in turn depends on the assumed cost of capital and the productivity of the research process; and
2. The worldwide revenues that can be expected from the drugs that result from that process.

As this and other chapters in this report illustrate, both worldwide revenues and the cost of R&D for each new NCE can change rapidly. If firms devote increasing resources to basic research, then the cost per success can increase dramatically, not only because of the actual outlays, but also because these expenditures are made early in the process and carry a high cost of capital. At the same time, worldwide revenues per NCE can also change dramatically over short periods of time, as figure 4-2 clearly demonstrates. The second-year U.S. sales of compounds that the FDA approved in the period 1984-88 were substantially higher than the sales of the drugs introduced in the 1981-83 period. Yet, future changes in methods of paying for prescription drugs, brought about by health insurance reform or health care cost containment in the United States and abroad, could adversely affect the sales curve for drugs introduced in the 1990s.

---

[25] The pretax net cash flows are reduced by only $5 million because higher initial capital expenditure means that a higher proportion of the cost of sales is devoted to depreciation expenses, which are subtracted from the estimate of direct manufacturing costs.

TOTAL PHARMACEUTICAL INDUSTRY RETURNS

The previous section described an analysis of investments in a specific group of new drugs, from their very beginning as R&D projects to their ultimate obsolescence and removal from the market. Although the analyses reviewed and presented above are imprecise, because some data on revenues and costs can be estimated only roughly, within the limits of data accuracy the analyses appropriately measure the net present value of investments in R&D.

Another more indirect way to assess returns on R&D is to estimate the profitability of research-intensive pharmaceutical companies. Audited financial data are available to estimate profitability at the company level for public corporations. Pharmaceutical firms invest in the discovery, development, production, marketing, and distribution of many products, including some that are not ethical pharmaceuticals. The total profit or return on a company's investment in a given period is a mixture of returns on past investments made over many previous years on many different projects.

At the company level, the return on investment is defined by the internal rate of return (IRR), the interest rate at which the net present value of all cashflows into and out of the firm equals zero. If the IRR across all companies in an industry is greater than the industry's cost of capital, then the industry returned more to its investors than was necessary to bring forth the investment dollars, and one would suspect that barriers to entry or other forms of monopoly power (perhaps obtained through patent protection) might exist in the industry (86). On the other hand, a low IRR relative to the cost of capital would, if companies invest efficiently, lead to disinvestment in the industry, including R&D.[26] Over the entire life of the industry (from its start to its dissolution), the IRR should be in the neighborhood of its cost of capital.

The annual financial reports of public companies contain estimates of total firm profit rates based on accounting records. For example, the net income as a percent of the total "book value" of assets[27] is a commonly used benchmark of firm profitability (301). Companies themselves report this ratio in their annual financial statements and compare their performance in specific years with that in previous years. Other commonly used profit ratios, such as net income as a percent of sales, are also easily computed from company financial statements.

It is not surprising, then, that analysts would compare the accounting profit rates of firms in the pharmaceutical industry with those of firms in other industries (301,457).[28] The ready availability of publicly reported and independently audited data, and the widespread use of these measures by companies themselves, invites such comparisons. But they are limited in two important ways. First, accounting-based profit measures can be poor approximations of firms' true IRRs. Second, comparing returns of the pharmaceutical industry with those of other industries is not a perfect substitute for comparing its returns with the industry's cost of capital. Risk differs among industries, so even if accounting-based profits were good proxies for IRRs, simple interindustry comparisons, without consideration of the riskiness of industries, would be misleading.

Accounting profits are poor measures of IRR for several reasons:

---

[26] Another possible explanation for persistently low IRRs in an industry is that the managers of firms in the industry do not adequately represent the interests of their shareholders (39,155,282).

[27] Book value refers to the end-of-the-year value of capital assets after depreciation expenses. Strict accounting conventions determine what kinds of investments create a capital asset. R&D, for example, is not recorded as an investment but is fully expensed in the year in which expenditures are made. This accounting convention, required since 1975 by the Federal Accounting Standards Board, is equivalent to depreciating the investment 100 percent in the year it is made.

[28] By these conventional measures the pharmaceutical industry would appear to be substantially more profitable than other industries.

- Accounting standards require firms to record as current expenditures all outlays for R&D, advertising, and promotion when in reality these expenditures are investments whose payoffs may be delayed or extended into future accounting periods. The value of the "intangible assets" produced by these investments is too uncertain for use in accounting statements. Thus, the book value of assets in a company's financial statement underestimates the true value of assets, especially when these investments are important components of the company's activities, as in the pharmaceutical industry (62,78,80).

- Financial statements often report income and expenses as they are accrued in accounting records, not as they are actually realized in cash flows. These differences between accrual accounting and cash flows can distort the timing of investments and revenues and therefore misrepresent the rate of return in a given period (27)

- Even if the above distortions are corrected, the accounting rate of return could still depart from the IRR because accounting profits do not adjust properly for the time profile of cash flows from various investments and are further distorted by growth or decline in investment over time (132,398,402).

■ Past Studies

OTA found six studies of pharmaceutical industry profits in which accounting rates of return to pharmaceutical firms were corrected by treating R&D (and sometimes advertising) as investments rather than as current expenditures. Each study makes assumptions about the useful life of these intangible investments and the rate at which their value depreciates. See table 4-7 for a summary of these studies. These studies are limited by small numbers of firms, virtually all successful and therefore likely to be more profitable than the industry as a whole, and few years of data. Nevertheless, they consistently find that correcting pharmaceutical industry profit rates for

investment in intangible capital reduces rates of return by roughly 20 to 25 percent (214).

Three research studies compared adjusted pharmaceutical industry profits with similarly adjusted profits in other industries. Table 4-8 summarizes the methods and results of these studies. Once again, these studies include a small number of pharmaceutical and nonpharmaceutical firms, virtually all successful, and examine a short time period. Nevertheless, these studies show that adjusting accounting rates of return for investments in R&D and advertising does not completely erase differences in computed profits between pharmaceuticals and the comparison industries.

Even if the corrections to accounting rates of return in these studies were sufficient to approximate IRRs (which they do only imperfectly), the differences in the rates of return might reflect differences in the riskiness (and, hence, the cost of capital) among industries. Thus, little can be said about the rate of return on investments in the pharmaceutical industry from these studies.

■ OTA's Contractor Report on Comparative Profits

OTA asked William Baber and Sok-Hyon Kang to compare the IRR of a sample of firms in the pharmaceutical industry with IRRs of non-pharmaceutical companies using a new technique that adjusts accounting data to obtain a closer approximation of IRRs. (27). The method, pioneered by Ijiri (199,200) and Salamon (359,360), calculates a "cash flow recovery rate" from accounting data, which can then be combined with assumptions about the time profile of cash flows to imply an IRR for the industry.

The time profile of cash flows (including the total life of investments and the shape of cash flows over time) is itself an unknown both for the pharmaceutical industry and for other firms. Consequently, Baber and Kang examined several alternative assumptions about the life of investments (including R&D as well as tangible capital facilities and equipment) and the shape of the cash flow curve in both pharmaceutical and nonphar-

Table 4-7—Accounting Rates of Return Corrected for Investment in R&D and Advertising

Researcher(s)	Sample	Time period	Data source(s)	Major assumptions	Accounting rate of return	Corrected rate of return	Corrected ROR ÷ Accounting ROR
Stauffer, 1975	6 major pharmaceutical firms	Varying across firms from 1953-72 to 1963-72	Compustat	1. No correction for inflation. 2. 4-year R&D gestation period with constant expenditures per unit of time. 3. Product sales reach constant level first year after introduction, remaining at that level for 15 years. 4. Sales decay rate = 0.7.	Varied across firms	Varied across firms; less than accounting rate of return for 5 out of 6 firms	Ranged from 0.72-1.23
Clarkson, 1977	1 pharmaceutical firm (Eli Lilly and Co.) (out of 69 firms in cross-sectional sample)	1965-74	Eli Lilly and Co. *Annual Reports*	1. Corrected for inflation using wholesale price index. 2. 3-year life for advertising. 3. Basic research = 16% of total R&D. 4. Basic research accumulates at 10% per year for 11 years and depreciates for 15 years. 5. Development accumulates at 10% per year for 6 years and depreciates for 11 years.	17.3% (average over time)	11.1% (average over time)	0.64
Grabowski and Mueller, 1978	7 pharmaceutical firms (out of 86 firms in cross-sectional sample)	1968	Compustat; previously collected R&D data for 1959-69; advertising expenditures for five major media "from individual media information sources."	1. Corrected for inflation using GNP price index. 2. Removed cyclical effects and financing effects. 3. R&D depreciates at constant proportional rate of either 5 or 10%. 4. Advertising depreciates at constant proportional rate of 30%.	14.1% (average over firms)	10.8% (using 10% R&D depreciation rate) 10.5% (using 5% R&D depreciation rate)	0.77 0.74
Bloch, 1973	4 pharmaceutical firms	1969	Annual reports	1. R&D depreciation schedule estimated by regression of sales on lagged R&D. 2. Advertising not capitalized. 3. After-tax returns.	Varied across firms 9.7-22.1%	7.6-16.1%	Ranged from 0.70-0.80
Ayanian, 1975	6 major pharmaceutical firms	1973 (for ROR)	Data on advertising and R&D expenditures provided by firms; *Moody's Industrial Reports.*	1. No correction for inflation. 2. R&D and advertising depreciated at same rate, assumed at either 9 or 13% per year.	17.7% (average over firms)	14.06% (average) (using 13% depreciation rate) 13.69% (using 9% depreciation rate)	0.79 0.77

(Continued on next page)

Table 4-7—Accounting Rates of Return Corrected for Investment in R&D and Advertising—(Continued)

Researcher(s)	Sample	Time period	Data source(s)	Major assumptions	Accounting rate of return	Corrected rate of return	Corrected ROR ÷ Accounting ROR
Megna and Mueller, 1991	10 major pharmaceutical firms	1975-85	Compustat	1. No correction for inflation. 2. Estimated firm-specific rates of depreciation of R&D and advertising by regression of sales on lagged R&D and advertising expenditures (assumed binomial lag functions).	14.81%	12.15% (average over time)	0.82

KEY: ROR = rate of return.

SOURCE: Office of Technology Assessment, 1993, based on E.J. Jensen, "Rates of Return to Investment in the Pharmaceutical Industry: A Survey," contract paper prepared for the Office of Technology Assessment, September 1990.

Table-4-8—Results of Studies Comparing Adjusted Pharmaceutical Industry Profits With Profits in Other Industries

Study	Pharmaceutical industry sample	Other industries sample	R&D capitalization assumptions		Advertising capitalization method		Results		Comments
			Pharmaceuticals	Other	Pharmaceuticals	Others	Pharmaceuticals	Other firms	
Grabowski and Mueller, 1978	7 companies 1968	79 firms in a national sample of industries performing R&D.	R&D depreciates in value at constant proportional rate of 5%.	R&D depreciates at constant proportional rate of 10%.	Depreciates at 30% per year	Depreciates at 30% per year	10.8%	7.2%	■ 1968 profits smoothed for cyclical effects ■ After-tax profits ■ Inflation adjusted
Clarkson, 1977	1 company 1959-73	68 firms in a national sample.	*"Basic" research:* 16% of R&D. Basic research has 26-year life, accumulates for 11 years (growing in value at 10 % per year); then depreciates for 15 years. *Development:* 84% of R&D. Development has a 17-year life, accumulates for 6 years (growing in value at 10 % per year) then depreciates for 15 years.	Development life and depreciation schedule estimated from industry sources. Varies across industries. Basic research assumed to accumulate for the development life plus 5 years.	3-year life	3-year life	12.9%	9.6%	■ After-tax profits ■ Inflation adjusted
Megna and Mueller, 1991	10 major firms 1975-88	Selected firms in advertising or R&D-intensive industries. 6 firms in toy industry; 4 distilled beverage firms; 9 cosmetic firms.	R&D depreciation rates estimated for each firm by regressing sales on lagged R&D. Maximum 8-year life.	R&D depreciation rates estimated for each firm by regressing sales on lagged R&D. Maximum 8-year life.	Same depreciation estimation technique as R&D with a maximum 4 year life.	Same depreciation estimation technique as R&D with a maximum 4 year life.	12.15%	■ Toys = 6.66%. ■ Distilled beverages = 11.44%. ■ Cosmetics = 11.51%.	■ After-tax profits ■ Not inflation adjusted

SOURCE: Office of Technology Assessment, 1993.

Figure 4-7—Cash-Flow Profiles Used in Internal Rate of Return Computations

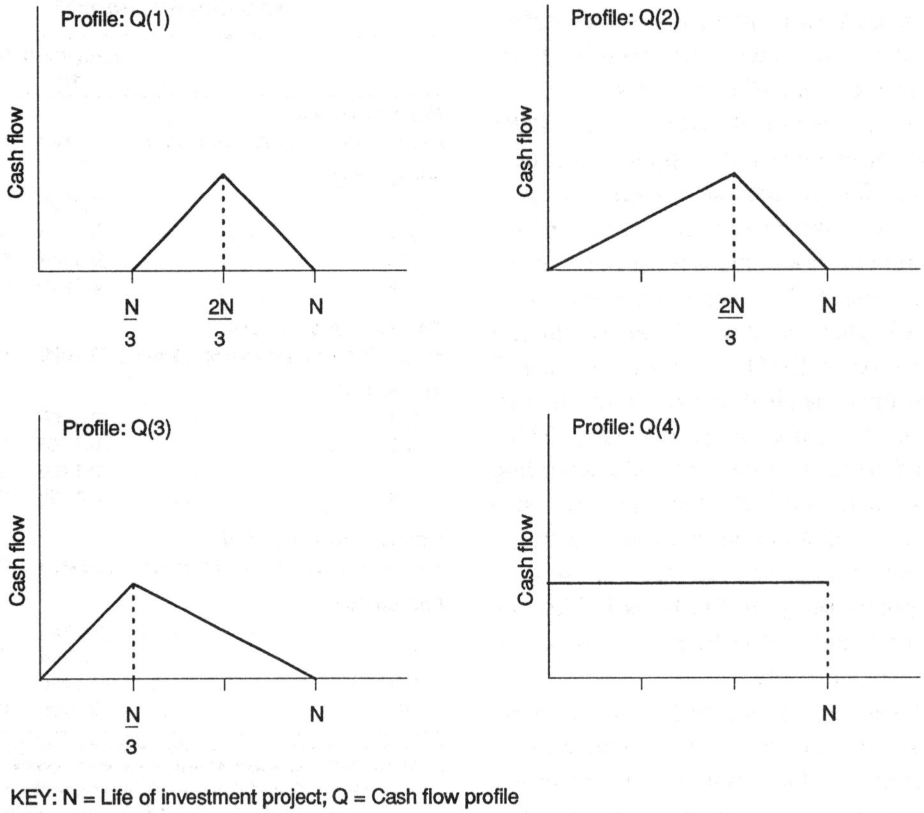

KEY: N = Life of investment project; Q = Cash flow profile

KEY: N = Life of Investment Project; Q = Cash-flow profile.

SOURCE: W.R. Baber and S-H. Kang, "Accounting-Based Measure as Estimates of Economic Rates of Return: An Empirical Study of the U.S. Pharmaceutical Industry 1976-87, draft report prepared for the Office of Technology Assessment, March 1991.

maceutical firms. Figure 4-7 shows four different cash flow profiles. Q1, an inverted v-shape profile with a substantial delay before revenues begin to accrue from an investment, has often been viewed as the most appropriate shape for an R&D-intensive industry like pharmaceuticals (160). (This profile is similar to the cashflow profile for new drugs shown in figure 4-1.) Other profiles may be more realistic for nonpharmaceutical firms. Because the productive life of investments may also be longer in the pharmaceutical industry, the contractors estimated IRRs for 20-year and 30-year investment lives.[29]

The contractors compared 54 research-intensive pharmaceutical firms listed at least once in the Compustat™ database between 1975 and 1987[30] with two "control" samples, each with 54 firms having financial characteristics similar to

[29] Other, shorter, investment lives were also considered, but the resulting calculated IRRs were unrealistically low for all samples and are not reproduced here. The difference in IRRs between pharmaceutical and nonpharmaceutical firms is even greater for shorter investment lives (27).

[30] Study of years prior to 1976 is infeasible because accounting practices for R&D were not standardized until 1975 with the publication of a Federal Accounting Standards Board rule on the treatment of R&D (29,74).

[31] The first control sample was obtained by matching nonpharmaceutical firms with pharmaceutical firms on the basis of sales and sales growth; the second control sample was obtained by matching nonpharmaceutical firms with pharmaceutical firms on the basis of sales and R&D intensity.

the pharmaceutical firms.[31] Table 4-9 shows the weighted mean IRRs between 1976 and 1987 for the pharmaceutical firms and each of the control samples under alternative assumptions about investment life and cash-flow profiles.

Differences in weighted mean annual IRRs between pharmaceutical and nonpharmaceutical firms of about 2 to 3 percentage points per year persist and were statistically significant regardless of assumptions made about investment life or cash-flow profile.[32] The same analysis for a sample of 88 pharmaceutical firms (including firms with ratios of R&D to sales lower than 5 percent) and their matched control firms showed differences of the same magnitude (27). Thus, while the differences in uncorrected accounting profits between research-intensive pharmaceutical companies and non-pharmaceutical companies over the period were as high as 4 to 6 percentage points per year, the IRRs implied by the contractors' study differ by much less, 2 to 3 percentage points per year.[33]

Baber and Kang's method for estimating industry-level IRRs is itself subject to measurement error, so the reliability of the measured rates of return for each industry group (pharmaceuticals and controls) is uncertain. Nevertheless, Baber and Kang applied the estimation method consistently across all firms in the three groups, so the **differences** in profit rates between pharmaceuticals and controls, which were stable across a wide range assumptions about their investments, are, in OTA's judgment, reliably estimated.

The contractor's comparative profit study is silent on the question of whether a 2 to 3 percentage point difference in rates of return is due to differences in the cost of capital between

Table 4-9—Mean Estimated Internal Rates of Return for Pharmaceutical Industry and Control Groups[a]

	Investment life (years)	
	30	20
Pharmaceuticals		
Mean accounting return on assets	0.1432	0.1432
Implied IRR[b]		
Q(1)	0.1382	0.1361
Q(2)	0.1413	0.1374
Q(3)	0.1434	0.1389
Q(4)	0.1460	0.1393
Control Group I (sales)[c]		
Mean accounting return on assets	0.1029	0.1029
Implied IRR[b]		
Q(1)	0.1143	0.1076
Q(2)	0.1147	0.1058
Q(3)	0.1150	0.1036
Q(4)	0.1155	0.1041
Control Group II (R&D)[d]		
Mean accounting return on assets	0.0875	0.0875
Implied IRR[b]		
Q(1)	0.1163	0.1117
Q(2)	0.1178	0.1113
Q(3)	0.1190	0.1109
Q(4)	0.1200	0.1111

[a] Based on a sample of 54 pharmaceutical companies listed in Compustat™ database at least once in the period 1975-87 with R&D-to-sales ratios of 5% or more. Constant growth rates of invested capital equal to the geometric mean sample growth rates from 1975-87 were used to calculate IRR estimates. Estimates based on actual growth rates in each sample are comparable.
[b] Cash flow Profiles, Q1 through Q4, are shown in figure 4-7.
[c] Firms matched with pharmaceuticals on the basis of sales and sales growth.
[d] Firms matched with pharmaceuticals on the basis of sales and R&D intensity.

KEY: IRR = internal rate of return; Q = cash flow profile.
SOURCE: Office of Technology Assessment, 1993, based on W.R. Baber and S.-H. Kang, 'Accounting-Based Measures as Estimates of Economic Rates of Return: An Empirical Study of the U.S. Pharmaceutical Industry 1976-87," contract paper prepared for the Office of Technology Assessment, March 1991.

---

[32] The estimates shown in table 4-9 are based on constant growth rates. In an extension of their study, Baber and Kang estimated IRRs with actual investment growth rates. The results were substantially the same (28).

[33] Because the study used new analytical techniques that are unfamiliar to many analysts, OTA solicited independent review and comment on the validity of its methods and findings from both its advisory panel and a selected group of academic experts in economics and accounting. The paper evoked considerable criticism from one outside reviewer, who questioned the validity of assumptions underlying the use of the method. OTA then submitted the detailed critique to the study authors, and both the critique and the authors' response were sent to two independent outside experts for further review. The results of the review process reinforced the conclusion that pharmaceutical industry IRRs were 2 to 3 percent higher than the returns on the control samples in the 12-year period under study. (A copy of the history of written reviews and comments is available upon request from OTA.)

pharmaceuticals and the control firms. If investment in the pharmaceutical industry is riskier than in the control firms, then the cost of capital will be higher. OTA examined differences in the cost of capital between the pharmaceutical industry and the two control samples.

The cost of capital is the rate of return investors require to induce them to invest in a company with a given level of risk. The weighted average cost of capital is the blended cost of the firm's debt and equity capital (285,409).

OTA estimated the weighted average cost of capital for the pharmaceutical industry and the two control groups. The cost of capital varies over time with changes in underlying interest rates; consequently, precise measurement of the cost of capital over the 12-year period of this study is impossible. In addition, OTA's method may be subject to biases in measurement. We used the same approach consistently across all samples, however, so the biases would tend to cancel themselves out when examining **differences** in the cost of capital between pharmaceuticals and controls. OTA is therefore confident that the measured differences in the cost of capital among the samples are reasonably precise. (The method and assumptions underlying the estimates are described in appendix C.)

The cost of capital for the pharmaceutical industry was slightly higher than that for control sample I (matched by sales and sales growth) but lower than that for the control sample II (matched by sales and R&D). (See table 4-10). Thus, it appears that the higher estimated IRRs of the research-intensive pharmaceutical industry cannot be explained by a higher cost of capital in the pharmaceutical industry.

Another possible explanation for the difference in estimated IRRs is the investment character of advertising and promotion. Baber and Kang did not convert advertising expenditures to invest-

Table 4-10—Cost of Capital Difference Between Pharmaceutical Industry and Control Firms (15 Largest Pharmaceutical Firms)

Pharmaceuticals - Control I	+.007
Pharmaceuticals - Control II	-.016

Control I: Firms similar to pharmaceutical industry in sales and sales growth.

Control II: Firms similar to pharmaceutical industry in sales and R&D intensity.

SOURCE: Office of Technology Assessment, 1993, based on data provided by S.-H. Kang, unpublished computations for firms listed in W.R. Baber and S.-H. Kang, "Accounting-Based Measure as Estimates of Economic Rates of Return: An Empirical Study of the U.S. Pharmaceutical Industry 1976-87," contract paper prepared for the Office of Technology Assessment, March 1991.

ments, but the pharmaceutical industry is characterized by high advertising and promotional expenditures that generate intangible capital. The life of these investments may be longer than the life of advertising in other industries, and longer than 1 year, although there is virtually no evidence to support this contention and some evidence against it (87,280).[34] In preliminary analyses, the contractors investigated the effect of capitalizing advertising expenses over a 3-year period for all firms; this action widened even further the gap in implied IRR between the pharmaceutical industry and the control firms (26).[35]

■ Other Studies

Another way of examining returns on pharmaceutical firms is to study the response of companies' stock and bond values to investments in tangible and intangible (i.e., R&D and marketing) assets. If the securities markets are efficient and accurately predict the future value of firms (at least over a long time frame), then the potential returns from new investments by a firm should, with random error, immediately be reflected in the market value of the firm.

Two unpublished research studies have used the relationship between investments and compa-

---

[34] Hurwitz and Caves (195) have suggested that advertising and promotion outlays may serve to realize the goodwill inherent in an innovation. The value lies in the innovation itself; promotion, like production and distribution, is necessary to unlock that value.

[35] Grossly longer investment lives for advertising in the pharmaceutical industry, such as 10 years or more would be required for the differences in implied IRRs between pharmaceuticals and the control firms to disappear.

nies' market values to estimate returns on different kinds of investments across industries. Results pertaining only to the pharmaceutical industry are reported here.

Thomas (422) estimated the relationship between market values and R&D, advertising, and working capital in 23 large pharmaceutical firms in 1984. Pharmaceutical industry stock market values rose with higher ratios of R&D to investment in plant and equipment, but pharmaceutical industry market values were unrelated to advertising expenditures.[36] Thomas used the estimated relationship between R&D intensity and the firm's market value to correct accounting rates of return for the value of the intangible capital built up from past R&D investments. The accounting rate of return declined from 20 to about 11 percent when the estimated value of the intangible R&D capital is added to the asset base.

As Comanor has observed, studies of stock market rates of return "indicate little about competition or monopoly in the pharmaceutical industry, [because] stock market values typically capitalize future returns into the value of the firm, which includes any prospective effects of monopoly power as well as other factors" (86). Thus, a high value of intangible R&D capital may reflect the monopoly-creating effect of R&D in an industry with relatively strong patent protection.

Mueller and Reardon (282) estimated the excess market rate of return for a sample of 21 pharmaceutical firms over their cost of capital in the period 1971-88. Mueller and Reardon observed changes in market prices from one period to the next can be related to changes in different kinds of investment. They found that investments in pharmaceutical R&D led to changes in market value that were more than twice as high as the cost of capital, while advertising did not raise market values at all, and investments in plant and equipment raised market values less than the cost of capital. High market returns on R&D relative to the cost of capital suggest that over the 18-year period of the study, pharmaceutical R&D paid off in the aggregate more than was necessary to bring forth the investment.

Mueller's and Reardon's conclusion that returns on R&D are well above the cost of capital in the pharmaceutical industry must be considered suggestive at best, because the method for estimating changes in market values required the researchers to estimate a rate of depreciation on existing assets (both tangible and intangible) that is the same across all kinds of assets. Yet, plant and equipment are likely to depreciate according to rates that differ greatly from those governing R&D and other intangible investments.

Other problems also cloud Mueller's and Reardon's findings. The benefits of R&D cannot be obtained without investments in plant and equipment that produce the products and, in the current market, without the advertising and promotion necessary to sell them. While R&D may be a necessary condition for obtaining high returns, firms must invest in those seemingly less profitable activities as well. Analysis of the market returns on investment as a whole in the seven largest pharmaceutical companies in Mueller's and Reardon's study found only three of the companies with stock market returns greater than the cost of capital.[37]

To summarize, studies of the impact of pharmaceutical investments on returns in the stock and bond markets do not prove, but are consistent with, the finding that R&D drives profitability in the industry and has produced returns over reasonably long periods of time that may exceed the cost of capital.

---

[36] Market values actually declined with the ratio of advertising expenditures to investment in plant and equipment, but the relationship was statistically insignificant. The failure to find a significant relationship could be due to very small variation among pharmaceutical firms in the advertising/plant and equipment ratio, but the paper did not provide information necessary to test this possibility.

[37] To calculate these returns, however, the authors had to assume that the market value of the firm's capital would decline at a rate of 10 percent per year in the absence of new investment. The validity of this assumption is questionable.

FINDINGS AND CONCLUSIONS

OTA's review of the evidence on the returns on R&D indicates that these returns were higher than was required to reward investors for the time and risks incurred. The net returns on NCEs introduced to the U.S. market between 1981 and 1983 are likely to exceed the cost of capital by an amount that would allow annual revenues from these drugs to be reduced across the board by about 4.3 percent.

These results conflict with findings of earlier studies, largely because the realized revenues from this cohort of new drugs were so much higher in real terms than the revenues from new drugs introduced in previous years. Very preliminary sales data on drugs approved between 1984 and 1988 suggest that the revenue curve from new drugs continues to steepen in real terms. OTA's assumptions about other key elements of revenues and costs also differed from those of previous studies but not consistently in ways that would increase returns. For example, OTA assumed a much higher cost of capital for R&D than did other studies and therefore used a relatively high cost of R&D against which to judge returns.

Estimates of returns on R&D are highly sensitive to changes in market conditions for drugs throughout their product life cycle. Actions by governments or insurers to control prices paid for new drugs or to encourage price competition among different drugs with similar therapeutic effects could rapidly reduce worldwide sales revenues. (See chapter 10 for a description of prescription drug pricing policies in the United States and selected foreign countries.) There is, however, no evidence that these effects have yet occurred at a scale that would seriously jeopardize the market for new drugs.

Evidence on the economic rate of return to the pharmaceutical industry as a whole over a relatively long period (1976-87) shows returns that were higher than returns on nonpharmaceutical firms by about 2 to 3 percentage points per year after adjustment for differences in risk among firms. This is a much lower differential than is suggested by conventional comparisons of profit ratios, but it is still high enough to have made the industry a relatively lucrative investment.

Together, the findings on returns on pharmaceutical R&D and to the industry as a whole explain why R&D expenditures have risen so dramatically in real terms throughout the 1980s. Investors have followed the promise of high returns on future innovations. Ultimately investment in research is determined by expected revenues. The dramatic increase in real revenues to new drugs throughout the 1980s has sent signals to the industry that more investment will be rewarded handsomely. The industry has responded as expected, by increasing its commitment to investment, including investment in R&D. The resulting rise in R&D investment may have dampened internal rates of return as more money is poured into projects that, if successful, must share revenues with other competing products on the market.

Trends in Science, Technology and Drug Discovery[1] | 5

S cience undergirds the growth of the pharmaceutical industry over the past century. The industry has long been highly research intensive. Its roots trace to the advances in physiology and organic chemistry at the end of the last century. In recent years, however, the investment in research and development (R&D) has reached new heights. Drug treatments have transformed medical practice; biomedical research has transformed the discovery and development of drugs.

The expanding science base for drug discovery has implications for the cost of developing new agents. Two implications of the rapid advance of science for the overall costs of discovery are the need to keep abreast of the expanding base of knowledge about disease mechanisms and the need to keep abreast of other competitors in the industry. Pharmaceutical firms compete on several fronts. Science and technology form one basis for competition. This chapter describes the process of pharmaceutical research, particularly the discovery of new drugs. It centers on research more than development and assesses how science and technology might change the process and its costs over the next decade. This chapter explains how a new agent is discovered, particularly how drug discovery is changing in the face of new developments in science and technology.

The focus is on changes in the discovery of new therapeutic drugs brought about by the explosion of knowledge about molecular biology and human genetics. The potential effects of new methods, materials, and instruments for *diagnosis* are not discussed here. The first fruits of many lines of research, including protein analysis and study of DNA (deoxyribonucleic acid) emphasized in this chapter, are likely to be new diagnostic tests.

---

[1]This chapter was prepared for the Office of Technology Assessment by Robert Mullan Cook-Deegan, M.D.

Improved diagnosis generally advances before treatment, often leading by a decade or more. Advances in body imaging, for example, have obvious implications not only for diagnosis, but also for measuring the efficacy of treatment (281).

Also not discussed in this chapter are new methods of drug delivery currently subject to extensive research efforts (218,333) and research on new assays to predict how the body responds to new agents. These and other topics are central to future directions in pharmaceutical R&D. Each has a rich literature. The discussion emphasizes molecular biology, however, because this best illustrates the shifting scientific foundations of drug discovery. This tack was chosen not because other topics are less important, or will have less impact, on future directions in pharmaceutical R&D. Rather, it was chosen as the most promising way to highlight the widening gulf between current and traditional research methods.

Finally, the emphasis on human genetics is only illustrative. Molecular biology has come to dominate other areas of research equally relevant to drug discovery. Molecular approaches to combat viral infections, to control the immune response, to understand cancer, to penetrate the brain and spinal cord, and to modulate responses to hormones and growth factors are all extremely active fields. A chapter of equal or greater length could be written for each field. The focus on human genetics was chosen in part because it touches on all these other fields, and because it also more starkly contrasts with more traditional approaches and thus emphasizes how the scientific foundations are shifting beneath biomedical research.

This chapter begins with a description of drugs and drug receptors. Next it considers proteins, the workhorses of biology that form structural elements within cells and that mediate biochemical reactions. The next section deals with DNA, the chemical basis of inheritance.

The study of DNA and proteins marks the advance of molecular biology. Pharmaceutical research increasingly relies on molecular biology, and it is here that science most directly joins drug discovery. Protein pharmaceuticals constitute an important new therapeutic class. Several protein drugs have had a dramatic impact on clinical practice in recent years, and many more are being prepared for the market. Novel protein drugs have, for example, constituted roughly half the new major introductions in the last few years; indeed the wealth of new prospects has raised concern that the regulatory pipeline may be overwhelmed by the flow of new biotechnology products (146,341). The direct use of DNA as a treatment constitutes the next logical step. This is currently a frontier of biomedical research, and this section is necessarily more speculative, and illustrates the uncertainty regarding a new treatment modality. A final section draws lessons from the various case histories, focusing on those elements most likely to influence the future costs of drug discovery.

DRUGS AND RECEPTORS

The notion of specific drug action is most often described by a lock-and- key analogy. The drug is seen as the key that acts specifically on a narrow range of locks. The lock is a drug receptor. A drug is a substance that causes a physiological response; the receptor is the molecule through which it works.

Paul Ehrlich formulated the idea of drug-receptor interactions in the first decade of this century. A.V. Hill modeled the interaction as the binding of a drug to its receptor in mathematical terms early in this century. This was embellished in the late 1920s by A.J. Clark who forwarded the idea of a drug "occupying" a receptor site, competing with natural agents that bound the receptor at the same site. Drugs were thereafter termed "agonists," those that caused the normal response (simulating the body's own action), or "antagonists," those that blocked normal action (105).

The model, in its simplest form, is that the drug binds to a receptor. The receptor has a binding domain that is specific for the drug, typically the same site sought by compounds normally found in the cell. Binding causes the receptor to respond, causing a cellular change. The receptor may open a gate for the influx or efflux of charged molecules through the cell membrane, for example, or it may catalyze a biochemical reaction. Many receptors act by causing the formation of ''second messengers,'' compounds that provoke cellular events such as the secretion of insulin or the synthesis of specific proteins. The site causing a cellular change is separate from, but signaled by, the binding site.

Many enzymes are drug receptors. Enzymes are proteins that mediate biochemical reactions.

They build cellular structures, degrade cellular byproducts, metabolize sugars, and perform the myriad chemical tasks that transpire in cells. Many drugs discovered in the 1970s and 1980s originated from understanding a metabolic pathway, finding the enzyme associated with a particular reaction, and studying how to inhibit its activity. The drug captopril, for example, was developed by tracing the biochemical pathway to produce angiotensin, a short protein (a polypeptide) that raised blood pressure. By slowing production of angiotensin, captopril helped treat high blood pressure (see box 5-A) (300).

Box 5-A—The Discovery of Captopril

Hypertension, or high blood pressure, is a highly prevalent condition. It predisposes to heart attack and stroke, and is a major cause of death and disability. A ''hypertensive principle'' was discovered in the kidney late in the last century. A theoretical model of hypertension was elaborated in the 1930s and 1940s. In this model, the kidney was a central actor. Blood volume and the resistance to blood flow, caused by contraction of smooth muscles in small arteries, were the main determinants of blood pressure. The kidney controlled blood volume by regulating how much water was retained in the body, in turn determined by how much salt was excreted.

The kidney also produced substances that directly caused contraction of smooth muscles in small arteries. These findings led to several treatment strategies. One long-standing approach entailed diuretics to reduce blood volume. Another involved relaxing smooth muscles in blood vessel walls by blocking the action of epinephrine and other chemicals present in blood. Drug researchers at Squibb discovered a wholly new class of antihypertensive agents through a logical set of steps that began early in the 1960s with the elucidation of one physiological pathway leading to high blood pressure. This line of research culminated in the discovery of captopril. The process was a prototype of rational drug design.

The physiological pathway began when a short protein, or peptide, angiotensin II was formed in the blood stream. Angiotensin II stimulated the release of a hormone, aldosterone, from the adrenal gland, which in turn caused the kidney to retain sodium. With more sodium in the blood, the body retained more water. Angiotensin also directly stimulated contraction of smooth muscles in blood vessels. By blocking the formation of angiotensin, one could pursue both paths to antihypertensive therapy in a single stroke.

Angiotensin II, the most active natural agent, consists of a short peptide—a chain of eight amino-acids. These 8 are cleaved from angiotensin I, which has 10 amino-acids. The enzyme that cleaves angiotensin I to II is Angiotensin Converting Enzyme (ACE). The path to captopril started by trying to inhibit the action of ACE.

Researchers at Squibb took several approaches. They started from the natural angiotensin I molecule and fashioned molecules that might have similar shapes but were more difficult to cleave. They also worked with a snake venom that inhibited ACE. The active components in the venom included several peptides, including one chain of 9 amino acids and another of 5 amino acids. These natural peptides were ACE inhibitors, but they had to be injected. The effort centered on finding an agent that could be administered

(Continued on next page)

Box 5-A—The Discovery of Captopril—(Continued)

orally, and would find its way into the bloodstream after surviving the brutal transit through stomach and intestines. The team screened a myriad of chemical compounds similar to the natural precursor and to the snake venom. They devised modifications of the venom peptides and the natural precursor. They altered the backbone of the five amino-acid venom peptide thinking that it might retain activity while resisting degradation. Of 2,000 compounds screened, only a few inhibited ACE and only one was specific to it. That one was a metal-binding molecule that promised to be toxic. Another approach was more successful.

The Squibb team also worked back from their conception of the receptor's shape, based on their knowledge of details of the cleavage reaction it performed. Since the ACE protein had not itself been structurally defined, they developed a hypothetical model based on the active site of another enzyme that performed a similar cleavage reaction, and whose structure was known from x-ray crystallography. The research team crafted compounds to fit into the hypothetical active site of ACE and discovered a compound with inhibitory activity that was similar in shape to two amino-acids in tandem. They performed further chemical modifications of this molecule and eventually found a chemical amenable to oral administration that was 1,000 times more potent than their initial "lead" molecule. The synthetic drug had greater activity than the nine-amino-acid venom peptide.

This new agent was named captopril. Squibb submitted a new drug application for captopril in 1979. Two years later, captopril was approved by the U.S. Food and Drug Administration for marketing under the brand-name of "Capoten." Captopril soon became a standard drug to treat hypertension, and also found clinical use in combating heart failure and other cardiovascular conditions. Its sales in 1988 exceeded $1.1 billion, joining only three other compounds with sales over $1 billion in a year. It also became the starting point for a round of new antihypertensive agents pursued by Squibb and other firms.

SOURCES: M.A. Ondetti, D.W. Cushman, and B. Rubin, "Captoril," *Chronicles of Drug Discovery*, J.S. Bindra and D. Ledniger (eds.)(New York: Wiley, 1983). M.R. Ziai and B. Beer, "Making Business Sense of Science with Rational Drug Design," *Pharmaceutical Executive* 10:40-46, October 1990.

■ Identifying a Receptor Expedites Drug Design

The first drugs were typically found by looking for chemicals that caused a particular clinical reaction. Extracts from the foxglove plant were long used to treat "dropsy" (congestive heart failure) and other ills. Digitalis was discovered by purifying chemicals out of those extracts and looking for the compounds that produced clinical improvement. Aspirin (acetylsalicylate) was found by testing chemical modifications of salicylate, a traditional remedy for fever and pain. Although aspirin had been synthesized in 1853, its clinical effects were not discovered until 40 years later. It has become one of the most commonly used drugs since the firm Bayer began making it on a large scale in the late 1890s (396). Screening compounds chemically similar to salicylate was an early example of a strategy that prevailed for many years, starting from chance observations of clinical effects of a known compound, with little or no knowledge of mechanism. This approach was refined until the synthesis of new compounds became a high art and screening tests a centerpiece of pharmacology. One pharmaceutical researcher described drug research in the early 1960s thus:

> There was a prevalent attitude in many places that the conduct of research should be of the man-and-a-boy type in which chemists would create molecules by the pound and send them to pharmacologists who would screen them for their activity in the hopes that luck would strike. It's what I characterize as 'research untouched by the human brain' (394).

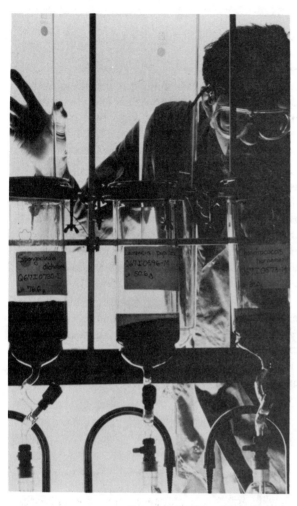

Photo credit: NATIONAL CANCER INSTITUTE

The first drugs were typically found by extracting chemicals from natural products and screening them for pharmaceutical activity. Though other methods of drug discovery have evolved, extraction remains an important ingredient of drug discovery even today.

Finding new drugs was not "irrational," but the rationale was not based in chemistry or knowledge of biological function. The purification and screening of natural products for antibiotics, for example, followed a reasonable strategy, but did not rest on knowledge of how the drugs worked. As attention turned to chronic diseases such as atherosclerosis, cancer, and neurological and psychiatric conditions, the development of drugs depended more on knowledge of the disease process. Rational drug design reversed the traditional process, working backward from a known receptor target. Rather than screening agents to serve specific functions, the molecular mechanism underlying a biological function was used to direct a search strategy.

Rational drug design is a general term that covers a broad range of approaches, but the underlying theme is a reliance on structural analysis of target molecules and deliberate design of agents to affect their function. One of the prototype successes was the development of cimetidine to treat peptic ulcer disease (see box 5-B). In this case, the first critical step was to define a class of receptors. The next step was to search for a compound that could at least partially block the action of histamine on these receptors. Once an initial "lead" antagonist compound was found, then chemical modifications of nearby atoms led to more potent and less toxic new compounds that could be tested for clinical effect. One of these proved effective in blocking acid secretion, dramatically tipping the scales in favor of medical management, as opposed to surgery, for most cases of peptic ulcer disease (140,394). Characterizing the H-2 receptor was a critical first step.

■ Structure-Activity Relationships

Having found a receptor, and compounds that act on it, the next step is to search for more potent chemical analogs, drugs that have a similar effect at lower concentrations. The standard way to do this is to synthesize compounds chemically similar to the "lead compound," altering one or a few key sites on the molecule by adding or taking away chemical groups, or by deforming its shape. Newly synthesized compounds are then screened for drug effect. The underlying premise is that the structure of the drug affects its activity. The process of chemical modification and searching for functional effects is called structure-activity relationships, or SAR (190).

In recent years, quantitative methods augmented SAR, and earned the name quantitative SAR, or QSAR. The refinements grew in part

Box 5-B—The Discovery of Cimetidine

In 1964, histamine was well studied for its role in allergic reactions, whose effects could be partially blocked by a group of antihistamine compounds still used in many over-the-counter cold remedies. James Black worked at the British pharmaceutical and chemical firm ICI, where he focused on drugs that affect the response to epinephrine (adrenaline), itself a large class of drugs now used to treat high blood pressure, disturbances of heart rhythms, diabetes, and many other conditions. The target molecule, the beta-receptor molecule, responded to epinephrine specifically, although its function varied in heart cells, blood vessels, and pancreatic cells, and other tissues.

Black moved to Welwyn laboratories, the British research arm of Smith, Kline & French. He worked to show the existence of a different class of histamine receptors, dubbed H-2 receptors, that caused stomach acid secretion. The task began by refining ways to measure H-2 receptor effects so that compounds could be screened rapidly. Initial tests were insufficiently sensitive; only improved screening procedures and higher doses of histamine enabled work to progress. Once the screening tests were in place, the search focused on finding antagonists, compounds that could block the action of histamine. The compound buriamide blocked H-2 activity.

In the late 1960s, administrators at Welwyn were ordered to stop working on the project to block acid secretion, as it duplicated work going on near corporate headquarters in Philadelphia. The British group persisted by finding a new name for their project, renamed the H-2 receptor program. Research administrator William Duncan resorted to subterfuge, adopting an "arm's length, isolationist policy in relation to headquarters R&D." Early in 1968, the new president of the company, Thomas Rauch, directly ordered that the project be preserved from drastic budget cuts "one more year," just long enough for success to squeeze through the door. He later reflected, "It's terrifying to think about it today."

In 1972, Black and other colleagues at Smith Kline & French published their data demonstrating the existence of H-2 receptors. They then searched for more potent antagonists, synthesizing and screening chemical modifications of buriamide, their "lead" compound. This led to metiamide and then to cimetidine. Metiamide was used in initial clinical trials, and showed promising results. In two patients, however, it suppressed production of neutrophils, white blood cells involved in inflammation. Cimetidine was already in early clinical testing, and work on it intensified. Cimetidine was approved for the market in November 1976, in the United Kingdom, and in August 1977 in the United States. Within a year, it was distributed to 90 countries, becoming king of the "blockbuster" drugs of the 1970s, and revolutionizing the treatment of peptic ulcer disease. Smith Kline & French's moribund stepchild became a robust prince.

SOURCES: C.R. Ganellin, "Cimetidine," *Chronicles of Drug Discovery*, J.S. Bindra and D. Ledniger (eds.) (New York, NY: Wiley, 1982). SmithKline & French International, *The Discovery of Histamine H2-Receptors and Their Antagonists* (Philadelphia, PA: SmithKline & French, 1982).

from the increased power and reduced cost of computers. Faster and better computers encouraged use of more complex but more accurate computational methods to predict the three-dimensional structure of small molecules, to display the shape of receptors and ligands using computer graphics, and to study the structure of large molecules including drug receptors. Quantitative methods also enabled simulations of chemical synthesis pathways, the design of agents that might fit into receptor sites, and high-resolution analysis of protein shape—all inputs to the QSAR process.

When multiple agents all work on the same receptor, their common features can serve as a core for seeking new agents to perform the same function. The process of defining entirely new drug agents, however, has no assured computational solution. A generic approach involving structural chemistry and biochemistry has emerged as a usually successful strategy. The process is far from a simple matter of defining the structure of a receptor, drawing a chemical that fits into it, and testing the result in a laboratory. Indeed, the process has become more complex rather than simpler. As one practitioner of QSAR noted:

> The incredibly rapid advances in biochemistry, molecular biology, theoretical chemistry, and computers along with the accumulated experience of the past 100 years must give drug research directors sleepless nights (179).

Indeed, even the technical advances are far from providing a cookbook to produce new drugs. The process remains too qualitative for precise predictions, and is better at finding agents similar to those discovered by others than in producing real innovation in the form of entirely new classes of agents. At a 1984 symposium called ''Drug Design: Fact or Fantasy,'' G. Jolles noted:

> The critical area of pharmaceutical innovation, the *de novo* lead generation, is unfortunately the area in which fantasy remains preponderant (217).

■ Frontiers of Rational Drug Design

Discovering drugs by design is a relatively new phenomenon, but it dominates the pursuit of new agents today. The logical strategy used to develop captopril is held up as a prototype of the new approach. The approach in its most refined form can be applied only to enzymes, however, and then only when the chemical reaction is well understood. The structure of the enzyme itself, or that of some enzyme with similar function, must first be determined by x-ray crystallography or nuclear magnetic resonance (NMR) spectroscopy (explained below).

Drug research is pushing back the frontiers of rational drug design in several directions. One direction is the structural analysis of receptor molecules. Most receptors are large proteins with multiple regions of interest. Determining their shape can be a first step to homing in on parts of the molecule that bind prospective drugs. Until recent years, the only hope of defining the shape of a molecule was x-ray crystallography. Crystal-

lography reconstructs the shape of molecules by analyzing how they deflect x-rays. This entails shooting x-rays through a crystal of a substance, and analyzing where they come out, in a process much like determining the shape of a sculpture by shooting balls off it and tracking where they bounce. One limitation of the technique is the necessity for a crystal.

Crystallizing large molecules, such as proteins, is a difficult art, and many molecules have proven refractory to crystallography for this reason. Even for the molecules that can be crystallized, the analysis of x-ray deflection patterns requires massive calculations. Defining a crystal structure can take years. The development of very high-intensity synchrotron radiation has given x-ray methods a new boost, with a particularly high-technology twist (183).

In recent years, a new technique of NMR has been applied to increasingly large molecules, permitting spatial resolution of small molecules, short peptides (small proteins), and regions of macromolecules (58,82). NMR spectroscopy reconstructs shape by analyzing the effects of very

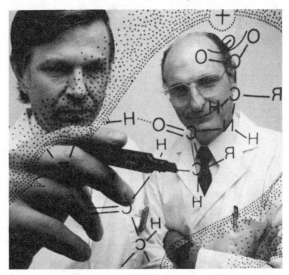

Photo credit: BRISTOL-MYERS SQUIBB COMPANY

Dr. David W. Cushman (left) and Dr. Miguel Ondetti (right) developed captopril using a new approach to drug discovery. The captopril team was able to design a molecule with the structure needed to block the active site of the converting angiotensin enzyme (see box 5-A).

high magnetic fields on the nuclei of atoms in the molecule.

Both NMR and x-ray crystallography require large investments in analytical instruments and computers to analyze the data, entailing multimillion dollar investments just to analyze the structure of potential drug receptors. The justification for such investments, made by many firms in recent years, is that defining the three-dimensional structure of receptor sites will improve the prospects for developing drugs that fit into those sites. The wisdom of the investments will only become clear in several years, if this approach bears fruit.

A second frontier is the analysis of molecules that are joined to proteins to give them distinctive shape, adhesive properties, or other attributes. Chains of sugars, called polysaccharides, project out from the surface of many proteins, for example, acting as antennae for chemical signals or providing structural stability on the outer surface of the cell. These polysaccharides often confer specificity to the receptor. The process of altering sugars, or attaching them to proteins, provides a possible mechanism to affect receptor function, but the chemistry and the biochemical pathways are far from being fully described, and the process of describing them is tedious and difficult.

Progress is nonetheless forthcoming. Modifying polysaccharide structure is a promising avenue to treating inflammation, autoimmune disease, and other disorders. It seems especially promising for diseases such as arthritis, diabetes, multiple sclerosis, and others that involve an inflammatory response that induces tissue destruction by the bodies' own defense mechanisms. As one of many possible examples, the molecule that attracts neutrophils (common white blood cells involved early in an inflammatory response to injury and some tumors) was recently shown to be a sugar chain (329,506). Drugs to control the production of the sugar chain, or to break it down, might temper the destruction by neutrophils, suggesting a path for drug development.

Cell surface molecules are the points at which cell-to-cell communication takes place. The process starts with binding of a molecule to the surface receptor. This entails specific binding, or recognition, that transmits a signal to alter cellular processes. The binding of a hormone from the bloodstream triggers the proliferation of cells, or the binding of a neurotransmitter causes an electrical signal to propagate along a nerve cell. A muscle contracts in response to a transmitter, or the immune system primes itself to fight a nascent infection. Viruses and other infectious agents also take advantage of cell surface receptors. The rabies virus homes in on nerve cells by binding to specific neurotransmitter receptors, for example, and the human immunodeficiency virus attacks cells bearing CD4, a molecule that projects from the surface of certain white blood cells. Cell surface receptors thus mediate many of the most physiologically important functions in the body and are extremely promising targets for future drug development. One serious problem is that there are so many cell surface receptors, and thus too many paths to follow for scientists to understand the structure and function of each.

Another major obstacle is that the methods of predicting three-dimensional structures are simply not up to the task for large molecules. New techniques to deduce the structure of large molecules are powerful but slow and not always successful. The ultimate solution would be predictive tools of sufficient power to predict shape from knowing the order of the building blocks, the amino acids in proteins and nucleotides in DNA. How long strings of amino acids emerge into shapely proteins is termed the "folding problem," and constitutes one of the most vexing and important fields in structural biochemistry today. Computational algorithms and theoretical chemistry are not yet powerful enough to make such robust predictions. All is not lost, however, as the structures determined for one protein can serve as a first approximation of the shape of another with similar function, as in the development of captopril described in box 5-A.

Cell surface receptors are clearly of great importance in understanding the function of the nervous system, the endocrine system, the immune system, cell proliferation, and targets for infection. The major chronic diseases such as cancer, diabetes, heart disease, arthritis, autoimmune disease, neurologic and psychiatric disorders, and endocrine dysfunction involve interactions with cell surface receptors. Understanding the structure and function of surface receptors has grown into one of the great thrusts of pharmaceutical R&D, pursued in the belief it will uncover as yet unknown approaches to treatment of diseases hitherto intractable.

▍ Organizing to Discover New Drugs

The wealth of new knowledge derived from basic biomedical research and the new power of rational drug design recast the drug discovery process, but there is no prototypical process that can be simply described. Pharmaceutical firms track research by talking to scientists and reading the scientific literature. They maintain in-house research teams, often doing research parallel to that performed in academic centers. New ideas may originate in corporate research efforts or in the academic ones; examples of both abound. This industrial research base is a source of new leads, and the stalking grounds for corporate "champions" of new drug ideas. Each firm has a somewhat different process to decide which leads to pursue. Some organize according to treatment category, assembling teams to focus on finding drugs to treat a disease or organ system; for example, entire firms are dedicated to research on cardiovascular drugs. Some firms make research-targeting decisions in committees, others delegate great authority to research directors who informally circulate in the firm and among academic groups, and still others have strong central direction. All attempt to manage innovation by balancing an endless supply of possible research directions against a need to produce salable products.

PROTEIN ANALYSIS AND PROTEINS AS PHARMACEUTICAL AGENTS

▍ Essentials of Protein Structure and Function

Proteins form structural elements in cells and perform a wealth of functions, including the catalysis of most biochemical reactions. Proteins are composed of linear chains of amino acids. There are 20 common amino acids in cells, each with a common chemical unit called the peptide group. The peptide group enables each amino acid to form a chemical bond with any other. Each amino acid in a protein serves as a chemical module: the peptide units confer structural stability and link the modules together, while chemical groups attached to the peptide backbone confer the distinctive structural and functional properties. The 20 amino acids have different chemical groups attached to the peptide core. The amino acid proline, for example, introduces turns into the protein backbone, while cysteine can form bridges with other cysteines located on different protein chains or remote parts of the same chain. Some amino acids prefer lipid (fatty) environments, providing stability in cell membranes, while others are highly soluble in water. Some are acidic and others basic.

Some proteins can be transported outside cells to lay down a matrix, such as the collagen that constitutes the bulk of bone and cartilage. Others act as enzymes to carry out the biochemical reactions taking place in cells at every moment. The enormous diversity that is possible when hundreds of amino acids are strung together produces a correspondingly large range of functions in the proteins they form, despite the simplicity of the constituent amino acid components.

▍ Proteins as Receptors

The vast majority of drug receptors in the body are proteins. Many are enzymes or cell surface receptors. Proteins are involved in virtually every cellular process and are components in most cellular structures. Protein chemistry is thus a dominant theme in current drug research.

Proteins have been a major preoccupation of biochemistry and molecular biology since the inception of those scientific fields. There are several ways to study proteins. Analysis of three-dimensional structure has been briefly described above. Biochemists have devised many ways to study enzyme function. One classic technique is to isolate an enzyme to near purity, then to attempt to study the chemical reaction it mediates in great detail. This is a key strategy in dissecting the biochemical pathways of energy metabolism, biosynthesis, and degradation. Another technique is made possible by modern molecular genetics.

The order of amino acids in a protein chain is specified by the genetic code laid down in DNA. DNA is composed of very long chains of four chemical bases linked through a sugar-phosphate-backbone. The information from DNA is ''transcribed'' and spliced in the cell's nucleus into a similar polymer, but in a somewhat less stable form called ribonucleic acid (RNA). RNA is transported from the nucleus to the cytoplasm, where it is translated to amino acids. The order of bases in DNA specifies the order of bases in RNA which in turn specifies the order of amino acids in the protein. A gene consists of a stretch of DNA that produces a functional product, either RNA alone or RNA that is subsequently translated into protein. The path from code to product thus typically involves three major steps: DNA, RNA and protein, with the possibility of modifications at each step. The linear order of DNA bases in a gene, modified by splicing out stretches of RNA and adding caps and tails to the message, thus directly determines the order of amino acids in the corresponding protein. In its simplest formulation, the cell translates a linear DNA code into a linear string of amino acids in proteins. The diverse shapes and chemical constituents that result from the chain of amino acids become proteins that form the structural supports and perform the biological functions for cells and tissues.

Through recombinant DNA technology, genes that produce a specific protein can be spliced into bacterial DNA. Large amounts of the protein can be produced in the bacteria, yielding enough DNA to precisely define the DNA sequence for the expressed part of the gene, from which the amino acid sequence for the resulting protein can be derived. Producing large amounts of the protein in bacterial cells is a boon to prospects of crystallizing proteins for crystallographic analysis; it also produces ample supplies for further biochemical analysis. One disadvantage of the process is that bacterial cells may not process the protein in exactly the same way as the cells in which the gene normally resides. Polysaccharides may not be added appropriately, for example, or the protein may fold somewhat differently because processing enzymes are not present in bacteria. The strategy nonetheless works for many proteins.

Manipulating the DNA code alters the order of amino acids in a protein. Scientists can exploit this effect by introducing a gene into bacteria or yeast by recombinant DNA with exquisite precision. They may thus introduce changes (mutations) in the native gene into the whole animal, where the mutation's effect can be observed. By introducing such mutations at specified sites, one amino acid can substitute for another at specific points in the protein peptide chain. To study the binding site of a receptor molecule, for example, the amino acids at that site can be replaced by those with similar, or with vastly different, chemical properties to assess the impact on ligand binding. The active sites for enzyme activity can be similarly studied by targeting just those amino acids thought to be important.

■ Proteins as Therapeutic Agents

Proteins also serve as chemical signals in the body. At the level of organ systems, proteins regulate immune responses, cell growth cycles, hormone responses, and many other functions. Blood proteins are involved in coagulation and dissolution of blood clots. Several hormones are short proteins, or polypeptides. Many polypeptides appear to be involved in modulating digestion, regulation of blood pressure, and other functions involved in many normal metabolic and disease processes. These proteins involved in cellular communication are prominent targets as drug receptors in many cases, but they can also be therapeutic agents in their own right. Proteins are thus of great interest to drug researchers, not only as drug receptors but also as drugs themselves.

As the tools to study proteins and protein-protein interactions have advanced, the importance of proteins and polypeptides has become increasingly clear. The production of large quantities of proteins became feasible with the advent of recombinant DNA techniques. Many companies were founded to exploit the potential of biotechnology and most established pharmaceutical firms have many projects underway to develop and market protein drugs. Michael Venuti of Genentech lists over 100 peptide products under development in 1991 (498). The first Food and Drug Administration approval to market a protein derived from recombinant DNA was granted on October 29, 1982, for human insulin (see box 5-C) (171). In 1985, the second approval was granted for human growth hormone, followed by various interferons beginning in 1986, tissue plasminogen activator in 1987, and erythropoietin in 1989. A recombinant DNA-derived hepatitis B vaccine was approved in 1986, and for Hemophilus B in 1988. A large number of protein pharmaceuticals have been recently approved, or are under active review (146,148).

Many of the products already on the market, and many yet to be approved, perform functions not achieved by other drugs. They represent

---

Box 5-C—Insulin

Charles Edouard Brown-Séquard postulated the existence of circulating factors whose absence caused disease in the late 1880s. William Bayliss and Ernest Starling worked on pancreatic secretions during the first decade of this century. In 1905, Starling proposed the term "hormone" for substances secreted into the blood by one organ to produce a response in another. In the period 1889 to 1920, many groups, most of them European, established the connection between cells in the pancreas, in the Islets of Langerhans, and the clinical presence of diabetes. The seminal work leading to the discovery of insulin began under Frederick Banting and his colleagues at the University of Toronto in May 1921.

Banting worked with physiologist John Macleod and Macleod's student Charles Best to tie off pancreatic ducts in dogs, to remove the pancreas, and to treat the resultant diabetes with pancreatic extracts. They quickly found a substance they called "isletin," because it was derived from cells in the Islets of Langerhans. The name was later changed to insulin. James Collip, a biochemist, joined the team to improve the extraction procedures, improving the potency and consistency of isletin. The University of Toronto's Connaught laboratories were brought in to scale up production of the substance, which met with strong clinical demand soon after the promising initial results were known. G.H.A. Clowes of Eli Lilly & Co. of Indianapolis then got involved. Lilly was already producing other glandular extracts, and Clowes had an excellent scientific reputation. Clowes met with Banting and Best after they presented preliminary results at a meeting in December 1921, and expressed interest in their work. He offered Lilly's services to scale up production.

In May 1922, the University of Toronto filed a patent on insulin for no other reason "than to prevent the taking out of a patent by other persons. When the details of the method of preparation are published anyone would be free to prepare the extract, but no one could secure a profitable monopoly." Soon thereafter, the University of Toronto and Lilly began a collaboration, sometimes rocky, to produce insulin for wider clinical use. George Walden, a chemist at Lilly, developed novel production methods that simplified production and further improved lot-to-lot consistency by the Fall of 1922. Lilly began to market

(Continued on next page)

Box 5-C—Insulin—(Continued)

its insulin as "Iletin," hearkening back to the original Banting and Best coinage, but with the dropping of a silent "s."

Insulin remains the main treatment for the most severe form of diabetes. Indeed, in current terminology this form is called insulin-dependent diabetes mellitus. Lilly remains the largest U.S. producer of insulin, and shares the U.S. market with Squibb. Outside North America, Novo of Copenhagen is the dominant producer. But the insulin story did not end with the production of insulin extracts. Insulin also became the target for assaults by molecular biology.

The importance of insulin made it the focus of Frederick Sanger's work in structural chemistry. Sanger applied chemist Emil Fisher's philosophy, using chemical principles to explicate protein structure and function. Sanger eventually established the order of amino acids that made up insulin, the first protein for which the amino acid sequence was determined. Knowing the sequence enabled comparison between insulins from different species, and discovery of the slight differences between them.

Recombinant DNA ushered in new hope for production of peptide hormones. As soon as recombinant DNA was discovered in the mid-1970s, the insulin gene became an early target. The gene for insulin was the first ever cloned from a mammal. Work on insulin emerged as the focus for product development at Biogen and Genentech, two prominent new biotechnology companies established during the late 1970s. The human insulin gene was introduced into bacteria by recombinant DNA, and the bacteria produced insulin. The City of Hope Medical Center synthesized DNA sequences for the gene that Genentech used to produce insulin in bacteria. Genentech licensed insulin produced through recombinant DNA to Lilly for large-scale manufacturing, marketing, and regulatory approval. In 1980, insulin was the first recombinant DNA product tested in humans. In October 1982, Humulin, trade name of the human insulin marketed by Lilly, became the first recombinant DNA drug approved for marketing.

SOURCES: S.S. Hall, *Invisible Frontiers: The Race to Synthesize a Human Gene* (New York, NY: Atlantic Monthly Press, 1987). F. Sanger, "Sequences, Sequences, and Sequences," *Annual Reviews of Biochemistry* 57:1-28, 1988. J.P. Swann, *Academic Scientists and the Pharmaceutical Industry: Cooperative Research in Twentieth Century America* (Baltimore, MD: The Johns Hopkins University Press, 1988). U.S. Congress, Office of Technology Assessment, *Commercial Biotechnology: An International Analysis* (OTA-BA-218) (Washington, D.C.: U.S. Government Printing Office, 1984).

---

entirely new classes of therapeutic agents. Erythropoietin, for example, stimulates the replenishment of red blood cells. It was approved in 1989 to treat the anemia that attends long-term renal dialysis (451). In the future, it could be used for many other purposes as well, and many are under investigation. A series of growth factors stimulates the proliferation of different kinds of white blood cells, and could be used to replenish them after cancer chemotherapy or in response to adverse drug reactions. A class of blood enzymes dissolve blood clots after heart attacks. Interferons and interleukins are promising in the treatment of cancer and infections, particularly viral infections for which there are relatively few effective treatments.

Proteins pose several problems as drugs, however. The necessity for parenteral, as opposed to oral, drug delivery is foremost among the limitations. Parenteral administration refers to techniques that break the skin surface, by injecting into veins, into muscles, under the skin, or elsewhere. These are more invasive and require sterile preparations. Proteins are readily degraded in the stomach and intestines, so that simple oral administration is impractical—the agent is destroyed before it can be absorbed. Insulin, the prototype of protein drugs, is still injected or administered by pumps installed in the body. It has been used as a mainstay of diabetes treatment since the 1920s, and has never been replaced by a smaller molecule. Decades of research have failed to uncover an oral formulation as effective as injectable insulin. The need for parenteral administration is nonetheless an immense impediment to widespread use of a protein drug.

The problems with parenteral administration include the pain of injections, immune reactions against the agent, local inflammation and scarring from repeated injections, the need for sterile preparations, and strong resistance from patients. Parenteral administration includes intravenous injection, intramuscular injection, subcutaneous injection, implantable pumps, and slow- release formulations placed just under the skin. Research along each of these avenues is proceeding apace. Research to introduce drugs through less invasive routes is also moving forward.

Coating peptide drugs with a shell to prevent digestion in the stomach, adding carrier molecules to permit rapid absorption, or formulating drugs with surfactants to promote absorption are all being pursued. Some peptide drugs can already be administered as suspensions for nasal inhalation for absorption by the rich network of blood vessels that can transport agents directly into the brain. Yet another line of research attempts to redesign peptide drugs into small organic molecules that can be administered orally rather than parenterally, making them much more attractive for general use.

For some applications, parenteral administration is not a major obstacle. Clot-dissolving agents, for example, are used mainly in the period immediately after a heart attack. The patient is typically in the hospital receiving intravenous fluids in any event, so that intravenous delivery is not a problem. This same feature will be shared by treatments for anemia from dialysis, cancer chemotherapy, and a few other uses. The clinical benefits of parenteral drugs must be significantly higher than oral drugs to overcome the inconvenience of parenteral administration for long periods.

Many potential drugs must be highly targeted to be useful. Highly potent cellular poisons, for example, would be useful if they could be induced to attack only cancer cells. One novel treatment approach is to affix poisons such as ricin, tumor necrosis factor, or diphtheria toxin to proteins recognized primarily by cancer cells. The recognition function can be served by antibodies raised against the target cells, or ligands that bind specifically to surface receptors on target cells. Antibodies have also been studied experimentally to coat lipid sacs containing anticancer drugs, as a means of delivering the drugs specifically to regions containing cancer cells (428). These developments are novel uses of proteins as means to target specific cells, but they remain limited by the range of specific recognition molecules, the need for parenteral administration, and a relatively narrow range of therapeutic applications.

Pharmaceutical research scientists are divided about the future significance of proteins as therapeutic agents. In interviews, they formed two camps with differing visions of the future of drug therapy. One camp believes that the problems of drug delivery will diminish over time as technological improvements overcome technical obstacles. They note that many of the promising protein agents have no small molecular counterparts—no small organic compounds have been found to serve the same function. Insulin is cited as a prototype. It is still used as a drug almost 70 years after its discovery (see box 5-C). The clot-dissolving enzymes, growth factors, and hormones approved for use in recent years are cited as other examples of new life-saving protein drugs that flowed straight out of molecular biological research. This group believes that many of the new proteins are so entirely novel in their action that small molecules may never be found to replace most of them, and at least for the foreseeable future proteins alone will be available. This group believes further that small biotechnology companies can grow into pharmaceutical giants through their successes in manufacturing protein drugs. They see protein pharmaceuticals as the technology that mediates a transformation of drug therapy and the pharmaceutical industry. Firms that fail to move aggressively toward protein drugs will lose out on many

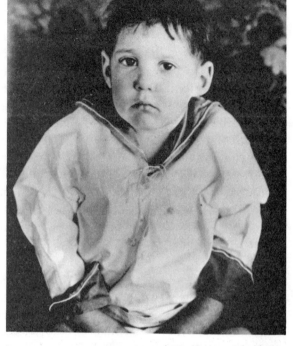

Photo credit: *ELI LILLY AND COMPANY*

Protein drugs accounted for over half of the major new drug introductions in the last few years. Insulin, the protoype for this class, remains in use 70 years after its discovery. Insulin was introduced to the medical profession in December 1922 in a *Journal of the American Medical Association* article illustrated with this photo of a mother holding her 3-year-old diabetic son before the child was treated with insulin. The photo on the right shows the same boy after treatment with insulin.

of the major drug innovations over the next few decades.

The other camp points to the immense difficulties of marketing drugs that must be administered parenterally. They acknowledge the importance of the new protein growth factors, hormones, and blood products, but believe that the markets for many protein drugs will be relatively small, seldom achieving the ''blockbuster'' status needed to sustain a pharmaceutical firm over the long run. The confinement to narrow therapeutic niches and a need for high prices because of a limited number of doses will limit the impact of protein drugs. This group maintains that protein drugs will be extremely important in a few therapeutic categories such as cancer or organ transplantation, but will rarely be commonly used outside the

hospital setting. In cases where proteins are the only available means to achieve a treatment goal, companies will concentrate their efforts to find a small organic molecule with the same function, developing drugs that do not require parenteral administration. This camp cites captopril (box 5-A) as the prototype. Here, a peptide drug was replaced by a small molecule that could be orally administered. While this model is only broadly possible today for enzyme drug receptors, the same principles could prove applicable to the full range of peptide drugs. Morphine itself appears to be a nonpeptide mimic of enkephalin, a naturally occurring peptide that modulates pain perception. Drug firms have recently discovered nonpeptide blocking agents for several other natural peptide hormones, such as cholecystokinin (which regulates function in the gastrointestinal tract and gall bladder), substance P (involved in pain sensation), and others. Drug firms may indeed pursue protein drugs, but mainly as stepping stones toward small molecules. Proteins will often serve merely as a research way station *en route* to more widely marketable drugs. These observers see the future pharmaceutical industry as an incremental extension of today's, with many of the same firms continuing to dominate the pharmaceutical market by incorporating new biological technologies. Biology will provide insights, but organic chemistry and the production of small molecules to substitute for the function of larger proteins will become the norm.

Disagreements about the importance of proteins as therapeutic agents does not extend to research. Here, all the experts agree that studying proteins is now central to developing new drugs. Rather, the disagreement among researchers centers on which problem will be solved first—finding small molecules to do what proteins do or finding ways to formulate proteins drugs for easier drug delivery.

Most large firms are hedging their bets, making substantial research investments and pursuing exploratory projects toward protein drug products. Other firms, generally smaller biotechnology companies, are betting a large proportion of their companies' assets on the success of protein drugs. Both strategies are being carried out, so the question will have an empirical answer in the next decade. Small companies may grow large, large companies may engulf them before they get large, or some instances of each may occur. These differing strategies exemplify the difficulties of making resource allocation decisions in pharmaceutical R&D. Both strategies are reasonable, and their success depends critically on factors that cannot be predicted: how many patients suffering from which conditions can benefit from a growth factor or immune modulator? Is it too soon to invest directly in developing a drug agent, based on current research results? Will it be possible to find small molecules to replace protein drugs? Can problems of drug delivery be solved? "There

are so many expensive avenues to explore that even with budgets in hundreds of millions of dollars it is no easy task placing bets'' (179).

GENETICS IN BIOMEDICAL RESEARCH

The study of DNA has been the second main thrust of molecular biology, paralleling analysis of protein structure and function. Proteins make up most cellular components; DNA contains the instruction set for when and how to make them. The other important function of DNA is to serve as the structural basis of inheritance.

∎ DNA as the Structural Basis of Inheritance

The DNA base pairs described earlier in this chapter are linked together in long chains. There are four nucleotide bases linked together in extremely long chains, coiled up and bound with proteins to form chromosomes. The information content of DNA is mainly contained in the order of these base pairs, the DNA sequence. DNA is the structure by which individual traits are transmitted from generation to generation. The linear code of four letters is analogous in some ways to the linear code of 0's and 1's in computer software, which also instruct hardware to carry out functions and can be copied faithfully for transmission.

Classical genetics, the study of inheritance, dates back to the 19th century. William Bateson's original definition of genetics presumed genes to be the hereditary "elements" discovered by Gregor Mendel in 1865 (230,261,336). Genes were units of inheritance, transmitting specific traits. The discovery of the structure of DNA by Watson and Crick in 1953 (509), spawned a field called molecular genetics. Classical genetics and molecular genetics came together in the study of DNA function, but this required some wobble in the exact meaning of the term "gene." The simple idea of a gene, an element of inheritance (in classical genetics) that coded for a protein had to be modified under assault from molecular genetics. Genes were not merely present or absent, but also subject to regulatory control.

Genes were expressed (i.e., produced a product) only at certain times, in certain tissues, and in certain amounts. Uncovering such complexities made it difficult to directly map inheritance, with its discrete particles of inheritance, to the exquisitely complex processes governing expression of genes. The complexity of molecular genetics was reflected in the changing face of human genetics.

■ Genetic Approaches to Disease

Human geneticist and physician Victor McKusick maintains a catalog of human genes, called *Mendelian Inheritance in Man*. The first edition in 1966 listed 574 well-characterized traits, and 913 partially validated ones; most were genetic diseases identified through inheritance patterns in human family pedigree studies. By the ninth edition in 1990, there were 2,656 well characterized traits and another 2,281 partially validated ones (266). This growth in knowledge of human genetics, already significant, understated the growth of knowledge about the contribution of genes to human disease. During this same period, human genetics moved from the backwater to the cutting edge of biomedical research. (Genetics in other organisms has been a central thrust of biology throughout the century, but its full application to humans awaited technologies developed in the 1970s and 1980s.) The genetic factors underlying the most common diseases, such as heart disease, cancer, Alzheimer's disease, diabetes, hypertension, and many others were becoming better delineated. Genetic approaches to understanding such illnesses emerged as a dominant research strategy. Entering the 1990s, genetics was poised to dissect complex diseases because of the growing power of genetic maps.

■ The Importance of Genetic Maps

Geneticists have been constructing maps of chromosomes since 1913, when Alfred Sturtevant found traits that were inherited together and inferred their corresponding genes were therefore located on the same chromosome. Geneticists labored for decades to construct maps of the chromosomes of fruit flies, yeast, bacteria, plants, mice, and other organisms (414). These efforts were greatly aided by controlled matings, an option obviously not available in humans. Constructing similar maps for humans relied on finding genes through indirect methods, a slow, uncertain, and tedious process. A global approach to genetic mapping in humans comparable to that enjoyed by geneticists for other organisms was greatly aided by the emergence of recombinant DNA techniques.

The first step toward isolating genetic factors for human traits is to find informative families. These are typically large families with a well-defined genetic character (trait), such as a genetic disease. The way in which the character is inherited provides a great deal of information about whether it stems from a single gene or many. Even single-gene defects vary in their inheritance pattern. A genetic disease may be dominant, expressed if an affected gene is inherited from either parent, or recessive, requiring affected genes from both parents. If affected fathers never transmit the character to sons, and women are only rarely affected, it is good evidence that the character is a recessive gene on the X chromosome (since males have only one copy of the X chromosome, inherited only from the mother). The inheritance pattern for multigenic diseases is even more complex. Yet another layer of complexity is added by genes that express themselves only in combination with environmental factors.

A genetic linkage map is the bridge from the study of inheritance in a family to establishing a gene's chromosomal location. Different individuals have, on average, over a million DNA differences in their genomes (a genome is defined as a complete set of chromosomes, one of each pair). Most variations have no clinical significance, but they can be used as markers on the chromosomes. The idea of a genetic linkage map is to find chromosomal sites that frequently vary among individuals, and to verify where on the chromosomes these common variations originate. Once this is done, the inheritance of bits of chromosomes can be tracked through families by tracing the fate of markers. The markers vary among individuals, so they are likely to differ between parents in each family. But the variations are present only at a specific site on the chromosomes. If markers from the same region of chromosome 7 are consistently inherited along with cystic fibrosis (CF) in different families, then this is strong statistical evidence the gene causing CF comes from that region (see box 5-D).

The way to construct a robust genetic linkage map in humans was first proposed in 1978 and published in 1980 (56). The first genetic linkage map of the human genome was published in 1987 (110). Other groups constructed genetic linkage maps of individual chromosomes, and the 1990s should see a major push to refine such maps sufficiently to find almost any gene, once family resources are good enough and the genetic character is well enough defined. (These are, however, significant limitations.)

Once the approximate chromosomal location of a gene is known, the next step is to obtain the DNA from that chromosomal region in hopes of finding the gene itself. A physical map is needed for this purpose. The order of genes or markers will always be the same between genetic linkage and physical maps, but the measure of distance is quite different. Genetic linkage maps measure how often markers stay together or separate during inheritance. This is a measure of the probability of being separated by genetic recombination, a DNA exchange process that occurs in the production of egg and sperm cells. The measure of distances in physical maps is the size of DNA fragments, ultimately translating to the number of DNA base pairs. The most useful physical map is a collection of cloned DNA fragments that span the chromosomal region in question and are arranged in order. With such a map, one can go from one end of the region to the other by picking out different clones of known orientation. Since the clones contain many copies of the DNA from that area, this allows direct study of DNA in search of a gene. Physical mapping was pioneered in viruses and bacteria. Groups

working on yeast (whose chromosomes are over 12 million base pairs in length) and the nematode Caenorhabditis elegans (100 million base pairs) scaled up to more complex organisms with larger genomes (99,299). Similar strategies are now being applied to individual human chromosomes (488).

■ Ways to Find and Study Genes

Once a region of DNA thought to contain a gene is in hand, then the hunt begins for a gene amidst the long string of DNA base pairs. There are many indirect methods to select DNA regions likely to contain ''candidate genes.'' All strategies ultimately entail extensive amounts of DNA sequencing from the region, and comparison of sequence differences among individuals.

In the hunt for the cystic fibrosis gene, for example, consistent sequence differences were found in affected children. The CF gene was located on chromosome 7 by genetic linkage in 1985 (425,504,518). Each parent of every CF child had to have ''normal,'' non-CF gene on one chromosome 7 and a CF mutation on the other. (If both copies were normal, parents would not have a CF child; if both were mutations, the parent would be affected.) Using genetic markers, scientists could trace which copy of chromosome 7 was passed on to the CF child from each parent, and this had to be the one with the CF mutation. Comparing ''normal'' to ''mutation'' sequences in DNA from this part of chromosome 7, taken from many affected children and their parents, revealed a consistent abnormality, the loss of three base pairs (229,351,353). This constituted the most common mutation causing CF. Once a small piece of a gene was identified, it was a straightforward matter to find the rest of the gene and the protein that it produced. Having found the gene, more than a hundred additional mutations causing CF were identified. The successful research strategy was thus: genetic linkage analysis of many families to find the gene's location, physical mapping of the region, DNA sequence analysis to identify the most common mutation (and thus the gene), and further analysis of

Box 5-D—The Search for the Cystic Fibrosis Gene

The search for the gene causing cystic fibrosis (CF) is a recent triumph of human genetics. The symptoms of CF are poor digestion of foods and recurrent lung infections. The main effects of the disease trace to the accumulation of thick mucus plugs in the duct systems of organs throughout the body. The organs most affected are the lungs and the pancreas. Proper lung function depends on clear airways. In CF, airways become obstructed, and pockets of infection develop. Pancreatic ducts normally drain digestive enzymes into the small intestine. When viscid mucus blocks pancreatic ducts, the enzymes are not delivered, and digestion is less effective. The digestive symptoms can be treated by enzyme supplements. Treatments for lung symptoms are primarily careful monitoring, efforts to physically dislodge mucus plugs, and frequent administration of antibiotics to stave off infections.

CF is the most common seriously disabling single gene defect among Caucasian populations. It is a recessive condition, present only when a child inherits defective copies of a gene on chromosome 7 from both parents. CF affects approximately 1 in 3,500 live births in the United States; 1 in 30 Americans has one copy of a CF mutation gene, but most are unaffected because it takes both copies of the gene to cause disease.

Until 1985, the main facts known about CF were its symptoms and its pattern of inheritance. That year, a group led by Lap-Chee Tsui at the University of Toronto found that CF was genetically linked to, i.e., frequently inherited with, a marker on chromosome 7. The marker was contributed by Collaborative Research, Inc., a small biotechnology company located near Boston. Other groups quickly confirmed the linkage.

Finding the gene itself took another 4 years. The process involved studying cloned DNA fragments from that region of chromosome 7, meticulously assembling a map, and then searching for differences in DNA structure that correlated with the presence of CF in patients. A large group of collaborators at several centers, led by Francis Collins, finally identified a common DNA defect, the loss of three DNA base pairs. Seventy percent of patients with CF had this mutation, which served to identify the gene. Once the DNA sequence surrounding this mutation was known, it could be used to find the rest of the gene, and to find the protein produced by the gene. With the gene in hand, it was possible to confirm that its dysfunction caused CF by introducing the normal gene into cells in tissue culture and reversing a molecular defect.

The molecular defect underlying CF involves the transport of chloride ions across cell membranes. Poor chloride transport leads to thick, sticky mucus. The CF protein now serves as a target for drug development. The fact that the CF protein regulates chloride ion flow raises hopes that a drug might successfully replace its function. Another possibility in the long run is to introduce the normal gene into the cells that line lung ducts (see gene therapy section in text), permitting production of normal mucus. This is technically difficult and will take years at best, although investigators took their first steps down this path in 1992 with the first CF gene therapy protocol. In the meantime, a wealth of other treatment possibilities center on increasing chloride flow by drug treatment, or on modulating the inflammation that actually causes tissue damage. Discovery of the gene has rekindled hope among CF families, and has renewed interest in clinical trials of new agents.

SOURCES: K. Davies, "The Search for the Cystic Fibrosis Gene," *New Scientist* 124:54-58, 1989. M. Dean, "Molecular and Genetic Analysis of Cystic Fibrosis," *Genomics* 3:93-99, 1988. E.D. Green, and M.V. Olson, "Chromosomal Region of Cystic Fibrosis Gene in Yeast Artificial Chromosomes: A Model for Human Genome Mapping," *Science* 250:94-98, 1990. B.-S. Kerem, J.M. Rommens, J.A. Buchanan, et al., "Identification of the Cystic Fibrosis Gene: Genetic Analysis," *Science* 245:1073-1080, 1990. S.T. Reeders, M.H. Breunig, K.E. Davies, et al., "A Highly Polymorphic DNA Marker Linked to Adult Polycystic Kidney Disease on Chromosome 16," *Nature* 317:542-544, 1985. D.P. Rich, M.P. Anderson, R.J. Gregory, et al., "Expression of Cystic Fibrosis Transmembrane Conductance Regulator Corrects Defective Chloride Channel Regulation in Cystic Fibrosis Airway Epithelial Cells," *Nature* 347:358, 1990. J.R. Riordan, J.M. Rommens, B.-S. Kerem, et al., "Identification of the Cystic Fibrosis Gene: Cloning and Characterization of Complimentary DNA," *Science* 245:1066-1072, 1989. L. Roberts, "The Race for the Cystic Fibrosis Gene," *Science* 240:141-144, 1988. J.M. Rommens, M.C. Ianuzzi, B.-S. Kerem, et al., "Identification of the Cystic Fibrosis Gene: Chromosome Walking and Jumping," *Science* 245:1059-1065, 1989. L.-C. Tsui, M. Buchwald, D. Barker, et al., "Cystic Fibrosis Locus Defined by a Genetically Linked Polymorphic DNA Marker," *Science* 230:1054-1057, 1985. B.J. Wainwright, P.J. Scambler, J. Schmidtke, et al., "Localization of Cystic Fibrosis Locus to Human Chromosome 7cen-q22," *Nature* 322:467-470, 1985. R.L. White, S. Woodward, M. Leppert, et al., "A Closely Linked Genetic Marker for Cystic Fibrosis," *Nature* 318:382-384, 1985.

pedigrees to find additional mutations of the same gene.

The polymerase chain reaction (PCR) is a simple technique that enormously expedites the study of DNA (283,358). It is, in essence, a way to make many copies of short stretches of DNA without having to clone it. PCR can be used to generate a DNA sequence directly, or as a "probe" to identify clones or cells that contain the sequence copied by PCR. It requires only a mix of chemicals, a DNA-synthesizing enzyme extracted from bacteria, and short stretches of DNA that define the starting points for DNA copying. PCR was first described in 1985 by investigators at the biotechnology company Cetus. By 1989, PCR was referenced in 860 publications, used in dozens of ways for a multitude of purposes (316). In searching for genes, and as an adjunct to use genes to study proteins, PCR replaces slower and more expensive processes and opens entirely new avenues for exploration.

The story of CF (box 5-D) is one of the most straightforward that can be expected, but it nonetheless required enormous effort. From 1985 to 1989, laboratories throughout the world labored to find the gene. One reason for the protracted search was that the physical maps and regional sequencing had to be done *de novo*. Once complete maps of the human genome are constructed, similar searches should be much faster and less costly.

Other diseases are much more confusing, and tracking them down may prove far more difficult. The gene causing Huntington's disease, for example, was mapped in 1983, but its gene (and consequently, its protein product) remained elusive after a decade. Even when a gene and a gene product are identified, however, it may not be obvious what the protein product does. To understand function, other methods from cellular biology and physiology are needed.

When a gene is found, it is often not readily apparent what it does. A newly discovered protein may be likewise inscrutable—merely a dot on a piece of filter paper or a product derived from DNA sequence. The most reliable tools of molecular biology and protein chemistry produce information about structure, but knowing structure does not guarantee an understanding of function. Genetics does provide tools to determine the function of a gene or protein, but the tools cannot crack open every lock. Genes can be introduced into bacteria, yeast, or animals to study the effects of a gene. As noted above, mutations can be made in the gene coding for a protein, in hopes that "breaking" the protein will clarify what it does when not broken.

The first step is to compare a new gene or protein to others already known, using databases that store the collected knowledge of researchers from around the world. There are databases for many kinds of structural information—crystallographic structure, protein structure, gene map positions, DNA sequence, and others (100). If a match is found—a protein that has a similar sequence of amino acids, for example—the matching protein may give clues to the function of the newly discovered one. Indeed, the "new" gene may not be new at all. Russell Doolittle and colleagues shocked the research community in 1983, for example, when they found an unsuspected similarity between a cancer-associated gene (a so-called oncogene) and a molecule that promoted cell growth (111).

To study the function of a disease-associated protein, such as the variant protein of cystic fibrosis, the abnormal gene can be introduced into cells in tissue culture, allowing much more precise experiments to be done quickly. The gene may also be introduced into another animal by recombinant DNA, making a transgenic animal. The effects of a gene mutation can thus be directly observed in the whole animal. This is a direct route to creating an animal model of a human genetic disease, with many of the complexities introduced by multiple organ systems, immune reaction, and other factors that are difficult to study in bacteria, yeast, or tissue culture cells. Until the advent of transgenic animal research, one had to hope that scientists had discovered an animal with an appropriate genetic defect similar to a human disease. Many human genetic diseases, however, had no animal counterpart, and for these, transgenic techniques were a godsend.

The technique has obvious implications for drug research. Most drug receptors are proteins with corresponding genes that can be introduced into animals to explore their functions and dysfunctions. Alterations of the drug receptor can be introduced, and their effects observed in animals, without having to put human subjects at risk.

Genetics as a Tool to Dissect Complex Disorders

Genetics may aid drug development by defining specific subpopulations of patients, thus simplifying the process of ascertaining the efficacy of new agents. Alzheimer's disease is an example of how genetics may help advance understanding of a disease by identifying subtypes (see box 5-E). Alzheimer's disease is the most common cause of dementia—loss of thinking ability. Symptoms typically begin only in middle age or later. It affects millions of Americans today, and is expected to afflict tens of millions early in the next century as the population ages (448). Alzheimer's disease is inherited as a single-gene dominant trait in some families, so that children of an affected parent in these families stand a 50-50 chance of developing it if they live long enough. The wide variation in symptoms and in age of onset have puzzled those studying the illness since it was first described in 1907. Indeed, only a small group of specialists were even aware that it could be inherited until recent years. Since 1987, studies of families affected by the familial form of Alzheimer's disease have revealed a genetic heterogeneity obscured by clinical and anatomical diagnosis. Even before the different genes in these families are found, it may be possible to categorize patients into subtypes, thus making it more likely to find effective drugs and other treatments (see box 5-E).

Genetics is but one of many approaches to disease. Following the trail down to a mutation in DNA cannot fully explain even most genetic diseases, and clearly genetic factors are only a part of most major diseases. The attraction of genetic approaches to disease, however, is that the tools are becoming so powerful. Most important diseases have been studied for decades. Those that could be easily explained by more traditional approaches have yielded; molecular genetics offers a strategy to crack those that have not.

The Implications of the Human Genome Project

The genetic approach dissects the genetic factors that conspire to cause disease. The basic tools needed to pursue the approach are genetic linkage maps, physical maps, and DNA sequencing capacity. These are complemented by an

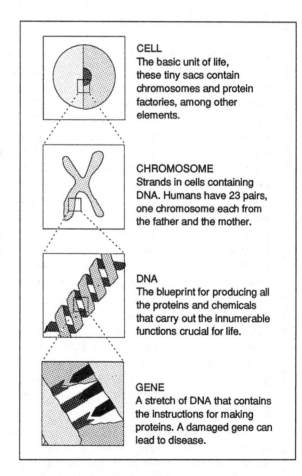

CELL
The basic unit of life, these tiny sacs contain chromosomes and protein factories, among other elements.

CHROMOSOME
Strands in cells containing DNA. Humans have 23 pairs, one chromosome each from the father and the mother.

DNA
The blueprint for producing all the proteins and chemicals that carry out the innumerable functions crucial for life.

GENE
A stretch of DNA that contains the instructions for making proteins. A damaged gene can lead to disease.

Reprinted from the May 28, 1990 issue of *Business Week* by permission. © 1990 by McGraw-Hill, Inc.

Box 5-E—The Complex Genetics of Alzheimer's Disease

Alzheimer's disease typically begins insidiously with loss of memory for recent events. It then progresses to more pronounced forgetfulness, loss of cognitive abilities, and frequently to behavioral symptoms such as irritability or depression. The course of the disease can extend for many years, even decades. Disease can begin to show as early as age 40, but most commonly begins after age 70. In 1907, Alois Alzheimer first described a 51-year-old woman with progressive loss of memory and distinctive microscopic changes in her brain. In the 1930s, many groups began to describe families in which many members developed Alzheimer's disease. By 1980, more than 80 such families were in the published literature, but the familial form of Alzheimer's disease was still not widely appreciated.

In some families, the disease travels as an autosomal dominant trait, so that the child of an affected parent has a 50-50 chance of developing it. In such families, a single gene best explains the pattern of inheritance. Getting the Alzheimer's copy of the gene from the affected parent translates to a very high probability of eventually developing Alzheimer's disease. Inheriting the normal copy means that one will not get Alzheimer's disease, or at least not the genetic form, and future progeny likewise will be spared. Several groups throughout the world attempted through the 1970s and 1980s to characterize the genetics of Alzheimer's disease. A picture began to take shape, but it was more complicated than a simple Mendelian disease caused by the same gene in all families.

The first breakthrough came from studies led by Peter Saint George-Hyslop. A large collaborative group studied several families with Alzheimer's disease, and in 1987 linked the disease to a genetic marker on chromosome 21. Another group in Europe confirmed the linkage. Over the next two years, however, other groups found families that seemed to have the same disease but did not show linkage to chromosome 21, even using the same markers. In 1991, a different group of families showed evidence of an Alzheimer's gene on a different chromosome, number 19; in 1992, another international collaboration found most familial Alzheimer families showed linkage to a region on chromosome 14. The story on chromosome 21 also became more complicated. Two groups found patients with a particular DNA mutation on chromosome 21 that correlated with the disease. Other families that showed linkage to chromosome 21 lacked this mutation, making it likely there were two or more causes of chromosome 21-linked Alzheimer's disease. A consensus emerged that more than two genes on chromosome 21 could cause the disease in different families. There was likely another gene on chromosome 19; and a set of families, called the Volga German families for their geographic origin in prerevolutionary Russia, that seemed to have a gene that did not map to either chromosome. There might thus be four or more subtypes: beta-amyloid mutant Alzheimer's disease, a distinct chromosome 21 Alzheimer's disease, chromosome 19 Alzheimer's disease; chromosome 14 Alzheimer's disease, and an unlinked (Volga German) familial Alzheimer's disease.

Time-honored clinical and anatomic classifications obscured the heterogeneity revealed by genetics. The hope was to find the genes, define their protein products, and use these to search for functional clues as to why nerve cells in the brain died prematurely. A similarly complex picture was beginning to emerge in complex diseases such as heart disease, schizophrenia, arthritis, diabetes, various types of cancer, and other disorders. Genetics, with its unique power to break diseases into precise subtypes directly correlated to molecular diversity, was likely to have implications for drug development. If different genes caused clinically similar diseases, different proteins were involved (or, perhaps, RNA products that regulated DNA expression).

All these different gene products are potential targets for drug development. If their function can be restored by drugs, then there is hope for therapy. Finding the gene may be the first step to finding the right target at which to aim. If the Alzheimer's gene produced a toxic product, for example, it might be possible to inhibit its production. If it resulted from lack of a growth factor, then agents to replace that factor might be synthesized.

(Continued on next page)

Box 5-E—The Complex Genetics of Alzheimer's Disease—(Continued)

The genetic factors involved in Alzheimer's disease underscore how little is known about its causes. The discovery of unsuspected subtypes of disease starkly points out how far medicine remains from a detailed understanding. Genetics is being pursued in hopes of getting a molecular "handle" on conditions for which little is known beyond the fact that they "run in families."

At the very least, being able to distinguish molecular subtypes can direct drug development for defined subpopulations. This could permit advances for diseases such as Alzheimer's that have to date proved refractory. Disease subtyping might also conceivably reduce drug testing costs. If it were possible to select in advance those subpopulations of patients likely to respond to a given drug, then it would be much easier to demonstrate efficacy. Proving efficacy is a major problem in developing drugs for complex chronic diseases. Drug effects apparent in only 20 percent of patients, for example, could easily be lost in the "noise"—random statistical variations in the other 80 percent. If genetic typing could select out only the 20 percent likely to respond, the effect would pop to the surface. Testing a small, molecularly defined population would amplify drug effects, lower testing costs, and speed regulatory approval.

PRINCIPAL SOURCES: A.M. Goate, A.R. Haynes, M.J. Owen, et al., "Predisposing Locus for Alzheimer's Disease on Chromosome 21," *Lancet* I(8634):352-355, 1989. P.H. Saint George-Hyslop, J.L. Haines, L.A. Farrer, et al., "Genetic Linkage Studies Suggest That Alzheimer's Disease Is Not a Single Homogenous Disorder," *Nature* 347:194-197, 1990. P.H. Saint George-Hyslop, R.E. Tanzi, R.J. Polinsky, et al., "The Genetic Defect Causing Familial Alzheimer's Disease Maps on Chromosome 21," *Science* 235:885-890, 1987. G.D. Schellenberg, T.D. Bird, E.M Wijsman, et al., "Absence of Linkage of Chromosome 21q21 Markers to Familial Alzheimer's Disease," *Science* 241:1507-1510, 1988. G.D. Schellenberg, T.D. Bird, E.M. Wijman, et. al., "Genetic Linkage Evidence for a Familial Alzheimer's Disease Locus on Chromosome 14," *Science* 258:668-671, October 23, 1992.

ADDITIONAL SOURCES: J. Constantinidis, G. Garrone, R. Tissot, et al., "L'incidence famiale des alterations neurofibrillaires corticales d'Alzheimer," *Psychiatrie et Neurologie* 150:235-247, 1965. W.H. English, "Alzheimer's Disease," *Psychiatric Quarterly* 16:98, 1942. E. Essen-Moller, "A Family with Alzheimer's Disease," *Acta Neurologica Scandinavica* 21:233-244, 1946. R.G. Feldman, K.A. Chandler, L.L. Levy, et al., "Familial Alzheimer's Disease," *Neurology* 13:811-824, 1963. F.E. Flugel, "Zur Diagnostik der Alzheimerschen Krankheit," *Gesamte Psychiatrie* 120:783-787, 1929. R.L. Friede, K.R. Magee, "Alzheimer's Disease," *Neurology* 12:213-222, 1962. L.L. Heston, D.L.W. Lowther, and C.M. Leventhal, "Alzheimer's Disease," *Archives of Neurology* 15:225-233, 1966. H. Jacob, "Muscular Twitchings in Alzheimer's Disease," *Alzheimer's Disease*, G.E.W. Wolstenholme (ed.)(London, England: Churchill, 1970). R. Katz, "The Prevalence and Malignancy of Alzheimer's Disease: A Major Killer," *Archives of Neurology* 33:217-218, 1976. P.J. Landy and B.J. Bain, "Alzheimer's Disease in Siblings," *Medical Journal of Australia* 2(18):832-834, 1970. H. Lauter, "Genealogische Erhebungen in einer Familie mit Alheimerschen Krankheit," *Archiv der Psychaitrie Gesamte Neurologie* 202:126-139, 1961. K. Lowenberg, and R.W. Waggoner, "Familial Organic Psychosis (Alzheimer's Type)," *Archives of Neurology and Psychiatry* 31:737-754, 1934. T. Luers, "Uber die familire juvenile Form der Alzheimerschen Krankhiet mit nerulogischen Herderscheinungen," *Archiv fur Psychiatrie und Nervenkrankheit* 179:132-179, 1947. R.T.C. Pratt, "The Genetics of Alzheimer's Disease," *Alzheimer's Disease*, G.E.W. Wolstenholme (ed.) (London: Churchill, 1970). T. Sjogren, "A Genetic Study of Morbus Alzheimer and Morbus Pick," *Acta Psychiatrica et Neurologica Scandinavica* [supplement] 82:9-63, 1952. L. Wheelan, "Familial Alzheimer's Disease," *Annals of Human Genetics* 23:300-310, 1959. G. Zawuski, "Zur Erblichkeit der Alzheimerschen Krankheit," *Archiv fur Psychiatrie Gesamte Neurologie* 201:123-132, 1960.

enormous diversity of ways to understand the function of genes, by introducing mutations in cultured cells, or by creating yeast models or transgenic animal models of a human disease. The Human Genome Project emerged in 1985 and evolved into a concerted effort to build the infrastructure for large-scale mapping, sequencing, and technology development which, in turn, were intended to lay the foundation for genetic explorations in biomedical research.

The underlying story was a convergence of technologies to analyze DNA, to clone large DNA fragments, to construct genetic linkage and physical maps, and to determine DNA sequences. These developments paralleled developments in computers that lowered costs and added computational power and flexibility. From these technological shifts, several individuals independently struck on the audacious idea of determining the sequence of all 3 billion base pairs in the human genome. The idea provoked considerable controversy, and the genome project was ultimately redefined to include genetic linkage mapping, physical mapping, as well as DNA sequencing. The goal of the Human Genome Project slowly and almost imperceptibly shifted from a complete DNA sequence of the genome to a complete structural catalog of human genes, which may not prove to be the same thing (91).

Work on model organisms is essential to interpret human gene maps, and has been incorporated into the project's goals (488). To accomplish its goals, the human genome project must develop new technologies to make mapping and DNA sequencing faster, less costly, and more accurate. These technologies will themselves be a boon to other investigations, as the analysis of DNA is central to biomedical research of almost every variety.

The objective is ambitious. An estimated 50,000 to 150,000 genes are dispersed through the human chromosomes, of which McKusick's catalog lists just over 2,000 that have been well characterized. The genome project should provide a molecular catalog for tens of thousands of genes that are as yet unknown. Genetic linkage maps with severalfold more markers are needed to locate genes known only by their pattern of inheritance. Most regions of the genome lack physical maps, and less than one percent of the genome has been sequenced as of 1991. The human gene map is only in its infancy (313,405). The physical and genetic linkage maps are slated to be near completion by mid-decade, with massive amounts of sequence data to be available in 15 years (488). The elaboration of these various maps, when combined with techniques to catalog the large mass of currently unknown genes, will undoubtedly reveal many genes that influence disease. Even in well studied organisms such as yeast and nematode worms, the direct approach of DNA structural analysis has uncovered many more genes than were known to exist. Each new protein is a potential drug receptor target; many will provide promising new leads for drug development.

DNA AS A THERAPEUTIC AGENT

▌Gene Therapy Is Just Beginning

One promising treatment strategy is deliberately to introduce genes into human cells to compensate for aberrant genes that cause genetic disease. The process is called human gene therapy. Gene therapy as a theoretical possibility was discussed widely for decades. In 1989, the first genes were introduced into the cells of cancer patients in order to *monitor* a novel anticancer treatment (354). The first gene insertion to *treat* a genetic disease, *bona fide* gene therapy, was performed in 1990.

Gene therapy falls into two major categories. It can be aimed at cells of the body, or somatic cells, so that it affects only that patient. The other, more controversial, alternative is to treat cells of an early embryo, egg cells, sperm cells, or their precursors. Any genes introduced into such cells would not only be present in the individual, but would also be passed on. Treatment of egg cells, sperm, or their precursors would lead to inherited changes in any babies resulting from fertilization. Treating an early embryo would affect not only somatic cells but also those giving rise to eggs and sperm. In each case, some fraction of future generations would carry the altered genes. This variety of gene therapy is termed germ line gene therapy.

The treatments approved to date, and anticipated in the near future, will involve bone marrow cells, white blood cells, skin cells, liver cells, lung cells, pancreatic cells or others that can be extracted from the body, treated, and reintroduced back into the patient. The first approved gene therapy clinical trial aimed to treat a rare genetic disease caused by a deficiency of the enzyme adenosine deaminase (ADA) known as "Bubble-Boy Syndrome." This is a recessive disorder, so both copies of the gene coding for the enzyme are abnormal. The result is that the enzyme fails to degrade the chemical adenosine. Adenosine accumulates, most notably in white blood cells, and the white cells responsible for fending off infections consequently function poorly. Untreated patients completely bereft of enzyme function generally die of infection before age 2. In an example of a protein used directly as a drug agent, the ADA enzyme has been chemically linked to polyethylene glycol and injected directly into patients. Patients have improved under this treatment. Another approach is to take white blood cells from such patients, insert the gene that produces ADA, and insert the cells back into the patient. This is the protocol approved as the first instance of human gene therapy (16,49). The first patient, a four-year-old girl, began treatment in September 1990; by the end of June 1992, there were 14 approved clinical protocols (with 35 patients) involving gene transfer in humans (15,194).

The original notion of human gene therapy was to treat single gene defects. The concept has since broadened considerably. Viewing gene therapy only as a way to compensate for defective genes in the patient's body has given way to seeing it as a way to introduce useful genes into cells that can act as drug delivery devices. This opens a far more diverse set of possibilities. Cells treated with inserted genes could conceivably be used to treat acquired immunodeficiency syndrome (AIDS), heart attacks, diabetes, and cancer (14). Several recent protocols approved or in preparation already illustrate the broader possibilities (305).

Several technical obstacles face gene therapy before it can be used as a standard treatment modality. First, the range of cells that can be targeted for gene insertion must be expanded considerably. Only white blood cells and certain types of bone marrow cells have been successfully treated to date. These cells die off over a period of months, and the treatment expires with them. The next step may be to get genes into the so-called "stem" cells that continually divide to produce whole populations of cells. If the gene were inserted into stem cells of the bone marrow, for example, then the treatment might not have to be repeated—there would be a steady stream of new cells expressing the gene, derived from stem cells. Second, the expression of the inserted gene must be sufficient to produce a clinical benefit and not too much as to cause toxicity. The amount of protein produced from artificially inserted genes is, in general, significantly lower than normal amounts. Third, for many applications it will be necessary to "aim" the gene insertion at specific organs or tissues.

For now, this problem is solved by extracting cells from the body before inserting the gene. This severely limits the types of cells that can be treated. It is not practical to remove cells from most organs before treating them. The ability to reliably insert genes only into nerve or muscle cells, for example, would greatly enhance prospects of treatment for intractable neuromuscular diseases. Those hoping to treat Duchenne muscular dystrophy have raised this possibility, and are working to fabricate DNA elements that express genes only in muscle cells (355). Finally, it would be a great boon to gene therapy if genes were not merely inserted, but instead new DNA sequences replaced old ones in the same gene. Current methods of introducing genes into cells insert whole new genes (attached to other genes and regulatory sequences). The chromosomal site of insertion is not predictable or controllable. The ideal treatment would instead excise "bad" DNA sequences while replacing them with "good" ones. This would require that the corrective sequence recognize the gene it was to replace with great specificity. This process is possible in yeast and bacteria, and is a standard tool of genetics. It has even been done in mammals; the problem is that it is successful only very infrequently. Before such techniques were clinically applicable, they would have to be much more reliable.

■ Prospects for Germ Line Treatments Are Remote

The prospects for germ line gene therapy are quite remote at present, for both ethical and technical reasons. Germ line gene therapy would be directly analogous to transgenic animal methods, in that a heritable gene would be introduced into a human. Changes could be inherited by subsequent generations. The technique is thus technically feasible, but there are extremely important differences between clinical application in humans and transgenic animal research. First, most transgenic animal experiments involve hundreds of animals, only a small fraction of which acquire the desired new gene (a percent or so at best). In many experiments, a fraction of animals become sterile or suffer genetic damage because of the new DNA inserts into critically important sites, disrupting another gene. To be clinically useful, the technique would have to successfully insert a gene almost all of the time and only very rarely cause adverse consequences. Clinical trials of germ line therapy would have to demonstrate, moreover, that the inserted gene had no demonstrable effect during embryonic and fetal development. Even contemplating how to demonstrate this in humans is a major task. Providing evidence of safety in humans without being able to target gene insertion is difficult to imagine.

Germ line gene therapy might be useful for conditions where damage accumulated during embryonic or fetal development, or if multiple organ systems had to be corrected. Germ line therapy would require techniques to insert genes into sperm or egg cells that currently do not exist (or into cells that produce them), or use of in vitro fertilization followed by treatment of early embryos. Prospective parents could more simply and safely choose to implant embryos that would not develop a disease, rather than treating embryos destined to do so. This alternative would not be available in one very unusual situation—if both parents had a recessive genetic disease. Both parents would carry double copies of a defective gene in this case, and so every embryo would

likewise have a double dose of a gene defect and would thus be affected. This clinical situation is not impossible, but it would be quite rare. These technical factors combine with a lack of consensus that germ line therapy is ethically acceptable to make germ line gene therapy unlikely in the foreseeable future, although it might resurface in the more distant future.

■ Uncertain Prospects for Gene Therapy as a New Treatment Modality

Those surveyed by the Office of Technology Assessment disagreed markedly about whether gene therapy would emerge as a major treatment modality over the next 10 to 20 years. Some saw gene therapy as the coming wave of therapeutics. They cited several advantages. First was that it could attack diseases that other methods could not. Most genetic diseases have only palliative treatments, or only partially effective ones. The optimists foresaw that the problem of getting cells into specific target cells and in specified chromosomal locations would be solved. If so, many single gene defects could be treated.

The most devastating symptoms of CF are due to lung problems. The cells that line lung ducts, for example, are constantly turning over. It might be possible to introduce normal genes into CF cells if the stem cells giving rise to them could be treated by gene therapy. But to treat a sufficient quantity, this would most likely have to be done without removing lung cells from the patient's body. A tamed virus, perhaps inhaled or injected, would have to home in on those stem cells. In addition, the introduction would have to be sufficiently controlled 50 that when many millions of cells were treated, the gene insertion did not induce mutations leading to cancer or cause other unwanted side effects. Gene therapy for CF is nonetheless being vigorously pursued, with the first clinical protocol approved in 1992.

Another advantage of gene therapy is that it might require many fewer treatments. Once stem cells were treated, it might not be necessary to continually administer drugs. In this sense, it would be more akin to organ transplantation or vaccination than to most drug treatments. One-time treatment is an appealing prospect for diseases such as diabetes, where it would obviate daily injections of insulin. Gene therapy also might restore the body's own feedback controls. Fluctuations in drug levels often fail to synchronize with normal regulatory controls. This is particularly important for hormones and other substances produced in response to environmental changes. Cells treated by gene therapy might be brought back into feedback control, either by including a gene's natural regulatory elements, or by repairing a defective gene in its natural chromosomal site.

Skeptics note the technical difficulties in targeting specific cell types, in getting genes into identified chromosomal sites, and in the high costs of clinical trials and safety testing. The range of diseases that can be attacked with current methods seems narrow. Gene therapy might be useful for cancer therapy, fatal genetic diseases of childhood, and other extremely serious conditions lacking better therapy. Some of those surveyed acknowledged that these revolutionary treatments were imminent, but questioned whether they would prove economically viable on a grand scale. If the number of affected individuals is small and the treatment is expensive to develop and to administer, the clinical advantages of a one-time treatment could prove a commercial disadvantage. The costs of R&D might fall on a small number of patients and single doses, limiting access and boosting the unit price. The range of disorders that can be approached by gene therapy will not broaden appreciably until better cell targeting and chromosome-site targeting are possible, and these make well take a decade of research to develop, if they develop at all. The unknown safety issues also raise concern that liability costs could be high.

Those working to develop gene therapy tend to be optimists. They view current protocols as analogous to Henry Ford's first primitive internal combustion engine, with prospects so revolutionary they cannot be predicted. The Federal Government is, for now, the main investor in gene therapy. The cost of the clinical trials has to date been funded directly by the National Institutes of Health, although this may change as more firms become involved in gene therapy development.

At least three small biotechnology companies were founded with gene therapy as part of their business plan, but these are viewed as long-term investments and the companies are now concentrating on research and new methods. They aspire to turn a profit from marketable therapeutic products in the next several years. These small startup companies have been joined by eight or more larger pharmaceutical firms pursuing gene therapy technology. Even if they cannot sell gene therapy itself, however, they may be able to sell reagents for gene transfer to other researchers. Gene transfer methods are widely applicable beyond gene therapy, and so this market, while not comparable to a major therapeutic agent, might nonetheless sustain a small firm during its formative years. Current work includes collaborative agreements with larger pharmaceutical firms, that fund small exploratory research efforts. For now, gene therapy is in its early exploratory phase.

■ Alternative Uses of DNA and RNA

In the future, DNA itself could serve as a therapeutic agent. There are several possible routes by which DNA (or RNA) could be used as drugs. The transcription of DNA into RNA can be blocked, for example, by proteins designed to bind to DNA. Short stretches of DNA introduced directly into the blood stream can last for hours, are actively taken into cells, and can also block the process of transcribing DNA into RNA. Short stretches of DNA or RNA can also inhibit the process of translating RNA into protein. This strategy of making "antisense" sequences to block the production of proteins is being explored by several pharmaceutical companies for its possible therapeutic value. These efforts closely parallel other drug discovery efforts, the main difference being that the physiological target is DNA or RNA rather than proteins. Like gene therapy, these alternative uses of DNA and RNA as therapeutic agents are in their preliminary research phase.

DISCOVERY INCREASINGLY DRIVEN BY BIOMEDICAL RESEARCH

An increasing reliance of drug discovery on biomedical research stands out as a salient theme of this chapter. Drugs uncovered by chance clinical observations or systematic refinement of folk remedies early in the century have given way to pharmaceutical firms with thousands of scientific workers pursuing drug research. The teams of organic chemists, specialists in pharmacological screening, and clinical experts have not been abandoned; they are still just as essential as they have always been. Rather, biologists have been added onto the front end of the drug discovery process.

■ The Foundation of Drug Discovery Is Biomedical Research

The first step along the pathway to discovering a major new drug is the understanding of what causes a disease. Many of the drugs that could be discovered by clinical happenstance have been developed in this first century of the pharmaceutical industry. Screening of microbes and plants is still important, but many of the classes of agents that can be discovered have already been. There are undoubtedly many clinically useful natural products yet to be found, but the process of discovering them has reached a point of diminishing returns. Pharmaceutical firms have turned their attention to understanding the mechanism of disease as a guide to discovering truly novel drugs.

The development of cimetidine and captopril illustrate the new approach. Dozens of other drugs could have served as equally valid examples. These drugs are already well established in the market. Many of the agents under investigation now will only come to market after the turn of the century. The differences of opinion belie an underlying, widely shared philosophy:

"Successful management of industrial research is dependent on rapid access to the latest discoveries in academic laboratories, the ability to recognize the importance of a given discovery, the ability to integrate the information into research programs within an industrial laboratory, and the ability to focus effort to allow maximum chance that the idea will bear practical fruit. It is vital for an industrial laboratory to have its own cutting edge basic research program at early stages of newly evolving fields'' (373).

The dominant strategy of modern pharmaceutical firms is to invest heavily in R&D, to form collaborations with academic laboratories and small specialized biotechnology companies, and to pursue the most promising leads with in-house research teams. Drug discovery research thus rests on a broad base of publicly funded basic biomedical research. It picks the fruits of basic research as new ideas emerge about disease mechanisms that suggest potential drug receptor targets.

■ Biomedical Research Turning to Larger Scale and More Complexity

Biomedical research is itself changing. The scale and complexity of problems are increasing. This is in part due to the massive accumulation of knowledge in the postwar era. Many of the simple problems have been solved, the simplest diseases understood. What remain are the conditions that could not be understood with past methods. Research methods grow more powerful at the same time as harder problems come into view. Structural understanding of proteins and DNA are at the forefront of innovative research methods and pose many of today's most tantalizing problems.

Genetics progressed from the study of viruses whose genomes are thousands of bases in length to those with hundreds of thousands, then to bacteria with millions of bases in their genomes. Only in the 1980s did DNA pioneers venture into genomes of tens or hundreds of millions of base pairs. As the 1990s began, they were poised to take on the human genome.

■ The Increasing Role of Instruments and Computers in Drug Research

A person picking up a scientific journal will open its pages to many advertisements aimed at biologists. In these advertisements, the stereotypical biochemist or molecular biologist holds a test tube in one hand and pipette in the other, focusing intently on transferring a fluid containing protein, DNA, or chemicals used to study such molecules. The image of biomedical research conjures up thousands of test tubes and hours spent moving reagents into and out of them, mixing them, and then analyzing the results. The image is accurate, but changing. In many advanced academic and industrial laboratories the test tubes have not gone away, but the person has been replaced by a robot or automated instrument. Sanger's work from 1945 to 1955 to determine the sequence of amino acids in insulin (see box 5-C) took almost a decade of intensive effort by a scientist who ultimately earned two Nobel prizes. Today, this can be done in days by a technician and a machine. The first 24 nucleotides of DNA sequence took many years effort in the early 1970s; today a single automated DNA sequenator can generate a thousand times as many in a day.

Extraordinary leaps in technological capacity open up new approaches to problems of larger scale. Instrumentation and automation thus dramatically increase the efficiency of doing the same experiments. In the 1970s, every well-to-do molecular biology laboratory had its own ultracentrifuge, used to spin test tubes very fast and enabling separation of proteins and DNA fragments according to weight, and a spectrophotometer, used to measure the color of liquids to determine the concentration of chemicals. These instruments cost tens of thousands of dollars each. Now, a laboratory must have not only these instruments, but others even more complex and expensive. To stay on the cutting edge of DNA or protein research, there are robots to do microchemical reactions, instruments to determine the sequence of amino acids in proteins and bases in DNA, machines to synthesize short proteins and

stretches of DNA with specified sequence. Some of these instruments edge over $100,000 in price. The percent of total Federal funding going to equipment has remained relatively stable over the past decade, indeed dropping somewhat from 6.2 percent in 1979 to 5.6 percent in 1988 (481). Within this stable base, however, there has been a shift from centrifuges and tissue culture needs to instruments that synthesize or sequence protein and DNA. Requests for preparative equipment, including centrifuges, dropped from 33 percent of requests in 1984 to 25 percent in 1988, while sequences and synthesizers increased from 11 to 14 percent (480).

Those surveyed by the Office of Technology Assessment agreed that the need for instruments had increased dramatically, and many offered the example of multimillion dollar investments in crystallography and computers as examples. These not only involve investments in instruments but also entail sustained commitments to specialized personnel to run the machines and cadres of support personnel to develop software and to analyze the data. Supercomputers are used and in the process of QSAR to analyze all the data emanating from protein structure studies. Virtually every firm has invested heavily in computers with sophisticated graphics displays for structural chemistry studies. Computer networks maintain and analyze the massive amounts of data flowing out of clinical studies. Many firms lease time on supercomputers. At least one drug company has purchased one outright, representing a several million dollar hardware investment, and has spent millions each year in personnel, software, operating, and maintenance costs.

IMPLICATIONS FOR FUTURE PHARMACEUTICAL R&D COST

■ Knowledge Better Specifies Targets for Drug Design, but Multiplies the Number

The large public investment in biomedical research since World War II has amply demonstrated how investment in research can translate to knowledge about disease and normal biology.

The mushrooming mass of medical facts has two major impacts on pharmaceutical R&D. Refined models of disease mechanism offer new insights into lines of research that might produce a new drug. Work can concentrate on the molecules that form the links in a causal chain leading to disease. Just as the targets become more precise, however, they proliferate in number.

Drugs to treat heart disease, for example, were until recent decades restricted to a few drugs that strengthened cardiac contraction (such as digitalis), sped heart rate (epinephrine), or constricted or relaxed small arteries (vasodilators and vaso-constrictors). These agents still exist, but drugs that modulate the flow of ions through cell membranes have been added to the list, including agents for calcium channels, potassium channels, sodium channels, and chloride channels. A wealth of drugs inhibit or stimulate cardiac muscle receptors selectively. Understanding diverse mechanisms that influence the contraction of heart muscle and blood vessels has uncovered a plethora of new drug receptor targets.

In general, each project undertaken now is far more precise and the mechanisms are better understood individually, but there are far too many avenues to pursue. This is perhaps the most significant change in drug discovery research over the past decade, and the trend is likely to continue.

■ Uncovering Disease Subtypes May Make Clinical Testing More Precise

As illustrated in box 5-E (on Alzheimer's disease) genetics may prove useful in identifying groups of patients more likely to respond to a given agent. If so, the process of demonstrating a drug's effect would be simplified and the drug approval process expedited. Refinements of drug receptor studies will frequently uncover tests for function that are more precise, capable of improving screening tests used to identifying promising chemical compounds for physiological effects. Narrowing the population that needs to be clinically assessed could dramatically cut costs of clinical trials.

The flip side of this coin is that tests of efficacy and safety could continue to proliferate. The number of tests that regulators could wish to see performed may increase to provide better evidence of safety and efficacy. If more population subtyping leads to an increased demand for studies of more refined groups that could not be distinguished before, then costs could go up rather than down. Here again, scientific advance is a two-edged sword. Each experiment or trial can be more precise, but the number and cost of experiments may go up as well. It is difficult to predict which effect will be greater.

■ Automation and Advances in Analytical Methods Can Make Research More Powerful

Some technologies clearly make essential steps faster and cheaper. The polymerase chain reaction (PCR) described above is a good case in point. PCR will have direct applications for diagnosis, and it also shortens or eliminates many steps in DNA research. This is a technology that clearly saves costs. The growing power of computers similarly makes old procedures practical for a much broader range of experiments. Dropping computer costs and improved instruments have enabled several drug firms to invest in facilities to do their own x-ray crystallography and high-field NMR analysis of proteins, for example.

■ Will New Technologies Speed the Discovery of New Drugs?

The new technologies of biomedical research clearly presage the development of new drugs. Whether the new approaches to drug discovery increase or reduce R&D costs depends in large part on whether the drug development cycle is shorter or longer as a result of the new technologies. A large fraction of the cost of any research-intensive enterprise, and especially drug development, is the cost of capital (see chapter 3). A dollar invested in drug discovery cannot be invested elsewhere, and its return can be known only many years later. The length of time from first investment to payback is a critical variable, since the costs compound each year.

Developing new therapeutic drugs will likely become more difficult over time, as the easiest to discover give way to more and more difficult tasks. Unless the new technologies expedite drug discovery sufficiently to compensate for the increasing difficulty of finding new agents, costs will rise. Most of the new investments in molecular biology appear to have been added to the "front end" of drug discovery, and thus represent an increased investment at the earliest stages of research, where the time-cost of capital is greatest.

As drugs move from discovery to clinical testing, the new technologies may make it easier to demonstrate efficacy. If the number of safety an efficacy tests increases at the same time, however, or if the testing process becomes slower, then costs will again rise. The critical factor is again how long trials take, how many new ones are added as a result of new technologies, how much the testing costs, and the duration of regulatory review. Molecular biology clearly promises to dramatically expand the repertoire of drug therapy in the coming decades. The prospects for cost reduction or cost escalation, however, are extremely difficult to gauge. Faster and cheaper methods may be offset by longer product development cycles and a need for more and better clinical trials.

Government Regulation and Pharmaceutical R&D | 6

T he pharmaceutical industry is one of the most highly regulated industries. Virtually all countries have established schemes to require the registration of products before they are offered for sale. The information companies are called upon to produce and registration mechanisms vary widely, but some form of evidence that the drug is safe, effective, of good quality, and suitable for the national market is typically required (302). The production of this information and the time required for regulatory authorities to review it contribute to the cost of bringing a new drug to market.

What are the origins of pharmaceutical regulation? Societal concern over the quality, safety, and value of medicinal therapies is not a new phenomenon. Documents dating to the Middle Ages contain the first recorded evidence of an organized community system to protect people from unsafe or adulterated medicines. The earliest systems focused on the local apothecary, the person who, throughout most of history, was responsible for the preparation of medicinal therapies. With the advent of commercial production and large-scale promotion of medicinal products during the 17th century, the focus of government interventions shifted to the control of quackery and fraud (114).

The next major change came roughly three centuries later as governments slowly began to recognize the value of premarket clearance programs. The early years of the 20th century produced a rapid expansion in the number of synthetic drugs available. Many of these products represented real and significant therapeutic advances, but many did not. Many posed a serious risk to the health of those who used them. Lacking the means to effectively police a large and rapidly growing market, governments set about to establish the administrative mechanisms necessary to identify unsafe or poor quality products prior to their being offered for sale.

Government concern over the effectiveness of pharmaceutical products is a relatively recent phenomenon. The emergence of clinical pharmacology[1] as a scientific discipline, along with the growing acceptance of controlled clinical trials, provided the tools necessary for governments to include proof of efficacy as a criterion for market approval decisions. In the United States, the Kefauver-Harris Amendments (Public Law 87-781) to the Federal Food, Drug, and Cosmetic (FD&C) Act (21 U.S.C. 301 et seq.) were passed in 1962. By the end of the 1970s most industrialized countries had added an effectiveness standard to their regulatory requirements for new pharmaceutical products (114).

In the United States, numerous laws and regulations at both the State and Federal level control the products of the pharmaceutical industry. But, within the patchwork of programs and policies, the FD&C Act has the greatest influence over the drug research and development (R&D) process. The agency responsible for implementing this body of law and regulation, the U.S. Food and Drug Administration (FDA), has slowly grown in importance since its inception in 1938. Every time Congress has amended the FD&C Act, the agency's control over the manner in which pharmaceutical products are developed and used has increased.

This chapter describes how compliance with Federal regulation has affected the cost of bringing a new drug to market. The first section provides a brief overview of studies on the impact of pharmaceutical regulation in the United States on the production of new drugs and the cost of development. The second describes the drug R&D process from the point at which a firm has identified a potential drug compound. The third section describes the regulatory review process. The fourth section describes FDA's recent efforts to improve the quality and timing of the review process. The fifth section reviews recent trends in rates of success and the timing of new drug development, and the last section briefly reviews recent trends in pharmaceutical regulation in Europe and Japan.

THE IMPACT OF PHARMACEUTICAL REGULATION ON R&D COSTS AND OUTPUT

Since the enactment of the 1962 amendments to the FD&C Act, researchers have studied the extent to which the regulation stifles, delays, or raises the cost of innovation in the pharmaceutical market. Many of these studies examined the impact of the 1962 event itself on the amount of time required for new drugs to receive approval, the cost of drug R&D, the rate of pharmaceutical innovation, and the level of competition among drug firms.

In the earliest estimate of the impact of the 1962 law on pharmaceutical R&D, Baily found that the law added significantly to the cost of bringing new drugs to market (32). Peltzman (315) used data on new drug introductions, prices, and quantities dispensed before 1962 to estimate what the demand for pharmaceuticals would have been in the absence of the 1962 law. By comparing these data with actual data on the post-1962 period, he concluded that the new regulation resulted in 50 percent fewer new drug introductions each year, increases in old drug prices, a doubling of the cost of bringing new drugs to market, but no decrease in "waste" on drugs that were not effective. In total, he estimated that the 1962 law was equivalent to a $300 million per-year tax on the users of pharmaceuticals.

Grabowski and colleagues (162) noted that Peltzman did not control for independent factors that may have affected the introduction of new

---

[1] Pharmacology is "the science of detection and measurement of the effects of drugs or other chemicals on biological systems (264).

[2] The terms "new chemical entity" (NCE) and "new molecular entity" (NME) both refer to new drugs, although their precise definitions are somewhat different. DiMasi and colleagues define NCE as "a new molecular compound not previously tested in humans" (109). NME is a term used by the FDA that, unlike NCE, includes some diagnostic agents and excludes therapeutic biologicals (109,474). In keeping with DiMasi's definition, this report uses the term NCE to refer to both therapeutic drugs and biologicals. OTA uses the term NME only when discussing work that specifically employs FDA's definition of that term.

chemical entities (NCEs)[2] after 1962, such as depletion of research opportunities, industry and physician restraint in the wake of the thalidomide disaster, or improvements in the science of safety testing. They compared the pre- and post-1962 NCE introductions in the United States and the United Kingdom, which did not have an efficacy standard in 1962. The United Kingdom had a threefold decrease in annual drug introductions between 1960-61 and 1966-70 compared with a sixfold decrease in the United States. Hence, they attributed about one-half of the U.S. decrease to the 1962 changes. They also suggested the 1962 law at least doubled the R&D costs of an NCE (162).

Wiggins (519) measured the longer-term effects of the 1962 amendments on the number of new drugs introduced to the U.S. market. He concluded that the 1962 law was associated with about 60 percent fewer new product introductions—but not until the 1970s—both directly as a result of the new regulatory requirements and indirectly as a result of company decisions not to proceed with R&D projects expected to be unprofitable.

Other researchers examined FDA regulation more broadly. In 1981, the Pharmaceutical Manufacturers Association (PMA) and nine of its member firms documented the costs associated with U.S. regulation by commissioning three studies, two of which were loosely related. Arthur Anderson and Company estimated the incremental financial and labor costs of complying with a series of FDA regulations that the PMA and its member firms labeled as "unnecessary" (20). These regulations cost the nine firms $117 million in 1978, including 1,600 person-hours of labor and 1 million pages of paperwork. Hansen estimated that these particular regulations were further associated with a 20 to 30 percent reduction in R&D productivity, or three to five fewer new drug introductions each year (177).

The third PMA-sponsored study, by Eisman and Wardell, compared the nine PMA-member companies' drug introductions in the United States with their introduction in other countries with "comparable regulatory standards." They

concluded that, on average, FDA regulation is associated with a 14-month delay in the introduction of new products with no evidence of greater safety or effectiveness (118).

Parker (307), however, came to a different set of conclusions. He studied the impact of regulation in 18 countries (including the United States) on the length of time between first and subsequent marketing application and introduction of 192 drugs in those countries. He found intercountry delays in product introductions decreased between 1954 and 1978 and countries with tougher regulation were not associated with longer lags in product introductions. However, the time between first and subsequent market applications increased over time. Because countries with tougher regulations tend to have larger markets, companies may take extra care in preparing those applications, thus accounting for the lack of a lag in ultimate introductions but more delay in filing applications (307).

Other authors examined the effect of regulation on competition in the pharmaceutical industry. Temin (420) studied the development of the industry in the 1950s and 1960s. Noting increased regulation usually acts as a "barrier to entry" for new firms, he argued that regulation in the drug industry should result in fewer larger firms with higher profits. Finding substantial growth in firm size but little consolidation or increased profitability over the period, Temin concluded that a variety of factors, especially technological opportunity and imperfect patent protection within particular classes of drugs, help explain the structure and performance of this industry.

In a 1990 study comparing the United States with the United Kingdom, Thomas concluded that additions to regulation between 1960 and 1980 (including the 1962 law) reduced innovation in small U.S. firms, but innovation in the larger U.S. firms largely mirrored that among U.K. firms. In addition, sales of NCEs introduced by large U.S. firms increased substantially while those of NCEs from all other U.S. and U.K. companies increased little or not at all. Thomas concluded regulation tended to reduce competition in the pharmaceutical industry (422).

Dranove and Meltzer (112) recently found that among all NCEs approved in the United States between 1950 and 1986, those of greater therapeutic importance (as measured by a variety of scientific and market-based indicators) progressed from first worldwide patent to U.S. approval more quickly than other drugs. (This finding is consistent with Office of Technology Assessment's (OTA) conclusion that higher U.S. sales revenues are associated with longer effective patient lives (see chapter 4)). They also found that almost all of the increase in the speed of drug development occurred prior to filing a marketing application. They concluded the acceleration in the speed of development was probably due to efforts of the firms rather than to efforts of the FDA to expedite review of important drugs.

One limitation of this conclusion is that the authors attribute to the FDA full responsibility for the length of time from submission of a marketing application until approval. In reality, the length of time necessary to review a marketing application may reflect the firm's earlier research efforts, its business decisions regarding when in the clinical research period to file an application to market the drug, the quality of its application, and the speed with which a firm responds to queries from the FDA as much as it reflects the FDA's own delays in reviewing applications.

Taken together, this literature indicates that increases in regulatory requirements and stringency increase the cost and time necessary to bring a new drug to market. However, because it is difficult to sort out effects of regulation from other factors that could affect drug R&D, the extent of such increases remains unclear. Also, most of the work to-date has focused on the impact of the 1962 amendments; little attention had been paid to more recent management and regulatory changes at the FDA. For example, recent attempts to identify and expedite the review of new drugs deemed therapeutically important may reduce the cost of developing some drugs but increase the cost of R&D on others. Increases in the variation in FDA review time for new drugs would lead to greater uncertainty and risk for drug sponsors.

THE U.S. REGULATORY REVIEW PROCESS FOR NEW DRUGS

Once a company identifies a compound or molecule with pharmaceutical potential, it enters a highly structured period of scientific inquiry that, if the agent is of value, culminates in the market launch of a new pharmaceutical product. Federal regulatory requirements act as a major organizing framework for these research activities, since they define a series of hurdles that companies must clear in order to gain access to the marketplace.

Because each pharmaceutical agent is different, there is much variation and uncertainty in the amount of data required to obtain FDA approval to begin clinical trials or to market new drugs (275). The company must wait until the FDA begins to review an application to find out if it offered enough information. Filing with too little information available about a drug may ultimately lead to a longer R&D process as the FDA tries to interpret the inadequate application and ultimately requests additional data.

On the other hand, some companies may collect more data than the FDA would require either because they are overly cautious or because the firm needs the data for other reasons (e.g., approval in another country or to market the drug more effectively) such firms spend money to pursue research questions not germane to the regulatory review process. Thus, the costs of clinical research in the regulatory phase cannot be attributed in its entirely to regulations.

Regardless of a company's decision about when to approach the FDA for authority to test a drug in humans or to market it, responsibility for reviewing the relevant documentation falls to one of two organizational units within the FDA: the Center for Drug Evaluation and Research (CDER) and the Center for Biologics Evaluation and Research (CBER).

Center for Drug Evaluation and Research

CDER is responsible for the premarket review and approval of all chemical pharmaceuticals, antibiotics, generic and over-the-counter drugs sold in the United States, as well as most hormones and enzymes. Once a drug is approved for marketing, the Center monitors companies to ensure their marketing claims comply with the drug's approved labeling, to guarantee the quality of manufactured drugs and to identify medications with unforeseen adverse reactions (471).

The work of CDER is divided among seven offices. The bulk of the work relating to the premarket review and approval of new drug products is carried out by two offices (Drug Evaluation I and Drug Evaluation II), each of which is divided into several review divisions with responsibility for different therapeutic classes. Although the other offices within CDER focus largely on the agency's post-approval regulatory responsibilities, several provide support for specific elements of the premarket review process as well as the statistical and manufacturing sections of a drug sponsor's application.

Center for Biologics Evaluation and Research

CBER is responsible for regulating "any virus, therapeutic serum, toxin, antitoxin, vaccine, allergenic product, or analogous product applicable to the prevention, treatment, or cure of disease or injuries of man," as well as blood, products derived from blood, and diagnostic reagents that use biotechnology-derived products.[3] In addition to monitoring the marketing and safety of approved products, CBER maintains closer surveillance of manufacturing processes for biologicals than does CDER for drugs, requiring manufactur-

ers to provide detailed documentation of production processes and regular samples of products that CBER can compare with reference standards kept at the FDA (40).

CBER has three offices: the Office of Compliance, the Office of Biological Product Review, and the Office of Biologics Research. The Office of Biological Product Review oversees the review of all applications to test investigational products in humans and to market new products, but staff in all three offices actually conduct the reviews.

Regulatory Review of Investigational New Drugs

To conduct clinical research on a drug (that is, to test the drug in humans), a sponsor must file an Investigational New Drug (IND) application with the FDA.[4] Federal law has required firms to file an IND application since 1962 (Public Law 87-781). Prior to 1962, sponsors could begin clinical investigations whenever they felt ready to do so, as long as they clearly labeled their new drug as an investigational product and limited its availability to qualified researchers who in turn guaranteed that they would use the drug solely for investigational purposes. Sponsors frequently submit more than one IND for the same investigational product if they hope to market more than one dosage form of the drug or claim the drug has more than one therapeutic benefit.

The IND process serves three purposes. First, it provides the Federal Government the opportunity to identify and bar from human use any investigational product that poses an undue risk. Second, the IND provides a mechanism for monitoring the actions of clinical investigators to ensure they protect the rights, safety, and welfare of individuals participating in any clinical investi-

---

[3] The CBER broadly defines a biotechnology-derived product as any product derived from a living source (human, animal, plant, or microorganism), made up of a complex mixture of proteins that are not easily identified or characterized, sensitive to heat, and susceptible to microbial contamination (40).

[4] In addition to commercial firms, individual researchers (such as those in academia) as well as noncommercial groups may seek and receive investigational new drug status to test investigational drugs in humans. Commercial and noncommercial INDs follow the same requirements and procedures outlined here.

gation involving the new product.[5] Third, the IND allows regulators to examine each clinical study a company plans to conduct and determine whether it is likely to produce the scientific and statistical information necessary to demonstrate the safety and effectiveness of the product when used as intended (21 C.F.R. 312.22). This review provides companies with an opportunity to revise their clinical research plans before spending money and time on inappropriate or inadequate trials, and it helps the FDA avoid tying up its staff with a flawed market approval application while products with strong scientific evidence await consideration.

CONTENT OF AN IND APPLICATION

An IND application contains the drug sponsor's clinical research plans, details of manufacturing processes, and the results of laboratory and animal tests to-date. The "clinical section" contains a detailed description of the initially planned clinical trials and a general overview of the studies that will follow; the "manufacturing section" describes the facilities, equipment, and techniques the sponsor will use to produce the drug (21 C.F.R. 312.23 (A)(7)). The "manufacturing section" of the IND for biological products is more important than for drugs, because biologicals tend to be molecularly more complex and more difficult to produce in quantity than are synthetic chemicals (40,399).

Although the laboratory and animal data the FDA requires in the IND varies, the R&D necessary to begin human clinical testing falls into four general categories (152,424):

- Laboratory tests to determine how the molecule reacts physiologically (in isolation from the rest of a human or animal) with the target disease or affected organ systems;
- Pharmacological animal tests using rodents to document what happens once the drug enters the body;

- Acute toxicological animal tests to determine the highest doses that two species of animals (including one nonrodent) can receive without risking overt toxic reactions and death; and
- Subacute and subchronic toxicological animal tests to determine whether repeated exposure to the drug changes any toxic effects discovered in the acute tests.

For toxicological tests requiring nonrodents, researchers choose species in which the organ systems of interest closely resemble those of humans. While the number of animals required also varies with each drug according to statistical principles (516a), table 6-1 shows the usual number for each type of toxicological test.

For biologicals, product integrity may be influenced by changes in temperature, equipment, handling, and other factors, so CBER encourages sponsors to produce the product for clinical testing in the same facility in which it will be manufactured once marketed. When this is not possible, the sponsor must validate the process and product following a physical change (40). Hence, the IND process for biologicals may, in essence, include approval of the manufacturing facility (43).

Once an IND goes into effect, drug sponsors must inform the FDA of modifications in clinical protocols, the drug's composition, or the processes used to produce it. The sponsor must submit new safety information to the FDA in a timely fashion, with data on serious adverse events sent to the agency immediately. Other information required of IND recipients by the FDA include the protocols for clinical trials not included in the original application, notification of the end of each phase of clinical research and of its key findings, and an annual progress report (21 C.F.R. sec. 312.22). An IND remains in effect until one of four events occurs: 1) the sponsor notifies the FDA it is no longer conducting clinical research

---

[5] Institutional Review Boards (IRBs) in each institution participating in a clinical trial must review and approve the study before it begins. Investigators must fully inform study participants about the purpose and nature of the research, the risks involved, the availability of alternative therapies, and their right to refuse to participate or withdraw from the study at any time.

Table 6-1—Toxicological Tests Used in the U.S. Regulatory Process

Type	Species	Number used	Measured outcome
Acute toxicity	Rats	50 per sex	Death
	Dogs	10 per sex	Morbidity
Subacute toxicity	Rats	50 per sex	Morbidity, histopathology, blood chemistry, body weight, organ weights, hematology
Subchronic toxicity	Rats	100 per sex	Same as subacute
	Dogs	20 per sex	Same as rats
	Monkeys	12 per sex	Same as dogs
Reproductive toxicity			
Segment I	Rats	50 per sex	Fertility and reproductive
	Rabbits	50 per sex	Performance
Segment II (teratology)	Rats	50 per sex	Malformed
	Rabbits	50 per sex	offspring
Segment III	Rats	50 per sex	Growth of
	Rabbits	50 per sex	offspring
Cancer bioassay	Mice	250 per sex	Tumors
	Rats	250 per sex	Tumors
Mutagenicity			
Dominant lethal	Rats	40 males	Dead implants (embryos)

SOURCE: G. Flamm, "Recent Trends in the Use of Animals in the Pharmaceutical Industry," contract report prepared for the Office of Technology Assessment, 1991.

using the drug; 2) the FDA approves the drug for marketing in the United States; 3) the FDA finds the sponsor has violated regulations governing investigational products; or 4) the FDA finds the product is unsafe for human use.[6]

FDA REVIEW OF IND APPLICATIONS

A company may begin clinical testing 30 days after the FDA receives the IND application, unless the firm receives notification from CDER or CBER of a "clinical hold" (21 C.F.R. 312.40). The FDA imposes clinical holds if the drug or trial design poses a significant health risk to participants, the clinical investigators named in the IND are not qualified to conduct the trials, the information the sponsor plans to provide to investigators conducting the trials is inadequate, the sponsor's research plan is not scientifically sound or would not meet the sponsor's stated research objectives,[7] or the IND application lacks sufficient information for the FDA to evaluate the study's risks to participants. CDER and CBER also use clinical holds to suspend ongoing clinical trials if new evidence suggests unforeseen risks to study participants or if the trials are not being conducted in accordance with Federal regulation (21 C.F.R. 312.42).[8]

To help it prioritize its work, CDER rates each drug for which an IND is received according to the drug's novelty and the agency's subjective judgment of the drug's therapeutic potential. Box 6-A describes these ratings schemes, which have recently changed.

---

[6] In reality, according to FDA staff, companies often do not formally inform the FDA of their decisions to end clinical research on an IND. The agency only learns of the company's decision upon pursuing tardy annual reports on the drug (269).

[7] This provision applies only to Phase II and Phase III studies.

[8] The FDA maintains administrative mechanisms for a sponsor to appeal a reviewer's decision to impose a clinical hold with which the sponsor disagrees.

Box 6-A—The Center for Drug Evaluation and Research's Classification of New Drugs

Between 1975 and 1992, the FDA assigned two ratings to each investigational new drug (IND) and new drug application (NDA) to determine the drug's place in the queue of applications to be reviewed. The agency introduced this system to identify and expedite the review of important new drugs. The first rating, which FDA continues to assign to INDs and NDAs, identifies the newness of the entity according to one of seven possible categories:[1]

Type 1: New Molecular Entity

The active moiety has not been previously marketed in the United States for use in a drug product, either as a single ingredient or as part of a combination product.

Type 2: New Ester, New Salt, or Other Derivative

The active moiety has been previously marketed in the United States, but this particular ester, salt, or other derivate has not been marketed, either as a single ingredient or as part of a combination product.

Type 3: New Formulation

The drug is marketed in the United States by the same or another manufacturer, but this particular dosage form or formulation has not.

Type 4: New Combination

The product contains two or more compounds which have not been previously marketed together in a drug product in the United States by any manufacturer.

Type 5: Already Marketed Product—Different Firm

The product duplicates a drug product already marketed in the United States by another firm.

Type 6: Already Marketed Product—Same Firm

A new use for a drug product already marketed in the United States by the same firm.

Type 7: Already Marketed Product, Without an Approved NDA

The product has received the first approved NDA for a drug product which has or is being marketed without an approved NDA.

The second rating, identified with letters, indicates the FDA's best guess of the drug's therapeutic potential. Since January 1992, the FDA has used a rating scheme consisting of only two categories:

"P" or "priority" for the most important drugs, and

"S" or "standard" for all other drugs.

Between 1975 and 1992, the FDA used a five-category rating scheme of therapeutic importance:

Type AA: Acquired Immune Deficiency Syndrome (AIDS) Designation

Drug is for the treatment of AIDS or AIDS related disease.

Type A: Important Therapeutic Gain

The drug is an effective treatment for a disease not adequately treated by any marketed drug, or represents a therapeutic advance over existing treatments for the target illness because it is more effective or safer.

---

[1] These categories are *not* mutually exclusive. A new formulation (Type 3) or a new combination (Type 4) might also contain a new molecular entity (Type 1) or a new salt (Type 2). In such cases, both numbers would be included in the classification.

Type B: Modest Therapeutic Gain

The drug offers a modest, but real, advantage over other drugs currently available to treat the same disease or condition. (FDA gave a drug a "B" rating if it expected the drug to improve patient compliance, eliminate annoying but not dangerous adverse reactions, reduce the cost of therapy, or be useful in the treatment of a specific subpopulation of those with the target disease, such as individuals who are allergic to currently available drugs.)

Type C: Little or No Therapeutic Gain

The drug essentially duplicates in medical importance and therapeutic usage one or more drugs already marketed in the United States.

Type V: Designated Orphan Drugs

The sponsor of the drug has officially requested and received orphan designation under the Orphan Drug Act (Public Law 97-414).[2]

Although made available publicly at the time of NDA approval, the subjective judgment of a drug's future therapeutic potential implicit in this earlier rating scheme had limitations when used for purposes other than the prioritization of the FDA's workload. First, ratings for investigational drugs could change over the course of their development. Because the FDA sometimes made early ratings on the basis of little or incorrect information, the agency often changed the drug's rating as it received subsequent research results. The FDA also lowered a drug initially rated as an "A" if another drug for the same indication received approval first or was shown to be safer or more effective.

Second, the FDA tended to be conservative in its allocation of "A" designations, reserving it for drugs that represented a major therapeutic advance, embodied an exciting pharmacologic concept that served as a prototype for still greater therapeutic advances, and those that offered a unique delivery system. Because of this conservative approach and the limited data available to the FDA, drugs that represented a real improvement over existing therapies could have received a "B" or "C" designation.

And finally, the agency based its final rating at the time of NDA approval on limited use of the drug during clinical trials, other investigational use, and any foreign use of the drug. Hence, drugs released to the market with a "1B" or "1C" designation might later have been found to be clinically much more valuable or more widely used than the agency's final rating would indicate. Despite these limitations, however, these ratings represented the only available measure of a drug's therapeutic importance and were often used in research trying to understand the effects of drug regulation in the United States between 1975 and 1992.[3]

---

[2] "A," "B," and "C" are mutually exclusive designations. Only one of these letters may be used to classify a drug. The other designations are *not* mutually exclusive. For example, an orphan drug may be classified as "1 B-V."

[3] See, for example, Wiggins (1981) and several analyses done by OTA and presented later in this chapter.

SOURCE: Office of Technology Assessment, 1993, based on *F-D-C Reports: Health News Daily*, "FDA changes Rating System for Drugs," *F-D-C Reports: Health News Daily*, p. 3, Jan. 7, 1991. M. Finkel, "The FDA's Classification System for New Drugs: An Evaluation of Therapeutic Gain," *New England Journal of Medicine* 302(3): 181-183, 1980.

■ Regulatory Review of New Product Applications

Once a drug sponsor gains permission to test an investigational drug in humans, it begins its clinical research. The principal goal of the research it to obtain evidence sufficient to submit a new drug application (NDA) and win approval of the FDA to market the drug in the United States. In addition to beginning the human clinical trials authorized by the IND, the sponsor also compiles laboratory data about a drug's chemical properties, descriptions of the facilities and methods the sponsor will use to produce, package, and distribute the drug, and evidence from additional animal tests.[9]

CLINICAL RESEARCH NECESSARY FOR NEW PRODUCT APPROVAL

Although drugs that enter testing in humans have all exhibited some potential as safe and effective therapies, there is a high chance of failure at some point in the clinical research period. Some drugs prove to be of limited or no clinical use, while others drop out because they are too poorly tolerated by patients. The FDA requires clinical trials be conducted according to formal protocols that the drug sponsor submits as part of the IND application. Pharmaceutical researchers commonly distinguish among three largely sequential phases of clinical trials necessary for regulatory approval:

- Phase I studies are small trials usually involving only healthy volunteers to map how the body absorbs and eliminates the drugs and to document the response it produces.
- Phase II studies test the drug's therapeutic effectiveness and note any adverse reactions in individuals affected by the target disease or condition.
- Phase III studies assess the drug's medical benefits and risks among a large number of patients under conditions of ordinary use. They often take more than 1 year.

Size of Clinical Trials—The number of people exposed to a drug during each phase varies widely. In interviews with OTA staff, pharmaceutical industry managers repeatedly emphasized the resource intensity of clinical trials and claimed regulatory demands have increased the size of clinical trials. OTA surveyed pharmaceutical firms that sponsored drugs approved for marketing by the FDA in two periods (1978-83

Photo credit: U.S. FOOD AND DRUG ADMINISTRATION

Drug sponsors submit to the FDA new drug applications to market new drugs. An NDA may contain many volumes of data. FDA staff review this complex array of data to make a recommendation for marketing approval.

and 1986-90) in three therapeutic classes: antihypertensives, antimicrobials, and nonsteroidial anti-inflammatory drugs (NSAIDs). For each drug, we obtained data from companies on the size and location of clinical trials conducted prior to FDA approval. Within each class of drug, we compared the size of trials in the earlier period with the size of those in the later period. Appendix H provides greater detail about the methods of this survey. Table 6-2 summarizes the results.

We found substantial increases between the early and later period in the number of clinical trial participants and number of studies per drug conducted to support the drug's first NDA. This

---

[9] Animal tests conducted concurrent with human trials usually include chronic toxicity tests designed to identify the drug's impact on living tissue when administered repeatedly for anywhere from 6 months to the lifetime of the animal; tests to determine whether the drug adversely affects the reproductive process over two successive generations of animals, whether it causes cancer, and whether it produces genetic changes that trigger tumors, other illness, and congenital deformities in offspring; and, for some drugs, tests to determine whether the intended dose form or route of administration causes any toxic effects.

Table 6-2—Trends in the Size of Clinical Research Supporting U.S. New Drug Applications for NCEs in Three Therapeutic Categories[a]

	Antihypertensives			Antimicrobials			Nonsteroidal Anti-inflammatory drugs		
	Year of NDA approval		Ratio of later to earlier period	Year of NDA approval		Ratio of later to earlier period	Year of NDA approval		Ratio of later to earlier period
	1978-83	1986-90		1978-83	1986-90		1978-83	1986-90	
	(number of drugs in parentheses)								
Mean number of therapeutic indications per drug.	1.2 (9)	1.4 (9)	1.2	5.1 (15)	3.2 (12)	0.6	3.3 (4)	2.7 (4)	0.8
Mean enrollment per drug.	2,020 (9)	3,520 (9)	1.74	2,326 (15)	4,972 (12)	2.14	3,608 (4)	7,031 (4)	1.95
Completed before NDA submission. . .	1,791 (9)	2,485 (9)	1.39	1,885 (15)	3,461 (12)	1.84	3,036 (4)	3,575 (4)	1.18
U.S. enrollment.	1,126 (8)	1,335 (8)	1.19	1,248 (15)	2,049 (11)	1.64	1,698 (4)	2,745 (4)	1.62
Foreign enrollment.	665 (8)	1,150 (9)	1.73	637 (15)	1,412 (11)	2.22	1,338 (4)	830 (4)	0.62
Completed after NDA submission. . . .	228 (9)	1,034 (9)	4.53	440 (15)	1,511 (12)	3.43	571 (4)	3,456 (4)	6.05
U.S. enrollment.	228 (9)	565 (9)	2.47	412 (14)	814 (11)	1.98	372 (4)	2,649 (4)	7.12
Foreign enrollment.	0 (9)	470 (9)	∞	60 (14)	734 (11)	12.17	199 (4)	807 (4)	4.05
Mean number of studies per drug. . . .	50 (9)	81 (9)	1.62	56 (15)	69 (11)	1.23	64 (4)	94 (4)	1.46
Completed before NDA submission									
U.S. studies.	29 (8)	25 (9)	0.86	31 (15)	29 (11)	0.93	38 (4)	30 (4)	0.79
Foreign studies.	22 (8)	34 (9)	1.54	13 (15)	18 (11)	1.45	23 (4)	19 (4)	0.83
Completed after NDA submission									
U.S. studies.	1 (8)	6 (9)	6.0	10 (11)	8 (11)	0.86	3 (4)	7 (4)	2.42
Foreign studies.	0 (8)	16 (9)	∞	1 (11)	13 (11)	24.50	1 (4)	38 (4)	38.00

[a] Number of drugs differs because some firms responded inconsistently or not at all to some questions. Parts do not sum to wholes because of item nonresponse.

KEY: NCE = new chemical entity; NDA = new drug application.

SOURCE: Office of Technology Assessment, 1993.

difference existed across all three therapeutic classes, although the magnitude of the differences was usually greater for NSAIDs than for the other two categories. The most dramatic increases occurred in clinical trials conducted outside the United States and in trials completed after the sponsor first submitted its NDA.

The apparent trend toward more and larger clinical trails could reflect both industrial business strategies and regulatory expectations.[10] The available data provide only a limited ability to distinguish among the potential explanations.

One potential explanation, for the increase often cited by industry managers in interviews with OTA staff, is that regulatory authorities have come to expect larger trials (i.e., greater statistical confidence in the results) or just more types of studies to support the marketing of new drugs in the United States. New guidelines for drug sponsors that the FDA adopted during the latter period could have led to a growth in studies by recommending sponsors study drugs' effects in special populations or potential interactions with foods or other drugs (48,499).

There are other possible explanations as well. First, the data are consistent with an increasingly global marketplace for pharmaceuticals. If firms have over time tried to market new drugs in more countries, one would expect to see an increase in the number of foreign trials, because foreign governments often expect marketing applications will be supported at least partly by clinical research conducted in their countries.

Furthermore, rewritten FDA regulations that went into effect in 1987 strongly emphasized the importance of worldwide safety data in the initial U.S. NDA and made it clear that an NDA could be based solely on foreign data (48). In addition, the FDA requires firms to file all clinical research data on a drug related to its safety, regardless of where the research was conducted or whether or not it was completed before the firm filed its NDA in the United States. The increase in clinical trial data provided to the FDA after the filing of the initial NDA could also reflect an increased tendency on the part of sponsors to file an NDA as early as possible.

Another possibility is that the later clinical trials were designed to support applications for indications other than those contained in the initial NDA. Even though the firm would file data on the efficacy of the drug for the additional indications in subsequent NDAs, the FDA would still expect the sponsor to file safety data from all completed trials for consideration of the first NDA. This explanation is consistent with the observation that in two of the therapeutic classes examined, the average number of indications contained in the initial NDA declined over time. In an effort to market the drug as early as possible, sponsors may be reducing the number of uses for which it seeks initial FDA approval.

Finally, it is possible that the work completed after the filing of the initial NDA reflects trials conducted to "seed the market" for the drug once it is approved by the FDA. "Seeding the market" means that the drug's sponsor attempts to enlist a large number of physicians into trial participation to acquaint them with the drug and its potential indications for use. Although such work may legitimately add to knowledge about the drug's safety and efficacy, its primary purpose may be to make physicians, especially those influential in specialties likely to prescribe the medication, familiar with its expected availability and therapeutic potential. Again, such data would appear in OTA's survey results as supporting the initial NDA because the FDA requires the sponsor to supply it with all available safety data.

---

[10] While OTA cannot rule out the potential presence of some measurement error in these data reflecting different interpretations by different companies of the definition of a clinical trial supporting their U.S. marketing applications, there is no reason to believe that such error could explain the observed increases between the two periods; any such measurement error should be present to a similar extent in both the early and later periods.

APPLICATIONS FOR MARKETING NEW DRUG PRODUCTS

When a drug sponsor seeks marketing approval, it files a formal application with the FDA. Sponsors seeking to market a new chemical, antibiotic, hormone, or enzyme drug product file a NDA with CDER. Companies with biotechnology-derived products file two applications with CBER, a product license application (PLA) covering the drug, and an establishment license application (ELA) covering the facilities manufacturing the product.

CDER Review of NDAs—CDER has 60 days from the date a company submits an NDA to decide if it contains sufficient information for the agency to conduct a substantive review. It refuses inadequate applications. Once CDER accepts an NDA, it logs the application into its management tracking system and refers it to the appropriate review division based on its intended use. This review division has primary responsibility for the application, but staff in other offices participate as well.

Each reviewer summarizes his or her findings in writing which the review division staff then compile for the division director together with a summary of the company's application and the proposed regulatory action (314). For nearly half of all NDAs the review goes no further than the division level. If the Division Director and review staff disagree on the strength of the scientific evidence and the appropriate regulatory action, the NDA moves up one level to the Office Director for consideration. If disagreements still remain, the director of CDER will review the application and proposed FDA decision (471). Some divisions routinely refer some or all NDAs to a standing advisory panel comprising outside experts. The decision of whether to approve a drug remains an FDA authority, however.

Once the agency reaches agreement, the review division director sends a letter to the company explaining its decision. The letter can either: 1) approve the product for market, 2) declare that the FDA would approve the drug once the company allays lingering concerns about effectiveness or safety (called an "approvable letter"), or 3) state that the drug is "unapprovable."

The sponsor must respond within 10 days to an "approvable" or "unapprovable" letter by providing information identified by the FDA as missing, stating its intent to provide such information at a future date, requesting a formal hearing on the matter, or asking that the FDA remove the application from further consideration. If the sponsor does not respond within 10 days, the FDA automatically withdraws the NDA (21 C.F.R. sec 314.105, 314.110, 314.120, and 312.125).

By law, FDA must complete its review of an NDA within 180 days,[11] but this deadline does not include time when the FDA is awaiting additional information from the company (467). Most NDAs require at least one such amendment by the company, and a recent analysis by CDER revealed that for the 68 NDAs for new molecular entities submitted to the FDA in 1984 and 1985, the sponsoring companies had filed a total of 1,141 amendments (496). Under law, each amendment allows CDER to extend its review time by an additional 180 days to ensure the agency can adequately consider the new information (21 C.F.R. 314.60).

Even with these extensions, however, actual review time of some drugs exceeds the statutory allowances (467). Data from the FDA do indicate that the 23 NDAs for new molecular entities approved in 1990 took an average of 30 months to approve with a median approval time of 26 months; however, these numbers do not indicate how many of the drugs had amendments filed to the original NDA, thus extending the statutory 6-month approval time. Data available from the FDA and other sources do not indicate the exact percentage of NDAs that violate statutory allowances.

---

[11] The law measures the start of this 6-month period from the day the FDA agrees to accept the application.

In interviews and informal discussions with company regulatory personnel and clinical researchers, OTA learned that many people involved in the process believe at least some reviewers in CDER use the ''application not complete'' notice to manage workloads. These sources claim that CDER staff can always find some additional information is necessary, so the agency can manipulate the starting date of its statutory time limit. To investigate this claim is beyond the scope of the study, but the very existence of this rather widespread belief suggests it is almost impossible to separate out delays in the approval process due to companies' inadequate applications from those due to the regulatory process.

CBER Review of PLAs and ELAs—The CBER review process for new products places added emphasis on the safety and quality of the processes and facilities used to produce a biological drug.[12] Also, in contrast to CDER's NDA process, there are no statutory limits on the amount of time CBER reviewers may take to complete their review of PLAs and ELAs (40). As with the CDER process, reviewers may refer the applications to a relevant FDA advisory committee before reaching a final decision.

In contrast to CDER, CBER does not routinely compile and publish statistical information on its workload, output, and review times for applications to market new products. OTA attempted unsuccessfully over the full course of this project to obtain such data from CBER. According to CBER staff, these statistics would be of limited value to the Center and potentially misleading to outside analysts because there is substantial variation in the products it reviews and the amount of time required for the FDA to ensure their safety and effectiveness (40).

Other published sources do shed some light on product approvals by CBER. According to data

Photo credit: U.S. FOOD AND DRUG ADMINISTRATION

As part of the new drug approval process of biologicals, FDA reviewers must inspect and approve the facilities to ensure the safety and quality of the processes that will be used in production.

recently compiled by the PMA, firms report 21 new biotechnology drugs awaiting PLA and ELA approval with another 111 currently in clinical trials (323).[13]

In a recent press account, one FDA official noted the review of biotechnology drugs has been relatively fast compared with synthetic chemical drugs, with a mean review time of 21.4 months, 10 months faster than the average CDER review time (146). However, the author also suggested that as the number of PLAs and ELAs grows[14] and the molecular complexity of these drugs increases, CBER's speed of review and approval will decrease substantially. For example, monoclonal antibodies are already experiencing significant delays. CBER has not approved any new monoclonal antibody products since 1986, and as

---

[12] The ELA review includes inspection and testing of the facility that will manufacture the drug and its component biological materials.

[13] PMA attempted to survey all firms that might have biotechnology-based drugs in development, not just companies belonging to PMA. However, they may have missed some smaller biotechnology firms with drugs in various (probably preclinical) stages of the R&D process.

[14] A total of 14 biotechnology-based therapeutic drugs were approved through October 1991, half of which had been approved since 1989.

Table 6-3—U.S. Food and Drug Administration Advisory Committees on Pharmaceuticals

Organization unit	Committee	Number of members	Number of meetings per year[a]	Year established
Center for Biologics Evaluation and Research	Allergenic Products	9	3	1984
	Biological Response Modifiers	9	3	1984
	Blood Products	11	4	1980
	Vaccines and Related Biological Products	11	4	1979
Center for Drug Evaluation and Research	Anesthesia and Life Support Drugs	13	2	1978
	Anti-infective Drugs	13	2	1980
	Antiviral Drugs	13	2	1989
	Arthritis	11	2	1974
	Cardiovascular and Renal Drugs	11	3	1970
	Dermatologic Drugs	11	2	1980
	Drug Abuse	15	2	1978
	Endocrine and Metabolic Drugs	11	2	1970
	Fertility and Maternal Health Drugs	11	2	1965
	Gastrointestinal Drugs	11	2	1974
	Oncologic Drugs	11	2	1973
	Peripheral and Central Nervous System Drugs	11	2	1974
	Psychopharmacologic Drugs	11	2	1974
	Pulmonary-Allergy Drugs	11	2	1972
	Radiopharmaceutical Drugs	11	2	1967

[a] Number is approximate. Committees meet only when the Director of the relevant center calls the members together. Some committees may not meet during the course of the year and others may meet more frequently than indicated in the table.

SOURCE: Office of Technology Assessment, 1993.

of October 1991, 58 drugs were awaiting FDA approval for marketing or for approval to enter various clinical testing phases (146).

ADVISORY COMMITTEES

FDA has 19 separate panels of 9 to 15 outside experts each that it can convene to advise CBER and CDER staff on drug approval decisions (see table 6-3). Each committee advises a specific review group within CDER or CBER. Although the FDA has used outside experts since 1964, the number of committees has grown steadily over the last 20 years, from 5 in 1972 to 13 in 1979, to

19 in 1991.[15] While some review divisions refer every NDA to an advisory committee before making a final determination, others refer only "problem" applications (173). Some divisions also involve advisory committees in the review of INDs, the surveillance of approved products, and the development of regulatory guidelines (467).

Topics for discussion at advisory committee meetings can run from technical questions about study methodology, to interpretation or adequacy of data, to potential changes in proposed labeling, to an overall assessment of a potentially controversial drug's net benefits (221,467). Committees may recommend approval, re-analysis of the data, further studies, or rejection of the application. Because these committees' reviews are purely advisory and not mandated by law, FDA staff need not follow their recommendations. To date, however, they almost always have done so.

Proponents of the advisory committee system see it as an important check on the thoroughness and quality of FDA reviews (467). However, the wide variation in the composition, operation, and questions considered by the committees have made observers of the agency skeptical that they achieve this objective. Critics suggest that they delay the approval of new drugs while adding little to the review process that the FDA does not provide on its own.

A recent study of 95 NCEs approved by the FDA between January 1983 and December 1987 compared NDA review times for drugs subjected to advisory committee review with those approved without such review (221). The researchers found that advisory committee review is associated with small delay (4.5 months).[16] The delay may reflect systematic differences between the drugs submitted to committees and those not submitted. For example, as shown in figure 6-1, there was substantial disparity among review divisions in the extent of their use of advisory committees (221). The researchers also noted on average it took the FDA 19 months to approve an NDA after an advisory committee recommended such approval (221). The FDA has commented that this delay reflects the need to respond to advisory committee recommendations for additional data or revised labeling and to give senior FDA management a last opportunity to review the application (471).

■ Post-Approval Research and Reporting Requirements

PHASE IV STUDIES

Because preapproval testing affords only a limited view of a drug's benefits and risks, the research process usually does not stop at the point of market approval. Post-approval research can involve both clinical trials, referred to as Phase IV studies, and new animal toxicity studies (21 C.F.R. 310.303).

One recent analysis of post-approval studies required by the FDA of drugs approved from 1970 through 1986 found the frequency of post-approval studies has increased significantly over the 1980s, with only 17 percent of approved drugs including FDA requests for post-approval research in 1983 compared with 45 percent in 1985-86 (350).

Most post-approval studies are less than a year in length and involve relatively small numbers of subjects. The Richard study found differences across therapeutic classes in the frequency of FDA requests for post-approval studies and the number of studies requested per drug.

The purpose of post-approval research has also changed over time. Fewer studies required in the more recent period examined additional uses or uses in children than did studies in the earlier years, while the number of post-approval studies of drug interactions has increased. Finally, the study found no evidence that postapproval re-

---

[15] The 1972 passage of the Federal Advisory Committee Act (Public Law 92-463), enabled the Federal government to make use of outside experts more easily than in earlier years (221).

[16] The p value for this difference was .054. The actual mean for the 45 drugs submitted to advisory committees was 36.9 months (median: 34.6), while the mean for the 55 not submitted to advisory committees was 32.4 months (median: 24.5).

Figure 6-1—Average Approval Times for NCE-NDA, by Therapeutic Category 1983-87: Reviewed by Advisory Committee Versus Unreviewed

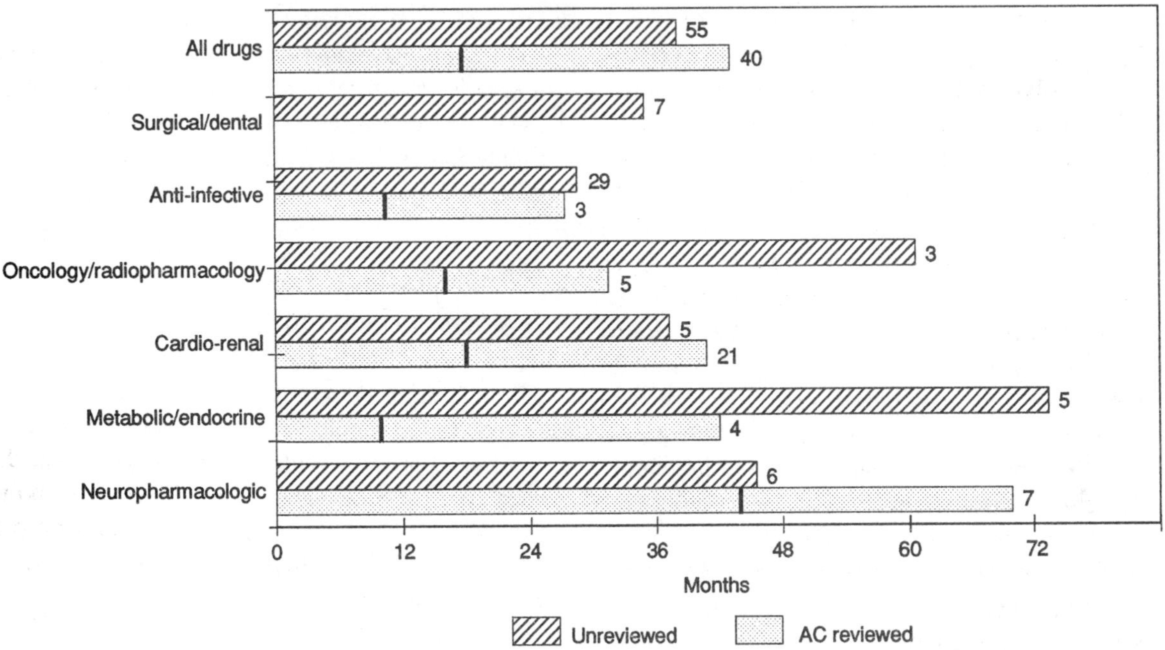

NOTE: Vertical lines across bars for AC reviewed drugs indicate point during the NDA review period when the AC, on average, made its recommendation to the appropriate FDA review division. Numerals at the end of bars represent the number of NDAs in each category.

KEY: AC = advisory committee; NCE = new chemical entity; NDA = new drug application.

SOURCE: Kaitin et al., "FDA Advisory Committees and the New Drug Approval Process," *Journal of Clinical Pharmacology* 29: 886-890, 1989.

search is associated with faster approval of NCEs, a commonly cited rationale for such requests (350).

POST-MARKETING SURVEILLANCE

Federal regulation requires manufacturers selling in the United States periodically to notify the FDA about the performance of their products. This surveillance is designed to detect uncommon, yet serious, adverse reactions typically not revealed during premarket testing. Manufacturers immediately notify the FDA of serious or unexpected side effects and annually send the agency data on all adverse reactions.[17] For frequent or serious side effects, the agency may seek additional animal or clinical research or use the

sponsor's surveillance data to revise the drug's approved conditions of use or notify medical practitioners of precautions they should take when prescribing. Sponsors can hold new information about the drug's therapeutic benefits gathered through surveillance until they file their annual report with the agency (21 C.F.R. 310.305, 312.85; 128a).[18]

EFFORTS TO EXPEDITE FDA NEW PRODUCT REGULATIONS

The regulatory system has been under almost constant attack since its inception in 1938. Numerous commissions, hearings, and studies conducted over the years questioned how the FDA enforces laws and regulations governing the

[17] During the first 3 years after market approval, the company provides this information quarterly to the FDA.

[18] To improve its ability to surveil marketed drugs, the FDA has recently conducted a successful educational demonstration program in Rhode Island to encourage physicians voluntarily to report suspected adverse reactions directly to the FDA or to the manufacturer. At the end of the 2-year project, adverse drug reports from this State were 17 times greater than the national average (374).

development and marketing of pharmaceutical products in the United States. There is some consistency to their themes and recommendations. Critics frequently cite the FDA for providing inadequate or untimely information about the processes and standards used by agency staff to judge the merits of an application (196,407). Poor working conditions within the agency, inadequate staffing, and low salaries are perennial criticisms, as is the need for better management. The agency is also regularly criticized for being slow to accept new scientific methods or to incorporate the latest advance in biomedical knowledge into the drug review process (196,197).

Against this backdrop of public debate over the appropriate role and effectiveness of government regulation of pharmaceuticals, the FDA has demonstrated its capacity to change when presented with opportunity, challenge, or mandate by modifying its programs and policies, issuing new regulations, or working with consumer groups or industry representatives to identify ways in which the drug development and regulatory review process might be made more efficient.

This section reviews these initiatives, including efforts to improve the conduct of research and regulatory review and to broaden or hasten the availability of important new pharmaceutical therapies. The review is purely descriptive, as an evaluation of how well these various programs have worked is beyond the scope of this report.

∎ Guidelines and "Points to Consider"

New drug regulation process is a labor-and document-intensive process. The typical IND is several hundred pages long and grows as researchers submit protocols for later clinical studies and other supplementary information. The typical NDA consists of 30 separate volumes of technical information totaling 100,000 pages of text, data tabulations, statistical analyses, and patient case report forms (469). For the drug development and regulatory review process to work efficiently, sponsors need to know what information the FDA expects to see in these applications and what standards reviewers will

use to evaluate the evidence submitted. Sponsors also need to understand how to organize and present the information. Reviews based on inadequate or poorly organized applications can be prolonged or unsuccessful, thus wasting both Federal and private sector resources (399).

Since 1977, CDER has periodically issued guidelines containing general information on preclinical and clinical testing procedures, manufacturing practices, product standards, ingredient standards, statistical methods, and product labeling. Although these guidelines are not legally binding, they represent the agency's official position about the nature and variety of information required by agency staff in judging the merits of new drug products. The agency maintains that a drug sponsor following the guidelines substantially increases its chances of producing an acceptable IND or NDA (assuming the firm conducts its scientific studies properly and the results are statistically significant). However, following the guidelines does not guarantee a favorable outcome. The FDA advises sponsors wishing to deviate from the R&D strategies laid out in these guidelines to meet with appropriate FDA review staff before acting on their plans. FDA describes these meetings as an opportunity for the drug's sponsor to describe and justify the alternative approach to the FDA staff who will later be responsible for reviewing the NDA and to discuss the strengths and limitations of the substitution (469).

Rather than issuing guidelines, CBER has written a series of memos, known as "points to consider," on subjects relevant to the R&D of biological products. CBER treats its "points" as more informal than CDER's guidelines, but they do allow CBER to react quickly to the rapid evolution of the science underpinning the biotechnology industry.

The "points to consider" memos do not represent official agency positions, nor do they require the agency to automatically accept manufacturing methods and research conducted according to the ideas laid out in the "points." Because they have no official standing within the agency, CBER can easily revise its "points to consider" to incorporate new knowledge and approaches to the development of biological products (116).

■ Rewrite of the IND and NDA Regulations

Because the Federal administrative rulemaking process, is cumbersome, the FDA rarely seeks to change the formal regulations that govern the review of INDs, NDAs, PLAs, and ELAs. After 1962, the agency changed these regulations only to implement new legislation and to make technical alterations that remedy deficiencies in language or modify specific requirements (274). By 1979, however, the FDA concluded that these changes had cumulatively rendered the agency's IND and NDA regulations inconsistent, unclear, and out of step with current scientific thinking. The agency began a review that resulted in new NDA regulations in 1985 and new IND regulations in 1987 (173). Among the changes instituted, the new regulations:

- Eliminated or simplified some prior regulatory requirements;
- Opened the door for improved communication between the agency and pharmaceutical sponsors;
- Established specific time limits for industry and agency action at various points in the regulatory review process;[19]
- Altered the format and content of the NDA and IND applications to facilitate review by the FDA; and
- Clarified or codified other FDA policies and practices (such as the conditions under which the agency issues approval and approvable letters and administrative procedures sponsors may use to resolve scientific disputes with FDA review staff).

Of particular importance is the increasing communication between the sponsor and the FDA throughout the course of the process. The revised regulations offer sponsors the option of meeting with FDA staff twice during the clinical research period to discuss scientific and medical issues pertaining to the development of the drug. Drug sponsors can request a meeting with FDA staff at the end of Phase II on the organization and content of Phase III testing, and to discuss any additional clinical or nonclinical information the agency may want to see in the NDA (52 FR 8798). FDA staff are responsible for keeping minutes of the "end-of-Phase II" meetings and any agreements reached. The minutes along with a copy of any written material the FDA provides to the sponsor serve as a permanent record of the meeting.

Sponsors may also elect to meet with agency staff at the conclusion of Phase III studies to discuss the organization and content of the NDA. The primary purpose of this meeting is to acquaint FDA reviewers with the information a sponsor plans to include in the NDA, to discuss appropriate methods for statistical analysis of the data, and to uncover any major unresolved research questions that may delay or preclude a favorable regulatory decision (21 C.F.R. 312.47).

■ Acceptance of Data From Other Countries

The FDA has permitted drug sponsors to include data from clinical trials conducted in other countries as part of a U.S. NDA since the early 1970s. Despite this stated policy, sponsors tended to use foreign data only to demonstrate product safety and to corroborate the outcome of U.S. effectiveness studies. FDA staff maintained that NDAs may include some foreign trial data, but there must be at least one U.S. trial conducted by a competent investigator in order to validate the foreign trial data (400). The FDA pointed to differences between the United States and other countries in preferred trial designs, a general lack of adherence to clinical protocols among foreign investigators, and difficulty in reviewing and

---

[19] Many analysts have suggested that the FDA does not necessarily adhere to some of these standards, such as the 180-day limit on the review and disposition of new drug applications (260).

verifying clinical records from foreign trials. In addition, the FDA argued that without the U.S. data it might approve a drug for the U.S. market based on a safety and effectiveness profile that had more to do with fundamental differences in population characteristics, diagnostic criteria, and therapeutic practices than the pharmacological potential of the drug. Although pharmaceutical sponsors believed they could control for such differences when designing foreign studies (399), they tended to interpret the FDA's position to mean that agency reviewers preferred U.S. data in making regulatory decisions (314).

European governments made efforts during the 1970s and 1980s to improve the quality of clinical studies and established pan-European standards for clinical research to support the move to a common market. These actions eliminated many of FDA's historical objections to the use of clinical trial data from the European Community (400).

FDA used the 1987 rewrite of the NDA regulations to indicate it was now willing to accept NDAs based solely on foreign data. Because there is still considerable variation in medical practice standards and the quality of clinical investigations throughout the world, the FDA still requires sponsors to prove that each foreign study used in an NDA was conducted by a qualified investigator in accordance with the U.S. regulatory requirements for the conduct of clinical trials and that the data are accurate and the findings apply to the U.S. population (21 C.F.R. 312.20).

▮ FDA Ratings of Drugs Under Review

CDER introduced a classification scheme in 1975, for new drugs based on their molecular novelty and therapeutic potential as an attempt to prioritize CDER's workload so that potentially important therapies might reach the marketplace more quickly than they had in the past. Box 6-A describes these ratings. In January 1992, CDER announced that, effective immediately, it would simplify this prioritization scheme to identify only two categories of therapeutic importance for drugs: "priority" for the most important drugs, and "standard" for all other drugs (127).

▮ The "NDA Day"

CDER is experimenting with the use of day-long meetings referred to as the "NDA Day," to forge an agreement among the FDA, drug companies, and advisory committee members on the final labeling of a new drug product. The "NDA Day" is usually faster than the traditional approach to approval of new drug product labels. Although scheduling difficulties and the preparation required by both the sponsor and the FDA somewhat limit their feasibility, CDER is considering use of similar meetings to speed up its review of INDs, clinical trial protocols, and technical sections of the NDA.

▮ Computerized Applications

In the late 1970s and early 1980s, drug companies developed computer systems to manage and analyze the large clinical research databases and began to explore the potential of computers to streamline the submission and review of NDAs, PLA/ELAs, and other aspects of the regulatory process. The FDA entered the computer age when it received the first computerized new drug approval application in 1985. CDER has since received over 40 computerized new drug applications (CANDAs) from over 20 sponsors, resulting in 12 approved drugs.[20]

The primary reason drug sponsors and the FDA agreed to experiment with computerized submissions was their potential for speeding up the review process. CANDAs do introduce a number of important efficiencies into the review process, but the agency has completed too few reviews involving CANDAs to determine whether their use actually results in shortened review times. The major advantage of CANDAs noted to date is that they allow review staff to search the application quickly for needed information using key words. CANDAs also facilitate comparison of

---

[20] Because CBER has had very limited experience with computer-assisted PLA reviews, this discussion focuses on CDER.

information across clinical trials and the search of individual patient records for specific data (376).

Industry views FDA's ability to do its own computations using data files and patient records as something of a double-edged sword. Some see this capability as a net benefit to companies, because it saves agency reviewers time when they have a question about information contained in the application (70). Other industry people are concerned that unfettered access to raw clinical research data gives FDA reviewers an opportunity to reprocess and analyze data in any way they see fit. Without the usual contact between sponsor and agency in interpreting each NDA, the sponsor may not know until very late that its application is in danger of rejection (399).

So far, the FDA has not established any standards for the organization of CANDAs or the hardware and software systems used in their preparation and review. To cope with the wide variation in computer literacy within the agency, each of the 20 sponsors submitting a CANDA met with the FDA reviewers prior to submitting their application so that they could tailor each CANDA to the computer skill and review requirements of the individual reviewers. This haphazard approach has produced a proliferation of hardware and software systems within the agency and general confusion among drug sponsors as to what the FDA will expect in the future.

■ Subpart E Regulations: Expedited Approval of Important New Therapies

Largely in response to the AIDS epidemic and the regulatory reform movement of the 1980s, the FDA issued new regulations, in 1988, known as "Subpart E," that substantially alter the research and regulatory review process for drugs to treat life-threatening and severely-debilitating illness.[21]

Subpart E is an attempt to expedite approval by encouraging close communication between the FDA and sponsors. Usually before filing an IND,

the drug's sponsor requests an expedited review designation. Once granted, the FDA and the sponsor meet to plan the animal studies necessary to initiate each phase of human testing, to discuss the organization and content of the IND, and to design the Phase I trials. Although traditional Phase I studies use only healthy volunteers, Phase I studies of expedited drugs may include individuals with the target disease, thus giving the sponsor some information on the drug's effectiveness early in the clinical research process.

At the end of Phase I trials, the FDA and the sponsor meet again to plan for Phase II studies. Data accumulated by the end of Phase II trials that are usually sufficient for an NDA. Although the Phase II trials may be bigger than usual in order to accomplish this goal, the total number of research subjects and amount of time involved in clinical testing should still be lower than for the combination of Phase II and Phase III trials under a traditional development scheme.

In reviewing a Subpart E NDA, the FDA considers the drug's benefits in relation to its known and potential risks, the severity of the disease, and the availability of alternative therapies. If the FDA believes important questions about the drug remain unanswered, it may opt to require Phase III studies before approval, or it may mandate Phase III tests to be done following market approval (21 C.F.R. (E)).

The FDA estimates that the Subpart E regulations are capable of cutting the time and money needed to develop and market a drug by one-third to one-half (258a). As of February 1992, 24 drugs with Subpart E designation had been approved, 3 others had NDAs under review, and 23 had active INDs (47).

■ Treatment INDs and Parallel Track: Expanded Access to Experimental Drugs

Although Subpart E regulations shorten the amount of time it takes to bring a select group of drugs to market, access to these drugs prior to

---

[21] The Sub-part E regulations, define a life-threatening disease or condition as one where "the likelihood of death is high unless the course of the disease is interrupted" or a disease or condition with a potentially fatal outcome, where the end point of clinical trial analysis is survival. Severely- debilitating illness is defined as a disease or condition that "causes major irreversible morbidity.'

market approval continues to be limited to people enrolled in clinical trials. The FDA established the Treatment IND program in 1987 in response to continuing demands of consumer groups for early access to potentially important new drugs. It followed 3-years later with the parallel-track program in order to provide access to promising experimental HIV-related therapies even earlier than was possible with a Treatment IND (55 F.R. 20656).[22]

Treatment INDs—The Treatment IND regulation essentially codifies a long-standing agency practice of releasing investigational drugs to general practitioners, on a case-by-case basis, for use in the treatment of immediately life-threatening diseases in instances where no satisfactory alternative treatment exists.[23] While the Treatment IND is most closely associated with the AIDS epidemic, it is available to any sponsor developing a drug for the treatment of a serious or life-threatening disease. Under a Treatment IND, sponsors can release experimental therapies to health care providers to treat people with life-threatening disease who are either too sick to qualify for a clinical trial or live too far from a trial site to be included (95,528).

A unique aspect of the Treatment IND is sponsors have the option of charging for drugs supplied under the protocol. A sponsor must notify the FDA of its intent to charge for a Treatment IND drug. This notice must include a justification for the amount to be charged,[24] tangible evidence the sponsor is well on its way toward securing market approval for the drug, and written assurance that the sponsor has no intention of creating a commercial market for the drug under the Treatment IND. Unless the FDA objects

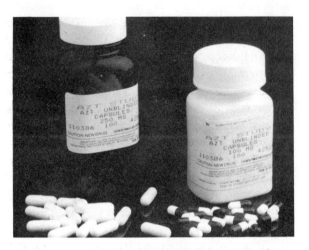

Photo credit: NATIONAL CANCER INSTITUTE

The regulatory review of drugs used in the treatment of life-threatening diseases such as AIDS has been expedited in recent years.

within 30 days, the sponsor may proceed to charge for the drug. The FDA can withdraw the authorization to charge if it believes the sponsor has failed to show due diligence in its pursuit of market approval, is using the Treatment IND to market its product, or the conditions underlying the Treatment IND no longer apply (21 C.F.R. 312.7(d)(2); 340).

So far, out of 23 drugs with Treatment INDs, only 5 have been supplied by the sponsor at a price (98).[25] This may reflect the industry's tradition of not charging for experimental therapies or a fear that sponsors who charge for their products are more likely to be sued should the drug be found to be associated with severe adverse effects. Or, drug sponsors might prefer giving up any revenue for these drugs to providing the Federal Government with data on research and manufacturing costs.

---

[22] The parallel-track program is limited to people with acquired immunodeficiency syndrome or Human Immunodeficiency Virus-related illness who have no therapeutic alternatives and cannot participate in conventional clinical trails. The Public Health Service announced it may extend the program to other life-threatening diseases in the future.

[23] The FDA has released investigational drugs for "compassionate use" purposes since the mid-1970s.

[24] The regulations specify the price charged cannot be more than the amount necessary to recover the "costs of manufacture, research, development, and handling of the investigational drug." The sponsor is required to supply the FDA with detailed information on these expenses to support the amount it plans to charge for the drug.

[25] All five of these pharmaceuticals are also designated as orphan drugs.

Between 1987 and 1991, the FDA received Treatment IND petitions for 37 drugs, allowed distribution to patients in 23 of these cases, and approved 14 NDAs or PLAs/ELAs for drugs with Treatment IND status (98). The modest number of Treatment INDs is partially explained by the few drugs under development at any time for the treatment of serious or life-threatening diseases and the even smaller number meeting the criteria set forth in the regulations. Furthermore, even if a drug potentially qualifies for Treatment IND status, the sponsor may decide that participation is not in its best interest.

Critics of the treatment IND program fear that making investigational drugs broadly available may decrease patients' willingness to participate in clinical trials. Others are afraid that because Treatment IND drugs are unproven, participating sponsors may subject themselves to a significant risk of product liability claims (95,232,279,340).

Parallel-Track Program—The parallel-track program, proposed in 1990 but not yet finalized, is designed to make experimental treatments for conditions related to Human Immunodeficiency Virus (HIV) available even if the evidence of their effectiveness is less than that required to receive Treatment IND status (55 F.R. 20656). Under this program, a drug sponsor would pursue two clinical research tracks for its investigational HIV-related therapies. The "scientific" track would comprise traditional Phase II and Phase III controlled clinical trials. The "parallel" track would comprise more open, loosely monitored studies. A sponsor could ask the FDA for permission to release a drug through a parallel-track program immediately following the completion of Phase I studies.

Physicians who provide patients with an investigational drug under a parallel-track program would be expected to function in a manner similar to clinical investigators in the scientific-track. They would provide the drug according to a protocol written by the sponsor, and they would provide the sponsor with data on adverse reactions and, if requested, evidence on the drug's effectiveness. The sponsor could use information from the parallel-track studies to support its petition for market approval of the new drug once the clinical trials are complete, but the FDA has stated it would continue to base its market approval decisions on data from the controlled clinical trials in the scientific track.

Critics of the proposed parallel-track program have cited potential liability, delayed market approval, and potentially higher R&D costs for drugs in the parallel-track programs. Because of the limited treatment options for the large number of HIV-infected people, participation in the parallel-track program might force sponsors to increase their production, distribution, and administrative capacities earlier than they otherwise would.

Unlike the Treatment IND program, the FDA does not expect sponsors to charge for drugs made available under a parallel-track protocol. Consequently, if a parallel-track drug ultimately proves to be unsafe or ineffective, the sponsor would face a larger loss on the project than it would under a traditional research program. However, sponsors facing economic hardship would be able to petition the FDA for permission to recover part of the cost associated with making the drug broadly available to those who need it (95,232).

Although the FDA has only issued proposed regulations governing the parallel-track program, drugs for HIV-related treatments already have made up a significant portion of the Treatment IND program. Of the 23 drugs receiving Treatment IND status by the end of 1991, 8 were for HIV or HIV-related infections, and 5 of these drugs have received NDA or PLA/ELA approval (98).

▮ Recent Initiatives to Expedite Drug Approvals

In November 1991, the White House Council on Competitiveness and the FDA proposed several initiatives aimed at further reducing the time required to move a drug from clinical testing through marketing approval.[26] Under these proposals:

- Drug sponsors could begin phase I clinical testing without receiving IND status from the FDA. Instead, Institutional Review Boards (IRBs) at hospitals or other medical institutions that administer the trials would review and monitor them.
- The FDA could approve drugs for life-threatening diseases and diseases for which no alternative therapy exists on the basis of limited evidence of safety and efficacy. Sponsors could collect and provide the full complement of such evidence after the drug is approved.
- The FDA would contract with outside experts in academic and other institutions to review pieces of NDAs submitted for antibiotics, allergy drugs, analgesics, and anti-inflammatory drugs, four therapeutic categories in which many drugs have already been approved and the FDA expects little scientific controversies.
- The FDA would look for foreign drug approval systems with sufficient high standards to warrant U.S. approval on the basis of an approval in these other countries.

Two of these proposals appear to be grounded in existing policy. Drugs for AIDS and other life-threatening illnesses reach patients through several programs prior to approval and through expedited approval. It is not clear how the new proposals would alter the substance or outcomes of these programs. As described later in this chapter, the FDA is already engaged in talks with other countries exploring the potential for some international harmonization of drug approval standards (380). But whether or not the search will result in the agency identifying acceptable

drug approval systems remains to been seen (147).

Proponents of external review of some NDAs suggest it is a natural extension of the FDA's current use of advisory committees and other outside experts and the agency still retains the actual approval decision. The FDA Commissioner has also said the agency would initially limit external review from 8 to 12 applications. Critics inside and outside the FDA claim that finding outside reviewers without conflicts of interests arising from financial stakes in the pharmaceutical industry may be difficult and scientists outside the FDA may lack the expertise found within the agency to provide a review in line with regulatory scientific standards (148,187).

Proponents of the proposal to allow phase I testing prior to IND status argue current policy needlessly requires double oversight of these clinical trials by both the IRBs at the institutions conducting the trials and the FDA. Critics argue that IRBs focus largely on the rights and safety of human subjects and lack the expertise or desire to oversee all FDA regulatory standards for investigational drugs receiving their first test in humans (147,187,203).

TRENDS IN THE R&D AND REGULATORY REVIEW PROCESSES

The time required to bring a new pharmaceutical to market depends both on the R&D strategy and competence of the drug's sponsor and on the efficiency and competence of FDA's review process. It is impossible to isolate the effect of each of these factors on the time it takes to develop an approved drug. It is also inappropriate to assign full responsibility or credit to the FDA for changes in the observed time from the first filing of an NDA to the approval decision. Changing company R&D development strategies can result in earlier or later submission of NDAs.

---

[26] In 1990 and 1991, two groups appointed by the President, the National Committee to Review Current Procedures for Approval of New Drugs for Cancer and AIDS (known as the Lasagna Committee) and the Advisory Committee on the Food and Drug Administration (known as the Edwards Committee), issued final reports suggesting changes in FDA policies regulating drugs for life-threatening diseases and FDA management procedures, respectively (462,467). Although the November 1991 initiative by the White House and the FDA was not a formal response to the recommendations of these two groups, the initiative does contain some proposals embodied in the committees' reports.

With these limitations in mind, OTA analyzed trends in the number of new drug candidates under development, their attrition rates, the amount of time they spend in the clinical R&D and regulatory processes, and the potential contributions of company actions and FDA actions in explaining these trends.

■ Trends in INDs and NDAs

Among the most basic measures of activity in the research and regulatory processes are the numbers of INDs issued, NDAs or PLAs received, and NDAs or PLAs approved by the FDA. These snapshots of the number of drugs in the development pipeline are of limited value in understanding the dynamics of the regulatory process. For example, they say little about trends in the probability of successfully bringing a new drug to market, the time required to do so, or the reasons for these trends. However, they do provide a window into the workload of the FDA and the output of companies' R&D efforts.

Figure 6-2 presents data compiled by Tufts University's Center for the Study of Drug Development (CSDD) on commercial INDs for NCEs filed in six different 4-year periods (107).[27] These data suggest that after declining through the 1970s, the number of NCEs entering clinical testing increased somewhat during the 1980s. For NCEs from U.S. sponsors, the number of self-originated drugs increased modestly in the late 1980s.[28]

Figure 6-3 shows NDAs received by the FDA in each year since 1975 (468,472,474). For the 1980s, the figure breaks out NDAs for new molecular entities (NMEs) from the total. NDAs submitted for NMEs have ranged fairly consist-

Figure 6-2—IND Applications for NCEs Received by the FDA in 4-Year Periods, 1963-86

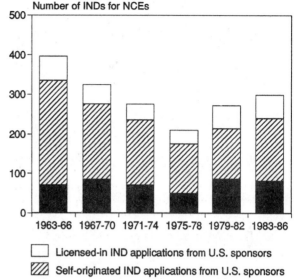

Number of INDs for NCEs

☐ Licensed-in IND applications from U.S. sponsors

▨ Self-originated IND applications from U.S. sponsors

■ IND applications from foreign sponsors

KEY: IND = investigational new drug; NCE = new chemical entity.

SOURCE: Office of Technology Assessment, 1993, based on data from J.A. DiMasi, N.R. Bryant, L. Lasagna, "New Drug Development on the United States," 1963-1990, *Clinical Pharmacology and Therapeutics* 50(5):471-486, 1991.

ently between 23 and 37 per year over the last decade with some decline in the last 3 years. By contrast, the total number of NDAs submitted peaked in the early 1980s and has declined fairly steadily since. Similar trends are apparent in data in NDAs approved each year (figure 6-4). A steady number of NMEs were approved, but the total number of NDA approvals declined. The decline in non-NME applications may reflect a tendency on the part of sponsors to forgo applications for new uses of drugs already on the market.

---

[27] These data come from 31 U.S.-owned and 10 foreign-owned firms. According to CSDD the data include 78 percent of NMEs from U.S.-owned firms and 63 percent of NMEs from foreign-owned firms that ultimately obtained FDA approval between 1963 and 1990 (107). Since the mid-1980s, CSDD has sought to include therapeutic biologicals in its surveys (106).

[28] A self-originated NCE is defined as one that was synthesized and developed by the sponsoring firm. The alternative is for the firm to "license in" or otherwise acquire an existing compound from another company or researcher. By the time sponsoring firms acquired licensed-in drugs, some R&D has already been done, so they should have a higher probability of approval and a shorter development time. CSDD does not give a breakdown between self-originated and licensed-in drugs for NCEs from foreign-owned firms because CSDD believes some of them to behave like licensed-in drugs. CSDD expects firms to file INDs in the United States only for drugs that have already shown a high potential for success in foreign research (107).

■ Trends in Time to Marketing Approval for New Clinical Entities[29]

A more revealing view of trends in the research and regulatory processes is obtained from analyses of drugs entering testing in specific periods.

Because the FDA's automated management information system does not permit tracking of NMEs from the point of first IND to market approval, all such data gathering must be done by hand. The FDA's Office of Planning and Evaluation (OPE) had compiled such data in 1988 for an analysis of NMEs whose INDs were first filed in

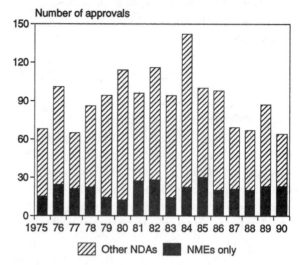

Figure 6-4—NDA Approvals by Year, 1975-90

Number of approvals

KEY: NCE = new chemical entity; NME = new molecular entity.

SOURCE: Office of Technology Assessment, 1993, based on data from U.S. Department of Health and Human Services, Public Health Service, Food and Drug Administration, Center for Drug Evaluation and Research, *Office of Drug Evaluation Statistical Report*, U.S. Department of Health and Human Services, Rockville, MD 1984, 1987, 1991, 1992.

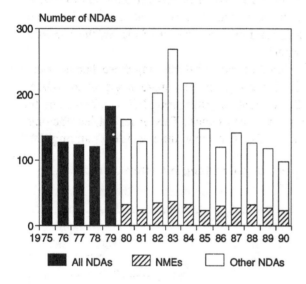

Figure 6-3—Original NDAs Received by the FDA for Review, 1975-90

Number of NDAs

NOTE: Breakdown of NMEs versus other NDAs not available prior to 1980.

KEY: NDA = new drug application; NME = new molecular entity.

SOURCE: Office of Technology Assessment, 1993, based on data from U.S. Department of Health and Human Services, Public Health Service, Food and Drug Administration, Center for Drug Evaluation and Research, *Office of Drug Evaluation Statistical Report*, U.S. Department of Health and Human Services, Rockville, MD, 1984, 1987, 1991, 1992.

the period 1976-78 (426). At OTA's request, OPE and CDER staff compiled similar data for the period 1984-86 (Appendix I describes methods used to compile these data). Figures 6-5 and 6-6 present the results of these analysis.

Figure 6-5 shows the cumulative percent of NMEs that result in an NDA in each period. Figure 6-6 shows the cumulative percent that resulted in a marketed product. The figures display data for the early cohort for 144 months and for later cohort for 54 months, the maximum amount of time elapsed after IND issuance for all drugs in the cohort over the time periods measured. More drugs in the 1984-86 group reached NDA submission and market approval than did drugs in the 1976-78 cohort at each month after clinical testing began. If these trends continue to

---

[29] In analyses presented in this section, data on the outcomes of more recent cohorts of drugs were available for shorter periods of time than were data on earlier cohorts. Hence, conclusions presented in this section about the lengthening or shortening of the time required for each cohort to achieve approval refer only to the amount of time necessary for a given percentage of drugs in each cohort to result in an NDA submission (or approval). For example, it may take 24 months for the first 20 percent of one cohort of NDAs to be approved, while it takes 36 months for a comparable percentage of another cohort of NDAs to receive approval. One cannot draw any conclusions about changes in the average time to approval for all ultimately approved drugs since the ultimate success of many drugs in the later cohorts is unknown.

Figure 6-5—Percent of IND for NMEs Entering Clinical Trials Resulting in NDA or PLA, 1976-78 and 1984-86

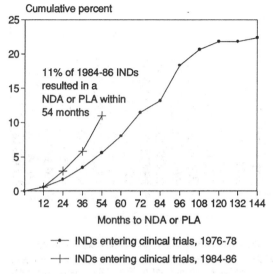

Cumulative percent

11% of 1984-86 INDs resulted in a NDA or PLA within 54 months

Months to NDA or PLA

—•— INDs entering clinical trials, 1976-78

—+— INDs entering clinical trials, 1984-86

KEY: IND = investigational new drug; NME = new molecular entity; NDA = new drug application; PLA = product license application.

SOURCE: Office of Technology Assessment, 1993, based on data supplied by FDA (see appendix I).

hold as time goes by, more NMEs that entered testing in 1984-86 may ultimately result in NDAs and marketed products than those in 1976-78.

Data supplied by CSDD to OTA permitted further analysis of trends in success rates and times from IND to market approval. Figure 6-7 shows the cumulative probability that an IND resulted in an NDA and that an NDA resulted in an approved product within a certain number of months after the first IND was filed. While the success of the IND to NDA submission phase for NCEs improved over successive IND periods, the opposite trend holds once those drug candidates made it to the NDA review phase. Because the CSDD database could track the latest cohort of drugs during NDA review for only 36 months, it is not clear whether the trends observed to date will continue over the remainder of the cohort's experience.

Another way of interpreting these data is to say that for any given percentage of approved NDAs, the amount of time from NDA submission to approval lengthened. This observed lengthening of the NDA review time is found among the

Figure 6-6—Percent of INDs for NMEs Entering Clinical Trials Resulting in Approved Products, 1976-78 and 1984-86

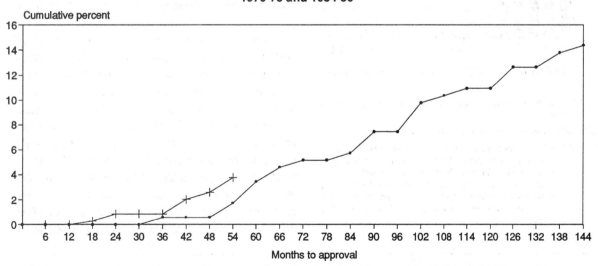

Cumulative percent

Months to approval

—•— INDs entering clinical trials, 1976-78 —+— INDs entering clinical trials, 1984-86

KEY: IND = investigational new drug; NME = new molecular entity; FDA = Food and Drug Administration.

SOURCE: Office of Technology Assessment, 1993, based on data supplied by FDA (see appendix I).

Figure 6-7—Percent of INDs for NCEs Resulting in an NDA/PLA and NDAs/PLAs for NCEs Resulting in Approved Products, 1965-82

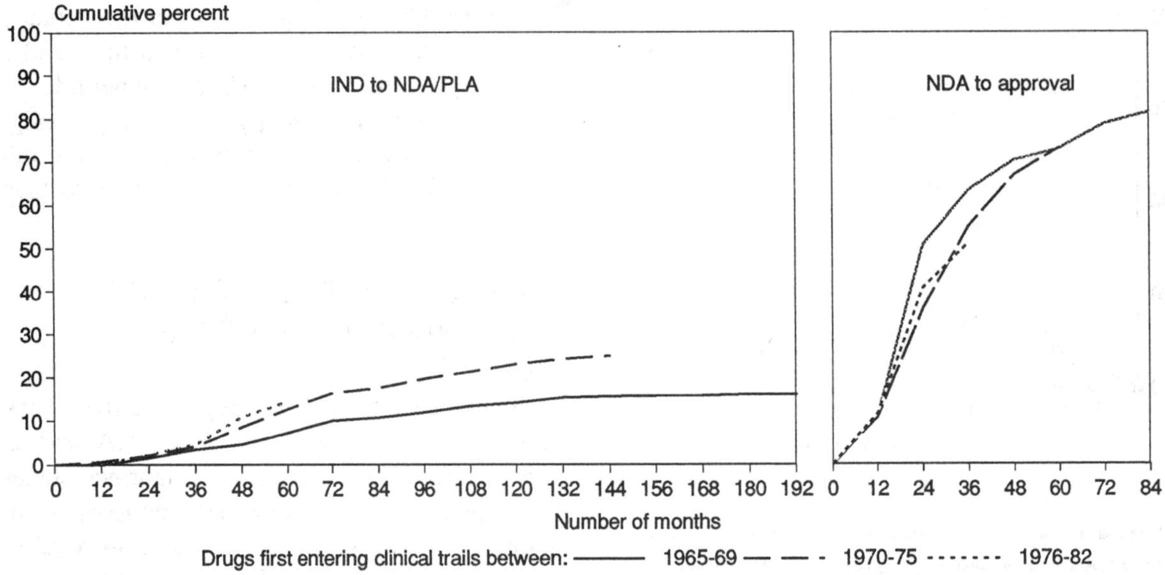

KEY: IND = investigational new drug; NCE = new chemical entity; NDA = new drug application; PLA = product license application.

SOURCE: Office of Technology Assessment, 1993, based on data supplied by the Center for the Study of Drug Development, Tufts University.

licensed-in NCEs, but not among self-originated drugs.

OTA also analyzed the FDA's published data on trends in the NDA review period. This analysis is similar to that of the CSDD data except that the cohorts of NMEs examined are defined according to the year in which their NDAs were submitted to the FDA rather than according to the year their INDs were first issued.[30] Figure 6-8 presents the cumulative probability of approval over time for all NMEs. Time to approval has increased for any given percentage of approved drugs, and the probability of approval within specified time intervals for all drugs reaching NDA submission has declined over time. Although the limited experience of the most recent NDAs (i.e., those submitted to the FDA between 1985 and 1988) suggests a possible increase in approvals compared with earlier cohorts, a breakdown of these

cumulative probabilities according to the FDA's rating of drugs' therapeutic potential (figures 6-9 through 6-11) shows all of the trend toward faster and higher approval rates among the most recent cohort appears attributable to drugs the FDA expected to be of modest or little therapeutic importance. Drugs with a rating of "A" show decreasing rates of success over time.[31] Additional experience with the most recent cohort of NDAs is needed to determine whether this trend will continue.

Reasons for the apparent decline in approval rates for drugs the FDA rated as having the highest therapeutic potential are not clear. Sponsoring firms may be submitting less complete or lower quality NDAs over time, or the FDA's expectations may have increased. It is also possible that increases in the FDA's responsibilities and the greater constraints on its resources

---

[30] These data exclude product license applications/establishment license applications reviewed by CBER (most of which would appear in the most recent period).

[31] The importance of this time trend is tempered somewhat by the fact that even with this decline over time, the approval of "A" drugs has been consistently higher and faster than those rated "B" or "C."

Figure 6-8—Approval Times for NME-NDAs Submitted in Three Periods

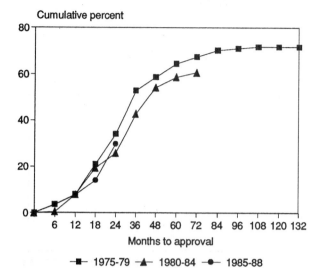

Cumulative percent

Months to approval

—■— 1975-79 —▲— 1980-84 —●— 1985-88

KEY: NDA = new drug application; NME = new molecular entity.

SOURCE: Office of Technology Assessment, 1993, based on data from U.S. Department of Health and Human Services, Public Health Service, Food and Drug Administration, Center for Drug Evaluation and Research, *Office of Drug Evaluation Statistical Report*, U.S. Department of Health and Human Services, Rockville, MD 1984, 1987, 1991, 1992.

documented elsewhere (436,462) have led to longer review times. Regardless of the reasons for this trend in the NDA phase, it still holds true that over time, greater proportions of drugs entering clinical research have reached the market in less time and that, on average, NMEs with a rating of ''A'' reach the market more quickly than other NMEs.

To summarize the above analyses:

- The percent of NCE drug candidates entering human trials that resulted in an approved NDA within 54 months increased during the 1980s compared with the 1970s.
- This improvement was confined largely to the pre-NDA period. Success rates once the NDA is submitted have actually declined. The lengthening of the NDA review period appears to be concentrated in NCEs acquired by license.

- Although the most recent group of submitted NDAs shows some improvement, drugs for which the FDA has tried to expedite approval times (category ''A'' drugs) actually showed a decline in approval rates and a lengthening of the NDA review period.
- Despite this disturbing trend, drugs designated by the FDA as category ''A'' are still associated with higher approval rates than others.

TRENDS IN THE REGULATION OF PHARMACEUTICALS IN OTHER COUNTRIES

Pharmaceutical industry representatives have stressed in both interviews with OTA and in public forums that because U.S. approval standards are the strictest, companies tend to establish clinical research strategies according to requirements of the U.S. FDA. Yet, drug sponsors must

Figure 6-9—Approval Times for NME-NDAs Rated A in Three Periods

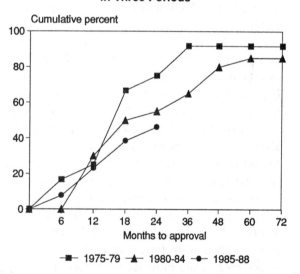

Cumulative percent

Months to approval

—■— 1975-79 —▲— 1980-84 —●— 1985-88

NOTES: NMEs rated "A" were deemed by the FDA to represent "important therapeutic gains."

KEY: NDA = new drug application; NME = new molecular entity.

SOURCE: Office of Technology Assessment, 1993, based on data from U.S. Department of Health and Human Services, Public Health Service, Food and Drug Administration, Center for Drug Evaluation and Research, *Office of Drug Evaluation Statistical Report*, U.S. Department of Health and Human Services, Rockville, MD, 1984, 1987, 1991, 1992.

Figure 6-10—Approval Times for NME-NDAs Rated "B" in Three Periods

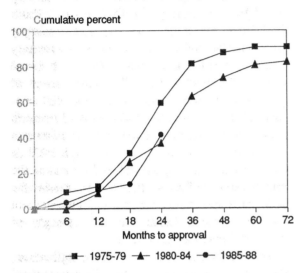

NOTES: NMEs rated "B" were deemed by FDA to represent "modest therapeutic gains."

KEY: NDA = new drug application; NME = new molecular entity.

SOURCE: Office of Technology Assessment, 1993, based on data U.S. Department of Health and Human Services, Public Health Service, Food and Drug Administration, Center for Drug Evaluation and Research, *Office of Drug Evaluation Statistical Report*, U.S. Department of Health and Human Services, Rockville, MD, 1984, 1987, 1991, 1992.

Figure 6-11—Approval Times for NME-NDAs Rated "C" in Three Periods

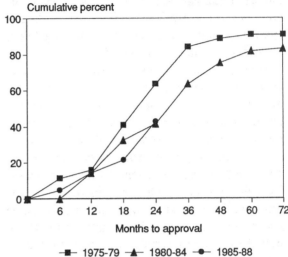

NOTE: NMEs rated "C" were deemed by the FDA to represent "little or no therapeutic gains."

KEY: NDA = new drug application; NME = new molecular entity.

SOURCE: Office of Technology Assessment, 1993, based on data from U.S. Department of Health and Human Services, Public Health Service, Food and Drug Administration, Center for Drug Evaluation and Research, *Office of Drug Evaluation Statistical Report*, U.S. Department of Health and Human Services, Rockville, MD, 1984, 1987, 1991, 1992.

also negotiate the regulatory approval processes of other countries to sell their drugs. OTA reviewed two major industrialized markets: Japan and the European Community. Europe, Japan, and the United States together account for 80 percent of the world's pharmaceutical sales. Hence, the size of these markets make them most important for the U.S. pharmaceutical industry's R&D activities and, potentially, for U.S. regulatory practices in the future.

▌ Drug Approval in Japan

The Japanese pharmaceutical industry traditionally was largely domestic. Japanese firms did little innovative R&D and thus did not produce many new drugs for potential introduction into other countries, nor did foreign companies market their own drugs in Japan. This situation, now changing, reflected Japanese trade policies, the organization of Japanese medicine, and principles governing Japan's clinical research requirements.

Until 1967, Japan did not require its own firms to conduct clinical trials for safety or efficacy in Japan for drugs licensed from foreign sponsors and already approved elsewhere. In contrast, until the 1980s, foreign sponsors were required to conduct trials on Japanese citizens and could not apply for marketing approval without entering into an agreement with a Japanese sponsor. These policies had the effect of encouraging Japanese sponsors to license foreign drugs rather than investing in their own R&D, and they effectively kept the foreign presence in the Japanese market to a minimum (344).

Other characteristics of the Japanese medical care system have affected its drug approval process and help explain the traditional isolation of the Japanese pharmaceutical market from the rest of the world. Among the significant features of this system are the primary role of the physicians in clinical practice and research and the deference shown them by patients and government. Until recently, the Japanese Government did not require researchers to obtain informed consent from research subjects, which made data from such studies unacceptable to the regulatory authorities in other countries (523).

In addition, physicians in Japan tend to own or have other financial stakes in the facilities that dispense drugs to their own patients. Because governmental approval of new drugs in Japan relies heavily on committees of outside physicians (with the government maintaining only a small staff to provide support for this process), individual physicians charged with review of new drug applications as well as the profession in general may face a conflict of interest by potentially benefiting financially from regulatory decisions they make or influence. This potential conflict of interest is compounded by the fact that committees charged with new drug review comprise leading researchers who may have conducted the clinical trials of pharmaceuticals under consideration for approval. Japan has relatively loose efficacy requirements for drugs to treat cancer and other life-threatening illnesses, leading to the availability of many treatments with no proven value. These practices have limited the acceptability of Japanese R&D results in other nations (523).

Regulation and approval of investigational pharmaceuticals falls to the Ministry of Health and Welfare's Pharmaceutical Affairs Bureau (PAB). Since the early 1980s, Japan has sought to establish tighter government control of the clinical use and investigation of new drugs to conform with R&D practices in other countries. PAB requires sponsors to receive approval to begin clinical testing, although the government does not review the drug's safety, the drug sponsor's research plans, or interim results in the same way the FDA does through its IND process. Since 1983 Japan has required investigators to comply with internationally accepted Good Laboratory Practices (GLP), and since 1990, with Good Clinical Practices (GCP). This latter group of guidelines include avoidance of potential conflicts of interest, an impartial review of research plans prior to beginning trials, and a requirement for informed consent (211). Although PAB is charged with auditing clinical trial records at the time the sponsor files an application to market the drug, early indications suggest that enforcement may be difficult because of the strength of traditional practices (211,523).[32]

When a sponsor files a new drug application, PAB refers it to the Central Pharmaceutical Affairs Council (CPAC), which is made up of outside medical and scientific experts. A subcommittee of CPAC's Committee on Drugs performs the bulk of the review, although the full Committee as well as CPAC's Executive Committee also approve the subcommittee's findings. CPAC sends its recommendation to the Minister of Health who formally grants approvals.[33]

The standard processing time for complete, sound new drug applications is 18 months. Once approved, Kosheibo's Health Insurance Board (HIB) enters price negotiations with the manufacturer (211).[34]

■ Drug Approval in the European Community

The decision by member countries of the European Community (EC) to create a single economic market by the end of 1992 has significant implications for the approval of new drugs

---

[32] In addition to a cultural taboo against government audits of physician records, physicians have criticized the informed consent requirement arguing that it goes against the Japanese practice of not fully explaining to patients the nature of their illness and treatment for fear any related anxiety will adversely affect patient and family. Critics also argue that adherence to these guidelines lowers patient willingness to participate in trials, thus raising development times and costs (523).

[33] Two other agencies, the National Institutes of Hygienic Sciences (NIHS) and the National Institutes of Health (NIH), must also validate the manufacturing quality of new drug products as well as validate the laboratory systems used in testing the drug. While NIHS tests drugs containing new chemical entities, NIH has charge of new biologics and antibiotics.

[34] Chapter 10 describes price regulation in other countries.

within the EC.[35] Currently, each national government has its own approval standards and process for allowing the marketing of new drugs within its borders. Beginning in 1979 (with modification in 1986), however, the EC established a process by which drug companies may apply for reciprocal approval in multiple EC countries once it has received formal approval for the drug within at least one EC nation. The other countries then have 4 months to either grant approval or state their grounds for not doing so. The Committee for Proprietary Medicinal Products (CPMP), made up of individuals from EC countries as well as members of its governing body, the European Commission, reviews individual nations' objections to reciprocal approval. The CPMP then issues a recommendation to the individual countries who still reserve the right to make a final decision on approval within 2 months (67). Because of differences in national standards and philosophies for new drug approval, this process has not led to timely reciprocal approvals (67). Only one drug has been approved without objection from individual countries, and few countries have made a final approval within the statutory 2 months following the CPMP's recommendation.

In 1988, the EC began to consider new options to streamline European drug approvals. Directives to be published in the next several years are expected to represent a compromise between those countries preferring a system of binding reciprocal approval and those preferring a single European regulatory body for drug approvals. Recent drafts suggest that the EC will adopt a three-tiered approval system:

- Companies could apply to a central Medical Evaluation Agency (MEA) to receive approval to market new drugs throughout the EC.[36]
- Alternatively, sponsors could apply to any single EC nation whose approval all other member countries would be required to

accept. The MEA would arbitrate any disagreements or objections, and its findings would also be binding throughout the EC.

- For drugs of limited geographic interest and for all generics, companies would continue to apply to national regulatory authorities for approval to market only within that country (67,210).

The net effects of these changes on the time and cost of bringing new drugs to market throughout the EC are not clear. On the one hand, standardization and centralization of the drug approval process will likely reduce the administrative and scientific effort currently necessary for sponsors to gain entry to 12 different national markets. On the other hand, the need to assure all member states of the quality of drug approval reviews throughout the EC may lead to an approval process (whether the central MEA or those in individual countries) that is more cautious, deliberate, and time-consuming than those currently employed in some of the individual EC members. In essence, a centralized MEA and binding mutual recognition may lead countries with relatively less burdensome regulatory reviews to bring their standards and processes up to the level of the more burdensome states, rather than the other way around. European observers expect this new process to go into effect sometime between 1993 and 1996 (210).

▌ Attempts to Harmonize International Drug Approval Regulation

In November 1991, representatives of the United States, the EC, and Japan met in Brussels for the first International Conference on Harmonization (ICH1) to formalize agreements reached during 18 months of negotiation. International harmonization of drug approval standards seeks to cut the cost of drug development by identifying duplicative studies required by multiple regulatory authorities. The results of ICH1 suggest

---

[35] The EC currently comprises Belgium, Denmark, France, Germany, Greece, Ireland, Italy, Luxembourg, the Netherlands, Portugal, Spain, and the United Kingdom.

[36] The MEA would automatically regulate all biotechnology drugs.

safety and quality-control studies are the most promising area for harmonization (63). In Brussels, the conferees agreed to reduce certain toxicity tests currently required in some countries and to adopt uniform guidelines for determining the shelf-life of pharmaceuticals, functions that are not the most costly R&D activities for drug sponsors. According to DiMasi's estimates, all animal toxicity testing represented 12 percent of all expected out-of-pocket expenditures for the R&D of a new drug in 1987 (109). Data from the PMA indicate that its member sponsors spent 7 percent of their total R&D expenditures in 1990 on toxicology and safety testing, another 7 percent on process development and quality control, and 9 percent on dosage formulation and stability testing (320). Less progress was made in harmonizing requirements for the more expensive clinical testing,[37] for which individual countries have been more reluctant to accept data from other countries. For example, Japan has traditionally argued that differences in diet, climate, and race make clinical results from Europe or the United States inappropriate for generalizing to Japanese patients (113,202,380). The three conferees will meet again in 1993 and 1995.

CONCLUSIONS

The time needed to establish the safety and effectiveness of a new drug represents a significant component of its R&D costs. The data presented in this chapter indicate that in recent years, the percent of drugs entering human clinical trials that can be expected to receive marketing approval in the United States has gone up. Furthermore, those approved at the time of OTA's analysis had moved from IND application to NDA approval faster than those that entered clinical trials in the 1970s. Most of this improvement came during the clinical research phase, because the time from NDA submission to approval has actually lengthened during the 1980s.

While these trends seem clear, their causes do not. The FDA's expectations of and actual advice to drug sponsors can determine the length of the clinical research period as much as drug sponsors' own decisions and research efforts. Likewise, the length of time required by the FDA to review and approve an NDA can reflect the completeness and quality of the sponsor's application as much as it reflects the FDA's resources and efficiency. As the literature reviewed in this chapter indicates, other market and scientific factors can also affect the amount of time required to move a drug into the marketplace.

Clinical trials are an especially resource-intensive component of drug R&D. OTA found that the number of people enrolled in clinical trials conducted prior to U.S. market approval has increased over time. This increase is especially large for trials conducted outside the United States and those completed after the filing of an NDA. While these increases could reflect increased regulatory expectations, there are also several other potential explanations including an increasingly global approach to drug R&D.

Since the mid-1970s, the FDA has tried to prioritize its review of NDAs so that drugs deemed therapeutically important may reach the market as quickly as possible. While drugs rated with the highest therapeutic importance have, on average, received the fastest NDA approvals when compared with other drugs, FDA's review of all drugs, no matter what the therapeutic importance rating, has become longer over time.

In recent years, the FDA has intensified its efforts to speed approval through programs to provide drugs for life-threatening illnesses to patients. While the Subpart E program attempts to speed actual NDA approval, the Treatment IND and proposed parallel-track programs allow expanded access to experimental treatments before approval. These efforts have resulted in greater or faster access to certain drugs, but it is possible the oversight they require may have slowed the

---

[37] Clinical testing represented 31 percent of PMA R&D expenditures in 1990 (320).

FDA's review of drugs not receiving high priority.

Recent anecdotal evidence raises some concern over a potential significant lengthening in the review of PLA/ELAs by CBER. Although there have been relatively few biological drugs to-date, the number of biological therapeutics expected to seek marketing approval from the FDA over the next few years is expected to grow substantially. OTA was unable to conduct quantitative analysis of recent trends in the review of biological drugs because CBER could not provide management data to OTA as CDER provided for OTA's analysis of the NDA review process.

Another initiative recently approved by Congress, the imposition of user fees on drug sponsors for the review of their drug marketing applications (Public Law 102-571) may offer additional opportunities to shorten regulatory review times. In exchange for fees of $100,000 for each NDA or PLA/ELA (rising to $233,000 in 5 years) and other fees, Congress and the FDA have agreed to augment the agency's staff of reviewers to speed the approval process. Whether the agency's faster approvals will justify the fees paid by sponsors can only be determined with time and experience.

Given the globalization of the marketplace for pharmaceuticals, regulation in other countries also can affect the cost of developing new drugs. To the extent that regulatory and scientific standards are roughly the same across countries and countries accept data gathered outside their borders, drug sponsors do not have to duplicate research to market their products in different countries. The two major marketplaces for drugs outside of the United States—Japan and Europe—have either changed or are in the process of changing their regulation of drug safety and effectiveness. While Japan has attempted to remove barriers to the marketing of drugs by sponsors from other countries and to improve standards for the conduct of scientific research including informed consent, significant differences appear to remain between Japan and the Western developed countries.

Across the Atlantic, the members of the European Community are in the process of consolidating and harmonizing their own drug approval processes. While a 1991 conference among the United States, the European Community, and Japan made some progress in harmonizing safety and quality-control testing, the development of mutually acceptable standards for effectiveness of new drugs remains a significant challenge for future conferences scheduled in 1993 and 1995.

Product Liability and the Pharmaceutical Industry | 7

What are the implications of product liability—the legal liability of a producer or seller for harm caused by a product—for the pharmaceutical research and development (R&D) process? Observers claim that over the past 20 years, the courts have broadened the circumstances in which injured parties may collect from manufacturers, a trend particularly cited regarding the pharmaceutical industry (250). They have also suggested that the frequency of large jury awards has increased for cases proceeding to trial, raising the degree of uncertainty surrounding expected liability losses for a manufacturer or its insurer (184).

While some argue that in the pharmaceutical sector these changes successfully protect the public from unsafe drugs (522), others suggest that increased liability, losses, and uncertainty affect R&D in two other ways:

- Costs associated with bringing a new pharmaceutical to market may rise as a result of additional research that firms may conduct to ensure the safety of new drugs (239).

- Firms may decide not to pursue areas of research or product development where they fear excessive liability costs will critically lower the potential return for a particular drug (236).

This chapter focuses largely on the second hypothesis, examining how product liability rules in the United States may affect the drug projects in which manufacturers choose to invest.

PRODUCT LIABILITY AND PHARMACEUTICAL R&D

The greatest impediment to understanding the effects of product liability on the drug R&D process is the lack of evidence on trends in pharmaceutical liability cases. Data on court cases are limited because the legal system adjudicates only a small fraction of all product liability claims and because there is no centralized database of all product liability cases filed and decided and no centralized record of settled claims.

The liability insurance industry is a poor source of information on the drug industry's product liability experiences because companies now largely self-insure for all but the highest liability losses. The best source of information on the costs and implications of product liability law in this industry are drug companies themselves. The Office of Technology Assessment (OTA) found no published data summarizing industry experience.[1]

Despite the lack of data, it is possible to sketch a rough picture of product liability trends in the research-based pharmaceutical industry from a variety of sources that are incomplete by themselves, including trends in law and insurance markets, a few in-depth studies of product liability litigation in particular jurisdictions, and anecdotal accounts of products particularly vulnerable to liability claims:

- Over the past 15 years, product liability claims and litigation against pharmaceutical manufacturers appear to have increased as measured by numbers of cases and changes in liability insurance. The legal circumstances under which courts hold pharmaceutical manufacturers responsible for injuries to consumers also broadened in recent years.
- The increase in liability claims is not uniform across all pharmaceutical products. Contraceptives, vaccines, and drugs taken during pregnancy appear to be particularly susceptible to liability claims. The vast majority of all product liability litigation in the health care sector over the past two decades is attributable to two products—the Dalkon Shield contraceptive and Bendectin,

a drug used to treat pregnancy-related nausea.

- While data suggest the average award per liability claim has increased substantially for pharmaceuticals, a very small number of cases with very large punitive damage awards explains the bulk of these increases. However, even excluding these very large cases, there has been a general increase in awards over time.
- Assessing the impact of increased product liability on pharmaceutical firms is difficult. No data exist to measure R&D and other business costs attributable to product liability. The little systematic research done to date on whether product liability affects the rate of pharmaceutical innovation has yielded inconclusive results. Evidence drawn from the experiences of particular products or from interviews with industry executives indicates liability may inhibit or preclude R&D or marketing of reproductive-related vaccines and products.
- Although the Federal Government has not adopted product liability reforms for therapeutic pharmaceuticals, several States have, and the Federal Government has adopted no-fault compensation schemes for swine flu and childhood vaccines that could offer potential models for Federal underwriting of other product liability risks. The U.S. Congress has also considered several proposals to adopt a Federal product liability law that would supersede current State law.

PHARMACEUTICALS AND PRODUCT LIABILITY LAW[2]

■ Establishing Legal Liability

Liability law in this country draws more from the common law precedents of previously de-

---

[1] A recent Institute of Medicine study of contraceptive R&D, however, conducted an informal survey of companies currently or formerly involved in researching new methods of birth control. The committee surveyed the companies about the implications of product liability on contraceptive business, but the committee report did not provide a wide range of survey results or any information about the representativeness of the sample (207).

[2] This section provides only a rough outline of some of the more important concepts of relevance to product liability for pharmaceuticals. These legal concepts have been described more fully elsewhere (250,371,413).

cided cases than from statute. Rather than having a single, uniform product liability system, the United States really has 51—one for each State and one for the Federal court system. The Federal system has jurisdiction only over product liability cases in which the parties reside in different States and one requests that the case be heard in Federal court (28 U.S.C. 1332). Hence, cases heard in different jurisdictions may operate under different theories and standards for establishing a pharmaceutical manufacturer's liability (265,443).

Even with these complexities, there are some common elements in pharmaceutical liability law. In determining whether the manufacturer is indeed liable for any injuries caused by the product in question, the courts tend to establish liability for pharmaceuticals in one of two ways:

1. The courts may consider whether a **design defect** makes the product unreasonably dangerous—i.e., whether the risk of a drug's use outweighs its utility. Although the American Law Institute (ALI)[3] recognized in its 1965 *Restatement (Second) of Torts* (Section 402A, Comment K) that pharmaceuticals have social value despite their potential to cause adverse reactions even when used as directed, some courts have applied the notion of **strict liability** to cases of injury associated with pharmaceuticals where there was no established negligence or malicious intent in the design and production of the drug[4] (247).

   According to this idea, liability lies with the party best able to prevent injury or absorb its costs—usually the manufacturer—even if that party was not responsible for causing the injury through negligence or intent (250). The courts may make this judgment independent of the U.S. Food and Drug Administration's (FDA) evaluation of the drug's safety and efficacy, although there is a great deal of uncertainty in how one establishes design defects in pharmaceuticals (142,413,416).

2. A more common means of claiming liability is to show a drug is "unreasonably dangerous as marketed" because the manufacturer has given inadequate warning of the drug's risks (413,416). Determination of a **failure to warn** focuses on information about the drug that the manufacturer targets to prescribing physicians. A warning may be inadequate because it is factually wrong or incomplete or because it is not conveyed in an effective way.

Even though the FDA must approve a drug's labeling, packaging materials, and advertising claims, courts have often found firms liable for adverse events that the FDA determined lacked a scientific basis for inclusion among the drug's warnings. Courts have also found inappropriate promotion can render warnings ineffective and the failure of a physician to consult materials describing a drug's risk (such as the *Physician's Desk Reference*) does not absolve the manufacturer of liability (413).

Once a court has determined that a manufacturer is liable for any injuries resulting from a pharmaceutical's use, the court must decide whether the product caused the specific injury in question. In cases where a class of plaintiffs (i.e., injured parties) cannot identify the specific manufacturer because of the passage of time, the courts of some States have adopted a "market share" theory to determine causality. Under this theory, plaintiffs may receive damage from all manufacturers of product in proportion to their market share (243,263).

---

[3] The ALI is a nonprofit membership association of judges, legal academicians, and lawyers. The institute's purpose is the "clarification and simplification of the law and its better adaptation to social needs."

[4] There have been relatively few cases where injured parties have established negligence in the *manufacture* of pharmaceuticals. Observers have suggested the FDA's tight regulation of Good Manufacturing Practices and quality control are the reason (416).

∎ Jury Awards

Across all types of liability (product, malpractice, and personal injury), in an average year only 2 percent of all insurance claims are resolved through litigation (i.e., a court case). Of these, only 5 percent (or 0.1 percent of all liability insurance claims) result in a trial verdict. The remainder are settled by the parties (247). Despite the relative infrequency of litigation, however, changes in judicial rules, decisions, and outcomes are important barometers of the total climate in which the U.S. product liability system exists.

In cases where courts establish a manufacturer's liability, juries' awards to the injured party have increased well in excess of the rate of inflation during recent years. While these verdicts comprise both compensatory and punitive awards, the bulk of the increase is attributable to punitive actions (192). A study by the Rand Corporation using data drawn from Cook County (Chicago) and San Francisco found substantial growth in the size of jury awards for all types of product liability suits.[5] From the 1960-64 to the 1980-84 period, the mean award for all product liability cases (not just pharmaceuticals) in San Francisco grew 1,116 percent in real terms and 312 percent in Cook County (318). In each city, the mean awards were substantially greater than the median, reflecting the small number of very large awards. The probability of actually winning a case that goes to court did not change over this period (318).

PRODUCT LIABILITY INSURANCE

Manufacturers traditionally protect themselves against the financial risk of product liability damage awards by buying insurance. Changes in pharmaceutical manufacturers' liability premiums, claims, and uninsured expenses provide a measure of the financial impact of product liability on a firm's cost of doing business and presumably reflect the changes in risk or expected losses posed by product liability claims.

Through the 1970s, most pharmaceutical firms protected themselves against liability losses with insurance that consisted of three pieces:

- The manufacturer paid a *deductible* for the first portion of each claim.
- Once the deductible was met, the *basic insurance* policy paid claims up to specified limits.
- Most companies also held *excess insurance* to pay claims above the basic policy up to another specified limit (443).

For the manufacturer, the total costs attributable to product liability include deductibles, any other losses not covered by insurance, any legal or administrative costs borne by the firm, and insurance policy premiums.

Most of the pharmaceutical firms interviewed by OTA indicated they can no longer get any basic insurance coverage in the traditional liability insurance market. The policies available today carry higher deductibles and premiums, with lower limits on how much they will pay per claim and in aggregate than did past policies (510). Some policies have excluded specific products or types of products thought to carry a higher than average risk of product liability loss. Consequently, pharmaceutical manufacturers have increasingly self-insured to compensate for lost basic insurance coverage by setting aside reserves to cover expected losses, establishing special lines of credit to cover unanticipated liability losses, and establishing "captured" insurance companies that are wholly or primarily owned by the insured pharmaceutical firm and have no other policyholders.[6]

Some companies also transfer a portion of their liability risk to insurance companies established in consortia with other manufacturers. Two exam-

---

[5] This research is limited. Variation between Cook County and San Francisco and between San Francisco and other California communities calls into question the representativeness of trends observed in these particular areas for product liability claims, suits, and awards to the country as a whole.

[6] Insurance industry observers have suggested that one reason for setting up a captured insurance company is some excess insurers require firms to have basic insurance in order to get an excess policy (510).

ples of such insurers mentioned to OTA by drug manufacturers are the American Casualty Excess, Ltd. (A.C.E.) and X.L. Insurance Company, Ltd. X.L. provides coverage below A.C.E., and A.C.E. insures against the highest losses suffered by a firm. Both insurers were established in the 1980s and are funded through premiums paid by manufacturers (243,490).[7]

PRODUCT LIABILITY CLAIMS AND R&D

Systematic attempts to determine product liability costs borne by the pharmaceutical industry, and the impact of product liability on firms' R&D decisions, innovation, and drug safety would require data from several sources, much of which is currently unavailable. Firms do not routinely report to the public on liability claims made on their products or settlements made by the firm or their insurers. Insurance companies collect data on claims made under their policies but do not report on claims associated with particular companies or products. For the minority of claims proceeding to litigation, court records exist but are not centralized across different State and local jurisdictions.

■ Overall Trends in Pharmaceutical Product Liability Litigation

TRENDS IN NUMBERS OF CASES

In 1988, researchers at the Rand Corporation analyzed product liability cases filed in the Federal District Courts between 1974 and 1986 to identify trends in the number of cases over time and their concentration within particular industries and products (115). They focused on the Federal court system because of the availability of a single computerized data system. However, these data have several limitations:

- Most product liability cases are heard in State courts, making the Rand analysis potentially unrepresentative of all litigation.
- The analysis is unrepresentative of product liability claims and settlements not resulting in litigation, which constitute the vast majority of all claims.
- The database records only the first named defendant in cases with more than one defendant.[8]
- Because this database does not mention the product involved in each suit, the Rand researchers classified defendants by the company's Standard Industrial Classification (SIC) code (which reflects the company's primary area of business activity). However, since many companies have diversified product lines, a suit against a firm with a pharmaceutical SIC code does not necessarily mean the suit itself concerns a pharmaceutical product.

The analysis found 85,694 different Federal product liability cases involving a total of 19,456 lead defendants. Pharmaceuticals and health care products represented 13.5 percent of the total cases but only 2.2 percent of the total number of defendants. Of the 11,292 suits for pharmaceutical and other health products filed, 72 percent are attributable to five firms, and 60 percent are attributable to two companies—A.H. Robins and Merrell Dow Pharmaceuticals.[9] Figures 7-1 and 7-2 show trends in these cases over time.

The Rand researchers concluded that A.H. Robins's Dalkon Shield contraceptive intrauterine device (IUD) and Merrell Dow's Bendectin antinausea medicine for pregnant women explained the bulk of liability cases for these two

---

[7] The Federal Government has tried to facilitate risk pooling by erasing barriers to firms or other organizations to form "risk retention groups" (RRGs) that write product and general liability insurance policies and collect premiums or "purchasing groups" (PG) that pool risk in order to get additional coverage or cheaper premiums than if they were purchasing insurance alone (Public Laws 97-45, 98-193, and 99-563). To date, firms have not made much use of these options (489,510), and pharmaceutical executives interviewed by OTA did not mention RRGs as part of their insurance protection against liability.

[8] The Rand researchers conducted a separate analysis of paper records of Federal product liability cases filed in California between 1977 and 1986. They found, on average, each case had 2.2 defendants, and codefendants (i.e., other than the lead defendant mentioned in the computerized Integrated Federal Courts Database) are sued infrequently in the Federal courts.

[9] A.H. Robins was the defendant in almost 5,700 cases, and Merrell Dow in just under 1,300.

firms. The dropoff in numbers of new cases involving these firms in 1985 and 1986 is attributable to a cutoff for new claims against the Dalkon Shield on April 30, 1986 (following A.H. Robins's bankruptcy in August 1985) and a district court ruling in favor of Merrell Dow in a February 1985 judgment involving 800 consolidated Bendectin suits. The Dalkon Shield and Bendectin cases are discussed further in the section that follows on products involving reproductive health.

Despite the overwhelming number of cases probably attributable to two products, the researchers noted a significant increase in the number attributable to other defendants during the 1980s and a contemporaneous increase in the number of defendants. The number of cases more

Figure 7-1—Filing Patterns of Federal Pharmaceutical Product Liability Cases, 1974-86

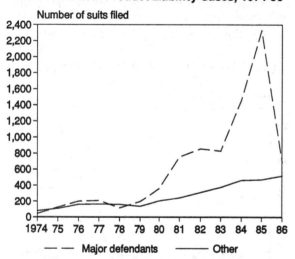

SOURCE: T. Dungworth, *Product Liability and the Business Sector: Litigation Trends in Federal Courts* (Santa Monica, CA: The Rand Corporation, 1988).

than doubled between 1981 and 1986, of a rate of increase greater than that for all Federal product liability cases during the same period.

In 1988, the U.S. General Accounting Office (GAO) published a study of its own examining trends in Federal product liability filings between

Figure 7-2—Federal Pharmaceutical Product Liability Patterns for Major Defendants, 1974-86

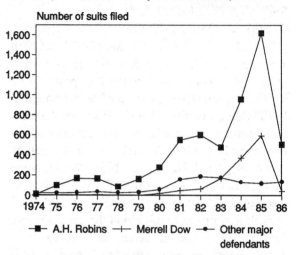

SOURCE: T. Dungworth, *Product Liability and the Business Sector: Litigation Trends in Federal Courts* (Santa Monica, CA: The Rand Corporation, 1988).

1974 and 1985 (432). Although GAO did not examine cases involving pharmaceuticals separately, it found that a few products—including the Dalkon Shield and Bendectin—were responsible for the bulk of the growth in filings during this period (432).

TRENDS IN JURY AWARDS AND JUDGMENTS AGAINST MANUFACTURERS

OTA found no systematic attempts to examine the monetary awards resulting from pharmaceutical product liability litigation. The Rand analysis of jury awards for all product liability cases (not just those involving drug companies) in San Francisco and Cook County showed that once sued, the number of claimants and the total amount claimed tended to be large and to have increased over time (318,388). Increases in the magnitude of the largest awards and in the probability of a plaintiff winning indicated manufacturers may have faced a greater expected loss if they allowed claims to proceed to trial.[10]

---

[10] Although there is no systematic analysis to date of jury awards specifically involving the pharmaceutical industry, the Rand Corporation is currently examining how product liability affects company decisionmaking and industrial economic performance (142).

■ Liability Claims Involving Reproductive Health Products

THE DALKON SHIELD AND OTHER CONTRACEPTIVES

The Dalkon Shield and Bendectin are both products intended to affect the reproductive health of women in childbearing years. A.H. Robins acquired the rights to the Dalkon Shield in 1970. Claims of the device's effectiveness as a contraceptive were based on a 1-year study of 640 women, which showed a 1.1-percent pregnancy rate during the trial period (103). At that time, Federal law did not require FDA approval of medical devices such as the Dalkon Shield.[11]

A.H. Robins began to market the contraceptive device in the United States in January 1971 despite questions among the firm's medical staff about the validity of conclusions drawn from the single effectiveness study (288).

During the first 3 years of marketing, A.H. Robins received evidence the Dalkon Shield could and did cause uterine infections and septic abortions, but it did not change the product or its labeling. In June 1974, A.H. Robins withdrew the device from the market after the U.S. Centers for Disease Control (CDC) had reported complications among 62 percent of women who became pregnant while wearing the Dalkon Shield (288).[12]

After the Dalkon Shield suits forced A.H. Robins into bankruptcy, the courts imposed an April 1986 filing deadline for new claims. By that time, about 320,000 claims had been filed against the firm for injury caused by the Dalkon Shield (206). Of the 4,400 claims resulting in litigation, A.H. Robins paid $250 million in out-of-court settlements and another $25 million in punitive awards imposed by 11 juries. As part of its bankruptcy plan, the courts required A.H. Robins set aside another $2.475 billion for unsettled claims (288).

Although the Dalkon Shield is not a pharmaceutical product, some observers have suggested that claims made against it have led to successful claims made against pharmaceutical products, including oral contraceptives (9,192). However, the data do not exist to measure whether there has been a significant increase in liability losses for contraceptives other than the Dalkon Shield. As measured in terms of decided court cases (i.e., not including those settled or otherwise resolved before completion of a trial), oral contraceptives show cyclical variation in numbers of cases over time, but the average number of cases within each cycle remained relatively constant between 1971 and 1988 (see figure 7-3).

BENDECTIN

First sold in the United States in 1956, Bendectin is a combination drug consisting of a vitamin, an antispasmodic, and a sedative. It is the only pharmaceutical ever approved in this country for the treatment of "morning sickness"

Figure 7-3—Yearly Reported Oral Contraceptive and IUD Liability Cases

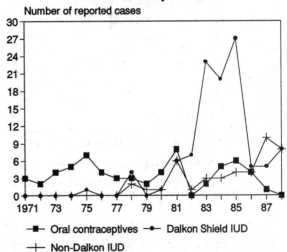

Number of reported cases

■— Oral contraceptives •— Dalkon Shield IUD

+— Non-Dalkon IUD

SOURCE: L. Mastroianni, P.J. Donaldson, and T.T. Kane (eds.), *Developing New Contraceptives: Obstacles and Opportunities* (Washington, DC: National Academy Press, 1990).

---

[11] Congress amended the Federal Food, Drug, and Cosmetic Act (21 U.S.C. 301 et seq.) in 1976 to require premarketing approval of medical devices (Public Law 99-295).

[12] Withdrawal from the market did not eliminate the potential for the IUD to cause new injuries, since many women kept implanted Dalkon Shields in place after 1974.

associated with pregnancy.[13] Beginning in 1969, the medical literature reported cases of congenital defects in babies born to women who had taken Bendectin during pregnancy. Because the number of deformities attributable to Bendectin was expected to be small if it *did* cause birth defects, establishing this relationship with any degree of statistical confidence was problematic.

Although the FDA concluded in 1980 that there was not enough evidence to ban Bendectin from the marketplace, it required the drug's manufacturer, Merrell Dow, to change its package insert to indicate while the drug had been carefully studied, it was impossible to prove it was without risk if taken as indicated (45 F.R. 80740).

As mentioned earlier, litigation proliferated despite the FDA's willingness to allow the drug's use. In the early 1980s, the courts consolidated 1,100 claims into a single, class-action suit that Merrell Dow offered to settle for $120 million. The plaintiffs rejected the offer, and the manufacturer successfully defended itself in a jury trial. Of the 17 Bendectin cases that had gone to trial by July 1987, Merrell Dow had prevailed in 12 (192). According to one source, total costs to Merrell Dow of defending itself against Bendectin's liability suits exceeded the $13 million in annual revenues the company received from sales of the drug, prompting the firm in 1985 to remove it voluntarily from the marketplace (61).

DES

First discovered in 1937, the synthetic form of estrogen called diethylstilbestrol (DES) was marketed as a generic product by over 300 manufacturers worldwide, especially during the 1950s, as a means of preventing miscarriages. However, research completed in 1971 showed a statistically significant association between DES use and clear-cell adenocarcinoma, a cancer of the glands, among daughters of women who had used the drug. This finding resulted in a large number of product liability suits against the drug's manufacturers.[14] Because of the large number of manufacturers involved and the long period between use of the drug and development of the cancer, the courts were unable to determine directly which manufacturer had caused each injury. The case of DES led the California Supreme Court to be the first to adopt the ''market share'' theory in attributing causality among drug manufacturers (142,192,263).

■ Liability Claims Involving Vaccines

Vaccines are another type of health care product frequently cited as prone to liability claims (9,239). Although they are usually not considered to be therapeutic pharmaceuticals—the type of health care product on which this report largely focuses—they are appropriately discussed in this chapter for several reasons:

- Because most vaccine manufacturers also produce pharmaceuticals, the behavior of firms responding to vaccine liability claims may be similar to their likely behavior in the face of pharmaceutical liability claims.
- The distinctions between vaccines and pharmaceuticals in terms of their underlying science and their R&D processes can be murky, particularly as more therapeutic pharmaceuticals rely on biotechnological techniques to replicate substances naturally found in living organisms as many vaccines traditionally have done.
- The Federal Government has attempted to absorb some of the product liability faced by vaccine manufacturers, potentially offering

---

[13] In 1972, as part of a review of drugs approved by the FDA before the imposition of the requirement that drugs show effectiveness to be marketed in the United States, the National Research Council and the National Academy of Sciences concluded there was no clinical evidence the antispasmodic contributed to the drug's therapeutic effect, and the manufacturer dropped this agent from the drug. This finding was unrelated to the claims that resulted in product liability litigation involving Bendectin (239).

[14] DES is not identified as a major product in the Rand analyses of Federal court cases described earlier in this chapter. This could reflect the fact that few DES cases were filed in Federal court (263). Alternatively, the number of DES cases in the Federal courts may be obscured because of a large number of DES manufacturers; the Rand analysis only identifies each case according to its ''lead'' defendant rather than by the product name or all codefendants (142).

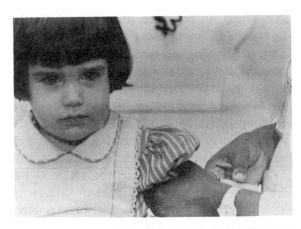

Photo credit: BRISTOL-MYERS SQUIBB COMPANY

Although vaccines can be an effective and cost-saving means of preventing diseases, manufacturers of these drugs have been the subject of many liability cases.

lessons and insights for policymakers considering greater Federal involvement in pharmaceutical liability.

All vaccines introduce some component of an organism that causes disease into the body in order to stimulate the immunized person's own system to produce antibodies against that disease.[15] For reasons not completely understood, some individuals exhibit reactions after receiving immunizations ranging from soreness in the arm to paralysis or brain damage (444). Determining the actual risk of serious harm for a given patient is difficult for two reasons: 1) they are rare; and 2) it is difficult to determine whether such harm would have occurred even if the patient had not received the vaccine (206).

The vaccine that has evoked the greatest liability concern to date is the pertussis compo-nent of the diphtheria-tetanus-pertussis (DTP) vaccine. The risk of encephalitic brain damage was estimated in a 1981 *British Medical Journal* article as 3.2 per million injections (9), although more recent U.S. epidemiological research has suggested the risk is actually much lower (165). Risks of serious complications from other vaccines appear to be even lower than that of DTP (9,444). Furthermore, vaccines are not mentioned as frequent subjects of lawsuits (115,432).

Why, then, are vaccines frequently cited as products bearing a heavy liability burden? The answer may lie in the nature of vaccine products and their differences from therapeutic pharmaceuticals, rather than in the risks or the absolute liability burden associated with vaccines. Vaccines are an effective and cost-saving means of preventing disease. Not only do the States require children to be immunized against the most serious childhood diseases, but the Federal Government supports vaccination activities for children and adults through a variety of grants and Medicare and Medicaid reimbursement (443,449). At the same time, however, some observers suggest vaccines have relatively low profit margins (239).

The legal burden for vaccine manufacturers also rests on somewhat different grounds than it does for drug manufacturers. While courts have found in most drug and contraceptive cases that companies have fulfilled their duty to warn of adverse reactions by adequately informing physicians of risks,[16] some courts have ruled that because there is no personalized relationship between physician and patient in mass immunization programs manufacturers must provide warn-

---

[15] There are four main strategies vaccines can adopt in producing immunity:

1) "Killed" or "inactivated" vaccines contain dead cells of the bacteria or virus that causes the disease to be prevented. Examples include the Salk polio vaccine and the pertussis vaccine.

2) "Live attenuated" vaccines contain living versions of a disease-causing virus that have been weakened in the laboratory. The Sabin polio vaccine and the vaccines against mumps, measles, and rubella are live attenuated.

3) "Toxoid" vaccines, such as those that prevent diphtheria and tetanus, contain weakened versions of poisonous toxins produced by the disease-causing bacteria (206).

4) Newer, "acellular" vaccines, which contain only pieces of the disease-causing bacteria, have been developed in the search for a safer means of immunizing against pertussis (239).

[16] This is sometimes referred to as the "learned intermediary" rule.

ings directly to patients.[17] Finally, many vaccines, especially the DPT immunizations, have relatively common, nonserious, but disquieting adverse reactions such as fever, inconsolable crying, localized soreness, rashes, and malaise (444). Such side effects may create the perception among health care consumers that the risk of serious injury is greater than it really is; patients may be more likely to claim that health problems occurring subsequent to vaccination occurred because of the vaccination.

■ Evidence Concerning Product Liability and Innovation

Given the discernible patterns of product liability claims and costs described above, what is known about their effects on the pharmaceutical R&D process? There are at least two hypotheses one could attempt to test:

- Product liability could increase R&D costs and lengthen the R&D process as firms perform "defensive studies" to help protect themselves from subsequent negligence claims and as they absorb the costs of liability for a drug administered during the clinical R&D phase.
- Product liability burdens could lead firms not to fund R&D in certain areas or ultimately not market certain products.

OTA found no studies or other evidence that allow one to test the first of these hypotheses. In addition, it was not cited by pharmaceutical industry officials in any of OTA's interviews at eight drug firms. Hence, OTA is unable to shed any additional light on this possible corporate response to product liability. However, there is evidence (albeit largely anecdotal) that bears on the second hypothesis.

PRODUCT LIABILITY AND FIRMS' WILLINGNESS TO CONDUCT R&D

OTA found only one attempt to bring together industrywide data to determine if product liability inhibits pharmaceutical innovation. In a 1991 study, Viscusi and Moore compiled data for pharmaceuticals and several other manufacturing industries for the first half of the 1980s on both product liability insurance experience and innovation (501). They concluded that during the period examined pharmaceuticals were both relatively innovative and subject to a volatile liability burden—that do not lend support to the hypothesis that product liability inhibits innovation. However, their study does not control for other factors that might have affected innovation.[18] In addition, their examination of industrywide data may obscure differences in access to various types of pharmaceuticals.

Much of the remaining evidence on product liability and pharmaceutical innovation is anec-

---

[17] The precedent-setting case was *Davis* v. *Wyeth Laboratories*, 399 F.2d 121 (9th Cir. 1968), which dealt with a polio vaccine administered in a mass immunization clinic. *Reyes* v. *Wyeth Laboratory*, 498 F.2d 1264 (5th Cir. 1974), reinforced this decision by ruling the manufacturer was liable because of inadequate warning even though it had manufactured the vaccine properly with printed warnings and there was good evidence the plaintiff's polio was caused by a virus not found in the vaccine. In this latter case, the court indicated firms should bear the cost of a potential vaccine-induced injury as a predictable business expense, passing the cost on to consumers in the price of the vaccine rather than placing the loss on the injured party (443). However, in another Federal case decided this year, *Mazur* v. *Merck*, the court actually ruled a manufacturer was *not* liable for an injury that occurred in a 1982 mass immunization program because a Federal agency, the U.S. Centers for Disease Control, had agreed to convey warnings to the patient (404).

[18] They point out several other limitations of the data they present:

1) The statistics on innovation are measured at the beginning of the period examined (1980), and almost no firm changed its responses in the subsequent annual surveys conducted. Hence, there is no measured variation in innovation over time in this database or any way to determine if innovation would have been different with less or more product liability burden.

2) The statistics on product liability are likely not to be an accurate reflection of product liability activity in the pharmaceutical industry because the authors depend on insurance data and much of the transition to self-insurance for drug manufacturers occurred before 1980.

3) The largest number of liability cases (as suggested in the Rand and GAO data) and the greatest amount of attention to product liability occurred during 1985 and 1986—after the collection of the data that Viscusi and Moore examine.

dotal and tends to fall into one of two lines of argument. One line of argument cites the discontinuation of products associated with high liability costs as evidence of how product liability directly limits the availability of products to consumers and as an indirect indication that liability could inhibit R&D for similar types of products. Among the products cited are the Dalkon Shield, Bendectin,[19] thalidomide as a sedative for nonpregnant women (239), and vaccines against DPT, Japanese encephalitis (254), and swine flu (293).

The second line of argument directly attributes certain changes in firms' R&D portfolios to product liability. The examples to support this argument are somewhat more general than those given above, perhaps because of the confidential nature of most firms' R&D portfolios.[20] Among the examples encountered by OTA:

- *Contraceptive R&D*—The number of large, U.S. research-based pharmaceutical firms engaged in contraceptive R&D has dropped in recent years from nine to two.[21] Product liability is the most-often cited reason for the decision to end such research programs (89).[22]

- *Pharmaceuticals Taken During Pregnancy*—Members of the legal staff at several pharmaceutical firms interviewed by OTA for this report indicated they would raise concerns about any potential product to be given to pregnant women. The lawyers tied their concerns specifically to the Bendectin expe-

rience. Other analysts have made similar findings (348).

- *Vaccines Against Human Immunodeficiency Virus (HIV)*—Legal staff at a firm engaged in R&D to develop a vaccine against HIV told OTA that liability was a significant consideration each time the company decided to continue this research. Furthermore, the firm's insurer was reluctant to provide any coverage for a potential product. Legal staff at two other companies indicated their liability insurers[23] asked the firms to inform them if they decided to engage in HIV vaccine R&D. In a recent case, Abbott Laboratories withdrew its participation in a planned NIH clinical trial that would have tested vaccine to ensure pregnant HIV positive women from passing the virus to their unborn children. Abbott cited fear of liability in its decision not to provide NIH with the vaccine, called HIV hyperimmune globulin (HIVIG) (81). Other groups have also cited potential liability problems surrounding the search for a product to prevent HIV infection (9,231).

Some observers suggest the impact of liability can be inferred from the complexity and extent of safety testing necessary to receive FDA marketing approval. According to this line of argument, these regulatory requirements are largely driven by public concerns that products not cause injury, the basis for liability (243).

---

[19] The liability experience of this drug and its withdrawal from the market has actually led one author to suggest that no company will *ever* again seek to market a drug to treat nausea associated with pregnancy (239).

[20] In OTA's interviews at eight research-based pharmaceutical firms, company officials offered specific examples of R&D projects abandoned or forgone because of liability concerns, but all firms asked that they not be identified by name with these decisions.

[21] Ortho Pharmaceuticals, a subsidiary of Johnson & Johnson, has had an ongoing contraceptive R&D program. Eight companies that have discontinued such R&D are: Syntex, Searle, Parke-Davis, Merck, Upjohn, Mead Johnson, Wyeth-Ayerst, and Eli Lilly (207). Wyeth-Ayerst, a subsidiary of American Home Products, has renewed its contraceptive R&D program in recent years, focusing on new forms of oral contraceptives (8,251). In addition, a relatively new, small firm, Gynco-Pharma, currently markets a copper IUD. Non-U.S. firms as well as universities and nonprofit foundations also carry on R&D on new forms of birth control (207).

[22] However, product liability is not the only reason cited. Others include limitations on patents that make potential products possibly unprofitable and perceived public pressure not to engage in contraceptive R&D (89).

[23] In each case, the firms had only excess product liability insurance and self-insured against lesser claims.

GOVERNMENT POLICY AND PRODUCT LIABILITY

To what extent has government intervened in recent years to alter product liability rules or to affect the outcomes of liability claims? This section reviews recent policy initiatives of potential relevance to pharmaceutical liability.

■ Tort Reform

As States have developed different case law, some have also enacted statutes designed to alter liability law, usually in response to the perceived ill effects of court decisions. Although some attempts at changing liability law have been found in most States, a Federal review of statutes adopted by State legislatures during 1986 alone revealed the actual provisions adopted vary greatly. The most common reform (enacted by 16 States) altered the doctrine of "joint and several liability" which allows multiple defendants named in a lawsuit all to be held responsible. Observers have suggested under this doctrine the wealthiest defendant often pays all or most of the damages whatever the defendant's actual degree of responsibility for causing the injury (265). Other provisions adopted by States include limitations on noneconomic and punitive damages, limitations on attorney's contingency fees, allowance for periodic payment of damage awards instead of requiring a lump sum, and modification of the "collateral source rule," which prohibits courts from considering other sources of compensation (such as personal health insurance benefits) a plaintiff may receive (490).

Over the past decade, Congress has considered several Federal product liability statutes that would supersede any relevant State statute or case law. The 101st Congress considered, but did not adopt, "The Product Liability Reform Act" (S. 101-1400).[24] Of particular importance to the pharmaceutical industry, the bill would bar punitive damages for drugs or medical devices receiving approval from the FDA unless the manufacturer had withheld or misrepresented relevant information from the agency. Among other provisions of the bill were limitations on punitive damages, limits on the amount of time in which a plaintiff can bring a claim, a limitation of joint and several liability[25] to compensatory (nonpunitive) damages only, and incentives for parties to settle the case prior to trial (442).[26]

One recent study suggests case law as well may be moving away from the expansion of liability and damages. In a quantitative analysis of recent State court decisions in product liability cases, Henderson and Eisenberg suggest that since the early to mid-1980s, courtroom decisions have subtly begun to favor manufacturers by placing limitations on injured parties' ability to receive damages. They show this change predates many of the statutory reforms described above. While such tendencies are becoming evident, the authors point out it still may be too early to assess their ultimate impact (182).

■ Federal Compensation for Injuries Associated With Health Care Products

To date, the Federal Government has not established any alternative or additional remedy for injuries associated with therapeutic pharmaceuticals.[27] However, on two separate occasions, Congress has adopted compensation schemes for vaccine-related injuries.

---

[24] Senate Bill 1400 (101st Congress) was very similar to several earlier product liability reform bills: S. 666 (100th Congress) and S. 2790 (99th Congress).

[25] "Joint and several liability" refers to the liability of each defendant for all damages even if more than one defendant is found liable.

[26] Introduced by Senator Robert W. Kasten in July 1989, the bill reached was reported out of committee (Senate Report 101-356), but not debated on the floor before the end of the session. Senator Kasten reintroduced this legislation in the 102d Congress (S. 640).

[27] As mentioned earlier in this chapter, Congress has considered adopting national tort law standards, including proposals to protect manufacturers from punitive damage awards for products approved by the FDA unless the manufacturer has acted fraudulently.

[28] In January 1976, several soldiers at Fort Dix (New Jersey) became sick with influenza found by the CDC to be caused by the swine flu virus responsible for the worldwide influenza epidemic in 1918-19 that killed 20 million (293).

THE SWINE FLU IMMUNIZATION PROGRAM

In August 1976, in the face of an epidemic of swine flu expected during the winter of 1976-77,[28] Congress established a national immunization program (Public Law 94-380). As part of this legislation, the Federal Government agreed to accept liability for vaccine-related injuries. Because insurers had excluded the vaccine from product liability policies, manufacturers were unwilling to supply it without Federal intervention. Under this law, people who believed themselves to have been injured could not sue, but were permitted to make claims against the United States within 2 years of the vaccination according to the theories of liability in practice in the State where the injury took place (169).

The U.S. Department of Health, Education, and Welfare (DHEW) (now the U.S. Department of Health and Human Services (DHHS)) halted the immunization program in December 1976 after several vaccinated individuals contracted Guillain-Barré syndrome, a condition that leads to paralysis.[29] About 40 million people had received the vaccine. In June 1978, DHEW announced that because the vaccine label and consent form did not warn recipients about the possibility of Guillain-Barré, those claiming injury did not need to prove fault (i.e., negligence by the government) in order to receive compensation. Out of the 4,179 claims and 1,604 lawsuits filed against the government under the swine flu program, the government paid a total of $90.1 million in 709 settled claims, 391 settled suits, and 105 judgments in favor of the claimants (169).[30]

THE NATIONAL CHILDHOOD VACCINE INJURY ACT OF 1986

In response to concern over the ability of the dwindling number of vaccine manufacturers to provide adequate supplies of vaccine for childhood immunization during the 1980s, Congress adopted a no-fault alternative to product liability litigation for people seeking compensation for injuries related to childhood vaccines administered up to 8 years prior to the enactment of the legislation (Public Law 99-660, Title III). Under the act, Congress determines which vaccines are included, and the Secretary of DHHS determines what types of injuries are eligible for compensation through regulation.[31]

Although claimants may still choose to pursue compensation, this statute essentially constitutes Federal tort reform for eligible childhood vaccine-related injuries. By establishing a no-fault compensation scheme as the first form of redress for injuries and limiting liability for manufacturers who have met FDA requirements, Congress has, in essence, nullified case law that had previously allowed liability findings based on theories of

---

[29] In addition, the epidemic of swine flu never occurred.

[30] According to Hagan, at the time these data were gathered in January 1989, 2 claims and 17 lawsuits were still to be resolved (169).

[31] Currently, the program includes vaccines for measles, mumps, polio, rubella, and diptheria/pertussis/tetanus (DPT). The law prohibits anyone from seeking awards of more than $1,000 or for an unspecified amount though civil litigation without first filing a petition for compensation with the U.S. Claims Court and the Secretary of DHHS.

Compensation can include nonlegal expenses incurred as a result of the injury, lost earnings, and death up to $250,000. The program allows compensation for attorneys' fees regardless of the outcome of the petition.

The compensation mechanism is "nonexclusive" in that claimants may choose to pursue remedies through the courts rather than accepting an award through the no-fault process. However, if a claimant sues, the law tries to protect manufacturers from claims of design defect if they have complied with all relevant FDA regulations in establishing a drug's safety and efficacy.

Compensation for vaccines administered before October 1, 1988 comes from appropriated funds which have averaged $80 million per year since Congress first funded the program in fiscal year 1989 (Public Law 100-436). A tax added to the cost of each vaccine funds a National Vaccine Injury Compensation Trust Fund, which pays damages awarded for vaccines administered after October 1, 1988. The tax rate is set according to evidence about the frequency and expected damages associated with each type of vaccine (169).

As of June 18, 1991, the U.S. Health Resources Services Administration, which is charged with implementing the compensation program within DHHS, had received 4,095 petitions for pre-October 1988 injuries and 127 for injuries on or after October 1, 1988. Of the 306 petitions acted on as of June 18, 1991, 66 were withdrawn or dismissed before being adjudicated, 188 were deemed compensable, and the remaining were ruled not compensable. The government has paid a total of $122.4 million in awards that individually ranged from $48,510 to $2.9 million. The average award for pre-1988 cases is $1.2 million (465).

strict liability and a failure to warn. The experience of this program could offer insights into the potential effects of adopting a similar no-fault compensation system for acquired immunodeficiency syndrome (AIDS) vaccines, as suggested by the Keystone AIDS Vaccine Liability Project (231), or into the implications of other product liability reform proposals like those mentioned earlier in this chapter.

CONCLUSIONS

Despite a lack of systematic data, it is possible to piece together the major implications of product liability on pharmaceutical R&D. Although health care products appear to be a part, if not a significant part, of the increase in product liability litigation over the last 20 years, the vast majority of health-care-related cases have involved only certain types of products, contraceptives, and other pharmaceuticals that affect reproductive health, and vaccines. Although some firms continue to pursue R&D in these areas, anecdotal evidence suggests liability concerns may significantly inhibit the overall level of industrial R&D effort in these areas. Both industry and government have implemented novel forms of underwriting health-care product liability risks, although no systematic evidence exists to evaluate the extent to which these programs enhance firms' willingness to conduct R&D for vaccines and reproductive health products. As suggested by recent experience, fear of product liability may be a particularly significant barrier to industry's willingness to develop, test, and market potential vaccines against HIV and may become a major policy concern for the Federal Government.

Federal Tax Policy and Drug Research and Development[1] | 8

T
he taxes paid by pharmaceutical companies alter both the net cost of pharmaceutical research and development (R&D) and the ultimate returns on R&D investments. This chapter examines U.S. tax code provisions that directly affect R&D or are of particular relevance to the pharmaceutical industry. It describes the incentives for taxpaying companies to alter their R&D behavior, and it estimates the actual impact of these provisions on the Federal Treasury and on drug companies.

ANALYZING TAX POLICY

Federal corporate income tax policy comprises laws and regulations that define income subject to taxation, adjustments to taxable income (deductions), tax rates, and adjustments to tax payments (tax credits and minimum tax payments). Tax code provisions are not just intended to raise revenue; they are also structured to provide taxpayers with incentives to spend or invest in desirable ways. Most of these incentives are either deductions from taxable income or credits against tax liability. For example, the tax code contains tax credits to encourage firms to perform more R&D and to make the United States competitive with other nations as a place to locate business. Similar tax deductions exist for some R&D expenses not eligible for these tax credits. Because each of these provisions reduces the taxes that the Federal Government collects from firms, they are sometimes referred to as "tax expenditures" (241). While any taxpayer theoretically could take advantage of any of these incentives, in reality many provisions have requirements that preclude their use except by certain types of taxpayers. This review focuses on components of the tax code that either directly affect industrial

---

[1] This chapter is based in part on two papers prepared under contract for the Office of Technology Assessment (7,245).

R&D expenditures or are used by the pharmaceutical industry more (in terms of Federal tax expenditures) than by other industries.

A common measure of the impact of tax policy on a firm's or industry's operation is the *average effective tax rate*, the ratio of actual income tax paid to the pretax income of a taxpayer or a group of taxpayers (such as the whole pharmaceutical industry). This measure of tax burden assesses the equity of taxes paid across different kinds of taxpayers or in examinations of corporate profits and profit rates.

Because the average effective tax rate combines the effects of all provisions of the tax code, it obscures differences in the tax rate that apply to different kinds of assets or across different firms within an industry (7). This chapter does not contain estimates of average effective tax rates in the pharmaceutical industry, but it does contain estimates of each tax credit in the U.S. Federal Tax Code as a percent of the pharmaceutical industry's taxable income. This measure is the difference between two average effective tax rates: the average rate without a credit minus the average rate with the credit.

To examine the effects of particular tax credits on pharmaceutical R&D investment, a more useful measure is the *marginal incentive effect* or *marginal credit rate* (5). This rate is the number of cents that a tax credit reduces the "cost" of an additional dollar that the taxpayer decides to spend on R&D. The "credit rate" is a negative tax rate. Because of limitations on particular tax credits, the effective marginal credit rate can be different from the "statutory rate."[2] This chapter reviews what is known about the marginal credit rate associated with each of the several tax credit provisions affecting pharmaceutical operations.

The *aggregate impact of a tax credit* is the extent to which it achieves its policy goal. For example, the goal of a tax credit is to increase corporate investment in R&D. The Office of Technology Assessment (OTA) did not measure policy impacts of the tax provisions affecting the pharmaceutical industry.[3]

Finally, a measure of the Federal Treasury's cost is the *net subsidy of a tax credit or deduction*. The value of tax credits claimed by taxpayers represents a dollar-for-dollar cost to the Federal Treasury. OTA estimated Federal tax subsidies associated with tax credits claimed by the pharmaceutical industry.

TAX DEDUCTIONS AND TAXABLE INCOME

■ Deductions of R&D Expenses From Taxable Income

Section 174 of the Internal Revenue Code permits businesses to fully deduct R&D expenditures in the year incurred—a practice referred to as "expensing."[4] In contrast, Federal income tax law does not permit expensing of outlays made on other kinds of investments such as machinery, equipment, or facilities that remain useful for a number of years.[5] The immediate expensing of R&D creates an incentive for a taxpaying firm to conduct R&D, because a tax deduction taken today is worth more than one that must be taken in the future. Firms do have the option to deduct R&D expenditures made in a particular year over a period of at least 5 years beginning with the month in which revenues first flow into the firm from the R&D. The deferral option is meant to benefit small or newer firms with little or no taxable income during their early years.

When it was written in 1954, section 174 gave little indication of what activities qualified as

---

[2] The statutory rate is the rate written into the internal revenue code.

[3] Analyses of the impact of the R&D tax credit on aggregate R&D investment, see (33,437).

[4] R&D is referred to in the tax code as research and experimentation (R&E). In this chapter OTA uses the term R&D to refer to R&E expenses covered under five tax code provisions.

[5] The cost of other investments is recognized over time through "depreciation allowances." The term "depreciation" refers to the allocation of the cost of a long-lived asset over its useful life.

R&D. Subsequent regulations, first adopted in 1957, provided more detailed guidelines (26 CFR 1.174). According to these regulations, the deduction is for "research and development costs in the experimental or laboratory sense," including all expenditures incident to the development of an experimental or pilot model, a plant process, a product, a formula, an invention or similar property, and improvements to existing property similar to these types. It also includes the cost of obtaining a patent.

Specifically excluded from the definition of qualifying R&D expenditures are those for testing quality control, management studies, advertising and promotion, market research, sales promotion, sales service, research in the social sciences or psychology, and other nontechnological activities or routine technical services. In interviews with executives at eight research-intensive pharmaceutical firms and with Internal Revenue Service (IRS) examiners responsible for auditing R&D deductions, OTA found that the IRS interprets these regulations to exclude the cost of developing software used in the R&D process as well as all management functions except the direct supervision of scientists and technicians. The regulations do permit firms to deduct the expense of qualifying R&D that the firm has commissioned and paid another organization to perform on its behalf.

In regulations proposed in 1989 (54 FR 21224), the IRS specifically discussed the application of section 174 to pharmaceutical R&D. The proposed regulations included the following very specific example:

> Example (9): C, a biotechnology firm developed a new drug that substantially lowers blood pressure. Prior to marketing the drug, C incurs costs to test the product and obtain U.S. Food and Drug Administration (FDA) approval of the drug.

The costs incurred by C to develop, test, and receive government approval of the drug are research and experimental expenditures within the meaning of section 174.

Although this interpretation has not yet been adopted as a final regulation, the IRS is currently interpreting the rules in this way.

If expenditures are disallowed by the IRS as qualifying R&D expenses under section 174, they can still be deducted as ordinary business expenses. However, the definition of R&D is the basis for allowing research expenses to count for a Federal R&D tax credit, which is discussed later in this chapter.

FOREIGN SALES AND DEDUCTION OF U.S. R&D EXPENSES

One provision of the tax code, currently suspended by congressional action,[6] could serve as a *disincentive* for multinational firms to locate R&D in the United States. A 1977 Treasury Department regulation (CFR 1.861-8) would limit the extent to which multinational firms could deduct expenses for qualified R&D conducted in the United States (CFR 1.861-8). The rationale for the regulation is that if a firm spends money for R&D in the United States and the resulting products or processes are sold abroad, then a portion of these R&D costs should be allocated against foreign sales. As discussed later in the section on foreign tax credits, foreign sales are subject to special U.S. tax provisions designed to provide some allowances for income taxes paid abroad. Because the U.S. tax rules governing income from foreign sources lead to higher effective tax rates on foreign income than on domestic income,[7] this regulation may provide an incentive for multinational firms to export a portion of R&D overseas (245). Because the research-intensive segment of the pharmaceutical industry is multinational, the incentive to locate

---

[6] In 1981, Congress passed a 2-year moratorium of U.S. Treasury regulation 1.861-8 (Public Law 97-34). Although Congress has never made the moratorium permanent, it has renewed the moratorium for a temporary period at each expiration. Most recently, the Omnibus Budget Reconciliation Act of 1990 extended the moratorium through the 1991 tax year (Public Law 101-508).

[7] Most other nations with provisions permitting the deduction of R&D expenses from taxable income do not disallow part of this deduction for foreign sales.

R&D outside the United States is especially important for the pharmaceutical industry.

■ Deduction for Contributions to Scientific Organizations

The internal revenue code allows corporations to deduct up to 5 percent of their taxable income for contributions to educational and scientific organizations held to be operating in the public interest (section 170a). The income of these scientific and educational organizations operated in the public interest is exempt from Federal income tax (section 501a-c). The operating standard for research in the public interest is that the work must result in information "published in a treatise, thesis, trade publication, or in any other form that is available to the interested public." If met, the research-performing institution qualifies for the tax exemption even if the research is performed under "a contract or agreement under which the sponsor or sponsors of the research have the right to obtain ownership or control of any patents, copyrights, processes, or formulae resulting from such research."[8] Under this provision, pharmaceutical firms that contract with academic institutions or donate R&D resources to such institutions can reap the commercial benefits of sponsored research at a cost that is net of taxes.

■ Depreciation of Capital Assets Used for R&D

In addition to resources that qualify for the section 174 deduction discussed earlier (such as salaries and depletable supplies), pharmaceutical R&D also requires the use of capital assets such as machinery, equipment, and facilities. The tax code requires companies to depreciate these costs instead of deducting the total investment in the year it was made.

Prior to 1981, firms were required to depreciate equal portions of a capital expenditure used in R&D (as well as assets used in other activities) each year over its whole useful life (which could be 10 or more years). The Economic Recovery Tax Act of 1981, or ERTA (Public Law 97-34), altered this practice by establishing an "accelerated cost recovery system" (ACRS). Under ACRS, firms can depreciate all capital expenditures for R&D over a 3-year period regardless of their useful lives.[9] Congress further enhanced this provision by giving companies a 6-percent tax credit for all new capital investment for tax years 1982 through 1986.[10] The Tax Reform Act of 1986 (Public Law 99-514) required firms to depreciate such investments over 5 years instead of 3.

Because tax savings realized sooner are worth more to pharmaceutical companies than those realized later, ACRS represents a net decrease in the cost of R&D-related capital investment and therefore an incentive for firms to expand their U.S. R&D efforts.

TAX CREDITS

■ R&D-Related Tax Credits

TAX CREDIT FOR INCREASING RESEARCH EXPENSES

A significant change in the tax treatment of R&D occurred with the enactment of ERTA in 1981. Among four major provisions related to

---

[8] As noted earlier, the section 174 deduction for qualifying R&D also permits firms to deduct the cost of R&D conducted by another organization. How then does the section 170(a) deduction differ from section 174 deduction? While it is possible that for a firm in the position of providing funds to another organization for research, the two deductions are, in practice, indistinguishable, it is also possible that the particular provisions of each deduction noted in the text may limit its usefulness to the firm. To use the section 174 deduction, the research performed must meet the definition of qualifying R&D discussed earlier in this chapter, whereas section 170(1) is less restrictive. Hence, the R&D expenses deductible under 170(a) may be greater than under 174. To use the section 170(a) deduction, however, the results of the research must be openly published, thus eliminating the possibility of trade secrets. Furthermore, for corporations the total amount of all 170(a) deductions must be less than 5 percent of taxable income.

[9] Capital expenditures for non-R&D assets are depreciated over 3 years or longer periods under ACRS (335). Hence R&D assets were advantaged by the system put in place in 1981 when compared with all non-R&D assets as a group.

[10] This investment tax credit was not renewed when it expired in 1986.

Photo credit: NATIONAL INSTITUTES OF HEALTH

The Economic Recovery Tax Act of 1981 allowed pharmaceutical companies to depreciate all expenditures for R&D facilities and equipment over a 3-year period. The Tax Reform Act of 1986 lengthened this depreciation period to 5 years.

R&D in ERTA was a new tax credit for *increases* in R&D expenditures.[10] The credit was originally equal to 25 percent of the difference between qualified R&D expenses in the current tax year and the average amount spent during the previous 3 taxable years, or 50 percent of current year expenditures, whichever is greater. Qualifying expenditures include company-financed expenditures for R&D wages and supplies, 65 percent of the amount paid for contracted research, and 65 percent of corporate grants to universities and scientific research organizations for basic research. Expenses must be paid by the taxable year and must pertain to the carrying on of a trade or business. Thus, the credit was originally not available to startup companies, certain joint ventures, or existing firms entering into a new line of business.

The credit has several important limitations. The requirement for "carrying on a trade or business" means that expenses incurred in connection with trade or business but not pertaining to the development of potentially marketable goods and services failed to qualify. For example,

development of new business accounting software would not qualify. Perhaps as important, the courts have interpreted this limitation to exclude research expenditures paid or incurred prior to commencing a trade or business (29). Only wages paid for doing actual research work qualified for the credit. Thus, wages for laboratory scientists and engineers and their immediate supervisors qualified, but wages for general administrative personnel or other auxiliary personnel (such as computer technicians working in a multipurpose computer and information-processing department) did not. Research done outside of the United States was also excluded.

Companies with insufficient tax liabilities to use credits in the year they are earned may "carryback" these credits for up to 3 years to offset past tax liabilities, or they may "carryforward" for up to 15 years to offset future tax obligations (26 CFR 38-39). Credits carried forward in time do not earn interest, making them less valuable than those that can be used in the year they are earned.

Since its enactment in 1981, the provisions of the R&D tax credit have changed several times. The Tax Reform Act of 1986 (Public Law 99-514) reduced the statutory credit rate from 25 to 20 percent. The law also narrowed the definition of qualified research to emphasize the discovery and experimentation stages of the innovation process, thus eliminating expenditures for product modifications after they reach their functional specifications (441). The legislative history of the Tax Reform Act clearly states that all R&D necessary to obtain approval from the FDA to market a pharmaceutical in the United States for one or more indications qualifies for the tax credit (Public Law 99-514, L.H. II-75).

Further changes in the tax credit enacted in the 1988 Technical and Miscellaneous Revenue Act (TAMRA) (Public Law 100-647) reduced the

---

[10] The other three provisions were: 1) an allowance for faster depreciation of R&D assets (discussed earlier in the text), 2) an increase in the deduction for newly manufactured research equipment donated to universities, and 3) a 2-year suspension of a 1977 Treasury Department regulation (FR 1.861-8) requiring a portion of R&D expenses for products or processes sold abroad to be allocated against foreign sales, thus reducing the value of the R&D deduction for U.S. taxes (also discussed earlier in the chapter) (357).

effective credit rate from 20 percent before TAMRA to 16.6 percent (233). The Omnibus Budget Reconciliation Act of 1989 (Public Law 101-239) extended the tax credit through September 1990 but also made changes that had important effects on its value to firms (33,233). In addition, as a company's rate of R&D growth (i.e., the annual percentage increase in R&D from one year to the next) goes up, so too does the probability that the credit will be subject to limitations. Baily and Lawrence (33) showed that a company first faces the limitations in the credit at growth rates above 36 percent. This provision of the law limited the ability of fast growing but small research intensive R&D firms (such as many biotechnology firms) to claim high credits.

Congress twice extended the version of the R&D tax credit as adopted in 1989 (Public Law 101-508; Public Law 102-227), although it expired in June 1992. Congress passed another extension as part of the Revenue Act of 1992 (H.R. 102-11) which President Bush vetoed November 1992.

A number of researchers have estimated the effective marginal credit rate (the percent reduction in the cost of R&D) implicit in the several incarnations of this tax credit using a variety of methods and assumptions; they have found effective credit rates that are substantially less than the statutory rates of 20 or 25 percent. The divergence between the effective and statutory rates stems from the way in which the credit is calculated, the interaction of the credit with other provisions of the internal revenue code,[11] the rate at which future savings are discounted to their present value, and the fact that not all firms have sufficient tax liability to use credits in the year they are earned.

Baily and Lawrence (33) estimated marginal effective credit rates for the R&D tax credit as it changed over the course of the 1980s. Assuming that a firm could take full advantage of the credit beginning in the first year it was available and assuming a (before-tax) interest rate of 12 percent, they calculated that the 1981 credit reduced the cost of qualified R&D by 9.3 percent. The 1986 changes in the credit and in corporate tax rates reduced this effective rate to 6.1 percent by 1988; alterations made in 1988 further reduced the marginal effective credit rate to 4 percent.

These calculations do not take into account the fact that not all firms could use the credit. Some were not expanding their R&D, making them ineligible for the credit since it was based on increases in research spending, while others did not have sufficient tax liability to use the credits. Other firms may have increased R&D spending so rapidly that they were subject to upper limits on the credit. To correct for these instances, Baily and Lawrence reduced the calculated rate by 30 percent, based on estimates that 30 percent of company-financed research expenditures across all industries from 1981 to 1985 did not qualify for the credit (437). After this correction, the marginal effective credit rate declined from 6.5 to 2.8 percent between 1981 and 1989. This marginal effective rate is an average across all firms in all industries. The pharmaceutical industry might have a higher effective credit because pharmaceutical R&D expenditures increased faster than R&D in most other industries in the 1980s (290). Individual pharmaceutical companies probably vary greatly in their marginal effective credit rate depending on their R&D expenditures.

Altshuler used a different approach to estimate marginal credit rates (5). Using data from the IRS, she modeled the extent to which any particular type of firm was able to use the R&D tax credit between 1981 and 1984. This model accounted for the carryforward and carrybacks of unused credits. Altshuler estimated the marginal effective credit rate for firms with different levels of R&D and different tax liabilities. Assuming an (after-tax) interest rate of 7 percent, she found a marginal credit rate of 1.3 percent for 1981 across all industries. When weighted by qualified re-

---

[11] For example, even without a tax credit, when the corporate tax rate was 46 percent, an additional dollar of R&D cost the firm only $0.54 because these expenses are deductible.

search expenditures,[12] this rate increases to 2.3 percent, a figure that is less than 10 percent of the statutory 25 percent credit rate in effect in 1981. For some types of firms that expand their R&D quickly and move from a nontaxable to taxable state, she found a negative credit rate, which suggests that the credit may create a counter-intuitive disincentive to expand R&D. (An earlier study by Eisner, Albert and Sullivan (119) that also used IRS data for the 1981-84 period but did not correct for carryforwards and carrybacks also found instances in which the incentive created by the credit to increase R&D is zero or negative.) A third study by Wozny (525) that uses similar data for the period and also accounts for the inability of some firms to claim credits in the year they are earned found marginal effective credit rates consistently below 6 percent. Taken together, these studies suggest that during the 1980s, this tax credit lowered the price of each extra dollar spent on R&D to a much smaller degree than the 25- and 20-percent statutory rates. However, none of these studies provide estimates of effective rates particular to pharmaceutical companies.

To date, only Baily and Lawrence have attempted to estimate the marginal effective credit rates of the 1989 version of the R&D tax credit, although this work also lacks any industry-specific estimates. Baily and Lawrence estimated that the marginal effective credit rate for firms able to fully utilize the credit is the statutory 20 percent, but for firms limited in using the credit, it may be as low as 10 percent. Assuming that 70 percent of company-financed R&D qualifies for the credit and no more than 10 to 20 percent of

R&D is in firms that face limitation, Bailey and Lawrence estimated that, on average, the marginal effective credit rate of the latest version of the credit is 12 to 13.5 percent. Regardless of the exact marginal rate, their calculations indicate that the 1989 version of the R&D credit provides incentives to increase R&D spending substantially greater than those of earlier versions.

THE BASIC RESEARCH TAX CREDIT

The Tax Reform Act of 1986 established a tax credit for support of university-based and nonprofit-based basic research. Like the R&D tax credit, its statutory rate is 20 percent, and it is given for increases in corporate cash payments to universities or nonprofit organizations for basic research over a base amount.[13] Basic research is defined as ''original investigation'' (in any area except the social sciences, arts, or humanities) undertaken ''for scientific advance without commercial objective'' (26 U.S.C. 41(e)).

OTA found no attempts to analyze the marginal effective credit rate of the basic research tax credit. Because of the complex structure of this credit, the marginal effective rate faced by any particular firm is lower than the statutory 20 percent and depends on the firm's overall qualified R&D expenditures during the tax year and previous years, its qualified basic research payments during the tax year, and its undesignated university contributions during both the base period and the tax year.

The IRS does not prohibit universities that perform basic research under this credit from assigning intellectual property rights (such as

---

[12] Because the marginal credit varies with the rate at which a firm is increasing its R&D over time, Altshuler (unlike Baily and Lawrence) weights research expenditures at the level of individual firms according to whether they were taxable in each of the 4 years she examined and according to whether their qualified R&D expenditures were growing at a low, normal or high rate. Baily and Lawrence weight at the level of all firms together, using the estimate that 70 percent of all R&D expenditures in the whole economy from 1981 to 1989 qualified for the credit. Using her method, Altshuler estimated that for the period 1981-84, 62 percent of all R&D expenditures qualified.

[13] The base amount is specific to each corporation and is the sum of two components. The first component is the greatest of three calculated amounts: 1) 1 percent of the average annual total qualified research expenses (as calculated for the R&D tax credit) during a 3-year base period; 2) all contract research payments made by the taxpayer during the base period; 3) 50 percent of the qualified basic research payments to universities and nonprofit organizations during the tax year. The second component is defined as the excess of the average annual nondesignated contribution to universities during the base period (updated for inflation) over nondesignated university contributions during the tax year. This second component is designed to reflect any decrease in nonresearch giving to universities during the tax year as compared with the base period. If this amount turns out to be negative, it is assumed to be zero in calculating the base amount.

patent ownership) resulting from such research to other parties, including the corporation that pays for the research. Because the pharmaceutical company may realize exclusive benefits from basic research it supports in universities, the basic research tax credit has created a new economic incentive for pharmaceutical companies to support research conducted in universities. However, such a decision is likely to depend on other factors in addition to the after-tax cost of such research, including where the scientific expertise resides, whether it is desirable to maintain secrecy of ongoing research, and what the firm's philanthropic policy is.

THE ORPHAN DRUG TAX CREDIT

The third tax credit designed to promote R&D is specific to the pharmaceutical industry. It is one of several incentives included in the 1983 Orphan Drug Act (Public Law 97-414) to encourage firms to develop new treatments for commercially unviable therapies in the United States.[14] Firms are entitled to a tax credit equal to 50 percent of qualified R&D expenditures for human clinical trials on therapies that have received official orphan drug status by the FDA. Firms can receive such status for drugs that treat diseases or conditions affecting less than 200,000 people in the United States.[15]

Clinical research expenditures for designated orphan drugs qualify for the orphan tax credit only if they otherwise meet the test for qualifying R&D expenditures under the R&D tax credit (26 U.S.C. 41(a-d)). This test excludes several types of expenses, including software development and management of R&D activities (except for direct supervision of R&D).

Is this tax credit an important incentive for pharmaceutical firms to engage in additional orphan drug R&D? Because it depends only on the amount of qualified clinical testing that a company does on a drug with orphan drug status, not on increases in R&D,[16] the cost of an additional dollar of qualifying orphan R&D is $0.50 for the company, a 24 percent reduction from the cost of the qualifying R&D without the tax credit.[17] However, not all firms can take advantage of this credit. To benefit, companies must have taxable income in the same year they make these clinical research expenditures, because there is no carryforward or carryback provision in the orphan drug tax credit. In addition, since some expenses associated with additional clinical orphan drug R&D do not qualify for the credit, the actual cost of additional clinical R&D for qualifying drugs is somewhat more than $0.50 on the dollar (but less than $0.66).[18] Even so, this analysis suggests that for

---

[14] See chapter 9 for a review of other incentives in the orphan drug law.

[15] Firms may also receive orphan drug status for therapies whose expected costs are high enough that no single firm would otherwise develop the pharmaceutical. However, since 1985 no firm has yet applied for orphan status under this provision. See chapter 9 for more information about how drugs receive designation as orphan drugs.

[16] There is one exception to this generalization. The orphan drug credit cannot reduce the taxes a firm owes below a calculated minimum amount (referred to as the "alternative minimum tax").

[17] Because taxpayers cannot deduct expenses eligible for the orphan drug credit from taxable income, one can figure the effective marginal rate as follows: Without the credit, the after-tax cost of a dollar of research is ($1.00 - 0.34) = $0.66 when the marginal tax rate is 34 percent. With the tax credit, the cost is ($1.00 - $0.50) = $0.50. Hence, the tax credit lowers the cost of the extra dollar of clinical orphan research from $0.66 to $0.50, a drop of 24.2 percent.

[18] OTA found no data on the percentage of pharmaceutical R&D spending that actually qualifies for the various tax credits. However, one study by the U.S. General Accounting Office (GAO) suggested that across *all* industries, qualifying R&D represented 70 percent of all R&D spending (437). *If* this figure applied to clinical orphan drug R&D as well, then the tax credit would reduce the cost of an additional dollar of such research (for a firm in the position to expand its clinical orphan R&D) by 17 percent. This figure is arrived at as follows:

Assuming a 34-percent tax rate, the cost of an additional dollar of clinical orphan R&D without the tax credit would be ($1.00 - $0.34) = $0.66. With the 50-percent tax credit and assuming that 70 percent of R&D expenses qualify for the credit, the cost would be 0.7($1.00 - $0.50) + 0.3($1.00 - $0.34) = $0.55. Hence, the tax credit would lower net cost per dollar of research from $0.66 to $0.55, a reduction of 17 percent. However, there is no evidence other than the single GAO study mentioned to indicate that 70 percent of clinical orphan R&D qualify for the credit.

a firm with a high percentage of its clinical orphan R&D qualifying for the credit, the potential tax savings may be substantial and potentially pivotal in the decision about whether to begin or continue clinical testing of an orphan drug.

■ Other Tax Credits

Among other tax credits of the Federal Tax Code, two provisions are of particular relevance to the pharmaceutical industry: the foreign tax credit system and the possessions tax credit. While these credits do not represent direct subsidies to the firm's R&D costs, there are at least two reasons to consider their importance for pharmaceutical R&D. First, they indirectly affect the location and amount of R&D. These credits affect the after-tax cost of doing business in political jurisdictions outside the United States. Second, they affect pharmaceutical firms' returns to R&D.

FOREIGN TAX CREDITS

All major U.S. pharmaceutical firms are multinational and are taxed under the U.S. tax code on the basis of their worldwide income.[19] This creates the potential for double taxation of foreign source income. Because most other nations have mechanisms to prevent double taxation, the United States would be at a competitive disadvantage without a similar policy here as well. For this reason, the United States has adopted a foreign tax credit system allowing multinational corporations to credit tax payments they make to foreign treasuries against their domestic income tax obligations (26 U.S.C. 861). Because the credit is limited to the amount of U.S. taxes a firm would owe on income derived from foreign sources, multinational firms would not receive the full credit if the taxes paid abroad are greater than the U.S. tax owed.[20]

Revenues from foreign sales (perhaps of a product resulting from foreign R&D) may be subject to both foreign and U.S. taxes. When the revenues are repatriated to the U.S. parent corporation, they are subject to U.S. taxes. Parent firms that already have excess foreign tax credits generate no additional U.S. tax liability, and parent firms without such an excess pay the difference between the rates at home and abroad. In the final analysis, both the former and latter parent corporations pay at least the U.S. tax on foreign income. However, for a firm that cannot use all of the credits earned on foreign income from a country whose effective tax rate is higher than the U.S. tax rate, the after-tax cost of business in the foreign country is higher than the cost of business in the United States. To the extent that firms are sensitive to such discrepancies between locations in the net price of investing, firms may be less likely to invest in the country with a higher effective tax rate. As suggested above, such considerations may influence the location, level, and financing of a firm's R&D investments. However, OTA's interviews with corporate and financial managers at eight U.S. research-based pharmaceutical firms indicated that tax considerations are much less important in determining where they locate R&D than are regulatory, marketing, and scientific considera-

---

[19] This system is called a "residence approach" to taxation and is not found in all countries. For example, many European countries use a "territorial" approach under which taxes are owed only on income earned within national borders. Mixtures of the two systems are also common.

In the United States, a multinational firm may organize an overseas operation as a branch or a subsidiary. The choice of legal form determines when it must pay U.S. taxes on income from foreign sources. Branches, which are not separately incorporated in foreign countries, are taxed when income (positive or negative) is earned. Subsidiaries, which are separately incorporated, pay taxes only when income is repatriated. This feature of the U.S. international tax system, called "deferral," creates a strong incentive to delay repatriations of subsidiary earnings indefinitely. In 1962, Congress enacted the Subpart F provisions that restrict deferral of certain types of unrepatriated income (Public Law 87-834). The Tax Reform Act of 1986 (Public Law 99-514) extended the classes of income subject to the Subpart F provisions. Within these limitations, a subsidiary may repatriate income from foreign sources in a variety of forms, each of which have different tax consequences. Although multinational firms are largely free to choose repatriation strategies that minimize their global tax liabilities, both the United States and foreign countries have passed laws that limit the scope of this activity.

[20] A firm's excess foreign tax credits may be carried back to offset tax obligations for up to 2 prior years or carried forward to offset future tax obligations for up to 5 years. However, unused credits do not earn interest over time.

tions. Like other multinational firms, pharmaceutical companies have an incentive to allocate their expenses among their international subsidiaries and divisions to the extent allowable by law to minimize their global tax liability.

THE POSSESSIONS TAX CREDIT (SECTION 936)

In an effort to encourage firms to locate operations in Puerto Rico, the United States altered the tax code to exempt qualifying income generated in Puerto Rico from U.S. taxation (7). In addition, Puerto Rico has designed its tax code to benefit U.S. firms that locate in the Commonwealth.[21] Section 936 of the U.S. tax code contains provisions that exempt qualifying corporations from U.S. taxes on Puerto Rico income. Corporations qualifying for this credit are called possessions corporations. U.S. companies are considered possessions corporations if they derive at least 80 percent of gross income from U.S. possessions such as Puerto Rico. Possessions corporations must earn at least 75 percent of their income from active business operations (such as manufacturing), and thus no more than 25 percent of income may be derived from financial mechanisms such as interest on bank investments.[22] The "possessions tax credit" is equal to 100 percent of the U.S. tax on income from Puerto Rico for subsidiaries or branches that meet the definition of a possessions corporation (6).

The pharmaceutical industry is a prime beneficiary of the possessions credit because of both the extent of its taxable revenues and its "intangible assets." Intangible assets include patents, licenses, trademarks, and corporate or brand names. Unlike tangible assets including buildings and machinery, intangible assets are not tied to any particular physical location. Hence, ownership of intangible assets such as patents may be transferred to subsidiaries or branches that qualify as possessions corporations according to guidelines established by the Federal Government.[23]

County NatWest's Washington Analysis Corporation (WAC) estimated the net tax savings from the possessions credit in 1989 for several companies using data from annual reports (248).[24] Table 8-1 summarizes the results of this analysis for eight research-based U.S. pharmaceutical firms. These are only rough estimates of net tax savings from the possessions tax credit, because the net income in that study was defined according to standard accounting practice and differs from taxable income as defined by the internal revenue code.

Because effective corporate tax rates in Puerto Rico are substantially lower than in the United States, this tax credit represents a major form of Federal tax expenditure for pharmaceutical firms. Although little actual pharmaceutical R&D is done in Puerto Rican locations (245), the credit may lead to more manufacturing jobs in the

---

[21] Puerto Rico has primary taxing jurisdiction over income earned within its borders. Although Puerto Rico has statutory corporate tax rates that range from 22 to 44 percent (and will drop to a maximum rate of 35 percent by 1993), the effective tax rates faced by most firms are much lower due to extremely generous tax exemptions. Corporations that engage in manufacturing or export services in Puerto Rico receive an exemption of current income of up to 90 percent. These exemptions take the form of grants and gradually expire over a 10- to 25-year period depending on the location of the plant. The Commonwealth usually grants extensions before expiration.

Structures and equipment located in Puerto Rico are also treated preferentially. Depreciation deductions are "flexible" which means that as long as the deduction does not make taxable income negative and the total amount depreciated does not exceed the value of the asset, any amount of depreciation may be claimed in any year.

Income repatriated to parent corporations in the form of dividends are subject to a Puerto Rican tax of 10 percent. However, if half the earnings from Puerto Rican investment are held in Puerto Rico for at least 5 years, the tax is reduced by one-half. In addition, interest generated from Puerto Rican financial instruments such as from bonds or banks is not subject to Puerto Rican taxes.

[22] For financial income to qualify for the credit it must be obtained from investments made in Puerto Rico.

[23] Possessions corporations must use one of several methods to allocate income derived from products protected by such patents between the U.S. possession and the U.S. mainland business. The most common method, called "profit splitting," allocates to Puerto Rico half the revenues generated from transferred intangibles (7,243).

[24] Statehood for Puerto Rico would lead to the repeal of the Possessions Tax Credit because the U.S. Constitution requires that Federal law apply uniformly across all States (430).

Table 8-1—Tax Savings for Selected Pharmaceutical Firms Attributable to U.S. Possessions Credit for Businesses in Puerto Rico, 1989[a]

Firm	Estimated tax savings attributable to possessions credit ($ millions)	Net income ($ millions)	Tax savings as a percent of net income
American Home Products............	$ 81	$ 1,102	7.3%
Bristol-Myers......................	64	747	8.6
Eli Lilly...........................	54	940	5.7
Merck............................	105	1,430	7.4
Pfizer Inc........................	106	681	15.6
Schering-Plough..................	49	399	12.3
Upjohn...........................	46	176	25.9
Warner-Lambert..................	40	413	9.6

[a] Data for Schering-Plough are for 1988.

SOURCE: Office of Technology Assessment, 1993. Based on data from I.S. Loss and A.D. Morgenstern, *Pharmaceuticals/Tax Policy: A Successful Puerto Rican Statehood Initiative Will Result in Higher Corporate Tax Rates for Many Companies* (Washington, DC: The NatWest Investment Banking Group, 1990).

commonwealth (430). In addition, the net tax savings improves pharmaceutical companies' after-tax returns.

■ Estimates of Federal Tax Credit Expenditures

At OTA's request the congressional Joint Committee on Taxation (JCT) estimated the size of all tax credits affecting the pharmaceutical industry in tax year 1987. These estimates come from the Statistics of Income (SOI) Database compiled by the IRS.[25]

The results of the analysis are presented in tables 8-2 and 8-3.

Table 8-2 shows the tax credits actually claimed by the pharmaceutical industry in 1987. In addition to the total dollar value of each credit, the estimated number of firms claiming them, and the pharmaceutical industry's credit as a percent of the credit's total dollar value for all industries, the table also estimates the credit as a percent of the industry's tax liability in the absence of any credits[26] as well as the credit as a percent of the industry's taxable income (a "negative tax rate"

on taxable income). As noted earlier, foreign tax credits differ somewhat from the other tax credits examined in this chapter in that they are a means to prevent double taxation of foreign source income rather than a provision to encourage certain types of taxpayer behavior. However, we include estimates of this credit here to underscore the multinational nature of the pharmaceutical industry and to show the size of foreign tax credits relative to the credits.

For the pharmaceutical industry, however, the possessions tax credit may be more important than the foreign tax credit.[27] More than half of the total credit was claimed by firms in the pharmaceutical industry, and, on average, it reduced each firm's tax liability by more than a third. The percentage deduction in tax liability was greater for smaller companies (those with assets $250 million) than for larger companies, which suggests size may not be a barrier to establishing a subsidiary in Puerto Rico.

The orphan drug credit had relatively little impact on either the Federal Treasury or the industry's tax obligations in 1987. As one would

[25] Appendix J describes how OTA and the JCT identified research-based pharmaceutical firms in the SOI.

[26] This statistic measures the extent to which the credit reduces the industry's tax obligations.

[27] Estimates of the possessions credit here represent tax expenditures for the Federal Treasury only and do not count taxes that firms must pay to the Commonwealth of Puerto Rico. Hence, the actual total tax savings to the industry is smaller than the subsidy provided by the Federal Government. As indicated earlier, however, effective tax rates in Puerto Rico are much lower than on the U.S. mainland.

Table 8-2—Tax Credits Claimed by the Pharmaceutical Industry in 1987[a]

	Aggregate credit claimed by pharmaceutical industry ($ thousands)	Number of firms claiming credit	Aggregate credit claimed as a percent of aggregate claimed by all industries	Aggregate credit claimed as a percent of taxes pharmaceutical industry would pay with no credits	Aggregate credit claimed as a percent of aggregate pharmaceutical industry income subject to taxes
Foreign tax credit					
Firms with assets less than $50 million	$ 469	2	0.1%	0.4%	0.2%
Firms with assets between $50 million and $250 million	287	6	0.1	0.1	0.0
Firms with assets of $250 million or more	928,089	20	4.6	26.6	10.7
All firms	928,843	28	4.5	23.4	9.4
Possessions tax credits					
Firms with assets less than $50 million	66,947	22	14.5	64.1	24.8
Firms with assets between $50 million and $250 million	313,536	20	40.3	81.9	33.0
Firms with assets of $250 million or more	958,100	11	67.8	27.5	11.1
All firms	1,338,800	53	50.4	33.7	13.6
Orphan drug tax credits					
Firms with assets less than $50 million	0	0	0.0	—	—
Firms with assets between $50 million and $250 million	0	0	0.0	—	—
Firms with assets of $250 million or more	4,665	6	90.5	0.1	0.1
All firms	4,665	6	90.5	0.1	0.0
General business tax credits					
Firms with assets less than $50 million	4,053	221	0.5	3.9	1.5
Firms with assets between $50 million and $250 million	2,355	7	0.7	0.6	0.2
Firms with assets of $250 million or more	79,240	20	1.2	2.3	0.9
All firms	85,648	248	1.1	2.2	0.9

[a]Estimates are for tax year 1987 from the U.S. Treasury's Statistics of Income (SOI) sample weighted to reflect relevant populations. Pharmaceutical industry is defined as SOI industry group 2830 minus firms with assets of $250 million or more and known not to be involved in pharmaceuticals.

SOURCE: Office of Technology Assessment, 1993. Estimates provided by U.S. Congress, Joint Committee on Taxation.

Table 8-3—Research Tax Credits Earned by the Pharmaceutical Industry in 1987[a]

	Aggregate credit claimed ($ thousands)	Number of firms claiming credit	Aggregate credit earned as a percent of aggregate earned by all industries
Research and experimentation tax credit[b]			
Firms with assets < $50 million...................	$ 6,455	147	3.1%
Firms with assets ≥ $50 million and < $250 million..	2,042	9	2.0
Firms with assets of $250 million or more..........	88,878	28	12.6
All firms.....................................	97,375	184	9.6
University-based basic research tax credits			
Firms with assets < $50 million...................	3	90	17.3
Firms with assets ≥ $50 million and <$250 million...	0	39	0.0
Firms with assets of $250 million or more..........	2,257	43	10.7
All firms.....................................	2,260	990	6.4
Orphan drug tax credits			
Firms with assets < $50 million...................	0	0	—
Firms with assets ≥ $50 million and < $250 million..	0	0	—
Firms with assets of $250 million or more..........	5,358	8	84.3
All firms.....................................	5,358	8	84.3

a Estimates for tax year 1987 are from the U.S. Treasury's Statistics of Income (SOI) sample weighted to reflect relevant populations. Pharmaceutical industry is defined as SOI industry group 2830 minus firms with assets of $250 million or more *and* known not to be involved in pharmaceuticals. Tax credits *earned* are not equivalent to tax credits *claimed* because the former does not reflect insufficient tax liability in current year, or carry-forwards from previous years.

b Research and experimentation credit estimates are net of university-based basic research credit.

SOURCE: Office of Technology Assessment, 1993. Estimates provided by U.S. Congress, Joint Committee on Taxation.

expect, virtually all (91 percent) of this credit was claimed by firms whose primary activity is pharmaceuticals.

Estimates of the R&D and university basic research credits claimed by the pharmaceutical industry are included in the ''general business credit.'' In addition to these two research-related credits, the general business credit includes other tax credits potentially available to corporations: a credit for newly created jobs, one for certain types of special investment, one for the use of alcohol as a fuel, and a credit for the provision of low-income housing. Because carrybacks and carryforwards are calculated on the general business credit *as a whole*, it is not possible to produce separate estimates of the R&D and university basic research credits actually claimed.

General business credits were claimed by firms of all sizes in this industry and reduced the taxes owed by the smallest companies (those with assets under $50 million) by almost 4 percent more than for larger firms. Although general business credits for drug companies cost the Treasury 17 times more than the orphan drug credit in 1987, it still totaled less than 10 percent of the foreign tax credit and only 6 percent of the possessions credit claimed by this industry.

Estimates of the R&D tax credit, the basic research credits and orphan drug tax credits *earned* by the pharmaceutical industry in 1987, are shown in table 8-3.[28]

Only eight companies, all large firms, earned an orphan drug credit in 1987.[29] Two-thirds of all orphan drug designations granted by the FDA

---

[28] For the R&D and basic research credits, the amount of each credit *earned* by a particular company is defined as 20 percent of the difference between qualifying expenses in the current year and the base amount. The amount of credit actually *claimed*, however, adds in credits earned in earlier years that are carried forward to the current year or subtracts credits earned in the current year but unused due to insufficient tax liability.

[29] The fact that only six firms claimed this credit (see table 8-2) indicates that two of the firms that actually had qualifying expenses in 1987 were unable to use it due to insufficient tax liabilities.

went to firms that are not members of the Pharmaceutical Manufacturers Association (generally the smallest companies in the pharmaceutical industry). Thus, the developers of most orphan drugs may not have been in a position to claim a tax credit or may not yet have reached the clinical stage of the R&D process.

The fluidity of tax laws during the latter half of the 1980s may make these 1987 estimates unrepresentative of the late 1980s. The Tax Reform Act of 1986 lowered the maximum corporate tax rate from 46 to 34 percent over a period of several years beginning in 1987. And, the structure of the R&D tax credit also changed substantially over time. Although the resources necessary to conduct the analysis presented in tables 8-2 and 8-3 limited OTA to examining a single tax year, the IRS publishes some summary statistics from the SOI database for Principal Activity Classification (PAC) codes, groups of firms organized according to the activity earning them the greatest proportion of their total receipts.

Table 8-4 presents estimates of tax credits claimed by firms in pharmaceutical firms (PAC 2830) in the 1984-87 period.[30] Whereas all of the credits increased in the 1984-86 period, the possessions, orphan drug, and general business credits dropped between 1986 and 1987, the first year after tax reform. Of these three, only the general business credit registered a major decline (48 percent). It is likely that the dramatic decline between 1986 and 1987 in this set of credits is attributable to the elimination of the Investment Tax Credit in the 1986 Tax Reform Act (297). The foreign tax credit actually increased between 1986 and 1987. Despite the evident trends, the numbers indicate that the relative magnitude of these credits remained roughly steady between 1984 and 1987.

In sum, the estimates in tables 8-2, 8-3, and 8-4 indicate that, in an effort to achieve a variety of

Table 8-4—Tax Credits Claimed by Firms in Statistics of Income Industry Group 2830, 1984-87 ($ millions)

	1984	1985	1986	1987
Foreign tax credit.	$621	$632	$747	$929
Possessions credit.	839	903	1,463	1,399
Orphan drug credit.	0	0	6	5
Research & experimentation tax credit[a].	86	88	—	—
General business credits[a].	135	125	180	86[a]

[a] Beginning in 1986, statistics of income (SOI) data subsumed the research and experimental tax credit within "general business credits" which also includes low-income housing, investment, jobs, alcohol fuel, and employee stock ownership credits.

SOURCE: Office of Technology Assessment, 1993. Based on Statistics of Income Division, Internal Revenue Service, U.S. Department of Treasury, *Source Books, Statistics of Income, 1984-1987, Corporate Tax Returns* (Washington, DC: U.S. Government Printing Office, 1984-87).

public policy objectives, the Federal Government makes substantial tax expenditures through credits claimed by the pharmaceutical industry. In 1987, not including over $900,000 for foreign tax credits, the Federal Treasury spent a total of $1.4 billion in tax credits for these firms (table 8-4). Taken together, they reduced the Federal taxes the pharmaceutical industry would have otherwise owed by over 36 percent.[31] The largest of these tax code provisions, the possessions credit, is also significant because the pharmaceutical industry makes more use of it than does any other industry, accounting for half of all the dollars claimed in 1987. Although this credit along with the foreign tax credit was designed to enhance the economic development of a U.S. possession and to avoid double taxation of foreign income, respectively, rather than to subsidize pharmaceutical R&D, they nevertheless do effectively reduce the tax liability of pharmaceutical firms. Hence, they raise net after-tax income achievable from pharmaceutical operations, including those arising from the development of new products.

---

[30] The data for PAC 2830 contain some large firms with multiple lines of business (and, hence, overestimate the industry's true assets and tax credits). Nevertheless, the summary statistics are useful for examining trends in the use of tax credits over time.

[31] Adding foreign tax credits raises this to 59 percent.

■ Firm Characteristics and the Use of Tax Credits

The tax credits available to businesses engaging in pharmaceutical R&D are of greater or less value to firms, depending on their specific financial and operating characteristics. The following stylized examples show how companies in various situations would stand to benefit from the various tax credits. Consider three types of research-based pharmaceutical companies:[32]

- A startup firm with no products or processes on the market, and hence, no income, but with a growing R&D budget financed by investment from sources outside the firm.
- An emerging firm with a few products on the market (either in the U.S. or abroad), some income, a growing R&D budget, and a very high ratio of R&D expenses to sales.
- An established, large, multinational firm with multiple products on the market and R&D expenditures that equal between 12 and 16 percent of sales (the same as that found among almost all existing large pharmaceutical firms).

For the startup firm, tax credits are not particularly useful since it usually does not pay income taxes. Such a firm is intent on identifying or moving a product or process to the point that investors may realize a return. To the extent that it can anticipate taxable income in the future, it can carry forward R&D tax credits to subsequent years, but the value of these potential future credits is diminished because of the time value of money. While the possessions and foreign tax credits can also theoretically be carried forward, a firm can earn these credits only by generating income (either abroad or in a U.S. possession).

The orphan drug credit has no carryforward or carryback provision at all. In practical terms, then, these credits are not useful to the startup firm.

The established firm cares most about the tax provisions having the greatest impact on its tax liability—the possessions and foreign tax credits. Although the established company will claim any R&D or orphan drug credit to which it is due, these have a smaller impact on taxes it pays: the total general business and orphan drug credits claimed by the largest pharmaceutical firms represented only 4 percent of the amounts claimed for possessions and foreign tax credits. In addition, the fact that the R&D credit is limited to expenses for research done in the United States diminishes its appeal for an established firm with multinational R&D facilities.

For the emerging firm, the R&D tax credit can be particularly important. Because the credit is for increases in R&D expenditures, its dollar value is higher for firms with relatively high annual rates of growth of qualifying research expenses. The higher the company's R&D-to-sales ratio, the more likely that tax subsidies from the R&D credit will reduce the company's Federal tax liabilities.[33]

OTHER NATIONS' R&D TAX INCENTIVES

To the extent pharmaceutical firms earn income in other countries, they are subject to the tax laws of the foreign countries in which they conduct business. While a full review of all foreign tax laws of relevance to the pharmaceutical industry and their implicit incentives is beyond the scope of this report, this section provides a brief examination of how other nations treat corporate R&D.

---

[32] The pharmaceutical firms visited by OTA staff over the course of this assessment included companies that resemble each of the three types described above. The perspectives of relevant corporate managers interviewed at these firms about the value of various tax subsidies closely fit these three generalizations.

[33] Although not considered in this chapter, OTA's interviews at pharmaceutical companies indicated that startup and emerging firms may care as much or more about the tax treatment of income generated for their investors as they do about taxes on their own income. Because such companies are likely to finance their R&D with funds from outside sources using novel mechanisms such as the R&D limited partnership, favorable tax treatment of investment income (particularly from high risk/high return financial instruments) may make it easier for firms to attract needed capital.

In a review of national tax policies in 23 developed or emerging high-technology countries,[34] OTA found that most nations permit R&D spending to be deducted from taxable income in the year incurred (245). In addition, most tax codes provide some mechanism to carry unused deductions forward into future years. Countries vary a great deal in the provision of tax credits tied to R&D spending. Currently, Brazil, China, Denmark, Hong Kong, Italy, South Africa, and Switzerland lack any R&D tax credits or other special allowances for R&D beyond the deduction of current expenses. Among other countries examined, Canada, France, Japan, Spain, Sweden, and Taiwan all provide a tax credit on increases in R&D spending similar to the United States. As shown in table 8-5, the statutory credit varies considerably but does not exceed 50 percent in any country. Remaining nations provide other incentives for R&D, including more specific types of tax subsidies as well as direct grants. These policies are also briefly summarized in table 8-5.

Although a complete understanding of particular tax subsidies and incentives faced by the pharmaceutical industry in other countries would require a more detailed analysis, this review suggests that most countries use some mechanism to subsidize private spending for R&D. In many cases, these mechanisms are similar to those employed by the U.S. Government. This general comparability of U.S. and international tax codes is reinforced by the recent trend in other countries to reduce corporate tax rates to levels near the maximum 34 percent rate adopted by the United States in its Tax Reform Act of 1986 (303). Corporate managers at the research-based pharmaceutical firms interviewed by OTA said that marketing and scientific considerations were much more important in deciding the location and level of R&D investment than were tax incentives. While specific research projects and programs may differ considerably in their tax implications, this perspective is consistent with an overall general comparability of national taxes across different countries.

CONCLUSIONS

Taxes paid by corporations are determined by numerous provisions of the tax code, each designed to achieve particular policy goals. Whether or not such provisions achieve their public policy goals, many lead to lower taxes for firms and to lower after-tax costs of R&D and higher after-tax returns to R&D.

In actual Federal dollars spent, Federal tax credits constitute one of the most substantial forms of government involvement in the operations of the pharmaceutical industry. In 1987, not including over $900,000 in foreign tax credits, the Federal Treasury made $1.4 billion in tax expenditures through credits to drug companies. Of this, only about $90 million was for credits whose specific policy purpose is to stimulate R&D. The major part, $1.3 billion, of the lost tax revenue was due to the foreign and possessions tax credits.

Overall, tax credits reduced the amount of taxes pharmaceutical firms would have otherwise owed the U.S. Government by 36 percent and equaled 15 percent of the industry's taxable U.S. income. Adding foreign tax credits raises these figures to 59 percent and 24 percent, respectively.

The relative importance of each credit varies among firms according to their financial characteristics. The incentives in the R&D tax credit may be stronger for emerging biotechnology companies who have some income on which to pay taxes but whose R&D budgets are growing more rapidly than they are for larger, more established firms. For the largest, most estab-

---

[34] The countries are Australia, Belgium, Brazil, Canada, China, Denmark, Germany, France, Hong Kong, Ireland, Italy, Japan, Netherlands, Norway, Singapore, South Africa, South Korea, Spain, Sweden, Switzerland, Taiwan, United Kingdom, and United States. The information gathered in this review does not capture tax policies at the regional or local level, which can be as important or more important than those at the national level. For example, in Switzerland, the individual cantons into which the country is divided have primary responsibility for collecting government revenue (334,335). Some countries, like Italy, may also have special incentives in their national tax codes that apply only to particular geographic regions where they wish to stimulate economic development.

Table 8-5—Research and Development Tax Incentives in Other Nations: Summary of Policies

Country	R&D tax credits	Other subsidies[a]
Australia		• 150% expensing of R&D • R&D tax "grants"
Belgium		• Special deductions for R&D personnel • Exemptions from tax of distributed profits
Canada	• 20% incremental	
France	• 50% incremental	• R&D grants in selected industries[b]
Germany	• Tax credits on R&D equipment	• Tax grants on capital investment
Ireland		• Tax exemption for royalty income from patent R&D done in Ireland
Japan	• 20% incremental	• Trade policies beneficial to R&D equipment[a] • R&D grants for selected technologies[b]
Netherlands		• Special allowances for R&D capital and labor
Norway		• Deductions for future R&D
Singapore		• 200% expensing of R&D
South Korea		• Deductions for future R&D
Spain	• 15% of R&D • 30% of R&D equipment	
Sweden	• 30% incremental	• Special allowances for R&D salaries
Taiwan	• 20% incremental	
United States	• 20% incremental on R&D • 20% incremental on university-based basic R&D • 50 percent of clinical orphan drug R&D	
United Kingdom		• Deduction of R&D facilities and machinery

[a] Beyond expensing of current R&D expenditures.
[b] These subsidies are provided directly to the qualifying firms; they are not administered through the tax code.

SOURCE: Office of Technology Assessment, 1993.

lished companies, the possessions and foreign tax credits are most likely more important. For the very newest startup firms, corporate tax credits may be of negligible value.

Quite apart from tax credits, the immediate deductibility of R&D expenditures reduces the cost of a dollar's worth of research performed today from $1.00 to about $0.66.

To summarize, the tax code includes numerous credits and deductions tied to firms' expenditures for R&D as well as several other tax code provisions that are especially important for drug companies and their profits. These tax policies are major avenues of U.S. Federal assistance to the research activities of the pharmaceutical industry. Although they were designed to achieve a variety of policy goals (most of which are not specific to the pharmaceutical industry), the tax policies reviewed here result in a substantial Federal investment in the industry in terms of foregone tax revenues.

Federal Support for Pharmaceutical Research and Development 9

Economic theory suggests that without help from the government, the private sector alone will underinvest in research (19,513). It makes sense for a firm to invest in research whose results lend competitive advantage to the company. But, much research creates knowledge that the firm cannot keep to itself. The patent system and the legal protections afforded trade secrecy are attempts by governments to confer exclusive ownership rights to knowledge, but not all discoveries can make use of these privileges. Basic research increases the storehouse of fundamental scientific understanding and is often necessary for commercial applications. Yet, a private industrial firm lacks the incentive to adequately support basic research because the firm cannot ensure it will capture all the benefits of such support. To realize the benefits of basic research and research training, the public sector must participate in its funding.

Underwritten largely by Federal and State Governments, research-intensive universities serve as the public sector's principal agents in the conduct of both biomedical research and training of biomedical researchers. The goal of this support is to realize the economic and public health benefits that can follow from the commercialization of research results (131).

The pharmaceutical industry is particularly adept at mining the motherlode of knowledge created by government-sponsored biomedical research and training. In a recent survey of firms in seven research-based industries, Mansfield (253) found over one-quarter of products and processes in use in the pharmaceutical industry could not have been developed without substantial delay in the absence of recent academic research (figure 9-1).

Photo credit: NATIONAL INSTITUTES OF HEALTH

The National Institutes of Health conducts targeted drug discovery and testing programs. The transfer of the scientific knowledge with commerical value from this agency to the pharmaceutical industry is one of the ways that pharmaceutical companies directly benefit from Federal research support.

Respondents to a survey of biotechnology firms conducted by Blumenthal and colleagues (52) reported that collaboration with academic institutions helped keep firms current with impor-

tant research (83 percent) and that it reduced the cost of mounting research and development (R&D) programs in new fields (60 percent). Indeed, most of the biotechnological techniques developed during the early 1980s, upon which the pharmaceutical industry now depends, came from academic laboratories (445).

The Federal Government provides even more direct subsidies to industrial pharmaceutical R&D than general support for biomedical research and training. The National Institutes of Health (NIH) and other Federal laboratories themselves conduct targeted drug discovery and testing in disease areas deemed particularly important. In addition, the Federal Government offers a series of subsidies specifically designed to encourage the development of orphan drugs, treatments that might not otherwise be commercially viable. And finally, the Federal Government may unintentionally defray some of the cost of clinical research through its Medicare and Medicaid programs.

Figure 9-1—Percent of New Products and Processes Based on Recent Academic Research, 1975-85

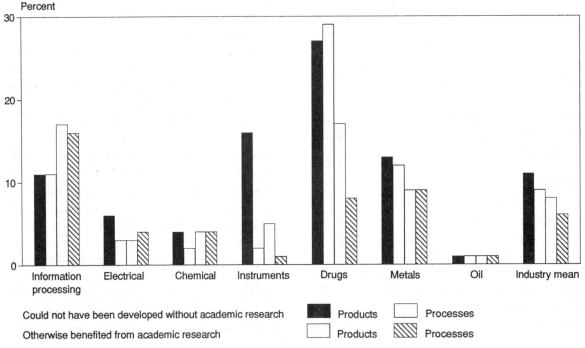

SOURCE: Office of Technology Assessment, 1993. Based on data from E. Mansfield, "Academic Research and Industrial Innovation," *Research Policy* 20:1-12, 1991.

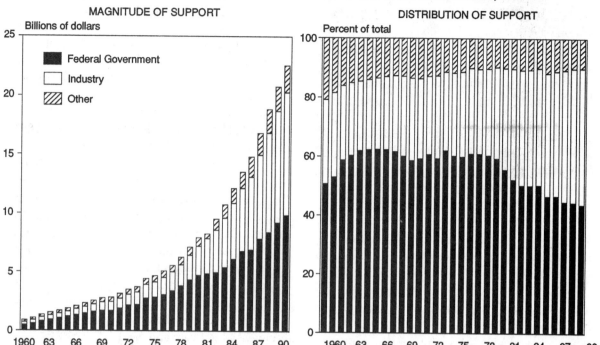

Figure 9-2—Sources of Support for Health-Related R&D in the United States, 1960-90

NOTE: Other sources of support include State and local government, private, and nonprofit support.

SOURCE: Office of Technology Assessment, 1993. Based on data from U.S. Department of Health and Human Services, Public Health Service, National Institutes of Health, *Data Book 1989* (Washington, DC: U.S. Government Printing Office, 1989).

This chapter describes direct Federal contributions to the pharmaceutical knowledge base as well as indirect support through its funding of the biomedical research and training infrastructure. In addition to assessing the extent of such Federal subsidies, this chapter describes how federally funded knowledge produced in academic institutes and government laboratories is transferred to pharmaceutical companies.

The transfer of scientific knowledge with commercial value to private companies that can develop and commercialize the resulting products or services unquestionably has benefits. This chapter describes powerful financial incentives recently put in place through Federal legislation to transfer technologies to the private sector. Whether the public pays too much for the resulting products, however, is a question that needs more attention from public policymakers.

FEDERAL SUPPORT FOR THE LIFE SCIENCES

In 1990, the Federal Government and industry each funded approximately 45 percent ($9.9 billion) of health R&D undertaken in the United States (483). Of the Federal portion, 75 percent came from NIH. In the post-World War II period as a whole, the contribution of the Federal Government to biomedical R&D has been much greater than that of industry. Figure 9-2 shows the Federal portion of health R&D conducted in the United States was consistently over twice that of industry throughout the 1960s and 1970s. NIH's investment in biomedical research continued to increase at 2.6 percent per year between 1981 and 1991, after adjusting for inflation. But, the dramatic spurt in industrial pharmaceutical R&D spending beginning in the early 1980s is responsible for the increase in industry's share of total biomedical R&D since 1980.

The Federal investment in R&D over the postwar period has created a physical and organizational infrastructure that continues to be productive today. Over 60 percent of all health-related academic and nonprofit research facilities built between 1958 and 1968 were financed with 50-50 matching funds available through the Federal Health Facilities Research Act (Ch. 779, 70 Stat 717).[1] The National Science Foundation (NSF) and several NIH institutes also had their own authority and appropriations to support building and renovation. Although Federal support for construction has fallen since the 1960s, the Federal Government's contribution over the entire period provided the necessary capacity to conduct subsequent research funded by government, industry and the nonprofit sector.

Industry, on the other hand, has never been a significant contributor of research facilities other than its own in-house laboratories (207).[2] When industry has provided research grants or contracts to academic institutions, its support for indirect and overhead expenses (which pay for facilities and administration) has generally been below the standard Federal contribution for such costs.

Dollars devoted to research and facilities do not fully reflect the importance of Federal support for the academic research infrastructure upon which industry depends. Not only did institutions of higher education receive 62 percent of NIH R&D funds and 53 percent of all Federal health R&D money, but colleges and universities receive virtually all Federal funds for research training (482).[3] Academia, in turn, has used these resources to produce one of the most important components of the R&D infrastructure—scientific talent. The Federal investment in training includes not only scholarship and fellowship support, but also research support to principal investigators who employ trainees in their laboratories, thus giving them a vital part of their education, a research apprenticeship.

Although data limitations preclude comprehensive measurement of Federal support for training,[4] the Office of Technology Assessment (OTA) estimates that in 1989 the Federal Government spent over $325 million on training support for over 14,000 postgraduate trainees in the biological sciences (see table 9-1).[5] (This does not include the billions of dollars spent on general training support for undergraduate and graduate education through the Federal student financial aid programs administered by the U.S. Department of Education.) About 25 percent of graduate students pursuing a doctoral degree in the biomedical sciences receive a training grant from NIH (207).

Over the last 10 years, the number of doctoral-level biomedical research jobs in industry has grown about 12 to 13 percent per year compared with an average 4.9 percent increase for biomedical research jobs in all sectors (207). Pharmaceutical companies make more intensive use of trained scientific personnel than do firms in other industries. While all industries together employ 27 trained scientists or engineers per 1,000 employees, the pharmaceutical industry hires 62 per 1,000 employees (figure 9-3).

---

[1] The other most common sources of funding for biomedical research facilities are State and local government and debt financing by the research institution itself (207).

[2] Well-publicized agreements between universities and industry in the health sciences that include the construction of new facilities are noteworthy for their size, but they have been limited to a few of the most research-intensive universities.

[3] Remaining Federal and NIH research money went to industry, Federal, State and local governments, and private nonprofit organizations not engaged in higher education.

[4] OTA published a more detailed discussion in 1991 of the strengths and limitations of data on scientific research and training in the United States (452).

[5] Most awards for training biomedical researchers are funded as National Research Service Awards (NRSAs). Most NRSA traineeships go to educational institutions that in turn award them to predoctoral trainees for up to 5 years and postdoctoral for up to 3 years. After completing their training, awardees must conduct biomedical research for 1 month for every month they received support. Those who do not provide this research ''payback'' must reimburse the government for their awards.

Table 9-1—Federal Research Training Support Targeted for the Life Sciences in 1989

Agency	Number of trainees supported			Funds for research training ($ millions)	Other characteristics
	Predoctoral	Postdoctoral	Total		
National Institutes of Health (NIH)	6,216	5,369	11,585	$256.0	For both NIH and ADAMHA, all but 1,150 awards require recipients to conduct research 1 month for each month supported after completing training.
Alcohol, Drug Abuse, and Mental Health Administration (ADAMHA)[a]	720	567	1,287	27.1	Includes approximately 630 awards for behavioral research training
National Science Foundation (NSF)	NA	NA	1,361	12.8	Training support is provided through research funds to principal investigator who hire trainees.
U.S. Department of Energy (DOE)	200	10	210	30.7	
Totals			14,443	$326.6	

[a] In 1992, the research institutes administering ADAMHA's training awards were made part of NIH under Public Law 102-321. The remainder of ADAMHA became the Substance Abuse and Mental Health Services Administration.

KEY: NA = not available.

SOURCE: Office of Technology Assessment, 1993.

Figure 9-3—Number of Trained Scientists and Engineers Per 1,000 U.S. Employees

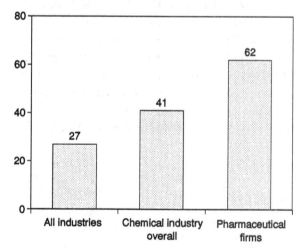

SOURCE: Office of Technology Assessment, 1993. Based on data from J.P. Swann, *Academic Scientists and the Pharmaceutical Industry: Cooperative Research in Twentieth Century America* (Baltimore, MD: The Johns Hopkins University Press, 1988).

Training support for graduate students and postdoctoral fellows comes not only through formal training grants, but also through employment as research assistants (RAs) on grants or contracts supported by Federal funds. About 52 percent of all graduate students with training support from DHHS in 1988 reported their work as RAs was the major form of such aid (289) compared with only 31 percent in 1981.

The Federal investment in R&D infrastructure outlined above made possible the fundamental knowledge and techniques upon which current drug discovery depends. The advances in molecular biology, which form the core of biotechnology (445), include recombinant DNA processes, monoclonal antibodies, and gene synthesis and splicing. Chapter 5 discusses the importance of these techniques in today's pharmaceutical R&D process. These advances were made, for the most part, in university laboratories and relied heavily on Federal support.

Private industrial firms also provide predoctoral or postdoctoral training in the life sciences through scholarships, fellowships, and other training grants as well as other research support in universities. About 6 percent of life science trainees (advanced graduate students and postdoctoral fellows) at six research-intensive universities surveyed by Blumenthal and colleagues in 1985 received training grants or scholarship support from industry (151).[6] Other types of involvement with industry also provided financial benefit to trainees. In all, about 19 percent of life science trainees in the six universities studied by Blumenthal and colleagues reported receiving research salary, training grants, or scholarships directly from industry; another 15 percent worked in the laboratories of faculty advisers who received industrial research support.

Industry support appears to be more restrictive than that of government. Of students and fellows reporting scholarships or training grants from industry, about 35 percent were required to perform some activity of direct benefit to the sponsoring firm, such as working for the company (151). And, while the average research training award at NIH in 1984 was $12,385 for graduate students and $22,425 for postdoctoral fellows, the mean award for training grants or scholarships from firms involved in biotechnology ranged from approximately $4,551 to $9,181 per award (150). Thus even when industry has provided training support for universities in the life sciences, the support is more restrictive than is Federal support.

COLLABORATION BETWEEN PHARMACEUTICAL FIRMS AND ACADEMIA

Collaborative arrangements between academic researchers and pharmaceutical firms represent an implicit transfer of federally supported research and knowledge to the private sector. As opportunities to commercialize research findings in the life sciences have grown, so too has interest in commercial relationships designed to make use of these results in the marketplace (445).

The pharmaceutical industry has a long tradition of cooperation with academia (415). When World War I eliminated the supply of pharmaceuticals from Germany, American drug companies realized the need to develop their own products. They established ties with universities in order to recruit scientific manpower and to capitalize on academic research with pharmaceutical potential.

Academics were receptive to such cooperation (415). During the postwar period, U.S. pharmaceutical firms established multifaceted strategies for cooperation with universities. They built ties with academic scientists by attending scientific meetings in force, visiting academic laboratories on a regular basis, sponsoring lectures by academic scientists at company facilities, sponsoring awards through academic societies, and developing lists of leading scientists within relevant fields to receive regular written updates on advances occurring within industrial laboratories. They also began to sponsor fellowships and trainees in universities. Between 1925 and 1930, for example, Squibb spent a seventh of its research budget on such fellowships (415).

Collaboration between academia and the pharmaceutical industry on *basic research* diminished steadily between 1940 and the 1970s as alternative sources of support for university research (mainly the government) increased and as the growth in industrial research laboratories reduced firms' reliance on academia (415). Yet, the amount of *clinical research* sponsored by the industry and conducted by academia grew significantly over this period, particularly after the 1962 amendments to the Food, Drug and Cosmetic Act (21 U.S.C. 301 et seq.) required drug sponsors to establish effectiveness as well as safety of new products.

Clinical research requires collaboration with academic medical centers that have the physician-

---

[6] Although these six universities are not representative of all institutions that train young biomedical researchers, the survey does provide insight into the role of industry in the training of students and fellows in very research-intensive universities. Such young researchers are likely to constitute the next generation of scientific leadership (151).

researchers, the patients, and the infrastructure to test new drugs. Hence, even as university-industry relationships revolving around laboratory research diminished in the 1950s to 1970s, pharmaceutical firms maintained formal and informal clinical relationships with academia.

Beginning in the late 1970s, the number of collaborations with universities during the discovery phase of research began to expand once more. Most observers have tied this trend to the development of biotechnology techniques in university laboratories (228,415,445). Large pharmaceutical firms turned to academia to learn these techniques. In many instances, the principal founders of new biotechnology companies came from academia and attempted to keep their university affiliations. In the 1980s academic scientists and venture capitalists, recognizing the value of these advances in the life sciences, sought to commercialize university research through startup firms that also maintained close relationships with academic laboratories (228).

Today's collaborations take place against a backdrop of pervasive government funding for biomedical research in academia. Even within the individual academic research laboratory, financial support from industry coexists with more extensive government support. As figure 9-4 indicates, in 1984 less than one-quarter of principal investigators in the life sciences who used biotechnological techniques[7] at 40 of the 50 most research-intensive universities received *any* support from industry (53). In addition, the vast majority of those faculty who received *any* research support from industry still get most of their research support from government and the nonprofit sector; only 10 percent of principal investigators receive more than 25 percent of their research support from industry. In comparison, faculty members in chemistry and engineering receive industrial funds almost twice as frequently.

■ Four Kinds of University-Industry Collaborations

There are at least four kinds of collaboration between academia and the pharmaceutical industry. The two most common are project-specific research support and consulting arrangements with pharmaceutical firms. Two less common forms of collaboration—large-scale, multiyear, investments in academic research centers by private companies and ownership or control of industrial firms by a university or its faculty—have received much more popular attention in recent years, perhaps because of their novelty in the life sciences and their potential impact on traditional academic values and norms of behavior (228).

Figure 9-4—Proportion of Faculty Receiving a Given Percent or More of Research Budgets From Industry, 1984

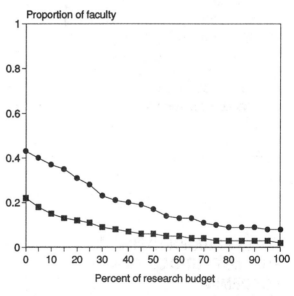

SOURCE: Reprinted with permission from D.B. Blumenthal, M.E. Gluck, K.S. Louis, et al., "University-Industry Relationships in Biotechnology Implications for the University," *Science* 232:1361-1366, 1986.

---

[7] The data also indicate that the vast majority of life scientists responding to the survey (81 percent) used biotechnological techniques.

Table 9-2—Large-Scale Pharmaceutical R&D Agreements Between Universities and Industry

Partners (university/firm)	Funds ($ millions)	Duration (years)	Year established	Area
Harvard University Medical School/Monsanto	$ 23.5	12	1974	Cancer angiogenesis
Leicester University/ICI	4.2	12	1978	Genetics
Massachusetts General Hospital/Hoechst	70.0	12	1981	Molecular biology
Scripps Institute/Johnson & Johnson	30.0	Open-ended	1981	Synthetic vaccine
Washington University/Mallink	3.8	5	1981	Hybridomas
Harvard University Medical School/Dupont	6.0	5	1981	Genetics
Yale University/Celanese	1.1	5	1981	Enzymes
Johns Hopkins University/Johnson & Johnson	1.0	Open-ended	1982	Biology
Rockefeller University/Monsanto	4.0	5	1982	Photosynthesis
Washington University/Monsanto	100.0	12	1982	Biomedical research
Yale University/Bristol Myers	3.0	5	1982	Anticancer drugs
Cold Spring Laboratory/Exxon	7.5	5	1982	Molecular genetic
Rochester University/Kodak (Sterling)	0.5	Open-ended	1983	DNA
Columbia University/Bristol-Myers	2.3	6	1983	Gene structure
Oxford University/Monsanto	20.0	5	1983	Glycoproteins
Georgetown University/Fidia	62.0	Open-ended	1985	Neurosciences
Harvard Medical School/Takeda	1.0[a]	Open-ended	1986	Angiogenesis factors
Oxford University/Squibb	32.0	7	1987	Pharmacology (central nervous system)
Johns Hopkins University/SmithKline Beckman	2.2	5	1988	Respiratory disease
Cambridge University/SmithKline French	4.0	5	1988	Molecular medicine
Oxford University/Beecham	8.0	10	1989	Neuropsychobiology
University of London P/Squibb	47.0	7	1989	Molecular biology: proteins
Massachusetts General Hospital/Shiseido	85.0	1	1989	Dermatology
University College London/Eisai	75.0	15	1990	Neuroscience
Harvard University Medical School/Hoffman-LaRoche	10.0	5	1990	Medicinal chemistry
Massachusetts General Hospital/Bristol-Myers Squibb	37.0	5	1990	Cardiovascular
University of California at San Diego/Ciba Ceigy	20.0	6	1990	Rheumatoid and osteoarthritis

[a] Harvard Medical School/Takeda contract is $1 million per annum (open-ended).

SOURCE: A.J. Webster and H. Etzkowitz, *Academic-Industry Relations: The Second Academic Revolution: A Framework Paper for a Proposed Workshop on Academic-Industry Relations* (London, England, Science Policy Support Group, 1991).

Support for specific research projects by firms that use the techniques of biotechnology in their R&D totaled between $85 and $135 million in 1984, or between 8 and 24 percent of all funds available for biomedical research in academia (51).[8] Spending per project was less than the average size of NIH grants, and they were typically of a shorter duration suggesting industrially supported research can be more focused and applied in nature than that funded by government (51,483).

Life science faculty at major research-intensive universities also receive support through *consulting arrangements* with private firms. About 40 percent of such faculty had consulted with industry for money at least once over the 3-year period ending in 1984 (53).

Large-scale collaborations between pharmaceutical companies and academia are largely a phenomenon of biology and pharmacology (511). Although these agreements may represent extensive support and collaborative opportunities for the faculty involved, they are relatively infrequent. Table 9-2 lists the bulk of such relationships of direct or indirect relevance to the pharmaceutical industry. In some cases, the industrial partner may create an entire physical structure in which industrially-supported work

---

[8] Because biotechnology has applications beyond biology and medicine, some of this estimated industrial support of academic research went for work in fields such as agriculture.

takes place; in others the company may support research in an existing academic facility.

Among other potential benefits to the industrial partner, some collaborations allow the placement of company scientists in university laboratories. Table 9-2 shows the industrial commitment in these relationships is often for a longer period than is industrial project-specific support. Though some systematic research about the structure, workings, and scientific or commercial outcomes of these large collaborations is currently underway, little is known about them today (228,512).

Private industrial ventures begun by universities or their faculty have created controversy about the appropriate limits of commercial activities on campus. Such startup ventures come in two main varieties: 1) commercial ventures established directly by the university to commercialize academic research and to benefit the school financially; and 2) firms founded by individual faculty members to commercialize their own research, usually for the financial benefit of the founders and other stockholders.

One of the earliest universities to try to capture the commercial benefits of its faculty's research is the University of Wisconsin, whose Wisconsin Alumni Research Foundation (WARF) dates from the 1920s. All faculty at the University of Wisconsin are required to assign the rights to patents arising from their work to the independent WARF, which then attempts to license the technology. Proceeds are shared by the university and the inventing faculty member. The vast majority of all its income is attributable to a single early patent of importance to the dairy industry, which suggests that such enterprises may be unable to generate much patent income for the university (50).

Despite the mixed success of the WARF example, during the 1980s a number of other research-intensive universities created similar institutions to commercialize campus research. The growth of these arrangements is partly due to the increasing opportunities to commercialize academic life science research and partly to a 1980 change in law that gave universities sole ownership of patents arising from government-sponsored research (Public Law 96-517)[9] (228).

An important feature of almost all these enterprises is that they are organizationally independent of the universities that own them. The separation is intended to prevent commercial considerations from perverting the traditional academic values of the university.

Critics of these arrangements have questioned whether true organizational separation is possible given the frequent involvement of individuals with strong ties to the parent university in the decisions of the commercial enterprise (50,228). Indeed, Harvard University soundly rejected a 1980 proposal to establish a firm to commercialize research because it was considered incompatible with the university's central missions of learning and the pursuit of knowledge (54). By 1988, the attitude had changed; the university reversed itself by establishing Medical Science Partners, an enterprise designed to commercialize biomedical research findings in a manner similar to WARF. In doing so, the university faced little of the faculty questioning or media attention that accompanied the 1980 proposal (514). To date, no evidence is available on whether these enterprises have in fact stimulated commercialization of research findings or whether the earlier fears of the critics were justified.

In the 1980s, many faculty in the life sciences founded companies with products or services based on their own research (445,450). Some early products based on biotechnology (such as diagnostic tests using monoclonal antibody technology) had a relatively fast R&D period, thus

---

[9] The Bach-Dole Patent and Trademark Act of 1980 (Public Law 96-517) gave universities, nonprofit organizations, and small businesses the rights to inventions resulting from research supported with Federal grants. It also required these institutions to share any royalty income from patents with the individuals responsible for the invention. Congress extended these patent rights in 1984 to Federal laboratories operated by universities and nonprofit corporations (Public Law 98-620).

generating early revenues and increasing interest in such enterprises among other faculty and the investment community (419).

Faculty-founded companies led universities to question how deeply involved in the commercial enterprise a faculty member should become while maintaining his or her university affiliations (228,415,511). In recent years, some universities have banned faculty equity holding in firms that support the faculty members' own research, while others have relied on faculty disclosure of such financial interests and a case-by-case consideration of their appropriateness (51,331).

Although individual cases have been controversial, the scanty evidence that exists suggests the phenomenon of faculty equity-holding in commercial enterprises is actually very infrequent. In 1985 only 8 percent of faculty involved in biotechnology at universities reported holding equity in a firm whose products or services were based on their research (53). In addition, only 0.5 percent held equity in firms from whom they also received support for their university research. Although responding faculty may have underreported these activities, the 8 percent no doubt includes equity ownership in nonstartup firms.

■ Issues in Current University-Industry Collaborations

During the early 1980s, as the frequency of industrial collaborations grew, so did questions about their ethical implications for the university and the appropriate balance between the potential risks and the benefits gained by the transfer of academic research to productive industrial applications (54,234). Among the most often-mentioned potential risks of university-industry collaboration are conflicts over faculty time commitments to the university, conflicts of interest for faculty who are in a position to benefit financially from their university laboratory research, and increased secrecy or other restrictions on the dissemination of industrial research results.

There is little evidence that the behaviors associated with these risks are at all widespread. Although one survey found that a minority of faculty has done some research in which the results could not be published without consent of the sponsor, the faculty who collaborate with industry tend to be among the most productive (53). They publish and teach more than their colleagues, so commitment to the academic institution appears not to be a big problem.[10] As indicated earlier, the potential for conflicts of interest arising from faculty involvement in startup firms appears to exist in only a very small minority of cases. Furthermore, in the last 2 years, the Federal Government and the research community itself have taken steps to prevent researchers from having any financial interest in the outcome of research they conduct.[11]

TARGETED FEDERAL PHARMACEUTICAL R&D PROGRAMS

In addition to the general research and training support that makes up the life science research infrastructure, NIH and other parts of the Federal Government have established 13 programs specifically targeted to fund pharmaceutical R&D.

---

[10] Data from the surveys conducted by Blumenthal and colleagues (52) suggest that while firms' expectations of their academic collaborators may vary, there is a general consensus about what constitutes acceptable behavior for academics who collaborate with firms. For example, patent rights arising from industrially supported research are expected to be owned by the university, although firms sometimes may have the right of first refusal for exclusive licensing for some period of time. Researchers have a right to publish and are usually not expected to protect trade secrets for a firm (52). A recent survey of graduate school deans suggests there has been increasing administrative attention to these ethical issues on campus as measured by the adoption and revision of university policies governing student and faculty communication of research results, teaching commitments, and interactions with industry (249).

[11] For example, in 1989, the *New England Journal of Medicine* (NEJM) adopted a policy that required authors to sign a statement that they had no personal financial interest in a firm that could benefit from the outcome of research reported in articles submitted to the journal for review and possible publication (347). The American Medical Association House of Delegates has considered the issue, and the *Journal of the American Medical Association* has adopted policies similar to those of NEJM (10). NIH is spearheading an effort for the Public Health Service to develop similar guidelines for the recipients of Federal health research funds. In April 1989, NIH solicited comments on proposed regulations (54 FR 17828), but has not yet issued a revised set of guidelines.

There are also cases in which federally supported research projects incidentally, but directly, influence pharmaceutical R&D, even though the government is pursuing research goals far removed from the discovery and development of new therapies. Consider a hypothetical research project:

> In an effort to understand the physiology of a particular disease, researchers test the hypothesis that the absence of a substance naturally produced by the body (such as an enzyme or protein), but largely lacking in patients suffering from the condition, actually causes the disease. The research involves administering to people with the disease a pharmaceutical compound that is used to treat another disease but is known to stimulate the body's production of the missing substance. The researchers' main objective is to understand whether providing the substance alleviates the disease. However, the research may also benefit the makers of the drug or biological who now have a potential new indication for which they may seek Food and Drug Administration (FDA) approval.

This mixing of basic research with more applied efforts that directly advance the development of new drug therapies makes it difficult to sort out the exact nature of any implied subsidy of private pharmaceutical R&D. OTA's discussions with Public Health Service (PHS) officials and its reviews of federally supported biomedical research projects suggest the use of potential pharmaceutical compounds in projects aimed at increasing basic understanding of diseases can be a common form of such hybrid work. Thus, it is difficult to assess how much of a research project represents targeted drug R&D as the private sector would perform it, how much merely aids such private efforts but does not mimic it, and how much is clearly unrelated to the drug R&D process. Box 9-A provides several examples of the link between federally supported basic research and the development of new drugs.

OTA identified 13 programs within the Federal Government whose specific mission is to conduct R&D involving actual or potential pharmaceutical products. There is no ambiguity in these

---

Box 9-A—Examples of the Link Between Basic Federal Biomedical Research and the Development of New Drugs

All basic research supported through the disease-oriented institutes of NIH and ADAMHA contributes to the ability to research and develop new pharmaceuticals by increasing fundamental understanding of normal and diseased functioning of living organisms. The line where untargeted basic research ends and targeted drug discovery begins is hazy at best. About $4.4 billion of the $6.9 billion appropriated for R&D at the Public Health Service in 1989 was for basic research.[1] The results of this public funding for basic research provide a necessary foundation for subsequent pharmaceutical R&D. The following three examples show how basic research in the biological sciences ultimately affects the introduction of new pharmaceutical products.

- In the early 1960s, scientists at the National Eye Institute (NEI) showed that cataracts (an obstruction of the lens of the eye) in animals with diabetes were due to the formation and accumulation of polyols (sugar alcohols). They discovered that an enzyme, aldose reductase, converts blood sugars (which are found in high levels in diabetics) into polyols. The sugar alcohols accumulate in cells, weaken the cell membrane, and eventually leak out of the cell, causing the cataracts. The discovery of aldose

---

[1] According to National Science Foundation definitions, "in basic research, the objective of the sponsoring agency is to gain fuller knowledge or understanding of the fundamental aspects of phenomena and of observable facts without specific applications toward processes or products in mind." Hence, this would exclude any research where the goal is to identify, characterize, or test an actual, potential pharmaceutical product.

(Continued on next page)

Box 9-A—Examples of the Link Between Basic Federal Biomedical Research and the Development of New Drugs—(Continued)

reductase and its role in diabetic cataracts led scientists to search for therapies that block the enzyme's action. The resulting class of drugs, aldose reductase inhibitors (ARIs), became the first therapies for diabetic complications that are unaffected by other treatments for diabetes itself (i.e., insulin used to lower blood sugar levels).[2] Current NEI research is intended to understand the role of aldose reductase and polyols in causing other complications of diabetes, including nerve and kidney damage.

- Since 1987, the National Institute of Allergies and Infectious Diseases (NIAID) has provided just under $3 million in grant support to three projects of research on the structure, functioning, and replication of rhinoviruses, which are estimated to cause 50 percent of common colds. The purpose of this support is to provide enough fundamental understanding of these viruses that pharmaceutical companies will be willing to invest in the development of preventive or therapeutic drugs. Laboratory analysis funded by NIAID has identified unique features of all rhinoviruses and has led to the development of drugs (called WIN compounds) that block viral replication in animals. Study of these drugs in animals (funded by NIAID) in turn increased fundamental scientific understanding of how the viruses behave in the body. At the same time, Sterling Winthrop pharmaceuticals has recently received investigational new drug (IND) status to test WIN compounds in humans.[3]

- Over the last 15 years, the National Institute on Drug Abuse (NIDA) provided sustained support for basic research to understand the specific mechanisms by which opiates affect brain cells and cause pain relief, addiction, and various side effects. In particular, NIDA-supported scientists have found that different opiate compounds attach themselves to brain cells at different places. This understanding has provided researchers with leads with which to seek medications to treat drug addictions. The NIDA-supported discovery of how opiates affect brain cells also provided scientists with a technique for rapidly screening potential pharmaceuticals that may act upon brain cells; researchers can determine if the pharmaceutical candidate "binds" to a desired "binding site" found on brain cells, and whether or not it also binds to undesired sites. This screening technique has been used by academic and industrial researchers in the development of new pain relievers and antipsychotic drugs among other types of pharmaceuticals.

---

[2] NEI also played a major role in clinical testing of these therapies by jointly designing, funding and conducting with Pfizer Pharmaceuticals a 5-year multicenter, randomized clinical trial of Pfizer's investigational ARI, Sorbinil™, in patients with diabetes. This Soribinil Retinopathy Trial (SRT) showed that this particular ARI compound was not significantly effective and caused adverse reactions in some patients.

[3] Neither NIAID or any other research agency of the Federal Government has provided support for these clinical studies.

SOURCE: Office of Technology Assessment, 1993. Based on data from: Dvornik D., Simard-Duquesne N., Kraml M., et al., "Inhibition of Aldose Reductase in Vivo," *Science* 182:1146-1147, 1973; Groft, S., Acting Director, Office of Science Policy and Legislation, National Institutes of Health, Public Health Service, U.S. Department of Health and Human Services, Bethesda, MD, personal communication, February 8, 1991; Heinz, B.A., Ruechert, R., Shepard, D.A., et al., "Genetics and Molecular Analyses of Spontaneous Rahino Virus #14 Mutants of Human Cells that are Resistant to an Antiviral Compound," *Journal of Virology* 63:2476-2485, 1989; Kinoshita, J.H., "Cataracts in Galactosemia," *Investigative Ophthalmololgy and Visual Sciences* 5:786-789, 1965; Kinoshita, J.H., Dvornik, D., Draml, M., et al., "The Effect of an Aldose Reductase Inhibitor on the Galactose-Exposed Rabbit Lens," *Biochimica et Biophysica Acta* 158:472-475, 1968; Kinoshita, J.H., "Mechanism Initiating Cataract Formation," *Investigative Ophthalmology and Visual Sciences* 13:713-724, 1974; National Science Board, *Science and Engineering Indicators-1989*, NSB Pub. No. 89-1 (Washington, DC: U.S. Government Printing Office, 1989); Pevear, D.C., Fancher, M.J., Felock, P.J. et al., "Confirmational Change in the Floor of Human Rahino Virus Canyon Blocks Adsorption to HeLa Cell Receptor," *Journal of Virology* 63:2002-2007, 1989; Rossman, M.G., "The Structure of Antiviral Agents that Inhibit Uncoating When Complexed with Viral Capsids," *Antiviral Research* 11(1):3-13, 1989; Sakamoto, N., Kinoshita, J.H., Kador, P.F., and Hotta N (eds.), *Polyol Pathway and its Role in Diabetic Complications: Proceedings of the International Symposium on Polyol Pathways and their Role in Diabetic Complications* (New York, NY: Excerpta Medica, 1988); *Science*, "The Microchip Microbe Hunters," *Science* 247:804-806, 1990; Van Heyningen, R., "Formation of Polyols by the Lens of the Rat with Sugar Cataract," *Nature* 184:194-196, 1959.

programs. They are intended to make new therapies available through public funding of R&D. Together, these 13 programs accounted for $387 million in spending in fiscal year 1989, about 55 percent of the total (preclinical and clinical) government-sponsored drug R&D estimated by OTA in the next two sections. It is impossible to estimate the proportion of these funds devoted to preclinical research, because most of the 13 programs support both clinical and laboratory research.

One program—National Cancer Institute's (NCI) Cancer Therapy Evaluation program, which accounts for 78 percent of the $387 million fiscal year 1989 funding—is devoted exclusively to clinical testing of cancer drugs. The NCI drug development programs together accounted for roughly 80 percent of all funds for Federal dedicated drug development programs in fiscal year 1989 (see table K-1 in appendix K). All but one of these programs, the Department of the Army's Antimalarial Program, are at NIH.[12]

The 13 programs vary in size, purpose, and methods of operation. Some have significant intramural laboratory programs; others are extramural grant and contract programs. Appendix K contains a summary of the 13 Federal dedicated pharmaceutical R&D programs.

What is the justification for direct public spending on targeted drug discovery? In certain cases, public health authorities have determined that national priorities necessitate public investment to speed the process of developing new therapies. Illnesses related to human immunodeficiency virus (HIV) is one example. There may also be barriers to private-sector involvement. The orphan drug programs exist because some conditions affect so few patients that the private sector might otherwise find investment in potential treatments financially unprofitable.

In another example, the National Institute on Drug Abuse suggested to OTA that private pharmaceutical firms have traditionally shown little interest in medications to treat substance abuse because of difficulties in getting clinical research subjects to comply with research protocols (343). It is also possible that firms perceive products for substance abuse treatment to represent relatively low potential returns, perhaps because of limited third-party coverage of such services.

Another reason the Federal Government conducts or supports targeted drug discovery is the difficulty of distinguishing basic from applied investigation. At least one long-time observer of science policy, Donald E. Stokes, has noted that most research projects have at once basic and applied qualities (410). Another observer has suggested that making such separations in the life sciences has become more difficult in the last 15 years as the development of new biotechnological techniques has "collapsed" the amount of time traditionally needed to move from basic scientific understanding to potential products, including drugs (306).[13]

▮ Federal Support for Preclinical Drug R&D

OTA asked NIH and the former Alcohol, Drug Abuse and Mental Health Administration (ADAMHA), which together make up the bulk of Federal health-related R&D, to estimate all of their expenditures for preclinical drug discovery, whether or not such expenditures were made as part of one of the targeted drug development programs described above.

The results must be considered rough estimates, because the institutes did not uniformly follow OTA's guidelines for classifying research projects, and some institutes were unable to

---

[12] One of the programs, the Drug Abuse Medication Development Program, is administered by the National Institute on Drug Abuse (NDA) which was part of ADAMHA until 1992. Recent legislation has moved this institute to NIH (Public Law 102-321).

[13] To make the division of labor between the Federal Government and private industry even less tidy, most industrial scientists interviewed by OTA during our visits to eight pharmaceutical firms stressed that while their primary mission is to bring new drugs to market, their work can also produce advances in basic scientific understanding. Such industrial contributions to the scientific literature are borne out by analyses of bibliographic and citation databases (286).

Table 9-3—Estimates of NIH and ADAMHA Research Support for Preclinical Pharmaceutical Screening, Synthesis, Evaluation and Development Activities, Fiscal Years 1988-90 ($ thousands)

	Fiscal year 1988	Fiscal year 1989	Fiscal year 1990
NIH			
NCI	$283,576	$308,851	$316,729
NHLBI[a]	28,324	31,983	28,350
NIAID[b]	46,603	52,358	64,897
NIDDK[c]	8,500	9,417	9,700
NICHD[d]			
NIA[a]	1,265	0	955
NINDS[e]	4,812	6,168	5,079
NIDR[f]	14,165	14,918	11,056
NCRR[g]	10,502	12,296	11,485
NIAMS[c]	284	275	618
NEI		6,420	8,557
ADAMHA[h]			
NIMH	N/A	N/A	N/A
NIDA	N/A	N/A	28,843
NIAAA	N/A	6,286	13,261
Total[i]	398,031	448,972	499,530

[a] NHLBI, NIA: Data are institutes' best estimates.
[b] NIAID: Based on narrow definition of drug development; may differ from earlier NIAID reports.
[c] NIDDK: Estimates include clinical research.
[d] NICHD: National drug development and clinical research cannot be separated; both included in clinical estimates (table 9-5).
[e] NINDS: Estimates prior to fiscal year 1990 with approximately 10 percent variance.
[f] NIDR: Fiscal year 1990 is the most accurate; others are likely overestimates.
[g] NCRR: Includes clinical research involving pharmaceutical development.
[h] ADAMHA: Data not available for following institutes and years: NIMH—fiscal years 1988 and 1989; NIDA—fiscal year 1988; NIAAA—fiscal years 1988, 1989, and 1990.
[i] Totals are only an approximation since data for several institutes are missing (counted as zero) and data for others include clinical activities.

KEY: ADAMHA = Alcohol, Drug Abuse and Mental Health Administration. NCI = National Cancer Institute. NCRR = National Center for Research Resources. NEI = National Eye Institute. NHLBI = National Heart, Lung and Blood Institute. NIA = National Institutes on Aging. NIAAA = National Institute on Alcohol Abuse and Alcoholism. NIAID = National Institute of Allergy and Infectious Diseases. NIAMS = National Institute of Arthritis and Musculoskeletal and Skin Diseases. NICHD = National Institute of Child Health and Human Development. NIDA = National Institute on Drug Abuse. NIDDK = National Institute of Diabetes and Digestive and Kidney Diseases. NIDR = National Institute of Dental Research. NIH = National Institutes of Health. NIMH = National Institute of Mental Health. NINDS = National Institute of Neurological Disorders and Stroke.

SOURCE: Office of Technology Assessment, 1993. Based on data provided by individual institutes of the Public Health Service, U.S. Department of Health and Human Services.

provide any estimates at all. Total estimated preclinical pharmaceutical R&D constituted approximately $450 million in 1988 (table 9-3), about 6 percent of the overall combined research budgets of NIH and ADAMHA. Such activity is highly concentrated at NIH, with a majority falling within the National Cancer Institute. OTA also estimated that NIH and ADAMHA's 1988 preclinical drug research spending of $400 million represented roughly 14 percent of the amount spent by private pharmaceutical firms for similar R&D functions (table 9-4).

Table 9-4—Estimates of NIH and ADAMHA Preclinical Pharmaceutical Research Support as a Percentage of PMA Firms' Expenditures for Preclinical R&D Activities, Fiscal Year 1988

	Estimate
A. PMA firms' R&D for human ethical pharmaceuticals[a]	$6.31 billion
B. Percent preclinical[b]	44%
C. PMA firms' preclinical R&D (A multiplied by B)	$2.77 billion
D. NIH/ADAMHA preclinical pharmaceutical R&D[c]	$ .40 billion
E. NIH/ADAMHA as a percent of PMA (D divided by C)	14%

[a] From Annual PMA Survey Reports, 1988-90.
[b] R&D functions included: "biological screening and pharmacological testing," "synthesis and extraction, pharmaceutical dosage, formulation, and stability testing," and "toxicology and safety testing." Excluded functions: "process development for manufacturing and quality control," all "clinical evaluation," "regulatory, investigational new drug and new drug approval preparation, submission and processing," and "other."
[c] Assumption for middle estimate is a rough approximation based on data from individual institutes of the Public Health Service, U.S. Department of Health and Human Services (presented in table 9-3); assumption of high and low estimates are 50 percent higher and lower than middle estimate.

KEY: ADAMHA = Alcohol, Drug Abuse and Mental Health Administration; NIH = National Institutes of Health; PMA = Pharmaceutical Manufacturers Association.

SOURCE: Office of Technology Assessment, 1993.

■ Federal Support for Clinical Drug R&D

OTA also requested NIH and ADAMHA to provide estimates of clinical research involving pharmaceuticals. Table 9-5 presents estimates

Table 9-5—Estimates of NIH and ADAMHA Support for Clinical Research Involving Pharmaceuticals, Fiscal Years 1988-90 ($ thousands)

	Fiscal year 1988	Fiscal year 1989	Fiscal year 1990
NIH			
NCI	$ 51,991	$ 55,072	$ 57,889
NHLBI	22,555	30,292	26,540
NIAID[a]	61,394	80,236	96,304
NIDDK			
NICHD[b]	11,252	12,512	11,107
NIA[c]	2,686	1,934	3,380
NINDS[d]	23,324	25,060	
NIDR[e]	9,193	8,127	5,246
NCRR	6,502	6,762	5,246
NEI	6,523	6,849	5,877
ADAMHA[f]			
NIMH	7,782	6,661	6,293
NIDA		16,500	17,500
NIAAA			1,227
Total[g]	203,202	250,005	237,977

[a] NIAID: Fiscal year 1990 is rough estimate.
[b] NIDDK and NICHD: Clinical and drug development activities could not be separated. NIDDK estimates were reported as preclinical (table 9-3). NICHD figures were reported here (as clinical research).
[c] NIA: Data are best estimates; not based on CRISP search.
[d] NINDS: Fiscal year 1990 unavailable; fiscal year 1989 based on examination of abstracts from CRISP search; estimates for earlier years based on fiscal year 1989.
[e] NIDR: Figure for fiscal year 1990 is most accurate, based on review of abstracts; others are rough estimates.
[f] ADAMHA: Data not available for following institutes and years: NIDA—fiscal year 1988; NIAAA—fiscal years 1988 and 1989.
[g] Totals are approximation since data for some institutes are missing (counted as zero) and data for others include nonclinical activities.

KEY: ADAMHA = Alcohol, Drug Abuse and Mental Health Administration. NCI = National Cancer Institute. NCRR = National Center for Research Resources. NEI = National Eye Institute. NHLBI = National Heart, Lung and Blood Institute. NIA = National Institute on Aging. NIAAA = National Institute on Alcohol Abuse and Alcoholism. NIAID = National Institute of Allergy and Infectious Diseases. NICHD = National Institute of Child Health and Human Development. NIDA = National Institute on Drug Abuse. NIDDK = National Institute of Diabetes and Digestive and Kidney Diseases. NIDR = National Institute of Dental Research. NIH = National Institutes of Health. NIMH = National Institute of Mental Health. NINDS = National Institute of Neurological Disorders and Stroke.

SOURCE: Office of Technology Assessment, 1993; based on data provided by individual institutes of the Public Health Service, U.S. Department of Health and Human Services.

provided by NIH and ADAMHA. The participating institutes estimated that between $200 million and $250 million per year was spent on research involving clinical pharmaceutical investigation in the fiscal years 1987-90. Together NIH and ADAMHA clinical research in 1988 represented roughly 11 percent of clinical research conducted by Pharmaceutical Manufacturers Association (PMA) firms in that year (table 9-6).

These estimates by themselves divulge little about the nature of clinical pharmaceutical research directly supported by the Federal Government. OTA reviewed federally funded clinical research projects for four drugs approved for marketing in the United States by the FDA in 1987—lovastatin, fluoxetine, zuidovidine (AZT), and tissue plasmiogen activator (TPA). The results indicated that the clinical projects supported by NIH and ADAMHA institutes span the pre- and post-FDA-approval periods. Projects involving drugs already approved for marketing include attempts to better understand the efficacy or safety of the drug as well as investigations into potential new indications for its use. Pharmaceu-

Table 9-6—Estimates of NIH/ADAMHA Support for Clinical Pharmaceutical R&D as a Percentage of PMA Firms' Expenditures for Clinical R&D Activities, Fiscal Year 1988

	Estimate
A. PMA firms' R&D for human ethical pharmaceuticals[a]	$6.31 billion
B. Percent clinical[b]	30%
C. PMA firms' clinical R&D (A multiplied by B)	$1.89 billion
D. NIH/ADAMHA clinical pharmaceutical R&D[c]	$ .20 billion
E. NIH/ADAMHA as a percent of PMA (D divided by C)	11%

[a] From Annual PMA Survey Reports, 1988-90.
[b] Clinical evaluation = phases I, II, III, and IV
[c] Estimate is based on data from individual institutes of the Public Health Service, U.S. Department of Health and Human Services (see table 9-5).

KEY: ADAMHA = Alcohol, Drug Abuse and Mental Health Administration; NIH = National Institute of Health; PMA = Pharmaceutical Manufacturers Association.

SOURCE: Office of Technology Assessment, 1993.

Box 9-B—NIH Clinical Trials Involving Cholesterol-Lowering Drugs

The class of cholesterol lowering drugs called HMG-CoA reductase inhibitors whose discovery and development is described in box 4-A has also been the subject of clinical research at NIH. In 1987, an advisory committee of the National Heart, Lung and Blood Institute (NHLBI) recommended that the institute fund a large-scale, multiyear trial to evaluate the long-term effectiveness and safety of this class of drug as a means of preventing fatal and nonfatal heart attacks among the elderly. Because the three drugs in this class currently on the U.S. market were approved on the basis of the short-term, "surrogate" measure of effectiveness—whether or not they lowered levels of cholesterol in blood—there was no available empirical evidence as to whether these drugs actually prevented death, particularly among the elderly. Given that as many as 60 million people are estimated to have high cholesterol, but fewer than 1 million people currently receive drug therapy, the results of this investment by NIH could have important scientific and economic implications. On the one hand, the trial could reinforce the effectiveness of this drug, thus maintaining or brightening their market prospects. On the other hand, if the research suggests the drugs are not effective or carry unforeseen risks for patients, the market for these drugs could evaporate.

Although funds were not available to mount a full-scale trial, which was expected to cost at least $60 million and involve 5,500 research subjects at 16 to 20 locations, NHLBI did fund a 2-year, $2.5-million pilot study to estimate the cost of the full-scale trial and to identify potential problems in carrying it out. The pilot study, called the Cholesterol Reduction in Seniors Program (CRISP), began in July 1990 at five sites (chosen by NHLBI through a competitive process) and involved 400 research subjects. In addition to measuring the rate at which potential subjects agree to participate in the trial and their compliance with the trial's protocol, the pilot study also collected data on side effects, the extent of cholesterol reduction observed, and a number of other measures of the drug's efficacy and long-term toxicity in elderly patients.

The three HMG-CoA reductase inhibitors currently available in the United States are manufactured by two firms: lovastatin and simvastatin by Merck, and pravastatin by Bristol-Myers Squibb. NHLBI invited each of the manufacturers to submit proposals to NIH for the use of their drugs in the trial. Because NHLBI considered the two companies' proposals to be equivalent, it suggested using both companies' products.

(Continued on next page)

tical firms typically provide the Federal Government with drugs used in federally supported trials at no cost; but the other costs of the trial are funded by the government.

The National Heart, Lung and Blood Institute's (NHLBI) potential support of a trial comparing the use of different HMG-CoA reductase inhibitors in treating high levels of serum cholesterol, described in greater detail in box 9-B, is an example of Federal support for clinical research on a drug—lovastatin—that is already marketed. Several other examples of federally supported investigations into new indications for drugs already marketed came from the National Institute of Mental Health (NIMH), which has supported trials testing new uses of a drug, fluoxet-

ine, that is already marketed as a treatment for depression.

As in the case of AZT, a drug whose use in treating HIV was demonstrated in research at NCI during the 1980s, the Federal Government also supports trials whose results ultimately yield evidence of efficacy and safety necessary for an FDA marketing application. NCI's involvement with AZT was the result of an urgent, specific Federal initiative to find therapies for HIV and its related illnesses (276,493). Because of data limitations, OTA was unable to make any better estimate of how frequently the Federal Government funds clinical work that later becomes part of a firm's new drug application.

When NIH supports clinical research, part of the total health care expenses incurred by patients

When one of the companies rejected this proposal, NHLBI chose to use Merck's lovastatin because it had received FDA marketing approval first and had experienced a low rate of serious side effects during its, by then, 3 years on the market. The pilot study's protocol involved two different doses of the drug and a placebo.

Merck bore the costs providing both the drug and placebo, including its distribution. All remaining costs associated with establishing the trial, administering the drug, diagnostic tests, related patient care, data collection, and analysis ($2.5 million) were paid by the Federal Government through NHLBI. According to NHLBI, industry scientists were not directly involved in planning the clinical trial or developing its protocol. They have participated in a steering committee for the pilot study convened by NHLBI, although they had no access to the study's data until its completion.

The pilot study ended in June 1992, and investigators expect to publish results in the medical literature during 1993. Plans are currently underway to make the full cholesterol-lowering trial part of a large Antihypertensive and Lipid-Lowering Treatment for the Prevention of Heart Attack Trial, which will begin in the fall of 1993. Of the 30,000 research subjects that will participate in this trial, 12,000 will meet researchers' criteria to receive an HMG-CoA reductase inhibitor. The study will follow these patients for 5 to 7 $\frac{1}{2}$ years, measuring heart attacks and long-term toxicity associated with the drugs. The researchers may also have sufficient statistical power to measure the potential effects of cholesterol reduction on overall mortality.

NHLBI has budgeted $78.3 million for the whole trial over 9 years. A protocol committee will convene in early 1993 to determine which drugs and what doses will be part of the trial. As of December 1992, NHLBI had entered into discussions with the relevant pharmaceutical manufacturers about their contributions to this effort. At a minimum, NHLBI hopes to receive drugs and placebos from the companies, but it may try to receive additional financial contribution as well in light of the importance of this research for the companies' markets. The role of pharmaceutical scientists (if any) in the design and administration of the trial is also yet to be determined.

SOURCE: Office of Technology Assessment, 1993. Based on information provided in personal communications from: S. Groft, NIH Office of Science Policy and Legislation, Feb. 8, 1991; C. Roth, Office of Policy and Legislation, National Heart Lung and Blood Institute, Dec. 22, 1992; J. Cutler, National Heart, Lung and Blood Institute, Dec. 22, 1992; David Gordon, National Heart, Lung and Blood Institute, Dec. 22, 1992; A. Garber, Assistant Professor of Internal Medicine, Stanford University, January 6, 1993.

enrolled in such trials is paid by the Federal Government. For those clinical trials conducted at the NIH clinical center, all services provided to patients are paid by the Federal Government (476). At other institutions, the cost of care associated with the research protocol is paid for by the Federal Government through research patient care rates established by the Department of Health and Human Services (DHHS). "Usual patient care" (e.g., items and services furnished ordinarily to patients by providers under the supervision of a physician or other certified health professional) are typically paid by the patient or the patient's health insurer.

INDUSTRY COLLABORATION WITH FEDERAL RESEARCH LABORATORIES

The Federal investment in biomedical research includes a substantial amount of intramural research conducted in Federal Government laboratories. In 1990, about $2.6 billion was spent on intramural health research at laboratories operated by the Federal Government (483).[14]

Over the last 10 years, Congress and the Executive Branch have paid increasing attention

[14] In addition to in-house research, this includes program management and direct operations attributable to health R&D. A total of $1.4 billion of this amount is for R&D that was performed at NIH. The remainder was performed at ADAMHA, FDA, CDC, Department of Defense, the Department of Veterans Affairs, the Environmental Protection Agency, the Department of Energy, and the National Aeronautical and Space Administration.

to the role of these Federal research laboratories in fostering commercial innovation. Legislation was enacted to encourage the transfer of research results from Federal laboratories to private firms when commercial applications are feasible. This section reviews Federal technology transfer activities within the Public Health Service, which contains NIH and other health research agencies.

■ Legislative History of Federal Technology Transfer Activities

Since 1950, the Federal Government has explicitly required Federal employees to report inventions created during the course of their work to the Federal Government (Executive Order 10096; 15 FR 389). Beyond this requirement, however, there was no uniform patent and licensing policy for all Federal agencies until 1980 when Congress passed the Stevenson-Wydler Technology Innovation Act (Public Law 96-480).

The Stevenson-Wydler Act made the transfer of Federal technology to the private sector a national policy and duty of Federal laboratories. Among its provisions, the act required that Federal laboratories spend at least 0.5 percent of their research budgets on ''Federal technology transfer activities.'' Additional legislation in 1984 directed the Department of Commerce to issue regulations governing licensing of technologies developed in Federal laboratories (Public Law 98-620; 50 FR 9801; 37 CFR 404).

These actions proved insufficient to bring about the intended level of formal interaction between government and industrial scientists (456), so Congress passed the Federal Technology Transfer (FTT) Act of 1986 (Public Law 99-502).

The FTT Act gives the Federal employee the right to his or her invention if the government determines the invention has no commercial value and does not intend to license it. The FTT Act also requires Federal agencies share at least 15 percent of royalties from any licensed inventions with the inventing scientists, and it directs agencies to establish cash awards for other personnel involved in productive Federal technology transfer activities.[15]

Most importantly, the legislation permits the establishment of formal cooperative research and development agreements (CRADAs) in which a Federal laboratory provides personnel, services, facilities, equipment or resources (but not funds), and a non-Federal party (e.g., a private company) provides funds, personnel, services, facilities, equipment or other resources for R&D.

The legislation does not provide any greater detail about the form or amount of resources each party must bring to a CRADA. It leaves implementation of a CRADA policy up to the relevant agency. As part of a CRADA, the Federal Government can agree in advance to grant licenses to the collaborating partner on any inventions resulting from research under the agreement. The use of CRADAs within the Public Health Service is discussed in greater detail later in this chapter.

■ Technology Transfer in the Public Health Service

NIH has taken the lead in implementing Federal technology transfer activities for PHS. Most of this responsibility has fallen to the Patent Policy Board (PPB), which recommends NIH policy, and to NIH's Office of Technology Transfer (OTT), which reports to the Board and carries on the administrative functions associated with technology transfer.[16] Federal technology transfer activities involving PHS laboratories and the private sector fall into three related areas: patenting policy, licensing policy, and CRADAs.

---

[15] The legislative history of the FTT Act stresses that it was not intended to alter any of the conflict-of-interest regulations that prevent current or former Federal employees from improperly benefiting from their government affiliation. At NIH, this includes limitations and prohibitions against renumeration from any outside source that has any formal agreement with an employee's laboratory or institute branch (478).

[16] The bulk of PHS technology transfer activity occurs at NIH. Although the Patent Policy Board and OTT are located at NIH, they now also recommend policy and administer CRADAs, patents, and licenses for ADAMHA and the Centers for Disease Control (CDC), the other PHS agencies with technology transfer activities.

PATENTING INVENTIONS OF FEDERAL BIOMEDICAL RESEARCH LABORATORIES

When an invention is created in a PHS laboratory or under a CRADA the Federal employee involved must report it to a technology development coordinator located in his or her institute so that patent applications may be filed before the discovery is published or discussed at scientific meetings. The coordinator determines whether the invention is patentable.

The number of patents filed annually by PHS has grown dramatically since 1987, the first year for which data on PHS patents are available. The number of applications more than doubled between 1987 and 1989 alone (figure 9-5). The number of patents awarded to PHS by the U.S. Patent and Trademark Office (PTO) in the same period did not increase, however, because of the substantial lag between application and award.[17] These trends indicate the financial incentives and organizational structure for patenting of inventions introduced in the FTT Act of 1986 had the desired effect.

LICENSING INVENTIONS FROM FEDERAL BIOMEDICAL RESEARCH LABORATORIES

Outside parties who want to use patented PHS inventions must obtain a license from the Federal Government. Under all PHS licensure agreements, the licensee must agree to make all efforts to develop a commercial product with the licensed invention. PHS monitors progress toward commercialization and can revoke the license under certain circumstances.

Royalties paid to the inventing PHS agency typically do not exceed 5 to 8 percent of the resulting product sales. The kinds of licenses available and the conditions under which they are given depend on the nature of the invention and whether or not it was developed as part of a CRADA (484,486). PHS grants *exclusive commercialization licenses* ''in cases where substantial additional risks, time and costs must be undertaken by a licensee prior to commercializa-

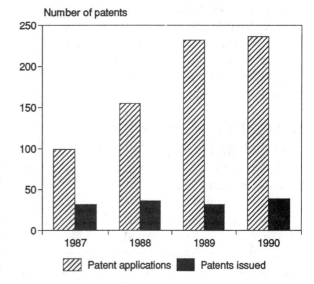

Figure 9-5—Public Health Service Patent Applications and Patents Issued, 1987-90

Number of patents

Patent applications   Patents issued

SOURCE: The Office of Technology Assessment, 1993. Based on data from U.S. Department of Health and Human Services, Public Health Service, National Institutes of Health, Office of Technology Transfer, 1991.

tion'' (484,486). Under CRADAs, collaborating firms may have the right to negotiate exclusive licenses to such inventions as part of the agreement itself.

Unless it receives a request for an exclusive license, PHS tries to negotiate *nonexclusive commercialization licenses* for inventions developed in its laboratories. Under such an agreement, PHS can license a single invention to more than one party. For both exclusive and nonexclusive licenses, PHS has developed a model agreement that is the basis for negotiations between it and the potential licensee.

PHS grants nonexclusive *research/evaluation licenses* to facilitate further research on the invention itself, but not for commercial production or as a substitute for commercially available research materials that the researcher could otherwise purchase. Research licenses are available even for inventions developed under a CRADA or

---

[17] The General Accounting Office found that the average time between patent application and issuance in 1988 was 21.0 months for all patents and 29.4 months for those involving biotechnology (433).

Figure 9-6—Licenses Issued by the U.S. Department of Health and Human Services, Fiscal Years 1977-91

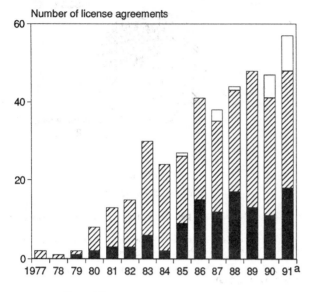

Number of license agreements

Type of license

☐ Research/evaluation   ■ Exclusive

▨ Nonexclusive

a Number in fiscal year 1991 annualized from the number of agreements reached during first 4 months of the year.

SOURCE: Office of Technology Assessment, 1993. Based on data from U.S. Department of Health and Human Services, Public Health Service, National Institutes of Health, Office of Technology Transfer, 1991.

already the subject of an exclusive commercial license by another party.[18]

Figure 9-6 shows the number of licenses issued by the DHHS through 1991.[19] These data indicate a fairly steady growth in licensing that predates the implementation of the FTT Act and CRADAs. Given the lag between patent application and issuance, the licensing data displayed in this figure do not capture any additional growth that might result from PHS's efforts since 1986 to promote technology transfer.

Pharmaceutical firms that license inventions from PHS laboratories receive economic benefits when the inventions are commercialized and lead to product sales. Private firms pay royalties to PHS (and its employees) that offset these economic benefits somewhat. Data on royalty income to PHS agencies suggest the royalties obtained by PHS are a small fraction of the total PHS intramural budget. In 1988, the total NIH royalty income (figure 9-7) was just 0.03 percent of total NIH intramural spending (76). Furthermore, the vast majority of all NIH royalty income in 1988 is attributable to a single institute and a single technology: NCI's HIV-antibody test kit, for which 12 nonexclusive licenses have been negotiated since 1984 (3,143). The patents on this

Figure 9-7—NIH/ADAMHA License Royalty Income, Fiscal Years 1987-90

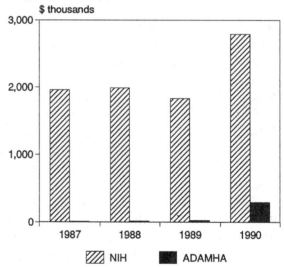

$ thousands

▨ NIH   ■ ADAMHA

KEY: ADAMHA = Alcohol, Drug Abuse, and Mental Health Administration; NIH = National Institute of Health.

SOURCE: Office of Technology Assessment, 1993. Based on data from U.S. Department of Health and Human Services, Public Health Service, National Institutes of Health, Office of Technology Transfer, 1991.

---

[18] In addition to licenses, the PHS also enters into materials transfer agreements, the most common formal relationships between a PHS laboratory and a private firm (3). Under such agreements (479) PHS provides biological research materials (such as a type of cell) not covered by a patent in return for a fee (479). The agreement also limits the scope the materials use, requires an acknowledgement of the PHS contribution in reporting research results, and absolves the government of liability associated with its use (Model MTA Agreement). PHS laboratories use the same agreement to obtain research materials from outside parties (3).

[19] Most DHHS patentable inventions, and hence licenses, are from NIH, ADAMHA, and CDC (72).

Figure 9-8—Distribution of NIH/ADAMHA Royalty Collections for Fiscal Year 1988

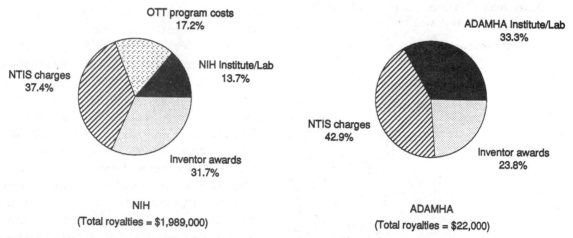

NIH
(Total royalties = $1,989,000)

ADAMHA
(Total royalties = $22,000)

a Net of $3.4 million in royalties from NCI's HIV antibody test kit licenses paid to private foundation as part of agreement with the French government. Inventor awards are calculated from gross revenue.

KEY: ADAMHA = Alcohol, Drug Abuse, and Mental Health Administration; NCI = National Cancer Institute; NIH = National Institute of Health; NTIS = National Technical Information Service; OTT = NIH Office of Technology Transfer; PHS = Public Health Service.

SOURCE: The Office of Technology Assessment, 1993. Based on data provided by the U.S. Department of Health and Human Services, Public Health Service, National Institutes of Health, Office of Technology Transfer, 1991.

one technology brought $1.76 million to NIH in fiscal year 1988, which represents 89 percent of all NIH royalties for that year.[20]

NIH takes the position that the purpose of royalties is to stimulate technology transfer by "offering an attractive incentive to encourage [PHS] scientists to participate in collaborations with industry ..." rather than to augment or replace funds appropriated by Congress for research (75). The distribution of royalties received by NIH and ADAMHA is consistent with this policy (figure 9-8). Almost one-third of NIH royalty income in 1988 went to the scientists responsible for the invention.[21] About 55 percent

of royalty income went to reimburse the government for the costs of negotiating and administering licenses themselves.[22] Only 14 percent (or $272,000) went back to the PHS division responsible for the invention.

The net returns to the licensee rise and fall directly with the ultimate cost to consumers of obtaining the product. The PHS policy governing exclusive licenses and licenses granted under CRADAs requires that prices of commercial products be commensurate with the extent of "public investment in the product, and the health and safety needs of the public" (486). The policy further states that licensees may be required to

---

[20] Royalties from licenses on these NCI patents actually totaled $5.16 million. However, under an agreement with the French Government settling a dispute over the discovery of HIV, $3.40 million was paid in 1988 to the nonprofit French-American AIDS Foundation to fund future work. A similar percentage of royalties from these licenses was paid in each of the other years, and is not reflected in the data.

[21] PHS policy directs inventing employees to get 25 percent of the first $50,000 of royalty income, 20 percent of the next $50,000, and 15 percent of the remainder up to $100,000 per employee per year from all patents for which they are inventors. NIH policy also allows some awards to go to noninventing employees that nonetheless contributed to the invention. After other expenses, the remainder is returned to the budget of the organizational unit responsible for the award (486).

In recent years (including 1988 as shown in figure 9-9), the amount of income to inventors for NCI's HIV-antibody test kit patents was calculated on the basis of gross revenues prior to the $3.4 million distribution to the French-American AIDS Foundation. Hence, final inventor awards in fiscal year 1988 totaled 32 percent of royalties actually turned over to the NIH.

[22] Until recently, the National Technical Information Service (NTIS) was charged with this function and received more than one-third of NIH royalties. The Office of Invention Development (now OTT) received about 17 percent to cover its costs. OTT has taken over the responsibilities previously carried out by NTIS.

Photo credit: *NATIONAL GAUCHER FOUNDATION*

After several years of treatment, this girl shows few visible signs of the Gaucher disease that afflicts her. The drug used in her treatment—Ceredase™—was originally discovered and developed by Federal scientists.

provide ''reasonable evidence'' to support their pricing decisions.

To date, PHS has implemented this pricing clause in only one case—the antiviral drug ddI manufactured under exclusive license by Bristol-Myer Squibb.[23]

Health consumers and activists have publicly questioned pharmaceutical pricing decisions for other products that have been developed at least in part through public investment (337). As mentioned earlier, the role of Federal laboratories in the development of one such drug, AZT, an antiviral drug used to treat HIV, has been the subject of public controversy and litigation stem-

ming, in part, from its price to consumers (276,493).

The case of Ceredase™, a treatment for the rare hereditary disorder Gaucher disease, also raises questions about the Federal Government's ability to protect the public's research investment in new drugs that come from our national laboratories. This drug, which is manufactured by Genzyme, Inc. of Massachusetts, was discovered in the early 1970s by NIH scientists and received FDA approval in 1991 on the basis of NIH designed, funded, and conducted clinical trials. An analysis by OTA[24] indicates that at Genzyme's current price and under accepted doses, this drug costs

---

[23] In a public hearing, representatives of patient groups at NIH in 1992 voiced no objections to Bristol-Myer Squibb's proposed price, which included a plan to give the drug free to those who could not otherwise afford it (3).

[24] OTA's analysis of the R&D leading to the Ceredase™ and the implications of the drug's costs is contained in a separately published OTA background paper prepared as part of this assessment (141).

patients between $71,000 and $550,000 per year, thus threatening the lifetime maximum insurance benefit of those with private insurance within a few years (455). Gaucher patients require this therapy for life. Because Ceredase™ is also a federally-designated orphan drug (as discussed later in this chapter), Genzyme has the right to market it without competition for 7 years.

While the pivotal discoveries for this drug predate current NIH technology transfer policies and procedures, it does suggest that the current mechanism of enforcing NIH's fair pricing policy alone might not be sufficient to protect the public's interest and ensure adequate compensation for the government's research investment. Even though OTA was able to infer a great deal about Genzyme's production costs and its own R&D investment in Ceredase™ from data provided by Genzyme, the company did not give sufficient information for OTA to determine independently the drug's ultimate profitability in the course of our year-long study of the drug (455). The Federal Government is likely to be faced with the same difficulties in gathering data upon which to make a confident judgment about the fair pricing of other drugs that come from its laboratories.

■ CRADAs

CRADAs give Federal laboratories the flexibility to accept industrial resources, including funds, and to provide Federal resources (except funds) for collaborative research. PHS encourages the use of CRADAs by Federal scientists who want to engage in collaborative R&D activities with outside parties (486). The disposition of intellectual property resulting from a CRADA follows the general PHS patenting and licensing guidelines described in previous sections of this chapter with the exception that the agreement may include a company's option to negotiate an exclusive license to any invention resulting from research under the CRADA.

Between fiscal years 1987 and 1990, 109 CRADAs were established within NIH and

Table 9-7—CRADAs Established by NIH and ADAMHA, Fiscal Years 1987-90

Year	Number of CRADAs established
1987	8
1988	21
1989	46
1990	34
Total CRADAs	109

KEY: ADAMHA = Alcohol Drug Abuse and Mental Health Administration; CRADAs = cooperative research and development agreements; NIH = National Institutes of Health.

SOURCE: Office of Technology Assessment, 1993. Based on data provided by U.S. Department of Health and Human Services, Public Health Service, National Institutes of Health, Office of Technology Transfer, 1991.

ADAMHA (table 9-7). An OTA analysis of CRADAs in effect in October 1990 in PHS (NIH, ADAMHA, CDC, and FDA) shows that CRADAs were heavily concentrated in the National Cancer Institute, which had 26 percent of all such agreements at that time (table 9-8).

Table 9-8—PHS CRADAs in Effect October 1990

CRADAs:	Percent[a]
in which the private collaborator is a PMA member	37%
in which NCI is the PHS collaborator	26
that are HIV- or AIDS-related	18
that involve the R&D of vaccines or other prophylactics	10
that involve the R&D of diagnostics	8
in which the private collaborator is a university or nonprofit institution	5

[a] Categories are not mutually exclusive or collectively exhaustive, and hence, do not add to 1.00.

KEY: AIDS = acquired immunodeficiency syndrome. CRADAs = cooperative research and development agreements; HIV = human immunodeficiency virus. NCI = National Cancer Institute. PHS = Public Health Service. PMA = Pharmaceutical Manufacturer Association.

SOURCE: Office of Technology Assessment, 1993. Based on data compiled from the U.S. Department of Health and Human Services, Public Health Service, National Institutes of Health, Office of Technology Transfer, *PHS Technology Transfer Directory*, October 1990.

Box 9-C—Examples of Two CRADAs at NIH

Thomas Kindt of the National Institute of Allergy and Infectious Diseases has been working with the gene for CD4—the protein that regulates the entry of HIV (human immunodeficiency virus) into cells—and wanted a good animal model for studying CD4 gene expression in lymphoid tissue. After reading one of Kindt's early papers, people from a Massachusetts company that makes transgenic animals called to propose a collaboration. They would make rabbits with the human CD4 gene, using their expertise at creating transgenic animals. Kindt would have the animal model he needed.

Says Kindt, "This is a nice, focused collaboration and provides my lab with resources we needed. I don't have the facilities for making rabbits." It does not cost Kindt a thing—the company pays for the breeding and care of the animals. And what does it get in return? The possibility that the rabbit will, in fact, turn out to be a good model for studying AIDS. Then, the company could make money selling these genetically special animals to people studying AIDS or testing AIDS drugs.

What would Kindt have done 3 years ago, before CRADA fever? He would have gone "hat in hand" to colleagues in academia who do research with transgenic animals. "I would have been asking for a favor," Kindt says, "and even if someone agreed, making animals for me would not necessarily be a top priority. With a CRADA I have a true collaboration."

Richard Jed Wyatt of the National Institute of Mental Health is another investigator who has made use of a CRADA to get needed research rabbits. A neuroscientist interested in how the AIDS virus gets into the brain, Wyatt began collaborating with a colleague at NIH who had developed an animal model. But the colleague did not have facilities for breeding and keeping rabbits. Neither did Wyatt. The solution: find investors to form a company that make rabbits. Wyatt did and RRI of McLean, Virginia, was formed. Then Wyatt and his colleagues signed a CRADA with RRI. The researchers have their rabbits, the company has a possible product. Another good idea.

But traditionalists worry. If CRADAs become common, will they really be true collaborations with intellectual, scientific input from both sides? Or will they just be another form of contract—one in which NIH benefits without having to pay?

Conversely, could CRADAs eventually turn NIH into little more than a giant contract lab if companies lure NIH scientists into cooperative agreements that serve the companies' need for NIH brain power at the expense of basic research?

SOURCE: Reprinted with permission from B.J. Cullition, "NIH Inc: The CRADA Boom," *Science* 245:1034-1036, 1989.

Although the idea for a CRADA can come from a variety of sources,[25] the first stage in establishing the arrangement is a research plan that includes the goals and activities of the CRADA, the respective contributions of each party, an abstract for public release, and identification of relevant patents and other NIH technology transfer agreements related to the CRADA (484). After review by legal counsel within the agency, a CRADA subcommittee of the Patent Policy Board must approve the CRADA before it is signed by the institute director and the private collaborator. Preference is given to CRADAs involving small businesses and firms that "agree to manufacture substantially in the United States" any inventions developed through CRADAs. Box 9-C describes two recent CRADAs.

---

[25] The Office of Technology Transfer has taken steps to make the private sector more aware of opportunities for collaboration with PHS agencies by sponsoring an annual conference for the past 3 years highlighting PHS research with potential commercial value. More recently, PHS has established an electronic bulletin board providing outside parties with information about specific collaborative opportunities.

According to the PHS Policy Statement on CRADAs and intellectual property licensing, "In certain areas of research, e.g., where the Government has the intellectual lead or where both scientific and commercialization capabilities are deemed essential at the outset, NIH/ADAMHA may competitively seek a collaborator through Federal Register notification. The Patent Policy Board has left to each institute the decision of when to publish in the Federal Register" (486).

As shown in table 9-8, the bulk of all CRADAs in 1990 (82 percent) are related either directly or indirectly to R&D on new human therapies, with vaccine or other prophylaxis research accounting for another 10 percent, and R&D on diagnostic tests accounting for the remaining 8 percent. At least 18 percent of all CRADAs are related to acquired immunodeficiency syndrome (AIDS) and HIV therapies or vaccines. This statistic reflects both a general emphasis on HIV-related research at NIH and an urgent interest in transferring knowledge about HIV into treatments or other products.

To what extent do private firms participating in CRADAS provide funds to the collaborating Federal research agency? All but 1 of the 14 NIH and ADAMHA institutes, centers, and divisions with CRADAs in fiscal year 1989 received some financial resources from their collaborations (table 9-9). At NIH, CRADA collaborators provided $1.8 million, of which $1.2 million went to support the salaries of 47 personnel. Over one-half of all support was centered in NCI. At ADAMHA, total financial support in 1989 under CRADAs was $187,000 with all but $10,000 going to support salaries of nine scientists at the National Institute of Mental Health. Even though the money received was only 0.2 percent of overall institute budgets for research within NIH and ADAMHA laboratories,[26] such support may be a catalyst for successful research. Furthermore, the data in table 9-4 are based on one of the earliest years of the CRADA program. Data for subsequent years may show more extensive financial support to Federal laboratories that have CRADAs.

ORPHAN DRUGS

Congress passed the Orphan Drug Act (Public Law 97-414) in 1983, providing strong incentives for private firms to discover and develop treatments for rare diseases and conditions. Amended

Table 9-9—Financial Resources Provided to NIH and ADAMHA Through CRADAs, Fiscal Year 1989

Institute	Personnel[a]		Program support[b]
NIH			
CC	$ 0		$ 5,000
DRS	0		0
NCI	623,288	(24)	325,635
NEI	0		0
NHLBI	0		2,625
NIA	0		25,000
NIAID	34,327	(1)	74,000
NIAMS	30,000	(1)	0
NICHD	127,028	(5)	20,000
NIDDK	57,000	(2)	0
NIDR	174,000	(7)	103,050
NINDS	177,500	(7)	20,000
Total	$1,223,143	(47)	$575,310
ADAMHA			
NIAAA	$ 0		$ 10,000
NIMH	177,250	(9)	0
Total	$ 177,250	(9)	$ 10,000

a Support for personnel; numbers in parentheses are numbers of persons supported.
b Travel, equipment, or supplies, used in conducting any part of the research effort.

KEY: ADAMHA = Alcohol, Drug Abuse and Mental Health Administration. CC = Warren Grant Magnuson Clinical Center. CRADA = Cooperative Research and Development Agreements Collaborators. DRS = Division of Research Services. NCI = National Cancer Institute. NEI = National Eye Institute. NHLBI = National Heart, Lung and Blood Institute. NIA = National Institute on Aging. NIAAA = National Institute on Alcohol Abuse and Alcoholism. NIAID = National Institute of Allergy and Infectious Diseases. NIAMS = National Institute of Arthritis and Musculoskeletal and Skin Diseases. NICHD = National Institute of Child Health and Human Development. NIDDK= National Institute of Diabetes and Digestive and Kidney Diseases. NIDR = National Institute of Dental Research. NIH = National Institutes of Health. NIMH = National Institute of Mental Health. NINDS = National Institute of Neurological Disorders and Stroke.

SOURCE: U.S. Department of Health and Human Services, Public Health Service, National Institutes of Health, Office of Technology Transfer, 1989.

three times since its initial enactment (Public Law 98-551, Public Law 99-91, Public Law 100-290), the law has three provisions (in addition to a tax credit described in chapter 8) designed to subsidize R&D costs or to remove other disincentives to developing drugs of limited commercial value:[27]

---

[26] Intramural (i.e., taking place on the PHS laboratories campus) research support totaled $782 million in fiscal year 1989 (482) and $103 million at ADAMHA in the same year (485).

[27] The Orphan Drug Act as first adopted excluded antibiotics from eligibility for orphan designation. Congress eliminated this restriction in August 1985 (Public Law 99-91).

- Food and Drug Administration assistance to orphan drug developers in protocol design for new drug approval (NDA) or product license approval (PLA) applications;[28]
- Research grants for clinical and preclinical studies of orphan products; and
- A grant of 7 years of exclusive U.S. marketing rights to the first firm that receives NDA approval for an orphan drug.

The FDA first published proposed regulations to implement the law in January 1991 (FR 1/29/91) (56 FR 3334). Prior to these proposed regulations, the FDA relied on interim guidelines that differed from the proposed regulations in important ways described later. Though the proposed regulations have not been adopted officially as final, the FDA has operated under these rules since they were published.

▌ Designation of Orphan Drugs

The first step in a request for orphan drug subsidies is to apply for official orphan drug status from the FDA's Office of Orphan Products Development (OPD) (468). Drug sponsors may seek this designation at any time between the granting of an investigational new drug (IND) exemption and the submission of an NDA.[29] In making such a request, the applicant must show the disease or condition that the drug is intended to treat:

- "Affects less than 200,000 persons in the United States; or
- Affects more than 200,000 persons in the United States and. . . there is no reasonable expectation that the cost of developing and making [the drug] available in the United States will be recovered from sales in the United States of such drug" (468).

Since 1985, virtually all orphan designations have met the first criterion. The exact interpretation of this provision has been subject to dispute. For example, the number of AIDS patients in this country has climbed above 200,000, but several AIDS drugs were designated as orphans early in the epidemic, when the prevalence of the disease was much lower (21).

In its recent proposed regulations (adopted as final in December 1992, the FDA makes clear that "the 200,000 prevalence figure means 200,000 affected persons in the United States at the time that the orphan-drug designation request is made (not 200,000 new cases annually)" and that a "drug would remain an orphan drug even if the disease or condition ceases to an orphan disease or condition because of increased prevalence" in order to "protect a sponsor's good-faith investment" (56 FR 3339);

More than one sponsor can receive orphan designation for the same drug for a single indication. For example, by December 1989, Biogen, Genentech, and SmithKline Beecham had all received orphan drug status for a single drug undergoing clinical research, human recombinant soluble CD4 for the treatment of AIDS (470). At most, only one of the three companies will ultimately be granted approval to market the drug for its orphan use.

Between January 1984 and the end of September 1992, the FDA granted orphan status to 494 drugs and biologicals (table 9-10). Of all the orphan designations ever given, 16 percent were granted during 1991 alone. Almost two-thirds of orphan designations (63 percent) went to sponsors who were not members of the U.S. Pharmaceutical Manufacturers Association. Because PMA membership is available only to companies marketing an FDA-approved pharmaceutical in the United States, this statistic suggests that a high

---

[28] NDAs and PLAs are formal applications made to the FDA by pharmaceutical sponsors to manufacture and market therapeutic drugs in the United States. NDAs are for synthetic chemical drugs and PLAs are for biological products. This chapter uses the term "NDA" to refer to both types of applications. See chapter 6 for additional discussion of the drug approval process in the United States.

[29] Prior to 1988, the orphan drug law did not specify exactly at what stage in the regulatory process the sponsor of an investigational drug for a rare disease or condition could seek an orphan designation from the FDA. Public Law 100-290, adopted April 18, 1988, clarified that this designation could be granted only prior to the submission of an NDA or PLA.

Table 9-10—Orphan Designations[a] Granted
January 1984 Through September 1992

	Number of designations[b]	Percent of total
Total	494	100
Given in 1991 only	81	16
Given to PMA members	183	37
Given to Non-PMA members ...	311	63

[a] As provided under section 526 of the Federal Food, Drugs and Cosmetic Act (21 U.S.C 30 et seq.) and amended by the Orphan Drug Act (Public Law 97-414).
[b] Includes both drugs and biologicals.

SOURCE: Office of Technology Assessment, 1993. Based on data supplied by the U.S. Department of Health and Human Services, Food and Drug Administration, Office of Orphan Product Development, 1992.

percentage of all orphan drug research is being sponsored by new (and probably small) firms or other organizations with little previous experience in researching and marketing drugs in the United States.[30]

An analysis of all orphan designations granted through November 1990 revealed that about 23 percent of all compounds granted orphan status by that date had more than one designation (table 9-11). Different sponsors can receive orphan designations for the same indication when they are simultaneously developing the same drug. As of November 1990, 66 compounds had orphan designations by at least two competing firms. A single sponsor may also receive multiple designators for a single drug, but for different potential uses of the compound. As of November 1990, 59 compounds had multiple designations by same sponsor.

■ Protocol Assistance

The FDA is required by law to provide written assistance upon request about the design of studies to support an NDA for an orphan drug. So far, the total number of such requests has been small compared with the total number of orphan drug designations issued (227). In 1985, FDA

Table 9-11—Multiple Orphan Designations[a] for the Same Generic Compound, January 1984 Through November 1990

A. Number of distinct generic compounds with orphan status	227
Percent of orphan compounds with multiple designations	23%

B. Multiple orphan designations for a given generic compound

Number of designations given	Number of compounds receiving that number of designations
2	45
3	8
4	4
5	4
6	2
7	1
9	1
10	1
Total	66

C. Multiple orphan designations for a given generic compound received by a single sponsor

Number of designations given	Number of compounds receiving that number of designations
2	44
3	8
4	4
5	1
7	1
10	1
Total	59

[a] As provided under section 526 of the Federal Food, Drugs and Cosmetic Act (21 U.S.C 30 et seq.) and amended by the Orphan Drug Act (Public Law 97-414).

SOURCE: Office of Technology Assessment, 1993. Based on data supplied by the U.S. Department of Health and Human Services, Food and Drug Administration, Office of Orphan Product Development, 1992.

received nine such requests; they have virtually disappeared in recent years.

The sponsor of any drug or biological has the option of requesting protocol advice directly from the FDA's Center for Drug Evaluation and Research (CDER) or the Center for Biological

---

[30] This statistic may underestimate the percentage of orphan drugs being researched at the initiative of PMA members since some academic or nonprofit "sponsors" may receive research funding from PMA firms. As discussed earlier in this chapter, the firm that supports such research may have the rights to market the drug if its succeeds.

Evaluation and Research (CBER). Because such meetings need not be requested formally and can involve iterative questioning and discussion, sponsors probably perceive this type of assistance as more flexible and useful than the formal interchanges mandated under the Orphan Drug Act (227). Some observers have suggested the FDA may actually discourage written requests for assistance (270).

■ Grants for Clinical Research

The Orphan Drug Act authorized grants for clinical research on potential orphan products, and one of its more recent amendments (Public Law 100-290) extended this authority to preclinical studies. These grants represent a direct subsidy for orphan drug R&D.[31] The Office of Orphan Products Development administers the program in a manner parallel to other Public Health Service grants.

Grants are given for single, discrete studies and are available to for-profit, nonprofit, and government organizations. In almost all cases, the grants have been limited to a maximum of $100,000 in direct costs per year for up to 3 years. Although recipients are not required to possess official orphan drug status for the drug or biological under study, the grants are designed for treatment of conditions affecting less than 200,000 patients in the United States.[32]

The orphan products grants program has grown steadily since 1983. In 1990, the Office of Orphan Products Development allocated a total of $7.6 million among 65 recipients (table 9-12).[33] For-profit organizations represent a very small part of the total grant program (table 9-12). The average size of each award each year (annual direct plus indirect costs for new and continuing grants) has increased from $79,000 in 1987 to $111,000 in 1990. This represents an increase of 6.5 percent per year in constant dollars.

■ Market Exclusivity

The first drug sponsor to receive NDA approval for a drug and indication with orphan status may market it exclusively for a 7-year period beginning on the day the FDA approves the drug.[34] This exclusivity prevents the FDA from approving an NDA for a drug for which another sponsor has already received marketing approval for the same indication.[35] Any patent protection covering the drug runs contemporaneously with the market exclusivity. Two or more sponsors may receive FDA approval for a single orphan drug if their approvals are for different indications and if they do not violate any patent protections.

ORPHAN EXCLUSIVITY VERSUS PATENT PROTECTION

In practice, the exclusivity clause is the strongest incentive in the orphan drug law, and for some drugs it may be more important than patent protection in effecting market exclusivity[36]:

- For some drugs orphan market exclusivity may extend beyond the expiration of the

---

[31] Because the Orphan Drug Act's grant authority has never received funding from Congress, the FDA has funded this program using money appropriated for orphan drug research under a general grants program of the Federal Food, Drug, and Cosmetic Act (21 U.S.C. 30 et seq.).

[32] Grants under this program are actually not limited to drugs and biologicals but are also available for medical devices and medical foods for rare diseases and conditions. In practice, almost all grants are for drugs and biologicals. For example, none of the new awards given in fiscal year 1989 were for medical devices or foods.

[33] These 65 recipients do not include 10 supplemental awards given to recipients of full grants in 1990 or earlier years who requested additional funds to cover unanticipated costs. In 1990, supplemental awards represented $388,332 of the total $7.6 million program.

[34] As first enacted in 1983, the Orphan Drug Act (Public Law 97-414) permitted market exclusivity only for orphan pharmaceuticals that were ineligible for a U.S. patent at the time of marketing approval. In August 1985, Congress removed this limitation making all orphan drugs eligible for the 7-year exclusive marketing period if no other sponsor has received approval for that therapy for that indication (Public Law 99-91).

[35] Because orphan drug status is given for a particular indication, market exclusivity is also limited to particular indications.

[36] In addition to patents and orphan drug market exclusivity for a specific indication, another potential barrier to competition for an orphan drug is FDA's regulatory approval process itself. A potential competitor must conduct R&D and receive FDA approval of an NDA or PLA for *each* indication for which it would like to market the drug (21).

Table 9-12—Orphan Products Development Grants for Clinical Research: Selected Statistics

	1983[f]	1984[f]	1985[f]	1986[f]	1987	1988	1989	1990
Number of awards								
First year awards[a]	8	11	21	21	27	18	19	30
Continuing (year 2 or >) awards[b]	—	—	—	—	21	32	31	35
Supplemental awards[c]	—	—	—	—	6	13	11	10
Total	8	11	21	21	53	63	61	75
Program outlays (in current dollars)								
Direct costs	—	—	—	—	$ 2,840,190	$ 3,473,561	$ 4,106,211	$ 5,470,428
Indirect costs	—	—	—	—	1,076,129	1,286,262	1,447,035	2,165,281
Total	$ 500,000	$ 1,030,000	$ 2,420,000[e]	$ 2,885,000	$ 3,916,319	$ 4,759,823	$ 5,553,546	$ 7,635,709
First year awards[a]	—	—	—	—	$ 2,110,008	$ 1,754,008	$ 2,093,254	$ 3,441,175
Continuing awards[b]	—	—	—	—	1,600,573	2,655,793	3,149,415	3,806,202
Supplemental awards[c]	—	—	—	—	205,738	350,022	310,577	388,332
Total	$ 500,000	$ 1,030,000	$ 2,420,000[e]	$ 2,885,000	$ 3,916,319	$ 4,759,283	$ 5,553,546	$ 7,635,709
Awards to for-profit organizations								
Number of first year or continuing awards	—	—	—	—	2	3	4	3
Number of supplemental awards	—	—	—	—	1	3	1	1
Total program outlays (in current dollars)	—	—	—	—	$ 153,135	$ 281,614	$ 393,082	$ 346,542
Mean award size[d]								
Mean direct cost per award	—	—	—	—	$ 57,356	$ 64,266	$ 77,586	$ 79,930
Mean indirect costs per award	—	—	—	—	21,592	23,931	27,267	31,569
Mean total costs per award	—	—	—	—	$ 78,948	$ 88,197	$ 104,853	$ 111,499
Mean total costs per award in 1987 dollars[g]	—	—	—	—	78,948	85,361	97,464	99,668

[a]Grants for 1-year awards or the first year of multiple-year awards.
[b]Grants for second, third, or fourth year of multiple-year awards.
[c]Supplemental awards given for existing grants upon application by investigators.
[d]Mean awards calculated net of supplemental awards; given in current dollars unless otherwise noted.
[e]1985 funds include $1 million provided by the National Institute of Maternal and Child Health, U.S. Department of Health and Human Services under interagency agreement.
[f]U.S. Food and Drug Administration, Office of Orphan Products Development, data systems can provide only limited information for years 1983-86.
[g]1987 dollars calculated using the GNP implicit price deflator.

SOURCE: Office of Technology Assessment, 1993. Based on data provided by U.S. Department of Health and Human Services, Public Health Service, Food and Drug Administration, Office of Orphan Products Development, 1992.

relevant patents. Because manufacturers usually receive their 17-year patents on potential new drugs early in the development process (220), the amount of time remaining on the patent at the time of FDA approval may be less than the 7 years guaranteed by the orphan drug exclusivity (21).

- Some drugs duplicate substances that naturally occur in the body (e.g., "biologicals"). For these, the state of patent law is currently so murky that the 7-year market exclusivity is a more certain means of protecting the product from competition (451).

Problems in Awarding Orphan Market Exclusivity Rights—Controversy has arisen over how different the molecular structure of two drugs must be in order for both to receive market exclusivity. Because biological pharmaceuticals tend to have relatively large and complex molecular structures, scientists can alter their makeup slightly without changing their clinical effects. If the Federal Government interprets any small clinically insignificant change as the creation of a "different" orphan drug eligible for its own market exclusivity, it effectively eliminates the incentives of the exclusivity clause for many biotechnology drugs. Since the orphan drug law was enacted, competitors have challenged the exclusivity of two approved orphan drugs by seeking approval of slightly different versions of the same pharmaceuticals.

Human Growth Hormone—In 1985, Genentech received FDA approval and exclusive marketing as an orphan drug for a human growth hormone (HGH) product to treat children whose bodies do not naturally produce enough of the hormone to ensure normal growth. Genentech's HGH product, Protropin™, contains one more amino acid than is found in the version usually produced by the body's pituitary gland, but this particular amino acid does not appear to alter the hormone's activity in the body.

Eli Lilly independently developed its own HGH product Humantrope™, with a molecular structure that is *identical* to the HGH produced by the human body. Eli Lilly applied for orphan drug status and marketing approval for Humantrope, arguing that because of the additional amino acid on Protropin, the Eli Lilly drug was "different" from Protropin. In 1986 the FDA agreed, giving orphan status to Humantrope.

Genentech subsequently challenged the FDA's decisions in court by arguing the FDA did not have the authority to grant orphan status to Eli Lilly. The courts ruled against Genentech. Currently, each manufacturer has orphan status for its version of HGH, and each drug is sold on the market.[37]

The results of the HGH case established that the FDA has the authority to determine when two therapies are sufficiently different from one another that each can receive its own orphan designation (240).

Recombinant Erythropoietin[38]—In June 1989, Amgen received approval to market its version of recombinant erythropoietin (rEPO) for the treatment of anemia in patients with chronic renal failure. EPO is a protein usually produced by the kidneys and necessary for the production of red blood cells. Amgen had first produced the drug in 1983 and had received orphan status for it in 1986. In September 1988, Chugai Pharmaceuticals of Japan, in a joint venture with Upjohn Pharmaceuticals, filed a PLA with the FDA to market its own version of rEPO in competition with Amgen.

---

[37] The orphan protection prohibits each manufacturer from marketing a version of HGH that is molecularly identical to the version produced by the other firm. For example, Genentech developed a new HGH that was identical to the HGH produced naturally by the body. However, because this new Genentech HGH was also identical to Lilly's Humantrope™, the FDA prohibited Genentech from marketing it (240).

[38] For a more complete discussion see chapter 3 of OTA's study on recombinant erythropoietin (451).

[39] Because amino acids are the building blocks of proteins, and because rEPO is designed to fulfill the function of the missing natural EPO, the drug's amino-acid sequence can be important in the effectiveness of the rEPO.

Although the Chugai/Upjohn drug has an amino-acid structure[39] identical to that found in the Amgen version, Chugai/Upjohn argued that the two drugs differed in glycosylation, the linkages of carbohydrates to the molecule, and that their version was therefore eligible for its own orphan designation and marketing approval. Although the FDA had not yet acted on the Chugai/Upjohn application for orphan drug designation at the time of the Amgen approval, then-FDA commissioner Frank Young stated publicly that the Chugai/Upjohn version appeared "different" from the Amgen drug (240). In October 1989, Amgen requested that the FDA develop regulations to determine the circumstances under which two molecularly similar orphans are eligible for shared exclusivity.[40]

Proposed Regulations—The FDA recently attempted to set forth general criteria for determining when two drugs are sufficiently different to warrant orphan status and exclusivity for both. In proposed regulations published on January 29, 1991 (56 FR 3338) and adopted as final in December 1992, the FDA would presume two orphan drugs to be the same "if the principal, but not necessarily all, structural features of the two drugs were the same, unless the subsequent drug were shown to be clinically superior." According to these guidelines, different glycosylation patterns in two protein drugs, the difference suggested to have been found in the two versions of rEPO, would not be sufficient to find the Upjohn/Chugai drug different from the Amgen drug. The proposed regulations identify three circumstances under which a subsequent drug could be deemed "clinically superior" to an already approved orphan, and hence, approvable:

- The subsequent drug is more effective than the first drug as shown in comparative clinical trials.
- The subsequent drug is safer than the first for a "substantial portion of the target population," including the case where the two

drugs have about the same therapeutic effect, the first drug has significant side effects, and the subsequent drug achieves its effect at a lower dose.
- The subsequent drug "makes a major contribution to health" as in the development of an oral dose form where the drug had only been available by parenteral administration.

While awaiting approval from the White House Office of Management and Budget to adopt a final version of the regulations, the FDA operated according to the draft regulations (227).

■ Impact of Orphan Drug Subsidies

The clinical research tax credit (discussed in chapter 8), protocol assistance, and clinical research grants theoretically lower the cost of orphan drug R&D; the market exclusivity provision increases the expected revenues to such R&D. In practice, the protocol assistance has had little effect, especially in recent years, and the tax credit and grants program represent, overall, a relatively small commitment of Federal funds to orphan products. This commitment may be critical for certain drugs, however, so it should not be discounted.

The 79 biological and drug applications approved for marketing by the FDA with orphan status as of September 1992 represent broad and extensive R&D efforts for rare diseases. The test of the Orphan Drug Act's effectiveness, however, is whether it has led to the approval and marketing of drugs for orphan conditions that would otherwise have been unavailable to patients. If pharmaceutical companies would have developed and marketed orphan drugs even without these subsidies, then their true effectiveness would be nil.

It is impossible to estimate how many of the new orphan drugs would have been made available since 1983 in the absence of these subsidies. Simple comparison of the number of such drugs approved and marketed before the passage of the act with those made available since its passage is

---

[40] Appendix E describes a controversy over patent rights for rEPO that took place at the same time as this dispute over orphan designation.

inappropriate because, many other factors, especially the state of scientific knowledge, may affect pharmaceutical innovation.

A recent analysis of the Orphan Drug Law's first 8 years concluded that while most orphan incentives have gone to the type of drugs Congress intended to subsidize, there is evidence that some drugs with orphan status would have been commercially viable without Federal help. Furthermore, the authors concluded there might have been sufficient information for the FDA to determine the drug's commercial viability in granting orphan status had the Orphan Drug Law permitted such consideration in awarding orphan drug incentives (389).

Concerns that the Orphan Drug Law has subsidized the development of commercially successful drugs which did not really need help from the Federal Government led to legislation in the 102d Congress that would have removed an orphan drug's exclusivity once cumulative net sales in the United States surpassed $200 million (S. 102-2060). Another piece of legislation (H.R. 102-1713) would tax "profits" on orphan drugs that exceed certain levels.[41]

Another measure of the law's effectiveness may be the extent to which orphan drugs have been sponsored by relatively small startup firms. As drug R&D costs go up, smaller firms may have a harder time mustering enough resources to bring new products to the market. By lowering barriers for such firms, the orphan drug subsidies may encourage competition in the industry and provide a new mechanism to realize the commercial benefits of biotechnological and other scientific discoveries, especially those originating in academia. As shown earlier, almost two-thirds of orphan designations have gone to drug sponsors that are not PMA members, a characteristic commonly found among startup firms.

MEDICARE AND MEDICAID SUPPORT FOR CLINICAL DRUG R&D

The Medicare and Medicaid programs are the sources of the vast majority of Federal spending for health services. Medicare and Medicaid payment for patient care rendered in association with clinical research on a pharmaceutical agent therefore constitutes a potential subsidy of pharmaceutical R&D. Nevertheless, there are no good estimates of clinical-trial-related health care costs paid for by Medicare and Medicaid (395).

By law, Medicare does not cover any drugs administered outside of the hospital or a physician's office, and the program does not pay for clinical research (487). Furthermore, to be covered by Medicare, drugs must be "reasonable and necessary," a criterion that the Health Care Financing Administration (HCFA) "has interpreted . . . to exclude . . . those medical and health care services that are not demonstrated to be safe and effective by clinical evidence" (487). HCFA has taken this to mean that "experimental" and "investigational" drugs are not covered.

"Group C" cancer drugs[42] represent the one exception to the statutory and regulatory exclusion of unapproved drug therapies from Medicare payment. Because Medicare does pay the costs associated with the administration of Group C drugs,[43] some patients have requested that Medi-

---

[41] There have been other congressional attempts to limit retroactively the use of orphan subsidies. In legislation passed by Congress in 1990, but later pocket-vetoed by the President, manufacturers would lose their exclusivity if disease prevalence grew more that 200,000. In addition, the legislation would have allowed more than one manufacturer to share an orphan market exclusivity if each reached certain regulatory hurdles contemporaneously (H.R. 101-4638).

[42] "Group C" cancer drugs are pharmaceuticals for which significant data on safety and efficacy are already available. These drugs are usually in phase III trials. NCI and the FDA jointly developed the concept of Group C drugs in 1976, although DHHS has never formalized the definition in regulations (NCI, 1990). Only physicians registered with NCI as clinical investigators can administer the drugs. Some of the drugs in the Group C category may never receive final FDA approval to market because firms consider them to be commercially unviable.

[43] NCI provides the Group C drugs free of charge.

care cover all drugs with Treatment INDs as well (69).[44]

In practice, there are other exclusions from Medicare coverage, particularly for drugs administered as part of a clinical research protocol. Prior to 1983 Medicare paid hospitals for the individual services they provided to patients. Anecdotal evidence suggests that Medicare's payment for clinical research was common in that period (446).

Since 1983, Medicare has paid hospitals a fixed amount per admission for a package of services based on a patient's primary diagnosis and major treatments. Medicare will now cover attendant hospital costs for patients receiving an experimental drug if the admission was not solely for the experiment. Some observers have suggested that adjustments to hospital payments allowed by Medicare to cover costs associated with medical education also underwrite some of the patient and faculty costs associated with clinical research. Medicare contractors, the companies that administer the Medicare program under contract with HCFA, interpret these policies differently in different parts of the country (395).

Although Medicare contractors screen claims submitted by hospitals to determine whether they are appropriate, and utilization and quality control peer review organizations (PROs) may screen and refuse payment for inappropriate services given Medicare beneficiaries by hospitals, it is likely that a great deal of patient care associated with pharmaceutical trials is paid for by Medicare because of the difficulty of screening claims to detect such services.

Because the Medicaid program, which pays for health services for individuals who are low-income, is administered by the States, decisions about coverage of pharmaceuticals (whether investigational or approved) are up to each State.

Medicaid is one of the biggest payers for prescription drugs in the United States, accounting for 10 to 15 percent of total spending.[45]

A recent informal DHHS survey of Medicaid drug program administrators found that while many States do not cover investigational drugs under any circumstances, some are willing to provide payment for investigational therapies under specific circumstances (487). Policy varies by State: a few States pay for investigational pharmaceuticals on a case-by-case basis; one State covered treatment IND drugs for treatment of AIDS, and the State legislature was considering codifying this practice. Another State requires prior approval for use of an investigational drug.

The results of this survey suggest it is possible (perhaps likely) that Medicaid is paying for some investigational pharmaceuticals and the attendant medical care costs of persons enrolled in clinical trials. However, the tremendous variation in Medicaid policies among States makes such subsidies impossible to estimate.

CONCLUSIONS

The Federal Government is the mainstay of support for the scientific infrastructure upon which advances in medical technology depend. The pharmaceutical industry makes use of this infrastructure through its hiring of scientists, its formal and informal interactions with federally-supported scientists in universities and in Federal laboratories, and informational resources that document research and its results. In addition, the government provides even more direct support to industry R&D through drug development programs in Federal laboratories, orphan drug policies, and Medicare and Medicaid reimbursements.

The public sector has been the major source of funds for training scientific personnel. Over the

---

[44] The Treatment IND program, established in 1987 and administered by the FDA, allows the release of investigational drugs to medical practitioners on a case-by-case basis for use in the treatment of immediately life-threatening diseases for which no satisfactory alternative treatment exists. Under this program, described in greater detail in chapter 6, the drug must be under investigation in controlled clinical trials and the sponsor must be actively pursuing marketing approval. With the permission of the FDA, sponsors may charge patients for Treatment IND drugs in order to recover production and R&D costs (21 CRF 312.34.(a)).

[45] See table 10-1 in chapter 10.

past decade, industrial demands for biomedical scientists have grown much faster than demands for biomedical scientists as a whole (12 to 13 percent per year versus 5 percent).

Collaborations with academic scientists have historically been an important component of the drug industry's R&D efforts and continue to be so today. Of all U.S. industries, innovation within the pharmaceutical industry is the most dependent on academic research and the Federal funds that support it. In recent years, advances in biotechnology that occurred within academic research laboratories added to the task of transferring basic scientific knowledge from academia and government to industrial applications.

The pharmaceutical industry's support for university scientists include consulting arrangements, funds for specific research projects, and to a lesser extent long-term support for entire laboratories or university research programs. The bulk of shorter-term research support from industry goes to laboratories that receive most of their support from the Federal Government.

A more direct form of Federal support for pharmaceutical R&D comes through the Federal Government's funding of research targeted to drug discovery and development. The Federal Government has 11 research programs devoted solely to the encouragement, funding, and coordination of nonclinical pharmaceutical R&D. At three institutes, these programs include the screening and characterization of potential medications submitted by outside researchers including pharmaceutical firms.

OTA's ability to measure the precise extent of different types of federally supported drug R&D is limited both by problems with defining relevant R&D and a lack of adequate data. But, a conservative estimate of research involving nonclinical drug discovery functions funded just by NIH and ADAMHA in 1988 is $400 million; this estimate represents 14 percent of the amount spent by firms in the PMA for the same R&D functions.

A conservative, likely underestimate of NIH- and ADAMHA-funded research in 1988 specifi-

cally involving clinical R&D is $200 million, which represents 11 percent of industry's expenditures for phases I, II, III, and IV clinical research. The Federal Government also indirectly supports clinical research by paying a portion of the health care bills of Medicare and Medicaid beneficiaries who are also enrolled in clinical trials. No data exist to measure the exact extent of this support.

In recent years, the innovation of the CRADA has allowed companies and Federal laboratories greater latitude for productive interactions. Although a comprehensive assessment of the benefits and risks of such arrangements for both parties is yet to be taken, the terms of such collaborations offer some preliminary indications. Through 109 CRADAs signed between 1987 and 1990, PHS gave pharmaceutical industry collaborators access to Federal research laboratories and potentially exclusive property rights for patentable commercial applications arising from the research. In return for such rights, PHS received just under $2 million in research resources from industrial and other CRADA partners in 1989.

In another form of technology transfer, DHHS issued 44 licenses (17 exclusive) for Federal patents in 1988. Income from licenses in 1988 netted NIH and ADAMHA research laboratories just $272,000 after expenses (.004 percent of NIH budget), the majority of which is attributable to a single technology (the HIV antibody test).

In the Orphan Drug Act, the Federal Government has created several potentially strong incentives for firms to pursue the R&D and marketing of pharmaceuticals for relatively rare conditions. In particular, designated orphan drugs are eligible for a 7-year exclusivity covering their approved indications and a 50-percent tax credit for clinical R&D that lowers the cost of qualifying clinical trial expenses by 76 percent. Researchers also received $7.6 million in grants from the Federal Government for 75 phase I and II clinical trials studying potential orphan drugs.

The policies and programs laid out in this chapter (and the one that precedes it) suggest that

Federal involvement can substantially lower the private sector's costs of bringing some new drug products to market. Furthermore, because this report does not examine any incentives provided by State and local governments to pharmaceutical firms located in their jurisdictions, actual public-sector involvement may be greater than that implied here.

Industry provides some compensation for its access to these resources, although such compensation is relatively limited. The true cost of pharmaceutical R&D is greater than just the private funds invested in this enterprise, and the Federal Government's support of the country's research infrastructure is critical to industry's ability to bring forth new drugs.

In the case of orphan drugs, some of the pharmaceuticals receiving help from the Federal Government might have been commercially viable anyway. Various proposals debated by Congress have attempted to target orphan drug subsidies more precisely on only those drugs that would not otherwise be available to patients.

When the fruits of Federal pharmaceutical research are transferred to the private sector for development and marketing, the Federal Government currently has neither sufficient incentive nor expertise to negotiate compensation or limits on prices that reflect the Federal investment in dollars or the technical risk of failure absorbed by the government during the R&D process. As the case of the drug Ceredase™ illustrates, this failure, along with extensive insurance coverage of pharmaceuticals described in the next chapter, creates the potential for the Federal Government to pay for such drugs twice—once through support of the R&D process and once again as a health insurer.

Trends in Payment for Prescription Drugs | 10

As soon as a new ethical pharmaceutical compound hits the market, revenues begin to flow to the drug manufacturer. These revenues depend on the decision of the physician to prescribe the drug and the decision of the patient to buy it, based on physicians' and patients' judgments of the drug's quality and price compared with those of other possible therapies.

The importance of price versus perceived quality depends on many factors, including the severity of the disease or condition for which the drug is intended, the availability of close substitutes, and the effectiveness of advertising and promotion in convincing doctors (and sometimes patients) that the drug is the right choice for the patient (86). Most important in tipping the balance between perceived quality and price, however, is health insurance.[1] When a medical service or product is covered under a patient's health insurance plan, the patient pays less and is less sensitive to price (516).

Like other medical services, pharmaceuticals are marketed in a world with a complex structure of health insurance. Health insurers offer different levels of insurance coverage for different kinds of services and products. Payment restrictions and regulations are as important as covered benefits in determining the demand for health care. As health care costs have increased, health insurers worldwide have adopted new methods to influence or control the use of health care products and services.

---

[1]Although ethical pharmaceuticals include some nonprescriptions items, health insurance coverage is typically limited only to prescription drugs. Consequently, the remainder of this chapter refers to prescription drugs.

This chapter documents recent trends in health insurance for prescription drugs beginning with a review of insurance coverage and payment controls for prescription drugs in the United States. The United States is not only the largest single national market for prescription drugs in the world, but it also has the world's most complex patchwork of insurance mechanisms. Americans are almost alone in the industrialized world in not having universal health insurance.

Virtually all other industrialized countries have national health insurance programs that include prescription drug benefits. Good examples, later in this chapter, are Australia, Canada, France, Japan, and the United Kingdom, which illustrate what other nations are currently doing to control expenditures for prescription drugs and what these controls mean for revenues from new drugs yet to be developed.

HEALTH INSURANCE FOR PRESCRIPTION DRUGS IN THE UNITED STATES

■ The Structure of Coverage

All public and private health insurers in the United States distinguish between inpatient, outpatient, and home health insurance benefits. So, whether or not an individual has insurance coverage for a prescription drug depends not only on whether he or she has health insurance but also on the setting in which the drug is prescribed and administered. *Inpatient benefits* cover services and products used in hospitals and sometimes in nursing homes. *Outpatient benefits* are for services or products obtained in clinics or offices of health professionals; *home health care benefits* are for services or products provided by certified personnel to patients at home.[2]

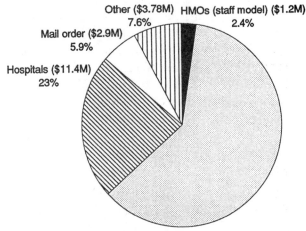

Figure 10-1—Pharmaceutical Sales in the United States by Trade Channel, 1991

Other ($3.78M) 7.6%
HMOs (staff model) ($1.2M) 2.4%
Mail order ($2.9M) 5.9%
Hospitals ($11.4M) 23%
Community pharmacies ($30.2M) 61%

SOURCE: IMS America, Inc., as cited in *F-D-C-Reports: Prescription and OTC Pharmaceuticals*, "Mail Order Grew 37% to $2.9 Bil. in 1991 IMS Survey; Growth May Slow Soon," p. 11, Mar. 16, 1992.

HOSPITAL COVERAGE

Most Americans—86 percent—have public or private health insurance, continuing a steady trend over the last decade (292). Virtually all health insurance plans cover hospital care, including drugs dispensed to hospitalized patients.

Sales to hospitals made up about 23 percent of total U.S. pharmaceutical sales in 1991 (128), a decline from about 29 percent in 1983 (291,320). (See figure 10-1 for a breakdown of pharmaceutical sales by type of buyer at the wholesale level.) A growing proportion of these sales represent drugs sold through hospital-based outpatient pharmacies,[3] so the inpatient hospital share of the pharmaceutical market today is actually below 23 percent.

---

[2] Insurance for health services provided in the home generally does not affect prescription drugs, because most drugs administered at home would be covered under outpatient prescription drug benefits. Home health benefits sometimes cover the professional care and device costs associated with administering an intravenous drug to patients at home, thereby making administration of such drugs at home (rather than in a hospital or clinic) a viable option (454). Sometimes Medicare will extend coverage for certain intravenous drugs as part of its durable medical equipment benefit to patients in the home even though the program lacks outpatient prescription drug benefits. Other insurers may also occasionally permit such "back door" coverage. Because such cases of extended coverage are relatively rare, however, they are not discussed in this report. See the Office of Technology Assessment's study of home intravenous drugs for more information (454).

[3] Virtually unheard of 10 years ago (369), this practice was carried on for profit by approximately 17 percent of U.S. hospitals in 1990 (120).

One reason for the decline in the inpatient hospital share of the overall pharmaceutical market is the major restructuring of hospital payment systems in the past decade. When Medicare adopted in 1983 a prospective payment system that pays by admission and not by specific service, Medicare created incentives for hospitals to reduce the services offered per stay and to reduce the length of stay for Medicare patients.[4] For drugs dispensed during the hospital stay in the 1980s, hospitals adopted stricter formularies,[5] aggressively used the cheapest generic drugs available, and closely scrutinized doctors' prescribing practices (411,412). Hospital use declined dramatically as well. Some of the shift from inpatient care to outpatient care means that medications that would have been prescribed on an inpatient basis are now prescribed to outpatients.

NURSING HOME COVERAGE

Pharmaceutical sales to nursing homes made up just 2.9 percent of total U.S. pharmaceutical sales in 1991 (128). Private insurance for nursing home care is very limited, but drugs dispensed to nursing home patients are typically covered under outpatient drug benefits if the patient has outpatient drug coverage. Medicare covers its beneficiaries for limited skilled care in a nursing home and covers drugs dispensed as part of a Medicare-covered stay as they would be in a hospital. If Medicare doesn't cover a patient's stay in a nursing home, Medicare would still pay for certain drugs that would be covered were the patient living at home (454).

Medicaid is a payer of last resort for nursing home residents whose personal funds are depleted, and virtually all State Medicaid agencies cover drugs as part of nursing home stays. Nursing home residents have a high probability (30 to 50 percent according to several studies) of becoming eligible for Medicaid while institutionalized, which then covers them for prescription drugs (137).

OUTPATIENT COVERAGE

Although fewer Americans have outpatient prescription drug coverage than hospital coverage, outpatient drug coverage grew in the 1980s. Most (67 percent) ethical pharmaceuticals in 1991 were dispensed through retail or mail-order pharmacies (128,324), so this growth in coverage has been an important stimulus to the demand for prescription drugs in the United States.

The proportion of outpatient prescription drug purchases paid for by insurance increased substantially, from 27 to 43 percent, between 1977 and 1987 (table 10-1).[6] The average expenditure for prescription drugs by individuals with any prescription drug costs increased 135 percent between 1977 and 1987 (from $69 to $162 in 1987 dollars) (277). Although Medicare does not pay for most outpatient prescription drugs, these same trends hold among elderly Americans, for whom private insurance paid for 36 percent of outpatient prescription drug expenses in 1987 compared with only 23 percent in 1977. People 65 and over are relatively heavy users of prescription drugs.[7]

---

[4] Medicare beneficiaries accounted for 45.2 percent of inpatient hospital days in 1989 and for 33 percent of the discharges (164).

[5] Formularies are lists of drugs that either include or exclude drugs that may be prescribed by physicians without special exceptions. The number of hospital pharmacies adopting formularies has steadily increased. Studies conducted by the American Society of Hospital Pharmacists show the percent of hospitals adopting a well-controlled formulary system increased from 53.9 percent in 1985 to 58.4 percent in 1989 (101,412).

[6] In 1977, and again in 1987, the Agency for Health Care Policy and Research (AHCPR), known until 1990 as the National Center for Health Services Research, collected data in a national survey of health care expenditures, payments, and insurance coverage. Both the 1977 study, called the National Medical Care Expenditure Survey (NMCES) and the 1987 study, referred to as the National Medical Expenditure Survey (NMES), included a household survey of expenditures and health care coverage for different types of health care products and services. Data on expenditures are available from both surveys. Data on coverage are not yet available from the 1987 NMES survey.

[7] In 1987, people 65 and over made up 12 percent of the U.S. population, but were responsible for 34 percent of the country's total expenditures on prescription drugs. Elderly Americans' per capita expenditure on prescription drugs in 1987 was $331, about twice that for the population as a whole (277).

Table 10-1—Sources of Payment for Prescribed Medicines in the United States

	Percent of expenditures 1977	1987
All prescribed medicines		
Family	73%	57%
Private insurance	14	28
Medicaid	8	10
Other sources[a]	6	6
Prescribed medicines for persons over 65 only		
Family	77	64
Private insurance	10	22
Medicaid	10	9
Other sources[a]	3	5

[a] Other sources include Workmen's Compensation, Medicare, other State and local programs, and any other source of payment.

SOURCE: Data from J.F. Moeller, Senior Project Director, U.S. Department of Health and Human Services, Public Health Service, Agency for Health Care Policy and Research, Rockville, MD, personal communication, Mar. 12, 1991; J.A. Kasper, Prescribed Medicines: Use, Expenditures, and Sources of Payment, Data Preview (Washington, DC: U.S. Department of Health and Human Services, National Center for Health Services Research, April 1982).

Insurance reimbursements alone do not reflect the full impact of outpatient insurance coverage on the use of prescription drugs. Coverage itself, though limited by deductible and copayment requirements, makes patients less sensitive to the cost of medical care than they would be without such coverage (294). Prescription drug costs frequently contribute to annual deductible amounts, and most privately insured people are protected from high expenditures by annual catastrophic limits on out-of-pocket costs.[8] Hence, people with health insurance, particularly those with chronic diseases or conditions requiring long-term medical treatment and medication, have relatively little incentive to minimize the cost of medical care, including drugs.

The Office of Technology Assessment (OTA) estimates private and public health insurance programs together provided at least some outpa-

tient drug coverage for 67 to 69 percent of the total noninstitutionalized civilian population in 1979. By 1987, this figure had increased to between 70 and 74 percent (table 10-2). Among people 65 and older, the proportion with outpatient drug coverage increased more dramatically, from 36 percent in 1979 to between 43 and 46 percent in 1987.

Not only has insurance coverage for outpatient prescription drugs increased over the past decade, but these benefits have become more generous over time, as insurance plans have moved toward policies with flat copayments for prescription drugs (see below). On the other hand, all third-party payers have tried to contain the costs of prescription drugs.

■ Private Health Insurance Benefits for Outpatient Prescription Drugs

EXTENT OF OUTPATIENT COVERAGE

Very few private outpatient prescription drug benefit plans pay for 100 percent of the allowed cost of drugs. Table 10-3 shows that only about 3 percent of employed people with prescription drug coverage had full coverage throughout the 1980s. Full coverage is most common in health maintenance organizations (HMOs),[9] whose enrollment grew from 4 percent of the population in 1980 to 14 percent in 1990 (209). In 1989, 10 percent of employees of medium and large firms who were enrolled in HMOs had full coverage, compared with only 1 percent of those enrolled in fee-for-service plans (35).

Limitations of coverage vary across plans and include restrictions applying specifically to prescription drug expenditures (e.g., copayments for each prescription) and restrictions affecting overall health expenditures (e.g., a single annual deductible for all covered medical services in a "major medical" policy). Policies with specific copayments for prescriptions increased substan-

---

[8] Most insurance plans (80 percent) have both an annual deductible and an annual maximum limit on out-of-pocket expenses (491).

[9] Unlike traditional fee-for-service insurance plans, HMOs (sometimes referred to as "prepaid health plans") collect a set premium for each member, but charge either nothing or a relatively small amount for each individual service. People enrolled in the HMO must receive their health care from providers designated by the HMO.

Table 10-2—Percent of U.S. Population With Outpatient Prescription Drug Coverage, 1979 and 1987[a]

I. ASSUMPTIONS

A. Total noninstitutionalized population

	Number of people (thousands)[b]	
	1979	1987
People under 65	198,966	212,700
People 65 and over	24,194	28,487
Total	223,160	241,187

B. Health insurance among people under age 65

	1979		1987	
	Number of people (thousands)[b]	Percent with prescription drug coverage	Number of people (thousands)[b]	Percent with prescription drug coverage
Group private health insurance	133,555	95[c]	140,909	95[c]
Other health insurance	35,765	41-54[d]	41,071	53-75[e]

C. Health insurance among people age 65 and over

	1979		1987	
	Number of people (thousands)	Percent with prescription drug coverage	Number of people (thousands)	Percent with prescription drug coverage
Medicare only (with no supplemental health insurance)	4,645[f]	0	5,877[g]	0
Group supplemental private health insurance	1,706[b]	71[h]	8,830[b]	45-53[i]
Other supplemental private health insurance	17,543[b]	43[j]	13,474[b]	61-67[k]

II. RESULTS

	1979	1987
Percent of total noninstitutionalized civilian population with outpatient prescription drug coverage		
People under 65	71-73	73-77
People 65 and over	36	43-46
Total	67-69%	70-74%

[a] A detailed memorandum describing OTA's methods in preparing this table is available upon request.

[b] From the Current Population Survey. C. Nelson, Census Bureau, U.S. Department of Commerce, Washington, DC, personal communication, Mar. 26, 1991; K. Short, Census Bureau, U.S. Department of Commerce, Washington, DC, personal communication, Nov. 15, 1991.

[c] From the U.S. Department of Labor, Bureau of Labor Statistics, surveys of employers; A. Blostin, U. S. Department of Labor, Bureau of Labor Statistics, Washington, DC, personal communication, Aug. 15, 1991.

[d] Weighted averages of percent of each type of "other health insurance" with outpatient prescription drug coverage: Medicare—0%; Champus—100%; nongroup private health insurance—0-24% (maximum 24% estimate from G.L. Cafferata, *Private Health Insurance of the Medicare Population*, Data Preview 18, Publication No. (PHS) 84-3362 (Washington, DC: U.S. Government Printing Office, 1984)); Medicaid—100%.

[e] Weighted averages of following percents: Medicare—0%; Champus—100%; Medicaid—100%; nongroup private health insurance—0-53% (maximum 53% from Market Facts, Inc. *Consumer Awareness of Medigap Insurance: Findings of a National Survey of Older Americans* (Washington, DC: American Associations of Retired Persons, 1990)).

[f] Based on estimates of Medicare only population in Cafferata, 1984 (footnote d).

[g] Based on estimates of Medicare only population in J. O'Sullivan, and D. Koitz, *Health Insurance That Supplements Medicare: Background Materials and Data*, 89-421 EPW (Washington, DC: Congressional Research Service, 1989).

[h] From Cafferata, 1984 (footnote d).

[i] From Market Facts, Inc., 1990.

[j] Weighted averages of percent of each type of "other health insurance" with prescription drug coverage: Medicaid—100%; Champus—100%; State pharmaceutical assistance programs—100%; nongroup private health insurance—24% (from Cafferata, 1984 (footnote d)).

[k] Weighted averages of following percents: Champus—100%; State pharmaceutical assistance programs—100%; nongroup private health insurance—45-53% (from Market Facts, Inc., 1990).

SOURCE: Office of Technology Assessment, 1993.

Table 10-3—Limitations of Prescription Drug Benefits Among Nonelderly People With Private Health Insurance Covering Prescription Drugs

	1977[a]	1989/1990[b]
Full coverage	3%	3%
Separate limits (copayments)[c]	9	30
Overall limits (major medical)[d]	88	61
Other limits[e]		7

[a] Results based on 1977 National Medical Care Expenditure Study Survey of employers and insurers of individuals under 65 years of age.

[b] Results based on U.S. Bureau of Labor Statistics 1989 and 1990 surveys of employers.

[c] "Separate limits" refers to restrictions applicable only to prescription drugs, such as a copayment for each prescription.

[d] "Overall limits" refers to restrictions applicable to a broader set of medical services. For example, a major medical policy may carry a $100 deductible and 20-percent coinsurance rate that applies to all covered services, not just prescription drugs.

[e] Other limits include policies that combine fixed copayments with overall limits.

SOURCE: Office of Technology Assessment, 1993, based on data from P.J. Farley, *Private Health Insurance in the U.S. Data Preview #23*, DHHS Publication No. (PHS) 86-3406, 1986. U.S. Department of Health and Human Services, National Center for Health Services Research and Health Care Technology Assessment, September 1986; U.S. Department of Labor, Bureau of Labor Statistics, *Employee Benefits in Medium and Large Firms, 1989*, Bulletin 2363 (Washington, DC: U.S. Government Printing Office, June 1990); U.S. Department of Labor, Bureau of Labor Statistics, *Employee Benefits in Small Private Establishments, 1990*, Bulletin 2388 (Washington, DC: U.S. Government Printing Office, September 1991); U.S. Department of Labor, Bureau of Labor Statistics, *Employee Benefits in State and Local Governments, 1990* (Washington, DC: U.S. Government Printing Office, February 1992).

tially between 1977 and 1989, roughly from 9 to 30 percent of the insured population. Copayments have substituted for other types of restrictions, such as the inclusion of drugs within the deductible and coinsurance framework of the major medical policy.

The trend in the 1980s away from inclusion of prescription drug benefits in major medical policies toward separate limits on drug benefits themselves represents a move toward a richer benefit structure for prescription drugs. The vast majority (95 percent) of employees facing fixed copayments per prescription in 1989 had a copayment of $5 or less (35). For people whose overall medical expenses lie below the deductible, a flat copayment for prescriptions means lower out-of-pocket prescription drug expenses than do the major medical restrictions. Even after a beneficiary covered under a major medical plan meets the deductible, he or she may be responsible for a 20 percent or higher coinsurance payment. For example, a $30 prescription would cost the employee covered under a major medical policy with a 20-percent coinsurance rate $6, whereas the typical cost under a flat copayment would be only $5.

REIMBURSABLE AMOUNTS

For policies providing prescription drug benefits, the actual insurance benefit depends on the allowed reimbursement level. The reimbursable amount is not necessarily equal to the price charged by a pharmacy for the prescribed medication, although it is usually tied to the drug's price. In 1977, 76 percent of those with outpatient prescription drug coverage had policies that based reimbursement rates for a given drug on the amount usually charged by the dispensing pharmacy or by other pharmacies in the geographic area (130). More recent data are not yet available, but informal OTA discussions with insurance plan administrators suggest the reimbursement base may have shifted during the 1980s to average wholesale prices (AWP). In either case, if the drug is a "single-source" drug,[10] the insurer essentially pays the manufacturer's price plus a retail markup.

REIMBURSABLE DRUGS

Private insurers generally cover all prescription drugs licensed for sale in the United States by the U.S. Food and Drug Administration (FDA) (35).[11] Thus, FDA approval is in essence a *de facto* coverage guideline for insurers. Indeed, pharmaceuticals are spared the additional insurance coverage hurdles that new medical devices must

---

[10] A single-source drug is a molecular entity that is marketed under a single brand name. After the patent on a drug expires, generic copies may be approved by the FDA, and the compound becomes a multiple-source drug.

[11] Most insurance plans do not cover nonprescription drugs, vitamins, medical supplies, dietary supplements, diabetic supplies other than insulin, and non-oral contraceptives (35).

often clear.[12] For drug manufacturers, the relatively uniform coverage of pharmaceuticals reduces the company's uncertainty about the expected returns from a drug once it has been approved by the FDA.

There is at least one exception to predictable coverage that may become more important in the future. Although virtually every prescription drug that the FDA approves is covered by private insurers, a pharmaceutical may not be covered if a doctor prescribes it for a use other than the one the FDA has approved. Insurers are typically not contractually obligated to provide coverage in these instances (278). Although some of these prescriptions are clearly experimental, others are standard therapies. Pharmaceutical manufacturers often do not seek approval to sell a drug for additional indications once it is initially licensed, because the process can be costly and time consuming (238). The practice of prescribing for unapproved indications, known as off-label prescribing, occurs in many branches of medicine.

There is little published data to show how many claims for off-label prescriptions are denied, but cancer patients report they have found it increasingly difficult to get reimbursement for off-label prescriptions and their associated costs (e.g., hospital stay) as insurers have begun to examine the prescriptions, mainly to control costs (395). About 33 percent of cancer chemotherapy prescriptions are off-label and about 56 percent of all cancer patients receive at least one off-label prescription in their drug regimen (238). Insurers are generally willing to reimburse for off-label uses that have been documented as effective in one of three major medical compendia[13] or in multiple independent published studies. Physicians have complained that there are often long delays between proof of effectiveness and approval in the compendia or other literature (278).

RECENT COST-CONTAINMENT TRENDS

In the past 5 years, many private health insurance plans have begun cost-containment measures that either directly or indirectly control or influence the use of, and prices paid for, prescription drugs. Chief among such provisions are incentives to purchase generic drugs, drug utilization review programs, and mail-order pharmaceutical programs. These provisions may represent a "second-tier barrier" to access to drugs beyond FDA licensing requirements (515). In addition, the rapid growth of HMOs over the past decade has added an indirect incentive to control the utilization of all services, including prescription drugs.

Incentives to Use Generic Drugs—The percent of enrollees in employer-based plans that encourage the use of generic drugs by reducing copayments when a generic is dispensed increased dramatically from 3 to 14 percent between 1985 and 1989 (35). The most common incentive is a lower copayment when a generic drug is purchased. In HMOs, where mandatory generic substitution can be enforced, the use of differential copayments appears to be just as effective as mandatory substitution in increasing the use of generics (515).

Formularies—A formulary restricts the doctor's choice of drugs to drugs on a list (or to those not on a list of excluded drugs) when more than one therapeutically similar compound is available to treat a condition. Except for HMOs, formularies do not exist in private health insurance plans. Recent surveys of HMOs indicate that between 28 and 55 percent of all plans have some type of formulary, but the nature and effectiveness of these restrictions have not been documented (515).

---

[12] Some private insurers subject medical devices and procedures to a rigorous review that can include cost or cost-effectiveness criteria in their coverage decisions. For example, the Blue Cross/Blue Shield Association of America has a Technology Management Program that undertakes such studies in order to make coverage recommendations to its individual insurance plans (12).

[13] These sources include the American Hospital Formulary Service's *Drug Information*, the U.S. Pharmacopoeia's *Drug Information*, and the American Medical Association *Drug Evaluations*. None of these sources are published with the intent that they should be used as guides for insurance coverage; they are references for doctors and hospitals concerning drug options and activities (395).

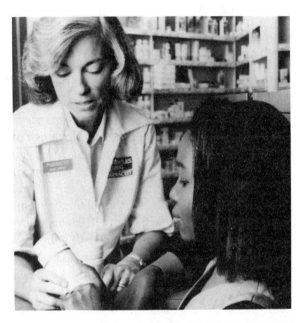

Photo credit: U.S FOOD AND DRUG ADMINISTRATION

The use of generic drugs is growing as health insurers give both patients and pharmacists incentives to substitute generic versions for brand-name versions of prescription drugs.

Drug Utilization Review (DUR)—DUR is the review of drugs prescribed or prescriptions filled to verify the drug's appropriateness, to identify potential interactions with other medications, or to identify alternative effective or cost-effective therapies for the patient (35,138,434,515).[14]

Data on the extent of DUR programs or their impact on the use of pharmaceuticals are limited. Among HMOs, about 70 percent report having a DUR program (515). OTA found no similar profile of DUR programs among fee-for-service insurance plans. A recent General Accounting Office (GAO) study described eight DUR programs, including some at retail chain pharmacies, one at a U.S. Department of Defense pharmacy, and one at a mail-order pharmacy (434). GAO

found that the identification of potential adverse drug reactions or adverse interactions with other drugs that a patient is using are the most common features of DUR programs, but the report also stresses that these systems could be linked relatively easily to insurance claims systems. Thus, although there is little evidence DUR is currently a major tool in attempting to control the use of, or total expenditures for, prescription drugs, insurers or others concerned with costs may try to use DUR more extensively for such purposes in the future.

Mail-Order Pharmacies—Another way in which insurers try to constrain prescription drug costs is by contracting with a "mail-order" pharmacy for drugs that patients need refilled on a regular basis. Unlike other cost-containment mechanisms, mail-order pharmacies do not necessarily restrict access to drugs or attempt to constrain use. These programs achieve cost savings through the economies of scale of a centralized mail-order operation and by providing incentives (usually through lower copayments) for patients to buy their medications in large quantities.

Mail-order pharmacy programs are also more effective than retail pharmacies in substituting less expensive generic versions of brand-name drugs when generic versions are available. One prescription drug insurance administrator with a large mail-order operation reported to OTA that between January and March, 1992, 44 percent of its mail-order sales of multisource drugs were for generic products. In contrast, only 31 percent of sales of maintenance multisource drugs purchased through the company's community pharmacy system were for generic products (255). Thus, the increasing use of mail-order pharmacies may appreciably reduce revenues for brand-name products that have lost patent protection.

---

[14] The now repealed Medicare Catastrophic Coverage Act (Public Law 100-360) included a mandated DUR program for the outpatient prescription drug benefit provided by that legislation. In 1990, the Congress required each State Medicaid program with a prescription drug benefit begin a DUR program by January 1, 1993 (Public Law 101-508). With the expectation that DUR may be a growing part of outpatient prescription drug dispensing, the Pharmaceutical Manufacturers Association (PMA), the American Pharmaceutical Association (APhA), and the American Medical Association recently adopted joint "principles" for DUR programs. This document stresses the importance of DUR in enhancing "the quality of patient care," but does not address its potential use by health insurers to constrain prescription drug costs (138).

Mail-order pharmacy programs appear to be growing rapidly among employer-based health care benefit plans. In 1989, about 13 percent of U.S. employees had a mail-order drug benefit; by 1990, 20 percent of employees had such a plan (135).

HMOs—The rapid growth in HMO enrollment over the past decade, from 3 to 14 percent of the population, means that incentives to economize on medical services are increasing dramatically. But, many HMOs do not give their doctors incentives to economize in drug prescribing. A recent review of seven HMOs found the plans were structured so that the prescribing physician never bore financial risk for prescription drug costs (515).[15] Rates of use of prescription drugs were actually higher in the seven HMOs studied than in traditional insurance plans (515). And, the enrollees in the HMOs used newly approved drugs at the same rate as did those in traditional fee-for-service plans.

Because HMOs are more suited than traditional fee-for-service plans to develop and enforce formularies, HMOs also are more able to negotiate discounts with makers of brand-name drugs. Some large HMOs have achieved substantial discounts on specific drugs for which close therapeutic alternatives exist.[16] Thus, the growth of HMOs has surely expanded price competition among single-source drugs and has reduced, though modestly overall so far, the returns to research and development (R&D).

▌ Medicaid Prescription Drug Benefits

Medicaid, funded jointly by the States and the Federal Government, provides health insurance to people of limited financial means.[17] Coverage of outpatient prescriptions is an optional Medicaid benefit offered by 49 States and the District of Columbia. Medicaid enrollees get their prescribed medications from a retail pharmacy usually at little or no charge to them. The pharmacy, in turn, is reimbursed by the State Medicaid agency according to payment limits and established dispensing fees set by Federal Medicaid regulations. Medicaid is responsible for about 10 to 15 percent of the Nation's outpatient prescription drug expenditures.[18]

EXTENT OF OUTPATIENT COVERAGE

To get a prescribed medicine from a pharmacy, a Medicaid beneficiary usually presents a Medicaid card verifying his or her enrollment, along with the doctor's written prescription. A total of 22 States require Medicaid enrollees to pay a part of the cost of medications (287). In most States with this provision, the copayment ranges from $0.50 to $3.00 (287). Federal law prohibits States from requiring copayments from important groups of beneficiaries: children under 18, pregnant women, residents of long-term care and hospice institutions, some HMO enrollees, and

---

[15] These HMOs were all Individual Practice Associations or Networks. These kinds of HMOs tend to have looser fiscal controls than staff model HMOs, where physicians are either employees or partners in the organization.

[16] The magnitude of such discounts has declined since 1990, when the Medicaid Rebate Law (Public Law 101-508) made it costly for pharmaceutical firms to offer such discounts (431).

[17] At a minimum, States must provide certain health services under Medicaid to the recipients of certain kinds of Federal financial assistance. In particular, recipients of Supplemental Security Income (SSI), Aid to Families of Dependent Children (AFDC), and several other groups of pregnant women and children meeting specific criteria are considered "categorically" eligible for Medicaid. States may also decide to provide these services to other low-income individuals without health insurance (sometimes referred to as "medically needy" individuals). States may also provide other services, including prescription drug coverage, to the categorically eligible only or to both the categorically and medically needy populations. In 1991, 17 States and the District of Columbia provided prescription drug coverage to the categorically needy only, while the remaining 34 States provided drug benefits to both the categorically and medically needy. Of the 17 States having no prescription drug benefits for the "medically needy," 16 offer Medicaid only to categorically eligible people (463).

[18] As shown in table 10-1, the 1987 National Medical Expenditure Survey of noninstitutionalized Americans indicated Medicaid accounted for about 10 percent of expenditures for prescription drugs in 1987. The National Health Expenditures Series, which estimates national spending on health care based on a variety of data sources, estimates the Medicaid share of pharmaceutical expenditures was 15 percent in 1990 (464).

recipients of emergency and family planning services (287).

REIMBURSABLE AMOUNTS

State Medicaid programs reimburse the pharmacist after a drug is dispensed to a Medicaid enrollee (235). States pay a fixed dispensing fee and an amount to cover the cost to the pharmacy of the prescribed drug. The median dispensing fee in 1990 was $4.10 (287).

Federal requirements for reimbursement of prescribed drug costs differ for single-source and multiple-source drugs. Until 1991, when a new Medicaid rebate law went into effect, State Medicaid agencies were required to pay no more for a single-source drug than either the pharmacy's estimated acquisition cost plus a reasonable dispensing fee, or the pharmacy's usual and customary charge to the general public (134). State Medicaid agencies generally discounted the published average wholesale price for the drug by a fixed percent (ranging from 5 to 11) to obtain the estimated acquisition cost (134). Since published wholesale prices are generally higher than the actual wholesale prices paid by retailers, Medicaid essentially paid the manufacturer's price plus a retail markup for single-source drugs.

Since the mid-1970s the Federal Government has tried to reap savings from price competition for multiple-source drugs by requiring that in the aggregate (i.e., across all multiple-source drugs) the State reimburse no more than 150 percent of the published price for the least costly product (134). States themselves have every incentive to pay as little as possible for multiple-source drugs. A big loophole in this regulation has been the exemption of any prescription from the upper limits if the physician has written by hand that a specific brand is medically necessary. When such an override occurs, the prescription is treated as a single-source drug even when generic competitors are available.[19]

REIMBURSABLE DRUGS

Until 1991, State Medicaid agencies had the authority to restrict the drugs that Medicaid covers. In 1990, about 22 States had restrictive formularies, which limited reimbursable drugs to a defined list. Another 28 States had "open formularies," under which all drugs are reimbursable except for those explicitly identified as ineligible.

The use of restrictive formularies can add a measure of uncertainty and delay to the drug development process and could affect manufacturers' returns to R&D. In the past, there were reports of long delays in the adoption of new drugs into Medicaid formularies after FDA approval. A study of delays in Medicaid formulary approvals for new drugs introduced between 1975 and 1982 in six States with restrictive formularies found the average delays in approval time for drugs eventually accepted ranged from about 1 to 4 years after approval by the FDA (153). An update of that study, which examined nine States over the period 1979 to 1984, found similar delays (156).

OTA examined the status of three newly approved drugs in States with restrictive formularies. Two of the drugs, AZT and gancyclovir, were approved in 1987 and 1989 respectively for treating AIDS patients. The third drug, fluoxetine, the first compound in a new class of antidepressants, was approved in December 1987. By September 1990, virtually all States had approved the three drugs for Medicaid reimbursement, although it had taken almost 2 years for some States to approve AZT. In addition, several States required prior authorization to fill prescriptions for these drugs (503).

Many State Medicaid programs restrict payment for off-label uses of prescription drugs; however, the restrictions are applied only to a few very costly drugs. Therefore, the overall impact of such Medicaid restrictions is minor.

---

[19] A study conducted in Florida in 1989 found almost 40 percent of prescriptions for multiple-source drugs were written with a physician's brand override and were filled with the originator's brand. In 1990, Florida issued a rule mandating the use of available generics and essentially refusing to pay for brand-name drugs regardless of the physician override when generic equivalents exist (517).

RECENT COST-CONTAINMENT EFFORTS: THE MEDICAID REBATE LAW

A new Federal Medicaid law enacted in 1990 rendered much of previous Medicaid prescription drug policy inoperative. The Omnibus Budget Reconciliation Act of 1990 (Public Law 101-508) required manufacturers selling prescription drugs to Medicaid patients to give States a rebate on their Medicaid purchases. In exchange, the law prohibited States from using formularies to restrict Medicaid patients' access to any FDA-approved drug in the manufacturer's product line. States *may* require doctors to get prior authorization for a drug but not for the first 6 months after FDA approval.

The required rebate on brand-name drugs[20] has two main components. The first is the Basic Rebate, which requires the manufacturer to effectively discount the price of each drug it sells to Medicaid by a specified amount. The second component is an Additional Rebate, which requires the manufacturer to pay money to Medicaid whenever the prices of its brand-name drugs increase more rapidly than price inflation. The Congressional Budget Office projected a total rebate for brand-name drugs (single-source and innovator multiple-source drugs) to the Federal Government of $637 million in fiscal year 1992 (431). Including the States' share brings this total to about $1.1 billion (317), or about 2 percent of total domestic manufacturer sales.

The Basic Rebate has two components—a flat discount off the average manufacturer's price[21] and a "best-price" discount that would equate the net Medicaid price with the lowest price offered by the company to any buyer. The required rebate is the higher of these two components. The flat discount increases over time as the law is phased in.[22]

The Additional Rebate operates one way until 1994, when it is slated to change in a manner that is potentially important for returns on new drugs. Through 1993, the average manufacturer's price of each brand-name drug product in any calendar quarter is compared with the price of the drug in the quarter ending October 1990. If the product's price has increased faster than inflation (as measured by the consumer price index (CPI)), then the manufacturer must give back to Medicaid the difference for each unit of the drug it sells to Medicaid. If a drug product is introduced after October 1990, then the price in the calendar quarter in which it was launched on the market becomes its baseline price.[23] Thus, while price increases to Medicaid are controlled, the launch price to Medicaid of a new drug is virtually unrestrained.

After 1993, the Additional Rebate for each drug is tied not to the pricing history of that drug alone but to the average manufacturer's price across the manufacturer's complete product line, weighted by the number of units of each product sold to Medicaid. The manufacturer's current weighted average price is compared with the manufacturer's weighted average price across its entire product line *as it existed in October 1990*. If the average price across drugs sold in a period after 1993 is higher than the average price as of October 1990, after accounting for general inflation, then the manufacturer must give back the

---

[20] Brand-name drugs are those available from only one manufacturer (i.e., single-source drugs) or, if generic competitors exist, the innovator company's brand-name product. The law also requires a rebate from generic manufacturers equal to 10 percent of the average manufacturer's price (increasing to 11 percent in 1994).

[21] The Average Manufacturer's price (AMP) is the average price charged by wholesalers for products distributed to the retail class of trade. The best price originally excluded depot prices and single-award contracts given any Federal agency. In subsequent legislation passed in 1992, prices paid by the Department of Veterans Affairs, the Department of Defense, Public Health Service Hospitals and other federally funded health providers, and certain hospitals that serve a disproportionate share of poor people were also excluded from the best price (Public Law 102-585).

[22] In the first 2 years, there are upper limits on the required rebate.

[23] The law does not specifically indicate what should be done about drugs introduced after October 1990, but the law has been implemented so far in this way.

Box 10-A—Medicaid's Additional Rebate After 1993: An Example

Suppose a company had two drugs on the market in 1990, with unit sales over the quarter ending October 30 and average manufacturer's prices as given below:

Drug	Price	Unit sales
X	10	100
Y	30	100

Suppose the consumer price index increased by a total of 10 percent between 1990 and 1995. Then, the inflation-adjusted baseline weighted average manufacturer's price in 1995 would be:

$$[(10(100) + 30(100)]/200] * 1.10 = \$22.00$$

Now, suppose in 1995 the firm introduces a new drug and its total sales now are as follows:

Drug	Price	Quantity
X	11	100
Y	33	100
Z	25	100

The weighted average price in 1995 for this manufacturer is now $23.

For every unit of each product it sells, the manufacturer must give back to the Medicaid program $1, the difference between the current weighted average manufacturer's price and the inflation-adjusted baseline weighted average manufacturer's price. This manufacturer would owe Medicaid $300 in additional rebate.

Without the new drug, the manufacturer would have owed Medicaid nothing, so the new drug pays a penalty of $3 per unit to Medicaid for having been introduced at a relatively high price.

SOURCE: Office of Technology Assessment, 1993.

difference for every unit of each drug it sells to Medicaid.

The baseline average weighted manufacturer's price as of 1990 would not contain any drugs introduced after that period, so as the law is currently written new drugs introduced to the market at high prices relative to pre-existing drugs will face additional rebates. (See box 10-A for an example of how this works.) At the same time, the law states that the Secretary of Health and Human Services (HHS) may exclude from the calculation of today's weighted average price any new drug that effectively would lower the rebate manufacturers must give to Medicaid. (A new drug product entering the market at a very low price, for example, might be excluded from the calculation of the weighted average manufacturer's price, but the per unit rebate would still be payable for each unit of the new product sold to Medicaid.)

The law *does* allow the Secretary of HHS to exclude from the weighted average price calculation, new products that increase the rebate to Medicaid, but only if their inclusion would impose "undue hardship" upon the manufacturer. The law also gives the Secretary the power to impose an alternative mechanism for calculating the Additional Rebate. No such alternative approaches have been published to date.

In the short term, the Additional Rebate gives firms the incentive to introduce new products at high prices. While a company's price increases for existing products are controlled, launch prices are not. And, the prohibition of restrictive formularies for participating manufacturers increases the potential for higher earnings in the early years after product launch.[24]

After 1993 the situation changes. If the Additional Rebate is implemented as designed, the effective launch price to Medicaid of a new drug will be constrained at or even below the inflation-adjusted weighted average price for 1990. Thus, new drug products launched at high prices will effectively face high Medicaid rebates, thus substantially reducing the revenues on this segment of the market.

The Post-1993 Additional Rebate as it is currently outlined in the law has implementation problems. Detailed data on the quantity of Medicaid drugs sold from June to October, 1990, necessary to compute the weighted average price of the manufacturer's products as of October 1990, do not exist in a usable form in most State Medicaid agencies. One technical solution to this problem would be to use a calendar quarter in late 1993 as the baseline date for quantity weights, because by that time Medicaid agencies would have better data on quantities of each drug product sold to their agency.

In the fall of 1992, technical amendments were introduced (but not passed) to change the post-1993 Additional Rebate (S.3274). Under the amendments, the baseline weighted average manufacturer's price would be calculated using the 1990 price for drugs already on the market in 1990 and the launch price of drugs introduced after that period. Importantly, it would weight those prices by unit sales in the current rebate period. This new rebate would not penalize firms when they introduce a new product at a relatively high price, although it would still control in-creases in prices to Medicaid after the introduction.[25] Thus, the effect on revenues obtained from newly introduced drugs would be less severe than under current law, which would effectively control the prices of new drugs to Medicaid.

∎ State Pharmaceutical Assistance Programs

During the past 15 years, 10 States have established State Pharmaceutical Assistance Programs (SPAPs) that extend pharmaceutical benefits mainly to people 65 years of age and older who do not qualify for Medicaid but cannot afford to purchase private health insurance. Four of these SPAPs also cover the permanently disabled. Together these programs currently spend about $500 million annually on prescription drugs (34,38,181,191,237,246,252,256,259). Eligibility in a SPAP is limited by personal income ceilings that each State determines and that usually fall between one and two times the Federal poverty line. In 1977, the first year of the programs, 43,000 people participated. By 1991, this figure had grown to approximately 936,000 people representing about 3 percent of the population age 65 and older. Five of the programs cover nearly all FDA-approved prescription drugs; the other five limit the classes of prescription drugs for which they will pay.[26]

Virtually all of the State programs have policies encouraging the use of cheaper generic drugs. Five States require dispensing generics if they exist, unless the physician specifically specifies the brand-name drug. Two of these States have also adopted other incentives to promote the use of generics. In Pennsylvania, a pharmacist who convinces a physician to change a prescription

---

[24] The Pharmaceutical Manufacturers Association (PMA) has complained that States are using the prior authorization rules as *de facto* formularies (371a), thereby undercutting the positive aspects for the industry of the restriction on formularies. Such tactics are illegal for only the first 6 months of a product's life.

[25] The technical amendments would also have removed the discretion of the Secretary of Health and Human Services to exclude new drugs from the weighted average price when such an action would lower the amount of the rebate. The Secretary also loses the discretionary power to change the overall approach.

[26] For example, Illinois, Maine, Vermont, and Rhode Island cover pharmaceuticals only for the treatment of chronic conditions including heart disease, diabetes, hypertension, and arthritis. Rhode Island also covers cholesterol-lowering drugs as well as treatments for cancer, glaucoma, and Parkinson's disease. Since 1991, Maryland has limited the drugs its SPAP covers to chronic disease treatments, anti-infectives, and drugs for a limited number of other diagnoses. None of the programs cover over-the-counter drugs.

from brand-name to generic receives an extra dollar of reimbursement from the State, while in Maine the patient pays a higher copayment for a brand-name prescription if a generic is available. The five States without a generic substitution requirement do require higher copayments from beneficiaries for prescriptions filled with a brand-name drug.[27]

Medicare Prescription Drug Benefits

Although Medicare generally does not cover outpatient drugs,[28] it does cover drugs that only a doctor or someone under a doctor's supervision can administer. Many drugs given by injection or intravenous (IV) administration fall into this category. Ordinarily, Medicare leaves it to its carriers[29] to determine whether specific drugs will be covered under this provision. If the drug is usually self-injectable or self-administered, the carrier can deny coverage (88).

Biotechnology drugs are frequently large molecules that must be administered by IV or injection. Thus, these drugs are more likely to be covered under Medicare than are other drugs. Nevertheless, at least two recently approved biotechnology drugs, Actimmune™ and Protropin™, were denied Medicare coverage by certain carriers because they were classified as self-injectables (43).

When Medicare does pay for outpatient prescription drugs, the carriers determine pricing policies. There is no official Medicare cost control strategy pertaining to the few outpatient drugs covered by Medicare.

PRESCRIPTION DRUG BENEFITS IN OTHER COUNTRIES

The existence of universal health insurance in other industrialized countries means patient demand for such drugs is not much affected by prices. Nevertheless, insurers in universal health systems more strictly control the use of drugs and the prices paid. Although data on drug utilization and prices paid in other countries for drugs are not generally available,[30] special studies conducted in recent years suggest some European countries pay less for drugs than do consumers in the United States (457).

OTA reviewed recent trends in payment methods for prescription drugs in five countries: Australia, Canada, France, Japan, and the United Kingdom. To a greater or lesser extent in each of these countries, drug payment policy is governed by two potentially conflicting objectives: to minimize health insurance prescription drug costs and to help the country's domestic pharmaceutical industry. Payment policies represent a blend between these objectives.

Australia

Australia's domestic pharmaceutical industry is very small, and the country represents a small proportion of the world market for prescription drugs.[31] Consequently, Australia has not had a major economic stake in promoting pharmaceutical R&D. Instead, the main objective of Australia's pharmaceutical payment policies has been to minimize the cost of drugs, both to the government and to its citizens. Recently, though, the government has made efforts to promote the

---

[27] A recent in-house study conducted by New York's SPAP suggests this type of consumer-based price incentive may have only modest effects. The study found that in New York, the lower copayment for generics led to the dispensing of generics for only 27 percent of prescriptions filled compared with 24 percent for all prescriptions filled nationwide (34).

[28] Medicare covers immunosuppressives after organ transplants, antigens, blood-clotting factors for hemophiliacs, and dialysis drugs such as erythropoietin.

[29] Medicare carriers are fiscal agents (typically Blue Shield/Blue Cross plans or other private insurance companies) under contract to the Health Care Financing Administration (under the Department of Health and Human Services) for administration of specific Medicare tasks. These tasks include determining reasonable costs for covered items and services, making payments, and guarding against unnecessary use of covered services.

[30] The U.S. General Accounting Office is currently engaged in an examination of European prescription drug price mechanisms to determine their applicability to the United States.

[31] Drugs subsidized by the Australian Government, which account for 75 percent of all prescriptions, were worth A$1.32 billion in 1990-91.

Australian domestic pharmaceutical industry through its pricing policies.

The Pharmaceutical Benefits Scheme (PBS) of Australia, adopted in 1950, originally made 139 life-saving and disease-preventing drugs available at no cost to patients. These drugs were supplied because the cost of treatment could be "most burdensome" to people in life-threatening situations (308). However, as this program grew to cover hundreds of drugs and 105 million prescriptions annually (75 percent of all Australian prescriptions), the government began to consider options for cost control.

One primary approach to controlling the government's pharmaceutical bill has been to enact copayment requirements, determined annually according to the Australian consumer price index (125,178). In August 1992, the patient copayment per prescription was A$15.90 for general beneficiaries (to a maximum per year of A$30, then A$2.60 to a maximum of an additional A$51.60 that year), and A$2.60 for retirees[32] (up to a maximum per year of A$135.20) (178).

Since 1963, the government has negotiated prices with manufacturers for any new chemical entity to be reimbursed by the PBS. After a drug is approved for efficacy and safety it must be admitted onto the list of products covered by the PBS. Legislation passed in 1987 requires the Pharmaceutical Benefits Advisory Committee (PBAC), the body responsible for recommending whether a new chemical entity should be listed for federal reimbursement, to consider not only effectiveness but also cost.

Guidelines implementing this legislation were not drafted until 1990; since then the rules have been subject to extensive debate. Revised guidelines were released in August 1992 and will be followed for all major submissions to the PBAC as of January 1993. The guidelines recommend the use of final outcome measures, such as cost per year of life saved, cost per death prevented, or cost per quality-adjusted year of life, to evaluate a drug's cost-effectiveness compared with alternative therapies. Because these measurements are difficult to make in many cases, estimated cost-effectiveness analysis may be based on intermediate outcome indicators such as the number of patients achieving a target blood pressure for a new antihypertensive agent.

Once a new chemical entity is admitted to the PBS list, manufacturers undergo price negotiations with the Pharmaceutical Benefits Pricing Authority (PBPA) (formerly the Pharmaceutical Benefits Pricing Bureau) to determine the PBS price for the product. Price negotiations were originally applied to multiple-source as well as single-source drugs entering the market; however, since 1990, only drugs identified as being without generic equivalents must enter price negotiations (see below).

The PBPA presently considers the following factors in the pricing negotiations: the prices of drugs in the same therapeutic group, cost information supplied by the manufacturer or estimated by the Authority, prescription volumes, economies of scale, product stability, special manufacturing requirements, prices of the drug in other comparable countries, the level of activity being undertaken by the company in Australia (see below), other relevant factors presented by the company, and other directions by the Health Minister of the Authority.

In 1988, as part of an Industry Development Plan, the government declared it would consider "the level of activity being undertaken by the company in Australia including new investment, production, research and development" in determining a company's price (308).[33] This provision, known as Factor-(f), granted further price increases "where a company can demonstrate that it is making a significant contribution to internationally competitive production in Australia" (308).

To enter the Factor-(f) scheme, companies are expected to increase their Australian production

---

[32] This category includes those with unemployment benefits, war veterans, and war widows, as well as pensioners.

[33] This plan also increased the length of Australian patents for drugs by 4 years and gave the drug industry representation in the PBPA.

and R&D activities by 3 percent. The actual price increase is based on the increase in local value added for a company's manufacturing, exports, and R&D. Companies receiving a pricing dividend under the Factor-(f) provision can apply it to any drug in their product line. The government has confirmed its commitment to expanding the drug industry in Australia by announcing an extension of the Factor-(f) policy through the year 1999.

Until 1990, drugs with generic equivalent competitors on the market underwent the same pricing negotiations as new chemical entities. Since then, drugs with generic equivalents are no longer subjected to the PBPA pricing process. Today companies may set their own prices for any drug having a generic equivalent on the market, but the government sets a benchmark reimbursement rate for each chemical entity equal to the lowest priced generic alternative (178). When a consumer purchases a drug, the PBS reimburses the pharmacist only up to the benchmark rate; if the doctor prescribes a more expensive brand, the consumer must pay not only the copayment but also the difference between the price and the benchmark. Patients can ask the pharmacist to substitute the benchmark product for a more expensive prescribed brand, but the pharmacist must contact the prescribing physician for approval (178).

The current benchmark pricing scheme was adopted to give consumers incentives to economize on the use of prescription drugs for which generic equivalents are available (178,408) and to make the marketplace more price competitive. Drug prices were freed subject to the benchmark pricing scheme late in 1990. In early 1991, of 651 brands subject to benchmark pricing, 131 (including the 65 most prescribed in Australia) have a price higher than the benchmark level (178). The

government reports that market shares decreased slightly for drugs priced above the benchmark level, while there has been an increase in market share for benchmark priced drugs and an increase in generic prescribing (408). However, it is likely that manufacturers would not price their drug above the benchmark price if they do not expect total revenues from the sale of the drug to be higher than they would be with a benchmark price. Thus, the freeing of prices means a potential shift of the burden of payment from the government to the consumer. Whether the consumer (or the physician) becomes more price conscious as the generic pricing system matures remains to be seen.

■ Canada

Like other countries OTA reviewed, Canada has sought a compromise between the two goals of pharmaceutical cost containment and development of a domestic pharmaceutical industry. Unlike other countries, Canada's national pharmaceutical cost control policy has used legislation that weakened the impact of patent protection on pharmaceutical sales in Canada.[34] This approach led to widespread penetration of generic products in the Canadian market, which in turn stimulated price competition among brand-name drugs in Canada. However, legislation passed in 1987 has restored a measure of patent protection to pharmaceutical products in exchange for the cooperation of multinational pharmaceutical companies in keeping pharmaceutical prices from increasing sharply and investing in R&D performed in Canada.

In the 1960s Canadian federal and provincial health programs did not yet include pharmaceutical benefits, so patients paid for nearly all drugs themselves. The early 1960s saw rapid increases in Canadian drug expenditures, which alarmed the public and created a national demand for price

---

[34] Canadian provinces operate independent programs to control the costs of pharmaceuticals. Control methods vary widely, using combinations of incentives for generics, restrictive drug lists, copayments, etc. Although this section focuses mainly on measures of the national government to control prescription drug expenditures, it should be recognized that provincial control over the prices of prescriptions sold through provincial drug plans (which make up 40 to 100 percent of drugs sold in individual provinces) gives Canada added leverage over market prices. One way most of the provinces exert downward pressure on prices is via a restricted benefits list; the manufacturers must negotiate prices with the provincial government to have a drug admitted to the list of those eligible for reimbursement in the province.

control. Three separate federal government studies conducted between 1963 and 1966 found drug companies had undue market power, allowing them to set unnecessarily high prices (90). The studies also concluded such market power would not exist if there were competition for many of the drugs protected by patents.

The legal right to bypass patent protection for pharmaceuticals has existed in Canada for quite some time. A statute enacted in 1923 permitted Canadian companies to apply for compulsory licenses to produce generic equivalents of drugs already protected by patents in Canada. This statute was not invoked often; since the Canadian market was small, it could not support a domestic manufacturing industry for generic drugs (244). However, in 1969, the Canadian Government extended the compulsory licensing provision to allow for import of generics from other countries.

In some Eastern European and South American countries, drug patent laws are either weak or nonexistent (90). Thus, when a company launches a new drug, manufacturers in these countries can reproduce the active ingredient and market the drug within about 2 years. The 1969 Canadian law allowed Canadian companies to apply for compulsory licenses to import and market these readily available generic products.

The government took other actions to support the growth of generic competition such as lowering the tariff on pharmaceutical imports, awarding large grants and loans to support domestic generic drug packagers and distributors, and setting up education programs for physicians (90).

By the early 1980s, generic drugs accounted for 10 percent of pharmaceutical sales. In 1968, the year before the law was enacted, Canadians paid, on average, 9 percent more than did Americans for 43 patented drugs. By 1976, Canadian prices for these drugs were, on average, 21 percent cheaper than in the United States (90). Imported

generics generally entered the Canadian market at prices 10 to 20 percent below their patented counterparts and maintained this margin if the price of the patented versions were reduced in response (30). When multiple generic products were available to compete with a single brand-name drug, the generics were sold at prices as low as 40 percent below the brand-name price (244). In 1983, savings of $211 million in a $1.6-billion market were realized as a result of compulsory licensing (244).

As the provinces adopted their own pharmaceutical benefits plans, they took advantage of the savings that generics offered. By the middle of the 1980s, most of the provinces had enacted measures to ensure generics would be used more frequently. All 11 provincial or territorial governments now have provisions encouraging or requiring pharmacists to substitute generics on reimbursed prescriptions whenever possible (30), unless the physician states otherwise.

The pharmaceutical companies selling patented products in Canada claimed that cost-control via compulsory licensing put an unfair burden on the most innovative companies (90). Although the ratio of Canadian R&D to sales increased moderately from 3.6 percent in 1960 to about 5 percent in 1980, manufacturers claimed Canada was punishing innovation because it lacked patent protection. In 1985, the United States put additional pressure on Canada to restore patent protection for drugs as part of negotiations on free trade (244).

Canada responded in 1987 with Bill C-22, a law that gives 7 or 10 years of conditional protection from compulsory licensing after a drug is approved for marketing in Canada.[35] If a new drug is invented in Canada, the protection lasts for the full 20 years of the patent (309). In exchange for this lengthened period of exclusive marketing, the multinational companies publicly committed

---

[35] If the generic equivalent of a patented drug is produced in Canada, the period of market exclusivity extends 7 years from the time of approval. Generics imported into Canada must wait 10 years after approval (244).

themselves to increase the ratio of Canadian R&D to Canadian sales to 10 percent by 1996 (244).[36]

The new law also created an independent quasi-judicial body, the Patented Medicines Pricing Review Board (PMPRB), whose main charge is to ensure prices of patented medicines are not excessive. The PMPRB does not set or approve prices; it monitors manufacturers' prices, evaluates whether those prices are excessive, and negotiates with companies to lower prices when they are considered too high. The Board has authority across all the provinces; in its own words, it is "investigator, prosecutor, and judge" (309), with the power to remove the market exclusivity of every patented drug.

The Board developed its own guidelines to determine what constitutes excessive pricing. Patented medicines are broken down by the Board into two categories: existing drugs and new drugs. Existing drugs are those sold in Canada before Bill C-22 was enacted and those whose introductory prices have been approved by the Board since Bill C-22 was enacted. The PMPRB will assume an existing drug's price is excessive if its rate of price inflation exceeds the cumulative change in the Canadian consumer price index over the same period.

To review the prices of new drugs entering the market, the PMPRB categorizes them into three subgroups, each with its own criteria for excessive pricing. Category (i), known as *line extension drugs*, includes product line extensions (such as new dosage forms). Line extension prices are judged excessive if the average price per kilogram does not bear a reasonable relationship to that of some other medicine or form of the same medicine with a comparable strength or dosage. Category (ii), *breakthrough drugs*, are deemed to have excessive prices if the price is greater than *both* all other Canadian drug products in the therapeutic class *and* the median price of the medicine in seven selected industrialized nations. Category (iii), *"other" drugs*, includes those that provide little improvement over their predecessors. Their prices will be judged excessive if they exceed the prices of other drugs in the same therapeutic class (309).

The Board has strong remedial powers at its command when a drug is found to have an excessive price. Although these powers have not been invoked since its inception, the PMPRB can order a drug's price lowered, or it can revoke the market exclusivity on both the drug in question and another of the manufacturer's patented drugs (the Board's choice) by granting compulsory licenses for the production of a generic equivalent of the patented medicine.

Both the price review measures and the efforts to stimulate R&D appear to have been successful in moderating price increases so far. From January 1987 to December 1991, patented drug prices increased at a rate of 2.9 percent annually, compared with an annual increase of 4.7 percent in the Canadian consumer price index.[37] The PMPRB reported that in its first 18 months of operation, compliance with the pricing limits was around 70 percent. Most of the cases where prices were deemed excessive were resolved, with a few exceptions where complicated circumstances delayed a solution. As of June 1992, the Board had not reported any incidents in which a patent was revoked in favor of compulsory licenses (311). The Board also reported that in the "existing drug" category, prices actually increased less rapidly than general inflation (309,310,311).

The PMPRB also monitors R&D conducted in Canada by firms selling drugs in Canada. The Board reported that by 1991 the ratio of R&D performed in Canada to sales in Canada had increased to 9.7 percent, up from around 5 percent in 1987 (311). Basic and applied research in-

---

[36] In comparison, in 1989, Sweden, the United Kingdom, and the United States had domestic R&D per sales ratios of 21.8, 20.9, and 14.2 percent, respectively (71).

[37] However, the 3.1 percent figure is for patented medicines only. When all Canadian pharmaceuticals are included, the annual rate of increase in pharmaceutical prices becomes 5.1 percent (244).

creased by 20 and 22 percent, respectively, from 1990 to 1991 (PMPRB 1992).

In January 1992, Canada proposed a bill to eliminate compulsory licensing as a punitive measure to further promote industrial growth as well as to maintain consistency with the draft text of a General Agreement on Tariffs and Trade released in December 1991.

Bill C-91, which was in the early stages of consideration by the Canadian legislature in the fall of 1992, proposes to amend the Patent Act to eliminate compulsory licensing during the entire course of a drug's standard 20-year patent life. The bill offsets the effects of this measure by enhancing the role of the PMPRB with extended judicial and punitive powers.

Under Bill C-91, PMPRB would have increased control over the introductory prices of new drugs entering the market. In the case of excessive pricing by manufacturers, the Board could essentially force manufacturers to roll back prices. If a manufacturer is found to be making a regular practice of continually pricing pharmaceuticals excessively, all fines and penalties could be doubled. Executives of pharmaceutical companies refusing to submit pricing and sales information or not willing to comply with the pricing orders of the Board would be subject to imprisonment for up to 1 year under the bill.

PMPRB has the authority to examine the prices of drugs being sold in all Canadian markets, public and private. The extended protection from compulsory licensing in Bill C-91 would essentially guarantee exclusivity for new drugs for a substantial period of time within a regime that monitors and, at least in principle, has the power to regulate excessive pricing of pharmaceuticals in all sectors of the market.

▌ France

French Social Security Funds subsidize about 74 percent of the prescriptions filled in France (381). When a French patient buys a drug, he or she generally pays up front for the medicine and then applies for reimbursement to the national insurance fund that covers all but the required patient copayments.

There are three different levels of reimbursement to the patient for different classes of drugs: "mainstream drugs," prescribed for common chronic and acute illnesses, are reimbursed at a rate of 70 percent. Medications "intended for the treatment of troubles and diseases usually not serious"[38] are generally reimbursed at a rate of 40 percent (386). The third category, single-source products for serious illnesses, is reimbursed at a rate of 100 percent.

Despite the seemingly high copayment requirements, the French have very low unreimbursed expenses. Numerous classes of people and chronic treatments are exempted from copayments. About 80 percent of the population belongs to supplementary insurance funds, or *mutuelles*, which pay for the bulk of the patient's drug costs, leaving only minimal copayments. Although 56 percent of prescriptions in France required some copayment in 1991 (381), most were very low. Thus, French consumers have little price sensitivity (67,174).

France boasts the highest per capita pharmaceutical consumption by volume in Europe (67) and the second highest per capita pharmaceutical expenditures among Organization for Economic Corporation and Development countries in 1990 (304). The high drug consumption rates at least partially explain why the French Government has found it necessary to regulate relatively strictly the price of pharmaceuticals. In 1990, the prices of medicines in France were the second lowest in the European Community (304). The government has focused its cost control measures on manufacturers' prices of the drugs that national insurance reimburses.[39] Although government efforts at

---

[38] Some examples are antinauseants, antipruritics, weight loss drugs, antispasmodics, antivaricose drugs, hormonotherapy drugs, laxatives, urologicals, and counter-irritants. There are a good number of other similar therapeutic categories included (386).

[39] The nationally reimbursed prescriptions make up 80 percent of drugs sold in France. About 11 percent are accounted for by hospitals, which negotiate prices on their own. The remaining 9 percent are sold privately, without any price constraints (386).

price control have been described as "piecemeal" and "fragmented" (174), they have clearly been successful in keeping drug prices comparatively low.

Any drug to be sold and reimbursed by national health insurance must work its way through a maze of French ministries and commissions (174,386). To reach the French market, a manufacturer must see its drug through a three-step process. First, the drug must win the French equivalent of U.S. FDA approval. Second, the drug must be approved for addition to the list of reimbursable drugs. Third, it must go through price negotiations to determine what the reimbursement price for the drug will be and whether national insurance will pay 40, 70, or 100 percent of this price when a patient receives the drug.

Through each of these steps, the drug is evaluated for its efficacy, safety, and risk/benefit ratio (406). The French equivalent of the U.S. FDA reviews drugs for marketing approval. This process is completed relatively quickly; the government has 120 days to make a decision after an application for marketing authorization is filed, with a 90-day extension available (406).

Once a drug gains marketing authorization, the manufacturer seeks the approval of the Transparency Commission, which decides whether to admit the drug onto a list of drugs approved for reimbursement by the national insurance funds. Although a drug can be prescribed without approval of the Transparency Commission, physicians rarely do so (406). The Transparency Commission is empowered to compare the drug's cost with that of alternative existing treatments. The Transparency Commission tries to keep the market clear of too many "me-too" drugs offering no real medical or economic advance (386).

Once a product is admitted to the list of drugs approved for reimbursement, its manufacturers must again document its benefits for a Pricing Committee, which negotiates both the price of the drug and its level of reimbursement (40, 70, or 100 percent). The Committee, made up of representatives from the Directorate of Pharmacy and Drugs, and the Ministries of Social Security, Industry, and Competition, enters into a two-step evaluation process. First, a "technical price" is set based on the effectiveness and economic efficiency of the drug. This price is set in relation to reimbursement rates for therapeutically similar drugs. "Me-too" drugs for which therapeutic equivalents are already on the market cannot receive a technical price higher than 90 percent of the price of existing therapeutic equivalents.[40] For breakthrough drugs with no close competitors, the price of the drug is compared with prices paid in other countries.

Second, the technical price is adjusted to an "economic price," the ultimate selling price. A bonus is added if the raw materials used to make the drug were produced domestically. Similar additions are awarded if the drug provides a positive French trade balance or creates French jobs. Finally, if the drug is a result of French research efforts, it may also receive price increases. Because these kinds of national incentives are banned under the European Commission's Transparency Directive, they no longer officially exist.

The price increases available in the Committee's adjustment of the technical price to the economic price are incentives to promote an active French pharmaceutical industry. But the magnitude of such incentives may not be great enough to spur research, especially when there are countries nearby that offer greater financial re-

---

[40] This rule also holds for generic equivalents of drugs already marketed. Manufacturers have actually used this 90 percent limit to slow the penetration of the French market by generics. When a brand-name manufacturer gets wind of a generic drug being developed for introduction into France, the manufacturer can quickly release a generic equivalent of its own. Multiple generic equivalents may be released by different subsidiaries of the company. With each generic accepted into the market, the price awarded decreases by another 10 percent. These generic copies are not marketed, but they ensure a competitor's generic entering the market will be granted a very low price, possibly not worth the trouble of importing or distributing. Low-priced generics may also be boycotted by pharmacists, whose profit margin is figured as a percentage of the drug's cost (174).

wards for R&D conducted within their borders. Between 1961 and 1970, France had the second highest rate of discovery of new chemical entities in the world; by 1981, France had slipped into fifth place (174). Although it is not at all clear what caused this decline, the French pharmaceutical industry blames the drop on 30 years of strict governmental price controls (174).

▌ Japan

To be sold on the Japanese market, a drug must be approved by the Japanese Pharmaceutical Affairs Bureau (PAB), an equivalent of the U.S. FDA. Once the PAB approves a drug, the Japanese Health Insurance Bureau (HIB), a branch of Japan's Ministry of Health and Welfare (MHW), must consider whether or not to add the drug to a national list of drugs that may be prescribed by Japanese doctors. Since the 1980s, the HIB has updated this list quarterly. Once a drug is admitted to the list, the HIB settles on the price that will be paid when the drug is prescribed.[41] Virtually the entire Japanese population is covered by some form of health insurance that adopts the HIB reimbursement rates, so these rates are applied to almost every prescription written throughout the country.

"Me-too" drugs entering the market are generally granted a price similar to those already held by therapeutic equivalents, although there has been no explicit policy to mandate or formalize this procedure (527). "Me-too" drugs in Japan include generics as well as drugs chemically different from ones already on the market but not considered medical advances.

Drugs without any therapeutic equivalent or chemical predecessor (known in Japan as "shin-ing new drugs") are evaluated for their therapeutic usefulness and priced accordingly: drugs already on the market that are viewed as equally innovative may be used as guidelines for setting the reimbursement rate.

All changes in reimbursement rates go through the HIB, which revises them once every 2 years. Pharmaceutical companies that want to participate in Japan's $35-billion domestic drug market must accept the HIB reimbursement rate as the final price their product will fetch when a doctor prescribes it.

Despite their virtually universal control over prescription reimbursement rates, the Japanese ranked first and second in per-capita pharmaceutical spending in 1987 and 1988, respectively (139,361). This spending seems odd because Japanese drug prices were drastically cut by a total of 52 percent from 1981 to 1990. To explain such high pharmaceutical expenditures in the face of the price cuts of the 1980s, one must look at how drugs are delivered in Japan.

Most drugs are dispensed to patients directly by the physicians who prescribe them. In fact, only 10 percent (by value) of drugs in Japan were sold by independent pharmacists in 1985; the rest were purchased from independent doctors or hospital pharmacies.[42] Most drugs are sold by manufacturers to hospitals and clinics (139,163,344), usually through wholesalers, at a discount off the rate set by the HIB; wholesalers receive similar discounts from the manufacturers.[43] Therefore, when the doctor or hospital pharmacy is reimbursed for dispensing a drug at the HIB rate, he or she (or the hospital) makes a profit. Discounts vary widely but typically run from 10 to 30

---

[41] Insurance generally pays between 70 and 100 percent of this rate; the patient makes up any difference. HIB reimbursement decisions are guided by policies drafted by the Chu-Ikyo, or Central Social Insurance Medical Council, an independent governmental advisory board.

[42] Doctors are found mainly in three settings in Japan. Private practices run by independent doctors are known as clinics as long as they have 20 or fewer beds. Private hospitals have more than 30 beds, but are also owned and managed by the doctors who work at the facility. The remaining doctors work in hospitals run by universities or the government. Hospital-based physicians are salaried, while independent doctors are reimbursed on a fee-for-service basis, with fees determined by the government (163).

[43] Wholesalers formerly were allowed to set their selling prices in collaboration with manufacturers, in exchange for price guarantees from the manufacturers. This allowed wholesalers to adequately gauge what discount they could offer hospitals and doctors without risking discounting at rates higher than the manufacturers' rebates. However, the Japanese Fair Trade Commission has ruled wholesalers can no longer enter into these collaborative agreements with the manufacturers, and must set their prices independently.

percent of the reimbursement rate. In certain therapeutic categories, such as antibiotics where product competition is relatively strong, discounts have traditionally run even deeper.

In a medical system where the reimbursement rate is set above the actual cost of drugs while reimbursement rates for physicians' services, which are also set by the MHW, are set below cost (344), doctors and hospitals have depended on the sale of pharmaceuticals to make money. Profits from drug sales made up about 37 percent of the independent doctor's wages in 1987 (344). Since the Japanese health system offers few additional subsidies (outside the doctor's salaries or fees) to help clinics and private hospitals purchase equipment or maintain facilities, the sale of pharmaceuticals has become a primary source of revenue to ensure the normal functioning of nongovernmental medical facilities. With no formal method to keep track of physicians' prescription habits,[44] the incentive is strong for doctors to prescribe unnecessary and excessive medications (139, 163,344).

The Japanese Government has struggled to combat physician-income subsidization by high drug price margins. Although the government has shown some support for "bungyo," the separation of drug prescribing from dispensing duties, most cost reduction measures have used pricing policies to try to erode or eliminate the industry's ability to grant discounts to doctors. The drastic reimbursement rate reductions that took place in the 1980s were enacted partially for this purpose.

Products with the largest discounts had their prices cut the most. Ostensibly, these cuts would reduce the reimbursement rate of heavily discounted products to the point where manufacturers would no longer be willing to undercut the HIB price to grant doctors their margins. Despite these strong efforts, discounts were still reported as prevalent in 1991, with many pharmaceutical companies granting doctors margins of 20 percent or higher (163).

Just as doctors have seized upon the sale of discounted drugs as a way to gain some control over their own incomes, so too have pharmaceutical companies. In a market where manufacturers have little control over the reimbursement rate, discounts to physicians have become an important tool in the competition to get one's product to those who prescribe drugs. Since drugs with higher profit margins are often more heavily favored by doctors, the ability to offer a large discount remains a significant factor in determining use. Although the discounts may have diminished somewhat in magnitude, drug companies continue to view discounts as a part of the normal cost of doing business.

A new landmark pricing policy took effect in April 1992 to limit doctors' discounts. Rather than trying to eliminate pricing discounts and the overuse of drugs that may accompany them, the regulations aim to reduce the discounts to a "reasonable level." This level, known in Japan as the "R-zone," would be effectively equal to 15 percent of the HIB price. When reimbursement rates are reviewed every 2 years, an average wholesale price of the drug over the past 2 years is calculated by dividing total sales for the drug by the number of units sold. The new reimbursement rate will be calculated by adding this AWP to 15 percent of the previous HIB rate for the drug.[45] This means that drug prices can be discounted at an average of 15 percent of the reimbursement

---

[44] The Japanese Government has direct access to detailed information regarding each doctor's prescribing history. Doctors must file claim forms describing exactly what dosage of what drugs were prescribed in order to receive reimbursement for medications provided to patients. However, the government does not frequently review or rebuke doctors for their prescription habits or overuse of drugs. According to one observer (527), only about a half dozen doctors in Japan are censured each year because of their drug prescribing habits.

[45] Here is an example of how this works. A drug has a current reimbursement rate of 100 yen. However, the AWP of the drug is 80 yen, leaving a 20-yen margin for the doctors. When the HIB recalculates the new rate for this drug, it adds the AWP (80 yen) to 15 percent of the old HIB price (or 15 percent of 100 yen=15 yen), giving a new HIB rate of 80+15 or 95 yen.

Now suppose the AWP for the drug is 90 yen. The new rate would be the AWP, 90 yen, plus 15 percent of 100 yen, or 105 yen. The policy requires that the new HIB rate cannot be higher than the old HIB rate; thus in this instance, the new rate would remain at 100 yen.

rate without suffering further price reductions (417). If a manufacturer discounts less than 15 percent on average, the revised HIB rate will remain the same.

The HIB plans to gradually reduce the R-zone rate from 15 to 13, 11, and 10 percent over the next 6 years (319). The gradual reduction of the R-zone is intended to ease companies into a system in which doctors' margins are reduced to a certain (arbitrary) level.

The plan will probably benefit newer products that have relatively little history of discounting; older products, which tend to be more heavily discounted to compete with newer drugs, will probably suffer as they are either forced to reduce the amounts of their discounts or to have their prices continually lowered until it is no longer profitable for the manufacturer to market them. It is not clear how this change will affect prescribing habits or overall pharmaceutical spending (345). It is possible that reduced profit margins could lead to even more excessive drug dispensation as doctors try to compensate for income no longer received from larger discounts.

There are also stipulations in the new scheme that extend beyond the reduction of doctors' margins and overall costs. These rules establish a consistent policy for increasing the reimbursement rates of so-called innovative or "shining new drugs" which are defined by the MHW as new chemical entities that are therapeutically as well as chemically innovative (2). In the rate revisions of "shining new drugs," a 20 percent R-zone will be added to the AWP instead of the normal 15 percent. This percentage will not decrease over time, so by 1998 innovative drugs will be granted an R-zone rate twice that of generic and "me-too" drugs that show no improvement in side effects or effectiveness.

Orphan drugs and "me-too" drugs demonstrating an improvement in efficacy or side effects over their predecessors and deemed "relatively useful" will be given prices 3 percent above the normal rate. With competition through discounting as strong as it is, these additional rate increases translate into a significant advantage for the "shining new" new chemical entities entering the Japanese market. The pricing policies encourage R&D in Japan. Although innovative new chemical entities were often spared to some degree in the price cuts of the 1980s, the new approach marks the first definitive policy to extend benefits to these products (345).

It appears the main objective of Japanese pro-innovation policy is health-related: to increase treatments for the diseases that the growing elderly population will face in increasing numbers. The development of the Japanese pharmaceutical industry is a secondary goal.[46] A proposed measure increasing the R-zone for Japanese-originated drugs was dropped, apparently to facilitate the import of significant new drugs from other countries (417). However, some Japanese policymakers and industry representatives believe the new directives will indeed foster a strong Japanese industry steeped in innovative R&D (319).

▌United Kingdom

In the United Kingdom, the government controls the cost of pharmaceuticals not by limiting individual product prices, but by setting a cap on the profit that individual pharmaceutical companies can enjoy from their business with the National Health Service. Each company negotiates with the Secretariat of Pharmaceutical Price Regulation Scheme (PPRS) a total rate of return on the capital employed in generating its sales to the British National Health Service (NHS).

---

[46] Historically, the Japanese pharmaceutical industry was not very active in developing drugs for the world market. Instead, Japanese drug firms grew mostly by serving a domestic market with generally high reimbursement rates for pharmaceuticals (508) and by the relative ease of government approval for marketing of domestically produced drugs (139,212). Between 1960 and 1980, only 10 Japanese drugs were approved as new chemical entities by the U.S. FDA (180). Only three "breakthrough" drugs developed in Japan between 1960 and 1990 were licensed for marketing in the United States (180). Finally, out of 1,234 globally marketed new chemical entities developed between 1940 and 1977, 46 (3.7 percent) were produced in Japan (332).

The PPRS is a nonstatutory arrangement in which confidential profit negotiations are held between individual companies and the PPRS Secretariat on behalf of the Ministry of Health. This plan, which has existed in various forms since 1957, was designed for two purposes: 1) to "ensure that safe and effective medicines are available to the NHS on reasonable terms" and 2) to "ensure that the Department of Health and Social Security acts as a sponsor for the drug companies" to maintain the industry as one of the United Kingdom's healthiest and most profitable (84).

The U.K. pharmaceutical industry is the fourth largest exporter of drugs in the world and the third leading export industry in the United Kingdom (22). How much of this success is due to the PPRS is a matter of conjecture, but the results are at least consistent with the second goal of the scheme. Whether British drug prices have been controlled by the system is also unclear. The Association of the British Pharmaceutical Industry reports that the U.K. retail price index increased by 29 percent between 1984 and 1989, while the pharmaceutical price index increased by only 22 percent. However, the Economist reported that drug prices outpaced the national inflation rate by more than 4 percent for the same time period (117).

All pharmaceutical companies with NHS brand-name drug sales over £500,000 are included in the Scheme, but only firms with sales over £4 million must submit financial records for a yearly assessment of their allowable profit rates (44). These 65 or so companies provide audited annual financial reports that document their total sales to the NHS including expenses for manufacturing, distribution, promotion, and R&D associated with those sales, and the capital employed in generating the NHS sales. At most, 9 percent of a company's total NHS sales may be claimed for promotional expenses, but an additional allowance is made for informational activities (386). The PPRS attempts to pay for its share of R&D by allowing firms to apply their worldwide ratio of R&D expenses to sales to their sales in the United Kingdom.[47]

An annual rate of return as a percent of capital employed is compared with the actual sales of brand-name drugs to the NHS. If revenues do not exceed cost plus an allowed profit rate, the firm's prices are deemed acceptable to NHS.

The procedure is different for *multinational companies* with scarcely more than an importing or marketing subsidiary in the United Kingdom. The PPRS attempts to apply the same standards to these companies; however, much of the information regarding a multinational company's expenses would not be applicable to the United Kingdom, so an allowed rate of return on sales is used instead of a return on capital employed (44,84).

The allowed profit rate has generally hovered between 17 and 21 percent of the allowed capital employed (386), though this range is by no means fixed. If a company exceeds the profit margin assigned by PPRS, it may attempt to justify the excess profits. Additional profits of up to 50 percent of the original rate can be awarded for expenses directed to innovation, new drug launches, improved drug efficiency, significant investment in the U.K. industry, and increased exports from the United Kingdom (44,84). Companies may attempt to justify profit rates outside of the limits on one or all of these grounds; they may also apply for future profit rate increases based on these criteria. These potential increases in profit rates are generally known as the "Grey Zone" of PPRS pricing. The final allowed profit remains confidential.

Both critics and proponents of the Scheme claim the PPRS provides many other opportunities for increased profits (84,117,174). The fact that the government must rely completely on the pharmaceutical company's own information on capital employed allows the industry a great deal of latitude (174). For example, in the past, many companies mutually agreed to sell each other ingredients at artificially high prices to make it

---

[47] In addition, any investments in R&D facilities and equipment in the United Kingdom are added to the estimated capital employed.

appear as though manufacturing costs were much higher than they actually were (84). Although some observers have suggested the close ties between industry and government have made for a fairly open relationship between the two (84), others believe the PPRS has no real power to question or investigate the claims of the drug companies (117,174).

The profit targets that the PPRS approves may become more difficult to attain in a market currently experiencing increased price competition with parallel imports and generic equivalents. A *parallel import* is a brand-name drug purchased by a middleman in a country where the price is relatively cheap and then is imported to other countries (possibly including the country of manufacture) where the drug's price is normally higher. The middleman sells the drug at a profit but undercuts the higher price. This practice is legal in Europe and is actually endorsed by the European Community. It is also growing in prevalence in Europe due to both wide variations in individual drug prices from country to country and the geographical proximity of the various markets (67). The United Kingdom is one of the largest targets for parallel imports, which currently hold about 8 percent of the British market (377). In addition, statistics for generics show they account for about 30 percent of British prescriptions and 9 percent of total sales (295).

Some experts claim the PPRS is responsible for the relatively successful containment of drug spending in the United Kingdom (17,376a). Low per capita spending (especially compared with countries such as Belgium, France, Germany, Italy, and the United States) is cited as an indicator that the PPRS is effectively managing pharmaceutical costs in the United Kingdom (304). However, data collected by Burstall indicate much of the cost reduction realized in the United Kingdom is due to the control of prescription volume, not prices (67). The per-person cost of drugs in the United Kingdom is the fifth highest in the European Community, 18 percent above the European Community average, and 170 percent higher than in France. Conversely, the consumption of drugs in the United Kingdom is quite low: two-thirds of the average European Community rate and one-third of the rate in France.

Because drugs bought through the NHS are paid for almost completely by the British Government, there has been almost no consumer-driven price competition in the U.K. market. Although there is a £3.75 copayment on each prescription a patient purchases through the NHS, so many classes of people are exempted from this charge that almost 80 percent of NHS ambulatory care prescriptions have this fee waived. Many of the poor in England are exempted from copayments; however, there is no formal method in existence to ascertain a patient's level of income. Tax records are confidential, and doctors have reportedly been unwilling to question patients on this matter (149). Thus, in practice, hardly anyone pays the prescription copayment. With no serious consumer interest in low market prices, pharmaceutical companies generally charge the NHS at least up to the limit of their allowed profits, assuring companies of the returns the PPRS has determined are acceptable (174).

Recently, new measures to influence prescribing and dispensing habits have been adopted as supplements to the PPRS. In 1988, the Department of Health formulated a list of drugs in therapeutic categories for which there are cheaper and/or more effective treatments. The NHS no longer pays for many of the most expensive brands. The therapeutic categories include antacids, cough and cold preparations, laxatives, vitamins, tranquilizers, sedatives, and analgesics. This effort may have saved as much as £70 million (117).

A more significant move was the exemption in 1985 of generics from the PPRS profit limits. Manufacturers were encouraged to promote generic drugs, since profits made from generics would no longer count toward a manufacturer's profit limit. To stimulate the prescription of generics by British practitioners, beginning in 1989 the NHS assigned each doctor an "indicative drug account" that monitors the cost of drugs he or she prescribes. A suggested per capita limit is a guideline for further action. Doctors who surpass their limit must defend their practices to a locally employed medical advisor to the Family Health Service Authority. If the case is not resolved, the doctor must appear in front of a specially convened three-person council. Physicians who consistently exceed the limit without justification are penalized[48] (117). Doctors may begin to favor cheaper generic alternatives if they believe the penalties (or the inconvenience of justifying overspending) are worth avoiding. Although it is too early to judge how effective this plan will be in the long run, the aggressiveness with which per capita spending is monitored will probably determine the success of this initiative in reducing the cost of prescribed drugs.

The current version of the PPRS policy expired in October 1992. In late October 1992, negotiations were underway between the National Health Service and the Association of the British Pharmaceutical Industry to reformulate and reauthorize the PPRS. It is expected that the PPRS will be reauthorized without any major structural changes (45). However, the future direction of the program is still unclear in light of potential changes occurring in the European Community with the advent of Europe 1992 (377).

CONCLUSIONS

In the United States insurance coverage for prescription drugs broadened over the 1980s, with almost three-quarters of the U.S. population having some private or public insurance coverage for prescription drugs.[49] These benefits have improved substantially in quality throughout the 1980s, as plans requiring a flat copayment for drugs replaced plans covering drugs only after a deductible amount has been spent. Today, roughly 30 percent of people with private prescription

drug insurance plans have fixed copayments, compared with 9 percent in 1977.

The improvement in insurance coverage for prescription drugs in the United States has led to attempts to control prescription drug costs through a variety of mechanisms. Different kinds of payers have different avenues open for cost control. These mechanisms, which include incentives to use cheaper generic drugs as well as attempts to control utilization directly through formularies, are most common in hospitals, HMOs and the Medicaid program. Traditional private health insurance plans have also used incentives for generic drug prescribing, but they have little power to restrict the availability of FDA-approved drugs and generally must pay their share of the manufacturer's price for single-source drugs.

The most effective cost-control mechanisms are available to those private-sector plans that can control prescribing through formularies. Hospitals and staff-model HMOs have used this power to exact price discounts from manufacturers even when the manufacturers are single-source producers of a specific compound. Some HMOs not only have a measure of control over drug prescribing through formularies, but they also can encourage price competition by encouraging (or even requiring) physicians to consider costs as well as effectiveness in the prescribing decision.

The power of certain classes of purchasers to exact discounts was recognized by the framers of the 1990 Medicaid Rebate Law, which attempts to piggyback on the negotiating power of HMOs and large hospital groups to obtain the same discounts for Medicaid. The strategy may have backfired, however, because manufacturers become unwilling to give discounts to HMOs if, by so doing, they stand to lose the amount of the discount on 10 to 15 percent of the total market for

---

[48] Penalties may take the form of fines, or the doctor may be asked to reduce his or her list of patients in order to reduce NHS expenses billed to that doctor.

[49] Still, roughly 16 million people 65 years of age and older and 53 million people under 65 years of age lack any insurance for prescription drugs (see table 10-2). For these people, many of whom have chronic illnesses, prescriptions drug expenditures can be a severe economic burden. Several pharmaceutical companies have recently announced programs in which certain expensive drugs will be made available without charge to people unable to pay for them (296,327,458).

outpatient prescription drugs. A coalition of large pharmaceutical purchasing groups recently called for the repeal of "best price" provisions because of the elimination of such discounts after the Medicaid rebate law went into effect (381a).

Trends in U.S. health insurance in the past decade have, on balance, provided an increasing potential market for prescription drugs, through more and richer third-party coverage, with modest downward pressure on the demand for such drugs or the price payers are willing to pay. The most comprehensive approach to prescription drug cost containment among third-party payers has been to encourage generic price competition for multiple-source drugs. Even there, the physician override provisions in both private and public insurance plans appear to have limited the loss of market share for originators. (See chapter 4 for recent trends in market shares for multiple-source, brand-name drugs.)

Under the universal health insurance found in other industrialized nations, the demand for drugs is not much affected by the price charged. Nevertheless, the utilization of specific drugs and the prices paid tend to be more strictly controlled by the insurers. To a greater or lesser extent, drug payment policy in other countries is governed by two potentially conflicting objectives: minimization of prescription drug costs and encouragement of the domestic pharmaceutical industry. National prescription drug payment policies are a blend of these objectives.

In the United States, there is no single coherent drug payment policy. To the extent cost-containment efforts exist, they are applied without regard to the country of manufacture or origin of a drug. Abroad, drug payment policy is generally developed with the two purposes mentioned above in mind.

Virtually all of the five foreign countries that OTA reviewed—Australia, Canada, France, Japan, and the United Kingdom—use some mechanism for controlling the price of single-source drugs as well as multiple-source drugs. Four of the five nations do so directly by setting payment rates for new drugs on the basis of the cost of existing therapeutic alternatives. The pricing policies in these countries do reward "breakthrough" drugs at a higher rate than "me-too" drugs, though they accomplish this result in different ways. The resulting prices of breakthrough drugs may still be low compared with those in the United States.

Appendix A
Method of Study

This assessment grew out of the continuing political debate over rising pharmaceutical prices in the United States. The House Committee on Energy and Commerce and its Subcommittee on Health and Environment requested in 1988 that the Office of Technology Assessment (OTA) provide an independent estimate of the "average" cost of bringing a new drug to market, in response to industry claims that the estimated cost of bringing a new drug to market was $125 million. The request was later endorsed by the Subcommittee on Antitrust and Monopolies of the Senate Committee on the Judiciary.

In preparing for a project proposal to OTA's Technology Assessment Board, OTA management concluded that focusing on research and development (R&D) costs alone would be too narrow and that these costs should be studied in the context of the financial returns that investors receive from pharmaceutical R&D. OTA also concluded that the study should examine how Federal policies affect both the costs of and returns on R&D. OTA submitted a proposal to the Technology Assessment Board in June 1989, which the Board approved for initiation in September 1989. (The project was not fully staffed until January 1990.)

The project had four components:

- Analysis of the cost of discovering and developing a new drug;
- Analysis of the financial returns on drug discovery and development;
- Analysis of financial returns in the research-intensive ethical pharmaceutical industry as a whole; and
- Review of the effect of external factors on costs and returns on pharmaceutical R&D, including new drug regulation, tax policy, product liability law, direct R&D subsidies by the National Institutes of Health (NIH) and other government research bodies, and reimbursement policies (both private and public) for prescription drugs.

■ Advisory Panel

Every major OTA assessment is advised by a panel of outside experts and representatives of relevant interest groups. The role of the Advisory Panel is to provide guidance in project planning and review of OTA's findings. The panel is not responsible for the final contents of an OTA assessment. OTA chose a 16-member Advisory panel comprising industrial pharmaceutical R&D managers, pharmaceutical industry executives, consumer advocates, physicians, accountants, economists and lawyers. Frederick M. Scherer, Professor of Economics at the John F. Kennedy School of Government at Harvard University served as panel chair. The Panel convened twice during the project, once early in 1990 to give advice about research priorities and directions for the project, and again in May 1991 to review a preliminary draft of the study. Six members of the Panel also participated in a workshop (discussed below), and the Panel was involved in every round of project review throughout the course of the study.

■ Site Visits

Early in the project, OTA visited eight pharmaceutical companies (listed in table A-1) to interview senior-level corporate and R&D managers about the R&D process and the economics of pharmaceutical R&D. These interviews were extremely useful in providing a qualitative appreciation for the complexity and cost of pharmaceutical R&D as well as an understanding of how companies track their R&D costs in internal management cost accounting systems. The meetings were not intended to, nor did they, produce actual cost data on new drug development.

■ Workshop on the Economics of Pharmaceutical R&D

To explore relevant economic methods and data, OTA engaged in intramural research and also contracted for several papers that were presented at a workshop held in September 1990 at the University of

Table A-1—Sites and Dates of OTA Visits to Selected Pharmaceutical Companies

Cetus Corporation Emeryville, CA July 19, 1990	Schering-Plough Corporation Madison, NJ February 12, 1990
Genentech, Inc. San Francisco, CA July 18, 1990	SmithKline Beecham Corporation Philadelphia, PA June 15, 1990
Eli Lilly and Company Indianapolis, IN April 17 and 18, 1990	Syntex Corporation Palo Alto, CA July 17, 1990
Merck & Company Rahway, NJ June 19 and 20, 1990	The Upjohn Company Kalamazoo, MI April 19, 1990

California, Santa Barbara. Workshop participants included paper authors, six members of the Advisory Panel with economic or financial expertise, and a small number of outside experts who reviewed and critiqued the papers for revision. (See table A-2 for a list of workshop attendees.) This review greatly enhanced the quality and clarity of the contract papers, some of which became essential pieces of the R&D assessment.

■ Review and Revision of Profitability Study

One contract paper, a comparative study of profitability of firms in the pharmaceutical industry with firms in other industries, utilized new methods for analyzing publicly available accounting data to infer economic profits. This study generated a great deal of discussion and critique at the workshop. Because of the potential policy importance of the subject matter and the technical nature of the methods and critiques, OTA initiated a thorough process of revision and review in collaboration with the contractors, William Baber (George Washington University) and Sok Hyon Kang (Carnegie Mellon University).

Baber and Kang submitted a second draft of their contract report to OTA in January 1991, based on the criticisms raised at the workshop. OTA contracted with two of the country's foremost experts on profit measurement, Franklin Fisher (Massachusetts Institute of Technology) and Gerald Salamon (Indiana University), as well as the panel chairman, to provide a thorough review and critique of the second draft. These two reviews formed the basis for a third revised draft of the profit study in March 1991, which was then submitted for further review not only to the Advisory Panel but also to Professors Fisher and Salamon and a

small number of outside economists who specialize in the pharmaceutical industry.

One outside economist who specializes in the pharmaceutical industry submitted a detailed critique of the third draft of the profit study in July 1991. OTA asked Baber and Kang to reply to the critique. The entire file of comments and replies was then sent back to the two contract reviewers and the panel chair for a final review. These reviews convinced OTA that the methods employed by Baber and Kang to measure profitability in the industry are sound and represent an important advance over previous methods. OTA compiled the entire history of review for the profit study into a single document that is available upon request to interested parties.

■ Other Research Activities

In addition to contracting for research on the pharmaceutical R&D process, OTA sought out other sources of data bearing on costs of R&D and returns to the industry from these activities. Data availability was a major problem, particularly data on domestic and worldwide sales of new drugs introduced to the U.S. market during specific time intervals. OTA was able to purchase limited data on domestic sales from IMS America, Inc., a market research firm specializing in surveys of pharmaceutical purchases and prescriptions, but was required to rely mainly on a sales data analysis conducted for other purposes by the Food and Drug Administration. OTA was also able to contract with Stephen Schondelmeyer of Purdue University to provide a report on pharmaceutical sales for drugs that have recently lost patent protection based on IMS America data.

OTA was never able to gain access to IMS data on worldwide sales. IMS International, Inc., quoted OTA a price of over $100,000 for specific data on the ratio of worldwide sales to domestic sales for drugs introduced to the market between 1981 and 1983. OTA used what data were available from existing literature and the sources available to us to conduct an independent analysis of returns on R&D.

OTA was assisted throughout the course of the study by contract papers on specific research issues and topics. Table A-3 contains a list of the major contract papers prepared under the assessment. Papers marked with an asterisk were presented and reviewed at the September 1990 Santa Barbara workshop. Other contract reports were reviewed as appropriate by outside experts and panel members.

Table A-2—Participants in the OTA Workshop on the Economics of Pharmaceutical R&D, Santa Barbara, California, September 1990

Robert B. Helms, *Workshop Chair*
Resident Scholar
American Enterprise Institute
Washington, DC

Rosanne Altshuler[a]
Assistant Professor of Economics
Rutgers University
New Brunswick, NJ

William R. Baber[b]
Associate Professor
George Washington University
Washington, DC

William S. Comanor
Professor Economics
University of California
Santa Barbara, CA

Paul Coppinger
Deputy Associate Commissioner for
    Planning and Evaluation
Food and Drug Administration
Rockville, MD

Richard Frank
Associate Professor of Health Policy
    and Management
Johns Hopkins University
Baltimore, MD

Ronald W. Hansen
Associate Dean for Academic Affairs
University of Rochester
Rochester, NY

Sok-Hyon Kang
Assistant Professor of Industrial
    Administration
Carnegie Mellon University
Pittsburgh, PA

Judy C. Lewent
Chief Financial Officer
Merck & Co. Inc.
Whitehouse Station, NJ

Albert Link
Professor of Economics
University of North Carolina
Greensboro, NC

Alison Masson Keith[c]
Assistant Director for Economic Analysis
Pfizer, Inc.
New York, NY 10017

David Salkever
Professor of Economics
Johns Hopkins University
Baltimore, MD

Frederick M. Scherer
Professor of Economics
Harvard University
Cambridge, MA

Stuart O. Schweitzer
Professor and Chair, Department
    of Health Services
University of California
Los Angeles, CA

Jacob Stucki
Vice President for Pharmaceutical
    Research (retired)
The Upjohn Company
Kalamazoo, MI 49008

Lakshmi Shyam-Sunder
Assistant Professor of Business
    Administration
Dartmouth College
Hanover, NH

Shyam Sunder
Professor of Accounting
Carnegie-Mellon University
Pittsburgh, PA

Steven N. Wiggins
Texas A & M University
College Station, TX

[a] Dr. Altshuler was with Columbia University at the time of the workshop.
[b] Dr. Baber was with Georgetown University at the time of the workshop.
[c] Dr. Keith was with the Federal Trade Commission at the time of the workshop.

Table A-3—Major Contract Papers Prepared for the Pharmaceutical R&D: Costs, Risks and Rewards Project

---

* **Roseanne Altshuler, Ph.D.**, Rutgers University, New Brunswick, New Jersey and **Henri Chaoul, Ph.D.**, Columbia University, New York, New York. *The Effect of Tax Policy on Returns to R&D in the Pharmaceutical Industry: A Methodological Review,* November 1990.

* **William R. Baber, Ph.D., C.P.A.**, George Washington University, Washington, DC and **Sok-Hyon Kang, Ph.D.**, Carnegie-Mellon University, Pittsburgh, Pennsylvania. *Accounting-Based Measure as Estimates of Economic Rates of Return: An Empirical Study of the U.S. Pharmaceutical Industry 1976-87,* March 1991.

William R. Baber, Ph.D., C.P.A., George Washington University, Washington, DC, **Ronald Ross, Ph.D.**, and **J. Raymond Apple, M.B.A.**, Georgetown University, Washington, DC. *Research and Development Accounting Issues With Specific Reference to the U.S. Pharmaceutical Industry,* December 1990.

Lester W. Chadwick, C.P.A., Ph.D., University of Delaware, Newark, Delaware. *Pharmaceutical R&D Study, Accounting for R&D.*

Robert Mullan Cook-Deegan, M.D., Consultant, Rockville, Maryland. *Trends in Sciences, Technology, and Drug Discovery,* (incorporated in edited form as chapter 5 of the final report) October 1991.

W. Gary Flamm, Ph.D., F.A.C.T., and **Michael Farrow, Ph.D.**, SRS International, Inc., Washington, DC. *Recent Trends in the Use and Cost of Animals in the Pharmaceutical Industry,* April 1991.

* **Richard G. Frank, Ph.D.**, and **David S. Salkever, Ph.D**, Johns Hopkins University, Baltimore, Maryland. *Pricing, Patent Loss and the Market for Pharmaceuticals,* December 1990.

Alan M. Garber, Ph.D., M.D., Palo Alto Department of Veterans Affairs Medical Center and Stanford University, Palo Alto, California, **Ann E. Clarke, M.D., Dana Goldman**, B.A., Stanford University, Palo Alto, and Michael E. Gluck, Ph.D., Office of Technology Assessment, U.S. Congress, Washington, DC. *Federal and Private Roles in the Development and Provision of Alglucerase Therapy for Gaucher Disease,* OTA-BP-H-104 (Washington, DC: U.S. Government Printing Office, October 1992).

* **Elizabeth J. Jensen, Ph.D.**, Hamilton College, Clinton, New York. *Rates of Return to Investment in the Pharmaceutical Industry: A Survey,* September 1990.

Albert Link, Ph.D., University of North Carolina, Greensboro, North Carolina. *Tax Incentives and the U.S. Pharmaceutical Industry,* November 1990.

* **Stewart C. Myers, Ph.D.**, Massachusetts Institute of Technology, Cambridge, Massachusetts and **Lakshmi Shyam-Sunder, Ph.D.**, Dartmouth College, Hanover, New Hampshire. *Cost of Capital Estimates for Investment in Pharmaceutical Research and Development,* January 1991.

Stephen W. Schondelmeyer, Pharm.D., Ph.D., University of Minnesota, Minneapolis, Minnesota, *Economic Impact of Multiple Source Competition on Originator Products,* February 1992.

Gordon Sick, Ph.D., University of Calgary, Calgary, Alberta, Canada. *Pharmaceutical Industry R&D and the Cost of Capital,* February 1992.

Ellen S. Smith, M.B.A., Woodcliff, New Jersey. *Third Party Payment for Unapproved Uses of Approved Drugs and for Medical Care Associated With Drug Clinical Trials,* January 1991.

Steven Wiggins, Ph.D., Texas A&M University, College Station, Texas. *Pharmaceutical R&D Costs and Returns,* December 1989.

NOTE: Contract papers marked with an asterisk were presented and reviewed at the September 1990 workshop held in Santa Barbara, CA.

In addition to other data collection and analysis tasks, OTA conducted a survey of clinical trial sizes for drugs approved in the late 1970s versus the mid-1980s.

■ Report Review Process

A preliminary draft of OTA's report was submitted for review and critique to the Advisory Committee in April 1991. The Panel meeting in May 1991 was devoted to a discussion and critique of that draft and suggestions for further research. OTA spent the next year continuing the research process outlined above, searching for data, verifying the accuracy of data, and conducting analyses. Sections of the draft were sub-mitted for special review to selected panel members and outside reviewers throughout the spring of 1992, and revisions were made in the draft before it underwent the general review. (A total of 43 people reviewed targeted sections of the report throughout this period.)

The full second draft of OTA's report was distributed for review to the Advisory Panel and a group of outside experts and interested parties in August 1992. A total of 122 people were sent the second draft, and 63 separate replies were received. OTA reviewed and revised the draft as appropriate in response to these comments.

Appendix B
Acknowledgments

O TA wishes to thank the Pharmaceutical R&D: Costs, Risks and Rewards Advisory Panel, its workshop participants, contractors, and the individuals and organizations listed below for their assistance over the course of this study. OTA also wishes to express appreciation to those who provided advice and information for its background paper, *Federal and Private Roles in the Development and Provision of Algucerase Therapy for Gaucher Disease*. These individuals and organizations do not necessarily approve, disapprove, or endorse this report. OTA assumes full responsibility for the report and the accuracy of its content.

Lois Adams
Office of Legislative Affairs
U.S. Food and Drug Administration
Rockville, MD

Reid Adler
Office of Technology Transfer
U.S. National Institutes of Health
Bethesda, MD

Gwynn C. Akin
Public Policy
Syntex (USA) Inc.
Palo Alto, CA

Fredrik Andersson
Battelle MEDTAP Europe
Battelle Institute, Ltd.
London, England

Naomi Aronson
Technology Evaluation
Blue Cross Blue Shield Association
Chicago, IL

Carolyn Asbury
Health and Human Services
The Pew Charitable Trusts
Philadelphia, PA

Wade M. Aubrey
Blue Cross Blue Shield of California
San Francisco, CA

Wiltse Bailey
Washington, DC

P. Etienne Barral
Rhone-Poulenc Rorer
Antony, France

Norman Barton
Clinical Investigation Section
National Institute of Neurological Disorders
   and Strokes
Bethesda, MD

Michael Beatrice
Center for Biologics Evaluation and Research
U.S. Food and Drug Administration
Rockville, MD

David W. Beier
Government Affairs
Genentech, Inc.
Washington, DC

Leslie Z. Benet
Department of Pharmacy
University of California
San Francisco, CA

Ernst Beutler
Department of Molecular and
    Experimental Medicine
Scripps Research Institute
La Jolla, CA

Douglas W. Bitz
Sandoz Research Institute
Sandoz Pharmaceuticals Corporation
East Hanover, NJ

Carla Bodaghi
U.S. Health Care Financing Administration
Washington, DC

Charles Booth
Office Payment Policy
U.S. Health Care Financing Administration
Baltimore, MD

Alan Blostin
Bureau of Labor Statistics
U.S. Department of Labor
Washington, DC

David Blumenthal
Medical Practices Evaluation Center
Massachusetts General Hospital
Boston, MA

Lawrence Brenkus
Arthur D. Little, Inc.
Cambridge, MA

John Brosan
Office of General Counsel
U.S. General Accounting Office
Washington, DC

Julie Cantor
Human Resources Division
U.S. General Accounting Office
Washington, DC

Douglas L. Cocks
Corporate Affairs
Eli Lilly and Company
Indianapolis, IN

Karen Cohen
National Gaucher's Foundation
Gaithersburg, MD

Joseph Collier
Department of Pharmacology and
    Clinical Pharmacology
St. Georges Hospital Medical School
London, England

Paul Coppinger
Office of Planning and Evaluation
U.S. Food and Drug Administration
Rockville, MD

Pedro Cuatrecasas
Pharmaceutical Research Division
Warner-Lambert Company
Ann Arbor, MI

Joan M. Curran
Merck and Company, Inc.
Rahway, NJ

Bruce Cwalina
Springfield, VA

Patricia M. Danzon
School of Business
University of Pennsylvania
Philadelphia, PA

Alfred B. Engleberg
Greenwich, CT

Alain Enthoven
School of Business
Stanford University
Palo Alto, CA

David Evans
World Health Organization
Geneva, Switzerland

Dee Fensterer
Generic Pharmaceutical Industry Association
New York, NY

Franklin Fisher
School of Management
Massachusetts Institute of Technology
Cambridge, MA

Scott D. Freedman
Pharmaceutical Division
Miles, Inc.
West Haven, CT

Jesse Friedman
Chevy Chase, MD

Steven Garber
Rand Corporation
Santa Monica, CA

Kevin Gaynor
Price Waterhouse, Inc.
New York, NY

William Glaser
School of Management and Urban Policy
New School for Social Research
New York, NY

Sarah Glavin
Human Resources Division
U.S. General Accounting Office
Washington, DC

Martin Glick
Genentech, Inc.
San Francisco, CA

Gregory Grabowski
Children's Hospital Medical Center
University of Cincinnati Medical Center
Cincinnati, OH

Henry G. Grabowski
Department of Economics
Duke University
Durham, NC

Stephen C. Groft
Office of Science Policy and Legislation
U.S. National Institutes of Health
Bethesda, MD

David Gross
Human Resources Division
U.S. General Accounting Office
Washington, DC

Charles Grudzinskas
Medications Development Division
U.S. National Institute on Drug Abuse
Rockville, MD

Marlene E. Haffner
Orphan Products Development
U.S. Food and Drug Administration
Rockville, MD

Ronald Hansen
School of Business Administration
University of Rochester
Rochester, NY

Edward Haas
Office of Planning and Evaluation
U.S. Food and Drug Administration
Rockville, MD

Jody Hessen
Pharmacy, Policy, and Education
Aetna
Minneapolis, MN

Michelle Hiltebeitel
IMS America
Plymouth Meeting, PA

Peter Barton Hutt
Covington & Burling
Washington, DC

David Jackson
Janssen Pharmaceuticals, Inc.
Piscataway, NJ

David C. Jones
Chapel Hill, NC

Robert Kaplan
School of Business Administration
Harvard University
Boston, MA

David Karlin
Institute of Clinical Medicine
Syntex Research
Palo Alto, CA

Alison Keith
U.S. Pharmaceuticals
Pfizer, Inc.
New York, NY

John V. Kelsey
Office of Orphan Products Development
U.S. Food and Drug Administration
Rockville, MD

William Kennedy
Drug Regulatory Affairs
ICI Pharmaceuticals Group
Wilmington, DE

Christiaan L. Khung
Policy Research and Development
Blue Cross and Blue Shield of Massachusetts
North Quincy, MA

Richard Kinny
Legislative Affairs
Schering-Plough Corporation
Washington, DC

Mary C. Knipmeyer
Office of Women Services
U.S. Substance Abuse and Mental
    Health Administration
Rockville, MD

Neil Kran
Internal Revenue Service
U.S. Department of the Treasury
New York, NY

Jacques Krasny
Bogart, Delafield, and Ferrier, Inc.
Morristown, NJ

Nancy J.W. Lewis
Institute for Pharmaceutical Economics
Philadelphia College of Pharmacy and Science
Philadelphia, PA

Harold S. Luft
Institute for Health Policy Studies
University of California
San Francisco, CA

Evan Marks
MEDCO Containment Services
Montvale, NJ

Kathleen McAvoy
Office of Planning and Evaluation
U.S. Food and Drug Administration
Rockville, MD

Jack McConnell
Hilton Head Island, SC

Robert T. McDonough
Public Policy Planning
The Upjohn Company
Kalamazoo, MI

Peter Merrill
Washington National Tax Service
Price Waterhouse, Inc.
Washington, DC

Gerald Meyer
Center for Drug Evaluation and Research
U.S. Food and Drug Administration
Rockville, MD

Abbey Meyers
National Organization for Rare Disorders
New Fairfield, CT

Ann Meyers
Center for Drug Evaluation and Research
U.S. Food and Drug Administration
Rockville, MD

Dann M. Michols
National Pharmaceutical Strategy
Ottawa, Ontario

Robert R. Miller
International Finance Corporation
Washington, DC

Andrew Mitchell
Pharmaceutical Evaluation
Department of Health Housing and
    Community Services
Canberra, Australia

John Moeller
Center for General Health Services
    Intramural Research
U.S. Agency for Health Care Policy and Research
Rockville, MD

Melissa Moncavage
Center for Drug Evaluation and Research
U.S. Food and Drug Administration
Rockville, MD

Lee Mortenson
Association of Community Cancer Centers
Rockville, MD

Dennis Mueller
Department of Economics
University of Maryland
College Park, MD

Michael Murray
Office of the General Counsel
U.S. House of Representatives
Washington, DC

Jane S. Myers
Patent and Trademark Office
U.S. Department of Commerce
Washington, DC

Maven Myers
Department of Pharmacy
Philadelphia College of Pharmacy and Science
Philadelphia, PA

John O'Hare
Joint Committee on Taxation
U.S. Congress
Washington, DC

Jonathan Peck
Institute for Alternative Futures
Alexandria, VA

Gary Persinger
Health Care Systems Division
Pharmaceutical Manufacturers Association
Washington, DC

Tim Proctor
Office of General Counsel
Merck & Company, Inc.
Rahway, NJ

Lisa Raines
Government Relations
Industrial Biotechnology Association
Washington, DC

Jonathan Ratner
Human Resources Division
U.S. General Accounting Office
Washington, DC

James W. Rayburn
Regulatory Affairs
Bristol-Myers Squibb Company
Evansville, IN

Larry Reed
Medicaid Non-Institutional Payment Policy Branch
U.S. Health Care Financing Administration
Baltimore, MD

Heinz Redwood
Suffolk, England

Michael R. Reich
School of Public Health
Harvard University
Boston, MA

Bryan G. Reuben
Department of Chemical Engineering
Southbank Polytechnic
London, England

Gerald Robertson
Department of Policy, Planning and Evaluation
Patented Medicine Prices Review Board
Ottawa, Ontario

Deborah Rogal
Alpha Center
Washington, DC

James B. Russo
Government and Public Policy
Smithkline Beecham

Gerald L. Salamon
Department of Accounting
Indiana University
Bloomington, IN

Jeffrey Sanders
Office of Legislation and Policy
U.S. Health Care Financing Administration
Washington, DC

Alice Sapienza
School of Public Health
Harvard University
Boston, MA

Janet Scheren
National Wholesale Druggists Association
Alexandria, VA

Stuart Schweitzer
Department of Health Services
University of California
Los Angeles, CA

James Shuttinga
Office of the Director
U.S. National Institutes of Health
Bethesda, MD

Richard Sweeney
School of Business Administration
Georgetown University
Washington, DC

Max W. Talbott
Lilly Research Laboratories
Eli Lilly and Company
Indianapolis, IN

Alison Taunton-Rigby
Biotherapeutics
Genzyme Corporation
Cambridge, MA

Albert Teich
Directorate for Science and Policy Programs
American Association for the Advancement of Science
Washington, DC

Henri Termeer
Genzyme Corporation
Cambridge, MA

Charles E. Van Horn
Patent and Trademark Office
U.S. Department of Commerce
Washington, DC

Jon E. Villaume
Drug Regulatory Affairs
Roche Pharmaceuticals
Nutley, NJ

Stuart Walker
Centre for Medicines Research
Surrey, England

Andrew J. Webster, Ph.D.
Faculty of Humanities, Arts, and Education
Anglia University
Cambridge, England

Roy Widdus
National Commission on AIDS
Washington, DC

Sidney Wolfe
Health Research Group
Washington, DC

Robert Wren
Bureau of Eligibility, Coverage and Reimbursement
U.S. Health Care Financing Administration
Baltimore, MD

James P. Yee
Institute of Clinical Medicine
Syntex Research
Palo Alto, CA

Aki Yoshikawa
Stanford University
Palo Alto, CA

OTA also acknowledges the assistance of individuals from the following pharmaceutical companies, without whom neither the survey on the size of clinical trials nor OTA's on-site interviews of pharmaceutical executives would have been possible.

Abbott Laboratories
Abbott Park, IL

Bristol-Myers Squibb Company
Princeton, NJ

Cetus Corporation
Emeryville, CA

Ciba-Geigy Corporation
Summit, NJ

Genentech, Inc.
San Francisco, CA

Hoffman-La Roche, Inc.
Nutley, NJ

Hoechst-Roussel Pharmaceuticals, Inc.
Somerville, NJ

ICI Pharmaceuticals Group
Wilmington, DE

Janssen Pharmaceutical, Inc.
Piscataway, NJ

Lederle Laboratories
Pearl River, NY

Eli Lilly and Company, Inc.
Indianapolis, IN

Mead Johnson & Company
Evansville, IN

Merck and Company, Inc.
Rahway, NJ

Miles, Inc.
West Haven, CT

Norwich Eaton Pharmaceuticals, Inc.
Norwich, NY

Parke-Davis
Ann Arbor, MI

Pfizer, Inc.
New York, NY

The R.W. Johnson Pharmaceutical
Research Institute
Raritan, NJ

Sandoz Pharmaceuticals Corporation
Hanover, NJ

Schering-Plough Corporation
Kenilworth, NJ

SmithKline Beecham Corporation
Philadelphia, PA

Syntex (U.S.A.), Inc.
Palo Alto, CA

Takeda U.S.A., Inc.
New York, NY

TAP Pharmaceuticals, Inc.
Deerfield, IL

The Upjohn Company
Kalamazoo, MI

Wyeth-Ayerst Research
Philadelphia, PA

Appendix C

The Cost of Capital[1]

Investors in pharmaceutical research and development (R&D) put up their money because they expect, on average, to get returns that adequately compensate them for the time and risk involved. Just as the interest rate on bank deposits is a payment for the use of depositors' money (or capital), the return on an investment in R&D is a payment the company or its investors get from the use of their capital. Riskier investments require higher dollar returns; otherwise, investors would put their money in safe investments like U.S. Treasury bills or bank certificates of deposit. The riskier the investment, the higher the required return. The rate of return that investors must be able to expect from money invested with a given level of risk is referred to as the investment's "cost of capital."[2]

▌ Risk and the Cost of Capital

How does one measure the riskiness of an investment? This is the key question in estimating the cost of capital for any project. Were there no risk, the cost of capital would be the same as the interest rate on U.S. Treasury bills.

Pharmaceutical industry executives often emphasize the particular riskiness of R&D. Analogies to drilling for oil are common: R&D involves dry holes and a few gushers. According to one industry executive, pharmaceutical R&D is like "wildcatting in Texas" (188). Data on the dropout rate for drugs under development support these notions that R&D is, indeed, an uncertain and risky undertaking.

The risk that is accounted for in the cost of capital is different from these conventional notions about the riskiness of R&D. Modern finance theory differentiates between two different kinds of investor risk: diversifiable risk and undiversifiable risk (59). The "wildcatting" risks of drug R&D are diversifiable; that is, the investor can diversify his or her portfolio across a large number of such projects (or firms undertaking such projects) and obtain, on average, an expected cash flow that is very predictable. Thus, the risk associated with low probabilities of successful drug development can be eliminated by diversifying the investment portfolio across a large number of projects.

The undiversifiable, or systematic, risk is the risk the investor cannot eliminate through diversification of his or her portfolio of investments. Suppose, for example, that prescription drug sales were closely linked to the state of the economy, perhaps because high unemployment produces more people without health insurance. Then, investment in pharmaceutical R&D would have a great deal of systematic risk because returns on R&D would depend on the state of the economy as a whole, and investors cannot diversify away these economywide risks.

The cost of capital for a given investment reflects only the portion of the investment's risk that is undiversifiable. The technical risks of project failure do not affect the required rate of return for an investment, though they do alter the potential cash flow expected from an investment.[3]

---

[1] This chapter draws heavily from a background paper on the cost of capital prepared by Stuart Myers and Lakshmi Shyam-Sunder (285).

[2] The cost of capital is also referred to as the "opportunity cost of capital," because the investor expects to get at least as much return as he or she can get from other opportunities to invest at the same level of risk.

[3] This concept of cost of capital is based on the Capital Asset Pricing Model (CAPM), which depends for its validity on the efficiency of capital markets. The validity of the CAPM theory is impossible to test (352a); consequently, the CAPM model has not been validated (96). Recently, researchers have presented analyses that question whether the CAPM is an adequate predictor of returns in the market (129). Nevertheless, the CAPM approach remains one of the most widely used models of expected returns, and no better practical alternatives to estimating the cost of capital presently exist.

AN EXAMPLE

Consider two hypothetical pharmaceutical R&D projects. Each project involves a newly synthesized compound with identical development costs and probabilities of being approved for marketing by the U.S. Food and Drug Administration (FDA). Clinical testing on each will take 2 years and cost $10 million (spent evenly over the 2-year testing period). Suppose also that the company's history with drug development suggests each drug has a 24-percent chance of ultimately reaching the market. The technical risks and R&D costs of the two drugs are therefore identical.

If either drug is successful in getting to market, it will produce net cash inflows (revenues less the costs of production, marketing, etc.) whose value is not known with certainty. To keep the example simple, suppose that the product life for either drug is just 1 year—after the first year of marketing, a new product replaces it and its revenues fall to zero. Each drug has the possible net cash inflows shown in table C-1.

Although both drugs have identical average or "expected" cash flows, the distribution of possible outcomes is different. Suppose project A is for a drug in a well-known family of analgesic products whose potential revenues are relatively certain. On the other hand, suppose project B is a very costly drug for patients with end-stage renal disease. It will be accepted and sold only if Medicare, which covers all end-stage renal disease patients regardless of age, agrees to pay for it. Once Medicare covers the drug, however, its revenues are completely certain. Although the "expected" net cash inflows from each drug are the same, the risk profile of the two drugs differs dramatically. Project B's cash flows are much riskier than project A's cash flows, because the firm can win big or lose big with that project, whereas once drug A is approved, its potential revenues vary in a narrow band.

Despite the fact that project B's expected cash flow is riskier than that of project A, that risk is largely diversifiable, because it is unique to the project and depends only on the Medicare coverage decision which, we can assume, is unaffected by the state of the economy. Project A's risk, on the other hand, may reflect undiversifiable, or systematic, risk because demand for analgesics may vary with the state of the economy. Although the total risk of project B is much

Table C-1—Potential Net Cash flows From Two Hypothetical R&D Projects

Project A		Project B	
Probability	Potential revenue ($ million)	Probability	Potential revenue ($ million)
0.33	$25	0.50	$0
0.33	50	0.50	100
0.33	75		
Expected net cash flow	50		50

SOURCE: Office of Technology Assessment, 1993.

larger, the cost of capital for project B would actually be lower than the cost of capital for project A.

How does the cost of capital affect decisions to invest in R&D projects? To assess whether the investment is worth its $10 million R&D cost, company managers (on behalf of their investors) would compute the net present value (NPV) of the investment by converting all future expected cash flows (both into and out of the firm) into their present value at the time the investment decision is made using the cost of capital appropriate to the project as the discount rate.[4] The algebraic sum of the present values of all the expected cash flows is the NPV of the investment. If the NPV is greater than zero, the investment is worth it and will compensate investors at a rate of return that exceeds the cost of capital.

Suppose we knew project A's cost of capital was 13 percent, while Project B's cost of capital was 10 percent. Then

$$NPV_A = -\$5 - \$5/(1+0.13) + 0.24[\$50/(1+0.13)^2]$$
$$= -\$0.03 \text{ million.}$$

and

$$NPV_B = -\$5 - \$5/(1+0.10) + 0.24[\$50/(1+0.10)^2]$$
$$= \$0.37 \text{ million.}$$

The NPV of project A is less than zero, so the project does not earn a high enough return to cover its cost of capital. Project B, on the other hand, does earn enough to repay its investment at its cost of capital. The company would decide to go forward with project B and forego project A, a result that would seem

---

[4] The present value (i.e., the value today) of $1.00 that an investor expects to receive 1 year hence, for example, is $0.91 when the cost of capital is 10 percent ($1.00/(1+1.10)).

counterintuitive to those who focus on total risks rather than on undiversifiable risks.

MEASURING UNDIVERSIFIABLE RISK

If the cost of capital is determined by the undiversifiable part of a project's risk, how can that risk be measured? At the level of the company (which can be considered a collection of investments), a standard approach to measuring undiversifiable risk for equity investors is to estimate the historical relationship between the firm's stock market returns and the returns from the stock market as a whole (59,96). If the firm's stock market returns are strongly associated with returns in the stock market as a whole, the relationship will be strong, and the firm has a high degree of undiversifiable risk. A measure of the strength of this relationship is referred to as the firm's "beta." If beta equals 1, the firm's equity has a risk profile that is average for the stock market. If beta is greater than 1, the firm's equity risk is higher than the average risk in the stock market. (In that case, swings in market returns are magnified in the company—when the overall stock market goes up, the company's stock market value goes up even more; when the market goes down, the company's stock market value goes down even more.) A beta of zero means that the firm has virtually no undiversifiable risk: its returns are completely uncorrelated with the stock market.

Although the riskiness of a company depends on how investors view its future performance, company betas are estimated from the historic relationship of the company's stock to the overall stock market. The assumption is that the systematic riskiness of a company today is probably similar to its riskiness in the recent past. Betas for individual firms and for industries are computed from stock market price and returns data available in several databases for publicly traded firms.

■ The Cost of Capital for the Pharmaceutical Industry

The cost of equity capital for a company as a whole is given by the following formula:

$$r_e = r_f + \beta(r_m - r_f)$$

where r_f is the rate of return to risk-free securities; $(r_m - r_f)$ is the risk premium for the equity market as a whole, and β (beta) is the firm-specific risk premium reflecting added or reduced risk of the firm's security in relation to a diversified market portfolio. The cost of equity capital for an industry can be estimated with the same formula, by weighting the individual firms' betas by the relative market value of each firm in the industry.

In a contract paper for OTA, Myers and Shyam-Sunder estimated that the risk-free rate in January 1990 was 6.8 percent and the market risk premium over the 70-year long period ending in December 1990 was 8.7 percent (285).[5] Myers and Shyam-Sunder also estimated market-value-weighted equity betas for a sample of 17 large U.S. pharmaceutical firms by regressing excess returns (over the Treasury bill rate) for pharmaceuticals against the excess returns on Standard and Poor's 500 composite index for 60-month periods ending in December 1979, December 1984, and December 1989. The estimated betas at those three points in time were 0.97, 0.66, and 0.98, respectively (285). Taken together, these estimates imply a nominal (i.e., unadjusted for investors' inflation expectations) cost of equity capital of 18 percent, 16.4 percent and 15.4 percent at the beginning of 1980, 1985, and 1990, respectively. After adjusting for inflation expectations at each time, the real cost of equity capital was 10.3, 10.9, and 10.4 percent.

Equity is only one kind of capital that companies raise. Debt financing is also used, and the cost of debt capital is generally lower than the cost of equity capital, because bondholders must be paid before stockholders are paid dividends.[6] The weighted average cost of capital, r^*, is the blended cost of the firm's debt and equity capital (285,409):

$$r^* = r_d(1-t_c)(D/V) + r_e(E/V)$$

where r_d and r_e are the cost of capital for debt and equity, respectively, D/V is the ratio of debt to market value of the firm, E/V is the ratio of equity to the market value of the firm, and t_c is the marginal corporate tax rate. The cost of debt is reduced by the amount of the corporate income tax because interest is

---

[5] The market risk premium has declined over the past 70 years. If the premium is measured over the post-World War II era, it is 8.3 percent, which would lower the cost of capital to the industry.

[6] The cost of equity capital increases as the firm takes on more debt (96). Empirical estimates of the cost of equity capital for an industry are therefore based on the observed capital structure (i.e., the ratio of debt to equity) in the industry. This approach assumes that the capital structure of firms in an industry is optimal.

deductible from business income and therefore costs the company less than it would without taxes.[7]

Myers and Shyam-Sunder calculated the cost of debt capital for a sample of 17 pharmaceutical companies. In January 1990, the market value weighted cost of debt for pharmaceuticals was 9.1 percent (285). The January 1990 cost of debt net of taxes, with a marginal tax rate of 34 percent, is therefore 6.0 percent. Before the Tax Reform Act of 1986 lowered marginal tax rates, the marginal tax rate was 46 to 48 percent, which would imply a net after-tax cost of debt of 4.9 percent.

Pharmaceutical firms have little debt, so the total cost of capital is close to the cost of equity capital. Based on all of the information given above, Myers and Shyam-Sunder estimated the real cost of capital for 17 pharmaceutical firms at the start of the year in 1980, 1985, and 1990 at 9.9, 10.7, and 10.2 percent respectively.

■ The Cost of Capital for Pharmaceutical R&D Projects

Companywide betas represent a weighted average of betas for the different individual investments that pharmaceutical companies make, including investments in R&D, manufacturing plant and equipment, and marketing.[8] Consequently, R&D investments are likely to have betas that differ from the companywide average. And, different projects will probably have different betas, as the stylized example above demonstrated. It is impossible to estimate a precise beta for each project, because historic data on returns to projects that are similar to it do not exist. Thus, while it is possible to make a reasonably accurate estimate of the companywide beta at any point in time for a pharmaceutical firm, it is not possible to directly estimate the beta for R&D projects.

Some general statements can be made about the cost of capital for R&D compared with the cost of capital for manufacturing or financial investments. Spending money on R&D can be thought of as buying an option, or opportunity, to invest in manufacturing a drug.

Without the R&D, there would be no opportunity to invest because a product would not exist. In order to actually manufacture the drug that the R&D produces, however, a company must make a fixed investment in plant and equipment. This necessary fixed investment is much like a fixed debt obligation—its claims must be met before the firm can actually reap the benefits of the R&D. Just as high fixed debts increase a company's riskiness to stockholders, who are last in line to be paid, so too does the fixed manufacturing investment increase the riskiness of the R&D investment. Consequently, the R&D is riskier than investment in plant and equipment (285).

Because the weighted average cost of capital for the firm as a whole includes investments in manufacturing and other operations as well as in R&D, the cost of capital for R&D must be higher than the weighted average cost of capital, while the cost of capital for investments in manufacturing and marketing must be less than the weighted average cost of capital.

R&D projects are in reality *sequential* investments that buy opportunities for further R&D along the way. Early in the R&D process there are high fixed obligations to be met before the company can actually begin to earn money, so the cost of capital is higher (other things being equal) for money invested very early in the process than for the money invested later, as the project approaches market approval. Therefore, early R&D projects are riskier than later projects and have a higher cost of capital.

Not only does early R&D produce an option on future investments and revenues, but it also produces information that reduces the uncertainty about the value of the project (96,330,352). Since R&D projects can be abandoned at any point in the process (or at least at certain project milestones), the investment in early R&D can be viewed as an investment in information that allows the firm to reduce the uncertainty of its later investments.

Suppose, for example, a new compound stands one chance in 100 of reaching the market, but $1 million

---

[7] Although debt interest is untaxed at the corporate level, it is fully taxed at the personal level. Equity returns, on the other hand, are taxed fully at the corporate level and lightly at the personal level to the extent that much of the equity returns are in the form of capital gains, which are taxed only when the gains are realized (391,392). At the investor level, the personal and corporate tax systems combine to largely eliminate the overall tax advantage of debt (273). This implies that at the firm level, the cost of equity should be lower than the cost of debt of comparable risk (392). Together, these findings imply that the cost of equity capital as calculated in the formulas given above may be overstated when beta is less than one and understated when beta is greater than one (391). Since the beta for the pharmaceutical industry was slightly less than one, the cost of equity capital in the pharmaceutical industry may be slightly overstated.

[8] Although R&D and advertising and promotion are treated as current expenditures in firms' accounting statements, if they lead to increases in revenues in later years, they are in principal investments, and stock prices would reflect this fact.

spent early on animal toxicology testing will either show it to be too toxic and therefore not worth additional R&D expenditures or increase its chances of success to, say, 1 in 10. Any money spent after the animal testing is completed would face vastly better odds than would be the case if the firm were required to commit to the full course of R&D at the very beginning of the project. The information produced by the $1-million expenditure is valuable and may justify early speculative R&D projects whose NPV, viewed from the beginning of the project, may appear to be negative (352).

This "information-producing" function of R&D essentially adds to the value of the R&D investment or, stated another way, dampens the effective cost of capital for R&D to more closely approximate the cost of capital for investments in manufacturing capacity for an approved drug. Although the betas and, therefore, the cost of capital for R&D projects are always higher than those for investment in ongoing operations, how much higher depends on the interplay between the information value of the investment and the fixed investment required to realize the returns from R&D.

To summarize, although the cost of capital for R&D must be higher than that for manufacturing, and it is higher the earlier in the research process the project is, there is currently available no practical approach to estimating just how high the cost of capital actually is for any set of R&D investments. The best that can be done to get a rough quantitative estimate of the cost of capital for pharmaceutical R&D projects is to examine the betas of firms that invest largely in R&D and that have relatively little investment in ongoing operations.

Stewart (409) estimated the cost of capital for business risk for 1,000 publicly traded companies in the United States and Canada. Companies whose main business was providing R&D services (R&D laboratories) had a cost of capital for business risk that was approximately 4.5 percentage points higher than the cost of capital for business risk for the drug companies in his sample. A recent update of the Myers and Shyam-Sunder paper by Shyam-Sunder found only a 2.7 percentage point difference in the net cost of capital between 30 biotechnology firms and 19 large pharmaceutical firms as of December 1990 (285). The results of these studies suggest that a 4-percentage point differential in the cost of capital from the beginning to the end of the research process provides a reasonable

outer boundary for calculation of the capitalized costs of R&D.

■ Comparing Pharmaceutical and Nonpharmaceutical Costs of Capital

This section describes OTA's procedures for estimating the difference between the cost of capital for the pharmaceutical industry and the cost of capital for the comparison firms used in the Baber and Kang study of pharmaceutical industry profitability (27).

At OTA's request, Baber and Kang estimated the internal rate of return (IRR) over a 12-year period (1976-87) for a sample of pharmaceutical companies and two comparison groups matched with the pharmaceutical companies according to sales, sales growth and R&D intensity (27). The IRR is the compound annual interest rate earned by investments in the companies over the period of study. Baber and Kang demonstrated that, after adjusting for distortions in financial accounting data, the difference in IRR between the pharmaceutical industry and the comparison groups over the period studied was 2 to 3 percentage points per year, a far smaller difference than traditional profitability analyses tend to show (27).

In their comparative profitability study, Baber and Kang did not address the question of whether a 2 to 3 percentage point difference in IRRs can be explained by a difference in risk (and, therefore, in costs of capital) between the pharmaceutical industry and other companies. To investigate this issue, OTA estimated the relative riskiness and differences in the cost of capital between the pharmaceutical firms and the nonpharmaceutical firms studied by Baber and Kang.

OTA's method for comparing the costs of capital is based in large part on procedures and information supplied by Myers and Shyam-Sunder in their OTA contract report (285). Although Myers and Shyam-Sunder laid out general procedures for estimating betas and weighted average costs of capital, they were asked by OTA to supply specific estimates only for the pharmaceutical industry. To estimate cost of capital differences between the pharmaceutical industry and the nonpharmaceutical firms sampled by Baber and Kang, OTA pieced together information provided by Myers and Shyam-Sunder as well as data provided by Baber and Kang on the specific samples of firms studied.

The Baber and Kang study examines nominal rates of return without adjusting for inflation. Therefore,

OTA's estimates of the cost of capital for each sample are nominal as well.

EVIDENCE ON BETAS

Estimation of beta, the correlation of a firm's returns with market returns, requires data that are available only for publicly traded firms. Hence, beta can be estimated only for a subsample of firms in the Baber and Kang study, although these firms represent a high proportion of total market values in these samples. Betas also vary over time, so the period over which they are estimated can affect the ultimate results.

OTA had two sources of evidence on pharmaceutical betas. First, as described earlier, Myers and Shyam-Sunder estimated market value-weighted equity betas for a sample of 17 large U.S. pharmaceutical firms by regressing excess returns (over the Treasury bill rate) against excess returns on Standard and Poor's 500 composite index for 60-month periods ending in December 1979; December 1984; and December 1989.[9] Estimated betas were 0.97, 0.66, and 0.98 respectively (285).

Second, Baber and Kang calculated market-value weighted betas for each year of the 12-year study period by regressing total firm returns against total market returns over the previous 240 months for companies for which data were available (24,224). Table C-2 shows the calculated betas and the number of firms included in each year's calculation. The calculated weighted average betas change slightly from year to year, as the sample of firms changes and as the market value weights change, but they are very stable.[10] The mean across all study years of the weighted average betas is 0.90 for pharmaceuticals, 1.00 for control firms matched by sales, and 1.29 for control firms matched by sales and R&D. OTA used these estimates of beta for the sake of consistency across samples.

EVIDENCE ON THE RISK-FREE RATE

Myers and Shyam-Sunder observed that the appropriate risk-free rate is the short-term Treasury bill rate, but this must be adjusted for forecasts that will govern the firm's long-term investments (285). The short-term Treasury bill rate averaged 5.76 percent in the period 1957-87 (23,223). Myers and Shyam-Sunder obtained a risk-free rate by subtracting an historical term premium (1.2 percent) from the 20-year Treasury bond yield. In December 1989, the net rate was 6.81 percent (285).

EVIDENCE ON THE MARKET RISK PREMIUM

The realized market risk premium (over the risk-free rate) is highly volatile over time, while expected risks are assumed to be stable over long periods. Therefore, the market risk premium is typically estimated over a long period of time (198). Myers and Shyam-Sunder found an arithmetic mean of 8.7 percent for excess market return over the Treasury bill rate for the period 1926-89 (285). The market risk premium declined in the post-war period, however, and the premium for the period 1947-88 was 8.3 percent (285).

In an unrelated study, Stewart estimated the market risk premium by comparing Standard and Poor's 500 stocks with long-term (20-year) U.S. Treasury bonds from 1925 to 1989 (409). He found that the risk premium was only 5.8 percent over the period. This would imply a risk premium over the Treasury bill rate (adjusted for long-term forecasts) of just 7.0 percent.

EVIDENCE ON THE AFTER-TAX COST OF DEBT

Myers and Shyam-Sunder calculated the cost of debt capital for a sample of 17 pharmaceutical companies based on Moody's industrial bond ratings. As of December 1989, the market value weighted cost of debt for pharmaceuticals was 9.1 percent (285).[11] The cost of debt net of taxes, with a marginal tax rate of 34 percent, was therefore 6.0 percent. At the pretax-reform marginal tax rate of 46 percent, the net after-tax cost of debt would have been 4.9 percent.

At OTA's request, Baber and Kang calculated the mean ratio of after-tax interest payments to the book value of long-term debt between 1975 and 1987 for the 15 largest firms in each of the three samples in this

---

[9] All of the firms included in Myers and Shyam-Sunder's analysis of the pharmaceutical industry are part of the Baber and Kang pharmaceutical sample.

[10] Betas estimated over a long period of observation tend to be more stable than those based on shorter periods. For example, Myers and Shyam-Sunder's estimate of betas for the pharmaceutical industry, which are based on 5 years' worth of data, vary more widely than do the estimates made by Baber and Kang. But, too long a period of historical observation can obscure the effects of changes in an industry's riskiness over time. Part of the variation in the estimates of Myers and Shyam-Sunder is probably random, but part may also be due to changes from the mid-1970s through the late 1980s in the riskiness of the industry.

[11] Overall, U.S. corporate bond yields averaged 10.87 between 1973 and 1989 (1).

Table C-2—Weighted Average Betas

| Year | Pharmaceuticals | | Control firms matched by sales and growth | | Control firms matched by sales and R&D | | Samples with R&D greater than 5% of sales | | | | | |
| | | | | | | | Pharmaceuticals | | Control firms matched by sales and growth | | Control firms matched by sales and R&D | |
	n[a]	beta	n[a]	beta	n[a]	beta	n[a]	beta	n[a]	beta	n[a]	beta
1975.	20	0.88	22	0.97	23	1.24	14	0.88	14	0.91	13	1.28
1976.	20	0.88	22	0.97	24	1.27	14	0.87	14	0.93	14	1.31
1977.	20	0.89	22	0.98	25	1.28	14	0.88	14	0.95	14	1.33
1978.	21	0.90	22	0.98	27	1.27	14	0.88	14	0.95	15	1.32
1979.	21	0.89	22	1.00	28	1.30	14	0.88	14	0.97	16	1.34
1980.	21	0.90	23	1.01	29	1.30	14	0.89	15	0.98	17	1.34
1981.	21	0.90	25	1.04	29	1.33	14	0.89	16	1.00	17	1.38
1982.	24	0.91	25	1.02	30	1.30	16	0.90	16	1.00	18	1.33
1983.	24	0.92	25	1.02	30	1.30	16	0.91	16	1.00	17	1.34
1984.	25	0.93	25	1.02	31	1.30	17	0.93	16	1.01	17	1.34
1985.	25	0.93	25	1.01	32	1.30	17	0.93	16	0.99	18	1.35
1986.	25	0.93	25	1.01	31	1.30	16	0.92	16	0.98	17	1.35
1987.	25	0.92	24	1.00	31	1.28	16	0.92	15	0.97	17	1.32
mean.		0.90		1.00		1.29		0.90		0.97		1.33

[a] n = number of firms in sample.

SOURCE: W. Baber and S.-H. Kang, "An Empirical Investigation of Accounting Rates of Return for Pharmaceutical Industry 1975-1987, draft report prepared for the Office of Technology Assessment, August 1990.

study. These ratios were 5.64 percent for pharmaceuticals, 4.92 percent for the control sample matched by sales and 5.72 percent for the control sample matched by R&D. Although these ratios are a crude measure of the cost of debt, the rate for the pharmaceutical sample is close to the after-tax rate estimated by Myers and Shyam-Sunder.

ESTIMATES OF COST OF CAPITAL

OTA estimated the weighted average cost of capital for the three samples based on the evidence summarized above. Because the control firms have much higher debt-to-equity ratios than do the pharmaceutical companies, OTA used parameter estimates that would tend to understate the cost of debt and overstate the cost of equity. The computed costs of capital are therefore biased in favor of a higher cost of capital in the pharmaceutical industry.

Specifically, OTA assumed the pretax cost of debt is 9 percent for all three samples, the risk-free rate is 6.8 percent, and the market risk premium is 8.7 percent. These parameters are consistent with those of Myers and Shyam-Sunder (285). Betas were assumed to follow those calculated in table C-2. Table C-3 summarizes the calculations for the pharmaceutical firms and the two control groups.

Because these estimates of the cost of capital are based on high estimates of the risk-free rate and the market premium, they should not be viewed as accurate estimates of the actual cost of capital over the period. Moreover, the cost of capital is a moving target over time; a single estimate provides only a rough approximation of its value. Yet, they do provide a reasonably accurate (indeed, a conservative) test of **differences** in the cost of capital among the samples of firms examined by Baber and Kang.

Table C-3—Weighted Average Cost of Capital, 1976-87

	Pharmaceuticals	Control sample I	Control sample II
Characteristics of industry[a]			
Market value of equity ($ million)	$1,288	$453	$562
Value of debt ($ million)	$ 85	$116	$129
Average firm value ($ million)	$1,373	$569	$691
Assumptions			
Beta	0.9	1.0	1.29
Cost of debt (pretax)	0.09	0.09	0.09
Marginal tax rate	0.46	0.46	0.46
Risk-free rate (r_f)	0.068	0.068	0.068
Market risk premium (r_m-r_f)	0.087	0.087	0.087
Results			
Cost of equity capital (r_e)	0.146	0.155	0.18
Cost of capital (r^*)	0.14	0.133	0.155

[a] Based on 15 largest firms in each sample.

KEY: Control sample I: Firms similar to pharmaceutical in terms of sales and sales growth.
Control sample II: Firms similar to pharmaceuticals in terms of sales and R&D industry.

SOURCE: Office of Technology Assessment, 1993.

Appendix D

Congressional Access to Proprietary Pharmaceutical Industry Data

I n the past, numerous congressional committees have expressed an interest in the research, development, and marketing costs of the pharmaceutical industry. While the industry is quite willing to disclose its own estimates, it guards the financial information that is used to derive these estimates, especially the data needed to determine overall industry profitability and profitability per product.

Without voluntary disclosure, Congress must resort to compulsory processes. Congress' auditing body, the U.S. General Accounting Office (GAO), which investigates "all matters relating to the receipt, disbursement, and application of public funds,"[1] is probably best equipped to do a financial analysis of the pharmaceutical industry. In addition, GAO is afforded special power to audit the expenditure of public funds through government contracts. Since 1951, almost all government contracts must contain a clause authorizing GAO to:

> . . .examine any directly pertinent books, documents, papers, and records of the contractor or any of his subcontractors engaged in the performance of and involving transactions related to such contracts or subcontracts.[2]

However, the pharmaceutical industry successfully battled GAO for a decade to prevent GAO from using these "access to records" clauses to obtain information about individual companies' research, development, and marketing costs. The following discussion outlines GAO's unsuccessful attempt to obtain research, development, marketing, and promotional costs from the industry, demonstrating the industry's willingness to fight disclosure.

Another avenue for obtaining this data would be through a congressional subpoena. It is clearly within congressional powers to subpoena this data; however, it appears that Congress has been reluctant to use this power against the pharmaceutical industry. The broad scope of congressional subpoena power summarized in this appendix demonstrates that legal constraints have not prevented Congress from obtaining proprietary data.

▮ GAO and the Pharmaceutical Industry

The controversy between GAO and several of the largest U.S. pharmaceutical companies began in 1967 when the Senate Select Committee on Small Business, Subcommittee on Monopoly, held a series of hearings on all aspects of the pharmaceutical industry, including its profitability and the amount of competition in the industry.[3] The intent of these hearings was to establish

---

[1] 31 U.S.C. Sec. 712.

[2] See, e.g., 41 U.S.C. Sec. 254 (1992) (civilian contracts); 22 U.S.C. Sec. 2586 (1992) (arms control and disarmament); 22 U.S.C. Sec. 2206 (1992) (atomic energy); 50 U.S.C. Secs. 1431, 1433 (1992) (military/national defense). Harvard Law Review, "The Controller General's Authority To Examine the Private Business Records of Government Contractors: *Eli Lilly & Co.* v. *Staats, Harvard Law Review* 92:1148-1159 (1979).

[3] "Competitive Problems in the Drug Industry: Hearings before the Subcommittee on Monopoly of the Senate Select Committee on Small Business (pt. 1) 90th Cong., 1st Sess. passim (1967), cited in note, "The General Accounting Office's Access to Government Contractor's Records," *University of Chicago Law Review* 49:1050- 1075 (1982).

a record in preparation for possible legislative action.[4] In 1971, the Comptroller General of the United States, the head of GAO, testified at one of these hearings.[5] The Subcommittee Chairman, Senator Gaylord Nelson, suggested that GAO use the "access-to-records" clause, found in a number of government contracts with the pharmaceutical companies, to "take a look at the costs" of the pharmaceutical industry.[6] After the hearings Senator Nelson's staff continued to urge GAO to use its powers under these clauses to obtain cost records "without any strings attached so that the high profits" of the drug industry could be made public by product and firm.[7]

Following the hearings, in 1972 GAO approached the Pharmaceutical Manufacturers Association (PMA) about doing a comprehensive study on the industry, including production process, efficiency, costs, and profits. PMA-member companies rejected GAO's request because the confidentiality of their cost and other data could not be protected.[8] GAO revised its plan and proposed a Phase I study that would examine the characteristics and methods of the industry. Six companies voluntarily cooperated with this initial phase: SmithKline Corporation, Bristol Laboratories, division of Bristol-Myers Company, Abbott Laboratories, Eli Lilly & Company, Merck & Company, Inc., and Hoffman La Roche.

In 1974, GAO published its Phase I findings[9] and proposed a second part to gather data that would illuminate "salient economic and operational aspects of the industry."[10] GAO originally proposed that the cost data from individual companies or drugs be kept confidential; however, Senators Nelson's and Edward Kennedy's staff insisted that the Committee's objectives could only be met if the data were made public.[11] The drug companies refused to cooperate, and in 1974 GAO decided to use its authority under the access to records clause to obtain the data.

Each of the six pharmaceutical companies GAO studied in Phase I had government contracts with the U.S. Defense Department and the U.S. Veteran's Administration. Relying on the access to records clauses in these contracts, GAO sent a letter to each company requesting:

...all books, documents, papers, and other records directly pertinent to the contracts, which include, but are not limited to (1) records of experienced costs including costs of direct materials, direct labor, overhead, and other pertinent corporate costs, (2) support for other information as may be necessary for use to review the reasonableness of the contract prices and the adequacy of the protections accorded the Government interests.[12]

As would later become apparent, GAO was seeking financial data that would allow it to estimate research, development, marketing, promotion, and distribution costs for individual products.

Each of the pharmaceutical companies' contracts was negotiated fixed price and the prices were therefore based on catalog prices, often with volume

---

[4] "Competitive Problems in the Drug Industry: Hearings before the Subcommittee on Monopoly of the Senate Select Committee on Small Business (pt. 1) 90th Cong., 1st Sess. passim (1967) (remarks of Senator Gaylord Nelson) cited in note, "The General Accounting Office's Access to Government Contractor's Records," *University of Chicago Law Review* 49:1050-1075 (1982).

[5] "Hearings on Competitive Problems in the Drug Industry before the Senate Subcommittee on Monopoly of the Senate Select Committee on Small Business," 92d Cong., 1st Sess., 8020 (1971) cited in note, "The General Accounting Office's Access to Government Contractor's Records," *University of Chicago Law Review* 49:1050-1075 (1982).

[6] *Bowsher* v. *Merck & Co., Inc.*, 103 S.Ct. 1587, 1591 n.4 (1983).

[7] *Bowsher* v. *Merck & Co., Inc.*, 103 S.Ct. 1587, 1591 n.4 (1983).

[8] *Eli Lilly & Co., v. Staats*, 574 F.2d. 904, 923 (7th Cir. 1978), *cert. denied*, 439 U.S. 959, 99 S.Ct. 362 (1978).

[9] *Eli Lilly & Co.* v. *Staats*, 574 F.2d. 904, 923 (7th Cir. 1978), *cert. denied*, 439 U.S. 959, 99 S.Ct. 362 (1978).

[10] *Bowsher* v. *Merck & Co., Inc.*, 103 S.Ct. 1587, 1591 n.4 (1983).

[11] GAO later asserted that its report to Congress would not identify particular companies or products, but rather it would be an industrywide report. *Eli Lilly & Co.* v. *Staats*, 574 F.2d 904 (7th Cir. 1978), *cert. denied*, 439 U.S. 959, 99 S.Ct. 362 (1978).

[12] Harvard Law Review, "The Controller General's Authority To Examine the Private Business Records of Government Contractors: *Eli Lilly & Co.* v. *Staats*", *Harvard Law Review* 92:1148-1159 (1979).

discounts. When the contracts were negotiated, the reasonableness of the prices was assessed on the basis of the contractor's established catalog or market price; no attempt was made to demand the manufacturer's actual costs.[13] A number of the companies believed any data relating to costs of the products were irrelevant to a fixed price contract, and to the extent any financial data were relevant, only direct costs (e.g., materials and labor) apply. Furthermore, the companies believed GAO was not authorized under the statute to conduct an audit for the sole purpose of doing a congressional study. They argued that the access-to-records clause was meant only to prevent fraud and abuse in government contracting and could not be used unless there was a reasonable basis for GAO to suspect fraud and abuse in pricing. Since the contract prices were at or below the catalog prices and were not negotiated, the companies claimed GAO should not be allowed to investigate their prices. Therefore, in answer to GAO's request, five of the six companies filed suit to prevent GAO from enforcing its demand.[14]

The fact that the catalog prices were not questioned during the contractual negotiations did not prevent GAO from auditing the prices paid. A previous case involving a fixed-price defense industry contractor had already established that GAO was not strictly limited in its investigation of government contracts to those items specifically negotiated. The word "contract," as used in the access-to-records statute, was interpreted to not only include the specific terms, but also the general subject matter of the contract which includes the business arrangements of the contract.[15] Faced with this precedent, the courts in the pharmaceutical cases were unwilling to narrowly limit GAO's ability to use access-to-records clauses to gather information on

prices even when the price was not specifically negotiated and was less than a catalog price. Moreover, although the courts recognized that GAO's request was motivated largely by the Senate Subcommittee on Monopoly's desire for a study on the pharmaceutical industry, the courts concluded that such mixed motivations did not limit GAO's stated statutory powers.[16]

After quickly disposing of these issues, the courts struggled with what became the main issue: what documents could GAO properly request? The only precedent, *Hewlett Packard* v. *United States*, had given GAO access to books and records related to the direct cost of materials, labor, and overhead but had not addressed the question of whether GAO's access extended beyond direct costs.[17]

The scope of GAO's power turned on the phrase "directly pertinent" in the statute authorizing GAO access to documents under government contracts. Interpreting the applicability of these two words became the subject of litigation for nearly a decade. No other court had interpreted this language, and the legislative history was ambiguous.[18] The original proposed bill allowed GAO access to all records that were "pertinent." The adjective "directly" was added at the end of legislative debate to limit "snooping' that may be carried out."[19] This amendment revealed that although Congress sought to give GAO broad enough powers to obtain data that would enable it to evaluate the reasonableness of Federal Government contracts and deter impropriety and wastefulness, certain Members also expressed concern about giving GAO overly broad access to private data.[20]

Between 1977 to 1983, 10 separate Federal court decisions were handed down in the cases between

---

[13] S.S. Garner, "GAO Right of Access and the Pharmaceutical Industry: *Bowsher* v. *Merck*," *Air Force Law Review* 24(2):125-156 (1984).

[14] Hoffmann LaRoche chose to settle with GAO. Letter from Thomas G. Stayton to the *Harvard Law Review* (Jan. 3, 1979) cited in "The Controller General's Authority To Examine the Private Business Records of Government Contractors: *Eli Lilly & Co.* v. *Staats*", *Harvard Law Review* 92:1148-1159 (1979). The terms of that settlement and the amount of information obtained from Hoffman La Roche do not appear to have been made public.

[15] *Hewlett Packard Company* v. *United States*, 385 F. 2d, 1013 (9th Cir. 1967), *cert. denied*, 390 U.S. 988, 88 S.Ct. 1184 (1968).

[16] See e.g., *SmithKline* v. *Staats*, 668 F.2d 201 (3rd Cir. 1981), *cert. denied*, *Bowsher* v. *SmithKline Corp.*, 461 U.S. 913, 103 S. Ct. 1891 (1983). For a more complete discussion of this issue, see Case Comments, "The Comptroller General's Authority To Examine the Private Business Records of Government Contractors: *Eli Lilly & Co.* v. *Staats*, *Harvard Law Review* 92:1148-1159 (1979).

[17] *Hewlett Packard* v. *United States*, 383 F.2d 1013 (9th Cir. 1967), *cert. denied*, 390 U.S. 988, 88 S.Ct. 1184 (1968).

[18] Note, "The General Accounting Office's Access to Contractor's Records," *University of Chicago Law Review* 49:1050-1075 (1982).

[19] 97 *Congressional Record* 13377 (1951) cited in *Merck* v. *Bowsher*, at 1602. The complete quote of Congressman Hoffman, who supported the amendment, was that "[t]he purpose is to limit 'snooping' that may be carried out under this bill which we do not have the votes to defeat." 115 *Congressional Record* 25800 (U.S. Senate - Sept. 17, 1969).

[20] *Bowsher* v. *Merck & Co. Inc.*, 460 U.S. 824, 103 S.Ct. 1587 (1983).

GAO and the pharmaceutical companies.[21] All of the courts agreed that GAO had the authority to see cost data even if the prices were not negotiated. The courts also agreed that direct costs, such as manufacturing costs, royalty costs, and delivery costs were relevant to the contract and were therefore subject to GAO review.[22] But, the courts were split on GAO's right of access to indirect costs (research and development (R&D), marketing, promotion, distribution, and administration costs). In most cases, the companies successfully argued that indirect cost data were not *directly pertinent* because only a small portion of indirect costs could be allocated to the Federal Government's contracts, and GAO would have to examine a large amount of data not related to the Government's contracts in order to discern this small amount.[23] The Government unsuccessfully argued that GAO would not have to go on a fishing expedition through all the company's unallocated costs, because the companies allocate costs to products and perform profitability studies for their own purposes.[24] That argument fell on deaf ears, and GAO was given access only to direct cost data that the industry was willing to provide.[25] From a practical point of view, these decisions left GAO with little meaningful data, since direct costs amounted to only about 9 percent of the cost of a particular pharmaceutical product. The access granted by these courts was, therefore, virtually useless as an auditing tool.

GAO did find a sympathetic ear in one judicial circuit. In *Eli Lilly & Co.* v. *Staats*,[26] the Seventh Circuit concluded that because R&D, marketing, and promotion costs constituted a major portion of the total price of the contracts, they were directly pertinent under both "common and legal understandings."[27] The court concluded that records were "directly pertinent" to a contract if it is "a significant input in the cost of the product purchased in the contract."[28]

The conflict between the courts was finally resolved by the U.S. Supreme Court, in *Bowsher* v. *Merck & Co. Inc.*[29] The Federal Government again argued that GAO had the right to examine records pertaining to every cost that the company used the Government's payments to defray.[30] The decision to make such a broad assertion of power may have been a strategic mistake because it gave no apparent recognition to the statutory limits imposed by the word "directly," and the Government's interpretation, "carried to its logical extreme. . . would dictate that few, if any, of private contractor's business records would be immune from GAO scrutiny."[31] Moreover, the Supreme Court cited GAO internal decisions and a memorandum to Con-

---

[21] *Bristol Laboratories Div. of Bristol-Myers Co.* v. *Staats*, 428 F. Supp. 1388 (1977), *aff'd per curiam*, 620 F. 2d 17 (2d Cir. 1980), *aff'd mem. by evenly divided court*, 451 U.S. 400 (1981); *SmithKline Corp.* v. *Staats*, 483 F. Supp. 712 (E.D. Pa. 1980), *aff'ds* 668 F.2d 201 (3d Cir. 1981), *cert. denied, Bowsher* v. *SmithKline Corp.*, 461 U.S. 913 (1983); *Eli Lilly & Co.* v. *Staats*, 574 F.2d. 904 (7th Cir. 1977), *cert. denied*, 439 U.S. 959, 99 S.Ct. 362 (1978); *U.S.* v. *Abbott*, 597 F.2d 672 (7th Cir. 1979). *Merck & Co.* v. *Staats*, 529 F. Supp. 1 (D.C.C. 1977); *aff'd*, 665 F.2d 1236 (D.C. Cir. 1981), *aff'd., Bowsher* v. *Merck & Co.*, 460 U.S. 824, 103 S. Ct. 1587 (1983).

[22] In one of the first cases decided, the Bristol-Myers Company offered to provide GAO with data on direct costs. This compromise position proved to be a useful strategy because the courts concluded that the company's offer reflected "a responsible and reasonable effort to distinguish 'directly pertinent' matter." *Bristol Lab. Div. of Bristol-Myers Co.* v. *Staats*, at 1391.

[23] *Bristol Lab. Div. of Bristol-Myers Co.* v. *Staats*, at 1391.

[24] *SmithKline Corp.* v. *Staats*, 668 F.2d 201 (1981), *cert. denied, Bowsher* v. *SmithKline Corp.*, 461 U.S. 913, 103 S.Ct. 1891 (1983) "we therefore adopt the standard formulated in *Bristol*, which for the most part relies on the distinction between direct and indirect costs"; *Merck & Co.* v. *Staats*, 665 F.2d 1236 (D.C. Cir. 1981), *aff'd, Bowsher* v. *Merck & Co.*, 460 U.S. 824, 103 S.Ct. 1587 (1983).

[25] *Merck* v. *Staats*, at 1247 (Mikva, J., concurring in part, dissenting in part).

[26] 574 F.2d 904 (7th Cir. 1978), *cert. denied*, 439 U.S. 959 (1978).

[27] 574 F.2d 904 (7th Cir. 1978), *cert. denied*, 439 U.S. 959 (1978).

[28] 574 F.2d 904 (7th Cir. 1978), *cert. denied*, 439 U.S. 959 (1978).

[29] 460 U.S. 824, 103 S.Ct. 1587 (1983).

[30] *Bowsher* v. *Merck & Co. Inc.*, 460 U.S. 824, 843, 103 S.Ct. 1587,1598 (1983).

[31] *Bowsher* v. *Merck & Co. Inc.*, 460 U.S. 824, 103 S.Ct. 1587 (1983).

[32] In a 1969 memorandum responding to Congress' interest in performing a profitability study of the defense industry, GAO wrote that "While GAO's legal authority would permit it to perform some to the work necessary in making a profit study. . ., to do a meaningful study of profitability. . ., legislation should be enacted broadening [GAO's] right of access to record. . ." Part of GAO's concern was that without specific authority it would be drawn into protracted litigation. *Memorandum on the Adequacy of the Legal Authority of the General Accounting Office To Conduct a Comprehensive Study of Profitability in the Pharmaceutical Industry*, reprinted 115 *Congressional Record* 25,801 (Senate 1969).

gress in which GAO appeared to acknowledge more limited authority.[32]

The Court followed the majority of the lower courts and drew the line between direct and indirect costs. The Court held that since Congress had drafted the limiting language ("directly pertinent"), arguments for change should be directed to Congress. The Court also noted that in the past Congress had found it necessary to pass legislation expanding GAO's powers to conduct a profit study of the defense industry.[33] In that case, Congress expressed its reservations about providing GAO with the authority to conduct a "fishing expedition" and limited this expansion of GAO's authority to a single study.[34] This past congressional action weakened the Government's argument that GAO had such broad powers under the access-to-records clauses.

■ The Availability of Congressional Subpoena Power

Although the Federal Government was willing to fight five separate cases through to the Supreme Court, Congress was not willing to use its subpoena power to obtain the data. A brief review of the scope of congressional subpoena power demonstrates that since the hearings were being carried out in anticipation of legislation, a congressional subpoena would have been a legal alternative, although perhaps not politically feasible.

Congress' power to legislate includes the power to investigate, to compel witnesses to testify, and to demand the production of documents. The power to investigate and issue subpoenas is, however, limited to the congressional committees.[35] There are few limitations on the scope of a congressional subpoena, provided it is carried out in the course of legitimate congressional powers. As the Supreme Court cases in this area demonstrate, legitimate congressional powers are quite extensive and congressional subpoenas are virtually immune from judicial challenge.[36]

The courts give congressional subpoenas deference because they fall within the protections of the Speech and Debate clause of the Constitution.[37] The Speech and Debate clause *literally* protects all Senators and Representatives from "questioning in any other Place for any Speech or Debate in either House." As interpreted, this protects members of Congress from judicial interference in legislative matters.

In *Eastland* v. *United States Servicemen's Fund*,[38] the Supreme Court reviewed a congressional subpoena issued during the course of an investigation of the United States Servicemen's Fund, Inc. (USSF). The USSF challenged the subpoena alleging it infringed upon the USSF's First Amendment rights.[39] The Court rejected the USSF claim, stating that since the congressional subpoena fell within the "sphere of legitimate legislative activity," the Committee's actions could not be questioned by the courts because the "prohibi-

---

[33] Military Appropriations Act of 1970, Public Law 91-121, Sec. 408, 83 Stat. 204, cited in *Merck* v. *Bowsher*, at 1595, n. 12.

[34] 115 Congressional Record 25795, 25793 (statements of Senator Ribicoff and Senator Proxmire, respectively), cited in *Merck* v. *Bowsher*, at 1595, n. 12.

[35] The power to investigate using compulsory process is derived from the U.S. Constitution, but Congress itself has limited subpoena power to the committees. Since 1946, each standing Senate Committee has had the power to issue subpoenas without obtaining specific permission from the Senate. See The Legislative Reorganization Act of 1946 (Public Law 79-901), cited in Congressional Quarterly, *Guide to Congress* (3rd Ed.) (Washington, DC: Congressional Quarterly Inc., 1982). In 1974, House Committees were given general subpoena power; however, each subpoena must be approved by the majority of the Committee or Subcommittee and can only be enforced by action of the full House. Congressional Quarterly, *Guide to Congress* (3rd Ed.) (Washington, DC: Congressional Quarterly Inc., 1982).

[36] *McGrain* v. *Daugherty*, 273 U.S. 135 (1927) (establishing that Congress must be able to obtain information to fulfill its legislative duties and may compel such disclosure). *Watkins* v. *United States*, 354 U.S. 178 (1957).

[37] U.S. Constitution, Art.I, Sec. 6, clause 1.

[38] 421 U.S. 491, 95 S.Ct. 1813 (1975).

[39] The USSF published an underground newspaper for American military persons and established coffeehouses near domestic military installations which were admittedly a "focus of dissent and expressions of opposition within the military toward the war in [Southeast Asia]." Congress was concerned that the activities of the USSF were undermining the moral of American servicepersons and issued a subpoena requesting all USSF documents and records to the bank in which USSF kept its account. The USSF protested that Congress was attempting to force the disclosure of "beliefs, opinions, expressions and associations of private citizens which may be unorthodox or unpopular," and that the sole purpose of the subpoena was to "harass, chill, punish, and deter [USSF and its members] in their exercise of their" First Amendment rights, particularly freedom of the press and freedom of association. *Eastland* v. *United States Servicemen's Fund*, 421 U.S. 491 (1974).

tions of the Speech and Debate Clause are absolute.''[40] Even valid constitutional objections are overridden by the absolute nature of the Speech and Debate clause.[41] To be within the protections of the Speech and Debate clause, the subpoena must be issued in ''a session of the House by one of its members in relation to the business before it.''[42] In addition, a court will not examine the motives for the subpoena, provided it can be related to possible legislative actions;[43] ''the wisdom of congressional approach or methodology is not open to judicial veto.''[44] The Supreme Court has stated that a legislative inquiry is valid even if there is ''no predictable end result.''[45]

Given this broad subpoena power, it is likely that a congressional committee could devise a legitimate subpoena to obtain R&D costs from the pharmaceutical industry. For example, Congress might investigate whether discounts should be required for pharmaceuticals purchased for Medicaid, Medicare, or other government programs, or look into whether current tax subsidies for R&D costs are warranted. The industry has cited its research costs in testimony during 1987 hearings on the consequences of the Drug Price Competition and Patent Term Restoration Act of 1984 (Public Law 98-417) and, therefore, has arguably made it a legitimate target for investigation.

Any subpoena directed at such data is likely to be met by protests about the proprietary nature of the data. Although business confidentiality arguments are not sufficient to block the subpoena,[46] such arguments can result in protracted negotiations over whether the information will be kept confidential and the scope of the documents that must be turned over.

In summary, Congress has the power to request R&D and marketing cost data from the industry. But, given the past history of litigation on the issue it is safe to predict that pharmaceutical companies are not likely to make such a request easy, and Congress has so far been unwilling to exercise this power.

---

[40] *Eastland* v. *United States Servicemen's Fund*, 421 U.S. 491, 95 S.Ct. 1813 (1975) (additional cites omitted).

[41] *Eastland* v. *United States Servicemen's Fund*, 421 U.S. 491 (1975) (additional cites omitted). However, three Justices wrote that in certain cases the constitutionality of a congressional subpoena may be reviewed by the Court, even if the subpoena is within the sphere of legitimate legislative activity. *Id.* (concurrence of Justice Marshall, with whom Justices Brennan and White joined).

[42] *Kilbourn* v. *Thompson*, 103 U.S. 168 (1881), cited in *Eastland* v. *United States Servicemen's Fund*, 421 U.S. 491 (1975).

[43] *Eastland* v. *United States Servicemen's Fund*, 421 U.S. 491 (1974); *Watkins* v. *United States*, 354 U.S. 178, 200, 93 S.Ct. 2018 (1957).

[44] *Doe* v. *McMillan*, 412 U.S. 306, 313, 93 S.Ct. 2018 (1973).

[45] *Eastland* v. *United States Servicemen's Fund*, 421 U.S. 491 (1974) (additional cites omitted).

[46] Conversation with Charles Tiefer, Office of the General Counsel, House of Representatives, U.S. Congress (September 4, 1991).

Appendix E

Patent Protection of Pharmaceuticals in the United States

Inventors have two mechanisms to protect the commercial value of their inventions: secrecy or patents. Trade secrets have legal protection if inventors make efforts to prevent the sharing or dissemination of their intellectual property (452). Patents prohibit others from making, using or selling the invention in the United States for 17 years after issuance without the inventor's permission.[1] Because of the relatively wide dissemination of pharmaceutical research results and production techniques through scientific literature and discussion, drug manufacturers rely on patents to protect potential and marketed drug products whenever possible. This appendix briefly examines the nature and limitations of pharmaceutical patent protection in the United States.

■ Pharmaceutical Patents and Products

Article I of the U.S. Constitution provides Congress with the power "to promote the Progress of Science and useful Arts, by securing for limited Times to Authors and Inventors the exclusive Right to their respective Writings and Discoveries," which Congress has implemented by allowing the Federal Government to issue patents. In contrast to many inventions, pharmaceutical products typically do not have a simple one-to-one correspondence with patents to which they relate. Several drugs can share the same patent, and some drugs may be protected by more than one patent. Other drugs are not eligible for patents at all.

According to Federal statute, an invention is patentable only if it is new, useful, and unobvious (35 U.S.C. §§101-103). The heart of a patent application is the "claims" that the filer makes. The claims succinctly define the subject matter that the inventor regards as the novel contribution. A patent examiner compares the claim against existing public information ("prior art") in deciding whether to award the patent. The claim defines the scope of protection granted to the patent owner and is the basis for future judgments of whether the patent has been infringed (11).

For most newly discovered pharmaceutical chemical entities, a patent applicant can make four types of claims:

- A *compound claim* covers the chemical entity, per se, including any and all formulations or uses of the chemical entity.
- A *composition claim* covers a chemical entity formulated for use as a pharmaceutical. These claims sometimes specify a particular dosage form (e.g., oral tablet, injectable drug) or carrier[2] although they rarely are limited to a particular carrier, dosage form or treatment of a particular ailment.
- A *method-of-use claim* covers the use of a chemical compound or composition in a specified way. For example, the applicant may claim compound X as an antibiotic when administered in an effective dose against bacterium Z.
- A *process claim*, or *method of manufacture claim*, covers the way in which a compound or composition is produced (124,284). These claims have been particularly important in recent years for drugs that rely on recombinant DNA (deoxyrbonucleic acid) technology, and because of

---

[1] Contrary to trade secrecy, the patent system actually contributes to the dissemination of scientific and technological advances through the publication of inventions and their details at the time the Federal Government issues their patent.

[2] A pharmaceutical carrier is usually an inert substance which allows or facilitates the active compound to be absorbed by and act upon the body (42).

a 1989 amendment to the patent laws that permits the holder of a U.S. patent to stop the importation of a product made outside the United States by the patented process (35 U.S.C. 271(g)).

Currently in the United States, all four kinds of claims are often found in a single patent. Prior to 1980, the U.S. Patent and Trademark Office (PTO)[3] usually granted three patents for the four types of claims: one for the compound claim, one for the composition and method-of-use claim and one for the method of manufacture claim. The transition to a single patent has occurred gradually over the past 10 years and reflects procedural changes within the PTO (284).

For a firm filing an application with a compound claim, there are tradeoffs in deciding how broad the claim should be. A broad claim may encompass thousands of compounds which share common structural characteristics that are thought to be responsible for providing a particular utility. However, the broader the claim, the greater the chance a patent already exists on some version of the compound, thereby defeating the novelty of the broad claim. If a patent already exists on a particular compound or composition, one can still apply for and receive a composition or method-of-use patent for a new use even though the proposed use would infringe the pre-existing patent claiming the compound. A patent, however, does not give its owner the affirmative right to make, use, or sell the claimed subject matter but rather only the right to exclude others from doing so. In granting patents the PTO is only concerned with the patentability of the claimed subject matter and has no authority to consider whether that subject matter infringes an earlier patent. Determination of whether or not an infringement has occurred and enforcement of a patent must be left to the court (124).[4]

Given the broadness with which an applicant can make a compound claim, each patent, in reality, may cover or protect multiple chemical compounds. The PTO estimates that the average pharmaceutical patent contains ten distinct chemical compounds (284). Assuming a single compound may have more than one composition or method-of-use claim, a single patent could be associated with an unspecified number of potential products. The ability to file new method-of-use claims on existing compound or composition patents (because of a newly discovered use or a new dosage form) increases the likelihood that the intellectual property protection of a single marketed drug product can rest on more than one patent (124,497).

Some drug products are not eligible for patent protection. Most of these have existed so long that all relevant patents have expired. A potential manufacturer can file a patent application for the new use of such a drug. However, the characteristics and actions of long available drugs (e.g., aspirin) may be so well known that it is difficult to establish the novelty (or lack of novelty) of a method-of-use claim. Even where a patent is obtained on a new method of use for an old drug with many shown uses, the patent may be difficult to enforce (497).

Until the 1980s, drugs discovered and developed in Federal laboratories rarely had patent protection because Federal policy dictated that they remain in the public realm. As a result of a series of legislative and policy initiatives developed during the 1980s, the Federal Government now patents drugs discovered in its laboratories and actively attempts to license them to the private sector.[5]

■ Patent Protection of Biotechnology Drugs

As discussed in chapters 5 and 6, major advances in the life sciences over the past 15 years have led to an increased number of biological drugs whose production is based on techniques of biotechnology. Biotechnology, particularly recombinant methods, allow manufacturers to produce sufficient quantities of these medicinal preparations for therapeutic use. Although the U.S. Supreme Court has held that living organisms are patentable, naturally occurring compounds and compositions themselves are not patentable because they are not considered "novel." Products that exist in nature may be considered patentable if they are given a form, quality or function they do not possess in the natural state or otherwise meet all other criteria for

---

[3] PTO is the agency within the U.S. Commerce Department charged with examining patent applications and issuing patents.

[4] If one inventor receives a patent on an improvement to another inventor's already patented invention, each inventor may find himself or herself blocked from using his or her invention by the other's patent. In such a situation, not uncommon among pharmaceuticals, the two inventors usually negotiate to cross-license their patents so both can use, produce, or sell their inventions (124).

[5] Chapter 9 describes in greater detail patent and technology transfer policies in the U.S. Department of Health and Human Services and their implications for pharmaceutical R&D.

patentability. Those who produce old drugs with the new techniques of biotechnology tend to seek patent protection for the methods by which they produce the drug; the bases for these patents are referred to as "process claims."

Because of the relative novelty of biotechnology drugs and their patent claims, they have been the subject of much legal uncertainty and dispute over the past few years. The drug recombinant erythropoietin (rEPO), which treats anemia by replacing a deficient enzyme vital to red blood cell production, is a notable example. In 1987, Amgen, Inc. and Genetics Institute each received a patent related to rEPOs. Genetics Institute received a patent on a method of purifying human EPO from natural sources (i.e., not rEPO) and applied for another patent covering the production of a recombinant form of EPO. Amgen's patent covered an intermediate product in this process. Genetics Institute also licensed its patent rights to Chugai Pharmaceuticals for the Japanese market and to a cooperative venture between Chugai and Upjohn Company for the U.S. market.

In subsequent litigation, a Federal court in Boston ruled that because Chugai produced its rEPO in Japan, it did not violate Amgen's patent; the court found that Amgen's protection of an intermediate product in the manufacture of rEPO did not cover production in another country. However, the judge did find that Amgen and Genetics Institute had each violated parts of the other's patent. In 1990, the court ordered these two firms to cross-license each other's patents without royalties (451). In March 1991, however, the Court of Appeals for the Federal Circuit reversed this decision, upheld Amgen's patent, ruled that Genetics Institute had infringed on Amgen's patent, and barred Genetics Institute from marketing rEPO in the United States (12,452).[6] This action ensured only Amgen's version

of rEPO would be available in the United States for the duration of its patent protection.[7]

■ Length of Patent Protection

Although the Federal patent statute provides for 17 years of exclusive rights to an invention, the actual amount of time a drug manufacturer is usually able to market its drug without competition is substantially less. Because firms usually seek patent protection once a potential drug compound is identified (284), a large portion of the patent period can be taken up by the sponsor's research and development (R&D) activities and the U.S. Food and Drug Administration's review of the marketing application (507). In 1984, Congress passed the Drug Price Competition and Patent Term Restoration (DPCPTR) Act (Public Law 98-417), which allowed PTO to add up to five years to the patent term of drugs when the patent term was eroded by regulatory review.[8] As of May 1992, the PTO had issued 142 patent extensions most often for a period of 2 years beyond the statutory 17-year exclusivity (497).

From time to time Congress has passed special legislation granting additional patent extensions for individual drugs.[9] In 1992 Congress considered, but did not enact, a bill granting patent extensions for Upjohn's nonsteroidal anti-inflammatory drug flurbiprofen (Ansaid™) (S. 102-1165) and U.S. Bioscience's antiradiation drug ethiofos or amifostine (Ethyol™) (S. 102-526). The PTO had already issued a certificate of patent term extension for 2 years though February 1993 under the DPCPTR Act on the patent for which Upjohn seeks a further extension, but the company claims that unwarranted delays by FDA in the approval of its drug justify a further 4+ years. U.S. Bioscience seeks a 10-year extension for ethiofos because of its claim that the U.S. Army prevented the drug's timely development for the potential treatment of persons with human immunodeficiency virus and cancer (439).

---

[6] Amgen received U.S Food and Drug Administration approval to market its rEPO for the treatment of anemia among patients with end-stage renal disease in June 1989.

[7] In another suit brought by Amgen, the U.S. International Trade Commission ruled that it lacked jurisdiction and sent the case to the Federal Circuit Court of Appeals which ruled in 1990 that Amgen's patent did cover a process for producing rEPO (13).

[8] This legislation represented a compromise that also allowed easier FDA approval for generic drugs after patent expiration. The law also allows two types of exclusivity not related to patent status--a 5-year exclusivity for new chemical entities not eligible for a patent and a 3-year exclusivity for new uses of approved chemical entities. This appendix discusses the 3-year exclusivity in greater detail in the following section.

[9] For example, in 1983, as part of the Federal Anti-Tempering Act (Public Law 98-127), Congress extended two patent terms covering an anesthetic drug to compensate for a delay in marketing approval while the firm conducted research at the request of the FDA that Congress deemed unnecessary (497). In another case, Congress granted a patent term extension for the drug gemfibrozil to Warner-Lambert Company after it was shown to have a new use in combating high cholesterol (Public Law 100-418).

■ Patents and "Follow-On" Products

Once relevant patents protecting the exclusive marketing rights of a drug expire, the manufacturer of the original form of the drug often seeks to maintain its market share by developing new, but related products. These new products may include previously unmarketed dose forms of the drug such as one that might require less frequent or easier administration. Once on the market, physicians and patients may prefer such a dose form over generic versions of the old dose form. Alternatively, the originator firm may develop a new (and patentable) drug product that is chemically related to the first but offers some clinical superiority. For example, the new drug may have fewer adverse reactions than the first generation product that is losing its patent protection. Although all companies theoretically may attempt to develop "follow-on" products to drugs losing patent protection, Federal law may offer the originator company an advantage in developing them more quickly. In a series of legal decisions, the Federal courts have determined that researchers may use patented materials and processes for noncommercial scientific inquiry, but that any research related to a possible commercial product constitutes a patent infringement. Hence, the originator may conduct R&D activities on follow-on products, while all other competitors must wait until any relevant patents expire before beginning to develop their own (452).

Furthermore, the DPCPTR Act (Public Law 98-417) contains a provision that may reinforce the advantage originator firms have in getting "follow-on" products to market. The law provides for 3 years of market exclusivity for companies receiving approval of an new drug application (NDA) that is not for a new chemical entity, or of a supplemental NDA for a new use of an already approved drug.[10] To be eligible, the new or supplemental NDA must be based on new clinical research (other than bioavailability studies) conducted or paid for by the drug's sponsor and essential to FDA approval (83).

---

[10] The law also allows for a 5-year market exclusivity for new chemical entities not otherwise guaranteed a period of market exclusivity through patent protection of their active ingredients (83).

Appendix F

Summary of Methods Used to Analyze Trends in Postpatent Revenues

The Office of Technology Assessment (OTA) contracted with Dr. Stephen Schondelmeyer to report on trends in sales revenue and unit sales volume for molecular compounds that lost patent exclusivity during the 4-year interval 1984-87 (368). The period 1984-87 was chosen because the Drug Price Competition and Patent Term Restoration Act of 1984 (Public Law 98-417) significantly reduced the barriers to market entry for generic manufacturers by allowing the U.S. Food and Drug Administration (FDA) to expedite the approval process for generic versions of drugs already proved safe and effective. Data were provided on sales of the sampled compounds from 1980 to 1990.

Dr. Schondelmeyers report to OTA is based on data from the IMS America, Inc. MIDAS system using the United States Drugstore and United States Hospital database. That database does not include sales made directly to mail-order distributors, health maintenance organizations, or Federal Government health purchasers (such as the U.S. Department of Veterans Affairs and the military.) In 1986, IMS America claimed the database reflected 98 percent of ethical pharmaceutical sales in the United States (368), but this share may be declining as mail-order pharmacies become more important.

■ Sample Selection

OTA supplied the contractor with a list of 83 pharmaceutical compounds which came off patent in the period 1984-87. This list was compiled from sources that included the FDA (262), trade publications and market research surveys. Products approved for over-the-counter sale during the period of study were excluded from the sample. Combination products were also excluded, except for two (methyldopa with hydrochlorothiazide and triamcinolone acetonide with nystatin).[1]

Drug products that would not be marketed in significant quantity through community-based pharmacies were also removed from the sample.[2] These included injectable, infusible, and diagnostic drug products. Injectible and infusible drugs make up a negligible part of the outpatient market but a larger proportion of the hospital market. Informal discussions with hospital pharmacists in a large voluntary hospital chain suggest injectible and infusible drugs constitute approximately 60 percent of dollar purchases of inpatient drugs.

After eliminating products not meeting the criteria for inclusion, 45 products were in the sample. The drugs on OTA's list also were compared with a drugstore database held by Purdue University (based on IMS data), and compounds with no recorded sales in any of the study years were eliminated. After this round, 41 drugs remained in the sample (see table F-1).

Further analysis of the IMS data showed some products with substantial generic sales in years prior to the assumed patent expiration date. We contacted the company marketing the brand-name product and also referred to a summary of patent issue dates produced in 1988 by the Pharmaceutical Manufacturers Associations (PMA) (322). Four products were removed from the list when the true patent expiration year was found to be earlier than the year obtained from the FDA. (These compounds are listed with a footnote in table F-1.) Two additional drugs (enflurane and dimethyl sulfoxide) met the selection criteria as noninjectable, noncombination drug products but were dropped from

---

[1] For these two products, only the combination products with specific ingredients identified were included.

[2] At the time the sample of drugs was selected, the contractor believed that data available from IMS included only drugstore sales. IMS America ultimately provided the contractor with sales data for both drug stores and hospitals.

the analysis, because they are used almost exclusively in hospitals. Enflurane is a general anesthetic and dimethyl sulfoxide is a urinary tract diagnostic aid. Table F-1 shows the final list of 35 products included in OTA's analysis.

The patent issue dates compiled by the PMA also revealed a number of discrepancies with the FDA patent expiration dates. Only 13 of the 35 drugs showed no discrepancy between the FDA and PMA sources. Of the remaining 22 compounds, 18 had PMA patent expiration dates that were earlier than the FDA patent expiration date. Choosing a later patent expiration date makes the rate of decline of originator revenues immediately following expiration look higher. Therefore, to be conservative, OTA took the FDA date in these 18 cases.

In the remaining four cases, the earliest PMA patent expiration date was either the same or earlier than the FDA date, but the PMA source showed a second patent that expired after the FDA year. (The earliest patent typically covers the compound, while subsequent patents often involve process or uses.) There were no generic sales in the study years following the FDA patent expiration date for two of the four drugs. OTA chose the FDA patent expiration date as the year of patent expiration in all of these four cases.

■ Data Analysis

The contractor provided OTA with a report containing unit and dollar sales for each compound in the sample. Because a drug may be produced in different strengths, dosage forms and package sizes, the contractor constructed a standardized measure of unit sales (368). This measure of sales volume, the defined daily dose (DDD), is based on the typical daily dose of a given drug product for an adult patient being treated for the drug's primary indication.

Dollar and unit sales data were compiled for the compound as a whole across all its dosage forms and strengths. We selected this orientation to examining generic competition because the returns to R&D depend on the entire history of the compound, including the exclusive opportunity to develop new dosage forms before the patents on the original compound expire.[3] Such product extensions bring with them 3 additional years of exclusive marketing rights from the FDA.[4]

Table F-1—Noninfusible Noninjectable New Chemical Entities Losing Patent Protection, 1984-87

Drug entity	Year of patent expiration
acetohexamide	1984
amiloride	1984
baclofen	1986
beclomethasone	1984
carbamazepine	1986
cefadroxil	1987
cephalexin	1987
cephradine	1986
clindamycin	1987
clonidine	1986
clorazepate	1987
danazol	1984
desipramine	1986
diazepam	1985
dimethyl sulfoxide[a]	1987
disopyramide	1985
doxepin	1986
enflurane[a]	1986
fluocinonide[b]	1986
flurazepam	1985
haloperidol	1986
lactulose	1986
lorazepam	1985
maprotiline	1986
meclofenamic acid	1985
mesoridazine	1985
methyldopa	1985
methyldopa hctz	1984
metoclopramide	1985
molindone	1987
oxazepam	1984
perphenazine	1986
propranolol	1985
sucralfate	1986
temazepam	1985
thiothixene	1984
tolazamide[b]	1985
trazodone	1985
triamcinolone[b]	
trifluoperazine[b]	1985
verapamil	1986

[a] Passed selection criteria as noninfusible, noninjectable, noncombination drug products, but not typically used in an outpatient setting; removed from analysis.

[b] Patent expiration year found to be earlier than year obtained from the FDA; removed from analysis.

SOURCE: Office of Technology Assessment, 1993, based on S.W. Schondelmeyer, "Economic Impact of Multiple Source Competition on Originator Products," contract paper prepared for Office of Technology Assessment, U.S. Congress, December 1991.

---

[3] Under this approach, the costs of R&D required to put the extended product on the market must also be included in an analysis of the returns to R&D. OTA included an estimate of such costs in its analysis of returns to R&D.

[4] The additional years of effective patent life obtained from new dosage forms were not reflected in OTA's estimate of effective patent life. That estimate is based on the effective patent life for the original compound.

Sales were reported to OTA in current dollars, but OTA converted them to constant 1990 dollars using the GNP implicit price deflator. OTA had 11 years of data which allowed examination of sales over a 14-year period relative to the year of patent expiration. Data on each compound were aligned according to the year of patent expiration. For example, sales in the first year after patent expiration for compounds whose patents expired in 1984 were those reported in 1985, whereas sales in the first year after patent expiration for compounds whose patents expired in 1987 were those reported in 1988. Thus, 1988 inflation-adjusted sales for the 1987 drugs were combined with 1985 inflation-adjusted sales of the 1984 drugs to obtain inflation-adjusted sales 1 year after patent expiration for the entire sample.

Data for the entire sample of 35 drugs were available from 4 years prior to patent expiration to 3 years after expiration. For earlier and later years, data were available for only a part of the sample. For example, data on dollar and unit sales in the sixth year after patent expiration were available for only eight drugs: those whose patents expired in 1984. The 6-year postpatent estimate is based on 1990 sales and volume data for these eight drugs. Also, 7 of the 35 drugs received FDA marketing approval after 1980. A drug was included in each year's analysis only when the product was marketed for the complete year.

∎ Summary of Results

Table F-2 shows the mean sales revenue (in constant 1990 dollars), and unit sales of originator products in each year relative to the year of patent expiration (year

Table F-2—Originator Sales of Compounds Losing Patent Protection, 1984-87

Year relative to patent expiration[a]	Sample size	Revenue per drug[b] (standard deviation)	Unit volume per drug[c] (standard deviation)
−7	5	$63,051 (79,645)	44,435 (45,950)
−6	14	41,887 (52,518)	60,346 (61,989)
−5	22	63,110 (86,663)	129,691 (195,887)
−4	32	60,258 (78,034)	118,697 (166,164)
−3	34	62,246 (77,934)	115,621 (156,440)
−2	35	68,194 (83,229)	115,823 (152,824)
−1	35	77,661 (91,620)	115,710 (143,258)
0	35	79,657 (84,010)	108,791 (126,585)
+1	35	69,810 (61,392)	90,513 (95,021)
+2	35	67,239 (66,448)	83,098 (98,475)
+3	35	66,012 (79,686)	73,771 (100,104)
+4	30	63,570 (94,340)	71,105 (108,036)
+5	18	50,832 (52,217)	49,181 (48,448)
+6	8	40,588 (59,995)	38,023 (51,406)

[a] Year 0 is the year of patent expiration.
[b] Measured in thousands, constant 1990 dollars.
[c] Measured in defined daily dose, in thousands. See text for explanation.

SOURCE: Office of Technology Assessment, 1993, based on S.W. Schondelmeyer, "Economic Impact of Multiple Source Competition on Originator Products," contract paper prepared for Office of Technology Assessment, U.S. Congress, December 1991.

0). Note that in the early and late years, only a subsample of drugs is included in the estimates. Year-to-year changes in revenues, shown later in this appendix, were calculated only for drugs for which data were available in both years.

The originator brand's market share in each year relative to the year of patent expiration is shown in table F-3. Originator products maintained almost 85 percent of the total market share (in dollars) as long as 6 years after patent expiration, but the originator product's market share in unit volume declined to 50 percent within 4 years of patent loss.

OTA examined changes in originators' dollar and unit sales over the years immediately preceding and following the year of patient expiration (figures F-1 and F-2.) Average year-to-year changes in revenues and unit sales were calculated only for drugs for which data were available in both years. Between the second year prior to patent expiration and the third year after patent expiration, all 35 drugs were in the sample. In contrast, only eight drugs were used to calculate the

Table F-3—Originator's Market Share

Year[a]	Dollar Sales	Unit Sales[b]
−7	100%	100%
−6	99	100
−5	99	100
−4	99	100
−3	99	100
−2	99	100
−1	99	100
0	95	94
+1	86	73
+2	84	65
+3	84	57
+4	85	51
+5	83	44
+6	85	62

[a] Year 0 is the year of patent expiration.
[b] Unit sales are measured in defined daily dose.

SOURCE: Office of Technology Assessment, 1993, based on S.W. Schondelmeyer, "Economic Impact of Multiple Source Competition on Originator Products," contract paper prepared for Office of Technology Assessment, U.S. Congress, December 1991.

Figure F-1—Originator Dollar Sales as Percent of Originator Dollar Sales[a] in Year of Patent Expiration for Drugs Losing Patent Protection, 1984-87

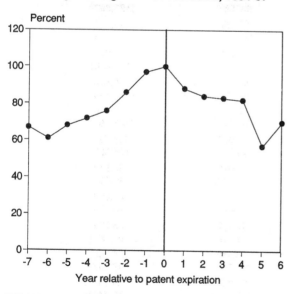

KEY: Year 0 is year of patent expiration.

[a] Based on 1990 dollars.

SOURCE: Office of Technology Assessment, 1993, based on S.W. Schondelmeyer, 'Economic Impact of Multiple Source Competition on Originator Products,' contract paper prepared for Office of Technology Assessment, December 1991.

Figure F-2—Originator Unit Sales as Percent of Originator Unit Sales in Year of Patent Expiration for Drugs Losing Patent Protection, 1984-87

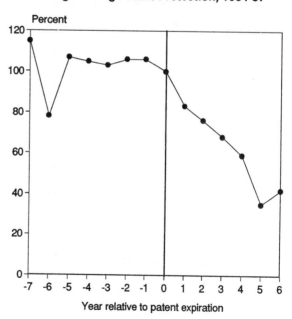

KEY: Year 0 is year of patent expiration.

SOURCE: Office of Technology Assessment, 1993, based on S.W. Schondelmeyer, 'Economic Impact of Multiple Source Competition on Originator Products,' contract paper prepared for Office of Technology Assessment, December 1991.

average percentage sales loss between the fifth and sixth year after patent loss.

The sharp decline experienced in year +5 revenue, as shown in figure F-2, is due primarily to the loss of data on verapamil, which came off-patent in 1986 and had 1990 revenue approaching $500 million. The originator market for verapamil actually grew after patent expiration because of the introduction by its manufacturer of a new sustained release dosage form shortly before its patent expired. Its loss to the sample in years 5 and 6 accounts for the substantial recorded decline in originator revenues in the figure.

Data on the history of revenues and unit sales volume for drugs coming off patent in each of the study years are presented in figures F-3 and F-4. Substantial differences were recorded in the pattern of revenue and unit volume loss across these subsamples, although originator sales and unit volume declined in all but one cohort of drugs. The sales volume for the 1986 cohort actually increased after patent loss. This was primarily due to verapamil's product line extension.

Figure F-3—Originator Dollar Sales for Drugs Losing Protection, 1984-87

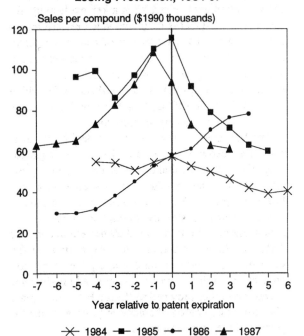

KEY: Year 0 is year of patent expiration.

SOURCE: Office of Technology Assessment, 1993, based on S.W. Schondelmeyer, 'Economic Impact of Multiple Source Competition on Originator Products,' contract paper prepared for Office of Technology Assessment, December 1991.

Figure F-4—Originator Unit Sales[a] for Drugs Losing Protection, 1984-87 ($ 1990)

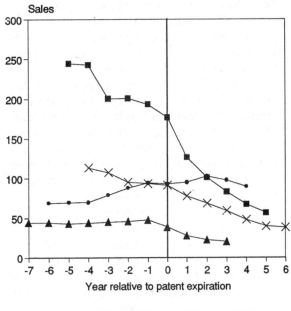

KEY: Year 0 is year of patent expiration.

[a] Unit sales are measured in defined daily dose.

SOURCE: Office of Technology Assessment, 1993, based on S.W. Schondelmeyer, 'Economic Impact of Multiple Source Competition on Originator Products,' contract paper prepared for Office of Technology Assessment, December 1991.

Some reviewers of OTA's draft report argued verapamil is an unusual case, both because it had a new sustained release form and because the indications for the drug were expanding over the period. Consequently, these reviewers believed OTA should remove verapamil from the sample of drugs.

The presence of verapamil in the sample of drugs does, indeed, have a large impact on the estimated rate of decline in originator sales following patent expiration. Verapamil had the highest inflation-adjusted dollar sales of all drugs in the sample by the third year after patent expiration, and its sales revenue in constant dollars grew over the period.

That there is wide variation among different compounds in their sales history and product life cycle is undisputed. In that sense, every drug is unusual. Manufacturers do depend on a few "big winners" to carry the fixed costs of R&D and marketing necessary to develop and sell drugs in today's market (159). OTA's analysis is at the industry level, however, and an accurate representation of the pattern of loss of revenues after patent expiration would be impossible if the big winners were excluded from the analysis. (The industry would appear to be losing great sums if the high selling drugs were removed.)

The practice of managing patent life by timing the introduction of new dosage forms is becoming more common, not less common, in recent years, as new drug delivery systems have become available. At least 4 of the 35 drugs in the sample had product line extensions that lengthened their exclusive marketing rights beyond the year in which the patent governing the compound itself expired. The extraordinary sales growth of verapamil's originator brand after its patent expired would probably have been substantially dampened without the extended release form.

One reviewer of OTA's draft report pointed out that one compound, chlorpropamide, whose patent expired in 1985 and whose 1985 inflation-adjusted sales were higher than all but four of the drugs in the sample, was not included in OTA's ultimate sample, even though it meets the inclusion criteria. Upon re-reviewing the selection process OTA discovered this drug had been eliminated from the sample because preliminary analysis of Purdue University's database had indicated many generic companies were manufacturing the product as early as 1981. This finding had suggested to us that the patent was not effectively barring generic competition and we therefore excluded it from the sample. As part of the re-review of this issue, we obtained rough estimates of sales of the originator's brand-name product, Diabenese™, and generic copies, which showed the generic sales in 1985 of chlorpropamide, were very small. Therefore, excluding Diabenese from the sample was probably a mistake.

Although OTA does not have access to the full history of sales of Diabenese and its generic competitors, we did obtain an estimate of its sales in 1985 and 1991. We assumed sales would decline at a constant percentage rate between 1985 and 1991. Using the resulting sales estimates for Diabenese, we recalculated the rate of decline in originators' revenues in the years after patent expiration. Table F-4 shows that the year-to-year decline in revenues after patents expire changes very little when Diabenese is included. Because OTA did not have access to the actual sales data for all years of the study, we did not recalculate any of the other tables presented in this appendix, but we did use the revised estimates of dollar sales declines in the analysis of returns on R&D.

Table F-4—Decline in Originator Dollar Sales With and Without Diabenese™ in Sample

Year relative to patent expiration[a]	Rate of change excluding Diabenese (percent)	Rate of change including Diabenese (percent)
0 to +1	−12.0%	−12.9%
+1 to +2	−4.0	−4.6
+2 to +3	−2.0	−2.7
+3 to +4	−5.0	−5.5
+4 to +5	−5.0	−5.3
+5 to +6	+3.0	+3.4

[a] Year 0 is the year of patent expiration.

SOURCE: Office of Technology Assessment, 1993.

The relatively slow postpatent decline in dollar sales of originator brands is surprising to many observers of the industry, because the impact of generic competition on the sales of some drugs and on the companies that manufacture them can be severe. OTA's analysis begins with the point at which the patent governing manufacture of the compound in its original form expires, not the point at which generic products enter the market. The entry of generics can be delayed by: 1) FDA's subsequent award of market exclusivity for follow-on products (as in the extended release example); 2) delays in FDA approval of generic copies of brand-name drugs; or 3) technical or market factors that discourage generic companies from entering the market at all. Drugs with small markets, or for which bioequivalence is difficult to achieve or demonstrate, may never have a generic competitor.

Another factor slowing down the decline in revenues is a steep increase in the price of the originator drug after patent expiration. OTA developed a price index for originator products using average sales per DDD as a proxy. The average price of the originator product increased steadily throughout most of the period (figure F-5). It increased 69 percent in constant dollars in the 6 years after patent expiration. At the same time, the ratio of the average price of generic products to originator products decreased rapidly over the course of the study period (figure F-6). Four years after patent expiration, the generic price was just 20 percent of the originator price.

Manufacturers continue to increase the real price of their drugs as their share of the market in unit volume falls. The real price increases dampen the rapid decline in unit sales that follows generic competition. Even with a very large price discrepancy between generic

**Figure F-5—Price Index for Originator Drugs[a]
($ 1990)**

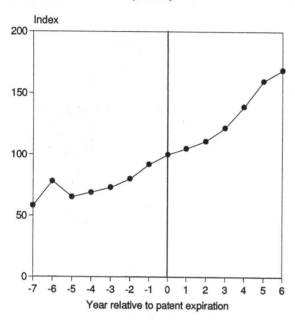

KEY: DDD = defined daily dose; Year 0 is year of patent expiration.

[a] Price is measured as average revenue (revenue/DDD).

SOURCE: Office of Technology Assessment, 1993, based on S.W. Schondelmeyer, 'Economic Impact of Multiple Source Competition on Originator Products,' contract paper prepared for Office of Technology Assessment, December 1991.

Figure F-6—Non-originator Price as a Percent of Originator Price[a] ($ 1990)

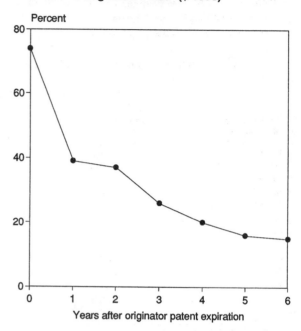

[a] Average revenue ($ Sales/DDD), of nonoriginator drugs divided by average revenue of originator drugs.

SOURCE: Office of Technology Assessment, 1993, based on S.W. Schondelmeyer, 'Economic Impact of Multiple Source Competition on Originator Products,' contract paper prepared for Office of Technology Assessment, December 1991.

product prices and the originator price, however, the originator product still maintains roughly a 40-percent market share in physical units 5 years after the patent expires.

■ OTA Estimate of Decline in Originator Sales Revenue

The data shown in figure F-1 are the backbone of the estimate of the year-to-year rate of decline in dollar sales to both hospitals and drugstores after patent expiration. Because the sample of drugs did not include injectible and infusible products, however, the rate must be adjusted for the probable impact of these hospital products on the rate of loss of sales.

Generic substitution is much more common in hospitals, where strong formularies and centralized pharmacies can control prescribing and dispensing more thoroughly, and where the incentives are strong to purchase the least expensive version of a drug for hospitalized patients.

OTA estimates about 60 percent of dollar sales to hospitals are for injectible and infusible products. About 23 percent of all ethical pharmaceutical sales are to hospitals, which would imply that about 14 percent of sales overall are for these products. But a proportion of sales to hospitals are made through hospitals' outpatient pharmacies, which have no incentives to encourage doctors to prescribe generics, so 14 percent is an overestimate of the size of the injectible-infusible market.[5] Nevertheless, OTA assumed 14 percent of total sales are for these hospital products. OTA also assumed that dollar sales of these products to hospitals

---

[5] About 2.4 percent of the market is made up of staff-model health maintenance organizations (HMO), which probably switch to generics much faster than the general community pharmacy market once generics are available. The overestimate of the injectible and infusible market compensates to an unknown degree for the failure of the IMS data to account for sales to these kinds of HMOs.

would decline at 50 percent per year from the year in which the patent expires. Table F-5 shows the resulting estimates of year-to-year changes in sales relative to the year of patent expiration. The year-to-year rates of change in the fourth column of table F-4 were used in

OTA's analysis of the returns to R&D for the 1981-83 introductions of new chemical entities outlined in chapter 4.

Table F-5—Change in Originator Brand Revenues for Drugs Losing Patent Protection, 1984-87

Year relative to patent expiration[a]	Rate of change excluding injectable and infusible drugs[b] (percent)	Rate of change in injectable and infusible drugs[c] (percent)	Blended rate of change[d] (percent)	Rate of change in OTA's analysis[e] (percent)
–7 to –6	1.7%	1.7%	1.7%	1.7%
–6 to –5	4.0	4.0	4.0	4.0
–5 to –4	6.6	6.6	6.6	6.6
–4 to –3	8.2	85.2	8.2	8.2
–3 to –2	12.7	12.7	12.7	12.7
–2 to –1	13.9	13.9	13.9	13.9
–1 to 0	2.6	2.6	2.6	2.6
0 to +1	–12.9	–50.0	–18.1	–18.0
+1 to +2	–4.6	–50.0	–8.5	–8.5
+2 to +3	–2.7	–50.0	–4.9	–6.0
+3 to +4	–5.5	–50.0	–6.6	–6.0
+4 to +5	–5.3	–50.0	–5.9	–5.0
+5 to +6	+3.4	–50.0	+3.1	–5.0

[a] Year 0 is the year of patent expiration.
[b] Rates based on figure F-5 and sources therein.
[c] OTA assumed the rate of growth would be the same as with other drugs until the year of patent expiration, when revenues would decline by 50 percent per year.
[d] Injectable and infusible drugs were assumed to make up 14 percent of the market in year 0.
[e] See chapter 4 for OTA's analysis of returns from R&D on drugs first introduced to the U.S. market in 1981-83.
SOURCE: Office of Technology Assessment, 1993.

Appendix G

Estimating the Cost of Producing and Selling New Chemical Entities

T o estimate the net returns on new chemical entities (NCEs) introduced in the period 1981-83, the cost of manufacturing, marketing and distribution in each year following market approval must be subtracted from net revenues. Precise estimation of such costs is impossible from published financial statements because companies produce a variety of products but report costs on a consolidated basis across all operations.[1] The Office of Technology Assessment (OTA) made assumptions about the costs of manufacture, distribution and marketing based on a variety of sources of data, including a review of the annual reports of six research-intensive U.S.-owned pharmaceutical firms,[2] as detailed below.

■ Manufacturing and Distribution Costs

The reported annual cost of goods sold for the six companies was used as an approximate estimate of the manufacturing and distribution costs of pharmaceuticals. The sales-weighted average ratio of cost of goods sold to total company sales for the sample of firms was 0.255. These costs include charges for depreciation on facilities and equipment used to produce, store, and distribute the firm's products. OTA estimated the cash outlays for construction of facilities and equipment separately; consequently the estimated depreciation charges associated with the cash outlays were deducted from the cost of goods sold. (The estimated construction costs of $25 million per NCE, for example, were assumed to generate depreciation charges over an average 20-year time horizon. Thus, $1.25 million per

year was deducted from the cost of goods sold in each of the 20 years of the product's life.)

■ Plant and Equipment Costs

Firms make investments in plant and equipment early in the product life cycle, typically before the drug receives approval for marketing. Additional investments may be necessary as time goes on, especially if the drug is one that has a high unit volume. OTA had little specific information to go on to estimate average expenditures for plant and equipment across all drugs. Such investments may vary systematically among types of drugs, especially between biologicals and synthetic chemicals.

One difference between traditional synthetic compounds and biotechnology and other biological drugs is the ease with which ''campaign'' product manufacturing can be undertaken. Product campaigning refers to the scheduling of production runs of different products on the same equipment and using the same facility. Campaign production generally reduces fixed facility costs because it allows different products to share the same facility and equipment and reduces down time of equipment. Costs are incurred in preparing the facility and equipment for new production runs, but the overall manufacturing process is generally cheaper when dedicated facilities do not have to be built.

The cost of sharing plant and equipment among different biotechnology drugs is much higher because of the more stringent U.S. Food and Drug Administration (FDA) requirements governing the manufacture of biological products. Although the FDA regulates the

---

[1] Companies themselves often have difficulty estimating the cost of producing and selling specific products or services (216). New methods for assigning costs to different products have been proposed but are not fully diffused into company practice (92,93,94,95).

[2] The six firms are Marion Merrell Dow (1989-90), Merck (1988-90), Schering-Plough (1989-91), Syntex (1989-91), Upjohn (1988-90), and Eli Lilly (1987-89).

manufacture of all kinds of pharmaceuticals, the requirements for facilities that manufacture biological products are more stringent (41). The potential for contamination is greater with biological products than with synthetic compounds, and containment areas may be necessary. Although the FDA does not prohibit biotechnology firms from manufacturing more than one product in a facility, many companies elect to build a dedicated facility to manufacture biotechnology products because of the stringent requirements (186). One biotechnology executive recently submitted a statement in congressional hearings that a dedicated bulk biopharmaceutical facility would cost approximately $25 million (31).

The drugs approved in the period 1981-83 included only a very few biotechnology drugs, so the special manufacturing problems with these products were not present. Anecdotal evidence about costs of building production facilities for two drugs, atenolol (Tenormin™) and loracarbef (Lorabid™) provides some information on synthetic chemicals. A recent bulk pharmaceutical plant for Tenormin™, an antihypertension drug, cost $60 million to construct (382). Tenormin had 1990 world sales of approximately $1.2 billion and was the fifth highest selling drug worldwide in 1991 (385). Eli Lilly and Company announced a $65-million plant to manufacture Lorabid (383). Although Lorabid™ was approved in December 1991 and launched in 1992, Kidder Peabody analysts forecast annual sales of at least $500 million for this antibiotic (384), which would place Lorabid™ near the top 25 selling drugs in 1991 (385).

These high-volume drugs can be expected to have higher capital expenditures for manufacturing plant and equipment. OTA estimates the mean worldwide sales of the drugs approved between 1981-83 in the fifth year after product launch were $170 million (in 1990 dollars). The few big winners are accompanied by many drugs with low sales. For example, if 1 out of 10 drugs is large enough to require $60-million manufacturing facilities, and the other 9 out of 10 drugs require $20-million manufacturing facilities, the average capital expenditure would be under $25 million.

OTA took the above information as a basis for estimating the costs of constructing plant and equipment to manufacture 1981-83 drugs. We assumed such facilities would cost $25 million, expended equally over a 3-year period beginning 2 years before market launch and ending in the year of market launch

approval. Because of the uncertainty associated with this estimate we examined the impact on the estimated returns on R&D of an average expenditure for plant and equipment of $35 million. (The results are presented in chapter 4.)

OTA's analysis of returns on R&D also included expenditures for capital facilities in other forms. The administrative and marketing cost estimates include charges for depreciation on facilities used in these functions. In addition, the cost of sales includes any charges for depreciation on manufacturing facilities in excess of the depreciation that would be charged for the $25-million facility. Also, manufacturers of drugs in finished form often buy their bulk chemicals from fine chemical producers. The cost of these materials to the pharmaceutical companies is included in pharmaceutical companies' financial statements as operating costs of goods sold. Thus, the estimate of cost of goods sold contains an implicit rental charge for the value of the manufacturing facilities used to produce bulk chemicals purchased from other producers. Therefore, if the capital expenditures on plant and equipment were in reality higher than $25 million, the extra costs would be at least partially captured in residual depreciation charges and cost of materials embedded in the cost-of-sales estimates.

▍Administrative Costs

Administrative costs are typically reported together with marketing costs in companies' annual financial statements. The marketing and administrative cost for the six firms was 33.6 percent of total sales in the years examined. One firm (Eli Lilly) reported over a 3-year period that 67 percent of marketing and administrative costs were for marketing. If this one firm is representative of the industry, administrative costs would be 11.1 percent of total sales. OTA used this estimate of administrative costs and assumed the percent would not vary over the life of the product. (A producer of generic drug products, Barr Laboratories, reported its annual general and administrative costs at 7.5 to 10.1 percent of sales in the period 1989-91.)

▍Marketing Costs

Marketing costs comprise promotion (advertising and detailing), sponsorship of symposia and other promotional events, and support functions such as market research. Between 1987 and 1990, in the six companies surveyed by OTA, 33.6 percent of sales were devoted to marketing and administrative costs. If Eli Lilly's cost structure is typical of the research-intensive industry, then 22.5 percent of pharmaceutical companies' total sales are devoted to marketing.

Another way of examining the ratio is to begin with advertising expenses, which are reported by companies, and estimate the ratio of advertising to other marketing expenses from published sources. Baber and Kang reported the average ratio of advertising to total sales for 88 pharmaceutical companies was 6.9 percent between 1975 and 1987, and the ratio for 54 research-intensive pharmaceutical companies was 4.5 percent (26).[3] Among the six U.S.-owned companies examined by OTA the ratio of advertising to sales averaged 4.3 percent in 1989 and 1990. In 1989, advertising comprised 26 percent and detailing activities comprised 74 percent of total promotional expenses for ethical pharmaceuticals (73). These facts together imply total promotional expenditures comprise between roughly 17 and 26 percent of sales.

OTA assumed 22.5 percent of pharmaceutical companies' total sales are devoted to marketing. These expenditures vary over the life of a product, however, and can be expected to be high in the early years of marketing and relatively low after a product loses patent protection. Caves, Whinston and Hurwitz reported on originator brand promotion expenses in the year of patent expiration for a sample of 21 drugs that lost patent protection between 1982 and 1987. Promotion comprised 6.5 percent of total sales in the year of expiration (73). OTA therefore assumed marketing expenses would be 6.5 percent of sales in the years subsequent to patent expiration.

OTA assumed marketing expenses in the first year after product approval would be equal to total worldwide sales; in the second year, they would be equal to 50 percent of worldwide sales (159). In the 3rd to 9th year (when patents expire), OTA assumed marketing costs would be equal to the percent that equates total marketing costs over the product life cycle to 22.5 percent of total sales over the life cycle. This calculated percent was 40.6.

Inventory Costs and Working Capital

The cost of producing inventory was calculated by assuming the company would build up inventory in each year equal to 12.7 percent of sales in the year (the average ratio of inventory to sales in the six U.S.-owned companies examined by OTA). If inventories are valued at the cost of goods sold, this percent is equivalent to 4.8 months of sales held in inventory. As sales decline at the end of the product life cycle, inventories decline accordingly. Working capital to finance accounts receivable was also charged against revenues. Accounts receivable comprised 17.2 percent of sales in the six pharmaceutical firms. This amount was used to estimate the working capital required in each year. As sales decline at the end of the product life cycle, accounts receivable decline as well.

Cost of Ongoing R&D

Since the revenue curve for a typical NCE is based on the total sales for the molecular compound for all indications and formulations, it is appropriate to include ongoing R&D that takes place after FDA approval and marketing to support new indications, new dosage forms, or routes of administration. Additional research may also be needed to obtain marketing approval in other countries. OTA estimated the cash outlays for ongoing R&D at $31.7 million (in 1990 dollars) per NCE over the product life cycle. This estimate was made for OTA by Dr. Joseph DiMasi from information obtained in his survey of R&D costs (109). In that study, the 14 surveyed companies reported that over the period from 1970 to 1986, research on self-originated NCEs comprised 73.7 percent of all R&D; research on licensed-in NCEs comprised 10 percent of all R&D; and existing product research totaled 16.3 percent of all R&D. OTA assumed existing product research is allocated proportionately between self-originated NCEs and licensed-in NCEs. DiMasi and colleagues also estimated the cash outlays associated with producing a self-originated NCE were $127.2 million (in 1990 dollars). Ongoing R&D costs associated with this expenditure based on these figures would be $20.7 million. Spending increased over the study period, however, and DiMasi estimated the time between spending on preapproval R&D and postapproval R&D requires an adjustment of the ongoing R&D estimate to $31.7 million (106). OTA used this estimate in its analysis of returns on new drugs.

Alternative Approach to Measuring Manufacturing and Distribution Costs

Because the estimates of production and other costs are imprecise, OTA compared the results of the above analysis with production and distribution costs calculated using an alternative method. This second method

---

[3] Pharmaceutical companies were identified as publicly traded U.S. registered companies reporting standard industrial classification (SIC) code 2834 (pharmaceuticals) as their principal line of business. Research-intensive firms were a subsample of the pharmaceutical firms whose ratio of R&D to sales was 5 percent or greater.

Table G-1—Ratio of Generic Price[a] to Originator Price by Year Relative to Patent Expiration[b] (for 30 compounds whose patents expired 1984-87)

Year relative to patent expiration	-3	-2	-1	0	+0	+2	3
Ratio	0.49	0.46	0.41	0.38	0.39	0.37	0.32

[a] Generic price is the average nonoriginator price in year 3, or in year 4 if no generic sales were recorded in year 3.
[b] Average price weighted by originator drug's physical volume as measured by defined daily dose.
SOURCE: Office of Technology Assessment, 1993, based on data from S.W. Schondelmeyer, "Economic Impact of Multiple Source Competition on Originator Products," contract paper prepared for Office of Technology Assessment, December 1991.

uses information about the price of generic drugs to infer the cost of manufacture and distribution of originator products.

As several researchers have noted, when a large number of generic suppliers have entered a market, the average price of the generic version of a drug can be taken as an upper bound on the long-run marginal cost of producing and distributing the product and providing general and administrative services in the running of the company (73,161). The pressures of price competition will, with entry of new firms, drive generic producers to charge prices that just cover the cost required to stay in business. This cost includes the required return on investment, or cost of capital. Thus, a brand-name product's markup over marginal production, distribution, and administrative cost can be roughly estimated by the difference between the brand-name price and the generic price.

The ratio of generic to originator price serves as a proxy for production, distribution, administrative, inventory, and working capital costs. It also includes the costs of facilities and equipment used to produce the product. These costs are recognized in the generic price as an effective rental or lease payment for such facilities.[4]

Generic companies also spend some funds to market their products, and they incur substantial R&D costs which also must be covered in the price they charge.[5] However, marketing and R&D costs for originator products are likely to be much higher than for generic products; consequently, the generic price does not fully cover these components of cost.

Although few if any of the compounds approved between 1981 and 1983 have faced any generic competition to date, OTA did have access to data on the sales of 35 compounds that lost patent protection in the period 1984-87 (368). For 30 of these compounds,[6] OTA calculated the ratio of the generic price obtaining in the third year after patent expiration (measured in 1990 dollars) to the originator's price in each year, from 3 years prior to patent expiration to 3 years after patent expiration.[7] Table G-1 shows the ratio of generic price (or marginal cost) to originator's price in the 7 years surrounding patent expiration for the 30 drugs in the sample. As expected, the ratio of generic price (marginal cost) to originator price declines as time passes. These results are consistent with the widely observed rise in average originator's price immediately before and after patent expiration (see appendix F) (73,161,195,368).

To compare the cost estimates from financial statements with those derived from the generic price ratios, a ratio of cost to price is required for the entire product life cycle. OTA had no data on originators' transaction prices in the first 5 years of product life for NCEs approved in the 1981-83 period. A review of published wholesale list prices for these compounds suggests that after adjusting for inflation, prices tended to rise in real terms in the first few years after introduction. (See table G-2.) The simple average annual rate of increase in price over the first 4 years of

---

[4] Although generic firms may build and own their own factories, the price they charge for the product must reflect the amount they must pay their investors for the use of the facility. This rental rate is implicit in the competitive price of the product and does not have to be explicitly estimated.

[5] Three generic companies whose annual financial statements were examined by OTA incurred R&D costs of 5 to 6 percent of sales in 1990. In addition, marketing expenses by one firm (that reported such expenses separately) amounted to 6.5 percent of sales, (36) the same as that estimated for originator firms in the year of patent expiration (73).

[6] Five of the drugs had no generic competitors in 1990, the last year of data collection.

[7] The generic price is measured by the total revenue across all generic producers of the same drug divided by the estimated volume of defined daily doses (DDDs) sold. The originator's price is total originator's revenue divided by the physical volume sold (measured in DDDs). The overall ratio of generic price to originator price in each year was calculated by weighting each drug's ratio by the volume of DDDs sold.

Table G-2—Changes in List Price of New Chemical Entities Approved Between 1981 and 1983

NCE name	U.S. trade name	Approval year	Dosage form	Rate of change in real price[b]			
				Year 1-2	Year 2-3	Year 3-4	Year 4-5
albuterol	Proventil	1981	Inhaler, 90mcgm	0.08	0.06	0.19	−0.03
alprazolam	Xanax	1981	Tab, 0.25mg, 100s	0.14	0.17	0.07	
alprostadil	Prostin VR	1981	Amp, 500mcgm/1ml, 5s	0.06	0.07		
amiloride	Midamor	1981	Tab, 5mg, 100s	−0.04	0.06	0.17	0.12
atenolol	Tenormin	1981	Tab, 50mg, 100s	0.08	0.00	0.15	
buprenorphine	Buprenex	1981	Amp, 0.3mg/1ml, 10s				
captopril	Capoten	1981	Tab, 25mg, 100s	−0.04	−0.04	0.19	0.05
cefotaxime	Claforan	1981	Via, 1gm, 10s	−0.04	−0.04	−0.17	−0.03
ceruletide	Tymtran	1981	Amp, 2ml, 5s		0.06		
estramustine	Emcyt	1981	Cap, 140mg, 100s	−0.04			
flunisolide	Nasalide	1981	Sol, 0.25%, 25ml	0.02	0.09	0.09	
gemfibrozil	Lopid	1981	Cap, 300mg, 100s		0.14	0.20	0.07
halazepam	Paxipam	1981	Tab, 20mg, 100s	0.24	0.06	0.29	−0.03
ketoconazole	Nizoral	1981	Tab, 60s				
latomoxef	Moxam	1981	Via, 1gm/10ml, 10s	−0.04	−0.04		
mezlocillin	Mezlin	1981	Via, 1gm/10ml, 10s		−0.03	−0.03	
nifedipine	Procardia	1981	Cap, 10mg, 100s		0.05	0.07	0.07
piperacillin	Pipracil	1981	Via, 2gm		−0.04	−0.03	−0.03
sucralfate	Carafate	1981	Tab, 100s		0.06	0.07	
temazepam	Restoril	1981	Cap, 15mg, 25s	0.10	0.10	0.06	
trazodone	Desyrel	1981	Tab, 50mg, 100s		0.22	0.11	
verapamil	Isoptin	1981	Tab, 80mg, 100s	−0.04			
aciclovir	Zovirax	1982	Oin, 5%, 15gm tube		0.07		
azlocillin	Azlin	1982	Via, 2gm/30ml, 10s			−0.03	
cefoperazone	Cefobid	1982	Via, 1gm				
cellulose	Calcibind	1982	Pow, 2.5gm, 90s			0.15	
ciclopirox	Loprox	1982	Cream, 1%, 15gm, tube		0.05		
diflunisal	Dolobid	1982	Tab, 250mg, 60s, uni	0.07	0.13	0.03	
diltiazem	Cardizem	1982	Tab, 30mg, 100s	−0.04	0.06	0.06	
econazole	Spectazole	1982	Cream, 1%, 15gm, tube		0.01		
etomidate	Amidate	1982	Syr, 2mg/1ml, 20gx1				
gonadorelin	Factrel	1982	Pow, 100mcgm	0.20	0.07		
guanabenz	Wytensin	1982	Tab, 4mg, 100s	0.06	0.03	0.07	
guanadrel	Hylorel	1982	Tab, 10mg, 100s		0.12	0.07	
isotretinoin	Accutane	1982	Cap, 10mg, 100s		0.07		
malathion	Prioderm	1982	Lotion, 20oz	−0.04	0.10		
niclosamide	Niclocide	1982	Tab, 500mg, 4s		0.07		
pindolol	Visken	1982	Tab, 5mg, 100s		0.22		
piroxicam	Feldene	1982	Cap, 10mg, 100s		0.08	0.09	0.09
praziquantel	Biltricide	1982	Tab, 600mg, 6s		0.07	0.07	
sodium phosphate		1982					
streptozocin	Zanosar	1982	Via, 1gm	−0.04	−0.03	0.04	
triazolam	Halcion	1982	Tab, 0.25mg, 100s		0.20	0.09	
acetohydroxamic	Lithostat	1983	Tab, 250mg, 120s				
atracurium	Tracrium	1983	Amp, 10mg/5ml, 10s				
bentriomide	Chymex	1983	Sol, 500mg, 7.5ml				
bumetanide	Bumex	1983	Amp, 0.25mg/2ml, 10s		−0.03		
ceftizoxime	Cefizox	1983	Via, 1gm/28ml, 1s				
cefuroxime	Zinacef	1983	Via, 750mg/1ml				
chenodiol	Chenix	1983	Tab, 250mg, 100s		−0.03		

(Continued on next page)

Table G-2—Changes in List Price of New Chemical Entities Approved Between 1981 and 1983—(Continued)

NCE name	U.S. trade name	Approval year	Dosage form	Rate of change in real price[b]			
				Year 1-2	Year 2-3	Year 3-4	Year 4-5
ciclosporin	Sandimmune	1983	Amp, IV, 50mg/5ml, 1s				
indapamide	Lozol	1983	Tab, 2.5mg, 100s		0.09		
netilmicin	Netromycin	1983	Syr, 150mg/1.5ml, 10s	−0.27			
ranitidine	Zantac	1983	Tab, 60s				

[a] Real prices calculated using GNP implicit price deflator; prices are retail or wholesale prices given in *Drug Topics Redbook*.
[b] Entries are blank when data are unavailable.
KEY: Amp—Ampoule; Cap—Capsule, IV—intravenous; Oin—Ointment; Pow—Powder; Sol—Solution; Syr—Syringe; Tab—Tablet; Via—Vial.
SOURCE: Office of Technology Assessment, 1993, based on data from *Drug Topics Redbook* (Montvale, NJ: Medical Economics Company, Inc., 1981-86).

product life was 5.5 percent for compounds in the sample for which list prices were available. OTA assumed this rate of increase in prices would continue throughout the first 5 years of product life, culminating in a ratio in year 6 of 0.49 (see table G-1).

For the last years of the product life cycle (4 and more years after patent expiration), OTA assumed originator prices would stabilize and the observed ratio (0.32) in the third year of patent life would hold in subsequent years.

This approach to estimating the marginal cost of the 1981-83 compounds (excluding marketing and R&D) is itself imprecise. The ratios are based on an entirely different set of drugs from the ones whose net returns are being analyzed. The approach assumes the average inflation-adjusted markup on a compound depends only on its age relative to patent expiration; drugs approved between 1981 and 1983 are assumed to have markups over cost that mirror those for drugs whose patents expired in 1984-87. Because this assumption is arbitrary, OTA did not use the method as a primary estimation procedure; rather, the cost estimates are merely intended to corroborate the estimates taken from companies' financial reports.

Table G-3 compares costs of production, distribution, and administration as a percent of sales in each year following market approval under the two methods of cost estimation. The marginal cost estimate, which represents an upper bound on actual costs, is higher than the financial statement estimates in most years. It is much higher (by up to 13 percentage points) in the early years. The marginal cost estimate includes both marketing costs for generic companies, which may be as much as 6 percent of sales, and an implicit rental cost of facilities and equipment, while the financial statement estimates given in the table do not include these costs. It also includes the cost of ongoing R&D for generic companies, which comprise approximately

5 to 6 percent of sales. If marketing and R&D costs were removed from the generic price ratio (at an assumed rate of 11 percent of sales), the resulting generic price ratio would be lower than the costs based on financial statements in almost every year. This comparison suggests cost estimates based on recent financial statements of research-intensive pharmaceutical firms do not underestimate actual costs over the product life cycle.

Table G-3—Cost of Production, Distribution, Administration, Working Capital and Inventories as Percent of Sales Under Different Estimation Methods

Number of years after approval	Financial statement estimates[a]	Generic price ratio[b] (marginal cost)
1	60.8%	62.8%
2	44.5	57.0
3	47.8	57.0
4	41.5	54.3
5	41.1	51.7
6	39.6	49.1
7	39.0	45.7
8	41.4	41.0
9	30.0	38.5
10	33.4	39.0
11	34.2	37.2
12	34.1	32.1
13	34.4	32.1
14	34.4	32.1
15	34.4	32.1
16	34.3	32.1
17	28.7	32.1
18	28.4	32.1
19	28.1	32.1
20	27.6	32.1

[a] This estimate *excludes* expenditures for capital facilities and equipment, marketing, and ongoing R&D costs.
[b] This ratio *includes* implicit costs of rental of capital facilities and equipment, ongoing R&D and marketing costs of generic producers, and return to investors.

SOURCE: Office of Technology Assessment, 1993.

Appendix H

Methods of OTA's Survey of Clinical Trial Size

The Office of Technology Assessment (OTA) conducted a survey of sponsors of new molecular entities (NMEs) that received U.S. Food and Drug Administration (FDA) marketing approval during certain years to estimate systematic changes over time in the number of participants in clinical trials conducted before new drug applications (NDA) approval.

To construct its sample, OTA began with 57 NMEs that had a first NDA approved between 1978-83 or 1986-90. OTA chose drugs approved during these periods to ensure the sample represented enough years to detect any trend in trial size while also ensuring all NMEs examined faced essentially the same regulatory guidelines. Because OTA hypothesized that there would be systematic variation in clinical trial size across product classes, OTA chose to focus on three very different therapeutic classes of drugs: antimicrobials, antihypertensives, and nonsteriodial anti-inflammatories (NSAIDs) in order to provide diversity in the analysis. (OTA analyzed data from each class separately). Before arriving at its final sample, OTA eliminated two NMEs from its sample because they were qualitatively different from other drugs in the class: one drug labeled by the FDA as an antihypertensive is not actually an antihypertensive, and another antihypertensive is actually a diagnostic agent rather than a therapeutic drug. This left a final sample consisting of 18 antihypertensives (9 for 1978-83 and 9 for 1986-90), 27 antimicrobials (15 for 1978-83 and 12 for 1986-90), and 8 NSAIDs (4 for 1978-83 and 4 for 1986-90).

OTA staff developed the survey instrument with the assistance of OTA project advisory panel members and Pharmaceutical Manufacturers Association (PMA) senior management. It contained seven questions pertaining to total clinical trial enrollment, total number of therapeutic indications for which the company sought FDA approval, the total number of clinical studies completed (both pre-and post-NDA), and the total number of trial sites. OTA asked companies to provide these numbers broken down by foreign and domestic research and by whether or not the clinical studies were completed before or after first FDA (NDA) marketing approval.

To ensure a timely response, OTA mailed identical survey packages to two contacts at the company manufacturing each drug. Each package contained a cover letter, a description of OTA's project and its advisory panel membership, a project fact sheet, a return envelope, and survey forms for each drug in the sample developed by that company. OTA made two followup calls to contacts that did not return their surveys. OTA received usable responses for all but two drugs—one antihypertensive and one NSAID (both from the 1978-83 period) for an overall response rate of 96 percent.

Appendix I

Methods Used in OTA's Study of Success Rates for New Molecular Entities

As described in the text of chapter 6, OTA used data from the U.S. Food and Drug Administration (FDA) to compare development times for two cohorts of new molecular entities (NMEs) with their first commercial investigational new drug (IND) applications submitted during two 3-year intervals: 1976-78 and 1984-86. The FDA had already compiled IND, new drug application (NDA), and final approval data on the 1976-78 cohort for their own previous analysis (426). For this analysis, the FDA updated the 1976-78 database to record approvals through July 1991. At OTA's request, the FDA compiled similar data for the 1984-86 cohort. Because the FDA's computer data systems do not link IND and NDA records for the same NME, the agency manually integrated these records.

Both cohorts exclude insulins, insecticides, sunscreens, vaccines and antitoxins from a biological source, and veterinary products from the analysis (426). For the 1984-86 cohort, the FDA added therapeutic biological entities evaluated by it's Center for Biologics Evaluation and Research (CBER). This step was not necessary for the 1976-78 cohort because the FDA did not establish CBER until 1988; prior to this date, all therapeutic drugs, no matter what their source, were reviewed by the predecessor of the FDA's Center for Drug Evaluation and Research (CDER). A total of 7 percent of the later cohort are biologics.

The FDA purged the 1984-86 cohort of INDs that did not represent a first commercial filing for the NME. Using available reference materials such as *Pharmaprojects* (328) and the *Merck Index* (267), the FDA verified each IND sponsor was a commercial firm and then checked the *Ingredient Dictionary*, the Drug Product Reference File microfiche, and its own management information system to confirm that no commercial INDs had been filed for a related compound (salt or ester) prior to the 1984-86 interval.

During the 3-year period 1976-78, commercial sponsors filed 174 first NME INDs. Of these 40 resulted in an NDA, and the FDA had approved 27 for marketing as of July 1991. During the 1984-86 period, commercial sponsors filed 344 NME INDs. By July 1991, 53 of these also resulted in an NDA, and 27 had received FDA marketing approval. All drugs in the 1984-86 cohort have at least 54 months experience following IND submission recorded in the database (the amount of time between December 1986 and July 1991).

Appendix J

Estimates by OTA and JCT of Federal Tax Credits Attributable to Pharmaceuticals

T his appendix describes how the Office of Technology Assessment and the congressional Joint Committee on Taxation (JCT) identified pharmaceutical firms in the Internal Revenue Service's (IRS) 1987 corporate Statistics of Income (SOI) database and used these samples to estimate Federal tax credits claimed by the drug industry in that year.

The SOI database consists of most elements from corporate tax returns. The sample is stratified by the size of firms so that 100 percent of the corporations in the United States with the greatest assets (approximately $50 million or more) are included. The bulk of companies are randomly selected for inclusion in each year's sample with a probability inversely proportional to their size as determined by several measures. The SOI database classifies each corporation according to a Principal Activity Classification (PAC) coding scheme that reflects the activity from which the firm derives the greatest proportion of total receipts (essentially gross income). Although similar in format to the U.S. Census Bureau's Standard Industrial Classification Codes (SIC), PAC and SIC codes are not equivalent. Each firm indicates on its tax return the PAC code it believes best describes its activities. However, to ensure consistency over time for some analyses that the IRS and other government agencies

conduct with the database, the IRS changes the PAC grouping for some firms (297). PAC code 2830 is described as "drugs."

In an effort to refine this industrial grouping so that OTA's analysis of tax credits would reflect only those parent firms and subsidiaries exclusively (or almost exclusively) involved in pharmaceutical R&D or production,[1] the JCT investigated each firm in PAC 2830 of the 1987 SOI sample with assets $50 million or more. Of 99 such firms, the JCT concluded from its research that 12 of them were not primarily drug companies[2] and should be dropped from the JCT/OTA analysis. The JCT did not investigate and eliminate nonpharmaceutical firms with assets of less than $50 million because these companies combined account for only 3 percent of total assets in PAC 2830 and less than 2 percent of the taxes paid by this industry group in 1987[3] (492). Because the bulk of corporations whose sales are diversified beyond pharmaceuticals have tax-filing subsidiaries that *do* fall into PAC 2830 and whose business is almost exclusively in pharmaceuticals, OTA also concluded that relatively little pharmaceutical business or tax payments fall *outside* of PAC code 2830 (297). Hence, OTA believes its analysis accurately and comprehensively captures the tax activity of the pharmaceutical industry in 1987.

---

[1] So called "generic manufacturers" of pharmaceuticals with relatively small research budgets are included in the analysis.

[2] According to the JCT, most of these companies did relatively little work in pharmaceuticals. These companies included manufacturers of medical devices, cosmetics, other chemical products, and nonpharmaceutical applications of biotechnology (297). OTA was unable to investigate the nature of these firms itself because confidentiality of tax return data precludes OTA from knowing the identity of firms included in the SOI database or the other information from the SOI database at the level of an individual firm.

[3] Because of the large number of such firms, an investigation of each one would require a commitment of resources beyond its value to the analysis.

Appendix K

Federal Programs Dedicated to Pharmaceutical R&D[1]

A s indicated in the text and summarized in table K-1, the Federal Government maintains 13 targeted drug research and development (R&D) programs. Eleven of these programs focus on drug discovery and testing, and two are devoted solely to clinical R&D. All but one, an antimalarial program run by the U.S. Walter Reed Army Medical Center, are located within the U.S. Department of Health and Human Services in its National Institutes of Health (NIH). This appendix describes the mission and organization of each program.

▮ Targeted Drug Discovery Programs

Cancer Development Therapeutics Program

Located within the National Cancer Institute's (NCI) Division of Cancer Treatment, the Developmental Therapeutics Program (DTP) uses both intramural and extramural funding to discover and develop new anticancer and anti-human immunodeficiency virus (HIV) agents. Under its current organization, DPT includes: 1) the Laboratory of Drug Discovery Research and Development for the expeditious development of agents given high priority in the treatment of cancer or HIV infection; 2) the Drug Synthesis and Chemistry Branch which acquires, screens, and evaluates the therapeutic potential of new compounds provided by outside researchers including pharmaceutical firms; and 3) an extramural program that supports preclinical drug discovery and development.

Biological Response Modifiers Programs

Begun in 1972, the Biological Response Modifiers Program supports intramural and extramural research (including some clinical investigation) on agents or approaches that alter the relationship between a tumor and the "host" patient by modifying the host's biological response to tumor cells in order to realize therapeutic benefits. In recent years, this program has included among the research it supports the development of new approaches to modify the body's response to HIV.

National Sickle Cell Disease Program

This program seeks to develop pharmacological agents that prevent or decrease the "sickling" of red blood cells in order to improve the quality and duration of life for persons afflicted with sickle cell disease. Because sickle cell disease is a hereditary disorder at the molecular level, research supported by this program over the past 20 years has attempted to use the developing tools of "rational drug development." In particular, laboratory investigation has focused on understanding the biochemical actions that underlie the disease and molecules observed to inhibit those actions. One particular approach, genetic modifiers that increase hemoglobin in the fetus, has moved close to clinical trials to determine efficacy.

Lung Surfactant Replacement Program

A component of the National Heart, Lung, and Blood Institute's (NHLBI) Specialized Center of Research Program, "Respiratory Disorders in Infants and Children," this drug development program has sought new therapies since 1979 for respiratory distress syndrome (RDS), a breathing disorder that affects about 40,000 infants per year in the United States. Caused by a deficiency in surfactant, a substance produced within the lung during the final trimester of pregnancy, research within the program has produced a number of synthetic surfactants as well

---

[1] Unless otherwise noted, the information on these programs were provided by the relevant agency (167,271,343).

Table K-1—Federal Targeted Pharmaceutical Development Programs

Program	Agency	Component	Year begun	Fiscal year 1989 budget ($ thousands)
Cancer Developmental Therapeutics Program	NIH (DHHS)	NCI		
Cancer Therapy Evaluation Program	NIH (DHHS)	NCI	1955[a]	$ 305,101[b]
Biological Response Modifiers Program	NIH (DHHS)	NCI	1975	
National Sickle Cell Disease Program	NIH (DHHS)	NHLBI	1972	742
Lung Surfactant Replacement Program	NIH (DHHS)	NHLBI	1979	1,506
National AIDS Drug Discovery Groups	NIH (DHHS)	NIAID	1987	18,908
Antimicrobial Chemistry Program	NIH (DHHS)	NIAID	1981	3,493
Antiviral Research Program (Non-AIDS)	NIH (DHHS)	NIAID	1969	9,722
Anticonvulsant Drug Development Program	NIH (DHHS)	NINDS	1968	4,188
Contraceptive Development Program	NIH (DHHS)	NICHD	1971	13,833
Drug Abuse Medications Development Division	NIH (DHHS)	NIDA	1972	30,216
Antimalarial Experimental Therapeutics Program	U.S. Army (DOD)	Walter Reed Army Institute of Research	1963	1,900
Total				389,609

[a] "Cancer therapies" programs began in 1955. No separate dates given for Cancer Developmental Therapeutics Program and Cancer Therapy Evaluation Program.
[b] All three NCI programs combined.
KEY: ADAMHA = Alcohol, Drug Abuse and Mental Health Administration; DHHS = U.S. Department of Health and Human Services; DOD = U.S. Department of Defense; NCI = National Cancer Institute; NHLBI = National Heart, Lung and Blood Institute; NIAID = National Institute of Allergy and Infectious Diseases; NICHD = National Institute of Child Health and Human Development; NIDA = National Institute on Drug Abuse; NIH = National Institutes of Health; NINDS = National Institutes of Neurological Disorders and Stroke.
SOURCE: Office of Technology Assessment, 1993.

as some derived from animals. NHLBI research has included testing of these compounds in both the laboratory and in humans through regular extramural grants and contracts as well as special grants to small businesses.

National Cooperative Drug Discovery Groups-AIDS

The National Institute of Allergy and Infectious Diseases (NIAID) set up its National Cooperative Drug Discovery Groups on Acquired Immune Deficiency Syndrome (NCDDG-AIDS) in order to promote collaboration among academic, industrial, and governmental scientists to increase the speed with which new and better AIDS treatments are discovered and developed. Although physically not centered in a single location, each NCDDG brings together three to seven senior scientists who represent expertise in different disciplines. As of February 1991, NIAID had established 34 NCDDGs with scientists drawn from 46 academic or nonprofit institutions and 27 for-profit firms. While some of the groups focus on HIV itself, others target their efforts toward treating opportunistic infections (OIs) to which people with HIV are susceptible and which represent the major causes of illness and death in this patient population.

These groups, which only conduct preclinical R&D, are part of a larger, coordinated effort within NIAID and other NIH institutes intended to bring about therapeutic developments in the treatment of HIV more rapidly than would otherwise occur.[2] NIAID has two clinical AIDS drug programs that are described in greater detail in the section below on Federal clinical drug R&D.

Antimicrobial Chemistry Program and the Non-AIDS Antiviral Research Program

NIAID has established these two research programs to develop new treatments for viral infections (other than HIV). Because viruses are parasitic organisms

---

[2] A recent report of the Institute of Medicine, *The AIDS Research Program of the National Institutes of Health* (208), describes the continuum of HIV research efforts within the NIH in much greater detail.

that exist within cells and whose replication is closely tied to that of the host cell, most antiviral agents have profound toxic effects on the host cell. While the Antimicrobial Chemistry Program focuses only on drug discovery and preclinical evaluation (including an intramural program to screen compounds submitted by researchers outside the government as well as research support for designing and testing new compounds), the Antiviral Research Program includes both laboratory and clinical R&D. Among the recent clinical trials supported by the Antiviral Research Program are a Phase I/II dose-response study of the drug ganciclovir in treating congenital cytomeglovirus infections in babies with central nervous system symptoms, and a Phase I/II study of acyclovir as a treatment for neonatal herpes simplex infections in infants in whom the disease is limited to the skin, eye and mouth.

Anticonvulsant Drug Development Program

The National Institute of Neurological Disorders and Stroke's (NINDS) Anticonvulsant (or Antiepileptic) Drug Development (ADD) Program supports both preclinical and clinical investigations into new therapies for the treatment of seizures in the hopes of finding drugs that are more effective and less toxic than existing interventions. In addition to supporting intramural and extramural research, the ADD Program serves as a clearinghouse for R&D efforts aimed at treating seizure disorders. It monitors worldwide patents on potential compounds, maintains regular contacts with pharmaceutical firms doing central nervous system (CNS) research, and facilitates collaborative arrangements between NINDS and commercial suppliers to evaluate potential compounds for anticonvulsant activity. NINDS and an *ad hoc* advisory committee meet to determine NINDS priorities for promoting the development of promising compounds.

Contraceptive Development Program

Since 1971, the National Institute of Child Health and Human Development (NICHD) has provided support largely through contracts (currently at about $1.3 million per year) for a Contraceptive Development Program to discover, develop, and clinically evaluate new potential pharmaceuticals. Included among the possible contraceptive strategies researched are drugs that block the production of viable ova (eggs) in women or spermatozoa in men or drugs that interfere in the ability of ova and spermatozoa to undergo

fertilization. This latter strategy includes spermicides for use in the female reproductive tract. Among the pharmaceutical approaches to contraception pursued by the NICHD are drugs that block the action of gonadtropin-releasing hormone (GnRH), which is necessary for the functioning of both the testis and the ovary. Development of contraception within this program may also provide advances in the treatment of diseases such as precocious puberty, endometriosis, and certain cancers that stem from improper GnRH activity.

Drug Abuse Medications Development Program

Although the National Institute on Drug Abuse (NIDA) has supported research for the development of medications to treat substance abuse since 1972, the current incarnation of the Drug Abuse Medications Development Program received its authorization from Congress in the Anti-Drug Abuse Act of 1988 (Public Law 100-690). The program draws a distinction between drugs to treat opiate and cocaine addition, although NIDA indicates the distinction may be somewhat artificial for several reasons: 1) some opiate compounds have shown promise in treating cocaine addiction; 2) co-addiction to both types of substances is not uncommon; and 3) many potential medications may be useful in treating both types of dependence. As mentioned earlier in Chapter 9, a major justification for Federal support of this program cited by NIDA has been the historical reluctance of pharmaceutical firms to invest in R&D for medications to treat drug abuse. In fiscal year 1989, this program funded $22.8 million in R&D, about two-thirds designated for narcotics dependence and one-third for cocaine. Of the total, about $16.5 million was for clinical investigations.

Antimalarial Experimental Therapeutics Program

Since the early 1960s, when U.S. military personnel stationed in Southeast Asia became infected with strains of malaria resistant to existing treatments, the U.S. Army's Walter Reed Army Research Institute has supported antimalarial research in its Division of Experimental Therapeutics (272). With an increase in the number of Americans traveling and living in parts of the world where such malarias are common, the public health need for new drugs has increased while pharmaceutical company interest in antimalarial R&D has remained historically minimal. The Walter Reed

Program maintains an in-house capability to study the malaria parasite itself, to discover, develop, and evaluate new compounds, and to develop collaborative agreements with other public organizations such as the World Health Organization (WHO) and private pharmaceutical firms for clinical testing and potential marketing successful compounds.

Among potential malarial treatments attributable to the program are: 1) mefloquine, 2) halofantrine, 3) artemisinin, and 4) a compound currently known as WR238605. Mefloguine was developed jointly by Walter Reed, WHO, and Hoffman-LaRoche, Inc., and was recently approved for U.S. marketing by the U.S. Food and Drug Administration (FDA). Halofantrine is a potential prophylactic jointly developed by Walter Reed and SmithKline Beecham that may be effective in parts of the world where malarias are proven resistant to mefloquine and is currently undergoing studies of chronic toxicity. Artemisinin is a drug based on traditional Chinese medicine and is in the early stages of development in cooperation with WHO as a treatment for severe forms of malaria. WR238605 will soon go into Phase I clinical testing as a replacement for the drug primaquine in treating malaria and possible Pneumocystis carinii pneumonia (PCP), a common opportunistic infection in HIV patients.

Pharmacological Research in the National Institute of General Medical Sciences (NIGMS)

Because NIGMS's sole research mission is to support work "in the sciences basic to medicine" (rather than to focus on a particular disease or organ system), it plays a unique role among agencies in the Federal Government supporting basic biomedical investigation. It "helps supply new knowledge, theories, and concepts" that can then be used in disease-specific research undertaken by other parts of NIH[3] (477). A large part of this fundamental scientific research portfolio is relevant to pharmaceutical R&D.

Among the institute's activities is the Pharmaceutical Sciences Program, which is charged with supporting "research and research training leading to increased understanding of the interactions of drugs with living systems in order to produce new, safer, and more efficacious therapeutic agents." While the program's work is interdisciplinary, drawing on the fields of genetics, molecular biology, chemistry, computer

science, and more traditional pharmacological investigation, most grants given by the Pharmaceutical Sciences Program are in three areas: anesthesiology, pharmacology, or bio-related chemistry (486a). The Pharmaceutical Sciences Program's extramural research budget totaled just under $86 million in fiscal year 1989, representing 15 percent of the institute's total extramural research funds.

■ Clinical Evaluation Programs

NCI's Cancer Therapy Evaluation Program

NCI is one of two NIH institutes that maintains targeted drug development programs focused solely on clinical testing. NCI's Cancer Therapy Evaluation Program is responsible for funding and coordinating most extramural trials within the NCI's Division of Cancer Therapy, including those involving anticancer and anti-HIV pharmaceuticals. Through a network of clinical cooperative groups the program's Investigational Drug Branch sponsors trials to determine the efficacy and toxicity of new investigational drugs and maintains close contact with the pharmaceutical industry to promote efficient, coordinated drug development.

The program also maintains a Regulatory Affairs Branch that has responsibility for preparing and submitting investigational new drug (IND) applications to the FDA for human trials (particularly for those drugs lacking a commercial sponsor to fulfill that function). The Branch also cooperates with pharmaceutical companies in providing data and other information needed for a pharmaceutical firm to receive approval of new drug applications (NDAs).

NIAID's AIDS Clinical Trials Groups Program and the Community AIDS Program

Begun in 1986, the NIAID's AIDS Clinical Trials Groups (ACTGs) involves active trials of drugs at every stage of clinical development at many research sites around the country (208). Because of the intense scrutiny of ACTG trial protocols by patient groups, trials are designed through a process of consensus coordinated by NIAID and involving NIAID staff, AIDS advocates, and the potential investigators. Data collection at multiple sites is similarly coordinated with the help of an NIAID research contract.

---

[3] NIGMS is also charged with supporting doctoral and postdoctoral training toward the same ends and coordinates many of the NIH-administered training programs outlined in chapter 9.

A more recent initiative within NIAID is the Community Programs for Clinical Research on AIDS (CPCRA), launched in 1989 in an attempt to involve a greater number and broader cross-section of people with AIDS in the clinical research process than was the case with the ACTGs alone. According to NIAID comments to the trade press at the time the program was begun, CPCRA also differs from the ACTG program in that while "many of the [ATCG] trials have clinical endpoints (e.g., development of opportunistic infection or death) and require stringent monitoring of immune responses to experimental drugs, CPCRA endpoints will include 'indications of drug efficacy that are relevant to and easily obtainable in the day-to-day practice of medicine' and which do not require the "sophisticated viral or cell-culturing capability or technically intense monitoring of typical ACTG studies" (375). In fiscal year 1990, CPCRA awarded $9 million to 18 community-based projects in 14 cities, leaving another $3 million to support statistical analysis and administrative coordination of the trials.

Appendix L

Acronyms and Glossary of Terms

Acronyms

AAALAC	—American Association for Accreditation of Laboratory Animal Care
ACE	—angiotensin conversion enzyme
ACRS	—accelerated cost recovery system
ACTGs	—AIDS Clinical Trials Groups (NIAID)
ADA	—adenosine deaminase (enzyme)
ADAMHA	—Alcohol, Drug Abuse, and Mental Health Administration (DHHS)
ADD	—Anticonvulsant (or Antiepileptic) Drug Development Program
AFDC	—Aid to Families of Dependent Children
AHCPR	—Agency for Health Care Policy and Research
AIDS	—acquired immunodeficiency syndrome
ALI	—American Law Institute
AMA	—American Medical Association
AMP	—average manufacturer price
ANDA	—abbreviated new drug application
APhA	—American Pharmaceutical Association
ARIs	—aldose reductase inhibitors
AWP	—average wholesale price
BPS	—Biophysics and Physiological Sciences Program
CANDAs	—computerized new drug applications
CAPM	—capital asset pricing model
CBER	—Center for Biologics Evaluation and Research (FDA)
CDC	—U.S. Centers for Disease Control
CDER	—Center for Drug Evaluation and Research (FDA)
CF	—cystic fibrosis
CMBD	—Cellular and Molecular Basis of Disease Program
CNS	

	—central nervous system
CPAC	—Central Pharmaceutical Affairs Council (Japan)
CPCRA	—Community Programs for Clinical Research on AIDS
CPMP	—Committee for Proprietary Medicinal Products (EC)
CRADAs	—cooperative research and development agreements
CRISP	—Computer Retrieval of Information on Scientific Projects system
CRR	—cash flow recovery rate
CSDD	—Center for the Study of Drug Development of Tufts University
CSOs	—consumer safety officers
DIS	—Drug Information System
DHEW	—U.S. Department of Health, Education, and Welfare (now DHHS)
DHHS	—U.S. Department of Health and Human Services
DNA	—deoxyribonucleic acid
DOE	—U.S. Department of Energy
DRG	—Division of Research Grants (NIH)
DTP	—diphtheria-tetanus-pertussis (vaccine)
DTP	—Developmental Therapeutics Program
DUR	—Drug Utilization Review
EC	—European Community
ED	—U.S. Department of Education
EDCs	—European Discovery Capability Units
ELA	—establishment license application
ERTA	—The Economic Recovery Tax Act
FDA	—U.S. Food and Drug Administration
FD&C	—Federal Food, Drug, and Cosmetic Act
FEDRIP	—Federal Research in Progress database
FTT	—Federal Technology Transfer Act
GAO	—General Accounting Office (U.S. Congress)
GCP	—good clinical practices

GLP	—good laboratory practices	NICHD	—National Institute of Child Health and Human Development (DHHS)
GSL	—Guaranteed Student Loan	NIDA	—National Institute on Drug Abuse (DHHS)
HCFA	—U.S. Health Care Financing Administration	NIDDK	—National Institute of Diabetes and Digestive and Kidney Diseases (DHHS)
HGH	—human growth hormone	NIGMS	—National Institute of General Medical Sciences (DHHS)
HIB	—Health Insurance Board (Japan)		
HIV	—human immunodeficiency virus	NIH	—National Institutes of Health (DHHS)
HMO	—health maintenance organization	NIHS	—National Institute of Hygienic Sciences (Japan)
HRSA	—U.S. Health Resources Services Administration		
ICH1	—International Conference on Harmonization	NIMH	—National Institute of Mental Health (DHHS)
		NINDS	—National Institute of Neurological Disorders and Stroke (DHHS)
IND	—investigational new drug		
IOM	—Institute of Medicine	NLM	—National Library of Medicine (NIH)
IPO	—initial public offering	NMCES	—National Medical Care Expenditure Survey
IRBs	—institutional review boards		
IRC	—internal revenue code	NME	—new molecular entity
IRR	—internal rate of return	NMES	—National Medical Expenditure Survey
IRS	—U.S. Internal Revenue Service	NMR	—nuclear magnetic resonance
IUD	—intrauterine device	NPV	—net present value
IV	—intravenous	NRSA	—National Research Service Awards Act
JCT	—Joint Committee on Taxation (U.S. Congress)	NSAID	—nonsteroidial antiinflammatory drug
		NSF	—National Science Foundation
LI	—licensed-in	NTIS	—U.S. National Technical Information Service
MACS	—Multiaxis Coding System		
MARC	—Minority Access to Research Careers program	OD	—orphan drug
		OECD	—Organization for Economic Cooperation and Development
MEA	—Medical Evaluation Agency (EC)		
MEDLARS	—Medical Literature Analysis and Retrieval System (NLM)	OIs	—opportunistic infections
		OMB	—U.S. Office of Management and Budget
MHW	—Ministry of Health and Welfare (Japan)	OPD	—Office of Orphan Products Development (FDA)
MIDAS	—Molecular Interactive Display and Simulation system,		
		OPE	—Office of Planning and Evaluation (FDA)
MSP	—Medical Science Partners program	OTA	—Office of Technology Assessment (U.S. Congress)
MSTP	—Medical Scientists Training Program		
NCE	—new chemical entity	OTT	—Office of Technology Transfer (NIH)
NCI	—National Cancer Institute (DHHS)	PAB	—Pharmaceutical Affairs Bureau (Japan)
NCRR	—National Center for Research Resources (DHHS)	PAC	—principal activity classification (codes)
		PBAC	—Pharmaceutical Benefits Advisory Committee (Australia)
NDA	—new drug application		
NDSL	—National Direct Student Loan program	PBPA	—Pharmaceutical Benefits Pricing Authority (Australia)
NEI	—National Eye Institute (DHHS)		
NEJM	—New England Journal of Medicine	PBS	—Pharmaceutical Benefits Scheme (Australia)
NHLBI	—National Heart, Lung and Blood Institute (DHHS)		
		PCP	—Pneumocystis carinii pneumonia
NHS	—National Health Service (United Kingdom)	PCR	—polymerase chain reaction
		PG	—purchasing groups
NIAID	—National Institute of Allergy and Infectious Diseases (DHHS)	PHS	—U.S. Public Health Service
		PIs	—principal investigators

PLA   —product license application
PMA   —Pharmaceutical Manufacturers
                Association
PMPRB   —Patented Medicine Prices Review Board
                (Canada)
PPB   —Patent Policy Board (NIH)
PPRS   —Pharmaceutical Price Regulation
                Scheme (United Kingdom)
PROs   —peer review organizations
PS   —Pharmaceutical Sciences program
PTO   —U.S. Patent and Trademark Office
PV   —present value
rEPO   —recombinant erythropoietin
RAs   —research assistants
R&D   —research and development
R&E   —research and experimental
RDS   —respiratory distress syndrome
RNA   —ribonucleic acid
RRGs   —risk retention groups
ROS   —return-on-sales
SATSU   —Science and Technology Studies Unit
                of Anglia College (England)
SBID   —Small Business Innovation
                Development Act
SBIR   —Small Business Innovation Research
                grants
SEC   —U.S. Security Exchange Commission
SEOG   —Supplemental Educational Opportunity
                Grants
SIC   —standard industrial classification
SOI   —Statistics of Income
SPAPs   —state pharmaceutical assistance
                programs
SRT   —Soribinil Retinopathy Trial
SSI   —Supplemental Security Income
TAMRA   —Technical and Miscellaneous Revenue
                Act
TDC   —Technology Development Coordinator
TPA   —tissue plasmiogen activator
UCSF   —University of California at San
                Francisco
USDA   —U.S. Department of Agriculture
USSF   —United States Servicemen's Fund, Inc.
WACC   —weighted average cost of capital
WARF   —Wisconsin Alumni Research
                Foundation
WHO   —World Health Organization

Glossary of Terms

Abbreviated new drug application (ANDA): A simplified submission to the U.S. Food and Drug Administration (FDA) for approval to market a copy of an already approved drug. An ANDA must contain evidence that the duplicate drug is bioequivalent (see ''bioequivalence'') to the previously approved drug.

Applied research: Research to gain knowledge or understanding necessary for determining the means by which a recognized and specific need may be met. While there is no standard definition of applied research for *pharmaceuticals*, it generally refers to all investigation targeted to the development and testing of actual pharmaceutical compounds.

Asset: Any owned physical object (tangible) or right (intangible) having economic value to its owners; an item or source of wealth with continuing benefits for future periods, expressed for accounting purposes in terms of its cost or other value (such as current replacement cost).

Average manufacturer price: The average price paid by wholesalers for products distributed to the retail class of trade.

Average wholesale price: The average price charged for a specific commodity to retailers by one or more wholesalers.

Basic research: Research performed to gain fuller knowledge or understanding of the fundamental aspects of phenomena and of observable facts, without specific applications towards products or processes in mind. Basic pharmaceutical research is aimed at understanding the underlying physiological causes, disease, or developing new techniques for use in developing pharmaceuticals.

Beta: A measure of a company's (or industry's) relative risk in capital markets. Beta measures the correlation between stock market returns to a company (or industry) and overall stock market returns. A value of beta close to 1 means that the company's stock has a risk profile that is average for the stock market. A beta higher than 1 means that the firm's risk is higher than the average risk of firms in the stock market.

Bioequivalence: Scientific basis on which generic and brand-name drugs are compared. To be considered bioequivalent, the rates at which the active ingredient of two drugs are absorbed by the body must not differ significantly when they are given at the same dosage under similar conditions. Some drugs, however, are intended to have a different absorption rate. FDA may consider one product bioequivalent to another if the difference in absorption rate is noted in the labeling but does not affect the drug's safety or effectiveness, or change its effect in a medically significant way.

Biological drugs: Drug products made from living organisms and their products, including viruses, serums, toxins, antitoxins, vaccines, allergenic or analogous products. Also included are blood, blood derivatives, and diagnostic reagents that use biotechnology-derived products.

Biopharmaceuticals: Pharmaceutical products produced by the application of biotechnology.

Biotechnology: Any technique that uses living organisms, or substances from those organisms, to make or modify a product, to improve plants or animals, or to develop micro-organisms for specific uses.

Book value: The current values of capital assets claimed by a company in its financial statements after depreciation expenses. Strict accounting conventions determine what kinds of investments create a capital asset.

Brand-name: The commercial name given to a drug product by an individual company for marketing and promotion purposes.

Breakthrough drug: A new therapeutic compound whose therapeutic effects and/or mechanism of action are substantially different from any previously marketed compound. Criteria for "substantially different" can vary among evaluators.

Capital asset: A tangible or intangible asset intended for long-term use.

Capital asset pricing model: An economic model of equilibrium in capital markets which predicts rates of return on all risky assets as a function of their correlation (or covariance) with the overall market portfolio.

Capitalized cost: The present value on a particular date of expenditures made in the past. The capitalized cost is measured by compounding the past expenditure to its present value at an appropriate interest rate.

Carryback: A tax provision that allows companies with insufficient tax liabilities in a tax period to apply credits earned during that period to tax liabilities incurred in a past tax year.

Carryforward: A tax provision allowing companies with insufficient tax liabilities in a tax period to save credits earned during that period for use in a future tax year.

Cash flow recovery rate: The rate of return on realized cash flows into and out of a firm over a defined time interval.

Clinical pharmacology: The study and evaluation of the effects of drugs in humans.

Clinical trials: Experimental research in which preventive, diagnostic, or therapeutic agents, devices, regimes, and procedures are given to human subjects under controlled conditions in order to define their safety and effectiveness. (See also phase I, II, III, and IV studies).

Constant dollars: Dollars expressed in terms of their purchasing power in a base year. Constant dollars adjust for changes in buying power due to inflation or deflation between the base year and the year of measurement.

Contribution margin: The percent of a company's sales that contributes to paying the fixed costs and profits of the enterprise after the direct costs of producing, marketing and distributing the product are deducted.

Cooperative Research and Development Agreements (CRADA): A formal agreement between a Federal laboratory and a non-Federal party (individual, university, or private firm) in which the non-Federal party provides resources in exchange for exclusive rights to license patents that result from the collaboration. Congress gave Federal laboratories the authority to enter into CRADAs as part of the Federal Technology Transfer Act of 1986 (Public Law 99-502).

Copayment: In health insurance, a form of cost sharing whereby the insured person pays a specified amount for the service or pharmaceutical. The copayment can be a fixed amount or a percentage of the bill.

Cost of capital: The interest rate required to induce investors to put up capital for an investment with a given level of risk.

Current dollars: The value of dollars spent or received at the time of the transaction, without adjusting for inflation or deflation since the transaction date.

Depreciation: The process of allocating the cost of tangible assets to operations over the expected life of the asset. Depreciation represents the gradual exhaustion of the service capacity of fixed assets. It is the consequence of such factors as use, obsolescence, inadequacy, and wear.

Discount rate: The interest rate used to convert future cash flows to their present value.

Drug: In this report, any chemical or biological substance that may be applied to, ingested by, or injected into humans to prevent, treat, or diagnose disease or other medical conditions.

Drug receptor: A site or structure in or on the surface of a cell which combines with a drug to produce a specific alteration of a cell function. The vast majority of drug receptors in the body are proteins.

Drug utilization review: A review system used by health insurers to monitor the frequency and usage of prescriptions by enrollees, to identify potential interactions with other medications, or to identify alternative effective or cost-effective therapies for the patient.

Effective patent life: In this report, the length of time during which a new chemical entity is formally protected from generic competition by patent or other statutory market exclusivity provision.

Effective tax rate: The ratio of actual income tax paid to the pre-tax income of a particular taxpayer or a group of taxpayers (such as the whole pharmaceutical industry).

Enzymes: Proteins that are produced by living cells and that mediate and promote the chemical processes of life without themselves being altered or destroyed.

Establishment license application: An application to the FDA for a license to produce a biological product at a given facility.

Ethical pharmaceuticals: In this report, biological and medicinal products for use in humans and promoted primarily to the medical, pharmacy and allied professions.

Expensing: In accounting, the practice of recording an expenditure in the period in which it occurs.

Fiscal year: Any accounting period of 12 successive calendar months, or 52 weeks, or 365 days, used by an organization for financial reporting.

Follow-on product: Any new combination, formulation, or dosing strength of existing therapeutic molecular compounds that must be tested in humans before market introduction.

Formulary: A list of selected pharmaceuticals and their appropriate dosages judged to be the most useful or cost-effective for patient care from which physicians are required or encouraged to prescribe. A formulary may also be a list of drugs that may not be prescribed without special appeals.

Gene therapy: See human gene therapy.

Generic drug: A "copy" of an existing pharmaceutical compound.

Health maintenance organization: A health plan that provides a full range of health benefits to a specified group of subscribers for a fixed prepaid fee, regardless of the expense of the care needed. The fee can either be paid by the subscriber or by an employer.

Human gene therapy: Treatment of disease by insertion of new genetic material or permanent modification of existing genes.

Innovator firm: A drug manufacturer that invents, develops, and in most cases, markets new chemical entities.

Internal rate of return: The interest rate at which the present value of all net cash flows into and out of a firm over a specified time interval equals zero.

Investigational new drug (IND) (application): An application submitted by a sponsor to the FDA before beginning human testing on an unapproved drug or on an approved drug for an unapproved use.

Joint and several liability: A legal term that refers to liability of each defendant for all damages even if more than one defendant is found liable.

Licensed-in NCE: A new chemical entity acquired from the originating company through a contractual agreement.

Line extension drug: See follow-on product.

Medicaid: A government medical assistance program that pays for medical expenses for the poor and certain other classes of uninsured people, established by the Title XIX of the Social Security Act of 1965. Each State administers its own program. Medicaid is funded by both the State and Federal governments.

Medicare: A Federally administered health insurance program covering the cost of services for people 65 years of age or older, receiving Social Security Disability Insurance payments for at least two years, or with end-stage renal disease. Medicare consists of two separate but coordinated programs—hospital insurance (Part A) and supplementary medical insurance (Part B). Health insurance protection is available to insured persons without regard to income.

Marginal credit rate: For tax credits, the percentage reduction in the cost of an extra dollar of spending for a taxpayer, holding everything else constant.

Marginal incentive effect: See marginal credit rate.

Me-too drug: A new chemical entity that is similar but not identical in molecular structure and mechanism of action to a pioneer NCE.

Molecular biology: The study of biology at the level of individual molecules, such as proteins and DNA.

Multiple-source drug: A drug product not protected by patents or other exclusive marketing rights and marketed by more than one company.

Net present value: The difference between the present value of all cash inflows from a project or investment and the present value of all cash outflows required for the investment.

New chemical entity: In this report, a new therapeutic molecular compound that has never before been used or tested in humans. The term refers to both drugs and biologicals. (See also new molecular entity.)

New drug application: An application to the FDA for approval to market a new chemical (nonbiological) drug for human use in U.S. interstate commerce.

New molecular entity: A term used by FDA in its published statistical reports to describe newly developed drug compounds. The FDA includes some diagnostic agents and excludes therapeutic biologicals in the definition.

Off-label use: The prescription or use of ethical pharmaceuticals for indications other than those specified in FDA approved labelling of the drug.

Opportunity cost of capital: The rate of interest that dollars invested must earn in exchange for being tied up in an investment with a given level of risk.

Orphan drug: A drug product discovered and developed for the treatment of a rare disease.

Overhead costs: Cost items that cannot be identified specifically with any one project or activity.

Over-the-counter drugs: Drugs available without a physician's prescription.

Parallel-track program: A FDA program, proposed in 1990, that would allow release of investigational drugs to medical practitioners, on a case-by-case basis, for use in the treatment of AIDS or HIV-related illness for which no satisfactory alternative treatments exist or patient participation in conventional clinical trials is not possible.

Patented drugs: Brand-name drugs that are marketed by a pharmaceutical company under exclusive marketing rights.

Phase I, II, III, IV studies: Specific phases of the clinical (human) testing of new drug products.

- Phase I studies are small trials usually involving only healthy volunteers to map how the body absorbs and eliminates the drugs and to document the response it produces.
- Phase II studies test the drug's therapeutic effectiveness and note any adverse reactions in individuals affected by the target disease or condition.
- Phase III studies assess the drug's medical benefits and risks among a large number of patients under conditions of ordinary use.
- Phase IV studies are clinical trials conducted after a product is already approved for marketing.

Pioneer drug: A new chemical entity that has a molecular structure and/or mechanism of action that differs from all previously existing drugs in a therapeutic area, such as the first therapeutic compound to inhibit the action of a specific disease or condition.

Preclinical research: Laboratory and animal research conducted prior to the clinical testing of a new chemical entity. Preclinical research may include basic research and applied non-clinical research.

Prescription drug: In the United States, a drug dispensed by a licensed pharmacist or medical practitioner on the written order (prescription) of a medical practitioner licensed by law to administer such drugs.

Present value: The economic value today (or at some specific date) of an amount paid or received at a later date discounted at an appropriate rate.

Protein: A type of molecule composed of linked amino acids in particular sequences, which determine the structure, function, and regulation of the various cells, tissues, and organs in the body.

Product license application: An application to the FDA to market a biological product in the United States.

Rational drug design: A process of drug research focusing on the physiological basis of disease and finding or creating new therapeutic agents that interfere with the course of disease at the molecular level. It is contrasted with random screening of existing molecules in search of empirically observed action against disease. A general term that covers a

322 | Pharmaceutical R&D: Costs, Risks and Rewards

broad range of approaches to the discovery of new drugs that rely on structural analysis of target molecules and deliberate design of agents to affect their function.

Real dollars: See constant dollars.

Receptor: See drug receptor.

Research and development: In the pharmaceutical industry, the process of discovering, and developing for the market new drugs and related products.

Self-originated NCEs: A new chemical entity discovered, developed, and brought to market by a single company.

Shining new drugs: A term used in Japan to refer to drugs without any close therapeutic competition or chemical predecessor.

Single-source drug: A drug marketed under one brand name usually by one company.

Standard Industrial Classification (SIC) Code: A numerical code used by the U.S. Department of Commerce to classify firms according to their primary line of business.

Strict liability: A legal concept that states liability lies with the party best able to prevent injury or absorb its costs even if that party was not responsible for causing the specific injury in question through negligence or intent.

Technology transfer: The process of converting scientific knowledge into useful products. This most often refers to the flow of information between public and private sectors or between countries.

Therapeutic class: A group of drugs intended to treat a particular disease or group of related diseases.

Third-party payers: Private insurance companies, government agencies, and self-insured business that pay medical providers for services given to a patient.

Treatment IND: An FDA program, established in 1987, that allows the release of investigational drugs to medical practitioners, on a case-by-case basis, for use in the treatment of immediately life-threatening diseases in instances where no satisfactory alternative treatment exists.

Vaccine: A preparation of whole or parts of living, attenuated, or killed bacteria or viruses, (or synthesized antigens identical or similar to those found in the disease-causing organisms) designed to produce or increase immunity to a particular disease.

Working capital: The excess of current assets over current liabilities. Where current assets and liabilities are cash and short-term securities and current liabilities are debts owed in the current accounting period.

References

1. Abauf, N., and Carmody, K., "The Cost of Capital in Japan and the United States: A Tale of Two Markets," Salomon Brothers Financial Strategy Group, July 1990.

2. Abe, M., Deputy Director, Economic Affairs Division, Pharmaceutical Advisory Board, Ministry of Health and Welfare of Japan, unpublished minutes from Board of Directors meeting, Siegel Associates, New York, NY, June 20, 1991.

3. Adler, R.G., Director, Office of Technology Transfer, National Institutes of Health, Public Health Service, U.S. Department of Health and Human Services, personal communications, February 8, 1990, February 21, 1990, February 26, 1990, April 12, 1991, and September 18, 1992.

4. Alderman, M.H., "Which Antihypertensive Drugs First—and Why!" [commentary] *Journal of the American Medical Association* 267(20):2786-2787, 1992.

5. Altshuler, R., "A Dynamic Analysis of the Research and Experimentation Credit," *National Tax Journal* 41(4):453-466, 1988.

6. Altshuler, R., Professor, Department of Economics, Columbia University, New York, NY, personal communication, November 26, 1990.

7. Altshuler, R., and Chaoul, H., "The Effect of Tax Policy on Returns to R&D in the Pharmaceutical Industry: A Methodological Review," contract report prepared for the Office of Technology Assessment, U.S. Congress, November 1990.

8. American Home Products Corporation, Annual Report, Filing With the U.S. Securities and Exchange Commission, Washington, DC, 1988.

9. American Medical Association, "Impact of Product Liability on the Development of New Medical Technologies," *Proceedings of the House of Delegates*, 137th Annual Meeting, Chicago, IL, June 26-30, 1988.

10. American Medical Association Council on Scientific Affairs and Council on Ethical and Judicial Affairs, "Conflicts of Interest in Medical Center/Industry Research Relationships," *Journal of the American Medical Association* 263:2790-2793, 1990.

11. Amernick, B.A., *Patent Law for the Nonlawyer: A Guide for the Engineer, Technologist, and Manager* (New York, NY: Van Nostrand Reinhold Co., 1986).

12. *Amgen, Inc. v. Chugai Pharmaceutical Co.*, 927 F. 2nd 1532 14 (Fed. Cir. 1990).

13. *Amgen, Inc. v. International Trade Commission*, 902 F. 2nd 1532 14 (Fed. Cir. 1990).

14. Anderson, W.F., "Whither Goest Thou, Gene Therapy?" *Human Gene Therapy* 1:227-228, 1990.

15. Anderson, W.F., "End-of-the-Year Potpourri," *Human Gene Therapy* 2:299-300, 1991.

16. Anderson, W.F., Blaese, R.M., and Culver, K., "The ADA Human Gene Therapy Clinical Protocol," *Human Gene Therapy* 1:331-362, 1990.

17. Andersson, F., Research Scientist, Battelle Medtap, London, United Kingdom, personal communication, April 1, 1992.

18. Aronson, N., Technology Manager, Blue Cross/Blue Shield Association, Chicago, IL, personal communication, October 9, 1991.

19. Arrow, K., "Economic Welfare and the Allocation of Resources for Invention," *The Rate and Direction of Inventive Activity: Economic and Social Factors*, R.R. Nelson (ed.)(Princeton, NJ: Princeton University Press, 1962).

20. Arthur Andersen and Company, "Executive Summary of the PMA Cost of Regulation Study," *Economic Costs of FDA Regulations*, Pharmaceutical Manufacturers Association, Mon-

ograph (Washington, DC: Pharmaceutical Manufacturers Association, March 1981).

21. Asbury, C.H., "The Orphan Drug Act: The First Seven Years," *Journal of the American Medical Association* 265:893-897, 1991.

22. Association of the British Pharmaceutical Industry, *Pharma Facts and Figures* (London, United Kingdom: The Association of the British Pharmaceutical Industry, 1992).

23. Baber, W.R., Professor, School of Business and Public Administration, George Washington University, Washington, DC, unpublished note to the Office of Technology Assessment, U.S. Congress, Washington, DC, July 1991.

24. Baber, W.R., Professor, School of Business and Public Administration, George Washington University, Washington, DC, personal communication, November 19, 1991.

25. Baber, W.R., and Kang, S.-H., "An Empirical Investigation of Accounting Rates of Return for the Pharmaceutical Industry 1975-1987," preliminary draft submitted to the Office of Technology Assessment, U.S. Congress, August 1990.

26. Baber, W.R., and Kang, S.-H., "An Empirical Investigation of Accounting Rates of Return for Pharmaceutical Industry 1975-87," draft paper prepared for the Office of Technology Assessment, U.S. Congress, December 1990.

27. Baber, W.R., and Kang, S.-H., "Accounting-Based Measures as Estimates of Economic Rates of Return: An Empirical Study of the U.S. Pharmaceutical Industry 1976-87," draft paper prepared for the Office of Technology Assessment, U.S. Congress, March 1991.

28. Baber, W.R., and Kang, S.-H., "Accounting-Based Measures as Estimates of Economic Rates of Return: An Empirical Study of the U.S. Pharmaceutical Industry 1976-87," draft paper prepared for the Office of Technology Assessment, U.S. Congress, July 1991.

29. Baber, W.R., Ross, R.S., and Apple, J.R., "Research and Development Accounting Issues With Specific Reference to the U.S. Pharmaceutical Industry," paper prepared for the Office of Technology Assessment, U.S. Congress, December 1990.

30. Bachynsky, J., "Government Control of Drug Prices in Canada," paper presented at "Government Influence in Pharmaceutical Pricing: Lessons from Home and Abroad," an invitational conference sponsored by the Institute for Pharmaceutical Economics, Philadelphia College of Pharmacy Science, Philadelphia, PA, September 26, 1991.

31. Bader, F., "Carrying Costs for Biotech Manufacturing Facilities: Impediment to Competitiveness," Executive Summary, Genetics Institute, Andover, MA, 1992.

32. Baily, M.N., "Research and Development Costs and Returns: The U.S. Pharmaceutical Industry," *Journal of Political Economy* 80(1):70-85, 1972.

33. Baily, M.N., and Lawrence, R.Z., "The Incentive Effects of the New R&D Tax Credit," unpublished manuscript, Brookings Institution, Washington, DC, July 1990.

34. Baird, S.J., Director of the Bureau of Program Development and Review, New York Elderly Pharmaceutical Insurance Program, Albany, NY, personal communication, October 30, 1991.

35. Baker, C., and Kramer, N., "Employer-Sponsored Prescription Drug Benefits," *Monthly Labor Review* 114:31-35, 1991.

36. Barr Laboratories, Inc., Annual Report, Filing With the U.S. Securities and Exchange Commission, Washington, DC, 1991.

37. Barral, P.E., *Fifteen Years of Results in Pharmaceutical Research Throughout the World, 1975-1989* (France: Fondation Rhone-Poulenc Sante, August 1990).

38. Barton, M., Staff Assistant, Vermont Department of Health, Waterbury, VT, personal communication, October 28, 1991.

39. Baumol, W.J., Heim, P., Malkiel, B.G., et al., "Earnings Retention, New Capital and the Growth of the Firm," *Review of Economics and Statistics* 52:345-355, November 1970; as cited in Mueller, D.C., and Reardon, E.A., "Rates of Return on Corporate Investment," Department of Economics, University of Maryland, College Park, MD, undated manuscript.

40. Beatrice, M.G., Acting Director, Center for Biologics Evaluation and Research, Food and Drug Administration, Public Health Service, U.S. Department of Health and Human Service, Rockville, MD, personal communications, October 18, 1990, and January 5, 1992.

41. Beatrice, M.G., "Regulation, Licensing, and Inspection of Biological Products," *Pharmaceutical Engineering* 11(3):29-35, May/June 1991.

42. Becker, E.L., Butterfield, W.J.H., Harvey, A.M., et al., *International Dictionary of Medicine and Biology in Three Volumes* (New York, NY: John Wiley and Sons, 1986).

43. Beier, D., Vice President of Government Affairs, and Glick, M., Treasurer, Genentech, Inc., Washington, DC and San Francisco, CA, personal communication, March 11, 1992.

44. Bennett, R.M., Director of Health Audit, National Audit Office, London, United Kingdom, letter to the Office of Technology Assessment, U.S. Congress, Washington, DC, November 29, 1991.

45. Bennett, R.M., Director of Health Audit, National Audit Office, London, United Kingdom, personal communication, October 23, 1992.

46. Berndt, E., and Griliches, Z., "Prices Indexes for Microcomputers: An Exploratory Study," *NBER Working Paper Series*, Working Paper No. 3378, (Cambridge, MA: National Bureau of Economic Research, 1990).

47. Bianucci, D., Food and Drug Administration, Public Health Service, U.S. Department of Health and Human Services, Rockville, MD, personal communication, February 5, 1992.

48. Bitz, D.W., Director of Drug Registration and Regulatory Affairs, Sandoz Pharmaceuticals Corp., East Hanover, NJ, personal communication, September 9, 1992.

49. Blaese, R.M., and Anderson, W.F., "The ADA Human Gene Therapy Protocol" [original covering memo] *Human Gene Therapy* 1:327-329, 1990.

50. Blumenthal, D.B., Epstein, S., and Maxwell, J., "Commercializing University Research: Lesson From the Experience of the Wisconsin Alumni Research Fund," *New England Journal Medicine* 232:1621-1626, 1986.

51. Blumenthal, D.B., Gluck, M.E., Epstein, S., et al., *University-Industry Relationships in Biotechnology: Implications for Federal Policy*, Final Report to the Assistant Secretary for Planning and Evaluation, U.S. Department of Health and Human Services, U.S. DHHS Grant #100A-83, March 20, 1987.

52. Blumenthal, D.B., Gluck, M.E., Louis, K.S., et al., "Industry Support of University Research in Biotechnology: An Industry Perspective," *Science* 231:242-245, 1986.

53. Blumenthal, D.B., Gluck, M.E., Louis, K.S, et al., "University-Industry Relationships in Biotechnology: Implications for the University," *Science* 232:1361-1366, 1986.

54. Bok, D., "Balancing Responsibility and Innovation," *Change* 14(6):16-25, 1982.

55. Bond, R.S., and Lean, D.F., "Sales, Promotion and Product Differentiation in Two Prescription Drug Markets," Staff Report to the U.S. Federal Trade Commission, Washington, DC, 1977.

56. Botstein, D., White, R.L., Skolnick, M., et al., "Construction of a Genetic Linkage Map in Man Using Restriction Fragment Length Polymorphisms," *American Journal of Human Genetics* 32:314-331, 1980.

57. *Bowsher v. Merck & Co. Inc.,* 103 S. Ct. 1587, 1591 n. 4 (1983).

58. Brauch, S.K., and Casy, A.F., "Applications of High-Field NMR Spectroscopy in Medicinal Chemistry," *Progress in Medicinal Chemistry* 26:355-436, 1989.

59. Brealey, R.A., and Myers, S.C., *Principles of Corporate Finance, 4th Edition* (New York, NY: McGraw-Hill, 1988).

60. *Bristol-Myers Co. v. Staats*, 428 F. Supp. 1388 (1977) *aff'd per curiam* 620 F. 2d. 17 (2nd Cir. 1980), *aff'd mem. by equally divided Court* 451 U.S. 400 (1981).

61. Brody, M., "When Products Turn Into Liabilities," *Fortune* 113:20-24, March 3, 1986.

62. Brownlee, O.H., "The Economic Consequences of Regulating Without Regard to Economic Consequences," *Issues in Pharmaceutical Economics*, R.A. Chien (ed.)(Lexington, MA: D.C. Heath and Company, 1979); as cited in Jensen, E.J., "Rates of Return to Investment in the Pharmaceutical Industry: A Survey," contract paper prepared for the Office of Technology Assessment, U.S. Congress, September 1990.

63. Burlington, D.B., remarks at "Drug Approvals in the United States and Abroad," seminar sponsored by the Institute for Alternative Futures Foresight, Washington, DC, October 7, 1991.

64. Burrill, S., and Lee, K., *Biotech 91, Changing Environment: An Industry Annual Report* (San Francisco, CA: Ernst & Young, 1990).

65. Burrill, S., and Lee, K., *Biotech 92, Promise to Reality: An Industry Annual Report* (San Francisco, CA: Ernst & Young, 1991).

66. Burrill, S., and Lee, K., *Biotech 93, Accelerating Commercialization: An Industry Annual Report* (San Francisco, CA: Ernst & Young, 1992).

67. Burstall, M.L., "Europe After 1992: Implications for Pharmaceuticals," *Health Affairs* 10(3):157-171, 1991.

68. Burstall, M.L., and Senior, I., *The Community's Pharmaceutical Industry* (Luxembourg, Belgium: Commission on the European Communities, 1985).

69. Buto, K., Director, Bureau of Policy Development, Health Care Financing Administration, U.S. Department of Health and Human Services, Baltimore, MD, personal communication, December 20, 1990.

70. Califre, R., "Marketing Applications in the 1990s, The Paper Dilemma—A Review of Alternative Technologies," conference sponsored by the Drug Information Association, Amsterdam, The Netherlands, November 9-11, 1989.

71. Canadian Drug Manufacturers Association, *The Straight Facts*, No. 5, September 1991, as cited in Lexchin, J., "Pharmaceuticals, Patents and Politics: Canada and Bill C-22," report prepared for the Canadian Centre for Policy Alternatives, Ottawa, Ontario, Canada, February 1992.

72. Carter, L., Special Assistant to the Director, Office of Technology Transfer, National Institutes of Health, Public Health Service, U.S. Department of Health and Human Services, Bethesda, MD, personal communication, February 28, 1991.

73. Caves, R.E., Whinston, M.D., and Hurwitz, M.A., "Patent Expiration, Entry, and Competition in the U.S. Pharmaceutical Industry," *Brookings Papers on Economic Activity Microeconomics: 1991* (Washington, DC: Brookings Institution, 1991).

74. Chadwick, L.W., "Pharmaceutical R&D Study," contract paper prepared for Office of Technology Assessment, U.S. Congress, Washington, DC, December 1989.

75. Chen, P.S., "Testimony on the Commercialization of Federal Laboratory Technology Before the Subcommittee on Regulation, Business Opportunities and Energy, Committee on Small Business," House of Representatives, U.S. Congress, Washington, DC, October 5, 1989.

76. Chen, P.S., Letter to the Honorable Ronald Wyden, U.S. House of Representatives in response to a request at hearings on October 5, 1989 before the Subcommittee on Regulation, Business Opportunities and Energy, Committee on Small Business, U.S. Congress, November 13, 1989.

77. Chen, P.S., "Testimony on Implementation of the Federal Technology Transfer Act Before the Subcommittee on Science, Research and Technology, Committee on Science," U.S. House of Representatives, U.S. Congress, Washington, DC, May 3, 1990.

78. Clarkson, K.W., *Intangible Capital and Rates of Return* (Washington, DC: American Enterprise Institute, 1977).

79. Clymer, H., "The Changing Costs and Risks of Pharmaceutical Innovation," *Economics of Drug Innovation*, J.D. Cooper (ed.)(Washington, DC: The American University, 1969).

80. Cocks, D.L., "Comment on the Welfare Cost of Monopoly: An Inter-Industry Analysis," *Economic Enquiry* 13:601-606, December 1975.

81. Cohen, Jon, "Did Liability Block AIDS Trial?" *Science* 257:316-317, July 17, 1992.

82. Cohen, N.C., Blaney, J., Humblet, C., et al., "Molecular Modeling Software and Methods in Medicinal Chemistry," *Journal of Medicinal Chemistry* 33:883-894, 1990.

83. Coleman, T.S., "Waxman-Hatch Exclusivity Provisions Not Related to Patent Status," *Food Drug Cosmetic Law Journal* 46:345-356, 1991.

84. Collier, J., "The Pharmaceutical Price Regulation Scheme: A Time for Change," *The Lancet* 1(8437):862-863, 1985.

85. Comanor, W.S., "Research and Technical Change in the Pharmaceutical Industry," *Review of Economics and Statistics* 47(2):182-190, May 1965.

86. Comanor, W.S., "The Political Economy of the Pharmaceutical Industry," *Journal of Economic Literature* 24:1178-1217, 1986.

87. Comanor, W.S., and Wilson, T.A., *Advertising and Market Power* (Cambridge, MA: Harvard University Press, 1974).

88. Commerce Clearinghouse, *Medicare and Medicaid Guide, 1990* (Chicago, IL: Commerce Clearinghouse, 1990).

89. Connell, E.B., "The Crisis in Contraception," *Technology Review* 90:47-55, May/June, 1987.

90. Consumer and Corporate Affairs Canada, *Compulsory Licensing of Pharmaceuticals: A Review of Section 41 of the Patent Act*, Canadian Catalog No. RG 15-2-1983 (Ottawa, Canada: Ministry of Supply and Services Canada, 1983).

91. Cook-Deegan, R.M., "The Genesis of the Human Genome Project," *Molecular Genetic Medicine, Volume 1*, T. Friedmann (ed.)(San Diego, CA: Academic Press, 1991).

92. Cooper, R., "The Rise of Activity Based Costing, Part I," *Journal of Cost Management*, Volume 6, Summer 1988.

93. Cooper, R., "The Rise of Activity Based Costing, Part II," *Journal of Cost Management*, Volume 7, Fall 1988.

94. Cooper, R., "The Rise of Activity Based Costing, Part III," *Journal of Cost Management*, Volume 8, Winter 1989.

95. Cooper, R., "The Rise of Activity Based Costing, Part IV," *Journal of Cost Management* Volume 13, Spring 1990.

96. Copeland, T.E., and Weston, J.F., *Financial Theory and Corporate Policy, 3rd Edition* (Reading, MA: Addison-Wesley Publishing Company, 1988.

97. Coppinger, P., "Overview of the Competitiveness of the U.S. Pharmaceutical Industry," presentation to the Council on Competitiveness Working Group on the Drug Approval Process, Washington, DC, December 12, 1990.

98. Coppinger, P., Deputy Associate Commissioner for Planning and Evaluation, Food and Drug Administration, Public Health Service, U.S. Department of Health and Human Services, Rockville, MD, personal communications, December 30, 1991 and January 6, 1992.

99. Coulson, A., Sulston, J., Brenner, S., et al., (eds.) "Toward a Physical Map of the Genome of the Nematode *Caenorhabditis elegans*," *Proceedings of the National Academy of Sciences* (Washington, DC: National Academy of Sciences, 1986).

100. Courteau, J., "Genome Databases," *Science* 254:201-207, 1991.

101. Crawford, S.Y., "ASHP National Survey of Hospital-Based Pharmaceutical Services—1990," *American Journal of Hospital Pharmacy* 47:2655-2695, 1990.

102. Dasgupta, P., and Stiglitz, J., "Uncertainty Industrial Structure, and the Speed of R&D," *Bell Journal of Economics* 11:1-28, 1980.

103. Davis, H.J., "The Shield Intrauterine Device," *American Journal of Obstetrics and Gynecology* 106(3):455-456, 1970.

104. *Davis v. Wyeth Laboratories*, 399 F. 2d 121 (9th Cir. 1968).

105. Dean, P.M., *Molecular Foundations of Drug-Receptor Interactions* (New York, NY: Cambridge University Press, 1987).

106. DiMasi, J.A., Research Associate, Center for the Study of Drug Development, Tufts University, Boston, MA, personal communications, November 3, 1992, September 1992, April 14, 1992, July 1991, and October 18, 1990.

107. DiMasi, J.A., Bryant, N.R., Lasagna, L., "New Drug Development in the United States, 1963-1990," *Clinical Pharmacology and Therapeutics* 50(5):471-486, 1991.

108. DiMasi, J.A., Bryant N.R., and Lasagna L., "Success Rates for New Chemical Entities (NCEs) Entering Clinical Testing in the United States," Poster Presentation, American Society for Clinical Pharmacology Annual Meetings, Orlando, FL, March 20, 1992.

109. DiMasi, J.A., Hansen, R.W., Grabowski, H.G., et al., "The Cost of Innovation in the Pharmaceutical Industry," *Journal of Health Economics* 10:107-142, 1991.

110. Donis-Keller, H., Green, P., Helms, C., et al. (eds.), "A Genetic Linkage Map of the Human Genome," *Cell* 51:319-337, 1987.

111. Doolittle, R.F., Hunkapiller, M.W., Hood, L.E., et al., "Simian Sarcoma virus *onc* gene, *v-sis*, Is Derived From the Gene (or Genes) Encoding a Platelet-Derived Growth Factor," *Science* 221:275-277, 1983.

112. Dranove, D., and Meltzer, D., "Does the FDA Accelerate or Delay the Approval of Important Drugs?" unpublished manuscript, Northwestern University and University of Chicago, Evanston IL, December 1991.

113. DuBose, M., and Moore, S.D., "Speedy Global Approval in Drug Tests Won't Be Implemented for Many Years," *The Wall Street Journal*, November 15, 1991, p. B5.

114. Dukes, G., *The Effects of Drug Regulations* (Lancaster, United Kingdom: MTP Press Ltd., 1985).

115. Dungworth, T., *Product Liability and the Business Sector: Litigation Trends in Federal Courts* (Santa Monica, CA: The Rand Corporation, 1988).

116. Eastep, R., Deputy Director, Division of Biological and Investigational New Drugs, Center for Biologics Evaluation and Research, Food and Drug Administration, Public Health Service, U.S. Department of Health and Human Services, Rockville, MD, personal communication, October 10, 1990.

117. *The Economist*, "A Tighter Prescription," *The Economist* 312(622):61-62, 1989.

118. Eisman, M.M., and Wardell, W.M., "Incremental Time Study: An Analysis of Time Spent in the Development and Approval of Drugs for the U.S. Market," *Economic Costs of FDA Regulations*, Pharmaceutical Manufacturers Association (ed.)(Washington, DC: Pharmaceutical Manufacturers Association, 1981).

119. Eisner, R., Albert, S.H., and Sullivan, M.A., "The New Incremental Tax Credit for R&D: Incentive or Disincentive," *National Tax Journal* 37:171-183, June 1984.

119a. Eli Lilly and Company, Annual Reports, Filing With the U.S. Securities and Exchange Commission, Washington, DC, 1987, 1988, 1989.

120. Eli Lilly, *Lilly Hospital Pharmacy Survey* (Indianapolis, IN: Eli Lilly & Co., 1991).

121. Eli Lilly & Co., "Eli Lilly and Company and Centocor, Inc., Form Strategic Alliance," July 16, 1992 [press release].

122. *Eli Lilly & Co. v. Staats*, 574 F.2d. 904, 923 (7th Cir. 1978) *cert. den.* 439 US 959, 99 S.Ct. 362 (1978).

123. Engelberg, A.B., "Patent Term Extension: An Overreaching Solution to a Nonexistent Problem," *Health Affairs* 1(1):34-45, 1982.

124. Engelberg, A.B., Attorney in private practice, Greenwich, CT, personal communications, February 26, 1991 and May 13, 1992.

125. Evans, D., Health Economist, Special Programme for Research and Training in Tropical Diseases, World Health Organization, Geneva, Switzerland, personal communication, April 1 and 2, 1992.

126. Executive Office of the President, Office of Management and Budget, *Standard Industrial Classification Manual* (Washington, DC: U.S. Government Printing Office, 1972).

127. *F-D-C Reports: Health News Daily*, "FDA Changes Rating System for Drugs," *F-D-C Reports: Health News Daily*, January 7, 1992, p. 3.

128. *F-D-C Reports: Prescription and OTC Pharmaceuticals*, "Mail Order Grew 37% to $2.9 Bil. in 1991 IMS Survey; Growth May Slow Soon," *F-D-C Reports: Prescription and OTC Pharmaceuticals*, March 16, 1992, p. 11.

128a. Faich, G., "Adverse Drug Reaction Monitoring," *New England Journal of Medicine* 314(24): 1589-1592, 1986.

129. Fama, E.F., and French, K.R., "The Cross-Section of Expected Stock Returns," Working Paper, Center for Research in Security Prices, Graduate School of Business, University of Chicago, Chicago, IL, January 1992.

130. Farley, P.J., *Private Health Insurance in the U.S. Data Preview #23*, DHHS Publication No. (PHS) 86-3406 (Washington, DC: U.S. Department of Health and Human Services, National Center for Health Services Research and Health Care Technology Assessment, September 1986).

131. Fein, R., "Economics of Health Research," *Horizons of Health*, H. Wechsler, J. Gurin, and G. Cahill (eds.)(Cambridge MA: Harvard University Press, 1977).

132. Fisher, F.M., and McGowan, J.J., "On the Misuse of Accounting Rates of Return to Infer Monopoly Profits," *American Economic Review* 73(1):82-97, 1983.

133. Flamm, W.G., and Farrow, M., "Recent Trends in the Use and Cost of Animals in the Pharmaceutical Industry," paper prepared for the Office of Technology Assessment, U.S. Congress, Washington, DC, April 1991.

134. Ford, M., *Medicaid: Reimbursement for Outpatient Prescription Drugs*, Congressional Research Service Report to the U.S. Congress, No. 91-235 EPW (Washington, DC: U.S. Government Printing Office, March 7, 1991).

135. Foster Higgins and Co., *1990 Health Care Benefits Survey. Report 1—Indemnity Plans: Cost Design and Funding* (New York, NY: A. Foster Higgins and Co., Inc., 1991).

136. Frank, R.G., and Salkever, D.S., "Pricing, Patent Loss and the Market for Pharmaceuticals," contract paper prepared for the Office of Technology Assessment, U.S. Congress, Washington, DC, December 1990.

137. Friedland R.B., *Facing the Costs of Long-Term Care: An EBRI-ERF Policy Study* (Washington, DC: Employee Benefit Research Institute, 1990).

138. Fritz, D.L., "Drug Use Review Principles Adopted by Key Organizations," *Journal of the American Association of Preferred Provider Organizations* 1(4):22-26, 1991.

139. Fukushima, M., "The Overdose of Drugs in Japan," *Nature* 342(252):850-851, 1989.

140. Ganellin, C.R., "Cimetidine," *Chronicles of Drug Discovery*, J.S. Bindra, and D. Ledniger (eds.)(New York, NY: Wiley, 1982).

141. Garber, A.M., Clarke, A.E., Goldman, D.P., et al., *Federal and Private Roles in the Development and Provision of Alglucerase Therapy for Gaucher Disease* (Background paper for OTA's Project on Government Policies and Pharmaceutical Research and Development), prepared for the Office of Technology Assessment, U.S. Congress, OTA-BP-H-104 (Washington, DC: U.S. Government Printing Office, October 1992).

142. Garber, S., Senior Economist, The Rand Corporation, Santa Monica, CA, personal communications, May 30, 1991 and September 17, 1992.

143. Gates, S., Associate Director for the Center of Utilization of Federal Technology, National Technical Information Service, U.S. Department of Commerce, Springfield, VA, personal communication, April 12, 1991.

144. Gaynor, K., Partner, Price Waterhouse, New York, NY, personal communication, April 1992.

145. Genentech, Inc., Annual Report, Filing With the U.S. Securities and Exchange Commission, Washington, DC, 1989.

146. Gibbons, A., "Biotech Pipeline: Bottleneck Ahead," *Science* 254:369-370, 1991.

147. Gladwell, M., "FDA Plans Reforms for Drug Process," *The Washington Post*, November 8, 1991, p. A1, A22.

148. Gladwell, M., "Critics Say New FDA Procedures for Approving Drugs Would Weaken Agency," *The Washington Post*, November 14, 1991, p. A3.

149. Glaser, W.A., Professor, New School for Social Research, Department of Management and Urban Policy, New York, NY, letter to the Office of Technology Assessment, U.S. Congress, Washington, DC, February 9, 1992.

150. Gluck, M.E., *University-Industry Relationships in Biotechnology: Implications for Society*, unpublished doctoral dissertation, Harvard University, Cambridge, MA, 1987.

151. Gluck, M.E., Blumenthal, D.B., and Stoto, M.A., "University-Industry Relationships in the Life Sciences: Implications for Students and Post-Doctoral Fellows," *Research Policy* 16:327-336, 1987.

152. Gogerty, J., "Preclinical Research Evaluation: Pharmacology; Toxicology; Drug Metabolism," *New Drug Approval Process: Clinical and Regulatory Management*, R.A. Guarino (ed.)(New York, NY: Marcel Dekker, Inc., 1987).

153. Grabowksi, H., "Medicaid Patients' Access to New Drugs," *Health Affairs* 7:102-114, Winter 1988.

154. Grabowksi, H., Professor, Department of Economics, Duke University, Durham, NC, personal communication, July 15, 1992.

155. Grabowski, H.G., and Mueller, D.C., "Life Cycle Effects on Corporate Investment," *Review of Economics and Statistics* 57:400-409, November 1975; as cited in Mueller, D.C., and Reardon, E.A., "Rates of Return on Corporate Investment," Department of Economics, University of Maryland, College Park, MD, undated manuscript.

156. Grabowski, H.G., Schweitzer, S.O., and Shiota, R., "The Medicaid Drug Lag Adoption of New Drugs by State Medicaid Formulas," unpublished paper, Durham, NC, July 1990.

157. Grabowski, H.G., and Vernon, J.M., "A Sensitivity Analysis of Expected Profitability of Pharmaceutical Research and Development," *Managerial and Decision Economics* 3(1):36-40, 1982.

158. Grabowski, H.G., and Vernon, J.M., "Pioneers, Imitators, and Generics—A Simulation Model of Schumpeterian Competition," *Quarterly Journal of Economics* 102(3):491-525, 1987.

159. Grabowski, H.G., and Vernon, J.M., "A New Look at the Returns and Risks to Pharmaceutical R&D," *Management Science* 36(7):804-821, July 1990.

160. Grabowski, H.G., and Vernon, J.M., unpublished appendix to "A New Look at the Returns and Risks to Pharmaceutical R&D," Department of Economics, Duke University, Durham, NC, 1990.

161. Grabowski, H.G., and Vernon, J.M., "Brand Loyalty, Entry and Price Competition in Pharmaceuticals After the 1984 Drug Act," *Journal of Law and Economics* 35(2):331-350, October 1992.

162. Grabowski, H.G., Vernon, J.M., and Thomas, L.G., "Estimating the Effects of Regulation on Innovation: An International Comparative Analysis of the Pharmaceutical Industry," *The Journal of Law and Economics* 21(1):133-163, 1978.

163. Graig, L.A., *Health of Nations* (Washington, DC: The Wyatt Company, 1991).

164. Graves, E.J., and Kozak, L.J., *National Discharge Survey: Annual Summary, 1989* (Vital Health Stat 13 (109)), DHHS No.(PHS) 92-1770 (Hyattsville, MD: National Center for Health Statistics, March 1992).

165. Griffin, M.E., Ray, W.A., Mortimer, E.A., et al., "Risk of Seizures and Encephalopathy After Immunization With the Diphtheria-Tetanus-Pertussis Vaccine," *Journal of the American Medical Association* 263(12):1641-1645, 1990.

166. Griliches, Z., "Search for R&D Spillovers," National Bureau of Economic Research, reprint 1758, 1992.

167. Groft, S., Acting Director, Office of Science Policy and Legislation, National Institutes of Health, Public Health Service, U.S. Department of Health and Human Services, Bethesda, MD, personal communication, February 8, 1991.

168. Haffner, M.E., and Kelsey, J.V., "Evaluation of Orphan Products by the U.S. Food and Drug Administration," *International Journal of Technology Assessment in Health Care*, 1992.

169. Hagan, C.F., "Vaccine Compensation Schemes," *Food Drug Cosmetic Law Journal* 45:477-486, 1990.

170. Hall, B.H., "Investment and Research and Development at the Firm Level: Does the Source of Financing Matter?" NBER Working Paper Series, Working Paper No. 4096 (Cambridge, MA: National Bureau of Economic Research, June 1992).

171. Hall, S.S., *Invisible Frontiers: The Race to Synthesize a Human Gene* (New York, NY: Atlantic Monthly Press, 1987).

172. Halliday, R., Lumley, C., and Walker, S., *Trends in Worldwide Pharmaceutical R&D Expenditure in the 1980s* (Surrey, England: Centre for Medicines Research, 1991).

173. Halperin, J., remarks at "Advisory Committees and the FDA," conference sponsored by the Food and Drug Law Institute, Washington, DC, March 15, 1990.

174. Hancher, L., "Regulating Pharmaceutical Prices and Corporate R&D Strategies in Britain and France," *Strategies for New Technology-Case Studies From Britain and France*, M. Sharp and P. Holmes (eds.)(New York, NY: Philip Allan, 1989).

175. Hansen, R., "The Pharmaceutical Development Process: Estimates of Development Costs and Times and the Effect of Proposed Regulatory Changes," *Issues in Pharmaceutical Economics*, R.A. Chien (ed.)(Lexington, MA: D.C. Heath and Company, 1979).

176. Hansen, R., Associate Dean, School of Business Administration, University of Rochester, Rochester, NY, personal communication, May 1, 1991.

177. Hansen, R.W., "Effects of Incremental Costs on Pharmaceutical Innovation," *Economic Costs of FDA Regulations*, Pharmaceutical Manufacturers Association (ed.)(Washington, DC: Pharmaceutical Manufacturers Association, 1981).

178. Harvey, K., "Australia: Pharmaceutical Benefits Scheme," *The Lancet* 337(738):418-419, 1991.

179. Hausch, C., and Blaney, J.M., "The New Look to QSAR" *Drug Design: Fact or Fantasy?* G. Jolles and K.R.H. Woolridge (eds.)(New York, NY: Academic Press, 1984).

180. Hawkins, E.S., and Reich, M.R., "Japanese-Originated Pharmaceutical Products in the United States from 1960 to 1989: An Assessment of Innovation," *Clinical Pharmacology and Therapeutics* 51(1):1-11, 1992.

181. Hazelwood, M., Manager of Ancillary and Pharmacy Sections, Medical Program, Illinois Department of Public Aid, Springfield, IL, personal communication, November 1, 1991.

182. Henderson, J.A., and Eisenberg, T., "The Quiet Revolution in Products Liability: An Empirical Study of Legal Change," *UCLA Law Review* 37:479-553, 1990.

183. Hendrickson, W.A., "Determination of Macromolecular Structures Form Anomalous Diffrac-

tion of Synchrotrom Radiation,'' *Science* 254:51-58, 1991.

184. Hensler, D.R., Vaiana, M.E., Kakalik, J.S., et al., *Special Report—Trends in Tort Litigation: The Story Behind the Statistics* (Santa Monica, CA: The Rand Corportion, 1987).

185. *Hewlett Packard Company v. United States*, 385 F. 2d, 1013 (9th Cir. 1967) *cert. denied* 390 U.S. 988, 88 S.Ct. 1184 (1968).

186. Hill, D., and Beatrice, M.G., ''Biotechnology Facility Requirements, Part I,'' *BioPharm*, October 1989, pp. 20-31.

187. Hilts, P.J., ''Top FDA Staff Members Oppose Looser Drug Approval System,'' *The New York Times*, December 20, 1991, p. A29.

188. Hilts, P.J., ''Seeking Limits to a Drug Monopoly,'' *New York Times* May 14, 1992, p. D1.

189. Himmelberg, C.P., and Peterson, B.C., ''R&D and Internal Finance: A Panel Study of Small Firms in High-Tech Industries,'' unpublished manuscript, Washington University, St. Louis, MO, July 10, 1992.

190. Hollenberg, M.D., ''Receptor Triggering and Receptor Regulation: Structure Activity Relationships From the Receptor's Point of View,'' *Journal of Medicinal Chemistry* 33:1275-1281, 1990.

191. Hopper, D., Pharmacy Specialist, Maine Bureau of Medical Services, Augusta, ME, personal communication, October 29, 1991.

192. Huber, P.W., *Liability: The Legal Revolution and Its Consequences* (New York, NY: Basic Books, 1988).

193. Huber, P.W, and Litan, R.E. (eds.), *The Liability Maze: The Impact of Liability Law on Safety and Innovation* (Washington, DC: The Brookings Institution, 1991).

194. *Human Gene Therapy*, ''Human Gene Transfer/Therapy Patient Registry—Summary,'' *Human Gene Therapy* 3:457, 1992.

195. Hurwitz, M.A., and Caves, R.E., ''Persuasion or Information? Promotion and the Shares of Brand Name and Generic Pharmaceuticals,'' *Journal of Law and Economics* 31:299-320, 1988.

196. Hutt, P.B., ''Investigations and Reports Respecting FDA Regulation of New Drugs (Part I),'' *Clinical Pharmacology and Therapeutics* 33(4):537-548, April 1983.

197. Hutt, P.B., ''Investigations and Reports Respecting FDA Regulation of New Drugs (Part II),'' *Clinical Pharmacology and Therapeutics* 33(5), May 1983.

198. Ibbotson, R.G., and Sinquefield, R.A., ''Stocks, Bonds, Bills, and Inflation: Simulations of the Future (1976-2000),'' *Journal of Business* 49:313-338, July 1976.

199. Ijiri, Y., ''Convergence of Cash Recovery Rate,'' *Quantitative Planning and Control*, Y. Ijiri, and A. Whinston (eds.)(New York, NY: Academic Press, 1979).

200. Ijiri, Y., ''Recovery Rate and Cash Flow Accounting,'' *Financial Executive* 48:54-60, March 1980.

201. IMS America, Inc., unpublished data prepared for the Office of Technology Assessment, U.S. Congress, Washington, DC, 1991.

202. Ingersoll, B., ''Drug Approvals to be Hastened Under New Pact,'' *The Wall Street Journal*, November 13, 1991, p. A3.

203. Ingersoll, B., and Stout, H., ''Plan to Reform Drug Approvals Has Opposition,'' *The Wall Street Journal*, November 14, 1991, p. B4.

204. *Inside Roche*, ''The Animal Research Debate: Is There a Common Ground?'' *Inside Roche* 13:2-11, 1989.

205. Institute of Management Accountants, *Management Accounting Glossary* (Englewood Cliffs, NJ: Prentice Hall, 1991).

206. Institute of Medicine, *Vaccine Supply and Innovation* (Washington, DC: National Academy Press, 1985).

207. Institute of Medicine, *Funding Health Sciences Research: A Strategy to Restore Balance* (Washington, DC: National Academy Press, 1990).

208. Institute of Medicine, *The AIDS Research Program of the National Institutes of Health: Report of a Study* (Washington, DC: National Academy Press, 1991).

209. Interstudy, *Managed Care: A Decade in Review, 1980-1990* (Excelsior, MN: Interstudy, 1991).

210. James, B.E., remarks at ''Drug Approvals in the U.S. and Abroad,'' seminar sponsored by the Institute for Alternative Futures, Washington, DC, October 7, 1991.

211. Japanese Pharmaceutical Affairs Bureau, *Pharmaceutical Administration in Japan, 5th Edition* (Tokyo, Japan: Yakuji Nippo, Ltd., 1991).

212. Japan Pharmaceutical Manufacturers Association, *Data Book 1990* (Tokyo, Japan: Japan Pharmaceutical Manufacturers Association, 1990)

213. Jensen, E.J., "Research Expenditures and the Discovery of New Drugs," *Journal of Industrial Economics* 36(1):83-95, 1987.

214. Jensen, E.J., "Rates of Return to Investment in the Pharmaceutical Industry: A Survey," contract paper prepared for the Office of Technology Assessment, U.S. Congress, Washington, DC, September 1990.

215. Joglekar, P., and Paterson, M.L., "A Closer Look at the Returns and Risks of Pharmaceutical R&D," *Journal of Health Economics* 5:153-177, 1986.

216. Johnson, H.T., and Kaplan, R.S., *Relevance Lost: The Rise and Fall of Management Accounting* (Cambridge, MA: Harvard Business Review, 1987).

217. Jolles, G., "Conclusions," *Drug Design: Fact or Fantasy?* G. Jolles and K.R.H. Woolridge (eds.)(New York, NY: Academic Press, 1984).

218. Jones, T.M., "Improved Drug Delivery: A Perspective From Industry," *Novel Drug Delivery and Its Therapeutic Application*, L.F. Prescott and W.S. Nimmo (eds.)(New York, NY: Wiley, 1989).

219. Kahn, H.A., and Sempos, C.T., *Statistical Methods in Epidemiology* (New York, NY: Oxford University Press, 1989).

220. Kaitin, K.I., Mathison, N., Worthington, F.K., et al., "The Drug Lag: An Update of New Drug Introductions in the U.S. and U.K., 1977 through 1987," *Clinical Pharmacology and Therapeutics* 4:121-138, 1989.

221. Kaitin, K.I., Melville, A., and Morris, B., "FDA Advisory Committees and the New Drug Approval Process," *Journal of Clinical Pharmacology* 29(10):886-890, 1989.

222. Kamien, M.I., and Schwartz, N.L., *Market Structure and Innovation* (Cambridge, NY: Cambridge University Press, 1982).

223. Kang, S.-H., Assistant Professor, School of Industrial Administration, Carnegie-Mellon University, Pittsburgh, PA, unpublished note to the Office of Technology Assessment, U.S. Congress, Washington, DC, July 1991.

224. Kang, S-H., Assistant Professor, School of Industrial Administration, Carnegie-Mellon University, Pittsburgh, PA, personal communication, November 19, 1991.

225. Kaplan, E.L., and Meier, P., "Nonparametric Estimation From Incomplete Observations," *Journal of the American Statistical Association* 53(282):457, 1958.

226. Katz, M., "The Birth Pangs of a New Drug," *Drug and Cosmetic Industry* 128:40, October 1980; as cited in Smith, M., *Principles of Pharmaceutical Marketing* (Philadelphia, PA: Lea & Febiger, 1983).

227. Kelsey, J., Special Assistant to the Director, Office of Orphan Products Development, Food and Drug Administration, Public Health Service, U.S. Department of Health and Human Services, personal communications, November 26, 1987, November 26, 1990, and May 10, 1991.

228. Kenney, M., *Biotechnology: The University-Industrial Complex* (New Haven, CT: Yale University Press, 1986).

229. Kerem, B.-S., Rommens, J.M., Buchanan, J.A., et al., "Identification of the Cystic Fibrosis Gene: Genetic Analysis," *Science* 245:1073-1080, 1990.

230. Kevles, D.J., *The Name of Eugenics* (Berkeley, CA: University of California Press, 1985).

231. Keystone AIDS Vaccine Liability Project, *Final Report* (Keystone, CO: The Keystone Center, May 1990).

232. Kiser, J.D., "Legal Issues Raised by Expedited Approval of, and Expanded Access to, Experimental AIDS Treatments," *Food Drug Cosmetic Law Journal* 45(4):363-376, 1990.

233. Klynveld Peat Marwick Goerdeler (KPMG), *Tax Treatment of Research and Development Expenditures* (Amsterdam, The Netherlands: International Tax Center, 1990).

234. Krimsky, S., "Corporate Academic Ties in Biotechnology: A Report on Research in Progress," *GeneWatch* 1:3-5, 1984.

235. Kuhlik, B.E., "The Medicaid Prescription Drug Rebate and Improved Access to Medicines Requirements of the Omnibus Budget Reconciliation Act of 1990," *Food Drug Cosmetic Law Journal* 46:363-390, March 1991.

236. Kuhlik, B.N., and Kingham, R.F., "The Adverse Effects of Standardless Punitive Damage Awards on Pharmaceutical Development and

Availablilty," *Food Drug Cosmetic Law Journal* 45:693-708, 1990.

237. La Pre, E., Eligibility Technician, Rhode Island Department of Elderly Affairs, Providence, RI, personal communication, October 28, 1991.

238. Laetz, T., and Silberman, G., "Reimbursement Policies Constrain the Practice of Oncology," *Journal of the American Medical Assocation* 266:2996-3000, 1991.

239. Lasagna, L., "The Chilling Effect of Product Liability on New Drug Development," *The Liability Maze: The Impact of Liability Law on Safety and Innovation*, R.E. Litan and Peter W. Huber (eds.)(Washington, DC: The Brookings Institution, 1991).

240. Lawton, S. "Controversy Under the Orphan Drug Act: Is Resolution on the Way?" *Food Drug Cosmetic Law Journal* 46:327-343, 1991.

241. Leonard, H.B., *Checks Unbalanced: The Quiet Side of Government Spending* (New York, NY: Basic Books, 1986).

242. Levin, R.C., Klevorick, A.K., Nelson, R.R., et al., "Appropriating the Returns From Industrial Research and Development," *Brookings Papers on Economic Activity* 3:783-820, 1987; as cited in Scherer, F.M., and Ross, D., *Industrial Market Structure and Economic Performance, 3rd Edition* (Boston, MA: Houghton Mifflin Company, 1990).

243. Lewent, J., Chief Financial Officer, Merck & Co., Rahway, NJ, personal communication, September 8, 1992.

244. Lexchin, J., "Pharmaceuticals, Patents and Politics: Canada and Bill C-22," report prepared for the Canadian Centre for Policy Alternatives, Ottawa, Ontario, Canada, February 1992.

245. Link, A., "Tax Incentives and the U.S. Pharmaceutical Industry," contract report prepared for the Office of Technology Assessment, U.S. Congress, Washington, DC, November 1990.

246. Lipenta, C., Human Resources Manager, The Nemours Foundation, Jacksonville, FL, personal communication, November 1, 1991.

247. Litan, R.E., Swire, P., and Winston, C., "The U.S. Liability System: Background and Trends," *Liability: Perspectives and Policy*, R.E. Litan and C. Winston (eds.)(Washington, DC: The Brookings Institution, 1988).

248. Loss, I.S., and Morgenstern, A.D., *Pharmaceuticals/Tax Policy: A Successful Puerto Rican Statehood Initiative Will Result in Higher Corporate Tax Rates for Many Companies* (Washington, DC: The NatWest Investment Banking Group, 1990).

249. Louis, K.S., Swazey, J.P., and Anderson, M.S., "University Policies and Ethical Issues in Graduate Research and Education: Results of a Survey of Graduate School Deans," unpublished manuscript, University of Minnesota, St. Paul, and Acadia Institute, Bar Harbor, ME, 1991.

250. Maedgen, B.J., and McCall, S.L., "A Survey of Law Regarding the Liability of Manufacturers and Sellers of Drug Products and Medical Devices," *St. Mary's Law Journal* 18:395-462, 1986.

251. Mahoney, R.J., and Littlejohn, S.E., "Innovation on Trial: Punitive Damages Versus New Products," *Science* 246:1395-1399, 1989.

252. Mains, M., Manager, ConnPACE, Connecticut Department of Aging, Hartford, CT, personal communication, October 30, 1991.

253. Mansfield, E., "Academic Research and Industrial Innovation," *Research Policy* 20:1-12, 1991.

254. Marcus, L.C., "Liability for Vaccine-Related Injuries," *New England Journal of Medicine* 318:191, 1988.

255. Marks, E., Vice-President, Medco Containment Services, Inc., Montvale, NJ, personal communication, October 27, 1992.

256. Marks, L., Staff Specialist for Pharmacy Services, Maryland Department of Health and Mental Hygiene, Baltimore, MD, personal communication, October 28, 1991.

257. Marovelli, F.D., *Effective Corporate Tax Rates 1987* (Arlington, VA: Tax Analysts, Inc., 1988).

258. Marovelli, F.D., Accounting Manager, Tax Analysts, Inc., Arlington, VA, personal communication, April 2, 1992.

258a. Marwick, C., "FDA Seeks Swifter Approval of Drugs for Some Life-Threatening of Debilitating Diseases," *Journal of the American Medical Association* 260(20):2976, 1988.

259. Mason, C., Supervising Administrative Analyst, New Jersey Bureau of Pharmaceutical Assistance, Trenton, NJ, personal communication, October 28, 1991.

260. Mattison, N., Trimble, A.G., and Lasagna, L., "New Drug Development in the United States, 1963 Through 1984," *Clinical Pharmacology and Therapeutics* 43:290-301, 1988.

261. Mayr, E., *The Growth of Biological Thought: Diversity, Evolution, and Inheritance* (Cambridge: Harvard University Press, 1982).

262. McAvoy, K., Chief, Economic Assessment Group, Food and Drug Administration, Public Health Services, U.S. Department of Health and Human Services, Rockville, MD, personal communication, October 1990.

263. McDonough, R.T., Public Policy Director, The UpJohn Company, Kalamazoo, MI, personal communication, September 8, 1992.

264. McGraw-Hill and Company, *McGraw-Hill Enclyclopedia of Science and Technology*, Volume 13 (New York, NY: McGraw-Hill and Company, 1987).

265. McGuire, E.P., *The Impact of Product Liability*, Research Report 908 (New York, NY: The Conference Board, 1988).

266. McKusick, V.A., *Mendelian Inheritance in Man* (Baltimore, MD: Johns Hopkins University Press, 1990).

267. Merck & Co., Inc., *The Merck Index: An Encyclopedia of Chemicals, Drugs and Biologicals* (Rahway, NJ: Merck & Company, 1989).

268. *Merck v. Staats*, 529 F. Supp. 1 (D.D.C. 1977) *aff'd per curiam Merck Co. v. Staats*, 665 F.2d 1236 (D.C. Cir. 1981).

269. Meyers, A., Chief, Document and Reporting Branch, Office of Drug Evaluation and Research, Center for Drug Evaluation and Research, Food and Drug Administration, Public Health Service, U.S. Department of Health and Human Services, Rockville, MD, personal communication, April 13, 1990.

270. Meyers, A.S., Executive Director, National Organization for Rare Disorders, Inc., New Fairfield, CT, personal communication, August 31,1992.

271. Milhous, W.K., Walter Reed Army Medical Center, Washington, DC, personal communication, October 29, 1991.

272. Milhous, W., and Shuster, B., "New Drugs for Multiple Drug Resistant Malaria," *U.S. Medicine* 26(15/16):27, 1990.

273. Miller, M., "Debt and Taxes," *Journal of Finance* 32:261-275, 1977.

274. Millstein, L.G, "Preparing a New Drug Application: General Considerations," *New Drug Approval Process: Clinical and Regulatory Management*, R.A. Guarino (ed.)(New York, NY: Marcel Dekker, Inc., 1987).

275. Millstein, L.G., "Specific Requirements, Content, and Format of an NDA," *New Drug Approval Process: Clinical and Regulatory Management*, R.A. Guarino (ed.)(New York, NY: Marcel Dekker, Inc., 1987).

276. Mitsuya, H., Weinhold, K., Yarchoan, R., et al., "Credit Government Scientists with Developing Anti-AIDS Drug', Letter to the editor, *New York Times*, September 28, 1989, p. A26.

277. Moeller, J., and Lair, T., *Prescribed Medicines: A Summary of Use, Expenditures, and Source of Payment*, U.S. Department of Health and Human Services, Public Health Service, Agency for Health Care Policy, and Research, tabulations, Rockville, MD, forthcoming.

278. Moertel, C.G., "Off-Label Drug Use for Cancer Therapy and National Health Care Priorities," *Journal of the American Medical Association* 266:3031-3032, 1991.

279. Montgomery, A.B., "How the Recent Changes in Expedited Drug Approval Procedures Affect the Work of a Clinical Investigator," *Food Drug Cosmetic Law Journal* 45(4):339-346, 1990.

280. Montgomery, D., and Silk, A., "Estimating Dynamic Effects of Market Communications Expenditures," *Management Science* 18(10):B485-B501, June 1972.

281. Moonen, C.T.W., van Zijl, P.C.M., Frank, J.A., et al., "Functional Magnetic Resonance Imaging in Medicine and Physiology," *Science* 250:53-61, 1990.

282. Mueller, D.C., and Reardon, E.A., "Rates of Return on Corporate Investment," Department of Economics, University of Maryland, College Park, MD, undated manuscript.

283. Mullis, K.B., "The Unusual Origin of the Polymerase Chain Reaction," *Scientific American* 262:56-65, 1990.

284. Myers, J.S., Director, Office of Electronic Information Products and Services, U.S. Patent and Trademark Office, U.S. Department of

Commerce, personal communications, February 8, 1990 and April 4, 1990.

285. Myers, S.C., and Shyam-Sunder, L., "Cost of Capital Estimates for Investment in Pharmaceutical Research and Development," contract report prepared for the Office of Technology Assessment, U.S. Congress, Washington, DC, January 1991.

286. Narin, F., and Rozek, R.P., "Bibliometric Analysis of U.S. Pharmaceutical Industry Research Performance," *Research Policy* 17:139-154, 1988.

287. National Pharmaceutical Council, *Pharmaceutical Benefits Under State Medical Assistance Programs* (Reston, VA: National Pharmaceutical Council, Inc., September 1991).

288. National Research Council and Institute of Medicine, *Developing New Contraceptives: Obstacles and Opportunities*, L. Mastroianni, P.J. Donaldson, and T.J. Kane (eds.)(Washington, DC: National Academy Press, 1990).

289. National Science Board, *Science and Engineering Indicators-1989*, NSB Pub. No. 89-1 (Washington, DC: U.S. Government Printing Office, 1989).

290. National Science Foundation, *Selected Data on Research and Development in Industry: 1990*, Selected Data Tables, NSF 92-317 (Washington, DC: National Science Foundation, 1992).

291. National Wholesalers and Distributors Association, *1989 Operating Survey*, (Washington, DC: National Wholesalers and Distributors Association, 1990).

292. Nelson, C., Survey Statistcan, U.S. Income and Statistics Branch, Census Bureau, U.S. Department of Commerce, Washington, DC, personal communication, March 26, 1991.

293. Neustadt, R.E., and Fineberg, H., *The Epidemic That Never Was: Policy-Making and the Swine Flu Affair* (New York, NY: Vintage Books, 1982).

294. Newhouse, J.P., Manning, W.G., Morris, C.N., et al., "Some Interim Results From a Controlled Trial of Cost Sharing in Health Insurance," *New England Journal of Medicine* 305:1501, 1981.

295. Norton, N.N., "Exploring Europe's Generics Market," *Pharmaceutical Executive* 11(9):46-56, 1991.

296. Oestreicher, P., Assistant Director of Public Policy and Communications, Hoffmann-La Roche, Inc., Nutley, NJ, letter to the Office of Technology Assessment, U.S. Congress, Washington, DC, June 22, 1992.

297. O'Hare, J., Economist, Joint Committee on Taxation, U.S. Congress, Washington, DC, personal communication, December 19, 1990.

298. Olson, M., "Pharmaceutical Firm R&D Strategy," working paper, Department of Economics, Washington University, St. Louis, MO, September 1992.

299. Olson, M.V., Dutchik, J.E., and Graham, M.Y., "Random-Clone Strategy for Genomic Restriction Mapping in Yeast," *Proceedings of the National Academy of Sciences* (Washington, DC: National Academy of Sciences, 1986).

300. Ondetti, M.A., Cushman, D.W., and Rubin, B., "Captopril," *Chronicles of Drug Discovery*, J.S. Bindra and D. Ledniger (eds.)(New York, NY: Wiley, 1983).

301. O'Reilly, B., "Drugmakers Under Fire," *Fortune* 124:48-61, July 29, 1991.

302. Organisation for Economic Co-operation and Development, *The Pharmaceutical Industry: Trade Related Issues* (Paris, France: OECD, 1985).

303. Organisation for Economic Co-operation and Development, Industry Committee, "Current Major Themes in Industrial Policy Tax Reform and Industrial Performance," unpublished document, OECD, Paris, France, September 1988.

304. Organisation for Economic Co-operation and Development, *OECD Health Data-Comparative Analysis of Health Systems* (Paris, France: CREDES-OECD, 1991).

305. Palca, J., "Changes Ahead for Gene Therapy Review Process? and Four Thumbs Up, One Thumb Down," *Science* 253:624-625, 1991.

306. Panem, S., *The Iterferon Crusade* (Washington, DC: The Brookings Institution, 1984).

307. Parker, J., "Regulatory Stringency and the International Diffusion of Drugs," *Arne Ryde Symposium on Pharmaceutical Economics*, B. Lindgren (ed.)(Stockholm, Sweden: Swedish Insititute for Health Economics and Liber Forlag, 1984).

308. Parry, T.G., and Thwaites, R.M.A., *The Pharmaceutical Industry in Australia—A Benchmark*

Study (North Sydney, Australia: Australian Pharmaceutical Manufacturers Association, 1988).

309. Patented Medicine Prices Review Board of Canada, *First Annual Report 1988*, Catalog Number RG79-1/1989 (Ottawa, Canada: Ministry of Supply and Services Canada, 1989).

310. Patented Medicine Prices Review Board of Canada, *Second Annual Report 1989*, Catalog Number RG79-1/1990 (Ottawa, Canada: Ministry of Supply and Services Canada, 1990).

311. Patented Medicine Prices Review Board of Canada, *Fourth Annual Report 1991*, Catalog Number RG79-1/1991 (Ottawa, Canada: Ministry of Supply and Services Canada, 1992).

312. Patterson, A., Chief of Drugs and Pharmacies, U.S. Department of Veterans Affairs, Washington, DC, personal communication, February 27, 1992.

313. Pearson, P.L., Lucier, R., and Brunn, C., "Databases to Serve the Genome Program and the Medical Genetics Community," *Etiology of Human Disease at the DNA Level*, J. Lindsten and U. Petterson (eds.)(New York: Raven Press, 1991).

314. Peck, C., "Testimony Before the U.S. Department of Health and Human Services Advisory Committee on the FDA, Subcommittee on Human Drugs and Biologics," Washington, DC, September 27, 1990.

315. Peltzman, S., *Regulation of Pharmaceutical Innovation: The 1962 Amendments*, AEI Evaluative Series (Washington, DC: American Enterprise Institute, 1974).

316. Perkin-Elmer Cetus, *PCR Bibliography Volume 1, No. 5* (Norwalk, CT: Perkin Elmer Cetus, 1990).

317. Persinger, G., Deputy Vice President of Health Care Systems, Pharmaceutical Manufacturers Association, Washington, DC, personal communications, January 28, 1991, March 31, 1992, and December 2, 1992.

318. Peterson, M.A., *Civil Justice in the 1980s: Trends in Jury Trials and Verdicts in California and Cook County* (Santa Monica, CA: The Rand Corporation, 1987).

319. Pharma Japan, "Chuikyo Scraps Bulk Line Method in Favor of Adding 15% of NHI Price to Weighted Average Value," *Pharma Japan* 1257:1-3, 1991.

320. Pharmaceutical Manufacturers Association, *Annual Survey Reports*, 1970-1991 (Washington, DC: Pharmaceutical Manufacturers Association, 1970-1991).

321. Pharmaceutical Manufacturers Association, *1981-1983 Statistical Report*, (Washington, DC: Pharmaceutical Manufacturers Association, 1983).

322. Pharmaceutical Manufacturers Association, "Patents on Medicinal Products," unpublished report, Washington, DC, 1988.

323. Pharmaceutical Manufacturers Association, *Biotechnology Medicines in Development*, (Washington, DC: Pharmaceutical Manufacturers Association, 1991).

324. Pharmaceutical Manufacturers Association, *1989-1991 Statistical Report: The U.S. Pharmaceutical Industry*, (Washington, DC: Pharmaceutical Manufacturers Association, 1991).

325. Pharmaceutical Manufacturers Association, advertisement in the *Washington Post*, January 30, 1992, p. A21.

326. Pharmaceutical Manufacturers Association, *Annual Survey Report 1992* (Washington, DC: Pharmaceutical Manufacturers Association, 1992).

327. Pharmaceutical Manufacturers Association, *Directory of Prescription Drug Indigent Programs* (Washington, DC: Pharmaceutical Manufacturers Association, 1992).

328. *Pharmaprojects* (Surrey, United Kingdom: P.J.B. Publications Ltd., 1991).

329. Phillips, L.M., Nudelman, E., Gaeta, F.C.A., et al., "ELAM-1 Mediates Cell Adhesion by Recognition of a Carbohydrate Ligand, Sial-Le[1]," *Science* 250:1130-1132, 1991.

330. Pindyck, R.S., "Irreversibility, Uncertainty, and Investment," *Journal of Economic Literature* 29:1110-1148, September 1991.

331. Porter, R.J., "Conflict of Interest in Research: Personal Gain—The Seeds of Conflict," *Biomedical Research: Collaboration and Conflict of Interest*, R.J Porter and T.E. Malone (eds.)(Baltimore, MD: The Johns Hopkins University Press, 1992).

332. Pradhan, S.B., *International Pharmaceutical Marketing* (Westport, CT: Quorom Books, 1983).

333. Prescott, L.F., "The Need for Improved Drug Delivery in Clinical Practice,' *Novel Drug Delivery and Its Applications*, L.F. Prescott and W.S. Nimmo (eds.)(New York: Wiley, 1989).

334. Price Waterhouse, *Doing Business in the United States: Information Guide and Supplement* (New York, NY: Price Waterhouse, 1987).

335. Price Waterhouse, *Doing Business in the United States: Information Guide and Supplement* (New York, NY: Price Waterhouse, 1989).

336. Provine, W.B., *The Origins of Theoretical Population Genetics* (Chicago, IL: University of Chicago Press, 1971).

337. Public Citizen Health Research Group, "Comments to the Office of Federal Patent Licensing, National Technical Information Service," unpublished memorandum, Washington, DC, April 29, 1988.

338. Quirmbach, H.C., "R&D: Competition Risk and Performance," MRG Working Paper No. M8742, University of Southern California, Los Angeles, CA, September 13, 1989.

339. Ragusa, C., Manager of Analytic Services, IMS International, Inc., Plymouth Meeting, PA, personal communication, May 13, 1992.

340. Randall, B., and McLaughlin, M., *Drug Approval: Access to Experimental Drugs for Severely Ill Patients*, Congressional Research Service Issue Brief No. IB90016, archived (Washington, DC: U.S. Government Printing Office, January 24, 1991).

341. Rathmann, G., Chairman and Cheif Executive Officer, ICOS Corp., Bothell, WA, personal communication, February 5, 1991.

342. Redwood, H., *The Pharmaceutical Industry: Trends, Problems, and Achievements* (Suffolk, United Kingdom: Oldwicks Press, 1988).

343. Regan, K., Director of Division on Planning and Evaluation, Office of Deputy Associate Administrator for Policy Coordination, Alcohol, Drug Abuse, and Mental Health Administration, National Insitutes of Health, Public Health Service, U.S. Department of Health and Human Services, Rockville, MD, personal communication, February 4, 1991.

344. Reich, M.R., "Why the Japanese Don't Export More Pharmaceuticals: Health Policy as Industrial Policy," *California Management Review* 32(2):124-150, 1990.

345. Reich, M.R., "Policy Challenges Facing the Pharmaceutical Industry in Japan," paper presented at the 1991 Pharmaceutical Manufacturers Association International Section Annual Meeting, Scottsdale, AZ, April 23-26, 1991.

346. Reinganum, J.F., "A Dynamic Game of R and D: Patent Protection and Competive Behavior," *Econometria* 50:671-688, May 1982.

347. Relman, A.S., "Economic Incentives in Clinical Investigation," *New England Journal of Medicine* 320:933-934, 1989.

348. Reuter, P., "The Economic Consequences of Expanded Corporate Liability: An Exploratory Study," The Rand Corporation, The Institute for Civil Justice, Santa Monica, CA. N-2807-ICJ, November 1988.

349. *Reyes v. Wyeth Labs*, 498 F. 2d 1264 (5th Cir. 1974).

350. Richard, B.W., Melville, A., and Lasagna, L., "Postapproval Research as a Condition of Approval: An Update, 1985-1986," *Journal of Clinical Research and Drug Development* 3:247-257, 1989.

351. Riordan, J.R., Rommens, J.M., Kerem, B.S., et al., "Identification of the Cystic Fibrosis Gene: Cloning and Characterization of Complementary DNA," *Science* 245:1066-1072, 1989.

352. Roberts, K., and Weitzman, M.L., "Funding Criteria for Research, Development, and Exploration Projects," *Econometricia* 49(5):1261-1288, 1981.

352a. Roll, R., "A Crituque of the Asset Pricing Therory's Tests," *Journal of Financial Economics* p. 129-176, March 1977.

353. Rommens, J.M., Iannuzzi, M.C., Kerem, B.-S., et al., "Identification of the Cystic Fibrosis Gene: Chromosome Walking and Jumping," *Science* 245:1059-1065, 1989.

354. Rosenberg, S.A., Blaese, R.M., and Anderson, W.F., "The N2-TIL Human Gene Transfer Clinical Protocol," *Human Gene Therapy* 1:73-92, 1990.

355. Rossiter, B.J.F., and Caskey, C.T., *Report of the MDA Gene Therapy Conference* (Tucson, AZ: Muscular Dystrophy Association, 1991).

356. Rovner, J., "Prescription Drug Prices," *The CQ Researcher* 2(26):599-604, 1992.

357. Ruscio, K., "Tax Incentives and Innovation," unpublished manuscript, 1981.

358. Saiki, R.K., Gelfand, D.H., Stoffel, S., et al., "Primer-Directed Enzymatic Amplification of DNA With a Thermostable DNA Polymerase," *Science* 239:487-491, 1988.

359. Salamon, G., "Cash Recovery Rates and Measures of Firm Profitability," *The Accounting Review* 57(2):292-302, 1982.

360. Salamon, G., "Accounting Rates of Return," *American Economic Review* 75(3):495-504, 1985.

361. Scheiber, G.J., Poullier, J.-P., and Greenwald, L.M.," Health Care Systems in Twenty-Four Countries," *Health Affairs* 10(3):22-38, Fall 1991.

362. Scheren, J., Vice President of Education Research Information, National Wholesale Druggists Association, Alexandria, VA, personal communication, May 7, 1992.

363. Scherer, F.M., "Research and Development: Resource Allocation Under Rivalry," *Quarterly Journal of Economics* 81:359-394, August 1967.

364. Scherer, F.M., "Inflation, Capital Budgeting and the Long View," School of Government, Harvard University, unpublished survey, Cambridge, MA, 1983.

365. Scherer, F.M., *Innovation and Growth: Schumpeterian Perspectives* (Cambridge, MA: The MIT Press, 1984).

366. Scherer, F.M., and Ross, D., *Industrial Market Structure and Economic Performance, 3rd Edition* (Boston, MA: Houghton Mifflin Company, 1990).

367. Schnee, J.E., "Development Cost: Determinants and Overruns," *Journal of Business* 45(3):347-374, 1972.

368. Schondelmeyer, S.W., "Economic Impact of Multiple Source Competition on Originator Products," contract paper prepared for Office of Technology Assessment, U.S. Congress, December 1991.

369. Schondelmeyer, S.W., "Economic Impact of Multiple Source Competition on Originator Products," contract paper prepared for Office of Technology Assessment, U.S. Congress, addendum, February 1992.

370. Schondelmeyer, S.W., Professor, University of Minnesota, Minneapolis, MN, personal communications, February 6, 1992 and March 15, 1992.

371. Schwartz, T.M., "Products Liability Law and Pharmaceuticals: Developments and Divergent Trends," *Food Drug and Cosmetic Law Journal* 43:33, 1988.

372. Schwartzman, D., *The Expected Return From Pharmaceutical Research* (Washington, DC: American Enterprise Institute, 1975).

373. Scolnick, E.M., "Basic Research and Its Impact on Industrial R&D," *Research Technology Management* 33:22-26, November/December 1990.

374. Scott, H.D., Thatcher-Renshaw, A., Rosenbaum, S.E., et al., "Physician Reporting of Adverse Drug Reactions," *Journal of the American Medical Association* 263:1785-1788, 1990.

375. *Scrip World Pharmaceutical News*, "US AIDS Research Grants Controversy," *Scrip World Pharmaceutical News* 1456:15, 1989.

376. *Scrip World Pharmaceutical News*, "Enormous Growth in U.S. CANDAs,' *Scrip World Pharmaceutical News* 1536:19-20, 1990.

376a. *Scrip World Pharmaceutical News*, "French Stress Efficacy/Cost Ratio," *Scrip World Pharmaceutical News* 1561:2-3, 1990.

377. *Scrip World Pharmaceutical News*, "UK PPRS as a Model in Europe," *Scrip World Pharmaceutical News* 1603:4-5, 1991.

378. *Scrip World Pharmaceutical News*, "Merck Drops Leukotriene Antagonist" *Scrip World Pharmaceutical News* 1612:22, 1991.

379. *Scrip World Pharmaceutical News*, "Leukotriene Research Making Progress," *Scrip World Pharmaceutical News* 1613:26-27, 1991.

379a. *Scrip World Pharmaceutical News*, "Prior Authorization as Bargaining Chip," *Scrip World Pharmaceutical News* 1617:18, 1991.

380. *Scrip World Pharmaceutical News*, "FDA Reforms Include Recognition of Non-U.S. Approvals," *Scrip World Pharmaceutical News* 1670:19, November 17, 1991.

381. *Scrip World Pharmaceutical News*, "French Reimbursement to November," *Scrip World Pharmaceutical News* 1692:4, February 14, 1992.

381a. *Scrip World Pharmaceutical News*, "Medicaid 'Best Price' Repeal Urged," *SCRIP World Pharmaceutical News* 1697:16, March 4, 1992.

382. *Scrip World Pharmaceutical News*, "ICI Invests More in Puerto Rico," *Scrip World Pharmaceutical News* 1700:9, March 3, 1992.

383. *Scrip World Pharmaceutical News*, "Lilly Constructing $65 Million Facility in Puerto

Rico," *Scrip World Pharmaceutical News* 1700:9, March 3, 1992.

384. *Scrip World Pharmaceutical News*, "Antibacterial Competition Intensifies in U.S.," *Scrip World Pharmaceutical News* 1709:26, April, 15, 1992.

385. *Scrip World Pharmaceutical News*, "Top 25 Products in 1991," *Scrip World Pharmaceutical News* 1717:28, May 13, 1992.

386. Sermeus, G., and Adriaenssens, G., *Drug Prices and Drug Legislation in Europe—An Analysis of the Situation in the Twelve Member States of the European Communities*, report prepared for the Directorate-General for the Environment, Consumer Protection and Nuclear Safety of Belgium, Number 112/89 (Brussels, Beligum: Belgian Consumers' Association, 1989).

387. Shanahan, B., Manager of University Programs, Standard & Poor's Compustat[1]Services, Inc., personal communication, January 31, 1991.

388. Shanley, M.G., and Peterson, M.A., *Comparative Justice: Civil Jury Verdicts in San Francisco and Cook Counties, 1959-1980* (Santa Monica, CA: The Rand Corporation, 1983).

389. Shulman, S., Bienz-Tadmor, B., Son Seo, P., et al., "Implemenation of the Orphan Drug Act: 1983-1991," *Food and Law Journal* 47(4):363-404, 1992.

390. Shyam-Sunder, L., "Estimates of Cost of Capital and Risk for Firms in the U.S. Pharmaceutical Industry," paper prepared for Pfizer Inc., New York, NY, December 1991.

391. Sick, G., "Pharmaceutical Industry R&D and the Cost of Capital," paper prepared for the Office of Technology Assessment, U.S. Congress, Washington, DC, February 1992.

392. Sick, G., "Tax-Adjusted Discount Rates," *Management Science* 36(12):1432-1450, 1990.

393. *SmithKline Corporation v. Staats*, 668 F.2d 201 (3rd Cir. 1981).

394. SmithKline & French International, *The Discovery of Histamine H2-Receptors and Their Antagonists* (Philadelphia, PA: Smith Kline & French, 1982).

395. Smith, E.S., "Third Party Payment for Unapproved Uses of Approved Drugs and for Medical Care Associated With Drug Clinical Trials," report prepared for the Office of Technology Assessment, U.S. Congress, Washington, DC, January 1991.

396. Sneader, W., *Drug Discovery: The Evolution of Modern Medicines* (New York, NY: Wiley, 1985).

397. Snedden, T., Director of PACE Program, Pennsylvania Department of Aging, Harrisburg, PA, personal communication, October 31, 1991.

398. Solomon, E., "Alternative Rate of Return Concepts and Their Implications for Utility Regulation," *Bell Journal of Economics* 1:65-81, Spring 1970.

399. Spilker, B., *Multinational Drug Companies: Issues in Drug Discovery and Development* (New York, NY: Raven Press, 1989).

400. Stanley, G.R., "Use of Foreign Data in a New Drug Application," *Food Drug Cosmetic Law Journal* 36:340-344, 1981.

401. Statman, M., *Competition in the Pharmaceutical Industry: The Declining Profitability of Drug Innovation* (Washington, DC: American Enterprise Institute, 1983).

402. Stauffer, T.R., "The Measurement of Corporate Rates of Return: A Generalized Formulation," *Bell Journal of Economics* 2: 434-469, Autumn 1971.

403. Stechschulte, D.J., "Leukotrienes in Asthma and Allergic Rhinitis" [editorial], *New England Journal of Medicine* 323(25):1769-1770, 1990.

404. Stein, R.E., Partner, Blicker, Futterman and Stein, Washington, DC, personal communication, August 7, 1992.

405. Stephens, J.C., Cavanaugh, M.L., Gradie, M.I., et al., "Mapping the Human Genome: Current Status," *Science* 250:237-244 [and wall chart], October 12, 1990.

406. Steru, L., and Simon, P., "French Drug Policy," *International Journal of Technology Assessment in Health Care* 2(4):637-642, 1986.

407. Stetler, C.J., "The Pharmaceutical Industry in Review: How We Got to Where We Are," *Medical Marketing and Media* 26:40-50, October 1991.

408. Stevens, A., Secretary to the Pharmaceutical Benefits Pricing Authority of Australia, Sydney, Australia, personal communication, December 11, 1991.

409. Stewart, G.B., III, *The Quest for Value: A Guide for Senior Managers* (New York, NY: Harper Business, 1991).

410. Stokes, D.E., "Perceptions of the Nature of Basic and Applied Science in the United States," *Science Policy Perspectives: USA-Japan*, A. Gerstenfeld (ed.)(New York, NY: Academic Press, 1982).

411. Stolar, M.H., "National Survey of Hospital Pharmaceutical Services—1982," *American Journal of Hospital Pharmacists* 40:963-969, 1983.

412. Stolar, M.H., "ASHP National Survey of Hospital Pharmaceutical Services—1987," *American Journal of Hospital Pharmacy* 45:801-818, 1988.

413. Stoll, R.R., "A Question of Competence: The Judicial Role in the Regulation of Pharmaceuticals," *Food Drug and Cosmetic Law Journal* 45:279-299, 1990.

414. Sturtevant, A.H., *A History of Genetics* (New York, NY: Harper and Row, 1965).

415. Swann, J.P., *Academic Scientists and the Pharmaceutical Industry: Cooperative Research in Twentieth Century America* (Baltimore, MD: The Johns Hopkins University Press, 1988)

416. Swazey, J.P., "Containing Risks of 'Unavoidably Unsafe' Products: Prescription Drugs and Product Liability," *The Liability Maze: The Impact of Liability Law on Safety and Innovation*, R.E. Litan and Peter W. Huber (eds.) (Washington, DC: The Brookings Institution, 1991).

417. Tachi, R., Chairman, Chuikyo (Central Social Insurance Medical Council of Japan), "The Self-Initiated Recommendations," unpublished typewritten summary of Chuikyo Special Committee on NHI Drug Prices meeting, Tokyo, Japan, May 31, 1991.

418. Tandon, P., "Rivalry and the Excessive Allocation of Resources to Research," *Bell Journal of Economics* 43:301-315, 1976.

419. Teitelman, R., *Gene Dreams: Wall Street, Academia, and the Rise of Biotechnology* (New York, NY: Basic Books, Inc., 1989).

420. Temin, P., "Technology, Regulation, and Market Structure in the Modern Pharmaceutical Industry," *Bell Journal of Economics* 10:429-446, Autumn 1979.

421. Thomas, L.G., "Regulation and Firm Size: FDA Impacts on Inovation," Columbia University Graduate School of Business, First Boston Working Paper Series, FB-87-24, September 1987.

422. Thomas, L.G., "Regulation and Firm Size: FDA Impacts on Innovation," *Rand Journal of Economics* 21:4, Winter 1990.

423. Tiefer, C., Deputy Counsel to the Clerk, Office of the General Counsel, House of Representatives, U.S. Congress, personal communication, September 4, 1991.

424. Traina, V.M., "The Role of Toxicology in Drug Research and Development," *Medical Research Reviews* 3(1):43-72, 1983.

425. Tsui, L.-C., Buchwald, M., Barker, D., et al., "Cystic Fibrosis Locus Defined by a Genetically Linked Polymorphic DNA Marker," *Science* 230:1054-1057, 1985.

426. Tucker, S.A., Blozan, C., and Coppinger, P., "The Outcome of Research on New Molecular Entities Commencing Clinical Research in Years 1976-78," OPE-Study 77, unpublished manuscript, U.S. Department of Health and Human Services, Public Health Service, Food and Drug Administration, Rockville, MD, May 1988.

427. Tufts University, Center for Study of Drug Development, unpublished data provided to the Office of Technology Assessment, U.S. Congress, Washington, DC, 1990.

428. Tyle, P., and Ram, B.P., "Monoclonal Antibodies, Immunoconjugates, and Liposomes as Targeted Therapeutic Systems," *Targeted Therapeutic Systems*, P. Tyle and B.P. Ram (eds.)(New York, NY: Marcel Dekker, 1990).

429. *United States v. Abbott*, 597 F.2d 672 (7th Cir. 1979).

430. U.S. Congress, Congressional Budget Office, *Potential Economic Impacts of Changes in Puerto Rico's Status Under S. 712* (Washington, DC: U.S. Government Printing Office, April 1990).

431. U.S. Congress, Congressional Budget Office, "Question and Answers: Medicaid Prescription Drug Rebates," unpublished report, Congressional Budget Office, June 1992.

432. U.S. Congress, General Accounting Office, *Product Liability: Extent of Litigation Explosion in Federal Courts Questioned*, GAO/HRD-88-36BR (Washington, DC: U.S. Government Printing Office, January 1988).

433. U.S. Congress, General Accounting Office, *Biotechnology: Backlog of Patent Applications*, GAO/RCED-89-120-BR (Washington, DC: U.S. Government Printing Office, April 1989).

434. U.S. Congress, General Accounting Office, *Prescription Drugs: Information on Selected Drug Utilization Review Systems*, PEMD-89-18 (Washington, DC: U.S. Government Printing Office, May 1989).

435. U.S. Congress, General Accounting Office, *ADP Planning FDA's Plans to Improve Processing of Medical Device and Drug Applications*, GAO/IMTEC-89-58 (Washington, DC: U.S. Government Printing Office, June 1989).

436. U.S. Congress, General Accounting Office, *FDA Resources: Comprehensive Assessment of Staffing, Facilities, and Equipment Needed*, GAO/HRD-89-142 (Washington, DC: U.S. Government Printing Office, September 1989).

437. U.S. Congress, General Accounting Office, *Tax Policy and Administration: The Research Tax Credit Has Stimulated Some Additional Research Spending*, GAO/GGD-89-114 (Washington, DC: U.S. Government Printing Office, September 1989).

438. U.S. Congress, General Accounting Office, *Tax Policy: 1987 Company Effective Tax Rates Higher Than in Prior Years*, GAO/GGD-90-69 (Washington, DC: Government Printing Office, May 1990).

439. U.S. Congress, General Accounting Office, *FDA Premarket Approval: Process of Approving Ansaid as a Drug*, GAO/HRD-92-85 (Washington, DC: U.S. Government Printing Office, April 1992).

439a. U.S. Congress, General Accounting Office, *Prescription Drugs: Companies Typically Charge More in the United States Than in Canada*, GAO/HRD-92-110 (Washington, DC: U.S. Government Printing Office, September 1992).

440. U.S. Congress, House of Representatives, Committee on Energy and Commerce, unpublished data, Washington, DC, 1983.

441. U.S. Congress, Joint Committee on Taxation, *General Explanation of the Tax Reform Act of 1986* (Washington, DC: U.S. Government Printing Office, 1986).

442. U.S. Congress, Library of Congress, Congressional Research Service, "The Product Liability Reform Act: S. 1400, 101st Congress," prepared by Henry Cohen, Washington, DC, August 1989.

443. U.S. Congress, Office of Technology Assessment, *A Review of Selected Federal Vaccine and Immunization Policies Based on Case Studies of Pneumococcal Vaccine*, OTA-H-96 (Washington, DC: U.S. Government Printing Office, September 1979).

444. U.S. Congress, Office of Technology Assessment, *Compensation for Vaccine-Related Injuries*, OTA-TM-H-6 (Washington, DC: U.S. Government Printing Office, November 1980).

445. U.S. Congress, Office of Technology Assessment, *Commercial Biotechnology: An International Analysis*, OTA-BA-218 (Washington, DC: U.S. Government Printing Office, January 1984).

446. U.S. Congress, Office of Technology Assessment, *Medicare's Prospective Payment System: Strategies for Evaluating Cost Quality and Medical Technology*, OTA-H-262 (Washington, DC: U.S. Government Printing Office, October 1985).

447. U.S. Congress, Office of Technology Assessment, *Alternatives to Animal Use in Research, Testing, and Education*, OTA-BA-273 (Washington, DC: U.S. Government Printing Office, February 1986).

448. U.S. Congress, Office of Technology Assessment, *Losing a Million Minds: Confronting the Tragedy of Alzheimer's Disease and Other Dementias*, OTA-BA-323 (Washington, DC: U.S. Government Printing Office, April 1987).

449. U.S. Congress, Office of Technology Assessment, *Healthy Children: Investing in the Future*, OTA-H-345 (Washington, DC: U.S. Government Printing Office, February 1988).

450. U.S. Congress, Office of Technology Assessment, *New Developments in Biotechnology, U.S. Investment in Biotechnology*, OTA-BA-360 (Washington, DC: U.S. Government Printing Office, July 1988).

451. U.S. Congress, Office of Technology Assessment, *Recombinant Erythropoietin: Payment Options for Medicare*, OTA-H-451 (Washington, DC: U.S. Government Printing Office, May 1990).

452. U.S. Congress, Office of Technology Assessment, *Federally Funded Research: Decisions for a Decade*, OTA-SET-490 (Washington, DC: U.S. Government Printing Office, May 1991).

453. U.S. Congress, Office of Technology Assessment, *Biotechnology in a Global Economy*, OTA-BA-494 (Washington, DC: U.S. Government Printing Office, October 1991).

454. U.S. Congress, Office of Technology Assessment, *Home Drug Infusion Therapy Under Medicare*, OTA-H-510 (Washington, DC: U.S. Government Printing Office, May 1992).

455. U.S. Congress, Office of Technology Assessment, *Federal and Private Roles in the Development and Provision of Alglucerase Therapy for Gaucher Disease*, OTA-BP-H-104 (Washington, DC: U.S. Government Printing Office, October 1992).

456. U.S. Congress, Senate, Report 99-283 in Legislative History to Public Law 99-502, 1986 U.S. CCAN 3442-63.

457. U.S. Congress, Senate, Special Committee on Aging, ''The Drug Manufacturing Industry: A Prescription for Profits,'' Comm. Pub. No. 102-50 (Washington, DC: U.S. Government Printing Office, September 1991).

458. U.S. Congress, Senate, Special Committee on Aging, ''A Status Report: Accessibility and Affordability of Prescription Drugs for Older Americans (Annotated),'' Serial No. 102-Q (Washington, DC: U.S. Government Printing Office, September 1992).

459. U.S. Department of Agriculture, Animal and Plant Health Inspection, *Animal Welfare Enforcement, FY 74*, report to the President of the Senate and Speaker of the House of Representatives, 1975.

460. U.S. Department of Agriculture, Animal and Plant Health Inspection, *Animal Welfare Enforcement, FY 87*, report to the President of the Senate and Speaker of the House of Representatives, 1988.

461. U.S. Department of Commerce, International Trade Administration, *U.S. Industrial Outlook '92* (Washington, DC: U.S. Government Printing Office, January 1992).

462. U.S. Department of Health and Human Services, Advisory Commitee on the Food and Drug Administration, *Final Report of the Advisory Committee on the Food and Drug Administration* (Washington, DC: U.S. Government Printing Office, 1991).

463. U.S. Department of Health and Human Services, Health Care Financing Administration, *Health Care Financing Program Statistics: Medicare and Medicaid Data Book, 1990*, HCFA Publication No. 03314 (Washington, DC: U.S. Government Printing Office, 1991).

464. U.S. Department of Health and Human Services, Health Care Financing Administration, Office of National Health Statistics, Office of the Actuary, unpublished data, Baltimore, MD, March 1992.

465. U.S. Department of Health and Human Services, Health Resources Services Administration, Vaccine Injury Compensation Program, unpublished data from *Weekly Status Report*, Rockville, MD, June 18, 1991.

466. U.S. Department of Health and Human Services, Office of Inspector General, *Promotion of Prescription Drugs Through Payments and Gifts*, DHHS Pub. No. (OEI) 01-90-00480 (Washington, DC: U.S. Government Printing Office, 1990).

467. U.S. Department of Health and Human Services, President's Cancer Panel, *Final Report of the National Committee to Review Current Procedures for Approval of New Drugs for Cancer and AIDS*, unpublished document, U.S. Department of Health and Human Services, Washington, DC, August 1990.

468. U.S. Department of Health and Human Services, Public Health Service, Food and Drug Administration, Center for Drug Evaluation and Research, *Office of Drug Evaluation Statistical Report: 1983*, unpublished document, U.S. Department of Health and Human Service, Rockville, MD, 1984.

469. U.S. Department of Health and Humans Services, Public Health Service, Food and Drug Administration, *Formatting, Assembling and Submitting New Drug and Antibiotic Applications* (Rockville, MD: U.S. Department of Health and Human Services, February 1987).

470. U.S. Department of Health and Human Services, Public Health Service, Food and Drug Administration, ''Orphan Designations Pursuant to Section 526 of the Federal Food, Drug and Cosmetic Act as Amended by the Orphan

Drug Act (Public Law 97-414) Through December 31, 1989," unpublished document, U.S. Department of Health and Human Services, Rockville, MD, 1989.

471. U.S. Department of Health and Human Services, Public Health Service, Food and Drug Administration, *From Test Tube to Patient: New Drug Development in the U.S., An FDA Consumer Special Report*, DHHS Pub. No. (FDA) 90-3168 (Washington, DC: U.S. Government Printing Office, 1990).

472. U.S. Department of Health and Human Services, Public Health Service, Food and Drug Administration, Center for Drug Evaluation and Research, *Office of Drug Evaluation Statistical Report: 1986*, U.S. Department of Health and Human Service, Rockville, MD, 1987.

473. U.S. Department of Health and Human Services, Public Health Service, Food and Drug Administration, Center for Drug Evaluation and Research, *Approved Drug Products, 10th edition* (Washington, DC: U.S. Government Printing Office, 1990).

474. U.S. Department of Health and Human Services, Public Health Service, Food and Drug Administration, Center for Drug Evaluation and Research, *Office of Drug Evaluation Statistical Report: 1990*, U.S. Department of Health and Human Service, Rockville, MD, 1991.

475. U.S. Department of Health and Human Services, Public Health Service, Food and Drug Administration, Center for Drug Evaluation and Research, *Office of Drug Evaluation Statistical Report: 1991*, U.S. Department of Health and Human Service, Rockville, MD, 1992.

476. U.S. Department of Health and Human Services, Public Health Service, National Institutes of Health, "Research Patient Care Costs Supported by NIH Sponsored Agreements," *NIH Extramural Research Manual* (Washington, DC: U.S. Government Printing Office, March 1986).

477. U.S. Department of Health and Human Services, Public Health Service, National Institutes of Health, *1987 NIH Almanac* (Washington, DC: U.S. Government Printing Office, 1987).

478. U.S. Department of Health and Human Services, Public Health Service, National Institutes of Health, "Outside Work and Activities," revision to *NIH Manual*, chapter 2300-735-4, mimeograph, September 1, 1988.

479. U.S. Department of Health and Human Services, Public Health Service, National Institutes of Health, Alcohol, Drug Abuse and Mental Health Administration, Office of Technology Transfer, Patent Policy Board, *Materials Transfer Agreement* (Bethesda, MD: National Institutes of Health, May 22, 1989).

480. U.S. Department of Health and Human Services, Public Health Service, National Institutes of Health, *Academic Research Equipment and Equipment Needs in the Biological Sciences: 1984-1987* (Bethesda, MD: National Institutes of Health, June 1989).

481. U.S. Department of Health and Human Services, Public Health Service, National Institutes of Health, *Extramural Trends: FY 1979-1988* (Bethesda, MD: National Institutes of Health, June 1989).

482. U.S. Department of Health and Human Services, Public Health Service, National Institutes of Health, *NIH Data Book 1989*, NIH Pub. No. 90-1261 (Bethesda, MD: National Institutes of Health, December 1989).

483. U.S. Department of Health and Human Services, Public Health Service, National Institutes of Health, *Data Book 1990* (Washington, DC: U.S. Government Printing Office, 1990).

484. U.S. Department of Health and Human Services, Public Health Service, National Institutes of Health, Alcohol, Drug Abuse and Mental Health Administration, *NIH/ADAMHA Technology Transfer: The Federal Technology Transfer Act and Collaboration With Industry*, NIH/ADAMHA training manual, sponsored by the NIH/ADAMHA Patent Policy Board and Office of Invention Development, November 1989.

485. U.S. Department of Health and Human Services, Public Health Service, National Institutes of Health, Alcohol, Drug Abuse and Mental Health Administration, Division of Program Analysis, Office of Extramural Program, *ADAMHA Data Source Book FY 1989*, Report No. 90-21 (Rockville, MD: Office of Extramural Programs, ADAMHA, 1990).

486. U.S. Department of Health and Human Services, Public Health Service, National Institutes of Health, Alcohol, Drug Abuse and Mental

Health Administration, Office of Technology Transfer, Patent Policy Board, "Policy Statement on Cooperative Research and Development Agreements and Intellectual Property Licensing, March 27, 1989," *PHS Technology Transfer Directory (NIH/ADAMHA/CDC)* (Washington, DC: U.S. Government Printing Office, 1990).

486a. U.S. Department of Health and Human Services, Public Health Service, National Institutes of Health, National Institute of General Medical Sciences, *Pharmacological Sciences Program's Biennial Report for Fiscal Years 1988-1989* (Bethesda, MD: National Institues of Health, September 1990).

487. U.S. Department of Health and Human Services, Public Health Service, Office of the Assistant Secretary for Planning and Evaluation, "Medicare Coverage for Investigational Drugs: Exploring the Options," unpublished document, U.S. Deparment of Health and Human Services, Washington, DC, 1990.

488. U.S. Department of Health and Human Services and U.S. Department of Energy, *Understanding Our Genetic Inheritance: The First Five Years, FY 1991-1995*, DOE/ER-0452P (Springfield, VA: National Technical Information Service, 1990).

489. U.S. Department of Justice, *Report of the Tort Policy Working Group on the Causes, Extent and Policy Implications of the Current Crisis in Insurance Availability and Affordability* (Washington, DC: U.S. Government Printing Office, 1986).

490. U.S. Department of Justice, Tort Policy Working Group, *An Update on the Liability Crisis* (Washington, DC: U.S. Government Printing Office, 1987).

491. U.S. Department of Labor, Bureau of Labor Statistics, Bulletin 2363, *Employee Benefits in Medium and Large Firms, 1989* (Washington, DC: U.S. Government Printing Office, June 1990).

492. U.S. Department of Treasury, Internal Revenue Service, Statistics of Income Division, *Source Book, Statistics of Income, 1987, Corporate Income Tax Returns*, IRS Publication 1053 (Washington, DC: U.S. Government Printing Office, 1987).

493. U.S. District Court, *People With AIDS Health Group, William Ceyrolles, and William Neithamer v. Burroughs Wellcome Company and the United States of America*, Civil Action No. 91-574, March 19, 1991.

494. U.S. District Court for the District of Columbia, "Memorandum in Support of Plaintiff's Motions for a Temporary Restraining Order and for a Preliminary Injunction," Civil Action 87-0605, 1987.

495. U.S. District Court for the District of Columbia, "Memorandum of Points and Authorities for Intervenor-Defendant Eli Lilly and Company in Opposition to Plaintiff's Motion for a Preliminary Injunction," Civil Action No. 87-0605, 1987.

496. Uzzell, J.K., and Meyer, G.F., "Learning Lessons at the School of NDA Submissions," *Pharmaceutical Executive* 10(6):82-86, 1990.

497. Van Horn, C.E., Special Assistant to the Assistant Commissoner for Patents, U.S. Patent and Trademark Office, U.S. Department of Commerce, personal communications, April 5, 1990, March 7, 1991, and September 8, 1992.

498. Venuti, M.C., "Molecular Genetics and Drug Discovery, *Molecular Genetic Medicine, Volume 1*, T. Friedmann (ed.)(San Diego, CA: Academic Press, 1991).

499. Villaume, J.E., Director, Drug Regulatory Affairs, Roche Pharmaceuticals, Nutley, NJ, personal communication, September 8, 1992.

500. Virts, J.R., and Weston, J.F., "Returns to Research and Development in the U.S. Pharmaceutical Industry," *Managerial and Decision Economics* 1(3):103-111, 1980.

501. Viscusi, Kip W., and Moore, Michael, J., "An Industrial Profile of the Links Between Product Liability and Innovation," *The Liability Maze: The Impact of Liability Law on Safety and Innovation*, Robert E. Litan and Peter W. Gruber (eds.)(Washington, DC: The Brookings Institution, 1991).

502. Wade, V.A., Mansfield, P.R., and McDonald, P.J., "Drug Companies' Evidence to Justify Advertising," *The Lancet* 1989, pp. 1261-1263.

503. Wagner, J.L., Senior Associate, Office of Technology Assessment, U.S. Congress, Washington, DC, "Statement," *Strategies for Containing Medicaid Prescription Drug Costs*, hearing

before the Senate Committee on Finance, U.S. Congress, Washington, DC, September 17-19, 1990.

504. Wainwright, B.J., Scambler, P.J., Schmidtke, J., et al., "Localization of Cystic Fibrosis Locus to Human Chromosome 7cen-q22," *Nature* 322:467-470, 1985.

505. *Wall Street Journal*, "Drug Costs Outstrip U.S. Consumer Prices New Report Discloses," *Wall Street Journal* September 11, 1992, p. B13.

506. Walz, G., Aruffo, A., Kolanus, W., et al. "Recognition by ELAM-1 of the Sial-Le[1] Determinant on Myeloid and Tumor Cells," *Science* 250:1132-1135, 1990.

507. Wardell, W.M., "The Drug Lag Revisited: Comparisons by Therapeutic Area of Patterns of Drugs Marketed in the U.S. and Great Britain From 1972 Through 1976," *Clinical Pharmacology and Therapeutics* 24:499-524, 1978.

508. Watanabe, T., "Japanese Pharmaceutical Industry Faces Growing—and Shrinking—Pains," *Business Japan* 31:71-74, 1986.

509. Watson, J.D., and Crick, F.H.C., "Genetical Implications of the Structure of Deoxyribonucleic Acid," *Nature* 171:737-738, May 30, 1953.

510. Weber, N., *Product Liability: The Corporate Response,* Research Report 893 (New York, NY: The Conference Board, Inc., 1987).

511. Webster, A.J., and Etzkowitz, H., *Academic-Industry Relations: The Second Academic Revolution: A Framework Paper for the Proposed Workshop on Academic-Industry Relations* (London, England: Science Policy Support Group, Monograph, 1991).

512. Webster, A.J., and Constable, J., "The Role of Hybrid Coalitions in Commercializing Public Sector Science," unpublished manuscript, Anglia College, Cambridge, England, 1989.

513. Weinberg, A.M., "Criteria for Scientific Choice," *Minerva* 1:159-171, Winter 1963.

514. Weiner, J., "Campus Capitalism: Harvard Chases BioTech Bucks," *The Nation* 248:12-16, January 2, 1989.

515. Weiner, J.P., Lyles, A., Steinwachs, D.M., et al., "Impact of Managed Care on Prescription Drug Use," *Health Affairs* 10(1):140-153, Spring 1991.

516. Weisbrod, B.A., "The Health Care Quadridilemma: An Essay on Technological Change, Insurance, Quality of Care, and Cost Containment," *Journal of Economic Literature* 29:523-552, June 1991.

516a. Weissinger, J., Center for Drug Evaluation and Research, Food and Drug Administration, Public Health Service, U.S. Department of Health and Human Services, Rockville, MD, personal communication, March 1991.

517. Wells, J., Pharmacy Program Manager, Division of Medicaid, Florida Department of Health and Rehabilitative Services, Tallahassee, FL, personal communication, 1990.

518. White, R.L., Woodward, S., Leppert, M., et al., "A Closely Linked Genetic Marker for Cystic Fibrosis," *Nature* 318:382-384, 1985.

519. Wiggins, S.N., "Product Quality Regulation and New Drug Introductions: Some New Evidence From the 1970s," *The Review of Economics and Statistics* 63(4):615-619, 1981.

520. Wiggins, S.N., *The Cost of Developing a New Drug* (Washington, DC: Pharmaceutical Manufacturers Association, 1987).

521. Wilkes, M.S., Doblin, B., Shapiro, M., "Pharmaceutical Advertisements in Leading Medical Journals: Experts' Assessments," *Annals of Internal Medicine* 116:912-919, 1992.

522. Wolfe, S.M., Director, Public Citizen Health Research Group, Washington, DC, "Statement," *Product Liability Reform Act*, hearing before the Subcommittte on the Consumer, Committee on Commerce, Science, and Transportation, Senate, U.S. Congress, May 10, 1990, Serial No. 101-743 (Washington, DC: U.S. Government Printing Office, 1990).

523. Wolski, K.P., remarks at "Drug Approvals in the United States and Abroad," seminar sponsored by the Institute for Alternative Futures Foresight, Washington, DC, October 7, 1991.

524. Woltman, R., "Reviewing the Bidding: R&D Costs and Profitability of New Chemical Entities," *Journal of Research in Pharmaceutical Economics* 1(3):49-65, 1989.

525. Wozny, J.A., "The Research Tax Credit: New Evidence on Its Effects," *Proceedings of the Eighty-Second Anuual Conference of the National Tax Association-Tax Institute of America* 1989, pp. 223-228.

526. Yoshikawa, A., Associate Director, Comparative Health Care Research Project, Stanford

University, Stanford, CA, personal communication, December 10, 1991.

527. Yoshikawa, A., Hayase Fellow, Asia Pacific Research Center, Stanford University, Palo Alto, CA, personal communication, March 5, 1992.

528. Young, F.E., Norris, J.A., Levitt, J.A., et al., "The FDA's New Procedures for the Use of Investigational Drugs in Treatment," *Journal of the American Medical Association* 259(15): 2267-2270, 1988.

Index

1000195906

WILKES UNIVERSITY LIBRARY